SOCIAL SECURITY REFORM

Options for China

SOCIAL SECURITY REFORM

Options for China

edited by

Jason Z Yin
Seton Hall University, USA

Shuanglin Lin
University of Nebraska at Omaha, USA

David F Gates
Exxon Company, International, USA

World Scientific
Singapore • New Jersey • London • Hong Kong

Published by

World Scientific Publishing Co. Pte. Ltd.

P O Box 128, Farrer Road, Singapore 912805

USA office: Suite 1B, 1060 Main Street, River Edge, NJ 07661

UK office: 57 Shelton Street, Covent Garden, London WC2H 9HE

British Library Cataloguing-in-Publication Data
A catalogue record for this book is available from the British Library.

SOCIAL SECURITY REFORM: OPTIONS FOR CHINA

ISBN 981-02-4104-6

This book is printed on acid and chlorine free paper.

Printed in Singapore by FuIsland Offset Printing

Contents

Part 4
Social Security Reform in the World: Lessons for China

PREFACE

Social security reform, particularly reform of the pension system, is one of the most urgent tasks of China's economic reform program. Put simply China's current pay-as-you-go pension system is becoming financially unsustainable. When it was established almost five decades ago there were more than 400 workers paying into the system for every retiree, so enterprise pension contributions of only 3 percent of the wage bill could fund a very generous retirement program. Subsequently, the ratio of workers to retirees fell to 30:1 by the time economic reform began in the late 1970s and to less than 5:1 by the mid-1990s. To maintain benefits the combined contribution rate of enterprises and their workers has soared to almost one-quarter, twice the rate of payroll taxes prevailing in other developing countries. The World Bank estimates that even under favorable assumptions the contribution rate would have to rise to almost 50 percent over the next three decades in order to maintain the existing pension system.

In response to growing financial pressure, the Chinese government now has embarked on an unprecedented transformation of its pension system. The government intends to dramatically curtail the role of the pay-as-you-go component of the retirement system. Fully funded individual retirement accounts, both mandatory and voluntary, will become the principle source of retirement income. The Chinese government faces complex problems in financing the transition to this new system. Once the bulk of ongoing contributions is allocated to funded individual accounts, the biggest challenge will be funding pensions of those who are already retired or will retire prior to accumulating sufficient assets in their own accounts. Another major challenge is expanding the scope of the system, which at present covers only about one-sixth of the labor force.

Ultimately the new pension system will require further reform of China's financial system. Funded pensions will be viable only if China develops a deeper capital market that offers longer term financial assets with positive, market-determined interest rates. It will also require the development of a competitive pension fund management industry. Eventually accumulated pension funds will become an important source of long-term financing, providing significant competition for banks, which now are the main source of long-term funding for enterprises. Thus the development of the funded pension system is closely linked to financial reform more broadly.

Nicholas R. Lardy
Senior Fellow
The Brookings Institution

INTRODUCTION

More than one fifth of the world population live in China, which has only seven percent of the world arable land. China is still a low-income country, with seventy percent of population lived in rural areas. China's population is aging faster than other countries due to the increase in the life expectancy at birth and a strict birth-control policy. As the economy moves from a centrally-planned economy to a market economy and becomes more and more integrated with the world economy, private enterprises and foreign enterprises are growing rapidly. China's current social security system mainly covers government employees and employees of state-owned enterprises and some large collective enterprises. To achieve the goal of stability and development, reforming the old social security system and establishing a new market-oriented social security system has become imperative for China. But how to reform the system remains as a question.

This book contains selected papers presented at an international symposium on establishing a market-oriented social security system in China. The symposium was sponsored by the Chinese Economists Society (CES), that consists of Chinese economists and China experts from North America, and the Chinese Academy of Social Sciences, China's leading research institute in social sciences and held in Beijing, China. This book addresses the issues such as what kind of social security system to establish, how to establish the system, how to manage the social security funds, and how to transform from the old system to a new system.

This is the first book that provides comprehensive analysis of the Chinese social security (old-age security and health care) reforms with a variety of views. The authors of the papers contained in this book include internationally well-known social security experts, Chinese policy makers, and scholars who have worked on Chinese social security for years. All papers were revised and updated in the light of comments made at the conference and by the referees.

It is the hope of the editors that the interests in this book will extend beyond those directly involved in social security reform in China, and that this book will increase the general awareness about Chinese economy and the general awareness of current debate on social security reforms around the world.

This book is made up of four parts, with a total of 24 chapters. The first part, consisting of eight chapters, deals with issue of what kind of old-age security system China should choose. The second part, consisting of four chapters, deals with the social security funds management and transition problems. The third part, consisting of six chapters, deals with rural social security reforms and medical care reforms. The fourth part consists of another six papers discussing international experience of social security reforms and policy implications to China.

Part I: The Choice of Old-age Security System

There are two basic social security systems: pay-as-you-go or unfunded system, fully-funded system, and partially funded system. Under the pay-as-you-go system, the government collects social security taxes from the current generation and transfers the revenue to the current retired generation. Under the fully-funded system, the individuals are forced to save by government during their working years, and receive the savings and interest during their retiring years. There are other social security systems which are the mix of the above two basic systems. China's social security system was established in the early 1950s as a nation-wide pay-as-you-go define benefit system for the staff and workers of the state-owned industrial enterprises and government agencies. The economic chaos and financial difficulties which resulted from the Cultural Revolution forced the government to shift the burden of social security benefits to the state-owned enterprises, although the government continued to finance social security benefits for its own employees. Since the advent of market-oriented reforms in 1978, private enterprise has reemerged in China and has grown at an extraordinary speed. In 1997, the share of total industrial output produced by the state-owned enterprises fell to less than 30%. The state enterprises, in addition to their other problems, have been heavily burdened by large social security payments to their retirees. Fear of losing health benefits now and losing social security benefits later makes many workers reluctant to move from state-owned enterprises to the private sector. Most of the private enterprises, which employ younger people, do not provide social security benefits. The economic and social reforms demand a rapid social security reform. What a new social security system China should adopt is the focus of the discussion in Part I.

In Chapter 1 of this book, **Martin Feldstein** provides his view on social security pension reform in China. He analyzes the economics of these two types of social systems, pay-as-you-go or unfunded system and fully-funded system, in the Chinese context and calculates the advantage to China of using an investment-based portion. The savings deposits in a funded system are less than tax required in a pay-as-you-go system to provide the same level of benefits. The increasing longevity of populations everywhere means the tax rates will have to rise in the future to maintain the current relation between retiree benefits and pre-retirement wages. For this reason, China is shifting from the pay-as-you-go system to a partially funded system. China also adopted a mixed system that combines defined benefits and defined contributions. It is shown that the funded system can provide the same level of benefits with a saving rate equal to only one fourth of the rate of tax required in the pay-as-you-go system. A transition is feasible with only a very modest increase in the combined tax-plus-savings rate in the early years and this combined burden would gradually decline and eventually become less than the initial pay-as-you-go tax rate. Regardless of the induced reduction in other saving, a funded plan still causes a higher national saving rate than an unfunded pay-as-you-go plan. He points out two alternatives options for the Chinese defined benefit plan which guarantee 25% of the average regional wage for those who have worked the full 40 years. The transition path to the recently legislated system is also discussed.

Different views are provided by **Henry Aaron** in Chapter 2. The author argues that particular forms of social insurance can spare active workers the burdens of growing economically inactive population. This burden can be reduced only by lowering the living standards of the economically active workers or by raising overall economic growth. The author shows that the promotion of economic growth is equally possible under a wide variety of pension systems. These systems differ greatly, however, in how they distribute the inescapable risks of pension systems across members of society. The author suggests that funded defined-benefit systems have important advantages in many circumstances over unfunded systems or defined contribution plans. The chapter starts with some basic propositions regarding social insurance, including a taxonomy of social insurance reforms, a basic social insurance identity, and certain principles of social insurance. The author raises two fundamental issues in the design of social insurance. The first one concerns who should bear the risks inescapable under very long term contracts. Social insurance requires individuals to make contributions or pay taxes and then provides benefits over a period that typically runs six decades or even longer. The second issue is whether to use social insurance to add to national savings. The author believes that the pension reform must be judged primarily on how well it advances the larger social and economic objectives of the economic transformation. The author argues that the new plan should place somewhat greater emphasis on the security of pension promises and protects workers somewhat more from financial uncertainties than the plan outlined in State Council Document No. 26, 1997. Such plan would combine a funded defined-benefit plan that is larger than the first tier plan outlined in State Council Document No. 26 and would rely less on a defined-contribution component than that of the second tier plan.

A Chinese government policy maker, **Li Tieyin** presents his view on how to establish a social security system with Chinese characteristics in Chapter 3. This chapter starts with a review of the history of Chinese social security. The Chinese social security system evolved from the wartime rationing system and it has experienced four stages: The establishment period (1949-1966) in which both workers and enterprises contributed to social security account, the paralyzed period (1966-1976) in which social security was taken over by enterprises, the early reform period (1978-1992) in which some regions started to require individuals to make contributions to social security accounts and some regions even started the experiment of a mixed system which combined a social account and an individual account, and the new era of social security reform (1992 -- present) in which China began to pursue a social security system which consistent with market economy. Establishing a social security system, which is independent of enterprises, will enable China to establish a real labor market to allow workers move from state enterprises to non-state enterprises. The objective of social security reform is to unify basic policy and regulations, to separate government and management of social security fund, to move from enterprises security to social security, and to cover all wage earners. Based on China's national situations, China should have a multi-pillar system which include basic social relief financed by government, old-age insurance financed by government, enterprises and individuals, and individual account financed by individuals. Unemployment insurance and medical insurance are also discussed in this chapter.

In Chapter 4, **Zheng Gongcheng** expresses his view on the rational choice of social security system in China. He characterizes Chinese social security system as six subsystems, social insurance, social relief and assistance, social welfare, military personnel security, public health security, supplementary security. The author discusses factors affect social security reforms, which include the political system, the traditional social security system, the population size, the stage of economic development, the inequality among different regions, and the Chinese culture. At the current stage of development, China should have a mixed system based on family security. The author believes social security reforms should not replace family security but supplement the family security. Social security design should take consideration of the differences among regions, and pursue social equality. Social security debt should be repaid through selling the state assets and reducing government spending.

In Chapter 5, **Shuanglin Lin** examines the effect of an expansion of the pay-as-you-go social security. He pointed out that China is in the process of industrialization with a large amount of the labor force moving from the agricultural sector to industrial sectors. An expansion of the pay-as-you-go social security system benefits current urban retirees, and may solve the social security payment problem faced by many state enterprises. Also, although facing a declining population growth rate, China may not have a social security crisis under a pay-as-you-go social security system just covering the wage earners, as many industrialized countries face. However, the expansion of the pay-as-you-go social security system may have an adverse effect on capital accumulation in the long run, hurting the rural old. Either benefiting or hurting the wage earners in urban areas before the completion of industrialization, it is likely to reduce wage earners' welfare after industrialization.

The efficiency and distribution effects of China's pension system were considered by **Dianqing Xu, Zhi Wang, Yan Wang** in Chapter 6. Given that the World Bank recommendation of a three-pillar social security system in China, this chapter quantitatively estimates the impacts of various schemes of financing pillar 1 (a universal benefit to all wage earners) on China's macroeconomic structure including GDP, GINI coefficients, aggregate demand, consumption, investment, labor demand and etc. It also examines the impact of social security financing on different industries in a newly defined computable general equilibrium (CGE) model.

In Chapter 7, **Haizheng Li and Janusz R. Mrozek** discuss efficiency and the mechanism for funding and provision of social security. They focus on efficiency issues related to different mechanisms of financing and providing social security benefits in China. This paper presents a theory of labor market equilibrium with alternative mechanisms for financing social security benefits and discusses the differences between mandated provision, public provision, and various intermediate mechanisms in terms of the linkages they create between the decision to work and the expected receipt of benefits. This incidence, whether it be of the tax that finance public provision or of the expense of the program compelled by mandated provision, determines the extent to which market decisions are distorted by the social security system. The author apply these ideas in discussing the mechanism of funding and provision in China, where the nature of the former provision mechanism is difficult to determine and various options exist for designing a new system. In an initial effort towards the goal of determining the appropriate mechanism, the authors provide a theoretical and empirical framework for identifying the incidence parameter, to be applied in the future empirical work using data from China.

Chapter 8, demographic underpinnings of China's old-age pension reform, by **Loraine A. West,** begins with a brief review of the features of China's emerging reformed old-age pension system, then focuses on future demographic trends and their implications for the social pension system. Changes in China's demographic variables, such as age structure and life expectancy, as compared to changes experienced by other countries are discussed. Finally the chapter addresses additional modifications to the social pension program suggested by the demographic factors.

Part II: Social Security Funds Management and Transitional Issues

The survival of the social security system relies heavily on the efficient management of the social security fund. Currently five ministries (labor, personnel, civil administration, public health and finance) are involved in administrating social security programs. Some regional, municipal, and industrial authorities have also created their own programs, each with their own policies and regulations. These social security programs are plagued with many problems. The following issues need to be addressed. Should social security be run by the central government or by the local government? Should the social security fund be invested in government bonds or in the stock market? How to use the modern technology to manage the fund? Does China have the financial system to manage the large social security fund?

Many suggest that China should move from the pay-as-you-go system to a fully funded system or partially funded system. The transition is not easy. The government must pay the current social security debt to the current retirees and the workers entitle for social security benefits. The next question is how to pay the debt. The Chinese government has had deficits for many years and does not have surpluses to pay the debt. The Chinese government faces the following options for the repayment of social security debt, collecting more taxes, issuing bonds, and selling assets of state enterprises. Which is the best option for China? If taxes must be collected, what kind of taxes should government collect, consumption tax or income tax?

In Chapter 9, **Jason Yin** discusses social security funds management. After reviewing the pension management system in China and analyzes the pros and cons of the pay-as-you-go and fully funded pension models, he outlines the institutional framework and organizational structure of a hybrid pension management program for China. The proposed program is composed of a small first-tier defined benefit plan run by the government in combination with a large second-tier defined contribution plan to be managed by private sector. This partially privatized program would provide better incentives for savings and bring market competition into the management of the pension system. The semi-decentralized decision-making structure in the program would eventually be able to maximize the return at a controllable risk level for the pensioners. He argues that privatization of social security fund management is an optimal choice for China.

In Chapter 10, **Anjali Kumar and Yan Wang** analyze pension fund management and China's financial sector. The Chapter begins with a discussion of the status of pension reform in China, and the drawbacks of the present system. It then analyzes the importance pension fund management in the success of China's current plans for pension reform, following by a discussion of broad regulatory and institutional principles for pension fund management, in particular, private and decentralized fund management, and describes how such funds operate elsewhere. China would do well to move towards a funded, and multi-pillar, with components that include decentralized and privately managed pension funds. But the institutions available are not ideally suitable. There are gaps in the regulatory framework and China still lacks a basic social insurance law and other regulations. This chapter also discusses the nature of financial instruments that are available to pension funds for investment and the structure of financial markets in which they operate. China's pension funds would also face difficulties in investing due to the limited array of capital market instruments available to investment. Thus, financial sector and capital market reform will have to proceed in parallel.

Estelle James provides a view on how China can move to a new social security system in Chapter 11. This chapter first summarizes the major problems of traditional social security systems, and proposals for structural reform. It compares three variations on the multi-pillar reform model: (1) Latin American Model, in which individual workers choose the investment manager for their retirement funds; (2) the OECD model, in which employers and or union trustees choose the investment manager for an entire company or occupation; and (3) the Swedish notional account model, in which there are no funds to invest. This chapter pays particular attention on how these countries to finance the transition and implications for China.

In Chapter 12, **George S-F Chu, Shunfeng Song, and Dasong Deng** make ten suggestions on how to establish a social protection system with Chinese Characteristics. Their suggestions include reform the social protection system gradually, broaden social assistance and welfare programs, encourage the development of private insurance, and establish a social protection system with multiple layers. They discuss models in determining insurance benefits based on the basic need, ensuring adequate funds for all social protection programs, and establish income recording, social protection trust fund commission, and unify the management and administration of social protection programs. Their view is based on the analysis of the US social security system.

Part III: Health Care Reforms, Rural Social Security, and Social Welfare

The government established a Labor Health Insurance for state enterprises and a Government Health Insurance for employees of government agencies in 1950s. Health care system in urban areas faces the similar problem as the old-age security in urban areas. The rural health care is different. During the cultural revolution, a system of rural health care cooperative was established in each village, which provides the basic health care to farmers. However, the system was eliminated with the break-down of the People's Commune in the rural China. The urgency of reforming the social security system for urban and town workers has been widely recognized. However, whether to establish a social security program for the rural residents is largely controversial. There are 860 million people living in rural China (excluding permanent residents of cities and towns), accounting for 70% of the Chinese total population. The number of people in rural areas is still growing despite the gradual decline in the share of rural population in the total population. There is no social security for the rural old. The existing social safety net in rural areas is targeted at poverty relief, special assistance to poor areas, and natural disaster relief. Villages and towns provide minimum old-age security to the old who do not have children. In rural China, people want to have more sons to support them at old age. As the control for the rural-urban migration getting loosing, more and more rural workers move to urban areas. Thus, the rural old-age security problem becomes more and more severe.

In Chapter 13, **D. Gale Johnson** provides his view on social security for the rural elderly in China. This chapter discusses current economic status of the rural elderly. Based on surveys of rural household in two provinces for 1990, the author concludes that the rural elderly had levels of income or consumption that did not differ significantly from those who are not elderly, rural families with elderly members received very little from the state budget, and the traditional Chinese family, as it existed in rural areas, met the needs of the elderly quite well, given the income less of the family. The current program of rural security is discussed. There exist a social program of welfare houses for the elderly who cannot take care of themselves and have no children to do so. Starting from 1993 a rural pension system has become available in most rural areas. The objective of the ratio of pension payment to earnings at time of retirement should be 40 to 50 percent of the income at the retirement age, assuming that the individuals still have a significant connection with agriculture. It is pointed out that the government so far has not made any commitment concerning the rate of return to be earned on the money that rural people pay into the fund given the negative rate of return on the money paid from 1993 to 1997.

Athar Hussian discusses social welfare and transition to a market economy in Chapter 14. The chapter outlines various social welfare programs in the broad context of social-economic changes. It begins with a discussion of socio-economic changes with direct implications for social welfare. It then analyses arrangements for income maintenance in rural and urban areas and their reform, including old-age pensions, unemployment insurance and poverty relief in rural areas. A brief outline of the rural social security system is presented. Finally the chapter discusses health-care and health insurance. The emphasis here is on the current situation and the likely trend of changes over next 25 years taking 1995 as the benchmark.

Yaohui Zhao and James Wen analyze Chinese rural social security and landholding in Chapter 15. They examine the rural old-age security under collective management of land and the household responsibility system, and discuss the factors affecting private savings and types of savings instruments available in rural China. They argue that current land collective ownership inadequate in providing support for the rural elderly.

In chapter 16, **Wei Yu** focuses on the issues on financing the China's urban health insurance reform. Starting from 1995, the government conducted a series of experiments in health insurance in 57 Chinese cities. In this chapter, the author examines the financial problems encountered in these experimental cities. The chapter begins with a review of the general background on demographics, the health care system, and health care facilities in the 57 experimental cities. It then focuses on three issues. (1) effects of economic reform on the labor health Insurance and government health insurance; (2) incentives of employers and employees in financing a community-based health insurance system: and (3) problems with a financing policy that combines an individual health care account with a social risk pooling account. The author believes that health care should be provided at a reasonable level to everyone in society. However, each person or employer has a strong incentive to achieve an optimum level of risk sharing, which is generally not consistent with the society's desire. Hence, a tax-based redistribution is needed to achieve the socially desired health care system.

Ake Blomqist, Susheng Wang, and Lijing Zhu postulate the issue of health care finance in China in Chapter 17. They argue that for countries at mediate income level, there is a strong case for a system of mixed public and private financing and provision of health services. More over, they argue that it may also be inequitable in the sense that a single-tier health care system represents an inefficient way of helping the poor. China's health care system is undergoing major changes, due to the reduction in the role of the state-owned firms that previously were responsible for financing the cost of their employees' health care, and in part because of the dismantling of the communes that had this role in rural areas. This chapter illustrate the consequences of different health policy choices by means of numerical simulations based on a simple general equilibrium model.

Myron J. Gordon discusses growth and social security under welfare-corporate capitalism and market socialism in Chapter 18. He reviews the historical development and examines the main current features of welfare-corporate capitalism and market socialism in providing economic growth and income security. He argues that welfare-corporate capitalism and market socialism are the systems that exist in the world now, and variations on them are what the future is likely to bring. The examination of market socialism relies on the Chinese experience.

Part IV: Social Security Reforms in the World: Lessons for China

Facing the situation of the population aging, many countries have started to reform their social security systems. Developing countries have been innovative on social security reforms. Chile abandoned the pay-as-you-go system and adopted a fully funded system in the early 1980s, with the social security funds managed by private firms. Other South American countries have also reformed their social security systems following Chile's example. With the Central Provident Fund (CPF), Singapore's social security system strictly relies on individual and family savings rather than on income redistribution. Taiwan's social security reforms aim at primarily of expanding and improving coverage of the first pillar of old age security to the entire population by the year of 2000. Social security reforms also took place in transitional economies such as Vietnam and Hungary. China is a developing country, it can learn the lessons from the experiences of other countries. In this part of the book, all contributions involve comparative analysis.

In Chapter 19, **Carmelo Mesa-Lago** provides a comparative analysis of the pension reforms introduced in eight Latin American countries from May 1981 to May 1997: Argentina, Bolivia, Chile, Colombia, El Salvador, Mexico, Peru and Uruguay. This chapter identifies seven principle issues or dichotomies in the world debate on pension reform. It discusses the two universal paradigms developed by the two principle international groups (IMF and the World Bank on one side and the International Labor Organization and the International Social Security Association on the other) and how the pension systems in the region fit into the two. The chapter then develops a typology of reforms and describes, in a systematic manner, the characteristics of the eight pension systems, noting its similarities and differences. The chapter also evaluates the performance of the eight reforms in relation to their most significant aspects. Finally, this chapter analyses the lessons of the reform for the region and the world.

Social security reform in Taiwan is discussed by **Sheng Cheng Hu** in Chapter 20. The Taiwan economy has sustained a long period of rapid growth, high savings rate, an equitable income distribution, near full employment and price stability. This chapter discusses Taiwan's existing social security system. Taiwan started to establish social security in the late 1950s and early 1960s. The system is fragmented and it covers only about two thirds of the population. The existing system is financed on the pay-as-you-go basis. Taiwan's existing social security system has three pillars. The first pillar has three programs: the public employees insurance program covers all regular government employees; the labor insurance program covers most workers in the private sectors; and a social assistance program provides assistance to the elderly poor. The second pillar consists of pension plans mandated by Basic Labor Law (for workers) and the Public Employees Retirement Law (for public employees). The third pillar consists of individual savings and commercial annuities. Social security reforms undertaken by the government consist primarily of expanding and improving coverage of the first pillar of old age security to the entire population. The first two pillars will provide around 60% of income replacement. Taiwan government plans to complete the reform by the year of 2000. Taiwan's experience with social security system and the current reform efforts provide useful lesson for the Mainland China.

In Chapter 21, **Daniel Goodkind** provides an analysis of Vietnam's old age security system and discusses recent transformations and their relevance for upcoming changes in China. Vietnam is not only China's neighbor but also has similar economic system. Prior to 1995, Vietnam's pension and disability benefits, the primary source of public support, were usually available only to state workers through an internal pay-as-you-go system (heavily subsidized with general government revenues). In 1995, a new social security administration was formally established which expanded such coverage to employees of non-state enterprises. Under the new system, employer contribution rates were raised, wage deductions added, and wage replacement ratios reduced to 75% or less of final wages. The author explores financial, ideological and demographic reasons for these reforms as well as Vietnam's market-oriented transition. The analysis draws upon survey data, reviews of public documents, and interviews with public officials. The author also compares the similarities and differences between the Chinese and Vietnamese contexts.

Ding Lu discusses the principles and institutional features of Singapore's social security system and its implications for the Chinese social security reform in Chapter 22. In this city-state of three million people, the backbone of the social security system is the Central Provident Fund (CPF), which was first established in 1955 and covers all those in the labor force. The CPF system strictly relies on individual and family savings rather than on income redistribution to provide basic social safety net. This feature serves not only to keep individuals' working and saving incentives intact but also to preserve the values of family cohesiveness. Despite that, the CPF proved to be flexible enough in the past decades to evolve itself into a comprehensive social-security savings scheme. The saving scheme not only takes care of a member's retirement, home ownership and health care needs, but also provides financial protection to CPF members and their families through its various insurance schemes. All the social insurance policies for personal catastrophic needs are fully funded by premium payment and managed separately from the limited state welfare subsidies and transfers to minimize moral hazard risks. The permitted uses of CPF savings before retirement are carefully designed to encourage demand for merit goods, such as housing and education, and other efficient use of savings. Singapore and China share the similar cultural roots and traditions. This makes the Singapore experience particularly appealing to China.

In Chapter 23, **Ying Yan** reviews the features of private pension systems in Chile, Mexico, and other countries and discusses lessons China can learn from these countries. The government-mandated retirement saving schemes in Chile and Mexico give pension participants a retirement income that is closely tied to the contributions they made. The Chapter discusses the two-tier systems of the United Kingdom and Japan. In this system, there exist two plans. One is a basic social security plan that provides the basic need for retirees, the benefit received may not be equal to the contribution made the individual, and participation is mandatory. The other one is a supplement plan which provides additional opportunity for old age security, the benefits received is equal to the contribution made in present discounted value, and the participation is voluntary. She suggests to increase mandatory contribution rate to the individual pension account that is defined-contribution oriented and similar to UK and Japan's supplement accounts. She also suggests to gradually reduce proportion of social security provided by government, and establishing a public managed pension scheme rather than an immediate move to a private pension management system.

Pension reform in Hungary and its implications for China is analyzed by **Antal Deutsch** in Chapter 24. The Author describes the setting and the process of pension reform in Hungary. Hungary was the first transitional economy to legislate the operation of private pension funds. Hungary is again the first transitional economy to legislated thorough-going social security reform. The lessons for China depend on both the present decentralized state of pension arrangements in China, and the degree of political determination to proceed to a multi-pillar system. Given that the multiplicity of local pension arrangements that now exist in China, a reconciliation of local interests may be necessary before a Hungarian style reform become acceptable in China.

Acknowledgments

We are indebted to many colleagues and friends for their insights, suggestions and support for this book. They include Henry Aaron, Nicholas Lardy, Min Tong, Justin Lin, James G. Wen, Daniel D. Xu, Shangjin Wei, Neng Liang, Shunfeng Song, Zhuliu Hu, Yuxing Zheng, Tieying Li, Jingwen Li, Shantong Li, and Chunze Jiang.

We would like to extend our special thanks to the organizations that provided the funds for organizing the social security conference and editing this book. They include World Bank, Asian Development Bank, Ford Foundation, the U.S. Chamber of Commerce, the Center for International Private Enterprise, Aetna International, Inc., China Talent Foundation, the China Center for Economic Research of Tsinghua University.

Finally, we would like to thank W. Paul Stillman School of Business of Seton Hall University, Department of Economics of University of Nebraska at Omaha and East Asian Institute of National University of Singapore for providing us an environment to work on this volume and general support.

Jason Z. Yin
Shuanglin Lin
David F. Gates
Editors

PART 1
THE CHOICE OF OLD-AGE SECURITY SYSTEM

CHAPTER 1

SOCIAL SECURITY PENSION REFORM IN CHINA

MARTIN FELDSTEIN*
National Bureau of Economic Research, 1050 Massachusetts Av.,
Cambridge, MA 02138-5398, USA

China has legislated a mixed social security pension system with a defined benefit pay--as-you-go portion and an investment-based defined contribution portion. This paper analyses the economics of these two types of systems in the Chinese context and calculates the advantage to China of using an investment-based portion. Several options for reform of the recently legislated system are considered.

The reform of social security pensions is a critical issue for China - a key to enterprise reform, sound pubic finance, and the well-being of current and future retirees. China has already begun to develop an investment-based system of individual accounts for urban workers, especially those in state owned enterprises. Looking to the future, China faces important issues both about improving the design and implementation of this system and about the transition from the existing unfunded system to the new arrangements.

---

* Professor of Economics, Harvard University, and President of the National Bureau of Economic Research. This paper is based on a talk given at the June 1998 Beijing conference of the Chinese Economics Society. Although my original plan for this lecture was to discuss the social security reforms occurring around the world (based on the information in Feldstein, 1998), I decided instead to talk about the current policies in China and some of China's options for the future. My decision is a risky one since I am certainly not a specialist on the Chinese economy. I recognize that some of my assumptions about the economy and about the current pension arrangements may be wrong, especially since those arrangements are changing rapidly and practice does not always correspond to the official rules. Several useful articles about the Chinese pension system are identified in the references to this paper.

1. Principles of Social Security Pension Design

A useful starting place for any academic discussion of pensions is the famous article by Paul Samuelson (1958) in which he showed that in equilibrium a completely unfunded pay-as-you-go (PAYGO) pension system has a positive real rate of return equal to the rate of growth of aggregate real wages, i.e., to the sum of the growth rate of the population and the growth rate of productivity. Samuelson's theoretical analysis assumed an economy with no capital stock and showed that in such a context a pay-as-you-go pension is a desirable policy.

Actual economies do have capital stocks and the marginal product of capital is greater than the growth rate of aggregate wages. This implies that a nation can buy retirement income with a funded pension system at a lower long-run cost than with a pay-as-you-go system, i.e., the savings deposits in a funded system are less than the tax required in a PAYGO system to provide the same level of benefits.

There is nevertheless a political temptation in any country to adopt a PAYGO system because doing so permits giving a windfall benefit to current retirees and to those who will soon be retired with the cost of that windfall deferred to future taxpayers. Many countries have succumbed to that temptation since Bismark introduced the first formal pension system in Germany in the nineteenth century. And countries with PAYGO systems have created new windfalls from time to time by increasing benefits and expanding coverage, thus maintaining the popularity and political support for the PAYGO system.

But now countries around the world with PAYGO systems are recognizing that there is no more scope for increased windfalls. There is a realization that the increasing longevity of populations everywhere means that tax rates will have to rise in the future just to maintain the current relation between retiree benefits and preretirement wages. As a result, we are seeing a shift from PAYGO to funded systems in a number of countries and the active consideration of such reforms in others.

China is already beginning the transition for workers in state owned enterprises from its unique PAYGO system to a partially funded system based on individual accounts. To the extent that China succeeds in this shift from a PAYGO to a funded system, it will keep future taxes lower than they would otherwise be, will help to develop a more efficient capital market, and will facilitate both the management and privatization of the currently state-owned enterprises.

The choice between a PAYGO system and a funded system is only one of the two important aspects of designing a pension system. The second key characteristic is the choice between a defined benefit and a defined contribution system. In a defined benefit program, retirees receive benefits based on a formula that typically involves the number of years of work and the past history of wages. In contrast, in a defined contribution program, employees (and/or their employers) make contributions to individual accounts during working years. The balances in these accounts earn a rate of return based on the assets in which those funds are invested. Retirees then receive an annuity based on the amount accumulated in their accounts.

It is of course possible to have a mixed system that combines defined benefits and defined contributions. In 1995 China adopted such a combined two-tier system. Participants will receive a defined benefit financed by pay-as-you-go taxes and also participate in a defined contribution program to which employers and employees both contribute. I return below to discuss both aspects of this system.

It is also possible to have a *conditional defined benefit system*, In such a system, individuals have defined contribution accounts but are also guaranteed a minimum amount (a defined benefit). Any shortfall between the annuity provided by the defined contribution account and the guaranteed defined benefit amount is made up by the government.

Around the world, social security reforms now generally involve moving from pay-as-you-go defined benefit systems to funded (investment based) defined contribution systems, often with some form of conditional defined benefit guarantee. Other combinations are possible. A government defined benefit plan can be financed by accumulating a centralized government fund that is invested in new capital. In yet a different approach, some governments are introducing defined contribution plans with individual accounts that are nevertheless operated as a pay-as-you-go system. Such unfunded defined contribution systems provide a notional rate of return, i.e., an accounting rate of return without any real capital accumulation. Such notional unfunded defined contribution systems provide a lower rate of return than a funded system; to be sustainable, the promised return in such an unfunded system must not exceed the rate of growth of total wages.

2. Potential Chinese (Gain from an Investment Based System)

Before discussing the specific features of the current Chinese system, I will use some estimated Chinese figures to discuss the magnitude of the advantage of an investment based system and the extent to which an investment based system can reduce the long-term cost of providing a given level of retirement benefits.

Consider the following example of a PAYGO system. Assume that there are 3 workers per retiree. The benefits given to retirees are 60 percent of the average wage. That implies that the tax rate must be 20 percent of wages. What does it cost to provide the same 60 percent benefit with a funded system? That depends on the future growth of aggregate wages and the future productivity of capital investments.

The World Bank estimates that over the next several decades as a whole real aggregate wages in China will grow at about 7 percent or less per year (World Bank, 1997). I do not know what the marginal product of capital will be in China in the future. But Gregory Chow (1993) estimates that the marginal product of industrial capital in China has been 17 percent, with a higher return on construction and a lower return on residential and retail capital. I will be very conservative and assume that in the future the real marginal return on capital will be only 12 percent. A higher rate of return would make a funded system even more attractive.

What do these two numbers imply? In a pay-as-you-go system the tax "contributions" earn an implicit rate of return equal to the rate of growth of aggregate wages which, looking ahead in China, can be taken to be approximately 7 percent. Consider an individual who contributes to the PAYGO system from age 25 to age 64 and then receives benefits from age 65 to 85. To simplify the calculation so that the nature of the result is transparent, assume that the contributions are all made at the midpoint of the working years (i.e., at age 45) and that the benefits are paid at the midpoint of the retirement years, i.e., at age 75. The funds are therefore earning a 7 percent implicit rate of return for the 30 years from age 45 to age 75. At 7 percent, one dollar saved at age 45 grows to $7.60 at age 75. In these calculations, all amounts are of course measured in the same price levels.

Compare this now with the effect of saving in a funded system with a 12 percent rate of return. One dollar saved at age 45 grows to $30 at age 75, about four times as much as in a PAYGO system in an economy with a 7 percent growth rate of aggregate real wages.

The implication of this is that the funded. system can provide the same level of benefits with a saving rate equal to only one fourth of the rate of tax required in the PAYGO system. If the PAYGO system requires a tax equal to 20 percent of wages to provide a given level of benefits (e.g., benefits equal to 60 percent of concurrent wages), a funded system with a 12 percent rate of return on capital (in comparison to the 7 percent rate of growth of aggregate real wages) can provide the same benefits with savings equal to 5 percent of wages.

This represents an enormous long-run "tax" saving, requiring individuals to set aside 5 percent of their wages during each working year instead of 20 percent. This not only increases the spendable income of future employees but also reduces the distortionary effect and deadweight loss of high marginal tax rates.

This calculation is about the long-run. What about the transition from a pay-as-you-go system to a funded system? Critics of such a transition argue that it would require current employees to "pay double". That seems to imply that if there is a tax equal to 20 percent of wages now, during the transition to a funded system the combination of the tax required to finance existing benefits and the saving required to fund future benefits would be double that or 40 percent.

Such a statement is wrong in two ways. Most important, the cost of funding future benefits is far less than the cost of the PAYGO system, a 5 percent saving rate in comparison to the 20 percent tax rate in the previous example. So the maximum additional cost to current employees would be the 5 percent required to fund their own future retirement annuities. Second, the PAYGO tax that starts at 20 percent would gradually decline over time during a transition as new retirees draw on their funded individual accounts as a source of retirement income.

As a result, a transition is feasible with only a very modest increase in the combined tax-plus-savings rate in the early years and this combined burden would gradually decline and eventually become less than the initial PAYGO tax rate (see Feldstein and Samwick, 1997, 1998).

3. The Current Social Security Pension System in China

Since 1995, most municipalities and provinces in China have adopted a two-part plan for workers in state owned enterprises. The first part of this plan states that retirees in the future will receive a defined benefit financed by a PAYGO system. More specifically, employees who have worked for 40 years are scheduled to receive benefits equal to 25 percent of the regional average wage, with a proportional reduction for those with shorter work histories in these state-owned enterprises. This benefit would be financed by a payroll tax that the authorities estimate will equal 9 percent of wages. This implicitly assumes that there will be about three workers per retiree (literally 25 workers per 9 retirees).

The second part of the plan is a defined contribution system. Current employees and their enterprises contribute 10 percent of wages to individual accounts managed by municipal or provincial authorities. Government calculations imply that the resulting annuity benefits would replace about 35 percent of individual's final year's earnings.

The official guidelines for this plan specify that 80 percent of the accumulated funds are to be invested in government bonds and 20 percent in bank deposits. In practice, some funds are said to be diverted into investments in local projects in pursuit of higher yields. The real returns on government bonds and bank deposits have been very low and in some recent years have actually been negative.

As one considers this new plan, an important question is whether the funding of the defined contribution part really represents new incremental capital? Or is it really just a notional PAYGO plan with no impact on national capital accumulation (as the World Bank implies in its 1997 report)?

This cannot be resolved by looking at the fact that the personal retirement accounts are invested primarily in government bonds. It depends on whether the bonds purchased for the personal retirement accounts would otherwise have been sold to the public (including the banks), thus crowding out other borrowing by enterprises.

If the existence of these defined contribution accounts causes the government of China to run correspondingly larger budget deficits, then there is no increase in capital accumulation and the defined contribution accounts are purely notional investments like any other PAYGO system. This would be true because the government would then have to raise future taxes to pay interest (and possibly principal) on these additional government bonds.

But while that is a logical possibility, I see no reason to believe that the existence of these defined contribution accounts does cause (or will cause) the government of China to run larger budget deficits. If my inference is correct, the additional saving that is accumulated in these defined contribution accounts represent increases in the nation's capital stock. The individuals and financial institutions that would otherwise buy the government bonds purchased by the defined contribution accounts will now buy other private market securities.

What is the rate of return earned on the incremental saving? If I am correct that the defined contribution deposits represent increased national saving and are not offset by increases in the government's budget deficit, the real rate of return on these incremental savings is the double digit marginal product of capital (assuming also that the imperfections and misallocations in the capital markets do not cause too much reduction in the effective rates of return.) This is true at the margin for changes in the defined contribution saving even if the government has a budget deficit and uses some of the defined contribution funds to finance that deficit as long as the amount of deficit financing does not increase with increases in the amount of defined contribution funds.

The fact that the defined contribution accounts are credited with much lower real rates of interest than the 12 percent marginal product of capital reflects an implicit tax that the government levies by requiring these defined contribution balances to be invested in government bonds and bank deposits with low rates of interest, a tax which reached 100 percent in recent years when the real rate of interest was driven to zero.

As restrictions on investments are relaxed in the future, these defined contribution accounts will invest in non-government securities - i.e., in enterprise stocks and bonds - and earn higher returns.

According to official Chinese projections, the 10 percent defined contribution rate is expected to provide an annuity equal to 35 percent of the pre-retirement wage. With a seven percent growth of real wages, this relation between the defined contribution rate and the replacement rate implies a real rate of return of only about 4 percent. If the defined contribution accounts could earn a real return equal to the 12 percent marginal product of capital, the proposed crediting of a four percent real return is equivalent to an effective tax rate of about 65 percent on the defined contribution return.[1]

If broadening the allowable set of investment options eventually allows a higher rate of return, the same benefits can be financed with a lower contribution rate or the same 10 percent contribution rate can be used to obtain a higher level of benefits. For example, doubling the return from 4 percent to 8 percent would permit cutting the contribution rate from 10 percent to 5 percent while simultaneously raising the replacement rate from 35 percent to 60 percent.

The promise of future social security pension benefits can induce households to decrease their own direct saving. The exact extent of this displacement is unclear but a credible promise of benefits equal to more than 60 percent of preretirement wages substantially reduces an individual's perceived need for other retirement income. Such a reduction in other saving can of course only occur if the individuals would otherwise have a high saving rate. As I understand the official Chinese statistics, households currently save a very large fraction of their incomes, an average of more than 25 percent. I do not know how that average is distributed

[1] Since the contribution rate in the individual account is fixed by law, the high tax rate on the return to that saving does not distort saving decisions. The tax is in effect a payroll tax rather than a capital income tax. It distorts work incentives rather than saving incentives. Whether this is a good way to collect such revenue in the Chinese context deserves a careful examination.

among different kinds of employees and between urban and rural sections of the workforce. But with overall saving so high, it is natural to consider the possibility that the provision of social security causes a substantial reduction in other household saving. In the extreme, a funded defined contribution plan could displace an equal amount of existing saving, leaving no net change in national saving. Similarly, a promise of benefits in a PAYGO system could reduce private saving with no offsetting rise in government or pension saving, thus causing a net decease in national saving.

The key point to note is that, regardless of the induced reduction in other saving, a funded plan still causes a higher national saving rate than an unfunded PAYGO plan. The PAYGO plan with the same benefits would displace an equal amount of household saving - but unlike a funded plan would have no pension saving with which to replace it.

4. Alternative Options for the Chinese Defined Benefit Plan

I return now to the first tier of China's new social security pension system: the flat rate benefit equal to 25 percent of the average regional wage for those who have worked the full 40 years.

The rationale for providing such a benefit in addition to the defined contribution annuity is clear: some individuals with low lifetime earnings would have unacceptably low retirement incomes if they had to depend only on the defined contribution plan. The uniform defined benefit part of the pension would raise the total pension income and guarantee that it is at least equal to 25 percent of the average wage in the region.

It is however possible to achieve this goal in a much more cost effective way by modifying this part of the pensions system in either of two ways (or in both ways).

The first possible modification would be to substitute a funded system for the currently planned PAYGO financing. According to official calculations, the PAYGO financing is expected to require a nine percent payroll tax on top of all of the others taxes and mandatory contributions. Substituting a *funded plan* - based on investments in existing government bonds or non-government enterprise securities - could cut the cost by a factor of three or four, from a 9 percent tax to just three percent or less. This would achieve a major reduction in the distortions caused by the Chinese tax system as a whole.

The second possible modification would be to focus or target the defined benefit pension on those with unsatisfactorily low Tier 2 defined contribution pensions instead of giving the full defined benefit payment to all retirees. Stated differently, this part of the overall pension could be a *conditional* defined benefit filling the gap between the defined contribution annuity and the level of retirement income that is regarded as acceptable. If such a reform has the effect of focusing these benefits on the lower income half of annuity recipients, the financing cost would be cut by more than 50 percent.

A targeted or conditional defined benefit pension would not be a general means tested program but would focus on the shortfall associated with the defined contribution plan. It would therefore not have adverse effects on work or other saving. The combined effect of both of these options would be to reduce the required tax from the projected 9 percent to less than 2 percent of earnings.

5. The Transition Path

China must deal with existing retirees and those who will soon retire as well as with the long-term problem of future retirees.

The magnitude of the existing unfunded liabilities to current retirees and workers are particularly difficult to assess in the Chinese context. In the past, retirement benefits were paid by the worker's enterprise without any explicit pension fund or accounting reserves. Often enterprises simply continued to pay the preretirement wage to workers when they reached retirement age and stopped working. These payments to retirees automatically reduced any surplus that the enterprise would otherwise have earned. And if it led the firm to a net loss, that loss would be absorbed by the central government or as non-performing bank loans. In effect, the past system of providing retirement income to employees of state enterprises was effectively a PAYGO system of defined benefits linked to the final wage and administered by the retiree's lifetime workplace.

Now China is adjusting to the change in enterprise ownership and in lifetime work patterns. Even state owned enterprises must face a more rigorous market test and are not supposed to incur losses. As part of this shift to' a more market based system, the enterprises' current pension obligations have been transferred to municipal or provincial governments. Enterprises as a whole are still taxed to meet these inherited obligations but the tax is no longer based on the specific retiree obligations of the particular enterprise.

Although such a shift of obligations from the enterprises to the government may help the transition to a more market based system of corporate management and facilitate greater employee mobility, it is not a necessary concomitant of the move to market based principles for corporate management and employment. In the United States, when companies have unfunded obligations for private pensions, this is reflected in lower share prices (reflecting lower future net earnings). If the unfunded pension obligations are so large that they imply losses in all future years and a negative present value of the company's future earnings, the company is technically bankrupt. Shareholders have no residual value. Pensioners are then paid by a government insurance fund (the Pension Benefit Guarantee Corporation). This is of course the extreme case. Usually, unfunded pension obligations are not that large, leaving a positive stream of future earnings and therefore positive but diminished share values. In Germany and certain other European countries, there is no external funding of private pensions and the unfunded company pension obligations are reflected in earnings and share values. China could in principle have followed this approach, leaving the unfunded obligations with the Chinese enterprises. In practice however this may be harder in present-day China than in the United States or Germany because it is harder to enforce a profitability test on state owned enterprises that lack the discipline of share prices and experienced arms-length banks.

Even with the shift of pension obligations from enterprises to government agencies, there is much talk in China about ways to provide collateral for these obligations. Although explicit government bonds might be a useful way to guarantee a future income stream to the pension beneficiaries, the discussion is generally about providing some form of real capital as collateral. Suggestions include transferring to the pension fund an explicit claim on land rents or on the income generated by some other state owned enterprises. In my judgement, the concern about collateralizing the existing pension obligations with a transfer of existing assets from the state is largely irrelevant. If the local or provincial government now owns an asset, there is no real difference between giving the associated income stream - e.g., the rental income on land or existing housing -- and giving a new government bond with the same stream of payments. Collateralizing the obligation of the government is largely irrelevant. This is particularly true if the obligations are regarded as ultimately the obligations of the central government that have been transferred to municipal and provincial governments for administrative reasons.

It would of course be different if designating some real asset as collateral causes it to be used differently, i.e., if the collateral owner is not merely the passive recipient of an income stream but is able to manage the use of the asset to achieve greater output and profitability. To the extent that the pension reforms can be used to put assets into the hands of better managers with clearer motives and incentives, the result will be to improve the use of China's resources.

But even if shifting assets to entities responsible for pension benefits causes them to be better managed, such a shift is economically efficient only if it leads to the best use of those resources among all the politically feasible options. If it is not, it would increase national income more if China privatized the state assets or land or housing in the most efficient available way and then gave bonds to current employers, employees or pension institutions to acknowledge the government's future obligations. If the World Bank is correct in its assessment of the value of these obligations, the bonds could be amortized over a 40 year period by a tax of about 1.5 percent of GDP.

6. Concluding Comment

China is noteworthy for its decision to develop a mixed system of defined benefit and defined contribution social security pensions. In doing so, it can provide protection for future retirees while strengthening national saving and expanding the market for enterprise securities. A greater emphasis on funded benefits and a shift from an unconditional defined benefit system to a conditional defined benefit guarantee would reduce the distortionary taxes and focus assistance on those in greatest need. The current system focuses on a limited fraction of the population, primarily urban workers in state owned enterprises. But the experience gained in doing this and thinking about this population can provide the basis for a stronger national system that can eventually provide retirement security for the entire Chinese population.

Cambridge, Massachusetts
June 1998

References

1. Chow, Gregory C. "Capital Formation and Economic Growth in China," *Quarterly Journal of Economics,* 1993, 108(3): pp 809-42.
2. Feldstein, Martin. *Privatizing Social Security,* Chicago: University of Chicago Press, 1998.
3. Feldstein, Martin and A. Sarnwick. "The Transition Path in Privatizing Social Security," in *Privatizing Social Security,* Chicago: University of Chicago Press, pp 215-65, 1998.
4. Feldstein, Martin and A. Samwick. "The Economics of Prefunding Social Security and Medicare Benefits," in NBER Macr I Annual 1997, (eds.) B. Bernanke and J. Rotemberg, Cambridge: The MIT Press, pp 115-147,1997.
5. Freidman, Barry and Leonard Hausman. "Sustainable Social Protection in China: Concluding the Reforms." Mimeo, 1998.
6. Hu, Aidi. "Reforming China's Social Security System: Facts and Perspectives," *International Social Security Review,* Vol. 50, No. 3, 1997, pp 45-60.
7. Hussain, Athar. "Social Security in Present-Day China and Its Reform," *American Economic Review,* 84:2,1994, pp 276-80.
8. Samuelson, Paul A. "An Exact Consumption Loan Model of Interest With or Without the Social Contrivance of Money," *Journal of Political Economy,* 1958, Vol. 66, pp 467-82.
9. Song, Shunfeng and G. Chu. "Social Security Reform in China: The Case of Old Age Insurance," in *Contemporary Economic Policy,* April 1997, Vol. XV, pp 85-93.
10. West, Loraine. "Pension Reform in China: Preparing for the Future," *Journal of Development Studies,* forthcoming.
11. The World Bank, *Old Age Security Pension Reform in China*, China 2020 Series, Washington, DC, 1997.

CHAPTER 2

CHINESE SOCIAL INSURANCE REFORM: PERSONAL SECURITY AND ECONOMIC GROWTH

HENRY J. AARON[1]
The Brookings Institution, 1775 Massachusetts Avenue N.W.,
Washington, DC 20036-2188, USA
E-mail: haaron@brook.edu

Throughout the world, nations are restructuring social insurance programs put in place many years ago under more congenial economic circumstances. The reasons for these reforms vary. In some nations, declining birth rates and rising life expectancies are causing large increases in the cost of social insurance. In other nations, a shift in political philosophy has led to modifications in social insurance, the design of which has always divided the political left from the political right. And in still other countries various forms of governmental mismanagement, such as rapid and sustained inflation or poor investment of accumulated pension reserves on ill-considered investments, have caused problems that have undermined the viability of pension systems.

Just as conditions vary from country to country, so also have the reforms that those countries have put in place. Nevertheless, some advisers have tried to lay down a single template to guide social insurance reform in all nations. The World Bank, for example, has set forth in *Averting the Old Age Crisis* (New York, 1994) a general pattern for social insurance reform to be applied everywhere[2]. This study expresses a fundamental confusion in suggesting that particular forms of social insurance can spare active workers the burdens of a growing economically inactive population. These burdens can be reduced only by lowering the living standards of the

---

1 Bruce and Virginia MacLaury Senior Fellow, The Brookings Institution: Chair, National Academy of Social Insurance. The author thanks Peter Heller and especially Peter Diamond for helpful comments and Stacey Carney for research assistance.

2 The World Bank applies this template to China in *China 2020: Old Age Security*, Washington, 1997.

economically inactive or by raising overall economic growth. As I shall show in the remainder of this paper, the promotion of economic growth is equally possible under a wide variety of pension systems. These systems differ greatly, however, in how they distribute the inescapable risks of pension systems across members of society. I shall suggest that funded defined-benefit systems have important advantages in many circumstances over unfunded systems or defined-contribution plans.

I shall begin with some basic propositions regarding social insurance—a taxonomy of social insurance reforms; a basic social insurance identity; and certain principles of social insurance. I shall draw attention to what I think are two fundamental choices in the design of social insurance. The first issue concerns who should bear the risks inescapable under very long term contracts. Social insurance requires individuals to make contributions or pay taxes and then provides benefits over a period that typically runs six decades or even longer. The second issue is whether to use social insurance to add to national saving. Then, I shall apply these observations to the general principles of pension reform as outlined in State Council Document No. 26 issued in July 1997.

1. A Taxonomy of Social Insurance

While quite elementary, the following taxonomy may prove helpful in analyzing the various approaches to reform of social insurance in common use around the world. These plans differ along four fundamental dimensions. Table 1 classifies pension plans according to three of them. Table 2 portrays a series of additional choices.

Table 1: A Partial Taxonomy of Social Insurance

	Funded		Unfunded
	Central Investment Control	Individual Investment Control	
Defined Benefit	Funded Social Insurance	(No system)	Traditional Social Insurance
Defined Contribution	Provident Fund	Personal Accounts	Notional Accounts

Starting with Table 1:

- Do plans call for accumulation of large reserves? Or are all or nearly all current revenues paid out as benefits—so-called "pay-as-you-go" or PAYG financing? Reserve policy can vary smoothly, of course. There may be no reserves at all. Reserves may be sufficient to cover gaps between revenues and benefits that might arise from economic slowdowns—so-called "contingency reserves." Or reserves may be sufficient to pay large benefits for a considerable period of time. Special problems arise when a country tries to move from PAYG to reserve financing. For a period of time, workers not only pay the cost of pensions for current retirees but also bear the cost of building reserves to pay for their own pensions. This phenomenon is often named "the transition problem," a rather misleading term, since the period may last fifty to seventy years, or even longer.
- Are pension benefits provided through so-called "defined-contribution" or DC plans in which pensions are tied to the amounts credited to individual accounts plus returns on investments in which balances in these accounts may be placed? Or are benefits provided through so-called "defined-benefit" or DB plans in which pensions are linked to a worker's earnings and the duration of the worker's career?
- To the extent that reserves are accumulated, who controls the investment of those reserves? Do individuals decide how to invest the reserves held in their names? If so, what rules restrict their choices? Or does some central authority, such as occupational or industrial boards, provincial boards, or the national government allocate savings among alternative investments and determine rates of return?

As Table 1 indicates, these three dimensions define the major types of social insurance. Tranditional social insurance is unfunded and defined-benefit. Chile and Argentina have recently replaced or supplemented traditional social insurance—unfunded, defined-benefit plans—with personal accounts—funded, defined-contribution plans, with individual investment control. Sweden is now converting its system to one that is based largely on notional accounts, an unfunded system under which benefits are based on amounts credited annually to an account for each worker, plus investment returns imputed on the basis of a complex formula. Singapore and several other nations have long provided retirement benefits through a provident fund, a system in which benefits are based on individual deposits plus the overall return on centrally managed investments[3].

Within each of these types of social insurance, various aspects of program design are of particular importance to pensioners, to workers, and to the government. One concerns rules governing the payment of benefits. Are benefits paid only as annuities? May pensioners take their payments as lump sums or pass them on to heirs? Are pensioners given limited choice among a small number of payment schedules? Another aspect concerns whether payments are indexed—that is, adjusted automatically for price changes. A third set of issues concerns the pension protections provided surviving spouses of workers who have died.

Table 2 shows a grid of possibilities for indexation and rules for the payment of benefits.

Table 2: Program Design Options

	Payment Options		
	Annuity Only	Limited Payment Option	Unlimited Payment Choice
Indexed	(1)	(3)	(5)
Not Indexed	(2)	(4)	(6)

Option 1 provides pensioners with greatest security—a pension guaranteed to provide a given real payment for as long as the pensioner lives. It corresponds to the rules governing pensions in most developed nations. Option 2 corresponds to the rules governing pension payouts under plans that require annuitization. Option 6 provides pensioners with the greatest choice, but least security. It corresponds to defined contribution plans in which saving is mandatory, but investments and withdrawals are unrestricted. I know of no real-world examples of option 5, which would correspond to a defined-contribution plan that required pensioners to invest in index bonds but imposed no restrictions on withdrawals. Option 3 and 4 correspond to defined-contribution plans under which pensioners are given several withdrawal options, but are neither permitted to withdraw funds as they wish nor required to accept an annuity. Defined-benefit plans all fall under options 1 or 2. Defined-contribution plans may fall under any of the six options.

3 Distinctions among these categories of plans are unclear. The Swedish system of notional account bears considerable resemblance to a defined-benefit plan in which benefits are based on total life-time earnings and the benefit formula is adjusted automatically for longevity and average earnings in the economy.

2. The Social Insurance Cost Identity

The cost of social insurance measured as a proportion of current income, *c*, is identically equal to the product of three ratios:

- a Demographic Ratio, equal to the number of social insurance beneficiaries (R) divided by the number of active workers (W);
- an Adequacy Ratio, equal to the average pension payments per beneficiary (B) divided by the average past income or earnings that beneficiaries received while active workers (E_P); and
- an Economic Growth ratio, equal to average past income or earnings of pensioners divided by average current income of active workers (E_W).

As economic growth slows, this ratio increases. In symbols:

$$c \equiv \underbrace{(R/W)}_{\text{Demographic Ratio}} \times \underbrace{(B/E_P)}_{\text{Adequacy Ratio}} \times \underbrace{(E_P/E_W)}_{\text{Economic Growth Ratio}}.$$

This formula provides a natural framework for explaining why the cost of social insurance in developed nations has risen in the recent past and is projected to rise much more in the future. Slowed earnings growth in developed countries means that changes in the Economic Growth ratio have also tended to raise costs. Replacement rates—the ratio of pensions to average earnings—have not changed much in developed nations in recent decades. It also clarifies why the existing pay-as-you-go system in China is unsustainable. The Chinese Demographic Ratio, R/W, has risen sharply as R has increased from 8.2 million in 1980 to more than 30 million today. This ratio is projected to rise still more, as falling birth rates lead inevitably to slowing growth in the labor force, and as rising life-expectancies increase the number of people who live to an age at which they are eligible to receive pensions. Replacement rates were projected to rise in China, as the proportion of retirees who had worked under the pension system long enough to qualify for full benefits increased.

In response to rising price of social insurance, most nations are proving once again the truth of the most fundamental law of economics, the law of demand. This law states, quite simply, that when price rises—in this case, the price is *c*—the quantity demanded—in this case, the desired quantity of social insurance per beneficiary—tends to fall. Total expenditures on social insurance may rise, as is possible in the face of any price increase, but the desired amount of coverage is falling.

2.1 Applicability of the Identity

The Social Insurance Cost identity, relating the cost of social insurance to three ratios, is simply an identity that decomposes changes in costs into three mutually exclusive and exhaustive components. The identity applies equally, therefore, to all of the pension variants shown in Table 1. The identity shows the proportion of current production that retirees consume under a funded, defined-contribution plan, just as it shows, for example, the cost of traditional social insurance—pay-as-you-go, unfunded, defined-benefit plans. When the number of beneficiaries increases, the replacement rate rises, or income (or earnings) growth slows, the amount of current production that retirees consume rises in exactly the same way under all forms of social insurance as it does under traditional systems. The only question is whether at some time in the past those who are currently retired added to national saving and investment enough to increase current production as much as their retirement consumption absorbs from current production. It is important to note that it does not matter whether this added saving takes place through social insurance, other taxation, or voluntary private saving—the critical quantity is the proportion of their incomes that retirees saved.

This identity provides a simple explanation of why the cost of the social insurance system under which China has operated for the past two decades would have reached such high levels if that system were not replaced. The Adequacy Ratio is very high by international pension standards. The Demographic Ratio and the Economic Growth ratio will both contribute to rising costs. Because these effects on costs are multiplied, they would have generated devastatingly heavy burdens. These high costs would have necessitated action, even if the costs had been distributed evenly across enterprises and regions. The unevenness of the distribution of burden would have made pension reform even more urgent as China moves to a market-based economy.

2.2 The Demographic Ratio

The Demographic Ratio is determined, over the long run, by three numbers:

- the birth rate,

- mortality rates, and
- the proportion of the adult population that works.

I assume that in light of the extended campaign to hold down birth rates in China, a policy of raising birth rates in order to lower future social insurance costs is not an instrument many Chinese would espouse. It goes without saying that intentionally lowering life expectancy is not an instrument for controlling the costs of social insurance that any civilized society would embrace, although the necessity of allocating given health care spending between children and the elderly can affect the relative life expectancies at various ages.

The only practical way of influencing the Demographic Ratio, therefore, is by changing the proportion of the adult population that works, especially by shifting the age of retirement. Changes in the age at which people retire can dramatically alter pension costs. In an extreme and hypothetical case, assume that all age cohorts are of identical size, everyone starts working at age 20, and everyone lives exactly to age 80. In such a situation, the cost of a given social insurance benefit is approximately 1.5 times larger if people all retire at age 60 than it would be if all retire at age 65[4]. Once again, the effect on cost of eligibility ages is the same whether the system is funded or not, whether it is defined-benefit or defined-contribution, and however investment is controlled[5]. In short, setting the age of initial entitlement is a critically important influence on program cost; but the effect is the same under any type of social insurance.

One new study suggests that pensions significantly influence people's decisions on when to retire in two ways[6]. First, because most people save little voluntarily in most of the countries covered in this study, people retire at sharply higher rates in the year pension benefits are first paid. The availability of the pension appears to make retirement possible for workers who wanted to stop

---

4 In fact, of course, mortality causes older age cohorts to be smaller than younger age cohorts, which tends to make the effect on cost of a higher retirement age ever larger. In addition, not everyone is working at "the retirement age" and no everyone who is working at that age retires upon reaching that age. To the extent that raising the age of entitlement causes some people to defer retirement, the reduction in pension cost from raising the age of entitlement is increased.

5 The statement in the text assumes that the economic consequences for the worker of deferring claim of benefits is the same in each case. Under defined-contribution plans, the lifetime expected value of benefits is usually unaffected by when the worker claims benefit. Under defined-benefit plans, the lifetime expected value of benefits may fall with continued work if the deferred benefit is not increased sufficiently to offset the reduced period over which the benefit will be paid. This feature of DB plans may raise or lower the effect on program cost of raising age of entitlement.

6 Jonahan Gruber and David Wise, "Introduction and Summary," Social Security Programs and Retirement Around the World, National Bureau of Economic Research, forthcoming.

working but lacked the financial means to do so. Second, the rate of retirement at the age of first entitlement rises still more if pensions for those who continue working do not compensate them for the loss of the pension payment while they work. If pension entitlements rise significantly for workers who delay claiming benefits, retirement is more gradual than if pensions do not increase when workers defer retirement. If pensions are not increased and are generous, as they are in many developed nations, most workers retire at the age of initial entitlement or soon thereafter.

2.3 The Adequacy Ratio

The effect of the Adequacy Ratio—the ratio of retiree benefits to their previous earnings—on program costs is obvious. Again, the transfer of goods from active workers to retirees is the same whether that transfer arises from a defined-benefit or defined-contribution pensions, from a funded or unfunded system, or from a system with centralized or decentralized management of investments. Pension replacement rates in developed countries range from as high as 70 percent of earnings, payable at age 60 (and earlier in a few countries) to as little as 40 percent payable at age 62. Once again, the total cost to active workers of supporting retirees is not limited to the pension, but depends on total living standards of pensioners.

2.4 The Growth Ratio

The focus of much debate on social insurance centers on how the form of social insurance affects the growth of earnings—that is to say, how social insurance contributes to or hinders aggregate economic growth. Earnings per worker depends on four factors:

- the level of training of workers;
- the quantity and quality of capital;
- the pace of technological advance; and
- the efficiency with which the means of production are organized and used — that is, on management or economic organization.

Some studies allege that social insurance affects workers' interest in securing training, but the effects are almost certainly small compared to other influences and easily overwhelmed by them. Social insurance could promote technological advance and the more efficient use of available resources by increasing the flexibility of labor markets and facilitating the transfer of labor from outmoded or inefficient enterprises to new and more efficient enterprises. Indeed, this justification for reform of social insurance in China is, perhaps, the most important reason for current action. To accomplish this purpose, pension portability is highly important. Defined-contribution plans can be portable, whether provided through government, through business enterprises, or by workers themselves. In contrast, defined-benefit plans can be portable only if publicly managed.

The most widely discussed channel through which social insurance can affect the Economic Growth ratio is by changing the rate of capital formation or affecting the allocation of investment. *Nonetheless, it is vital to recognize that it is the volume of aggregate national saving that counts for economic growth—not whether that saving is generated by the centralized accumulation of social insurance reserves, individual saving accounts, enterprise profits, or government budget surpluses outside pension accounts.* And it is how efficiently those savings are allocated to high-productivity investments that determines whether additions to capital produce growth in overall ("total-factor") productivity or simply contribute to the accumulation of large volumes of capital goods.

While accumulation of social insurance reserves *may* boost saving and raise economic growth, such a result is not assured. Individuals may offset some or all of the accumulation of reserves (whether in central reserves or individual accounts) by reducing other forms of saving. Governments may offset some or all reserve accumulation by running larger deficits or smaller surpluses than they would otherwise do on other operations of government. And state-owned enterprises may find themselves with smaller retained reserves from which to finance investment because of the costs of contributions to create social insurance reserves.

In the case of China, one cannot help wondering whether building social insurance reserves will actually increase the extremely high current rates of capital accumulation. Might not the accumulation of social insurance reserves cause reductions in saving elsewhere in the economy? Should such offsets occur, building social insurance reserves would add nothing to capital formation, however large social insurance reserves might become. And even if total national saving is increased, it would be important to consider whether productive outlets for such enormous saving flows could be found on a sustained basis. The experiences of several other Asian nations suggest caution. Extremely high saving rates supported rapid growth in national output for many years in several Asian nations, but evidence is now accumulating that much of that saving was misallocated to projects of marginal value.

3. Risk and Returns

All long term commitments are risky. Social insurance plans are very long term, lasting six decades or more. They begin when workers first enter the labor force and continue until the last retirement pension is paid to the worker or the worker's surviving dependents. Any such plan, in which cumulative benefits cannot exceed cumulative taxes and other revenues, is extremely risky.

The risks are of three general kinds:

- Risks arising from the emergence of imbalances in the system as a whole that require modifications in overall benefits or taxes,
- Risks external to the pension system that affect its sustainability, including exchange rates and withdrawal of political support, including a failure to honor pension commitments and confiscation of reserves, and
- Risks confronting individual worker-pensioners from factors that affect them directly.

Economic and demographic variables that affect balance in the overall system include average interest rates, growth of labor productivity, labor-force participation rates, birth rates, and mortality rates. Each worker may be affected by his or her experience with each of these variables.

3.1 System Risk

No defined-benefit pension plan can credibly promise to sustain a particular ratio of benefits to earnings under all circumstances. No defined-contribution plan can promise to sustain a given contribution or tax rate under all circumstances. These two statements mean that periodic adjustments in replacement rates, tax rates, or both are inescapable under both DB and DC plans if economy-wide variables relevant to pension costs differ from those on which the plans are based. The political circumstances in which these adjustments are made will differ, possibly in important ways, but the belief that either type of pension system will be free of the need for periodic legal changes is a delusion.

Why DB Plans Require Adjustments. A simple example indicates why DB plans that promise constant replacement rates are almost certain to require change.

Consider a population in which everyone begins work at age 20, retires at age 65, and dies at age 75. Each retiree receives an annual pension of 100 percent of his or her average lifetime earnings. The average birth rate is initially 3 children per woman and earnings grow at an annual rate of 3 percent. The payroll tax on active workers necessary to pay for the promised benefit under these assumptions is 5.8 percent.

Now assume that the birth rate falls to 1.5 children per woman, earnings growth slows to 1 percent, and people live to age 80. The tax rate necessary to pay benefits under these new conditions will eventually reach nearly 58 percent, a ten-fold increase. Put another way, it would be possible to maintain the initial tax or contribution rate only if the replacement rate were cut 90 percent. Confronted with the news that it will take a tax rate of this size to sustain benefits, people are likely to conclude that benefit cuts and tax increases are both desirable.

This example, although highly artificial, bears considerable resemblance to the shift in circumstances some western European social democracies have experienced and will experience. *These examples illustrate why some long term variation in tax (or contribution) rates, replacement rates, or both under any DB plan is unavoidable, in practice.*

Why DC Plans Require Adjustments. DC plans require periodic adjustment because the contribution rate necessary to build a sufficient fund to support retirement pensions varies with wage growth and real interest rates[7].

Table 3: Actual Replacement Rates as Percent of Target Replacement Rate

	Germany	Japan	United Kingdom	United States
Pension contribution based on interest rates and wages rate growth during first half period	261	255	233	342
Pension contribution based on interest rates and wages rate growth during second half period	41	40	43	30

Source: Lawrence Thompson, "Risks of Mid-Career Economic and Demographic Changes, *Issue Brief #9*, The Stockholm Initiative, International Social Security Association, September 1997

7 I ignore the adjustment problems that would arise if interest rates change just before an older worker buys an annuity, which could convert what seemed to be the "right" amount of savings into a grossly excessive or insufficient accumulation.

One study has calculated the ratio of actual to intended benefits that would have been generated in four industrialized countries—Germany, Japan, the United Kingdom, and the United States—if they had enacted defined-contribution pension plans in 1953 that remained in place until 1995. The calculations shown in Table 3 are done under two assumptions.

The first set assumes that the pension plan is calibrated to achieve a target replacement rate of 50 percent based on completely accurate forecasts of real interest rates and the growth of real earnings in the period from 1953 through 1973, the first half of the 42-year period over which the pension plan would have operated. Given actual interest rates and wage rate growth over the entire 42-year period, such a plan would have provided replacement rates ranging from 2.3 to 3.4 times as large as intended. The second set of results shows replacement rates that would have resulted if the plan had been based on actual interest rates and growth of real wages over the period from 1974 through 1995. Such projections are of interest because interest rates and growth of earnings could easily have followed a pattern that was the reverse of the time sequence actually observed. The second set of projections shows that replacement rates would have been 30-43 percent of what was intended. *These examples illustrate why some long term variation in tax (or contribution) rates, replacement rates, or both under any DC plan is unavoidable, in practice.*

3.2 Risks External to the System

Pension systems everywhere are subject to political risks originating outside the pension system. Because of a foreign exchange crisis, for example, a government may force pension fund managers or banks—private or public—to invest pension reserves in government bonds, the real value of which, subsequent devaluation and ensuing inflation seriously erode. Governments may require that pension reserves be invested in assets that have low yields or, in extreme cases, may force interest-free loans.

Both defined-benefit and defined-contribution plans are subject to such risks, but they arise in different forms. Under unindexed defined-benefit plans, the government may fail to adjust benefits for inflation in order to cut budget costs when plans are unfunded or to provide additional reserves for investment in designated projects under funded plans. Indexing defined-benefit plans therefore establishes a political commitment, visible to the entire population, that may limit the ability of the government to renege on pension commitments. Commitments under defined-contribution plans, in which reserves are invested in government bonds, deposits in state-owned banks, or other designated investments, are particularly easy to escape because the government can lower pension obligations by its control over interest rates paid on reserves. The obstacles to reneging on defined-contribution pension commitments are greater if assets are invested by individuals in assets of their choice, but such systems are also vulnerable, as governments can—and, in practice always do closely regulate the investments of individual accounts.

Although any pension fund established by government can be modified by government, the political economy and long-term evolution of defined-benefit and defined-contribution plans under conditions of political or economic adversity may be rather different. Once again, the obligations of neither defined-benefit nor defined-contribution plans are immune to erosion from external economic and political forces. The best protection for pensioners is clear and unequivocal commitment by the government to provide identified benefits so that failure to deliver on those promises entails high political costs. On this criterion, indexed defined-benefit plans probably rank highest.

3.3 Summary on System and External Risk

Both defined-benefit and defined-contribution plans are subject to uncertainties that make it impossible as a practical matter permanently to hold constant the key variable each type of plan purports to stabilize—replacement rates, in the case of DB plans, and contribution rates in the case of DC plans. In both types of plans, periodic legislative corrections are almost certain to be necessary to assure that the programs come close to achieving stated objectives. *The claim often made that DB plans are inherently unstable, while DC plans are self-correcting and stable is false. Both are inherently unstable. Neither system is self-correcting. Both require periodic legislative changes. Both are therefore subject to political risk.* But the political conditions in which these adjustments occur may be rather different.

It is easy and gratifying for political leaders to deal with outcomes that are more favorable than expected. Dealing with the consequences of unfavorable developments can be extremely divisive—as French premier Jacques Chirac recently discovered when he proposed to cut back on social insurance benefits or as President Suharto recently found out in much more extreme conditions. The absence of a promise to deliver a specific benefit under defined-contribution plans means that gradual erosion of promises is not a clearly definable event, as it is under defined-benefit plans. All that a defined-contribution plan promises is a given contribution; if benefits turn out lower than originally indicated, no pledge has been broken. All that defined-benefit plans promise is a given benefit; if costs of meeting commitments turn out to be higher than anticipated and taxes or contributions must be increased, no pledge has been broken.

From the standpoint of government, provisions that permit easy escape from pension promises if conditions turn out less favorable than anticipated have important attractions. From the standpoint of workers and pensioners, these provisions have major drawbacks. Choosing the proper balance between credible commitment to pay benefits and retention of fiscal flexibility by the government is a difficult and subtle matter. The new Swedish system of notional accounts, for example, automatically lowers initial retirement benefits when the growth of earnings slows or life expectancy increases. Each age cohort receives a benefit based on its life expectancy, and benefits are increased after payments begin only to the extent that aggregate wage growth exceeds a specified threshold. As a second example, many U.S. analysts favor cutting retirement benefits in proportion to the increase in life expectancy so that the present expected value of lifetime benefits is unchanged. It would be possible to automatically raise the age of initial entitlement to benefits to achieve the same result. These rules provide a modest measure of flexibility.

The requirement under State Council Document #26 that reserves accumulated through the second tier of the plan be invested in government bonds or state banks, in contrast, provides the government with much greater control over benefits than does either the Swedish or U.S. systems. The requirement that all reserves in the mandatory saving plan must be invested in government bonds would mean that the government can control pension costs by varying the interest rate it pays on these bonds. Variations in interest rates can be used to raise or lower benefits if key economic or demographic variables differ from those assumed in the design of the plan.

Unfortunately, this same provision places workers and pensioners at risk. It also would create a continuing temptation to government officials, who could raise large sums for state purposes without the need to raise taxes or explicitly cut government spending. Officials could simply hold down the interest rate paid on pension accumulations, whether or not underlying conditions warrant larger payments. On balance, I believe that if individuals are required to invest only in government bonds, the statute establishing personal accounts should state clearly and unequivocally that interest rates paid on those accounts should be tied directly to market rates of interest. Depositors should be informed clearly that the government is committed to paying these rates, and that this policy will not be modified.

3.4 Personal Risk

Even if a pension plan never becomes unbalanced in the aggregate, individual workers face risks that will influence the size of the pension they eventually receive. Their wage rates may be higher or lower than expected. Similarly, a worker may encounter more or less unemployment, die earlier or live longer, experience higher or lower interest rates, or experience more or less inflation than expected. Defined-benefit and defined-contribution plans handle these risks in different ways. In general, defined-benefit plans spread risks more broadly across current and future workers and retirees than do defined-contribution plans. In general, defined contribution plans require workers and retirees to shoulder more risk as individuals than do defined-benefit plans, although defined-contribution plans differ in how much risk they permit (or encourage) workers to bear.

Interest Rates and Asset Prices. Fluctuations in interest rates and asset prices are unimportant in unfunded plans, unless they affect tax revenues that indirectly support the pension plan. Under funded DB plans, variability in interest rates or asset prices affects pensioners only as it necessitates changes in overall benefit formulas or tax rates. In these cases, benefits or taxes for most people covered by a system are likely to be affected by a small amount. Under DC plans, however, fluctuations in interest rates and asset prices, even if they occur around some correctly forecast economy-wide trend that does not cause system changes, will affect the pensions that individual workers receive. The effects can be quite large. One U.S. study has simulated the replacement rates that would have resulted if workers had contributed a constant fraction of their earnings to a personal pension fund that earned the average return generated by common stocks in the United States and that was used to buy an annuity when the worker retired. This study finds that the replacement rates of workers who reached retirement age in 1976 would have been 60 percent smaller than the replacement rates of workers who retired just seven years earlier. This huge difference arises for three reasons:

- workers under this hypothetical plan purchased assets at different prices, depending on their age;

- they sold their assets at different prices depending on when they reached retirement age; and
- their savings purchased annuities of different value depending on interest rates when they retired.

All workers in this example are assumed to follow the same investment strategy. If workers are permitted to invest in different assets, as they may do in the United Kingdom, additional variation in pensions for workers of the same age and with the same earnings will also result. If the goal of a retirement system is to assure a basic income on retirement, it is difficult to understand the purpose that is served by such variability in benefits. A defined-benefit plan enjoys a clear advantage if the goal is to make sure that retirees have access to a pension of a given size.

Individual Management of Investments. Individual funds management not only raises the risks that workers face, it also lowers average returns because of administrative costs. Workers who invest funds themselves will earn the same rates of return, exclusive of administrative costs, as would be earned if funds were managed centrally and invested in portfolios roughly similar to those selected by individuals as a group. However, defined-contribution accounts are more costly to administer than are defined benefit plans.

The differences in pension accumulations can be quite large, as experience in the United Kingdom and Chile shows. Even a 1-percent annual charge reduces the amount that a person can accumulate over 40 years by roughly 25 percent. A 2-percent annual charge reduces the accumulation by roughly 41 percent.[8] Administrative costs in the British system of individual accounts, for example, have generated annual administrative costs averaging roughly 1.6 to 2 percent of fund balances for typical savers[9]. The Chilean system has been sullied by enormous waste generated through frequent shifting of funds among accounts which

---

8 The precise reduction depends on the investment return before deduction of administrative costs. The higher the return before administrative costs, the larger the percentage loss inflicted by a given charge.

9 Peter Diamond, "Macroeconomic Aspects of Social Security Reform," *Brookings Papers on Economic Activity*: 2, 1997. The estimate of 2 percent is based on average administrative charges as estimated by the chief actuary of the United Kingdom, as reported by Peter Diamond, assuming that each depositor saves 5 percent of earnings equal to what a median U.S. worker covered by the United State Social Security system earns. Since U.S. incomes are approximately 60 percent higher than those in the United Kingdom, British median earnings would be lower and administrative costs higher, because of fixed costs. The 1.6 percent estimate assumes that earnings are 2,5 times as high as in the former case.

advertising campaigns carried out by large sales staffs financed by approved investment organizations have encouraged[10].

The average investment returns, apart from administrative costs, on funds invested through individual accounts cannot differ much from the average returns on funds channeled into similar assets through a central fund. If reserves are held to help finance a basic, assured replacement rate, giving individuals discretion to shift funds among alternative investments simply raises administrative costs and, for that reason, raises the tax rate necessary to sustain that benefit. *Furthermore, in countries where capital markets are not developed sufficiently to provide a wide range of investment assets, meaningful choice cannot be exercised by individuals in any event.* State Council Document No. 26 recognizes this simple fact by requiring that balances held in mandatory individual accounts, beyond those necessary to cover benefit payments for the succeeding two months, be invested in government bonds. No other domestic investment option is now feasible, given the state of development of Chinese capital markets. Even if a wider range of assets should become available in the future, individual management of investments would remain inadvisable under any pension plan intended to reach a modest target replacement rate.

Longevity Risk. Defined-benefit plans in practice all provide annuities. Defined-contribution plans may require that retirees convert accumulations into annuities, but many do not do so. Pensioners may be permitted to withdraw funds according to one of several prescribed schedules. Or retirees may withdraw funds after retirement as they wish or retain them for bequests to children or other relatives.[11] It is hard to see why voluntary savers should be subject to any significant restrictions on withdrawals. But the purpose of mandatory saving—apart from a possible goal of raising national saving—is to make sure that individuals have

---

10 The average annual cost of United States mutual funds, in which most retirement funds held in individual accounts are invested, is currently approximately 1.25 percent, and these costs are rising.

11 If the purchase of annuities is optional, those who wish to buy pension will encounter additional costs, based on experience in the United States. Insurance companies' administrative costs average approximately 10 percent of the price of annuity. In addition, insurance companies must take account of the fact that people who expect to die soon are unlikely to wish to buy annuities. For that reason, the life expectancy of people who buy annuities is higher than average. To take account of this fact, insurance companies must charge an additional fee to cover this so-called "adverse selection." This fee adds an additi0onal 10 percent to the price of annuity. For U.S. information, see Olivia S. Mitchell, James M. Poterba, and Mark J. Warshawsky, "New Evidence on the Money's Worth of Individual Annuities." National Bureau of Economic Research Working Paper, No. 6002.

adequate incomes after retirement or some adversity. The only way to assure that this target is met is to limit withdrawals to annuities or some other fixed schedule.

Spouse Protection. In most nations, men earn more than women on the average, but women's life expectancy is higher than men's. Since pensions are related directly to earnings under both defined-benefit plans and indirectly under defined-contribution plans, many women are at risk of ending their lives with insufficient income, unless pension rules protect them. It is possible to protect women fully only by providing explicit widows protection under a defined-benefit plan or requiring that accumulations under defined-contribution plans be converted into annuities that continue until both spouses have died. If funds can be withdrawn freely from defined-contribution plans, women are unprotected.

4. Funded *versus* Unfunded Plans

The returns to funding may be measured at the level of the nation or of the individual worker. These returns need not be the same and, in fact, almost always differ.

4.1 Returns to the Nation

When *national* saving is undesirably low, accumulations of pension reserves—under either DB or DC plans—can raise saving in a politically sustainable way. As is always the case, an increase in saving lowers consumption in the near term and raises potential consumption in the future. Compared to unfunded plans, funded plans—defined-benefit or defined-contribution—lower living standards in the short run, but increase them in the long run. Both require sacrifices from the current population. Either retirees must forego pensions so that reserves can be accumulated, or workers must pay taxes sufficient not only to support pensions but also to build pension reserves. There is a difference between funded and unfunded plans in their effects on national saving, but no difference between funded DB and funded DC plans.

The Chinese national saving rate—now over 30 percent of gross domestic product—is already among the highest in the world. In addition, China is an attractive focus of foreign investment. Continuing to find productive outlets for so much domestic saving and imported capital will pose major challenges. Whether further increases in the national saving rate are desirable is unclear, because of the difficulty, which grows as saving increases, of investing in ways that will yield high rates of return. Experience in other Asian nations that have generated very high rates of saving over extended periods suggests caution. While high domestic saving and capital imports fueled rapid growth in those nations for many years, they also led to ill-considered investments that have precipitated economic crises.[12]

The choice is straightforward—if China does not want still higher rates of capital formation than those already achieved, the accumulation of sizeable reserves in the social insurance system loses much of its rationale. The accumulation of social insurance reserves, might well lead to reductions in saving elsewhere—smaller saving through enterprises or reduction in individual saving, for example. If China wishes still higher rates of capital formation than the very high levels already achieved, the accumulation of social insurance reserves is a way of doing so that should be considered along with alternative means. Furthermore, the decision to build reserves can be achieved under either defined-benefit or defined-contribution systems.[13]

---

12 Paul Krugman was among the first to point out that he rapid growth of investment accounted for nearly all of the growth in output per worker in certain south Asian countries. Studies of western countries have shown, in contrast, that most growth in output per worker arises not from increases in the quantity of capital but from improvements in overall productivity that is distinct from additional quantities of capital. Since he potential for added saving to add to growth declines if overall productivity does not increase, this issue is central for sustained growth of living standards. In mathematical terms, assume a linear production function where output (O) depends on labor (L), capital (K), and a productivity indicator (A) that varies over time and with changes in public policy, of the form $O=Af(K,L)$. The increase in output per unit of capital is simply dO/dK. This term falls as capital per worker increases, unless offset by increases in A.

13 Defined-contribution accounts may have one political advantage over funded defined-benefit systems. The ownership of a savings account may serve a function similar to the one envisaged by the Tsarist agrarian reformer, Pyotr Stolypin, who provided Russian peasants with the opportunity to buy and sell land in the hope of creating a prosperous, stable and loyally conservative class of farmers. While this efforts failed for a variety of reasons, the political insight behind he reform, which bears some resemblance to the creation of personal retirement accounts, may well be sound.

4.2 Returns to Workers

A decision to build pension reserves is a decision to lower consumption of workers during the period when reserves are built in order to increase the consumption of workers in the more distant future. The effects are the same under funded defined-benefit and funded defined-contribution plans. It is essential not to confuse the question of whether or not to build reserves to support future accruals of pension rights with the question of how to deal with the unfunded liability created by China's previous unfunded pay-as-you-go system. If that unfunded liability is honored, it will have to be met by some combination of taxes or contributions. The size of the unfunded liability depends on the part of benefits promised by the old system that the government is determined to honor.

The immediate return to workers under a *new* PAYG system would be very high, as it is under all newly established unfunded systems. Eventually workers would receive a rate of return equal to the rate of growth of the revenue base used to pay for the new system. World Bank projections of labor-force and real wage growth indicate that the urban wage base will grow at the following rates

Decade	***Average Annual Real Growth Of Urban Wage Base***
2000 — 2010	7.6 percent
2010 — 2020	5.4 percent
2020 — 2030	3.6 percent

In later years, the World Bank projects slower growth in the urban wage base. Whether returns to workers would be higher or lower under a funded system than they would be under an unfunded system depends on the real returns generated by the assets in which reserves are invested. *Since reserves, by State Council Document No. 26, are to be invested exclusively in government bonds, the real return to workers is under the control of the government.* This return may well differ from the social return to added investment. I shall return to this feature of the proposed Chinese system presently.

5. Applications to Chinese Pension Reform

State Council Document #26 follows proposals of the World Bank rather closely. It calls for the creation of a rather small first tier unfunded, defined benefit plan that would pay pensions equal to approximately 20 percent of the average earnings in a worker's province, region, or city. In addition, a mandatory second tier funded, defined-contribution saving plan would be created to which 11 percent of earnings (3 percent by enterprises, 8 percent by workers) will *eventually* be contributed and on the basis of which an annual benefit equal to 10 percent of the fund balance will be paid. In addition, there would be a third tier made up of voluntary private saving. Tax rates would be uniform across the nation except for small variations in rates allowed in areas where retirees constitute an especially large proportion of the population. While this proposal holds important implications for the pension system, its most important roll will be as an instrument to facilitate the transformation of the Chinese economy into a market-based system. Based on the principles I have examined in this paper, I will conclude by posing certain questions that the government may wish to consider in deciding the specific provisions of pension reform.

5.1 Personal Security

The combined first and second tier will provide rather generous benefits—at least for workers with lengthy working careers during good economic times. The first tier benefit, however, is quite meager by international standards. The heavy dependence on second tier benefits could expose workers to serious risks, as shown in table 4.

A worker who is employed and contributes to the second tier account for 40 years, experiences annual increases in real earnings of 3 percent throughout his career, and earns a real annual interest rate on deposits of 5 percent will receive a second tier pension equal to 53 percent of final earnings. In combination with the first tier, this pension would replace approximately 73 percent of earnings, a quite generous replacement rate, provided that the third tier of the World Bank plan is significant. A 35-year worker earns a total combined first tier and second tier benefit of 66 percent—still a high replacement rate.

Table 4: Illustrative Replacement Rates under Alternative Circumstances
(percent of earnings during final working year)

	40 year Career	35 year Career
3 percent real annual earnings growth, 5 percent interest rate	73	66
3 percent real annual earnings growth, 3 percent interest rate	57	53
---with unanticipated 10 percent annual inflation during last ten working years	39	38
---with unindexed second tier benefits and 10 percent annual inflation, ten years after retirement	27	27
---with unindexed second tier benefits and 10 percent annual inflation, twenty years after retirement	23	23

Unfortunately, these benefits are not secure. If inflation strikes unexpectedly in the last ten years of the worker's career and the government bonds in which pension reserves are invested are not inflation-indexed, the second tier benefit will be worth only 19 percent of final earnings and the combined replacement rate will be only 39 percent. If inflation continues at 10 percent annually after the worker retires and the second tier pension is not indexed for inflation, the retiree will see the value of his second tier pension erode, until it has a real purchasing power equal to only 7 percent of final-year earnings. Even if the first tier benefit is indexed, the combined replacement rate would fall to only 27 percent. After an additional ten years in retirement, the replacement rate would be only 23 percent.

I have gone into some detail regarding the effect of inflation to illustrate the sensitivity of defined-contribution pension plans to unanticipated events. Smaller problems could arise if workers are forced to retire with thirty or fewer years of contributions. On the other hand, favorable surprises could easily push benefits much higher than the most favorable example shown in table 4. For example, an unexpected decline in inflation could leave bond holders with very high real rates of return that would result in replacement rates well over 100 percent, as the examples in table 2 showed. *The point of this illustration is to pose the question of whether it is wise social policy to rely on pension rules that result in such large uncertainty regarding the pensions that workers will receive.* Such uncertainties are inherent in defined-contribution plans. This uncertainty can be reduced if a larger part of a worker's pension is derived from defined-benefit plans where benefits are related to lifetime earnings, rather than to financial market variables, and are adjusted automatically for inflation.

5.2 Economic Growth

I have noted that reserve accumulation serves little purpose if saving from other sources is abundant. In that case accumulation of social insurance reserves may well lead to offsetting declines in saving in other parts of the economy. And, even if it does not, excessive saving can lead to poor project selection, as it has done in some Asian countries.

On the other hand, if reserve accumulation is to be used to increase national saving, there is no good reason why only the defined-contribution part of the plan should build reserves. Since the Chinese draft plan calls for investing all second tier reserves in government bonds or state banks, government-designated financial agencies or the government itself will determine the real assets in which the resulting deposits are invested. Individuals will exercise no control over how funds are invested. Individual control of the investment of pension reserves will not really be possible, even if it were desirable, until Chinese financial markets are more fully developed. Even then, as I have pointed out, individual control over investment of pension reserves, on the Chilean or British models, generates large administrative costs that seriously erode pension accumulations. In general, it makes as much sense to build reserves under the first tier plan as under the second tier plan.

5.3 Build-in Flexibility

In order to make clear to the public that changes in replacement rates or tax rates are inevitable if economic or demographic conditions change, it would be prudent to consider enacting provisions that make such adjustments automatic under certain conditions. The Swedish model of adjusting pension amounts for anticipated longevity and actual economy-wide earnings growth illustrates such automatic adjustments. Alternatively, the age of initial pension eligibility could be raised automatically as longevity increases. Since increases in longevity are virtually certain in China as incomes rise and public health measures improve, a commitment to fixed initial age of eligibility for pensions can prove costly. This problem threatens both first tier and second tier benefits under provisions outlined in State Council Document No. 26.

6. Conclusion

The Chinese pension reform is part of the most extraordinary effort at economic transformation in world history. The effort to introduce the market into the Chinese economy while sustaining rapid economic growth and improved living standards for 1.2 billion people is of epochal significance. The final test for pension reform, therefore, is not the establishment of a pension system that meets some ideal of pension planners. The pension reform must be judged primarily on how well it advances the larger social and economic objectives of the economic transformation. I believe that a plan which places somewhat greater emphasis on the security of pension promises and protects workers somewhat more from financial uncertainties than the plan outlined in State Council Document No. 26 may serve those objectives better than the draft plan. Such a plan would combine a *funded* defined-benefit plan that is larger than the first tier plan outlined in State Council Document No. 26 and would rely less on a defined-contribution component than does the draft plan. By assuring workers improved retirement security, the plan I am describing would facilitate the many adjustments that economic transformation will require.

CHAPTER 3

ESTABLISH A SOCIAL SECURITY SYSTEM WITH CHINESE FEATURES

LI TIEYING
The Chinese Academy of Social Science, President,
Beijing 100732, P.R. China

Social security is a system, which maintains social stability and is closely related to the interests of the general public. Social security system reform is one of the most important reforms China is undertaking today. The Third Plenary of the Fourteenth Congress of the Communist Party passed a resolution to establish a socialist market economic system and set clear guidelines concerning the goals and the principles of social security reform. Since 1994 I have discussed ways to carry out this resolution with some experts and scholars. Here I will present some of my own opinions.

1. The History of Social Security

Social security is a social economic system, which maintains social stability, promotes economic development, and is related to the interests of all members of the society. Social security is a product of industrial development and mass production. In the late 19th century, the German government passed perhaps the first social security law. Several other European countries followed suit. In 1935, the U.S. congress passed a social security law to set up a social security administration in the federal government, marking the establishment of a modern social security system. After World War II, many European industrialized countries carried out a "universal welfare" policy. East Europe and other socialist countries adopted a so called "government security" policy. Now, social security systems exist in more than 160 countries.

Entering the 1970s and 1980s, many countries encountered difficulties with social security payments, and therefore, began to reform their social security systems.

The Chinese social security system evolved from the rationing system during the war. It evolved through four stages:

(1) The 1949-1966 period. This period saw the establishment of the Chinese social security system. In 1951, the government issued "The Labor Insurance Provisions of the People's Republic of China (Draft)", which covered illness, injury, pregnancy, medical retirement and death and unemployment, etc. The National Workers Union was in charge of labor insurance, and the Labor Department of the central government served as an overseeing agency. Part of the social security benefits was paid by enterprises and part of it was paid by the National Workers Union.

(2) The 1966-1976 period. During the ten years of chaos, which began in the mid-1960s, the social security system was paralyzed. The National Workers Union was shut down and was no longer in charge of social security. Social security was taken over by enterprises.

(3) The 1978-1992 period. As reforms in other areas proceeded, China began to put social security on a reform schedule. In 1984, some regions started old-age security reform, requiring individuals to make contributions to social security accounts and allowing state and collective enterprises to distribute social security benefits to retirees. Some areas even started to experiment with a mixed system which combined a social account and an individual account. In 1988, Premier Li Peng in his Government Work Report highlighted the importance of speeding up social security reform and establishing a social security system with Chinese features. In 1990, he pointed out on several occasions that housing reform, insurance reform and medical reform were to be the most important reforms over the next ten years.

(4) The period after 1992. The Fourteenth Congress of the Communist Party first announced that China would establish a socialist market economic system. It also noted that social security system reform was one of the most significant elements in economic system reform.

2. The Role of the Social Security System in China

A social security system is crucial to a country's economic development and social stability. In particular, it plays an important role in a socialist market economic system, like China's. For example, without a complete social security system, it is very difficult for workers to move from state enterprises to non-state enterprises and vice versa; and therefore, it is very difficult to have a real labor market.

Reform of the social security system forms an important basis for further reform of state-owned enterprises. State owned enterprises face many problems, such as bankruptcy, mergers and acquisitions, structural adjustment, capital movement, competitiveness and technological advancement, etc. An incomplete social security system is one of the major problems. There are many redundant employees in these firms, about 20-30%. Some economists call it "hidden unemployment", I call it "transitional employment". With "five persons doing the job of three persons", how can a firm be efficient? Without a new, complete social security system, China cannot prevent enterprises from remaining a small closed society, and China cannot improve firms' operating systems.

Social security is also a redistribution system. It redistributes income among different income groups. In the long run, the social security system has a direct effect on a country's development.

3. Establishing a New Social Security System with Chinese Features

To establish a social security system, China must learn from foreign experience, and China must also consider its own situation. The latter is more important.

3.1 Starting from Reality

China is a heavily-populated, less-developed low-income country. China's population is over 1.2 billion, and will reach 1.3 billion by the end of this century. By the 30s of the next century, it may reach 1.6 billion. Because of the baby boom during the period of the 1950s to 1970s, China will become an aging society very soon. Western countries' transition into aging societies took about 100 years. It will take less than 20 years for China. By estimate, 7.4% of China's population will be 65 years and older by 2000, which is the sign of an aging society. By 2030, those retired will reach a peak, which is more than 40% of the total employment force (17.6% in 1992), and the fee for those retired will be 44% of total salaries (17.6% in 1992). Those numbers are clear evidence of the size of the challenge. Social and economic development within China is quite uneven. There is a huge difference between the southeast coast and the mid-west inland regions, and the gap has increased in recent years. Currently the rural population accounts for 74% of the total population. Based on this situation, China's social security system not only should be based on uniform principles, but also should be flexible and adaptable. Different areas may have slightly different systems. China also needs to take care of the current generation as well as future generations.

China's national situation is that it is in the primary stage of socialist society. The first thing is to develop China's economy. This is the starting point of all our work.

3.2 The Level of Social Insurance

The purpose of establishing a new social security system is economic development. If the level of social security is too low, it will hurt workers' incentives to work. But this is not socialism. China can not spend too much on welfare. Based on China's national situation, China may secure the basic standard of living. For example, China does not have the economic strength to include all rural people within the social security system. China can not pay too a high level of social security benefits to city workers either. Furthermore, social insurance needs to be complemented by commercial insurance.

From the past experience of other countries, China can see that high welfare and equalitarianism have no future. After World War II, Western countries' social welfare coverage became higher and higher, causing many social and political problems. The once popular "universal welfarè" system is now very hard to continue. From 1960 to 1990, social security expenditures in the OECD countries, including the major industrialized countries, increased from 7% of GNP to 15.4%. Medical expenditure increased from 3.9% to 7.8%. Looking at the increase in government expenditures, 25% was for social security. Large expenditures on social security contributed to huge government budget deficits.

3.3 Social Security Contributions and Benefits

Currently, in China's social security system, individuals pay very little, while government and enterprises pay most of the cost. Social security payments have become a burden for government and state enterprises. Under this system, individuals lack the awareness and the obligations of self security. In 1993, government social security and housing expenditures were 185.89 billion yuan and more than 130 billion yuan, respectively. The two items accounted for 67.8% of total salaries of workers and staff, and accounted for 10% of GNP. Individual contributions were very small, at 2% of an individual's salary for social security, and 6% for housing. Obviously, the benefit an individual received was far from equal to the contribution made. In the new social security system, China should reduce government contributions and increase individuals' contributions.

3.4 Efficiency and Fairness

Different programs of social insurance have different purposes. Social welfare, veterans benefits, and some other benefits are paid by the government. Anyone who meets the criteria is eligible to receive the benefits. These programs are for fairness. The major programs in social security should be based on the principle of "efficiency first, fairness second", and should be financed by individuals, enterprises and government. The government guarantees a minimum level of living standard. The additional social security benefit received by an individual should be connected with the individual's contribution in order to provide the individual with an incentive to work and save. Commercial insurance should be based on the principle of efficiency.

China is a developing country, and is in transition to becoming a socialist market economy. To increase individuals' awareness of participation and self reliance, as well as provide an incentive to work hard, the new system requires that employees put a small part of his or her salary into social security funds. Once an employee retires, government will pay social security benefits which will be in addition to personal savings and interest earnings on those savings.

Overall, when choosing a social security system, China should consider whether it can provide incentives for workers to raise productivity, given China's level of economic development.

4. The Objective and the Principle of Social Security Reform

The objectives of China's social security system reform are: by the end of this century, China should establish a social security system that fits the socialist market economic system, has many channels for fund raising, has multi-levels of security, connects contributions to benefits, and is run by the government instead of individual enterprises.

To realize those goals, China has to follow the following principles:

(1) Unified Policy and Unified Guiding Organization. The basic policy and regulations should be the same all over the country. China should manage the system according to the law. China has to establish various laws, regulations and supervisory systems for the new social security system. In this way, the system will function according to and be protected by laws. Right now China has different

government agencies managing social security, resulting in high operating cost and inconsistencies in carrying out policy. China has to change this.

(2) Separation of Government and Management. China should separate government administration and social security fund management, and also separate executive and supervisory agencies. The administrative agency of social security is for making policy, regulation standards and supervision. Social security fund collection and management should be carried out by a special agency according to the law, and under the supervision of the government. China has to stop misusing social security funds by using them for other purposes.

(3) Socialization of Old-age Security. Right now old-age security is provided by enterprises and can be called "enterprise security." China must change the current system to a unified social security system. This will help to equalize the social security burden among new and old enterprises, equalize the social security burden among firms in different industries, and promote fair competition.

(4) Universal Coverage. Every member of society has to face retirement, medical care, and other problems. Everyone has the obligation to work with others in dealing with accidents and disasters. Therefore social insurance should cover all members of society. The current social security system only covers about 80 million employees of government, state-enterprises and some collective enterprises. There are 83 million workers in collective, private, and other enterprises which are not covered by social security provisions. Such a situation has to be changed.

(5) Rural and Urban Areas. Currently there exist huge differences between urban and rural areas in terms of productivity, employment structure, income level and consumption. Therefore, the social security systems of urban and rural areas must be different. The majority of rural areas do not have the conditions to establish social security. But in some places where living conditions are better, farmers can voluntarily develop (with government's help) old-age security insurance.

(6) Gradualism. To establish a new social security system requires the efforts of several generations. During this process, China needs a transitional policy to maintain social stability. China should have different policies for current retirees, employees with long working experience, and new employees. China needs to move to the new system step by step.

(7) All Sides Work Together. All programs of social insurance need the support of government organizations, enterprises, families, and individuals. China has to utilize all available forces to change the current situation in which only the government and enterprises are involved.

5. The Basic Structure of China's Social Security System

China's social insurance system includes social security, social relief, social welfare, veteran benefits, and mutual help, as well as individual savings.

There are different social security systems. China can define different systems according to the methods of raising funds, or according to the purpose of the insurance. I will put all the criteria together. Our social security system has three major parts, involving 13 separate items. One part is supported by government revenues, and includes social relief, social welfare, veteran benefits, and community service. Another part is social insurance which is enforced by law, and includes retirement, unemployment, medical, injury, pregnancy and housing. The third part is voluntary commercial insurance, and includes individual insurance, enterprise insurance, and mutual insurance. These are the components of social insurance.

5.1 Social Security Programs Financed by the Government

In China, social relief, social welfare, and veteran settlements are financed by government, which results in a redistribution of national income. Government is responsible for helping those who cannot reach the basic living standard and those who need special assistance. This reflects the principle of fairness.

(1) Social Relief. The objective of social relief is to help those who are weak, including those with low incomes and those facing great difficulties. The low income group comprises those who cannot meet basic living standards through working. These include the handicapped, widowed, etc. People having great difficulties are those who suffer from natural disasters, or other disasters, and who temporarily cannot meet basic living standards. Through government financial support, they can reach basic living standards. Statistics show that the Chinese government now supports about 86.69 million people, at an expenditure of 600 million yuan per year. The purpose of social relief is to eliminate absolute poverty in a short period of time, and help to reduce relative poverty in the middle or long run. This is the basic requirement of social insurance.

(2) Veteran's Benefits. Veteran's benefits are a government special program. It is for those who gave special service to the country. The beneficiaries include the direct family members of veterans (alive or dead), disabled veterans, retired veterans and former members of the national guard.

Currently 39 million people receive veteran's benefits, including 3.96 million who receive benefits from the government. In 1993, government expenditure on veteran's benefits reached 2.01 billion yuan, inclusive of, 1.32 billion for family members of veterans and family members of those who died in military service. Every year government creates jobs for 60,000 veterans and their family members. Since 1949, the government has found jobs for 30 million retired veterans.

(3) Social Welfare. Social welfare programs help orphans, the elderly, the disabled and their children, the mentally-ill, etc. By the end of 1993, there were 43,681 social welfare communities and 56,843 welfare enterprises providing jobs for 842,000 disabled people. In China, 60% of the disabled have a job. The proportion reaches 80% in the big cities.

Social welfare needs to be reformed. Government cannot do it all. China should rely on the participation of public, social organizations, and enterprises.

(4) Community Service. The goal of community service is to establish social welfare service networks, to take care of the elderly and the disabled, to help the poor and those with great difficulties, and to provide child-care, as well as care for orphans. China should encourage public participation, improve service quality, and reduce the cost of these services. China needs a systematic community service policy and China needs to manage the community services according to laws.

5.2 Social Insurance Items Financed by Government, Employers and Individuals

Currently our social insurance includes retirement, unemployment, medical, injury and pregnancy, which are enforced by laws. During the period 1995-2000, the major targets of reform are retirement, unemployment and medical insurance for city workers.

Presently, China has a combined public general account and an individual account for retirement, which is the continuation of the traditional system. The reform will have seven parts:

(1) Expand the coverage from government and part of the collective ownership work force to all workers in the cities, including all workers employed in all kinds of ownership entities.

(2) Social security for retirement is to be financed by firms and individuals. The current contribution of 2-3% of salary is to be increased one percent annually to half paid by the individual and half paid by the firm.

(3) Set up a reasonable level of insurance, capital accumulation and rate of accumulation. · According to our country's economic development, individual incomes and the level of savings, a basic replacement rate, i.e. the proportion of retirement fund vs. salary level, of 60% is reasonable standard.

(4) All the employees should have an individual account. A combined public and individual account is suitable for China.[1]

(5) China needs to adjust social security payments for retirees to maintain their standard of living against inflation. Some experts suggest an increase of 50-80% of average salary increases each fiscal year; while others suggest an adjustment to 70% of the basic salary increase rate.

(6) Establish many different levels of social security for retirees, such as employee's basic social security, firm's supplementary security, and individual retirement savings. Employee's basic social security is mandatory under the law; firm's supplementary security is based on the profitability of each firm under government's guidelines, and firms can choose their own insurance agency; individual retirement saving is based on individual's ability to save and needs according to the voluntary principle.

(7) Increase public service and management for social security. Emphasize the service side of social security agency. The social security fund should be distributed by banks. The system could increase community service, separate the linkage between retirees and their employers, and increase community service. Currently, China has to set up public service arrangements for those retirees whose employers went bankrupt.

In order to smoothly pass the peak of population aging, China cannot adopt the "pay-as-you-go" social security system. By 2033, the population in cities aged 60 and above would reach 22.06%, and the retirement fee will be 39.27% of the salary. Such a high percentage is very hard for firms to sustain, and will cause a social security payment crisis, which will severely harm economic development and cause social instability. When considering affordability, China cannot adopt the private accumulation system completely either. According to such a system, by 2000, the rate for retirement fee will be 34%, while during the period of 2004-2031, it will be 37%. Under this system, the economy would suffer in the initial stage whilst the burden would be gradually lightened. Although it is good for getting through the period of peak aging, the initial burden for firms is so big that they cannot accommodate it. Based on the situation China is facing, China should adopt a partial accumulation system by establishing a suitable rate for firms and individuals. The rate can be adjusted later according to economic development. This is an important part of the government's macro control.

---

[1] See Announcement about Further Reforms of the Social Security System for Workers in the State Enterprises," State Department, March 1995.

At the beginning of the reform, the individual account is small, while social funding is large. Social security funding for most retirees or those who will retire soon would still come from the general fund paid by the firms. Therefore, some have said it is "an empty account". I think, since the pay-as-you-go system does not have an accumulation, it is an empty account itself, or "no account". This is not due to the new system. In the old system, there was no prepaid social security for retirement, and all accounts were empty. It depends on the next generation to pay for the current one. Second, now that China puts individual payments into individual accounts, and therefore has some actual funds, the risk is reduced. Third, the current workers are all in the accumulation stage before retirement and will not encounter the problem of an empty account. It is just like putting money into the bank--although the bank circulates money all the time, depositors can withdraw money when they need it.

According to Shanghai's experience, when the old generation dies out, the money which firms contribute to retirement can be transferred to current employee's individual account and increase the accumulation. Therefore firms with high retirement payments can gradually reduce their share.

Based on recent years' experience, the combination of public and individual accounts is good for China. Now Shanghai, Shenzheng, Ningppo, and Wuhan have implemented such a policy. They chose this model over other models. Shanghai and Wuhan also held public debates on the new system. The model of combined public and individual accounts is practicable and suitable for China.

In the rural areas, there is a tradition, also an advantage, that the family takes care of the elderly, which is a good moral practice. The social security system is determined by the means of production, the way of living, and level of economic development. Rural areas in China need to continue such practice. China can also have some other forms of taking care of the elderly. Such as community help. In some places, farmers can put individual savings into social security account based on the voluntary principle. They can also set up the combined public and individual accounts, just like urban employees. The final objective is to establish a social security system with self security as the major part, combined with community and government help, along with rural economic development and increases in farmers income. The social security system in the countryside must be suitable for the local situation, help the current family-based production system and maintain its stability. All have to be based on the voluntary principle and help in rural development. China cannot implement coercion, egalitarianism and equal sharing.

6. Unemployment Insurance Reform

It is important to establish unemployment systems to help the unemployed to secure their living.

(1) Expand the coverage of unemployment insurance. The current system only includes workers in public ownership. China should extend the system to cover all employees in all kinds of ownership including collective, stock, private, and foreign invested.

(2) Unify the collection of the unemployment insurance fund and standardize the management. The unemployment insurance fund collection should be based on spending, and maintaining certain insurance savings. There should be universal standards and collection. The current plan is that employers contribute 0.6 to 1% of all employees' salary to the unemployment insurance. Since an individual employee may become unemployed because of the factors related to the individual, firm or society, each individual should also contribute a small amount to unemployment insurance.

(3) Adjust the applications of the unemployment insurance. Most (at least 80% or more) should be used for unemployed workers and their families. China should strengthen public inspection.

(4) Actually do a good job in helping the unemployed. For all workers enrolled in the unemployment insurance program, as long as they are involuntarily unemployed, and have worked one year or more prior to unemployment and registered as unemployed, they should receive unemployment benefits. China should raise the unemployment benefits a little bit. Right now the standard is 120-150% of social relief benefits. It can be changed to 70-80% of local legal minimum wage and made adjustable according to the minimum wage. The period of unemployment benefits should have different levels according to the length of prior employment, with the maximum of 24 months, with transfer to the social relief program after that.

(5) Establish good connection between unemployment benefits and the social relief program. After the unemployment benefits period is over, those still unemployed should get into the social relief program if they are eligible, and obtain social relief benefits from the public affair department. Since they are not the standard objects of the social relief program, their benefits should be paid by government financing.

(6) Explore all kinds of job opportunities to help the unemployed to get a job. China should encourage training programs and setting up employment agencies, using unemployment funds to finance those firms to develop self help programs as

long as it meets the market needs. China needs to emphasize the profitability and social benefits while using the funds under public scrutiny.

7. The Reform of Workers Medical Insurance

The objective of reforming workers medical insurance is to establish a social security system which combines public funding and individual medical accounts, gradually covering all workers. The range of medical insurance is the same as the retirement insurance, which only covers basic medical expenses. However, it does not include all medical expenses, which is impossible. Some medical expenses and health care, etc. should be covered under commercial insurance.

The major content of medical insurance reform which was carried out in Jiu Jiang and Zhen Jiang provided that the government, firm and individual pay their respective parts of the medical insurance. The individual payment was 1% of the salary, while the largest part of the firm's payment (above 50%) went into the individual account, and the rest came from public funding. Medical expenses were paid first using the individual account. When the individual account did not have sufficient funds, the individual would pay a small part, while public funding would pay most of it.

The cooperative medical system is for rural residents. It has different ways of collecting money and managing the system. Usually, there is a special medical fund, which is a supplemental payment for a portion of the medical and health care expenses incurred by farmers, supported by the community and individuals. The reform of the rural cooperative medical system has to be based on the actual conditions of each region. The objective is, from now till the end of this century, to establish a primary health care system over all the rural areas, with establishment of the cooperative medical system in most areas. The rural medical and health care system cannot be sponsored solely by the community as before. The illegal collection and illegal spending of rural medical health care fund have to be stopped as well.

CHAPTER 4

THE RATIONAL CHOICE OF SOCIAL SECURITY SYSTEM IN CHINA

ZHENG GONGCHENG
The Institute of Social Security Research
Wuhan University,
Wuhan 430072, P.R. China

This paper summarizes the characteristics of China's social security reform and the factors that may affect the choice of the system. The author argues that at the present stage the new system should be based on family security and protection. Progresse and problems in establishing the new social security system are also addressed.

1. Introduction

The Chinese social security system has the following three characteristics. First, it is of welfare nature. That is to say, what the beneficiaries gain is surely larger than what they pay. Second, it is organized and implemented by the government or social groups. Third, it aims fundamentally at ensuring and improving the national living conditions. The Chinese social security system is in the course of reform and the framework of the new social security system is forming. The new system is composed of the following six subsystems:

(1) Social Insurance. It is the most important subsystem which consists of pension insurance, medical insurance, unemployment insurance, industrial injuries insurance and child-bearing insurance. It is mainly provided for workers in the cities and towns.

(2) Social Relief and Assistance. It is a basic subsystem which offers the lowest level security comprising poverty relief, poverty assistance and disaster relief. Each of them is respectively provided for the lower income families, the poverty stricken areas and the disaster victims.

(3) Social welfare. It is a steadily growing subsystem which consists of old age welfare, disability welfare, women and children welfare, housing welfare, education welfare, vocational welfare, etc. It provides many kinds of welfare services and allowance.

(4) Military personnel's Security. It is a comprehensive subsystem which comprises military personnel's pension, medical security, compensation, welfare

and employment security. It is provided for servicemen, retired military personnel and their families.

(5) Public Health Security. It is a subsystem which covers specific health risks. It comprises the national health care, the cooperative medical service in the rural areas and the medical assistance as well as the medical insurance.

(6) Supplementary Security. It refers to other social security items which are not mentioned above but also play a role in ensuring the basic need of people. It comprises the uncompulsory supplementary insurance programs, mutual security and the charities. It is an addition to the fundamental security system and is supported and guided by the government. Thus, it is an important part in the new Chinese social security system.

The subsystems mentioned above and their own specific items altogether constitute a new Chinese social security system. In spite of the imbalance of development nowadays, the subsystems will develop coordinately during the course of reform and play their own important roles in the system.

2. Factors that Affect the Choice of Chinese Social Security System

It's well known that social security systems usually vary in different countries as a result of the differences of specific national conditions among them. There is no uniform set of standards for the social security system around the world. Consequently, except for several internal development laws, the choice of the social security system in one country ultimately depends on the specific conditions of that country. The experiences from other countries which have turned out to be successful should be carefully examined to ensure their applicability in China.

For China, the current conditions require that the Chinese social security system have its own steps of reform and development. That is to say, China needs the modern social security system which has Chinese characteristics. In the present stage, there are several factors which restrict the Chinese social security system.

(1) The political factor. China is a socialist country with its own characteristics. So the socialist system requires a social security system that reflects the interest of the whole nation. In other words, the government should keep maintaining the living rights and interests of the most people in the economic reform instead of abandoning its main responsibility in the construction of the social security system.

(2) The traditional security system. Due to the nature of continuity and inertia in the development in social security, the traditional social security system which was based on the planned economy will not completely disappear at once after the establishment of the new economic system. Some specific items and

relating contents will remain. It needs a period to accomplish the substitution of the new social security system which can fit in with the needs of the market economy system.

(3) The population. China has the largest population in the world which will hit 1.3 billion by the end of this century and has to face the approaching of the peak of aging. That is an important factor which determines that low level of social security in China. And the pension and old age welfare will become the key items in the new Chinese social security system.

(4) The economic strength. China is a developing country. Although it has greatly increased its economic strength through nearly 20 years of continuous rapid development, its per capita GDP is only $729 in 1997 and also in that year the state revenue is just nearly $92 billion. The facts show that China has a weak economic power to support the social security system, and it's necessary for the government to arouse the national initiative.

(5) The different levels of development among different regions. China is a large country and has an uneven regional development. There co-exist the advanced southeastern coastal areas and the backwardness of the poor areas. The development levels greatly vary in the east, central and western parts, which are hard to change in a short period. Therefore, it is very difficult to hold the wholly unified social security system at the present stage in China. And it requires some diversity in the social security system in different regions.

(6) The differentiation of the socioeconomic structure. China is now in transition, which brings changes not only in economic structure but also in social structure and leads to a trend of complexity and diversity. For example, the proportion of the output produced by the state enterprises is on a decline while the output produced by the private enterprises is in a rapid growth. In the social structure, there are more and more people working in industry, commerce, and services. Furthermore, there have been changes in the government employees and the institutional workers. All these indicate that the dramatic change and instability in the socioeconomic structure of China will inevitably bring important influence on the government choice of the social security system.

(7) The national tradition, history and culture factor. China has a long history and has its own special national tradition, history, and culture. For instance, as a fundamental function of the Chinese family, raising the young and supporting the old has become a matter of ethics and law. The government bears the main responsibility of social security nowadays as in the ancient time. This is obviously different from the social security of the western countries which had been affected deeply by the religion and had made full use of the non-governmental organizations. The above factors will surely influence the reform and development of the social security system in present stage.

3. The Rational Choice of the Chinese Social Security System in Present Stage

The desirable social security system in China should meet the following requirements: 1. Consistent with the market economy. 2. Based on the specific conditions and economic strength of China. 3. Avoid the social security crisis.

The desirable Chinese social security system in the present stage is a new mixed system based on the family protection. It has the following basic components:

(1) The basis is the family security. The stability of family relations and the security provided by the family members is not only the Chinese tradition, but also a strength in stabilizing the social relations and building the new social security system. Consequently, the reform in Chinese social security system is not to replace the family protection, but to offset the weakness of the family security. It is still necessary to keep the family stability.

(2) Adopt social insurance as the key point in the system, and improve social relief and assistance, improve social welfare programs, boost the development of various supplementary social security programs. In the new Chinese social security system, due to the rapid progress of industrialization, the social insurance, especially the pension insurance and medical insurance, should be adopted as the focal point. Meanwhile, the social relief and assistance is still an important part in the whole system because China is a developing country with frequent natural disaster which causes more than one hundred million disaster victims every year, and tens of millions of poor people. And it also requires the development of various social welfare programs for more and more aged people, 60 million disabled people as the economy grows. Furthermore, it needs to develop various supplementary security arrangements to make up for the deficiency of fundamental security provided by the government.

(3) Embody the co-existence of a multi-tiered and a multi-polar structure in the system design. On one hand, the multi-tiered structure of the social security system embodies in the classification of three parts as the basic security, the supplementary security and other security. Among them, the basic security focuses on the low level and broad coverage, and pursues the equality of the whole society. The supplementary security is expected to reflect the differences and realize the equality among regions, professions and enterprises. And other security is used to meet with some special security demands. The goal of such a multi-tiered structure is to partly reduce the direct responsibility of the government, and reflect the differences among regions, professions and enterprises. On the other hand, since different social strata have different social economic backgrounds, seeking the highly unified social security system in present stage will not only directly add to the burden of the government but also

rule out the differences among the strata. It must embody the characteristics of the multi-polar structure in the security system design, because it is obviously a rather long way to realize the unified system. As a result, the new social security system features the coexistence of multi--tiered and multi-polar structure.

(4) Consider the differences among regions and form a system which reflect both the national characteristics and regional characteristics. Chinese social security system ought to have Chinese characteristics. There should be differences in item structure, coverage, and security level among regions because of the uneven development among regions and the existence of tax-sharing system and the fiscal responsibility system. Inevitably, the new social security system should reflect both national characteristics and regional characteristics.

(5) Allow the co-existence of the socialized security and the community security, and supplementary welfare programs. Undoubtedly, the new social security system needs socialization. Nevertheless, many security programs can be organized and implemented by the communities. The traditional idea among Chinese of belonging to a working unit can be easily replaced by idea of belonging to the community. So the communization must be taken into account in the new system, and the community security can become the base for a higher level social security. In the past, enterprises ran welfare programs in China. Although now it is necessary to reduce the social affairs of the enterprises in establishing the modern enterprise system, the moderate welfare level will be more suitable for the nation and help to adjust the relations between the enterprises and labor. Accordingly, the new Chinese social security system need not just socialization but the co-existence of the socialized security and the community security, and supplementary group welfare altogether to form a inseparable security network.

(6) Allow the co-existence of the central governemnt programs and the local government programs and the co-existence of programs of government and non-governmental organizations in the new social security system. On one hand, the social security is a national project and also a local project, it requires the direction of central principle to ensure that the development of the new social security system is on the right track, and also the direct responsibility of the local government to boost the development of the new system. In other words, the local governments should have certain rights of self-determination under the framework provided by the central government in funding the social security. On the other hand, the government should fully encourage the development of the non-governmental security (for example, the charity in Hong Kong is the important partner of the government social security), because the continuous increase of income has formed the corresponding economic base for the development of the non-governmental security. Therefore, it will be an

actual and rational choice to accept the combination of government security and non-governmental security.

(7) Pursue the social equality as the main objective of the system. As far as the macro situation of Chinese social economy is concerned, it is correct to take efficiency as the priority and care about the equality in the policy making. However, the ultimate goal of the social security system is to create and maintain the equality. It is a demand of the market economy and also determined by the social security system. For instance, as a transfer program, the social relief and assistance subsystem ought to fully embody the equality. In the social welfare subsystem, some welfare items should embody the social equality, while others should embody the moderate combination of equality and efficiency. Though the social insurance focuses on the combination of equality and efficiency, it adopts the equality as its base during the establishment. And the supplementary security and mutual security also manifest the equality. Accordingly, it requires the creation and maintenance of the equality as the base of the new Chinese social security system. It should be known that either equality without efficiency or efficiency without equality is bound to fail. We must set the balance between social equality and economic efficiency as the goal of social security.

(8) Consider the specific conditions of China. For example, it is necessary to adopt the independent and parallel styles in the Chinese social security legislation. As to the management system, we need to accept the Department of Labor and Social Security and the Department of Civil Affairs as the two major departments and adopt the cooperation of related departments, and pay close attention to the functions of the semi-governmental and non-governmental organizations such as the Chinese Disabled Association, the Labor Union, the charities, etc. As to the execution system, we need to establish the socialized and community network and make full use of the basic political organizations in the cities and villages such as the Resident Committee in the cities and the towns, the village committee in villages. As to the supervisory system, we need to build a multi-layered and authoritative supervisory system which represents the interests of different strata besides the general judicial supervision and the administrative supervision. Inevitably, the operation of the Chinese social security system will demonstrate the features of Chinese political and administrative structure.

(9) Adopt the mixed financing system in raising funds. At the present stage, we need to not only pay the expenses of present retirees and repay the historic debts formed in the past, but also accumulate funds for the current workers. Consequently, it is necessary to expand the government expenditure and collect the premium from enterprises and individuals, moreover, sell parts of state assets and advocate the civil donation. As to the pension insurance and medical

insurance, it is rational to choose the funding pattern of combining the social plan and the individual account. In one word, China needs a mixed social security system with Chinese characteristics corresponding to the conditions mentioned above.

4. Progresses and Problems in Establishing the New Social Security System

Social security reform has lasted for more than a decade, and we have made great progress.

(1) The basic principles of the new system have been established. For example, the principle of social equality and socialization, the multi-layered principle, the cost-sharing principle, the low level of benefit and broad coverage principle are now guiding the further reform of the system.

(2) Great success in assisting the poor has been achieved. The population in extreme poverty has dropped to 57 million in 1997 from 250 million in 1978, and the elimination of the regional poverty has entering the last stage.

(3) A big stride in the reform of social insurance has been made. The pension insurance system characterized by the combination of social plan and personal account has been basically established. Experiments of medical insurance reform have been conducted in many regions. It is estimated that the pattern of the new social insurance subsystem will be fixed in 5 years.

(4) Rapid progress has been made in the construction of the new social relief and assistance subsystem. The security system which aims to help the poor has been established in more and more cities and villages. And the new system of different responsible levels in aiding the disaster victims has already been set up.

(5) The new administrative system has been basically set up. The Department of Labor and Social Security is in charge of the national social insurance, and the Department of Civil Affairs is in charge of the social relief and assistance, the social welfare, and the military personnel's security.

(6) The various supplementary security has been developed. For example, the Disabled Welfare Funds, the Charity Funds, the Mutual Aid Association and the "Hope Project" have had positive effects in China. Furthermore, the reform has set the target for the construction of the new system by revealing the conflict and the discrepancy of different interest groups. Therefore, up to now, the traditional social security system, run by each enterprise and complemented with state security and rural collective security, has been entirely broken. A new social security system has been partly set up through the development of a certain items and constructing the subsystems separately.

Nevertheless, many problems arose in the establishment of the new social security system and, as the reform proceeds, the problem become more complex. The main problems are as follows.

(1) The large debt which has been accumulated in the past can not be repaid through the normal way. Thus, it is a rational choice to sell parts of the state assets to repay the debt. But up to now the government has not announced any measure to repay the debts. However, the rapid expansion of the social security expenditure (especially in the pension insurance) calls for the rational solution as soon as possible.

(2) The government lacks understanding of the diversified structure of the social security system. Generally, government focuses on the workers of the state enterprises in the cities and towns, but lacks attention to other social strata. For example, the non-urban and non-rural population apart from the villages has formed a special social group which has reached an amount of about 0.2 billion. However, the government hasn't made any corresponding social security plan for them. This indicates that China has a huge potential social risk.

(3) Important social security laws have not been laid down. China has hitherto laid down several laws relating to the living rights and interests security of the nation such as "Disabled Security Law", "Aged Rights and Interests Security Law", "Women Rights and Interests Security Law", "Labor Law", etc. It also has issued several decrees, such as "Rules of the Military Personnel's Compensation and Privilege", "The Working Rules of Five Provisions in Villages", "Unemployment Insurance Rules for Workers in State Enterprises", etc. However, the fundamental laws such as "Social Insurance Law", "Social Relief and Assistance Law", "Social Welfare Law" have not yet been laid down. Thus, the framework of the law system of the Chinese social security have not been established. If this situation does not change, the new system could not be implemented.

(4) There exist serious problems in implementation of the nationwide program and in coordination among subprograms. For example, social insurance is subject to a low level of planning. The conflict between the regional interests and the interest of industries controlled by central government result in an insurmountable block for transferring social insurance to a higher level--the provincial planning level. There are a great deal of difficulties, such as insufficient funds and the transformation from enterprise welfare to community welfare. The social insurance, the social relief and assistance, the social welfare and the supplementary security is confined by the way of financing and discordant relationship among various ministries and industries.

(5) It lacks attention to the development of the social security system in the countryside. On one hand, the traditional collective security system in the village has no longer existed because of the dissolution of collective farms. For example, the cooperative medical service system, which has covered more than

95 percent of the rural population, has entirely broken down and need to be replaced by a program under the new system. Also, the government has not made a corresponding pension plan as the aging trend of the rural population is getting more serious. On the other hand, since the government neglects the construction of the rural social security system, most villages either lack necessary social security programs, or still utilize the traditional security which was used in cities and towns before. This will undoubtedly increase the costs of social security reform, and slow down establishment of the new social security system.

(6) The other related reforms have not kept the pace with the social security reform. For example, the reform of the medical insurance system in cities and towns has reached the critical stage that depends on medical system reforms. That is to say that the establishment of the new medical insurance system requires the synchronous medical reform. But the medical reform is still seriously lagging. Also, the delayed reform of the governmental organizations causes confusion in the social security administration and will surely affect the reform of the social security. The delay in the reform of the financing and tax system relating to the social security is now affecting the whole social security system. Therefore, we must change the guiding ideology that the new social security system should simply serve for the economic reform, and realize that the establishment of a new social security system is a major part of economic reforms. Other related reforms will affect social security reform, so we must accelerate the reform of the related system.

There are several ways to solve the above problems. 1. Repay the historic debt of social security by increasing taxes, selling the state assets, and issuing government bonds. 2. Design a general (or a bundle) reform plan to ensure the coordinated development of the social security reform. 3. Transfer enterprise welfare to community welfare.

5. Concluding Remarks

China has found the right direction of the reform and development of social security system and has established several correct principles. However, it needs more efforts to put the new social security system in practice.

It should be pointed out that we can count on the new social security system to solve various problems related to social security, however, we can not expect to solve every problem. Just as China can not entirely copy the social security system of other countries, the social security system which is based on the Chinese specific national conditions can not be imitated by other countries.

Once the new Chinese social security system, which can solve the social security problem of this developing country with 1.3 billion population, is set up, it will be a great contribution to world development.

References

1. Zheng Gongcheng, 1997, *On the Road of Social Security of Chinese Special*, Wuhan University Press.
2. Bureau of State Statistical, 1998, *A Statistical Survey of China*, The Statistical Press of China.
3. Gou Jingchong, 1995, *The Readings of Chinese Social security system*, The Democratic and Legal System Press of China.

CHAPTER 5

THE EFFECT OF AN EXPANSION OF THE PAY-AS-YOU-GO SOCIAL SECURITY SYSTEM IN CHINA

SHUANGLIN LIN
Department of Economics
University of Nebraska
Omaha, NE68182, USA
E-mail: slin@shuanglin_Lin.unomaha.edu

China is in the process of industrialization with a large amount of the labor force moving from the agricultural sector to industrial sectors. An expansion of the pay-as-you-go social security system benefits current urban retirees, and may solve the social security payment problem faced by many state enterprises. Also, although facing a declining population growth rate, China may not have a social security crisis under a pay-as-you-go social security system, which just covers the wage earners, that many industrialized countries face. However, the expansion of the pay-as-you-go social security system may have an adverse effect on capital accumulation in both the short run and the long run, hurting the rural old and either benefiting or hurting the wage earners in urban areas before the completion of industrialization and is likely to reduce wage earners' welfare after industrialization.

1. Introduction

As economic reforms in other areas proceed in China, social security reform has become urgent. China has a pay-as-you-go social security system which covers only a small portion of the population. The social security reform can go in different directions: expanding the existing system to cover more people, or privatizing the present system by establishing individual accounts, or a combination of the two.

This paper analyzes the effect of an expansion of the current pay-as-you-go system on the Chinese economy.

Many countries in the world provide social security to their residents. Most social security systems are pay-as-you-go in nature, i.e., government collects taxes from the working generation to finance the benefits to the retired generation. This system is also called an "unfunded system" because the benefits received and the taxes paid may not be the same. Under this system each generation will benefit by population growth since there will be more young people supporting the retirees. Problems arise when the population growth rate begins to decline, i.e., each generation has to pay more and more to keep the parent generation as well provided for as their grandparent generation. As capital markets become better developed, it is also possible for a person to provide old-age security for him- or herself. When working, each individual deposits a portion of his or her salaries into a fund. Over time the fund accumulates interest, and on retirement, each individual receives the principal and accrued interest as social security benefits. This form of old-age security can be called "individual security," and it is a fully-funded system because individuals receive exactly what they paid in terms of the present value.

Recent research on Chinese social security reforms have identified two major problems that the new social security system must solve. One is to reduce the social security burden of the state enterprises, and the second is to avoid a social security crisis due to the decrease in the population growth rate [Zhou and Wang (1994) and the World Bank (1997)]. To solve these problems, a social security system which combines a social account (pay-as-you-go in nature) and an individual account (fully-funded) has been recommended. On the one hand, this proposed system is an expansion of the current pay-as-you-go system since more workers are covered; on the other hand, the system is a partial privatization of the existing system since each worker has his or her own forced saving account. The relative sizes of the social account and the individual account are essential determinants of the social security system. At present, the social account is the major part. Thus, the social security system is largely pay-as-you-go in nature.

This paper argues that a pay-as-you-go social security system can easily solve the social security payment problem in the state enterprises. China's current social security system only covers the employees of state enterprises, state institutes, and government agencies. Each state enterprise takes care of its own employees and the government pays social security benefits to the employees of state institutes and government agencies. Most non-state employees are not covered by the current system. Expanding the pay-as-you-go system to all wage earners will enable the government to collect enough funds to pay social security benefits to the retirees in the state enterprises.

This paper also argues that, unlike the industrialized economies China may not have a social security crisis in the near future with the pay-as-you-go system covering all wage earners. Due to decreasing population growth rates, the U.S. and other industrial countries will have a social security account deficit around 2030. Facing the imbalance of social security accounts in the future, some countries, such as the U.S., now have adopted a partially funded system, i.e., reserving some of the tax revenues to pay social security benefits to future retirees. China is in the process of industrialization, as more and more rural laborers become wage earners. Thus, there should be more and more young workers supporting retirees in industries, even though the growth rate of the total population is declining.

One problem prior studies on Chinese social security have disregarded is the effect of a social security system on capital accumulation. Most prior studies on social security have shown that social security has an adverse effect on private savings and capital accumulation [see, for example, Feldstein (1974, 1996), Blinder, Gordon, and Wise (1981), Diamond and Hausman (1982), and Kotlikoff (1979)].[1] China is a developing country which needs a large amount of capital goods. This paper shows that a pay-as-you-go social security may reduce capital accumulation in both the short run and the long run.

Another problem which has not been addressed is the differential effects of social security systems on urban wage earners and rural farmers. If a pay-as-you-go system is established, the young workers who have just migrated to cities will face double social security burden, i.e., pay social security taxes to finance benefits to city retirees and make transfers to support their rural parents; the rural old might be worse off since their children who migrated to the cities may transfer less to them; the current retirees will be better off due to the increase in social security taxes while future generations may be worse off due to lower capital stock.

This paper is organized as follows. Section 2 describes the stage of Chinese economic development and the social security system from a historical perspective. Section 3 presents an overlapping generations model. Section 4 provides a comparative static analysis of the effects of a pay-as-you-go social security system

[1] However, Barro (1978) found that social security had no effects on the economy based on the time series data from 1929-1940 and 1947-1974, and Kopits and Gotur (1980) found that social security had positive effects on savings based on the data from fourteen industrial countries for the period of 1969-1971. Many economists, including Feldstein and Samwick (1996) and Kotlikoff (1996), called for privatization of the pay-as-you-go social security system. Others including Diamond (1996) suggested less radical adjustments to the current system.

on the real interest rate, the real wage rate, and capital accumulation. Section 5 analyzes the effect of a pay-as-you-go social security system on industrial workers and rural farmers. Section 6 discusses the effects of declining population growth on the pay-as-you-go social security system. Section 7 provides concluding remarks.

2. The Stage of Chinese Economic Development and Current Social Security System

When discussing social security reforms in China, we must take into consideration the stage of Chinese economic development. China is a low-income developing country. The population increased from 0.55 billion in 1950 to 1.22 billion in 1996.[2] In 1990, the life expectancy at birth was 68 for men and 71 for women. The per capita GDP in 1996 was 5,605 Chinese yuan, equivalent to $700 based on the official exchange rate. In 1996, 0.86 billion people, or about 70% of the population, lived in rural areas, while 0.35 billion people, or 30% of the population, lived in urban areas.

China is in the process of industrialization. Table 1 shows China's total GDP, per capita GDP, and GDP of the agriculture industry (including farming, forestry, animal husbandry, sideline production and fishery) from 1978 to 1996 at the 1978 constant price, as well as the agricultural GDP share in total GDP and data on urban and rural populations. It can be seen that the agricultural GDP share declined from 33.27% in 1982 to 20.24% in 1996. The growth rate of the population is declining. The annual growth rate of the population was 1.93% from 1952 to 1980, and dropped to 1.34% from 1980 to 1996. However, due to industrialization, the annual growth rate of the population in urban areas has been rising. The annual growth rate of the population in urban areas was 3.51% from 1952 to 1980, and rose to 3.94% from 1980 to 1996. In 1952, the share of rural the population in the total population was 87.54%, it was 82.85% in 1978, and it decreased to 70.63% in 1996. The annual growth rate of the population in rural areas was 1.64% from 1952 to 1980, and was only 0.52% from 1980 to 1996. In fact, the rural population even declined from 1991 to 1993. The decline in the population growth is not caused by a decrease in the rural birth rate, but by growth of rural-urban migration. As industrialization proceeds, the decline in the agricultural population is inevitable.

Table 1: Some Indicators of Economic Development *

[2] *A Statistical Survey of China*, 1997.

Year	GDP (100 million)	Agriculture GDP (100 million)	Agriculture Share in GDP (%)	Population (10000)	Per-Capita GDP (yuan)	Urban Population (10000)	Rural Population (10000)	Rural Population Share (%)
1978	3624.10	1018.40	28.10	96259	376.49	17245	79014	0.820848
1979	3959.02	1234.22	31.17	97542	405.88	18495	79047	0.810389
1980	4179.28	1257.54	30.09	98705	423.41	19140	79565	0.806089
1981	4392.41	1396.21	31.79	100072	438.93	20171	79901	0.798435
1982	4693.88	1561.70	33.27	101541	462.26	21480	80174	0.789573
1983	5182.97	1712.49	33.04	102495	505.68	22274	80734	0.787687
1984	6092.61	1950.30	32.01	103475	588.80	24017	80340	0.776419
1985	6997.97	1984.07	28.35	105851	661.12	25094	80757	0.762931
1986	7512.67	2035.27	27.09	107507	698.81	26366	81141	0.754751
1987	8210.36	2199.25	26.79	109300	751.18	27674	81626	0.746807
1988	8644.06	2218.30	25.66	111026	778.56	28661	82365	0.741853
1989	8313.27	2078.66	25.00	112704	737.62	29540	83164	0.737898
1990	8930.14	2415.50	27.05	114333	781.06	30191	84142	0.735938
1991	10115.96	2474.78	24.46	115823	873.40	30543	85280	0.736296
1992	11828.64	2550.62	21.56	117171	1009.52	32372	84799	0.72372
1993	13587.45	2699.92	19.87	118517	1146.46	33351	85166	0.718597
1994	15073.95	3048.74	20.23	119850	1257.73	34301	85549	0.713801
1995	16421.82	3367.87	20.51	121121	1355.82	35174	85947	0.709596
1996	18156.11	3675.01	20.24	122389	1483.48	35950	86439	0.706264

Source: *Statistical Yearbook of China*, various issues.

* Values of GDP, GDP in agriculture, and GDP per-capita are calculated by the author at the 1978 price

Every society has its own old-age security. Like other traditional societies in which agriculture dominates, for a long time in China, several generations of a family lived together, and people raised children to support them in old age. This can be called "family security."[3] The old-age security had a great impact on Chinese culture. People wanted to have sons to support them in their old age.[4]

[3] The system can also be considered as a funded system in the sense that parents invest on their children first and then receive the returns from their children.

[4] The views of "raising sons for old-age security" and "more sons and more happiness" were widely spread in rural areas. Children were disciplined in a way to respect the old and take care of their parents. This kind of old-age security was a result of labor immobility, and it in return further restrained the labor mobility. The young were taught that, "Do not travel far away from home when father and mother are alive." The young should unconditionally respect and serve their parents. Also, parents value sons higher than daughters (zhong nan qing nu). In rural China, when daughters get married, they normally live with the husbands' home and take care of the husbands' parents.

China's social security system was established in the 1950s. In the early 1950s, China undertook a socialist reform, i.e., eliminating all private enterprises in the industrial sectors, and collectivizing individual farmers. A nation-wide pay-as-you-go social security system was established for staff and workers in all state enterprises and some collective enterprises, as well as government agencies.

In 1966 China began the ten-year Cultural Revolution, which resulted in severe economic hardships. The government was unable to pay the committed social security benefits, and therefore, shifted to the state-owned enterprises the responsibility of paying social security benefits to their own workers, while the government paid social security to other government employees using tax revenues.

In 1978 another reform started, aimed at bringing market mechanisms into the economy. Although much progress has been made in other areas, China's social security system remains largely unchanged. Table 2 shows the social insurance and welfare funds by ownership (state units, collective units, and other ownership) in 1996. The social insurance and welfare funds include pensions, medical care, funeral expenses and pensions for survivors, transportation and other subsidies. Retirement pensions are the largest item among social insurance and welfare payments. In 1996 total social insurance and welfare funds were 179.768 billion yuan, and retirement pensions were 119.927 billion yuan. Medical care ranked second, with 26.561 billion yuan in 1996. Funeral expenses and pensions for survivors were only 2.66 billion yuan. Unlike the U.S. where a retiree (no matter whether they worked or not before retirement) receives at least half the spouse's social security benefits, in China only the person who worked receives social security benefits.

In 1996, the share of social insurance and welfare funds for state units was 84.4%, for urban collective units 12.8%, and for all other enterprises only 2.7%.[5] Meanwhile, the state-owned enterprises in industry produced less than 30% of total industrial output, while other enterprises produced about 70% of industrial output in 1996. While shares of w\employment show higher shares for SDEs, many non-state employees are not covered by the social security system.

The state enterprises, in addition to other problems, have been heavily burdened by large social security payments to their retirees. The ratio of retirees to workers was 7.8% in 1980, 16.4 in 1990, and 21.7 in 1996.[6] Thus, the ratio of

---

[5] Calculated based on the data from Table 2.

[6] See *China Labor Statistical Yearbook*, 1997, pp. 466-467. Officially, the retirement age for a man is 60 years old and for a woman is 55 years old.

retirees to workers is growing. Most of the private enterprises employ younger people and do not have large social security payments.

Table 2: Social Insurance and Welfare Funds in 1996 (billion yuan)

	Total	Pensions for termination	Retirement pensions	Resignation allowances	Medical care	Funeral Expenses & Pensions for Survivors	Trans-portation	Other subsidies
Total	179.768	13.776	119.927	1.710	26.561	2.660	1.416	14.000
Enterprises	127.804	6.559	87.874	1.303	18.509	1.961	0.889	10.600
1. State Units	151.778	12.847	99.248	1.196	22.974	2.28	1.253	11.981
Enterprises	101.689	5.735	68.526	0.823	15.168	1.611	0.737	9.090
Local	66.569	3.534	46.142	0.637	10.528	0.974	0.437	4.318
Institutions	34.537	3.711	22.549	0.221	5.234	0.459	0.335	2.027
Local	27.887	2.884	18.507	0.195	4.092	0.38	0.261	1.568
State Organs	15.553	3.400	8.173	0.152	2.572	0.21	0.181	0.864
Local	14.187	3.107	7.566	0.138	2.274	0.19	0.163	0.749
2. Urban Collectives Units	23.08	0.731	17.32	0.473	2.685	0.306	0.133	1.433
Enterprises	21.628	0.653	16.262	0.444	2.509	0.289	0.123	1.346
3. Other Ownership	4.901	0.198	3.359	0.0402	0.903	0.0712	0.0314	0.307
Enterprises	4.488	0.170	3.086	0.0353	0.832	0.0620	0.0290	0.273

Sources: *China Labor Statistical Yearbook*, 1997, pp. 456-457.

Table 3 shows the level of pensions for retirees. In 1978, total pensions were 1.73 billion yuan; while 1996 total pensions increased to 40.38 billion yuan at the 1978 constant price, 23.3 times as large as in 1978. In 1978 the average pension for all retirees covered by the social security system was 551 yuan, and 574 yuan for retirees of state units; in 1996, the average pension for all retirees covered by the social security system was 1,280.84 yuan, and 1,384.07 yuan for retirees worked for state units at the 1978 constant price. The average pension per retiree in 1996 was 2.3 times that in 1978. The large increase in total pensions was caused by the large increase in the number of retirees.

In 1997, the population over age 60 in cities and towns accounted for 10.2% of the total population. Morevoer, China is entering the population aging period.[7] It has been estimated that the ratio of the population 60 years or over to the total population will be 12.7% in the year 2000, and will reach 36.6% in 2040.

Recently efforts have been made to reform the system by pooling many enterprises together at the county, municipality, and province level. This pooling of responsibility is intended to help the heavily indebted state enterprises fulfill their social security obligations, although it may also spread risk. Through this reform, the government implicitly transfers the funds from new enterprises (which have smaller social security burdens) to old state enterprises (which have heavy burdens of social security payments). The effect is to help save the old state enterprises at the expense of the young private or collective enterprises. This pooling approach is an expansion of the pay-as-you-go system.

Can this reform solve the short-run social security payment problem for state enterprises and government institutes? Will the declining population growth cause a social security crisis? How will the expansion of the pay-as-you-go system affect industrial workers and farmers? How will the pay-as-you-go system affect current and future generations? We intend to discuss these issues based on an overlapping generations model.

3. The Model

The economy consists of two parts, cities and rural areas. There are two types of individuals in each generation, industrial workers and farmers. Farmers are in rural areas and industrial workers are in urban areas. Each individual lives for two periods. Industrial workers work, earn wages, and save in the first period, and retire in the second period. Each industrial worker is endowed with one unit of labor in the first period, which is supplied inelastically. Each farmer is endowed with a fixed amount of output in the first period, which is used for his own consumption and for support of his parents. Farmers are supported by their children in the second period of life. Government lives forever, collecting taxes to finance its spending and social security.

Table 3: Pensions for Retirees * (100 millions yuan unless specified)

---

[7] Generally, a country's population is said to be aging if the population over age 60 accounts for more than 10% of the total population.

Year	Total Pensions	Pensions for State Units			Pensions for Urban Collective	Pensions for Other Ownership	Average pensions (yuan)	Average pensions for State Units (yuan)
		Sub-total	Paid by Units	Paid by Civil Admin. Dept				
1978	17.30	16.30	14.10	2.20	1.00	0.00	551.00	574.00
1979	31.86	28.33	25.59	2.75	3.53	0.00	700.00	749.02
1980	46.62	40.15	37.10	3.05	6.48	0.00	660.50	722.48
1981	56.28	48.15	45.17	2.98	8.13	0.00	637.76	699.19
1982	64.80	55.05	52.22	2.84	9.75	0.00	628.55	686.17
1983	76.24	64.63	61.83	2.79	11.62	0.00	634.06	687.34
1984	90.14	71.88	69.33	2.55	18.01	0.25	650.81	692.44
1985	113.66	90.63	87.74	2.89	22.72	0.31	729.90	814.21
1986	124.52	101.25	98.82	2.43	22.83	0.44	723.86	820.32
1987	140.22	115.44	112.70	2.75	24.91	0.55	743.31	846.26
1988	156.46	124.84	121.02	3.82	30.75	0.87	765.49	841.34
1989	153.98	124.24	120.55	3.69	29.06	0.69	712.88	783.19
1990	187.10	150.84	147.38	3.47	35.44	0.82	831.01	899.37
1991	214.55	174.50	170.94	3.56	38.98	1.08	905.94	980.81
1992	252.49	206.79	202.71	4.09	44.18	1.51	1003.55	1087.03
1993	293.17	240.45	235.74	4.71	48.02	4.71	1090.23	1168.69
1994	331.04	277.72	272.08	5.64	46.52	6.80	1159.57	1264.67
1995	360.52	301.66	296.21	5.45	50.55	8.31	1197.14	1297.39
1996	403.81	340.23	334.91	5.32	53.15	10.43	1280.84	1384.07

Sources: *China Labor Statistical Yearbook*, 1997.
* Excluding funeral expenses and pensions for survivor, medical expenses and health care.
Figures for 1985-1988 do not include price subsidies.

The population growth rate is η. Farmers can become industrial workers. The portion of farmers who become laborers in each period is q. Thus, the number of farmers in period $t + 1$, F_{t+1} is: $F_{t+1} = (1+\eta-q)F_t$, and the growth rate of farmers is: η - q. Assume that η - $q < 0$.[8] The number of industrial workers in period t+1, L_{t+1} is: $L_{t+1} = (1+\eta)L_t + qF_t$, and the growth rate of laborers in period t+1, n, is: $n_{t+1} = (L_{t+1} - L_t) / L_t = (\eta L_t + qF_t) / L_t = \eta + qF_t / L_t$. The

[8] The rural population in China in 1992 and 1993 was lower than that in 1991, but started to increase slowly again (Statistical Yearbook of China, 1997, p. 69). If the birth control policy and the rural-city migration continue, the number of farmers will decline in the future.

total population in period $t+1$, P_{t+1} is: $P_{t+1} = (1+\eta)(L_t + F_t)$, and the growth rate of total population is η.

The production function in industry exhibits constant returns to scale in both capital and labor. The output, Y_t, is given by: $Y_t = F(K_t, L_t)$, where K_t is capital and L_t is labor. Letting $y_t = Y_t / L_t$, the output-labor ratio, we have: $y_t = f(k_t)$, $f'(k_t) > 0$, $f''(k_t) < 0$, where $k_t = K_t / L_t$, is the capital-labor ratio. Assume that capital is fully depreciated after one period's production. Factor markets are perfectly competitive, thus the rate of return to each factor is its marginal product, i.e.,

$$1 + r_t = f'(k_t) \tag{1}$$

$$w_t = f(k_t) - r_t k_t \tag{2}$$

where $1+r_t$ is the rate of return on physical capital in period t, and w_t is the rate of return to labor.[9]

The optimization problem for a representative non-migrant industrial worker in industry is as follows:

$$\text{Max } u = u(c_t^t, c_{t+1}^t)$$

$$s.t.$$

$$c_t^t + c_{t+1}^t / (1 + r_{t+1}) \le (1 - \pi_t) w_t + z_{t+1} / (1 + r_{t+1})$$

where c_{t+j}^t is consumption in period $t+j$ of an agent born in period t (called generation t), $j = 0, 1$; π is the tax rate on labor income; z_{t+1}, is social security benefits from the government.

Migrant industrial workers care for their parents by giving them a fixed portion of their income as gifts. For simplicity, we assume that this kind of transfer yields utility to the migrants. Using a "^" to indicate the variable for a migrant worker, the optimization problem for a representative migrant industrial worker in industry is as follows:

$$\text{Max } \hat{u} = u(\hat{c}_t^t, \hat{c}_{t+1}^t) + \gamma(1 - \pi_t) w_t / \sigma$$

$$s.t.$$

$$\hat{c}_t^t + \hat{c}_t^t / (1 + r_{t+1}) \le (1 - \pi_t) w_t + z_{t+1} / (1 + r_{t+1})$$

where $\gamma(1 - \pi_t) w_t$ is the transfer a migrant gives to parent, and σ is the altruistic parameter.

---

[9] If capital does not depreciate, it is better to use r_t for the rate of return on capital.

Farmers receive gifts from their children migrating to industry, as well as gifts from their children remaining in rural areas. The optimization problem for a representative farmer is as follows:

$$\text{Max} \quad u = u(c_t^t, c_{t+1}^t)$$
$$s.t. \quad c_t^t \leq e_t - \lambda e_t$$
$$c_{t+1}^t \leq (1+\eta-q)\lambda e_{t+1} + \gamma q(1-\pi_t)w_{t+1}$$

where $e_{t+1} = (1+\omega)e_t$ is the endowment in period 1 (ω, η, and q are constant); $\lambda e_{t+1} = \lambda(1+\omega)e_t$ is the gift each old receives for old-age security from each young; λe_t stands for transfers to the parent by the young remaining in the rural area; and $\gamma q(1-\pi_t)w_{t+1}$ is the gifts received from their children migrating to urban areas.[10]

To obtain explicit solutions for savings and other endogenous variables and keep the model tractable, assume that $u(c_t^t, c_{t+1}^t) = \ln(c_t^t) + \rho \ln(c_{t+1}^t)$ where $\rho < 1$ is the (constant) pure rate of time preference.[11]

Solving the representative non-migrant industrial worker's maximization problem yields:[12]

$$s_t = \frac{\rho(1-\pi)w_t}{1+\rho} - \frac{z_{t+1}}{(1+\rho)(1+r_{t+1})}$$

(3)

where s_t represents savings in period t of a non-migrant industrial worker born in period t, which is the difference between the first-period income and the first-period consumption.

Solving the representative migrant industrial worker's maximization problem yields:

$$\hat{s}_t = \frac{\rho(1-\gamma)(1-\pi)w_t}{1+\rho} - \frac{z_{t+1}}{(1+\rho)(1+r_{t+1})}$$

(4)

---

[10] There might be other reasons why the young support their parents. The first one is government laws. In countries such as China, the law requires the young to support his or her parent. The second one is social pressure. If a young person does not support his or her aged parent, he or she will be criticized by the society. The third reason is that the young wants to be an example for his or her kids, so that his or her kids will support him or her in the future.

[11] Previous studies using this type of utility functions include Lin (1998).

[12] A detailed derivation is available on request.

where $\hat{s}_t$ represents savings in period t of a migrant industrial worker born in period t.

The government can finance its spending and social security by collecting labor income taxes. The government budget constraint is as follows:

$$G_t + L_{t-1}z_t = L_t \pi_t w_t$$

where G_t is government spending, $z_t \equiv Z_t / L_{t-1}$ where Z_t is the per capita social security payments in period t. Dividing both sides of the above equation by L_t gives:

$$g_t + z_t / (1+n_t) = \pi_t w_t \tag{5}$$

where $g_t \equiv G_t / L_t$.

A competitive equilibrium for the economy is defined as a set of sequences $\{k_{t+1}, s_t, \hat{s}_t, r_t, w_t, g_t, z_t, \pi_t\}$ satisfying equations (1)-(5), and

$$\frac{(1+\eta)L_t s_t + qF_t \hat{s}_t}{L_t} = (1+n_{t+1})k_{t+1} \quad \text{or}$$

$$\frac{[(1+\eta)L_t + qF_t]\left[\dfrac{\rho(1-\pi)w_t}{1+\rho} - \dfrac{z_{t+1}}{(1+\rho)(1+r_{t+1})}\right] - qF_t \dfrac{\rho\gamma(1-\pi)w_t}{1+\rho}}{L_t} = (1+n_{t+1})k_{t+1}. \tag{6}$$

Equation (6) indicates that savings in the current period must be equal to the physical capital or investment in the next period.[13]

4. Pay-as-You-Go Social Security and Capital Accumulation

This section examines the effect of an introduction of a pay-as-you-go social security system on the interest rate, the wage rate, and capital accumulation in both the short run equilibrium and the steady state equilibrium.

4.1 Short-Run Effect

[13] In the OG model, the ownership of capital changes every period. Thus, capital stock is equal to investment from an individual's perspective.

In the short run equilibrium (or momentary equilibrium as described by Persson 1985), the wage rate is predetermined. The government increases the labor income tax rate to finance the social security benefit. Totally differentiating equations (5) and (6) with w_t being predetermined, and collecting terms yields the impact of an increase in the labor income tax on the real interest rate:

$$\frac{dr_{t=1}}{d\pi} = \frac{\Delta}{\Omega} \tag{7}$$

where $\Delta \equiv \dfrac{[(1+\eta)L_t + qF_t]\left[\dfrac{-\rho w_t}{1+\rho} - \dfrac{(1+n_{t+1})w_{t+1}}{(1+\rho)(1+r_{t+1})}\right] + qF_t \dfrac{\rho\gamma w_t}{1+\rho}}{L_t}$

$$\Omega \equiv (1+n_{t+1})\frac{dk_{t+1}}{dr_{t+1}}dr_{t+1} - \frac{[(1+\eta)L_t + qF_t]\left[-\dfrac{(1+n_{t+1})\pi \dfrac{dw_{t+1}}{dr_{t+1}}}{(1+\rho)(1+r_{t+1})} + \dfrac{z_{t+1}}{(1+\rho)(1+r_{t+1})^2}\right]}{L_t}$$

Ω is negative by the stability condition, and Δ is negative since $\gamma < 1$. Thus, $dr_{t+1} / d\pi > 0$, which implies $dk_{t+1} / d\pi < 0$ and $dw_{t+1} / d\pi < 0$.

Therefore, in the short run, an increase in the labor income tax rate to finance a pay-as-you-go social security will increase the real interest rate, reduce capital accumulation, and reduce real wage rate.

An increase in the labor income tax rate reduces disposable income which tends to reduce savings; an increase in social security benefits in the second period resulting from higher payroll taxes also tends to reduce savings. Thus, savings [the left side of equation (6)] will decrease at the initial interest rate. Meanwhile the demand for funds (investment and government bonds) remains unchanged at the initial interest rate. Therefore, there is an excess quantity demanded for funds and the interest rate must increase to clear the market. An increase in interest rate will lower the wage rate and capital accumulation.

4.2 Long-Run Effect

Next we consider the long-run effect of a pay-as-you-go social security on capital accumulation. In the long run, the growth rate of wage earners is equal to the growth rate of population, i.e., $\lim_{t\to\infty} n_{t+1} = \eta + \lim_{t\to\infty} qF_t / L_t = \eta$. Recall that $F_t = (1+\eta-q)^t F_0$ and $1+\eta-q<1$. The steady-state version of equation (5) and (6) can be written as:

$$g + z/(1+\eta) = \pi w \qquad \text{or} \qquad z = (\pi w - g)(1+\eta) \tag{8}$$

$$s = \frac{\rho(1-\pi)w}{1+\rho} - \frac{z}{(1+\rho)(1+r)} = (1+\eta)k \tag{9}$$

Substituting $z = (\pi w - g)(1+\eta)$ into equation (9) and differentiating the resulted equation yields:

$$\frac{\rho(1-\pi)}{1+\rho}\frac{dw}{dr}dr + -\frac{\rho w}{1+\rho}d\pi - \frac{w(1+\eta)}{(1+\rho)(1+r)}d\pi - \frac{\pi(1+\eta)}{(1+\rho)(1+r)}\frac{dw}{dr}dr$$

$$+\frac{(\pi w - g)(1+\eta)}{(1+\rho)(1+r)^2}dr = (1+\eta)\frac{dk}{dr}dr$$

Rearranging terms gives: $$\frac{dr}{d\pi} = \frac{\Lambda}{\Pi}$$

where $\Lambda \equiv -\dfrac{\rho w}{1+\rho} - \dfrac{w(1+\eta)}{(1+\rho)(1+r)}$

$$\Pi \equiv (1+\eta)\frac{dk}{dr} - \frac{\rho(1-\pi)}{1+\rho}\frac{dw}{dr} + \frac{\pi(1+\eta)}{(1+\rho)(1+r)}\frac{dw}{dr} - \frac{(\pi w - g)(1+\eta)}{(1+\rho)(1+r)^2}$$

The numerator is negative and the denominator is negative by the stability condition. Thus, $dr/d\pi > 0$, implying that $dk/d\pi < 0$ and $dw/d\pi < 0$. Thus, *in the steady-state equilibrium, introduction of a pay-as-you-go social security financed by labor income taxation will increase the real interest rate, reduce the wage rate, and reduce capital accumulatio.*

The intuition is as follows. An increase in the labor income tax rate, π , will not affect investment [the right side of equation (9)] at the initial interest rate and unambiguously decrease savings [the left side of equation (9)]. Therefore, there will be excess quantity demanded for funds, and the real interest rate must increase to clear the market. As the real interest rate increases, the capital-labor ratio and the real wage rate will decrease.

5. The Impact of the Pay-as-You-Go System on Industrial Workers and Farmers

This section compares the benefits to non-migrant workers, migrant workers, and farmers, under a fully-funded social security system and the pay-as-you-go social security system.

5.1 Gains by Industrial Workers

Consider a forced savings social security system. The government forces every industrial worker to save part of their income when young, and everyone receives savings plus interest rate when old. Assume that the forced saving rate is π . The net rate of returns to savings is the interest rate. Table 4 shows the costs and benefits received by non-migrant industrial workers.

The net returns to a representative industrial worker in generation *t*-1, generation *t*, and generation *t*+1 are $r_t \pi w_{t-1}$, $r_{t+1} \pi w_t$, and $r_{t+2} \pi w_{t+1}$, respectively. In China, the savings rate for time deposit for 5 years was 9% on April 21,1991,

Table 4: Gains under a Fully-Funded System

Generation	*Costs and Benefits in Time Period*				*Gains*
	t-1	t	t+1	t+2	
t-1	$-\pi w_{t-1}$	$(1+r_t)\pi w_{t-1}$			$r_t \pi w_{t-1}$
t		$-\pi w_t$	$(1+r_{t+1})\pi w_t$		$r_{t+1} \pi w_t$
t +1			$-\pi w_{t+1}$	$(1+r_{t+2})\pi w_{t+1}$	$r_{t+2} \pi w_{t+1}$

12.06 % on May 1, 1996, and 9% on August 23, 1996.[14] From 1978 to 1996, the annual inflation rate was about 9.41% based on GDP deflators, and was 7.384% based on general retail price indices.[15] In 1996, the inflation rate was 6.1% based on the general retail price index, and 9.6% based on the GDP deflator. Thus, the real interest rate in China was between 3%-6%.

Now consider a pay-as-you-go social security system. As shown in section 4, a pay-as-you-go social security system will lower the capital stock and the wage rate, i.e., $w_t > \tilde{w}_t$. Each young non-migrant industrial worker at time *t* pays a payroll tax $\pi\tilde{w}_t$ when young, where π is the tax rate and $\tilde{w}_t$ is the wage rate. The total amount of taxes are $L_t\pi\tilde{w}_t$. The tax revenue is used to finance the social security benefit for the current retirees in urban areas. The labor force is growing at the rate of n_t. Assume that the real wage rate is growing at the rate of λ_t, i.e., $\tilde{w}_t = (1+\lambda_t)\tilde{w}_{t-1}$. Table 5 illustrates the contributions and benefits of a representative industrial worker. Recall that $n_{t+1} = (L_{t+1} - L_t)/L_t = (\eta L_t + qF_t)/L_t = \eta + qF_t/L_t$. The old in period t (generation t–1) contributes nothing but receives $(1+n_t)(1+\lambda_t)\pi\tilde{w}_{t-1}$. Each old in generation *t* contributes $\pi\tilde{w}_{t-1}$, and receives $(1+n_{t+1})(1+\lambda_t)\pi\tilde{w}_t$. Thus, the net rate of returns to generation *t* is $(1+n_t)(1+\lambda_t) - 1 = n_t + \lambda_t + n_t\lambda_t$. Similarly, the net rate of returns to generation *t* is $(1+n_{t+i})(1+\lambda_{t+i}) - 1 = n_{t+i} + \lambda_{t+i} + n_{t+i}\lambda_{t+i}$, for $i = 1, 2, \ldots$.

Now let's compare the net returns under the fully-funded system and the pay-as-you-go system. Recall that under the fully-funded system, the net return for a

Table 5: Gains under a Pay-as-You-Go System

Generation	*Costs and Benefits in Time Period*				*Gains*
	t-1	t	t+1	t+2	
t-1				0	$(1+n_t)(1+\lambda_t)\pi\tilde{w}_{t-1}$
$(1+n_t)(1+\lambda_t)\pi\tilde{w}_{t-1}$					
t				$-\pi\tilde{w}_t$	$(1+n_{t+1})(1+\lambda_{t+1})\pi\tilde{w}_t$
$(n_{t+1}+\lambda_t+\lambda_t n_{t+1})\pi\tilde{w}_t$					

[14] See *Statistical Yearbook of China*, 1997, p. 625.
[15] See *Statistical Yearbook of China*, 1997, p. 42, 267.

t+1 $-\pi\tilde{w}_{t+1}$ $(1+n_{t+2})(1+\lambda_{t+2})\pi\tilde{w}_{t+1}$

$(n_{t+2}+\lambda_{t+2}+\lambda_{t+2}n_{t+2})\pi\tilde{w}_{t+1}$

---

worker of generation *t* is $r_{t+1}\pi w_t$ and the net return under the pay-as-you-go system for a worker of generation *t* is $(n_{t+1}+\lambda_t+\lambda_t n_{t+1})\pi\tilde{w}_t$. Thus, theoretically, whether workers will be better off or worse off under the pay-as-you-go system is unambiguous, depending on whether $(n_{t+1}+\lambda_t+\lambda_t n_{t+1})\pi\tilde{w}_t$ is greater or less than $r_{t+1}\pi w_t$.

Recent data indicate that industrial workers can be better off under the pay-as-you-go system in the short run. The urban population growth rate from 1978 to 1995 was about 4.081%,[16] and thus, the growth rate of wage earners, n_t, was about 4.1%. The growth rate of real wage rate is λ_t. The growth rate of the real wage rate was about 5.462% from 1978 to 1996, but was 8.12% from 1991 to 1996.[17] Thus, rate of returns to each retiree was more than 13%! Recall that under the fully-funded system (the forced savings system), the rate of return was only about 3-6%. Thus, wage earners will receive higher returns under a pay-as-you-go social security system than a forced-saving system. As industrialization proceeds, eventually there will be less and less labor migrating from rural areas to cities. The decrease in the migration rate, together with the decrease in capital accumulation and wage rate, may reduce the urban wage earners' welfare in the long run.

Like a non-migrant industrial worker, the rate of return to a migrant industrial worker is the real interest rate. As mentioned earlier, the real interest rate in China was between 3%-6%. Migrant industrial workers must take care of their rural parents when young, i.e., transferring an amount of $\gamma(1-\pi)q\tilde{w}_{t-1}$ to their rural parents. With the same wage rate, migrant industrial workers will have less income left for consumption and saving than a non-migrant worker.

It should be mentioned that, if the pay-as-you-go system is introduced in period *t*, then the generation *t*-1 will receive a windfall benefit without paying anything, and will be clearly better off. However, the debt will be transferred to the future generations.

5.2 Losses by Farmers

---

[16] Urban population was 172.45 million persons in 1978 and 359.5 million persons in 1996. See *Statistical Yearbook of China*, 1997, p. 69.

[17] General retail price index was used to calculate the real wage rate. See *Statistical Yearbook of China*, 1997, p. 123, 267.

As mentioned, farmers rely on family security. Old farmers receive gifts from their children who migrate to industry, as well as gifts from their children who remain in rural areas. Table 6 shows benefits to farmers under a fully-funded system and a pay-as-you-go system for urban workers.

Table 6: Benefits to Farmers under Alternative Social Security System for Urban Workers

Generation	*Costs and Benefits in Time Period*				*Gains*
	t-1	t	t+1	t+2	
t-1	$-\beta e_{t-1}$	$(1+\eta-q)(1+\omega)\beta e_{t-1}$ $+\gamma(1-\pi)qw_t$			$[(\eta-q)+\omega+(\eta-q)\omega]\beta e_{t-1}$ $+\gamma(1-\pi)qw_t$
t		$-\beta e_t$	$(1+\eta-q)(1+\omega)\beta e_t$ $+\gamma(1-\pi)q\tilde{w}_{t+1}$		$[(\eta-q)+\omega+(\eta-q)\omega]\beta e_t$ $+\gamma(1-\pi)q\tilde{w}_{t+1}$
t+1			$-\beta e_{t+1}$	$(1+\eta-q)(1+\omega)\beta e_{t+1}$ $+\gamma(1-\pi)q\tilde{w}_{t+2}$	$[(\eta-q)+\omega+(\eta-q)\omega]\beta e_{t+1}$ $+\gamma(1-\pi)q\tilde{w}_{t+2}$

Each young farmer in period *t*-1 contributes βe_{t-1} amount out of his endowment to his parent, and receives $(1+\eta-q)(1+\omega)\beta e_{t-1}$ amount from his rural children and $\gamma q(1-\pi)w_t$ amount from his migrant children when old (time period *t*). Recall that η is the population growth rate, q is the rate of migration from rural areas to cities, and ω is the growth rate of endowment. Population growth is beneficial to farmers. Rural-urban migration may or may not be beneficial to farmers. While migration results in less young in the rural areas to support the old, it also results in more migrant workers to give their rural parents gifts.

Suppose that a pay-as-you-go social security system for the urban workers is introduced in period t. As mentioned earlier, a pay-as-you-go system may reduce capital accumulation and the wage rate, i.e., under a pay-as-you-go system, the wage rate is lower than that under a fully funded system. Letting the real wage rate under the pay-as-you-go system, we have $\tilde{w}_{t+1} < w_{t+1}$ for $t > 0$.

An introduction of pay-as-you-go social security for the urban workers will hurt the rural old. The reason is clear. The rural old partially depend on transfers from their children who migrated to urban areas. The transfer is part of the migrant worker's disposable income. When a social security system financed by labor income is introduced, the disposable income of migrant workers will decrease. Thus, they will transfer less to their rural parents. Thus, an introduction of pay-as-you-go social security benefits the current urban retirees, while hurting the rural old.

6. The Impact of the Decline in Total Population Growth

Since the early 1970, China has adopted a population control policy. The policy was more strictly carried out in cities than in rural areas. As a result, China's population growth rate has declined significantly. The annual growth rate of population was 2.02% from 1952 to 1975, and 1.33% from 1978 to 1996. From 1952 to 1975, the annual growth rate of population was 3.327% for urban areas and 1.7% for rural areas. From 1978 to 1996, the annual growth rate of population was 4.1% for urban areas, and 0.50% for rural areas. [18] Although there was a decrease in the growth rate of total population, the growth rate of the population in urban areas has increased.

The increase in the city population was caused by the labor migration from rural areas to urban areas. In 1995, the annual natural growth rate of population was 1.06% for the nation, 0.923% for cities, and 1.109% for rural areas; meanwhile, the total city population increased by 2.55%; thus, the annual migration rate from rural areas to cities was about 1.44%. [19]

Many economists and policy makers in industrialized countries are concerned with the social security crisis that resulted from the decrease in the population growth rate.[20] Their concern is justified since there will be fewer young people to support the old. Without raising the social security tax rate, the future retirees will have lower social security benefits. Some Chinese policy makers and economists

---

[18] See *Statistical Yearbook of China,* 1997, p. 69.

[19] See *Statistical Yearbook of China,* 1996.

[20] It was estimated that in the year of 2030 a deficit will appear on the social security account.

also predict that a similar social security crisis will occur in China under a pay-as-you-go system due to a decline in the population growth rate.[21] This concern might be unwarranted. If the pay-as-you-go social security system covers only wage earners (the population in cities), there will be no social security crisis. The growth rate of wage earners has been increasing.

Thus, the decrease in the growth rate of population may not cause a pay-as-you-go social security crisis in China as would happen in the industrialized countries since more and more farmers will move to urban areas and become wage earners.

7. Concluding Remarks

China is in the process of industrialization with a large amount of the labor force moving from the agricultural sector to industrial sectors. An expansion of the pay-as-you-go social security system benefits current urban retirees, and may solve the social security payment problem faced by many state enterprises. Also, although facing a declining population growth rate, China may not have a social security crisis under a pay-as-you-go social security system, which just covers the wage earners, that many industrialized countries face. However, the expansion of the pay-as-you-go social security system may have an adverse effect on capital accumulation in both the short run and the long run, hurting the rural old and either benefiting or hurting the wage earners in urban areas before the completion of industrialization and is likely to reduce wage earners' welfare after industrialization.

Expanding the individual account and gradually privatizing social security will increase capital accumulation and benefit Chinese economic development. The difficulty of privatizing social security lies in financing social security debt (the obligation to current retirees and workers who have made contributions under the pay-as-you-go system). Since China's social security system only covers a small portion of the population, the social security debt is not too large. International experience indicates that pension debt is about 20-30 times of the current pension payment. In 1996, pensions for retirees were 152.55 billion yuan. Thus, the social security debt should be between 3,051.2 billion and 4,576.8 billion yuan, the social security debt should be about 44-66% of GDP (China's GDP was 6859.38 billion yuan in 1996). In 1996, pensions for state enterprises were 128.54 billion yuan, implying that the social security debt should be between 2,570.8 billion yuan and 3856.2 billion yuan.[22] Chinese government has run budget deficits since 1985, and

---

[21] See The World Bank (1997) and Zhou and Wang (1994).

[22] *Labor Statistical Yearbook of China*, 1997.

there is no budget surplus to be used for social security debt finance. The asset of state enterprises was about 3,452 billion yuan, which might be enough to pay the social security debt.[23] Government can issues bonds to finance the social security debt. It can be shown that asset finance and debt finance are equivalent, both transferring the burden to future generations. Tax finance, particularly consumption tax finance, is beneficial to capital accumulation and economic development.

China's major social security problem may occur in the rural areas. The birth control policy has resulted in a decline in the birth rate, and industrialization has caused large rural-city migration. Thus, the ratio of the rural old to the rural young is increasing. The income for rural residents is still rather low. In 1996, the average annual cash-receipt of a rural resident was 2,309.4 yuan, the cash expenditure was 2,137.4 yuan, and the surplus was only 172 yuan (about $20 based on the official exchange rate).[24] The pay-as-you-go system does not work in rural areas since the government cannot collect enough taxes. The forced saving system also may not work since in most rural areas farmers may not have much cash left for savings. The rural young provide their old parents with a lot of services which would be very costly through the market. There exist large external benefits in a rural family with the young and the old being together. The family security may have to last a long time in many rural areas. The government must raise funds to provide basic supplies for those rural old people who do not receive transfers from their children.

References

1. Barro, Robert J., 1978, *The Impact of Social Security on Private Saving: Evidence from the US Time Series,* Washington, D.C.: American Enterprise Institute.
2. Blinder, A., Robert Gordon, and D. Wise, 1981, Life Cycle Savings and Bequest: Cross-Sectional Estimates of the Life Cycle Model, in *The Determinants of National Savings and Wealth*, edited by Modigliani, London and New York: Macmillan.
3. China's Ministry of Finance, 1997, *Finance Year Book of China*, Beijing: China's Finance Journal Publishing House.
4. China's National Statistical Bureau, 1997, *Labor Statistical Yearbook of China*, Beijing: Statistical Publishing House.
5. China's National Statistical Bureau, 1997, *A Statistical Survey of China*, Beijing: Statistical Publishing House.

[23] *A Statistical Survey of China*, 1997.
[24] *A Statistical Survey of China*, 1997.

6. China's National Statistical Bureau, 1997, *Statistical Yearbook of China*, Beijing: Statistical Publishing House.
7. Diamond, Peter A., 1996, Proposals to Restructure Social Security, *Journal of Economic Perspectives* 10, 67-88.
8. Feldstein, Martin, 1996, Social Security and Saving: New Time Series Evidence, *National Tax Journal* 49, 151-164.
9. Feldstein, Martin, 1974, Social Security, Induced Retirement and Aggregate Capital Accumulation, *Journal of Political Economy* 82, 905-926.
10. Feldstein, Martin, and Samwick, Andrew, 1996, "The Transition path in privatizing social security," National Bureau of Economic Research (Cambridge, MA*) Working Paper No. 5761.*
11. Gruber, Jonathan, and David Wise, 1997, Social Security Programs and Retirement Around the World, NBER *Working Paper Series* No. 6134.
12. Kopits, George, and Padma Gotur, 1980, The Influence of Social Security on Household Savings: A Cross-Country Investigation, International Monetary Fund, *Staff Papers* 27, 161-190.
13. Kotlikoff, Laurence J., 1996, Privatizing Social Security at Home and Abroad, American Economic Review 86, 368-372.
14. _______, 1979, Testing the Theory of Social Security and Life Cycle Accumulation, *American Economic Review* , 396-410.
15. Lin, Shuanglin, 1998, Labor Income Taxation and Human Capital ccumulation, *Journal of Public Economics* 68, 291-302.
16. World Bank, 1997, Old Age Security, Pension Reform in China, Washington D.C.
17. Zhou, Xiaochuan, and Wang, Lin, 1994, Social Security: Economic Analyses and System Suggestions, *Reform*, Nos. 3 & 4.

CHAPTER 6

THE EFFICIENCY AND DISTRIBUTION EFFECTS OF CHINA'S PENSION REFORM

DIANQING XU
Department of Economics, Huron College, University of Western Ontario
London, Ontario N6G 1H3, Canada
E-mail: xu2@sscl.uwo.ca

ZHI WANG
Agriculture Department of U.S.A., 5225 Pooks Hill Road, #1709N, Bethesda, MD 20814, USA
E-mail: zwang1@worldbank.org

YAN WANG
The World Bank, 1818 H St., NW,
Washington, DC 20433, USA
E-mail: ywang2@worldbank.org

The purpose of the paper is to quantitatively estimate the impacts of various schemes for financing the basic pension component to keep retirees above the poverty line (Pillar I plan), using a newly defined computable general equilibrium (CGE) model. The authors found that it is better if the financial burden of Pillar I is shared by the state, enterprises, and employees than by enterprises only.

1. Introduction

One of the most serious impediments to further progress in the continued transformation of China's centrally-planned economy into a market oriented economy is the lack of an effective social security system. If the momentum of economic reform is to continue, the development of a new social security system compatible with the emerging market economy is now a matter of urgency. In the past few years there have been many research projects on China's social security system reform, however, there is not enough quantitative analysis on how to design a social security system that meets the needs of China's new economic realities, or how to manage the transition from the present industry-controlled social security system to a new state-sponsored system.

Our research will address some of the important and urgent problems that need to be resolved. As pointed out by the World Bank report, "Old Age Security: Pension Reform in China", the social security system should combine social pooling with funded individual accounts. It should provide for a basic pension component to keep retires above the poverty line (Pillar 1) and for large mandatory individual accounts (Pillar 2) to obtain the advantages of funding, supplemented by voluntary accounts (Pillar 3). "In China's case it is recommended that this pillar (Pillar 1) provide universal benefits, financed out of payroll contributions and covering all formal sector workers in urban areas and employees in large township enterprises." The report proposed that Pillar 1 could be financed through general taxes or payroll taxes. (p44) However, the report did not discuss the differences between a general tax and a payroll tax when financing Pillar 1. In fact, the impacts of various schemes for financing Pillar1 are precisely different.

The purpose of this research is to quantitatively estimate the impacts of various schemes for financing Pillar1 on China's macroeconomic structure based on a newly defined Computable General Equilibrium (CGE) model. The research will focus on the impacts of varies schemes for financing Pillar 1 on the GDP, GINI coefficients, aggregate demand, consumption and investment. Furthermore, the research will investigate the impacts of pension reforms on output, labor demand, investment on various sectors as well as the impacts on consumption of various groups of citizens with different income levels.

Using the CGE model we have obtained some promising results from preliminary simulations of various schemes for financing Pillar 1. We found that, the aggregate investment, social demand will be higher, and social inequality will be lower if Pillar 1 is financed via payroll taxes instead of general taxes. It is better if the financial burden of Pillar 1 is shared by the state, enterprises and employees rather than by enterprises only.

Financing Pillar 1 via general taxes will increase the GINI coefficient and the inequality of the society will be granter. Financing Pillar 1 via payroll taxes is better than via general taxes. Financing Pillar 1 will induce sectoral output and demand for labor increase in construction, building materials, mechanical manufacturing, road vehicles and metal products. The output and demand for labor in processed food, apparel, electronic machinery, leather and services will decrease. Labor will move from light industry and services to construction and heavy industry. Moreover, the research suggests new ways to organize the economic data in the transition process which could be used as a base for economists to exchange their knowledge and analyze various reform proposals.

2. Financing Basic Pension Component

There are many options for the design and implementation of Pillar 1, and each is associated with risks and tradeoffs. To be concrete, there exist at least three alternative approaches to finance Pillar 1: (1) To increase general tax rate (for example, sales tax or value added tax) and finance Pillar 1 from the aggregate tax revenue pool. (2) Enterprises contribute 9% of each worker's total wage from their profit. This would be similar to an increase in the enterprise income tax. (3) An individual contribution of 9% of total wages. Each individual has to pay not only personal income tax but also social insurance tax.

The advantage of approach 1 is easy of implementation and no notable distortion to labor market. However, it is unfair to use general tax revenues to finance Pillar 1, because current social security reform has been designed to cover only all formal sector worker in urban areas and employees in large township enterprises and disregards workers in the rural area who are almost 70% of total population. The redistribution will take place from uncovered sectors to the formal sector.

Approach 2 is also easy to implement in the current stage but may be difficult after tax and financial reforms are implemented in China. Collecting funding for Pillar 1 through enterprise profits directly but not through neither direct tax nor indirect tax is not favourable for firm's development and financial administration. In addition, the problems of scenario 2 is includes questions on the definition of worker's total wage.[1]

The major advantages of approach 3 are (a) If the definition of a worker's wage is clean it is easy to collect 9% of that wage as social security tax. (b) It is fair to collect a fixed proportion of the wage for social security because high income workers will pay more and low income workers will pay less. This is helpful to narrow social inequality. (c) To collect the same amount of tax revenue, the social

---

[1] The worker's wage is only around 50% of their net income currently in China. The total value of bonus, subsidies, housing allowance and other benefit received by worker may be no less than their nominal wage. Most economists agree that it is much better to reform the payroll system and merge all welfare payment with wage as in western countries.

welfare will be better if the tax is collected directly from consumers instead of from producers.

At the current stage, the major problem of approach 3 is if workers contribute 9% of their wages to Pillar 1 it will significantly slim down their standard of living. In order to keep worker's standard of living stable in the reform process, it is possible to ask enterprise to increase worker wages first. For example, if worker wages increase 9%, then they pay the same amount for social security tax. Because the nominal wage and social security tax burden are increased in the same amount, the worker's standard of living will remain at the same level. The burden to the enterprise will be the same as approach 2. It is suggested to ask government to reduce enterprise income tax to lessen financial burden for enterprises. The burden of Pillar 1 could be shared evenly by all three: government, enterprises and individuals if workers pay 9% of their wage for social security tax, their wage increases 6%, and the enterprise income tax is cut 3%. In such case, the net contribution from government, enterprises and workers is 3:3:3. Obviously, there are many different ways to split the financial burden among government, enterprises and workers, for example, 4:3:2, 4:2:3, 2:3:4 etc. In order to determine which weight is best the quantitative simulation is essential.

In approach 2 the social security tax is paid by enterprises based on the total amount of the wage bill. The changes in firm's cost will alter the relative prices among their productive factors. In approach3 the social security tax is collected from worker incomes, and does not affect relative prices, therefore, even the amount of social security tax collected from two scenario is the same, the impact of the two schemes on the macroeconomic structure will be totally different. It is necessary to check the following macroeconomic variables when the optimal scheme of funding Pillar 1 is discussed:

(1) the effect on GDP;

(2) the effect on GINI coefficient ;

(3) the aggregate demand;

(4) aggregate consumption;

(5) aggregate investment.

In addition, we also need to examine the effect of social security reform on the welfare of residents with different income, the effect on sectoral output, sectoral labor demand and sectoral investment, consumption etc.

According to the World Bank report, the sustainable contribution rate should be 9% of a worker's monthly wage paid as pension insurance premium to pension fund. We have reservations on the amount of contribution rate in above recommendation. Moreover, the remaining question is what is the reasonable share contributed by workers, employers and government in Pillar 1 and 2? Due to the limited scope of our research, the amount of the sustainable contribution rate will be studied in the next stage of our research.

3. Theoretical Framework and Literature Review

There has been a great deal of academic interest in analyzing and evaluating the pension reform policies quantitatively in the transition processes. M. Feldstein (1974) pioneered the use of mathematical tools for describing aggregate capital accumulation in social security systems. Thomas J. Sargent and his colleagues (1995) used rational expectation model to examine the impact of a pension fund system. Laurence Seidman (1986), Patricio Arrau (1990), Laurence Kotilkoff (1997) and many others have significantly advanced the study of pension system in recent years. Dr. Kangbin Zheng at the World Bank has developed a menu-driven computer program to calculate the effects of pension fund collection. While their research has provided important theoretical guidelines in this area, there have been repeated calls for more quantitative studies to assist in the design of reform strategies.

Most of those that have been done, however, rely only on partial equilibrium analysis. For example, they investigated the pension system but with an assumption that prices and wages are fixed. They assumed that changing the pension system would have no effect on the price levels of products and input materials, no effect on wage levels of various groups of workers, no effect on labor demand of various sectors, no effect on the structure of the economy etc. In addition, most current researches do not investigate substitution effects between sectors and factors, without allowing for the subsequent intersectoral reactions. Clearly, the partial equilibrium approach has serious limitations for analyzing complex and dynamic issues of pension reform.

The Computable General Equilibrium model (CGE), which incorporates the fundamental general equilibrium links among production structure, incomes of various groups and the pattern of demand, has been widely used for macroeconomic analysis. Recent literature indicates a rapidly growing interest in these models. For instance, CGE models are being used to analyze the effects of various trade policies (J. Shoven and Whalley, 1992), tax and fiscal policy (J. Piggott, 1985), energy policy (T. Kehoe, 1992), etc. Ayse Imrohoroglu, S. Imrohoroglu and Duglas Joines used CGE model to do a life cycle analysis of social security. Obviously, in order to study pension reform in China some significant modifications of the CGE model are necessary and possible because of the flexibility of the CGE model.

4. Description of Proposed CES Model

The proposed CGE model includes multiple sectors, factors and institutions. This multisectoral model captures not only multisectoral supply-demand interactions but also the nonlinear substitution possibilities between the inputs in production processes, between imports and domestic sales, and between exports and domestic sales. It also incorporates macro variables and mechanisms that are essential to achieving a balance among various economic aggregates. The proposed CGE model can be used to simulate the different approaches to finance Pillar 1 and to analyze the impact on macroeconomic structure.

The basic structure of the proposed CGE model is an extension of the Cameroon model (Devarajan B. N. S. and R. Weiner (1989), the U.S. model (S. Robinson, 1989), the Chinese model (D. Xu, 1996) and the world trade model (Z. Wang, 1997). The proposed framework could facilitate the analysis of the casual chain process by which an "exogenous shock" works its way through the economic system. This obviously is an improvement over the partial equilibrium approach used in other investigations in the field. There are 22 sectors, 12 groups of citizens with different income levels, 5 productive factors including capital, land, agricultural labor, un-skilled labor and skilled labor with around 2500 equations in the proposed CES model. These modifications make this CGE model much more complex but much more useful for discussing pension reform in the transition process than the earlier versions of CGE models.

The CGE model is based on a 22 sector Social Accounting Matrix (SAM) estimated for 1992 data. Production is characterized by two-level nesting of constant elasticity of substitution (CES) function. At the first level, firms are assumed to use two types of inputs: a composite primary factor and an aggregate intermediate input according to a CES cost function. At the second level, the split of intermediate demand is assumed to follow a Leontief specification, therefore, there is no substitution among intermediate inputs. The five primary factors also substitute smoothly through a CES cost function. The degree of substitutability between the composite primary factor and the aggregate intermediate as well as among the five primary factors depends on their base year share in production and on the elasticity of substitution that is assumed to be constant.

The private household maximizes a Stone-Geary utility function over the 14 composite goods, subject to their budget constraints, which leads to the Extended Liner Expenditure System (ELES) household demand function. Household saving are treated as demand for future consumption goods with zero subsistence quantity. An economy-wide consumer price index is specified as the price of savings. It represents the opportunity cost of giving up current consumption in exchange for future consumption. Government spending and investment decisions are based on Cobb-Douglas utility functions, which generate constant expenditure shares for each composite commodity. The firm intermediate inputs, household consumption, government spending and investment demand constitute total demand for the same Armington composite of domestic products and imported goods from different sources. A two-level nested CES aggregate function is specified for each composite commodity. The total demand is first divided between domestic produced and imported goods, then the expenditure on imports is further divided according to geographical origin under the assumption of cost minimization. Sectoral import demand functions are derived from the corresponding cost function according to Shephard's lemma.

A software package GAMS (General Algebraic Modeling System) designed by the World Bank has been used for constructing and solving large complex mathematical programming models. This software has been used widely by the World Bank, U.S. government agencies and academics in CGE modeling and computation.

5. Simulation and Results

We have designed four sets of counterfactual experiments to investigate the impacts of various pension schemes on GDP, income, government savings, GINI coefficient etc.

(1) In the first scenario we increase general tax by an amount equal to 9% of total worker's wage bill to finance Pillar 1. The weight of financial burden among government, enterprise and worker is 9:0:0.

(2) In the second scenario, we assume social security collects the same amount of funds for Pillar 1 but the money comes directly from enterprise profit, similar to an enterprise income tax. The weight among government, enterprise and worker is 0:9:0.

(3) In the third scenario, we assume all these funds come from workers wages after the enterprises increase workers wage at the same amount. The weight is 0:9:0,

the same as scenario 2.

(4) In the last scenario, the social security burden will be evenly shared by government, enterprises and workers. The workers have to pay 9% of their wages as social security taxes after their wages have been increased 6%, meanwhile the government reduces the enterprise income tax which is equal to 3% of the wage bill. The weight is 3:3:3 among government, enterprise and workers. The workers, employers and state will contribute one third of the fund for Pillar 1.

Table 1 presents the percentage changes in GDP, aggregate domestic demand, GINI coefficient, total consumption and total investment.

Table 1: Impacts of pension fund collection on Macroeconomic structure

	Base year	Scenario 1	Scenario 2	Scenario 3	Scenario 4
GDP	0.00000;	0.00083;	0.00007;	0.00008;	0.00012;
Domestic demand	0.00000;	0.08561;	0.02943;	0.02708;	0.05037;
GINI coefficient	0.00000;	0.01564;	-0.00089;	-0.00691;	0.00227;
Total consumption	0.00000;	-3.15699;	-0.37289;	-0.43558;	-2.11489;
Total Investment	0.00000;	12.05653;	7.82289;	7.90725;	10.42875;

In the simulation, household has been defined as 12 groups: 7 groups in rural area: lowest, low, middle low, middle, middle high, high, highest; and 5 groups in urban area: low, middle low, middle, middle high, and high. Table 2 presents the impacts on welfare for above 12 groups of citizens with different income levels (EV).

Table 2: Impacts on household welfare gains

	Base year	Scenario 1	Scenario 2	Scenario 3	Scenario 4
Rural lowest	0.00000;	-0.67177;	-0.16293;	-0.08849;	-0.39675;
Rural low	0.00000;	-0.59040;	-0.15174;	-0.03785;	-0.32290;
Rural middle low	0.00000;	-0.65614;	-0.17002;	-0.03498;	-0.36605;
Rural middle	0.00000;	-1.20154;	-0.34217;	-0.10339;	-0.71289;
Urban low	0.00000;	-0.48202;	-0.17122;	-0.26811;	-0.32482;
Rural middle high	0.00000;	-0.87879;	-0.27717;	-0.11184;	-0.55681;
Rural high	0.00000;	-1.02934;	-0.36963;	-0.19882;	-0.70751;
Urban middle low	0.00000;	-0.49758;	-0.25500;	-0.34517;	-0.38535;
Urban middle	0.00000;	-0.99966;	-0.56322;	-0.77677;	-0.83593;
Rural very high	0.00000;	-0.80873;	-0.37918;	-0.31905;	-0.67608;
Urban middle high	0.00000;	-0.98658;	-0.60109;	-0.83520;	-0.88841;

Urban high	0.00000;	-1.55349;	-1.08877;	-1.62956;	-1.69178;

* Table 2 presents the equivalent variation (EV) of different types of households affected by financing pillar 1 under four scenarios. Equivalent variation is the Hicksian measure of the change in consumer surplus. It is a money matric measuring how much better or worse off is the representative household in the equilibrium after a policy change than it was in the initial equilibrium using the base year price as reference.

Table 3-6 present the impacts on sectoral output, labor demand, household consumption and investment in 22 sectors.

Table 3: Impacts on sectoral output

	Base year	Scenario 1	Scenario 2	Scenario 3	Scenario 4
Crops	0.00000;	-0.42733;	-0.04614;	-0.03602;	-0.08963;
Other agriculture	0.00000;	-0.02116;	-0.51853;	-0.52698;	-0.91047;
Mining	0.00000;	-0.09098;	0.13092;	0.19095;	0.19596;
Processed food	0.00000;	-7.40391;	-0.88286;	-1.06592;	-1.46866;
Textiles	0.00000;	-0.45791;	-0.37673;	-0.40615;	-0.65445;
Apparel	0.00000;	-1.32983;	-1.36309;	-1.52557;	-2.33173;
Leather	0.00000;	-0.35087;	-0.70985;	-0.78879;	-1.24480;
Other non-durable goods	0.00000;	-0.80975;	-0.38965;	-0.41814;	-0.67361;
Energy	0.00000;	-0.37074;	-0.19168;	-0.17803;	-0.34560;
Chemicals	0.00000;	-1.12228;	-0.45548;	-0.38040;	-0.84353;
Build materials	0.00000;	2.91163;	1.35380;	1.41321;	2.35464;
Basic metals	0.00000;	1.57082;	0.91261;	0.99100;	1.56528;
Metal products	0.00000;	0.55031;	0.30263;	0.36376;	0.50712;
Machinery	0.00000;	2.13013;	1.19087;	1.28679;	2.04321;
Road vehicles	0.00000;	1.68305;	0.85345;	0.90059;	1.47734;
Electronic machinery	0.00000;	-0.30789;	-0.38790;	-0.46634;	-0.63671;
Electronics	0.00000;	-2.02970;	-0.85011;	-0.77246;	-1.52398;
Other Industries	0.00000;	1.69952;	0.76281;	0.78838;	1.33060;
Construction	0.00000;	7.08148;	3.18312;	3.25902;	5.57382;
Infrastructure	0.00000;	-0.91289;	-0.58684;	-0.55200;	-1.04683;
Commerce	0.00000;	-0.02790;	-0.17285;	0.17344;	-0.30130;
Service	0.00000;	-0.97374;	-0.70650;	-0.79232;	-1.20205;

Table 4: Impacts on sectoral labor demand

	Base year	Scenario 1	Scenario 2	Scenario 3	Scenario 4
Crops	0.00000;	-0.43670;	-0.04865;	-0.03838;	-0.09406;
Other agriculture	0.00000;	-0.11983;	-0.48382;	-0.49546;	-0.84683;
Mining	0.00000;	-0.35560;	0.02545;	0.08789;	0.00870;
Processed food	0.00000;	-7.69052;	-1.00378;	-1.18363;	-1.68207;
Textiles	0.00000;	0.19718;	-0.48032;	-0.50766;	-0.83746;
Apparel	0.00000;	-1.56979;	-1.46029;	-1.62098;	-2.50202;
Leather	0.00000;	-0.54597;	-0.78779;	-0.86510;	-1.38206;
Other non-durable goods	0.00000;	-1.06891;	-0.49364;	-0.51997;	-0.85737;
Energy	0.00000;	-0.69156;	-0.31464;	-0.29688;	-0.56424;
Chemicals	0.00000;	-1.42176;	-0.57307;	-0.49485;	-1.05168;
Build materials	0.00000;	2.62217;	1.24122;	1.30321;	2.15475;
Basic metals	0.00000;	1.26203;	-0.79343;	0.87512;	1.35205;
Metal products	0.00000;	0.29328;	0.20134;	0.26484;	0.32706;
Machinery	0.00000;	1.87092;	1.09134;	1.19017;	1.86478;
Road vehicles	0.00000;	1.37066;	0.73365;	0.48443;	1.26289;
Electronic machinery	0.00000;	-0.57988;	-0.49359;	-0.56888;	-0.82409;
Electronics	0.00000;	-2.28695;	-0.94938;	0.86830;	-1.69959;
Other industries	0.00000;	1.45151;	0.66581;	0.69372;	1.15754;
Construction	0.00000;	6.93227;	3.12650;	3.20383;	5.47110;
Infrastructure	0.00000;	-1.21401;	-0.70637;	-0.66883;	-1.25791;
Commerce	0.00000;	-0.25549;	-0.28280;	-0.28018;	-0.49650;
Service	0.00000;	-1.12944;	-0.75508;	-0.83563;	-1.29008;

Table 5: Impacts on sectoral investment

	Base year	Scenario 1	Scenario 2	Scenario 3	Scenario 4
Crops	0.00000;	0.00000;	0.00000;	0.00000;	0.00000;
Other agriculture	0.00000;	5.05068;	4.73607;	4.92445;	6.13284;
Mining	0.00000;	0.00000;	0.00000;	0.00000;	0.00000;
Processed food	0.00000;	0.00000;	0.00000;	0.00000;	0.00000;
Textiles	0.00000;	0.00000;	0.00000;	0.00000;	0.00000;
Apparel	0.00000;	0.00000;	0.00000;	0.00000;	0.00000;
Leather	0.00000;	0.00000;	0.00000;	0.00000;	0.00000;
Other non-durable goods	0.00000;	11.17332;	6.36292;	6.42402;	9.15283;
Energy	0.00000;	0.00000;	0.00000;	0.00000;	0.00000;
Chemicals	0.00000;	0.00000;	0.00000;	0.00000;	0.00000;

Build materials	0.00000;	0.00000;	0.00000;	0.00000;	0.00000;
Basic metals	0.00000;	0.00000;	0.00000;	0.00000;	0.00000;
Metal products	0.00000;	12.01965;	6.57869;	6.62104;	9.55357;
Machinery	0.00000;	11.68595;	6.50073;	6.55309;	9.40591;
Road vehicles	0.00000;	11.48221;	6.43268;	6.48830;	9.28075;
Electronic machinery	0.00000;	11.79699;	6.51545;	6.56248;	9.43591;
Electronics	0.00000;	11.58407;	6.46867;	6.52235;	9.34667;
Other industries	0.00000;	11.48820;	6.44955;	6.50522;	9.31240;
Construction	0.00000;	12.25309;	6.68104;	6.72398;	9.73974;
Infrastructure	0.00000;	11.95378;	6.55042;	6.59424;	9.50160;
Commerce	0.00000;	11.71291;	6.48504;	6.53255;	9.38100;
Service	0.00000;	11.74580;	6.46343;	6.49820;	9.34855;

Table 6: Impacts on household consumption by sector

	Base year	Scenario 1	Scenario 2	Scenario 3	Scenario 4
Crops	0.00000;	-5.02783;	0.26170;	0.66637;	-1.84809;
Other agriculture	0.00000;	-3.05113;	-0.00307;	0.14825;	-2.13256;
Mining	0.00000;	0.88712;	1.29458;	1.40379;	0.15774;
Processed food	0.00000;	-13.34526;	0.12677;	-0.05335;	-1.74176;
Textiles	0.00000;	-0.28967;	0.70773;	0.76987;	-0.82525;
Apparel	0.00000;	0.40505;	0.57288;	0.29333;	-0.89230;
Leather	0.00000;	0.52604;	0.52640;	0.16970;	-0.95562;
Other non-durable goods	0.00000;	0.60546;	0.48342;	0.22725;	-1.05290;
Energy	0.00000;	-0.86107;	-0.41256;	-0.67352;	-2.65716;
Chemical	0.00000;	-1.47385;	0.04670;	0.40651;	-2.14370;
Build materials	0.00000;	-1.20060;	-0.16412;	0.15627;	-2.47129;
Basic metals	0.00000;	-1.65139;	-0.13580;	0.41571;	-2.52890;
Metal products	0.00000;	-0.81708;	-0.28649;	-0.24603;	-2.53598;
Machinery	0.00000;	-1.46862;	-0.56989;	-0.46317;	-3.07274;
Road vehicles	0.00000;	-6.86221;	-1.14280;	-2.62055;	-3.30831;
Electronic machinery	0.00000;	-0.31900;	-0.83416;	-1.44507;	-3.18738;
Electronic	0.00000;	-1.14064;	-0.64116;	-0.71860;	-3.10124;
Other industries	0.00000;	2.19932;	-0.52184;	-0.22579;	-3.14531;
Construction	0.00000;	0.00000;	0.00000;	0.00000;	0.00000;
Infrastructure	0.00000;	-2.25119;	-0.88025;	-0.75299;	-3.65357;
Commerce	0.00000;	-1.73088;	-0.90851;	-1.04543;	-3.56817;
Service	0.00000;	-1.15577;	-1.10447;	-1.71036;	-3.70196;

6. Findings

We have obtained some interesting results from the preliminary simulations. Obviously, none of the scenarios have strong effect on real GDP but the impacts on domestic demand are various. Scenario 1 (financing Pillar 1 by general tax) increases domestic demand 0.08561%, Scenario 2 (by firm's profit) increases domestic demand 0.02943%, scenario 3 (by payroll tax) increases domestic demand 0.02708%, scenario 4 (by evenly share tax) increases domestic demand 0.05037%. Sharing social security taxes among government, enterprise and workers is better than asking firms to finance Pillar 1 alone in term of increasing domestic demand.

The GINI coefficient increases 0.01564 in Scenario 1 and decreases 0.02943 and 0.02708 respectively in scenario 2 and 3. Financing Pillar 1 by general tax may be worse than by payroll tax in term of inequality in the society. It seems the GINI coefficient will increase in scenario 4 because we increase the general tax rate for all residents, however, if taxing urban resident only then the GINI coefficient will remain the same. If we introduce aggressive tax rate instead of flat general tax rate, then the GINI coefficient will be decreased in scenario 4.

Because all pension funds collected in our simulations will be used for investment, collecting funds via a general tax is better than via payroll tax in term of investment. Sharing the financial burden among state, enterprise and workers is also better than asking enterprises to take care of financing Pillar1 alone.

Financing Pillar 1 will benefit sectoral output in construction, construction material, mechanical manufacturing, road vehicles and metal industries. Sectoral output will decrease in processed food, apparel, electronic machinery, leather and service industries.

Because the simulations are based on an assumption of full employment, the changes in sectoral labor demand indicate the trend of labor movement. From the Table 4, scenario 1 will cause the labor demand in processed food decrease 7.69052% and in Electronic machinery 2.28695%, in apparel sector 1.56979%. Meanwhile, the labor demand increase 6.93227% in construction sector, 2.2217% in building materials. The labor demand in machinery, road vehicles, other industry also increase. Reforming social security system will cause the labor force to move from light industries to construction and heavy industries.

Social security reform is beneficial to construction, manufacturing and other heavy industries because the relative prices in those sectors will increase.

References

1. Devarajan B. N. S. and R. Weiner "The 'Dutch' Disease in a Developing Country", *Journal of Development Economics*, 30: p71-92, 1994.
2. Feldstein, M, "Social Security, Induced Retirement and Aggregate Capital Accumulation", *Journal of Political Economy*, 82, No.5, p905-26, 1974.
3. Holzmann Robert, "Financing the Transition to Multi-pillar", HDNSP, Working paper, February 23,1998,
4. Imrohoroglu, Selahattin, He Huang and Thomas J. Sargent, "Two Computational Experiments to Privatize Social Security", *Mimeo*, March, 1995.
5. Imrohoroglu, Ayse, S. Imrohoroglu and Duglas Joines, "A Life Cycle Analysis of Social Security", Working paper of University of Southern California, 1992.
6. Kotilkoff, Laurence J., "Generational Accounting in Europe - An Economic, Social and Moral Imperative", Working paper of NBER, May, 1997.
7. Kotilkoff, Laurence J., "Simulating the Privatization of Social Security in General Equilibrium", Martin Feldstein, ed., Forthcoming in NBER volume Social Security, The Chicago University Press, 1997.
8. Robinson, S., M. Kilkenny and K. Hanson, "The USDA/ERS Computable General Equilibrium (CGE) Model of the United States", U.S. Department of Agriculture. Staff Report No. AGES 9049, 1990.
9. Seidman, Laurence S. "A Phase-Down of Social Security: The Transition in a Life Cycle Growth Model," *National Tax Journal*, vol. XXXIX, no.1, March 1986.
10. Wang, Zhi, "China and Taiwan access to the World Trade Organization: implications for U.S. agriculture and trade", *Agricultural Economics*, 17, p239-264, 1997.
11. Xu, Dianqing, "The Chasm in the Transition: A CGE Analysis of Chinese Economic Reform", *Journal of Policy Modelling*. Vol.18, p117-140, 1996.

CHAPTER 7

EFFICIENCY AND THE MECHANISM FOR FUNDING AND PROVISION OF SOCIAL SECURITY IN CHINA

HAIZHENG LI
School of Economics, Georgia Institute of Technology, Atlanta, GA 30332-0615, USA
E-mail: Haizheng.Li@econ.gatech.edu

JANUSZ R. MROZEK
School of Economics, Georgia Institute of Technology, Atlanta, GA 30332-0615, USA
E-mail: janusz.mrozek@econ.gatech.edu

An earlier version of this paper was prepared for presentation at the International Symposium on Establishing a Market-Oriented Social Security System in China, Beijing, June 24, 1998. We are thankful for the valuable comments we received from an anonymous referee, participants in the Symposium, and Keyong Dong and Wenruo Hou.

1. Introduction

Observers generally agree that China's further economic reform necessitates adoption of a market-oriented social security system. In a broad sense, social security includes not only income supplements for the elderly, the disabled, and for survivors of deceased workers (as in the Social Security system in the United States), but also medical care and unemployment compensation.[1] These benefits were traditionally provided to state workers by the Chinese government, through its

[1] For this study, income assistance for low-income individuals and families is not included in the scope of social security.

control of state-owned enterprises (SOEs). As state-owned industries shrink or are privatized, and as non-state sectors boom, the Chinese government faces new challenges in providing social security for state workers, and for the growing number of non-state workers. These challenges are heightened in the short run because of significant layoffs and early retirements of state workers following bankruptcies and contractions of state-owned enterprises.

In establishing a new social security system, a fundamental question is the need for government intervention. Although some would advocate no action from the government and a pure market system for social security, most observers agree that optimal provision of social security requires government action.[2] The most obvious arguments for government intervention are to correct various forms of market failure (Summers 1989) and to create a mechanism for redistribution of market outcomes. Individuals may value certain services too little and may irrationally underestimate the probability of catastrophic losses, or may be inept at making intertemporal decisions for their retirement. To the extent that individuals enter their retirement years with few resources, they will require publicly funded support services, creating an externality on society as a whole. Rothschild and Stiglitz (1976) also discuss the adverse selection problem for market provision of health benefits. Because of information asymmetry, such benefits will be under-provided and overpriced by the market. In addition, the social security system can also provide a means to redistribute incomes.

In choosing government intervention, one important concern is the loss of efficiency when existing market outcomes become distorted. The extent of these efficiency losses depend on the nature of the financing and benefit provision mechanism, so the choice of this mechanism is crucial in determining the social security program's economic effects. Two types of mechanisms discussed in the literature include mandated provision, in which the government compels employers to provide the benefits as part of their compensation packages, and public provision, in which the government provides benefits directly to the citizenry out of revenues from taxation. An important characteristic distinguishing provision mechanisms is the linkage between the decision to work and the provision of benefits. We argue below that the strength of the linkage determines the economic efficiency of the provision alternative.

Most countries provide social security through some form of public provision, and these public programs have generally expanded over time. For example, in

---

[2] We use the term "liberal" in the sense commonly used in China (and parts of Europe) today, which is somewhat opposite to the usage in the United States.

1997, 34% of US federal revenues were raised by social security payroll taxation, compared to 12% in 1960 (*Economic Report of the President* 1998). Among the Organization for Economic Cooperation and Development (OECD) nations over the 1965-88 period, social security payroll taxation grew from 19% to 25% of national tax revenue and from 5.2% to 9.9% of gross domestic product (GDP), on average (Gruber 1997).

However, public provision mechanisms have been criticized for their efficiency losses and their potential for financial imbalance. For example, the pay-as-you-go defined benefit pension system, a typical mechanism of public provision, is facing financing problems in the United States. As a result, interest in mandated provision mechanisms has risen, such as pension systems with defined contributions though individual accounts (James 1996, World Bank 1994). In Chile the pension system was privatized in 1981, with mandated contributions to individual accounts by employee and employer, and numerous proposals to privatize social security in the United States are currently being debated.

In this study, we will focus on efficiency issues related to different mechanisms of financing and providing social security benefits in China. This paper presents a theory of labor market equilibrium with alternative mechanisms for financing social security benefits and discusses the differences between mandated provision, public provision, and various intermediate mechanisms in terms of the linkages they create between the decision to work and the expected receipt of benefits. The strength of this linkage can be measured by the incidence of the cost burden of providing the benefits. This incidence, whether it be of the tax that finances public provision or of the expense of the program compelled by mandated provision, determines the extent to which market decisions are distorted by the social security system. We apply these ideas in discussing the mechanism of funding and provision in China, where the nature of the former provision mechanism is difficult to determine, and various options exist for designing a new system. In an initial effort towards the goal of determining the appropriate mechanism, we provide a theoretical and empirical framework for identifying the incidence parameter, to be applied in future empirical work using data from China.

Section II explains the differences in how public and mandated provision affect the equilibrium in the labor market, and the importance of the incidence of the costs, arising from the linkage between compensation and benefits. In Section III the principle of linkage is applied to the provision of social security benefits in China. To provide evidence on the key incidence parameter, Section IV proposes a method for estimating it empirically. Previous empirical specifications are criticized, and a new specification is derived in which the incidence parameter is correctly identified statistically. Section V introduces an estimation procedure for the new specification, Generalized Method of Moments (GMM). We demonstrate the procedure using Panel Study of Income Dynamics (PSID) data from the United States, and explain how the methodology can be applied when data from China become available. Section VI describes the policy implications of the theoretical and empirical work for a future social security system in China.

2. Mechanisms for Financing and Provision of Social Security Benefits

Government provision of social security must be financed by taxation, but such taxation can result in significant deadweight losses. Estimates of the marginal deadweight loss from a $1 increase in taxes is about $1.21 in the US (Browning, 1987). Furthermore, such taxation can cause total employment to decline, which is an important concern for China. The magnitudes of employment reductions and deadweight losses depend on the relative elasticities of labor supply and demand, and, of particular consequence, on the form of provision.

Summers (1989) describes two general types of provision of social security. Public provision entails the government collecting revenues, and using them to pay for various types of social security programs: retirement benefits, disability insurance, unemployment insurance, medical services, and so forth. For example, the US system for provision of retirement benefits and medical services to the elderly involves the collection of payroll taxes from workers and from employers, and the subsequent transfer of those monies to retirees and to their medical care practitioners.

Under the second form, mandated provision, the government commands employers to provide social security benefits to employees. No monies flow through the government. Rather, expenses are paid for by employers (and to some extent employees, as in the deductibles under most health care plans in the United States). Sometimes these expenses are incurred contemporaneously, as in health care, while in other cases the employer sets certain funds aside for future expenses, as in a pension. In turn, the employers consider these expenses as part of the cost of hiring workers, and workers consider these expenses as part of the compensation they get for their labor.

This study uses the term provision in a slightly different way than the literature as a whole. Here, the term will indicate the combination of the mechanism for distributing benefits (by government vs. through employers), the formula by which benefit entitlements are calculated, and the means by which funds to pay for the benefits are gathered. Such usage is broader in scope than current usage, but will allow for precise exposition of the factors that affect the efficiency of social security programs. Extreme versions of the two general types of provision described above can be viewed as extreme points on a continuum of possible provision mechanisms. This continuum is defined by the extent to which potential recipients of social security benefits perceive a linkage between the magnitude of those benefits and their work decisions.

At first glance, mandated provision appears to directly link an employee's expectation of social security benefits to their decision to work. Summers (1989) argues that a mandate acts much like a benefits tax. In either case the costs of the program are paid for by employees and employers in some combination, in a way that shifts supply and/or demand in the labor market. If employees value the benefits that they are receiving, then they should be willing to accept a lower wage in exchange for the mandated social security benefits. Therefore, the cost of the social security benefits will shift back to workers and there will be less increase in the labor cost for employers, lowering efficiency losses. If workers fully value the benefits, the cost of providing social security shifts completely to wages, so there will be no efficiency loss and no reduction in employment. Thus, the efficiency of mandated provision depends on the value employees assign to the expected benefits, which determines the incidence of the costs.

These values may be less than the cost of providing such benefits, however. First, employees may recognize that the future is uncertain, and that problems may arise which lead to a reduction in or loss of benefits. For example, company sponsored pension plans may invest their monies poorly, or managers may divert funds to other uses. Second, employees may not value certain types of benefits to be worth the cost of provision. They may not accurately perceive the need for long term care insurance, for example. Finally, to the extent to which the government provides social security benefits to unemployed individuals, the value of receiving such benefits as part of one' compensation for working is diminished. In such cases the value to employees of a mandated compensation package will be less than the costs of provision, so labor market outcomes will be distorted.

The linkage between the decision to work and the receipt of social security benefits may be much weaker in the case of public provision. In the extreme case, individuals may be entitled to certain benefits regardless of their employment status or work history. In that case the linkage is broken. Since revenues must nonetheless be collected, to pay for the benefits, distortionary taxes must be applied to the economy, resulting in inefficiency.

The strength of the linkage between work decisions and benefits also depends on the rule used to distribute benefits. For example, in the United States, retirement income benefits (Social Security) are determined using a formula based on the worker's contributions to the retirement trust fund over their working life. Since for many older workers the expected benefits have exceeded the present value of lifetime contributions, the linkage has been incomplete.

A linkage may also arise from the way in which the public perceives the public provision mechanism. For example in the United States the Social Security system collects payroll taxes from current workers and spends the revenues on benefits for current retirees and on reductions in the true budget deficit of the federal government. Individual claims on retirement benefits are not binding on future governments; the benefit formula can be, and has been, revised at any time. To the extent that workers perceive a binding contract that links their taxes to their eventual receipt of retirement income, however, they will not view the tax payments as reducing the size of their compensation package, and labor market distortions will be reduced. In the extreme case where the public pension system is fully privatized, there is a direct linkage between the mandated payments and the subsequent retirement benefits.

These arguments are illustrated in the Figure 1. Either an imposition of a social security tax on employers or a mandate of social security benefits on employers will shift the labor demand curve from D to D′. If the government uses the tax revenues to create a universally accessible social security system (public provision), employees will not consider the value of retirement benefits in their work decisions. Thus, the labor supply curve does not change, and employment will fall from E to E′, as employers cannot pass on all the cost for social security to workers. However, in the case of mandated provision, workers may perceive their benefits to be linked to their place of employment. Thus, they are willing to accept a lower wage, because they evaluate the entire compensation package. Therefore, the labor supply curve will also shift, to S′, and employment will fall only to E″.

Clearly the reduction of employment and the deadweight loss are both smaller in the latter case. If workers value the benefits fully (equal to the cost of providing them), they will accept a wage decrease that exactly offsets the benefits provided, so the entire cost of social security is passed on to workers. There is no efficiency loss and no reduction in employment. Thus, the extent to which the costs of social security are passed on to workers, the incidence of the costs, becomes a significant empirical issue, since it acts as an indicator of the efficiency of the financing system.

Figure 1: The Mandated Provision of Social Security

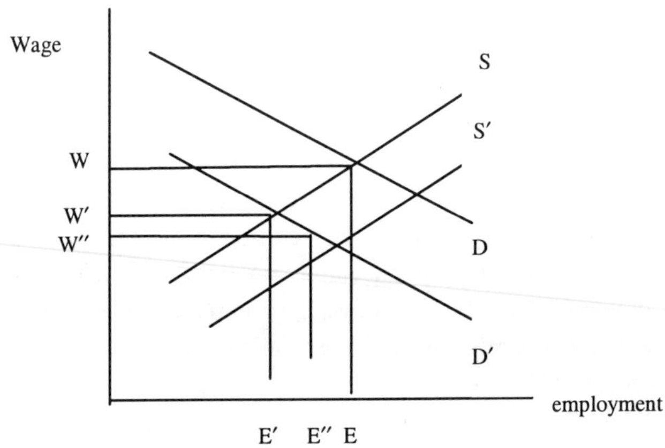

3. Financing and Provision of Social Security Benefits in China

Unlike the Social Security system in the United States, the traditional Chinese social security system provides a very broad range of benefits. These benefits include housing, health care, and retirement income, but they are limited to state workers. In the past these benefits were distributed through state-owned enterprises (SOEs). Before economic reform, these firms were not independent profit seeking production units, and it was even difficult to distinguish employees and employers. Compensation packages, including wages, were mainly determined by the government and varied little across the country. Labor mobility was quite limited. Because it was difficult to distinguish between firms and the government, and furthermore the linkage between compensation and benefits, it is difficult to say whether the system used mandated or public provision. Thus, the notion of the incidence of the costs of social security was also difficult to define.

The profound economic reform is largely changing the structure of the SOEs. They are being required to become more profitable, so they are striving to reduce labor costs. Compensation structures are changing, with greater emphasis on wages, which are increasingly being determined in labor markets, in which mobility is rising. This process is still underway, however, and labor markets are still incomplete. Thus, the burden of the social security costs can still only be shifted partially to workers; the incidence must fall to a significant extent on employers. Thus, to avoid employment and efficiency losses due to social security provision, it is important that a new provision mechanism be chosen that allows the maximum possible shifting of costs, by enabling a linkage between compensation and social security benefits.

For the growing numbers of non-state-owned firms in China, whether private or joint venture enterprises or town and village enterprises (TVE), this linkage is likely to be stronger. Labor markets in this sector of the economy are more complete, and thus workers will be more responsive to the provision of benefits at their place of employment. Employers in this sector are not expected to receive government subsidies to pay for social security benefits, and yet are more concerned about avoiding the burden of the costs themselves. Thus, the selection of a mandated provision mechanism for this part of the economy should yield a particularly large gain in terms of avoided efficiency losses.

An important problem that has arisen during the reform process is the lack of profitability for SOEs. Further restructuring is inevitable. Nonetheless, other ways are being sought to increase profits. A strong consensus exists for relieving SOEs of their requirement to provide social security programs. Social pooling is being considered as an alternative to enterprise-based social security financing and provision. Under social pooling, benefits no longer would be provided by SOEs to the workers, as the benefits transfer mechanism is to be transferred to either government or private agencies. While SOEs still have a financial burden in making their employer contributions, they would no longer have the significant administrative burdens involved in handling benefit transfers themselves.

The key issue is how to design the social pooling mechanism. Currently in China it seems that many policy makers consider social pooling and public provision to be the same type of mechanism. It is important to realize that the social pooling mechanism need not, and in fact should not, be set up as a public provision mechanism. For example, in China an experimental system of individual retirement accounts has existed for several years, and the Chinese government is in the process of establishing such a system throughout the country, through an agency called the Social Security Bureau, from which workers will receive their retirement benefits. However, this system suffers from several flaws, reducing its efficiency. First, employer contributions into an individual's account may not be carried over if the individual changes his place of employment. Thus, the employee will reduce his valuation of that benefit by the extent to which he foresees changing his place of employment, and thus the linkage will be weaker. Second, while employers make substantial contributions toward retirement benefits, currently totaling about 21% of a worker's wage, only 3% enters individual retirement accounts, as the rest enters a public, pooled account. Thus, most of the employer's contribution is not completely linked to the work decision, and so it is difficult for the employer to shift the costs to workers.

Alternatively, the retirement system could allow the portability of employer contributions to individual retirement accounts, and could direct a greater share of total contributions into individual accounts. These changes would transform the social pooling system into more of a mandated provision system, in that the linkage between compensation and benefits would be significantly strengthened.

The arguments in this section apply the principle of linkage to the design of social security provision in China. Maximum efficiency in the labor markets requires that the linkage between compensation and benefits be as strong as possible. Implementation details for individual components of the social security system are important in determining the strength of this linkage.

4. Identifying the Incidence of Social Security Costs

The argument above makes clear that the incidence of the social security funding mechanism, determined by the linkage between compensation and benefits, determines its efficiency. In many instances, however, the true nature of this linkage can only be revealed through empirical analysis that estimates the incidence. Economists and policymakers may also be concerned with the incidence of a social security program because of the employment effects, measured separately from the efficiency effects. Therefore, good estimates of the incidence are fundamental to policymaking.

Estimation of the incidence is not an easy task, however, and previous attempts have sometimes come up short. Several estimates of the incidence of the Social Security payroll tax in the US were published in the 70s (Brittain (1971), Vroman (1974), Hamermesh (1979)). These studies were controversial in their identification strategy, and some of them received specific criticism in the literature. For example, Feldstein (1972) has criticized the Brittain (1971) study for not being grounded in theory, while Asher (1984) criticizes Hamermesh (1979) for not identifying the parameter of interest (see also Hamermesh 1984).

Other estimates of incidence have been more successful. Recently, several such studies have used difference-difference estimation to estimate the incidence of mandated provision. For example, Gruber (1994) investigates the incidence of mandated maternity benefits and finds that the cost is completely shifted back to workers. Gruber (1997) finds that the cost of social security in Chile also fully shifts back to workers. These full shifts indicate an efficient outcome because they imply that there is no labor market distortion and no reduction in employment. Unfortunately, the difference-difference method places strong requirements on the data, and thus cannot always be applied.

We propose a new method for estimating incidence. Our approach differs from these recent studies in that we estimate a reduced form wage equation. In doing so we account for an important feature of the US system that may be adopted by China: the threshold on the maximum income level upon which taxes are payable, above which the marginal rate is zero. Treating this system as a non-linear but continuous tax affecting all income levels, as Hamermesh (1979) does by combining observations above and below the threshold, causes model misspecification. The model is misspecified because the estimation procedure imposes an additional restriction that the functional form specification is the same for both cases.

Asher (1984) points out the specification problem, using a hypothetical data set to demonstrate the spurious relationship that Hamermesh treats as tax incidence. But in that data set, working hours are assumed to be constant across individuals. The above models show that when working hours do not vary, the incidence is not identified. Thus, Asher implicitly assumes that labor supply is perfectly inelastic, and so the incidence parameter is restricted to 1.

In our approach, we split our sample of employees into two subsets, according to whether job incomes are above or below the threshold for payment of the marginal payroll tax. This allows us to identify the parameter of interest, using cross-section data for one subset and panel data for the other subset. To correctly deal with certain estimation problems, we will apply General Method of Moments (GMM) estimators, as explained below. Our approach can be applied to estimate both the incidence of the tax that supports public provision and the effect of mandated provision on wages.

We believe the method may be readily applied to data from China before a new social system is established. For China's non-state industries, policies on social security vary considerably across cities. This variation may provide useful information allowing the identification of the incidence.

Model Specification

To identify the incidence of social security funding, we use data on individual workers to estimate a reduced-form wage equation incorporating two elements. The first element consists of the usual supply and demand determinants for wages. The second element specifies the precise relationship between the incidence of payroll taxes on pre-tax and after-tax wages, including the effects of a threshold on the income subject to taxation. Figure 2 illustrates the components of this specification, which we now derive formally. While Figure 2 is drawn to show the general case in which workers will value the benefits to a partial extent, the following procedure also applies when the labor supply curve does not shift at all, as in a standard taxation case.

Figure 2. The Incidence of Social Security

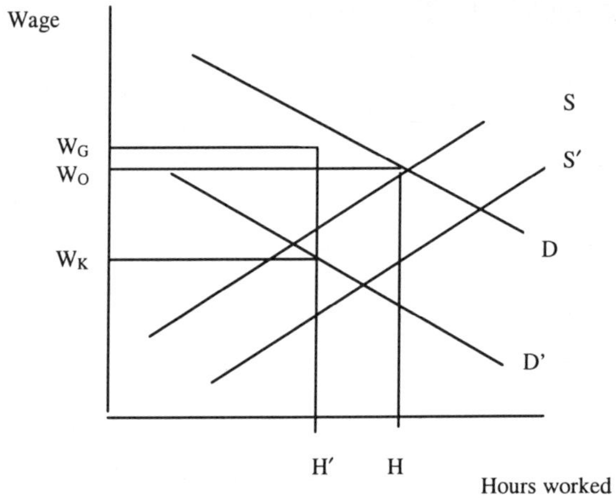

The basic variable definitions are as follows. First, t_f and t_e represent the employer and worker social security tax rate or mandated provision rate (which, for simplicity, we will call the "tax rate" in either case) on incomes below the maximum taxable annual salary, the "threshold," S, respectively. Thus, $(t_f + t_e)$ is the total payroll rate (we assume the payment is deducted from payroll directly).[3] H is the observed

[3] In the US, the total payroll tax rate is currently 15.3%, of which employers and employees each pay half.

annual hours worked. If the annual salary lies above the threshold salary, then one can calculate the average tax paid per hour as $T = (t_f + t_e)\cdot S/H$. W is the observed taxable hourly wage, and W_O is the hourly wage that would prevail in the absence of the payroll tax. W_G is the employer's hourly cost for an employee when the payroll tax is present, and W_K is the after-payroll-tax "take home" hourly income.

Assume τ is the incidence of the tax on the employee; the proportion of the tax burden that falls on the employee in terms of reduced wages. Its definition depends on how the total tax is calculated, and thus is defined differently for each of the two cases presented below. However, $\tau = 0$ when the after-tax wage rate W_K equals the no-tax wage rate W_O, and so the take home ware rate does not change when the tax is implemented. Similarly, $\tau = 1$ when the employer's hourly cost does not change: the no-tax wage rate W_O equals the employer's hourly cost under the tax, W_G. Note that, for a tax incidence τ of less than 50% ($\tau < 0.5$), the observable hourly wage W is actually higher than the no-tax wage W_O, although of course the "take home" pay is lower, $W_K < W_O$.

The relationships between the unobserved no-tax hourly wage, the observed wage, and the tax incidence depend on whether the annual wage $W\cdot H$ is above or below the salary threshold S. Thus, we consider the two cases separately.

Case 1: W < S / H

The (combined employer and employee) amount of social security taxes paid, per hour of employment, is $(t_f + t_e)\cdot W$ (since taxes are calculated based on some "declared" wage rate, and not the take home wage rate). The incidence of the tax τ is the fraction of the tax borne by the employee, as follows.

$$\tau = (W_O - W_K) / ((t_f + t_e)\cdot W)$$

For this case $W_K = (1\text{-}t_e)\cdot W$ and $W_G = (1+t_f)\cdot W$. Rearranging,

$$W_O = W_K + \tau\cdot(t_f + t_e)\cdot W$$

Substituting for W_K:

$$W_O = (1\text{-}t_e)\ W + \tau\cdot(t_f + t_e)\cdot W, \text{ and thus}$$

$$W = W_O / (1 + \tau\cdot t_f - (1\text{-}\tau)\ t_e)$$

For small values of $(\tau\cdot t_f - (1 - \tau)\ t_e)$, the following mathematical approximation holds:

$$\ln(1 + \tau\cdot t_f - (1\text{-}\tau)\ t_e) = \tau\cdot t_f - (1\text{-}\tau)\ t_e\ .$$

Taking the log of W and substituting in the approximation,

$$\ln W = \ln W_O - \tau\cdot t_f + (1\text{-}\tau)\ t_e. \qquad (1)$$

Substituting the usual specification for a wage equation, $\ln W_O = X'\beta + \varepsilon$, for $\ln W_O$ in (1), we get the following empirical equation,

$$\ln W = X'\beta - \tau \cdot t_f + (1-\tau)\, t_e + \varepsilon, \tag{2a}$$

where ε is the error term. The above empirical equation has a natural constraint on parameters (the parameter on t_e minus the parameter on t_f should equal 1), which can be used in estimation and to test the robustness of estimates.

If $t_f = t_e = t$, as the payroll tax in the US, the above equation becomes,

$$\ln W = X'\beta + (1-2\tau) \cdot t + \varepsilon. \tag{2b}$$

Thus, the observed hourly wage consists of two parts. The second part is determined by the incidence of the payroll tax. The first part, the no-tax wage rate, is determined both by human capital model factors and by supply and demand factors. These factors can be measured empirically by a vector of individual and job characteristics X.

Equation (2a) is different from the one posed by Asher (1984), because it allows the payment rate to vary for employees and employers: t_e need not equal t_f. This is important because the payment from employers and employees is different for many mandated benefits. Also, this makes clear that the relevant tax rate to be included is the combination of that payable by the employer and that payable by the employee. Hamermesh (1979) tries to estimate the incidence of the US social security tax paid by employers and implicitly assumes full valuation of employees for their own contribution. This may not be the case, especially when many younger Americans believe that they will not receive any social security benefits after their retirements.

In this specification, τ cannot be identified with cross-section data if t_f and t_e are constant, as in the US, and thus collinear with the constant element of X. Thus, in a cross-sectional data set consisting solely of observations for people below the income threshold, incidence cannot be estimated. In a panel data set, however, t_f and t_e may vary over time, as the tax rate in the US has increased a number of times since the Social Security program began. For example, both t_f and t_e have risen in steps from 4.4% in 1967 to 7.65% for 1998. Thus, one can estimate the incidence of social security costs if a panel data set is available. This identification problem can be avoided when using data on workers in China. There, the policy on social security for non-state enterprises varies across cities and/or provinces. This variation will allow identification of the incidence using cross-section data.

Case 2: W > S / H

When annual wages are greater than the taxable income threshold S, the average tax paid per hour, and thus the average tax rate, depends on annual income. The (combined employer and employee) amount of social security taxes paid per hour of employment is the tax rate times the part of annual pay that is taxable, divided by annual hours worked: $(t_f + t_e)\cdot S/H$. Then, the incidence of the tax τ is again expressed as a fraction of the total amount of Social Security tax:

$$\tau = (W_O - W_K) / ((t_f + t_e)\cdot S/H).$$

Rearranging:

$$W_O = W_K + \tau\cdot(t_f + t_e)\cdot S/H$$

For this case $W_K = W - t_e\cdot S/H$ and $W_G = W + t_f\cdot S/H$. Substituting for W_K:

$$W_O = W + [\tau\, t_f - (1 - \tau)t_e]\cdot(S/H)$$

and

$$W = W_O + [(1-\tau)\, t_e - \tau\, t_f\,]\cdot(S/H)$$

In this specification, if working hours vary across individuals, the incidence is identifiable, even if t_f and t_e do not vary in cross-section. If there is variation in t_f and t_e and H, the above empirical equation becomes:

$$W = W_O - \tau\cdot t_f\cdot(S/H) + (1-\tau)\cdot t_e\cdot(S/H). \qquad (3)$$

When $t_f = t_e = t$,

$$W = W_O + (1- 2\tau)\cdot t\cdot(S/H).$$

Therefore, in a data set consisting solely of observations for people above the income threshold, τ is identified for both cross-section data where working hours vary and for panel data where both tax rates and working hours may vary. However, several complications arise in estimating this model. First, normally the wage equations is specified as log-linear, but the derivation above compels linearity. One solution to the problem is to assume $W_O = X'\beta + \varepsilon$ instead of $\ln(W_O) = X'\beta + \varepsilon$. Substituting for W_O in (3) yields the following linear empirical equation,

$$W = X'\beta - \tau\cdot t_f\cdot(S/H) + (1-\tau)\cdot t_e\cdot(S/H) + \varepsilon. \qquad (4a)$$

Another solution is to use the log-linear function form for wages, and then substitute the transformation of that form, $W_O = e^{X'\beta} + \varepsilon$, in (3).[4] This yields the following, alternative specification,

$$W = e^{X'\beta} - \tau\cdot t_f\cdot(S/H) + (1-\tau)\cdot t_e\cdot(S/H) + \varepsilon. \qquad (4b)$$

Doing so comes at a cost: a non-linear estimator must be used.

---

[4] Changing the functional form also changes the assumptions made on the distribution of the error term.

Second, and more importantly, the variable 1/H is endogenous because unobservable factors that affect wages, such as motivation, may also affect working hours. As this endogenous regressor is non-linear in form, the traditional estimation approach, two-stage least squares, is inconsistent, because the predicted value of working hours H will not remove the endogeneity of 1/H.

5. Estimation Method, and Results Using US Data

To address the endogeneity and non-linearity problems, we adopt the Generalized Methods of Moments (GMM) estimator (Hansen 1982, Davidson and MacKinnon 1993). The GMM estimator is robust to non-linearity of endogenous regressors and does not require construction of reduced form equations for each endogenous variable to produce fitted values. Furthermore, GMM estimation is more efficient than general instrumental variable estimation in the presence of heteroskedasticity and autocorrelation. The GMM estimation can be applied to both empirical models above, for cross section and panel data.

Since we lack data from China, we only demonstrate the procedure of identifying the incidence of social security funding, using US data applied to the model described in Case 2 above. For simplicity, we use a linear wage model: $W_O = X'\beta + \varepsilon$. Since $t_e = t_f = t$ for the US data, the model takes the simplified form of (4a):

$$W = X'\beta + (1\text{-}2\tau)\cdot t(S/H) + \varepsilon. \qquad (4a')$$

Our source of data is the 1992 wave of the PSID (Duncan et al., 1995). Our sample consists of 521 men and women whose incomes fall above the 1991 social security tax threshold (S) of \$53,400.[5] We follow Hamermesh (1979) and Gruber (1994) in choosing the explanatory variables represented by X. Thus, we include sex, age and age squared, race, gender, experience and experience squared, 5

---

[5] We combine information from the Individual (gender, schooling, income, and age) and Family (all other variables) files. To eliminate outliers and erroneous data, we restrict the sample to individuals over the age of 19 whose hourly wage is less than \$150. We also eliminate government workers because they are covered by a different retirement system. We eliminate observations for which certain information is missing, including hours worked, experience, schooling, SMSA size, race, age, and number of jobs worked.

industry dummies, 4 schooling dummies, a dummy for the South, and a dummy if the person lives in an SMSA (urban area).[6]

For the general form of the empirical equation (4a), the sample orthogonality condition is:

$$\frac{1}{n}\sum_{i=1}^{n} [W_i - X_i'\beta + \tau \cdot t_{fi} \cdot (S_i/H_i) - (1-\tau) \cdot t_{ei} \cdot (S_i/H_i)] \cdot IV_i = 0,$$

where t_f, t_e, S, and H are variables and IV_i is the instrument vector. This general form is suitable for application to data from China, where different places may have different policies on tax rate and threshold levels. The criterion function of GMM estimator is then given by

$$Q_n(\gamma) = F_n(\gamma)' A_n F_n(\gamma),$$

where

$$F_n(\gamma) = \frac{1}{n}\sum_{i=1}^{n} [W_i - X_i'\beta + \delta_1 \cdot t_{fi} \cdot (S_i/H_i) + \delta_2 \cdot t_{ei} \cdot (S_i/H_i)] \cdot IV_i,$$

A_n is a weighting matrix, γ is a combined parameter vector, $\gamma' = [\beta', \delta']$, and $\delta' = [-\tau, (1-\tau)]$. One parameter restriction for the model is $\delta_2 - \delta_1 = 1$, which can be tested in the estimation. For the payroll tax system in US, as $t_e = t_f = t$, the empirical moment function has the following simpler form:

$$F_n(\gamma) = \frac{1}{n}\sum_{i=1}^{n} [W_i - X_i'\beta + \delta \cdot t \cdot (S/H_i)] \cdot IV_i,$$

and $\delta = 1-2\tau$. The GMM estimator is defined by

$$Q_n(\hat{\gamma}_n) = \inf_{\gamma \in \Theta} Q_n(\gamma),$$

where Θ is the parameter space. GMM estimation proceeds, using appropriate instrument variables.

The OLS results and the GMM results are reported in Table 1.[7] Because the sample size is small, relative to the size needed for precise results using GMM estimation, the results should be interpreted with caution. The main purpose of presenting this result is to demonstrate the implementation of our identification framework.

---

[6] The instruments include all the variables listed plus years of schooling ("schooling"), schooling quared, schooling interacted with experience, schooling interacted with gender, and a graduate school dummy interacted with gender.

[7] The reported GMM estimates are obtained using the identity matrix as the weighting matrix. The data file and GAUSS program are available from the authors upon request.

Table 1: Determinant of the wage rate for US workers above the social security payroll tax threshold, Dependent Variable: Hourly Wage

Variable	OLS		GMM	
	Estimate	T-Stat	Estimate	T-Stat
tS/H *	16.4	11.8	0.72	0.059
Gender	-3.6	1.7	0.64	0.16
Age	-0.52	0.54	1.4	0.90
Age^2	0.011	1.0	-0.0084	-0.47
Experience	0.00048	0.0010	-0.67	-1.03
$Experience^2$	-0.0058	0.50	0.0096	0.53
High School Graduate	6.0	1.51	9.1	1.09
Some College	5.6	1.43	6.9	0.87
College Graduate	7.4	1.91	10	1.33
Some Graduate School	9.7	2.46	11	1.43

- tS/H is the variable to which the parameter $1\text{-}2\tau$ is associated. The estimate for the tax incidence parameter, τ, is easily derived.

Clearly the OLS estimate of the tax incidence parameter $(1 - 2\tau)$ is unreasonable, as it is of the wrong sign and magnitude. The GMM estimation of the incidence parameter, converted from the value in the table, yields a sensible estimate for τ of 0.14. The interpretation of this estimate is that workers bear about 14% of the total social security tax, whereas employers bear 86%.

This result indicates that workers in the United States do not much value the program paid for with payroll taxes. This result is consistent with the observation that many young workers in the United States believe that the social security system will go bankrupt, leaving them without any benefits when they retire. This result may also hold because the high-income individuals represented by this sample have reason to fear both benefit cutbacks and obligations to pay taxes on some of their social security benefits, which would reduce the value of their benefits.

The estimating equation also included a constant term, 5 industry dummies, a region dummy (South), and an SMSA dummy, results for which are not reported here.

Another interpretation is suggested by the fact that the t-statistic shows that the estimated parameter is insignificant. Then, the estimated value for τ is insignificantly different from 50%, indicating that both employees and employers share the burden equally. Much caution should be used in interpreting the significance of the GMM estimates. For relatively small data sets, the GMM estimation can be very inefficient, as reflected here in the insignificance of all of the parameters.

One additional concern for this estimation framework is that, even for GMM estimation, some kind of spurious relationship may also affect the estimate of the parameter of interest -- the incidence of the funding mechanism. With US data, controlling for spurious correlations is difficult, because one cannot find a control group not affected by the payroll tax. Natural experiments in China, however, may offer a unique opportunity to identify the incidence, because social security policies have varied across cities and over time. Such variation can allow for adequate control of spurious relationships (see Gruber 1994).

Nonetheless, no evidence exists that the public provision mechanism of the social security system in the US results in full shifting of costs to workers. The remaining cost burden on employers creates a distortion in the labor market. If our estimate of the incidence is correct, that 86% of the payroll tax burden falls on employers, then the efficiency losses are likely to be substantial. In contrast, for the mandated provision pension system in Chile, Gruber (1997) finds that the cost of social security is fully shifted back to workers. Furthermore, Gruber (1994) finds the costs of mandated maternity benefits in the US are also completely shifted back to workers. These full shifts indicate that there is no labor market distortion and no reduction in employment under the mechanism of mandated provision.

These empirical findings are consistent with our theory on the different financing and provision mechanisms for social security benefits: mandated provision is at least as efficient as public provision because of the more direct linkage between the benefits and working decisions. Such a direct linkage facilitates the shifting of program costs from employers back to employees, and thus results in lower efficiency and employment losses. As a result, the mandated provision mechanism should be a preferred mechanism of financing and providing social security in a new social security system for China.

6. Policy Implications

This paper considers efficiency issues arising from the choice of mechanism for provision of social security benefits, and applies the theory to the Chinese situation. We demonstrate that a mandated provision mechanism for social security is generally more efficient, with less labor market distortion and lower deadweight losses, than a public provision mechanism. In doing so, we demonstrate that the extent of the efficiency differences between the two alternatives is determined by the linkage between compensation and benefits, and thus the incidence of program costs. These concepts apply whether benefits are funded with a tax, as under public provision, or through financial contributions imposed by government, as under mandated provision. We then apply the concept of linkage in discussing the provision mechanism in China. In doing so, we argue that the primary social security system in China should be based on mandated provision.

We emphasize that the incidence of social security funding is the key parameter to be estimated in making a policy decision for social security. Toward this end, this paper introduces a new estimation framework to statistically identify the incidence, and presents illustrative results based on US data. Our empirical finding shows that in the pay-as-you-go public provision system in the US, employers cannot completely pass on the cost burden to employees. Thus, this public provision system must cause efficiency losses and reduction in employment. Other studies indicate that mandated provision indeed results in full shifting of the social security costs to employees, and then causes no labor market distortion and losses in efficiency.

These findings are consistent with the theory of the financing and provision of social security programs. The main difference between public provision and mandated provision is the linkage between compensation for workers and their social security benefits. This linkage affects workers' valuation of their compensation packages, and thus their labor supply decisions. Mandated provision generally creates a much stronger linkage than public provision, and at worst, cannot create a weaker linkage. Therefore, mandated provision should be a preferred mechanism choice in a social security system. This is true not only for a developing country like China but also for a developed country like the US.

While we recommend the mandated provision mechanism for most applications, there is a limited need for the public provision mechanism. In particular, it is still necessary to finance social security benefits in China for retired workers, especially in the short run, because the former pay-as-you-go system did not accumulate sufficient funds. The public provision mechanism is attractive for this application because it transfers the financial burden for the transition costs, supporting current retirees and other needy individuals who are no longer able to work productively, across individuals and generations.

Additional factors should be considered in choosing a provision mechanism. First, the efficiency argument for mandated provision may be weakened if wage rigidities exist, such as those caused by the minimum wage law and the anti-discrimination requirement on wages (where firms pay different workers the same wage even though the cost of providing social security varies). Second, mandated provision may cause employment discrimination against certain demographically identifiable groups, such as older workers and women of child bearing age. Finally, and importantly, the provision of benefits to unemployed workers must balance the social desire to provide support against the effects that such support will have on employment incentives. Future research should investigate these issues, and should also gather empirical evidence on the incidence of the costs of various programs. The framework for identifying cost incidence presented in this study is ready for application to data from China, as it becomes available.

References

1. Asher, Martin A., 1984, "On the Estimation of Payroll Tax Incidence: Comment," *Southern Economic Journal*, 50:4 (April), pp. 1225-1230.
2. Brittain, J., 1971, "The Incidence of Social Payroll Taxes," *American Economic Review*, 61:1 (March), pp. 110-125.
3. Browning, Edgar, 1987, "On the Marginal Welfare Cost of Taxation," *American Economic Review*, 77, pp. 11-23.
4. Davidson, R. and J.G. MacKinnon,1993, *Estimation and Inference in econometrics*, Oxford University Press, pp. 583-620.
5. Duncan, Greg J., Martha S. Hill, James N. Morgan and Sandra J. Hofferth, 1995, *Panel Study Of Income Dynamics 1968-1992 (Waves I-XXV)* [computer file]. Ann Arbor, MI: Survey Research Center [producer], Ann Arbor, MI: Inter-university Consortium for Political and Social Research [distributor].
6. *Economic Report of the President*, 1998, Washington DC: US Government Printing Office.
7. Feldstein, Martin S., 1972, "The Incidence of the Social Security Tax: Comment,"*American Economic Review*, 62:4 (September), pp. 735-738.
8. Gruber, Jonathan, 1994, "The Incidence of Mandated Maternity Benefits," *American Economic Review*, 84:3 (June), pp. 622-641.
9. Gruber, Jonathan, 1997, "The Incidence of Payroll Taxation: Evidence from Chile," *Journal of Labor Economics*, 15:3 pt.2, pp. S72-S101.
10. Hamermesh, Daniel S., 1979, "New Estimates of the Incidence of the Payroll Tax," *Southern Economic Journal*, 45:4 (April), pp. 1208-1219.
11. Hamermesh, Daniel S., 1984, "On the Estimation of Payroll Tax Incidence: Reply," *Southern Economic Journal*, 50:4 (April), p. 1231.
12. Hansen, L. P., 1982, "Large Sample Properties of Generalized Method of Moments Estimators," *Econometrica*, 50, pp. 1029-1054.

13. James, E., 1996, "New Systems for Old Age Security-Theory, Practice, and Empirical Evidence", Working Paper, World Bank.
14. Krueger, A. and Pischke, J., 1992, "The Effect of Social Security on Labor Supply: Cohort Analysis of the Notch Generation,"*Journal of Labor Economics*, 10, pp. 412-437.
15. Li, Tiayin, 1995, "Establishing a Social Security System with Chinese Characteristics," paper presented at the International Symposium on Establishing a Market-Oriented Social Security System in China, Beijing, 1998.
16. Madhur, Srinivasa, 1998, "Pension Reform in the People's Republic of China: Recent Initiative and Future Challenges," paper presented at the International Symposium on Establishing a Market-Oriented Social Security System in China, Beijing, 1998.
17. Pechman, Joseph A., 1987, *Federal Tax Policy*, 5th ed., Washington, DC: Brookings Institution.
18. Rothschild, Michael and Joseph E. Stiglitz, 1976, "Equilibrium in Competitive Insurance Markets: An Essay on the Economics of Imperfect Information," *Quarterly Journal of Economics*, 90 (November), pp. 629-650.
19. Summers, Lawrence H., 1989, "Some Simple Economics of Mandated Benefits," *American Economic Association Papers and Proceedings*, 79, pp. 177-183.
20. Vroman, W., 1974, "Employer Payroll Tax Incidence: Empirical Tests with Cross-Country Data," *Public Finance*, 29, pp. 184-200.
21. World Bank, 1994. *Averting the Old Age Crisis: Policies to Protect the Old and Promote Growth.* World Bank and Oxford University Press.

CHAPTER 8

DEMOGRAPHIC UNDERPINNINGS OF CHINA'S OLD-AGE PENSION REFORM

LORAINE A. WEST
International Programs Center
U.S. Bureau of the Census
Washington DC 20233-8860, USA
E-mail: lwest@census.gov

After a brief review of the features of China's emerging reformed old-age pension system, the paper focuses on future demographic trends and their implications for the pension programs. Changes in China's demographic variables, such as age structure and life expectancy, as compared to changes experienced by other nations are discussed.

1. Introduction

The weaknesses and limitations of China's old-age pension system established in the 1950's became apparent as the country shifted towards a market-oriented economy in the early 1980's. The enterprise-based system was increasingly unable to meet present obligations, and prospective analyses revealed that pay-as-you-go financing clearly would be unsuitable to meet the challenge of the next century with an aging population. Furthermore, the pension system, which was limited primarily to employees of government and party organizations, state-owned enterprises, and large urban collectives, was shrinking in its coverage of the labor force as self-employment and employment in private enterprises grew. The changing structure of China's economy and population led researchers and officials to examine the existing system and propose major changes. Various reforms of the pension system were underway on a trial basis in a number of cities by the mid-1980's. Pension reform gained momentum in the early 1990's when experiments became more widespread, and social security reform began to focus on expanded coverage and uniformity in design details.

In the near term, economic factors may well dominate demographic factors in driving the revamping of China's old-age security system. The effect of longer term demographic processes, however, will need to be considered in shaping a sustainable old-age social security system. The one-child family planning policy and declining mortality rates will accelerate the aging of the population, especially in urban areas. Aging of the population, in turn, will exert increasingly stronger downward pressure on the workers-to-retirees ratio in the future.

After briefly reviewing the features of China's emerging reformed old-age pension system, the paper focuses on future demographic trends and their implications for the social pension system. Changes in China's demographic variables, such as age structure and life expectancy, as compared to changes experienced by other countries are discussed. Finally, the paper addresses additional modifications to the social pension program suggested by the demographic factors.

2. Features of the New Pension System

Following a decade of trial pension reforms throughout the country, the Third Plenary Session of the 14th Communist Party Central Committee in 1994 specified an overall framework for the establishment of an old-age security system. It called for a multi-pillared system combining a social basic pillar with supplemental enterprise-sponsored pensions and individual savings for old age. At present, emphasis continues to be placed on designing the social pillar which is to provide a minimum standard of living for retirees and to be financed by the enterprise, employee, and government through a combination of pooled funds and individual accounts. Work on the other two pillars has just begun and is expected to proceed slowly. [1]

In an effort to increase uniformity in the design of the new social pension scheme, the State Council issued Document Number 6 (*State Council Circular on the Deepening of Reform on Enterprise Worker's Pension System*) in 1995, which

---

[1] By mid-1995, only 12,000 enterprises nationwide were offering supplemental insurance plans that covered 3 million employees. At the same time, 700,000 workers had established individual retirement savings accounts, with accumulated funds reaching 50 million yuan [Wang J., 1995]. In some cases, foreign-funded and private enterprises and self-employed individuals have purchased commercial pension insurance policies, primarily from the People's Insurance Company of China, which dominates the commercial insurance market. Commercial pension insurance, however, accounts for a small fraction of total benefits with disbursements averaging 1.5 billion yuan in the early 1990's as compared to nearly 72.5 billion yuan in pension payments made through the government-sponsored pension system in 1994 [China State Statistical Bureau, 1995: 580, 676].

outlined two models for the social pension. The decree required that city and prefecture governments select one of the two models or design a third variant. Province governments were given the responsibility of approving the design choice of the local governments. More recently, the State Council issued *Decisions on the Establishment of the Unified Basic Pension System for Enterprise Workers* (State Council Document Number 26, 1997), which provides more specific guidelines for achieving greater uniformity in local programs. While the reformed pension system varies regionally in its details and the system can be expected to continue to evolve as the central government strives for more uniform standards, the general characteristics of the social pillar are already evident.

A combination of plans has replaced the former single defined-benefit plan. The social pillar has two components: a defined-contribution plan with an individual account established for each worker and a defined-benefit plan known as the base pension, which is funded by a social pooling account. The State Council has called for the relative emphasis on the two components to be fairly balanced, with 11 of the suggested 20 percent contribution rate allocated to the individual accounts and the remaining 9 percent contributed to the social pooling account.

Unlike the provident funds of Singapore and Malaysia, savings in the individual account can only be withdrawn as a pension after retirement.[2] In retirement, the worker will receive the accumulated principal and interest in the individual account. Because the individual accounts are largely notional, the State Council has called for an interest rate based on bank savings rates to be credited to these accounts. Workers who have participated in the new scheme for a total of 15 years will also qualify for the defined-benefit base pension [State Council, 1997]. This component of the social pillar will pay beneficiaries a monthly pension equivalent to 20 percent of the average local wage, according to the State Council (1997).[3]

A regionally-based pension pool system formed along administrative lines (county, city, prefecture, or province) is replacing the work unit as the focal point of the social pillar. The State Council has called for the gradual expansion of pools to higher administrative levels. Once provincial level pooling has been achieved nationwide, the various pools formed along industry lines are to be disbanded and

---

[2] Singapore and Malaysia allow workers to use a portion of the savings in their provident accounts prior to retirement for the purchase of a home or to cover expenditures for a major illness.

[3] The average local wage includes bonuses and subsidies and is based on the average for the province, municipality, or prefecture in which the enterprise is located. Usually the choice corresponds to the administrative boundaries of the social pool.

workers in these industries are to join their respective province pool.[4] The goal is to create a nationwide uniform program with a single pool and thereby eliminate the drawbacks of multiple pools, such as inhibiting labor mobility, placing disparate burdens on enterprises based on their location, and failing to maximize gains of risk sharing and economies of scale in administration.

Pension financing is being diversified, with the employer (work unit) no longer the sole contributor to the pension fund. Employees now also make contributions, and the government is to contribute as needed in its role as pension guarantor. Employee and employer contribution rates are levied on total wages. Workers' contributions are to be a minimum of 4 percent of their wages by 1997 and are to increase one percentage point every two years from 1998 onwards, until reaching 8 percent. As the worker's contribution rises, the employer's contribution rate is to decline. According to State Council guidelines, all of the worker's contribution is to be allocated to the individual account.

3. Demographic Underpinnings

Population aging is forcing many developed countries to examine the structure and financing of their pension programs. Because developed countries generally will face the ramifications of population aging in advance of China, China has the advantage of being able to learn from the experiences of these countries. However, owing to both faster declines in birth rates and faster increases in life expectancy, China will experience much more rapid growth of its elderly population than most developed countries.

Past and current trends in fertility are the primary factors determining the speed of population aging in China, although improvements in mortality are also important driving forces. The level of fertility declined dramatically in the 1970's, falling from 5.8 births per woman in 1970 to 2.8 in 1978 [Chen, 1984]. Further declines in fertility have occurred since 1987 with the total fertility rate falling from 2.8 in 1987 to about 1.8 presently [Banister, 1996; Bureau of the Census, 1997]. Stricter family planning controls, rapid economic development, and urbanization likely contributed to recent reductions in fertility rates. Mortality rates fell and life expectancy increased rapidly in the first few decades following the founding of the People's Republic of China. Life expectancy increased from less than 50 years prior to 1949

---

[4] The State Council has allowed 11 central ministries and industries, including the non-ferrous metals and coal industries, to set up their own pension pools. Workers in these ministries and industries do not participate in local pools.

to more than 60 years by the early 1970's [Banister, 1997]. Improvements in mortality have continued in recent decades, raising life expectancy to an estimated 70 years in 1998 [Bureau of the Census, 1997].

Presently, China still has a pyramid-shaped population age structure, although the narrowing of the youngest cohort is already evident. Assuming continued low levels of fertility hovering around 1.8 children per woman per lifetime and trending down to 1.7 by 2050, fewer children will be available to support future generations of older persons. Continued gradual improvements in mortality rates among the older population will contribute to larger future cohorts of the elderly. In 2025, the three largest 5-year age cohorts will be in the working ages, but the base will have narrowed considerably. By 2050, any resemblance the population age structure had to a pyramid shape will have disappeared, and the single largest 5-year age cohort is projected to be ages 60-64.

During the next several decades, the percent elderly is projected to rise substantially in China. What sets China and many of her Asian neighbors apart from the developed countries of Europe and North America is the speed of the demographic aging process. In the latter nations, population aging has been a gradual process that allowed societies and economies time to adapt to their demographic evolution. For instance, it took 81 years for the elderly (60+) share of total population to rise from 10 percent to 20 percent in the United States. This same increase will be compressed into just 27 years for China (Figure 1). The speed of population aging in China will be comparable to that recently experienced by Japan but not as fast as the rate projected for Singapore.

The share of China's population aged 60 and over is presently only 9.9 percent as compared to 16.5 percent in the United States and 22.1 percent in Japan. By 2025, however, China's share will have doubled and one of every 5 persons will be at least 60 years old (Figure 2). In absolute numbers China will see its 60-and-over population explode from 123 million in 1998 to 278 million by the year 2025. The "oldest old" (persons aged 75 and over) will be the fastest-growing segment of China's population, increasing by 141 percent from now to the year 2025 (Figure 3). The health and long-term nursing care needs of the oldest old will have major implications for China's society and economy.

Figure 1: Speed of Population Aging

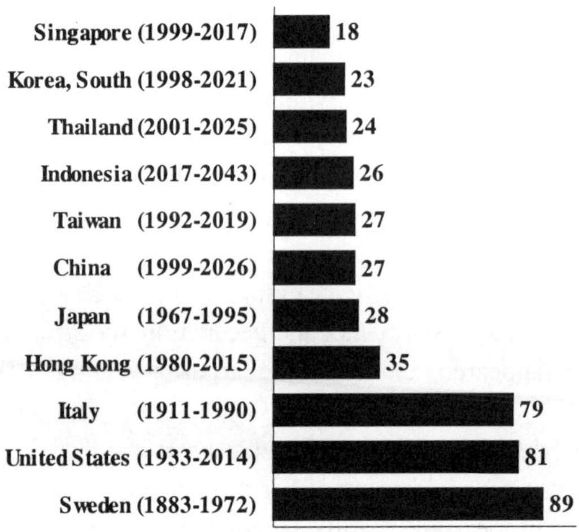

Source: U.S. Bureau of the Census, International Programs Center, International Data Base.

Figure 2: Percent of Population Aged 60 and Over: 1998 and 2025

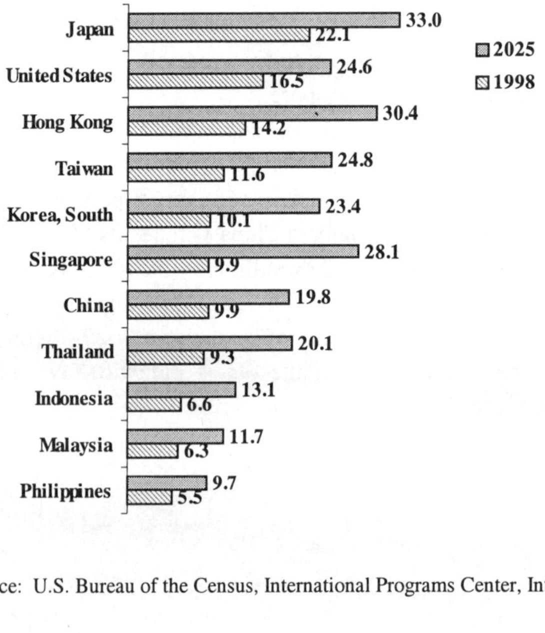

Source: U.S. Bureau of the Census, International Programs Center, International Data Base.

The elderly support ratio (the number of persons aged 60 and over per 100 persons aged 20 to 59) will increase from 17.6 presently to 34.8 in 2025 and to 64.7 in 2050. Thus, unless there is an increase in the labor force participation rate or an increase in labor productivity, each economically-productive person will have to support twice as many people of retirement age by 2025. While other Asian countries, such as Japan and South Korea, will experience even higher elderly support ratios (Figure 4), China already has high labor force participation rates and, therefore, more limited options for dealing with the rising burden of the elderly.

Figure 3: Percent Increase in Total, Elderly and Oldest - Old Population: 1998 to 2025

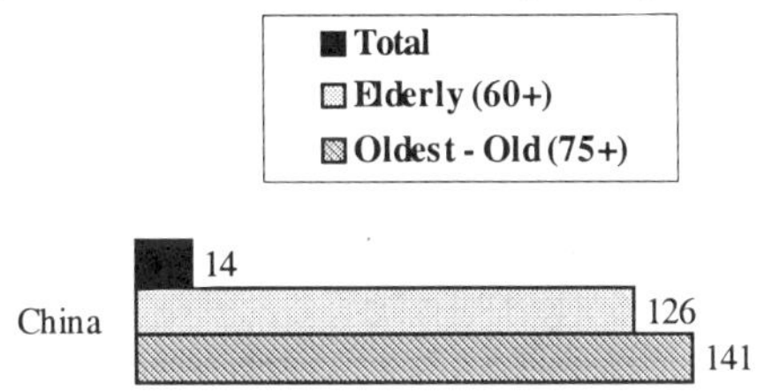

Source: U.S. Bureau of the Census, International Programs Center, International Data Base.

Figure 4: Elderly Support Ratios in Four Asian Nations: 1990 to 2030

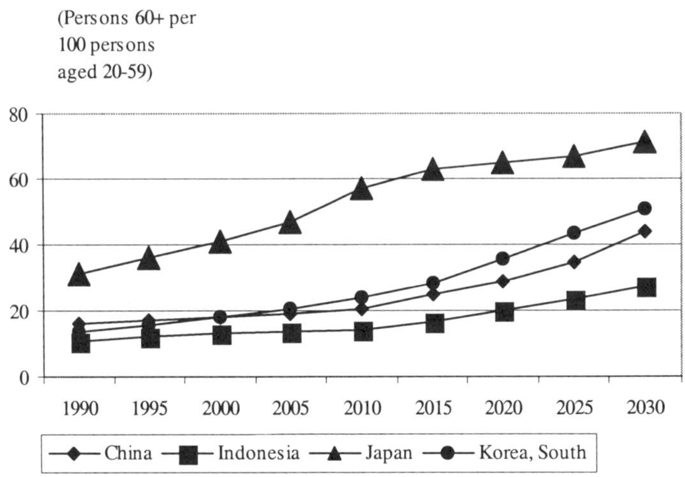

Source: U.S. Bureau of the Census, International Programs Center, International Data Base.

4. Further Reforms

Reforms, thus far, have successfully established a new framework that incorporates the insurance principle of risk sharing and has further eased the financial burden on enterprises by introducing worker contributions. Reforms have initiated coverage expansion beyond state-owned enterprises and urban collectives and introduced indexing for protection of the standard of living after retirement. In many respects, reforms have gone a long ways towards addressing the weaknesses of the former system. However, several key issues remain to be addressed in achieving an old-age pension system suited to China's future. One issue is the affordability of the new system both today and in the first half of the next century when the aging of the population will peak. Currently, many enterprises are struggling to meet their contribution obligations, and in spite of the State Council call for partial accumulation, 80 percent of the localities have no surplus in their pension pools. Individual accounts are largely notional accounts because these contributions are needed to pay current retirees. A second issue is the level of pooling and its effect on labor market development. The multiplicity of pools – administrative- and industry-based pools as well as separate pools for different ownership types within a number of administrative pools [Hussain, 1994; World Bank, 1996] – is unsatisfactory for a number of reasons. This section focuses on these issues and options for addressing them.

Reforms call for the pension system to shift from pay-as-you-go financing to partial accumulation in preparation for the future, when the number of beneficiaries (retirees) will increase because of both the maturation of the expanded coverage under the system and the aging of the population. Building up a reserve will require even higher contribution rates, which many enterprises that are struggling to meet obligations now may be unable to afford. Aggregate fund reserves are estimated to have reached 79 billion yuan by the end of 1997 [Ministry of Finance, 1998].[5] Because of rising pension expenditures, reserves were still less than one year's annual expenditure. Moreover, reserves are concentrated in only 20 percent of all pools.

The next stages of reform will need to focus on making the system more affordable and, therefore, sustainable. Several measures are already being implemented or are under discussion. The first is to reduce benefits by gradually lowering the income replacement rate of the pension program to around 50-60

---

[5] Aggregate fund reserves are difficult to measure because funds are scattered across numerous pools and under the supervision of different levels of government and departments.

percent [Du, 1997]. The timing of reductions in the replacement rate is to be determined in large measure by the pace of development of supplementary old-age pension support.

A second measure is to raise the retirement age which, if applied to workers under the former system as well as workers hired after implementation of the new system, will effectively reduce accrued liabilities and future liabilities. Given high life expectancy – 68 years for men and 71 for women in 1998 – retirement ages in China are relatively and absolutely low by international standards. The retirement age for workers covered by the new old-age pension scheme remains at 60 for men and 55 for women in salaried cadre positions and 50 for women in blue collar jobs.[6] For women in these two categories the weighted average retirement age is 51 [Research Team, 1996: 44]. Younger retirement ages apply to those working in conditions designated as harsh or dangerous. Early retirement (5 years before the normal retirement age) can be granted in special circumstances. In recent years, it has become common practice for workers within 5 years of retirement in bankrupt enterprises to be required to take early retirement. Most recently, many civil servants within three years of retirement are being forced to retire early as part of the restructuring and downsizing of the government, although they will continue to draw their full salaries until reaching official retirement age.

Because of the relatively young retirement age and the use of early retirement, China's urban old-age pension system has a higher system dependency ratio than demographic old-age dependency ratio. In 1996, among enterprises covered by the social pension system, there were only 4.6 workers to every retiree, while there were 5.7 persons ages 20-59 to every person age 60 and over [China State Statistical Bureau, 1997: 751; Bureau of the Census, 1997]. With fewer workers contributing to the system and more beneficiaries (retirees) drawing from the system, the contribution rate is necessarily higher.

In the short term, China faces an excess labor situation, especially with ongoing reform of state-owned enterprises, and increasing retirement ages at this time is not viewed as a viable option by most officials.[7] However, the present surplus labor situation in China may change to one of a labor shortage in the not too distant future. After the year 2000, the growth rate of the population ages 15-59 is projected to slow down, and after 2015, the growth rate turns negative (Figure 5). In contrast, the growth rate of the population ages 60 and over increases at an average annual

---

[6] Thus far only the retirement age for female government civil servants has been raised from 55 to 60.

[7] Delayed retirement for workers possessing special skills in high demand is being implemented in pilot areas and is viewed as a first step towards raising the retirement age [Hu, 1996].

rate exceeding 2 percent until 2035, when the growth rate slackens but still remains positive. Finding additional workers through increases in the urban labor force participation rate is of limited scope given China's already high labor force participation rate. [8] It is possible that in the future labor force participation rates may even decline. Rising income levels and less generous enterprise benefits, such as maternity leave and child care, may lead one spouse to drop out of the labor force for more extended periods of time. If the latter happens, the problem will be compounded.

Figure 5: China Population Ages 15-59 and Age 60 and Over, 1998-2050

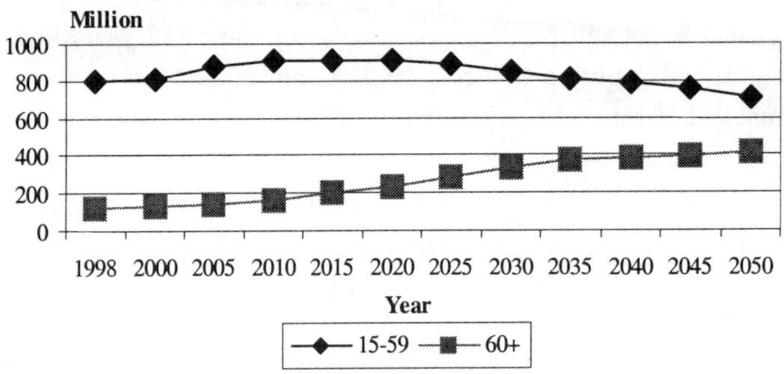

Source: U.S. Bureau of the Census, International Programs Center, International Data Base.

Disbursement of benefits from the individual account are inconsistent with China's current retirement age and life expectancy. The State Council has stated that the accumulated savings in the individual account should be disbursed monthly over a 10 year period after the worker retires. However, a male retiring at age 60 today has a life expectancy of 17 years and will, therefore, exhaust his individual account and receive only the base pension (20 percent of the average wage) from the social pillar for nearly half of his retirement period. Women will be dependent on the base pension after exhausting their individual account for an even longer period of time because of their younger retirement age and longer life expectancy.[9] Continued increases in life expectancy mean that a male retiring at age 65 in 2020 can expect the same period of retirement as a male retiring at age 60 in 1990.

---

[8] In 1990, the employment participation rate among urban males ages 25-49 exceeded 90 per cent and for urban females ages 25-44 it exceeded 80 per cent [Harbaugh and West, 1993]. In 1993, women accounted for 44 per cent of the employed urban labor force [Lu, 1994].

[9] In 1998, a 55 year-old woman has a life expectancy of 24 years.

Therefore, it may be both feasible and desirable to begin increasing the retirement age early next century with an advance announcement so that workers may prepare and adjust their plans for retirement.

A third measure is to expand the coverage of the reformed old-age security system. The central government has announced that the new system aims to cover all urban workers, including the self employed, by the year 2000 [State Council, 1995]. Because most state-owned enterprises and urban collective enterprises have already been brought into the new scheme, future expansion will primarily bring in workers without accrued liabilities and these workers will make contributions for a period of time before they become vested and eligible for retirement. In addition, the foreign-invested, private, and township and village enterprises tend to have younger labor forces than the state-owned and large urban collectively-owned enterprises [Hu, 1996]. Their inclusion will lower the old-age dependency ratio for the social old-age pension insurance scheme.

Some township and village enterprises located in urban areas are starting to be included in the basic pension scheme. An International Labor Organization (ILO) and Ministry of Labor survey of 300 industrial enterprises in Beijing, Shanghai, Guangzhou, Tianjin, and Shenyang in 1995 found that 9.5 per cent of surveyed township and village enterprises were participating in the reformed social basic pension system [Lim and Sziracki, 1995: 19]. Contracted rural migrant laborers in urban enterprises are supposed to be covered as well. While the inclusion of rural migrant labor in urban areas would also reduce the dependency ratio because of the concentration of migrant laborers in the young working age groups, present weaknesses in administrative capacity make it questionable whether these workers will ever draw benefits, especially if they return to rural areas or move on to other urban areas. In some cases, the pension contribution is simply an added tax from which the migrant will derive no benefits.

All three measures – lowering the income replacement rate, raising the retirement age, and expanding coverage – would extend the financial viability of the new scheme over a longer time horizon.

While pooling at the county and city level is an improvement over the former enterprise-based system, there are further gains that could be achieved through pooling at the provincial or national level. The persistence of numerous pension pools, whether geographically- or industry-based, serves to inhibit labor mobility. While it was not unusual in the past for a worker to have the same employer throughout his/her working life, today China has an increasingly mobile labor force. In the past decade, a number of workers have left the state or collective sector to join foreign-invested enterprises or to go into business for themselves. Workers also are switching industries within the state sector, many moving into the growing service sector.

Even greater labor mobility can be expected as the restructuring of state-owned enterprises progresses. It is inevitable that a number of state-owned enterprises will need to shed redundant labor if they are to be competitive and estimates of surplus labor are sizable, ranging from one-fifth to one-third of state-owned enterprise employees [Lim and Sziraczki, 1995: 4-5]. It is increasingly likely that in the future new entrants to the labor force as well as redundant laborers will be absorbed by the non state sector. The portability of pension benefits across administrative boundaries, sectors, and ownership types will become increasingly important.

The State Council supports consolidation of pools. It has called for city and county pools within a province to merge and for a single province wide pension plan and pool to be established. The longer term goal is the creation of a nationwide pension program. In order to reach this end, the State Council is seeking to narrow the differences across pools by issuing regulations dealing with more details of the basic old-age pension scheme. For example, industry pools have been told that if their schemes are more generous than the average of local pools, the additional benefits should be converted to supplementary insurance and not be considered part of the basic old-age pension insurance.

However, achieving convergence on a single old-age pension model with uniform standards and higher level pooling is not proving to be easy. Regional variation in the inherited obligations and relative burden under the former pension system presents a formidable stumbling block to unifying the system at a higher level, even at the province level. Regions with higher concentrations of state-owned enterprises and older state industries have relatively high pension burdens and consequently tend to require higher contribution rates. For example, Shanghai has a large number of old industries and consequently a very low workers-to-retirees ratio of only 2.3 in 1996 [China State Statistical Bureau, 1997: 751]. Shanghai also has one of the highest contribution rates of 25.5 per cent for enterprises and 4 per cent for workers in 1996 [Shanghai Finance Department, 1996]. Some government officials argue that a province or national pool would lead to the underdeveloped areas subsidizing the developed regions [Hu, 1996]. While it is the case that several of the poorer provinces – Tibet, Inner Mongolia, and Ningxia – are among provinces with the lightest pension burden, several wealthier provinces in the coastal area are also in this group – Shandong and Fujian, for example. In fact, the very wealthy Pearl River Delta region in Guangdong province, which has a very favorable ratio of workers to retirees and hence low contribution rates, objects to joining a province pool and subsidizing state-owned enterprises and older enterprises through higher contribution rates.[10]

It should be noted that the wide range of contribution rates across administrative pools within a province, across provinces, and across industrial sectors reflects differences in both pension benefit design and pension burden.[11] Once a standardized pension benefit design has been adopted, the range in contribution rates will narrow. If unifying pooling at the province and ultimately the national level results in an unacceptable redistribution, the system design could still be uniform so as to facilitate labor mobility and the government could choose to explicitly subsidize selected regions, enterprises, or individuals.

A number of other important issues remain to be tackled. It is critical that regulations and supervision catch up with the new system. In common with other countries, China needs to safeguard pension funds and yet achieve sufficient growth to meet the demands of future retirees. Contributors and beneficiaries alike need to be assured that accurate records are being maintained and that funds are properly managed. In addition, if pension reform is to be successful, it is imperative that state-owned enterprise reform proceeds. There are many aspects to state-owned enterprise reform, including the establishment of unemployment insurance, housing reform, and a determination of how to value and sell off state assets while preserving a portion of assets from bankrupt enterprises to cover pension obligations. Delay in completing state-owned enterprise reform runs the risk of causing the reformed pension system to unravel, especially if the current need to bail out state-owned enterprises and excuse their pension contributions continues indefinitely. At the same time, a reformed pension system has an important role to play in increasing labor efficiency through labor mobility and thus enterprise efficiency. Finally, China may find that informal old-age support systems, such as family and mutual aid societies, which are presently the mainstay of the social security system, weaken and lose their traditional effectiveness as development and urbanization advance. Under

---

[10] Zhuhai, a Special Economic Zone in the Pearl River Delta of Guangdong province, has a contribution rate of only 12 per cent while Guangzhou, the province capital, has a rate of about 26 per cent [Guangdong Finance Department, 1996; World Bank, 1996: 10].

[11] Contribution rates ranged from 19 to 32 per cent across 70 county and city level pools in Hubei province in 1996 [Hubei Finance Department, 1996]. Among the industrial pools, there also is a wide range with a contribution rate of 7.5 per cent for China National Construction and Engineering Corporation and a rate of 22.7 per cent for the coal industry [Xin, 1997].

these circumstances, a sound, well-functioning social pillar for the old-age security system will be increasingly critical as population aging progresses.

References

1. Banister, J., 1996, "The PRC: End of Century Population Dynamics", *PRC Tomorrow Development Under the Ninth Five-Year Plan*, edited by Chong-Pin Lin, Kaohsiung, Taiwan: National Sun Yat-Sen University, Graduate Institute of Political Science.
2. Banister, J.,1997, "Perspectives on China's Mortality Trends", processed mimeo.
3. Bureau of the Census, International Programs Center, 1997, International Data Base.
4. Chen, S., 1984, "Fertility of Women During the 42-Year Period from 1940 to 1981", *Analysis on China's National One-per-Thousand-Population Fertility Sampling Survey*, Beijing: China Population Information Center.
5. China State Statistical Bureau, *China Statistics Yearbook* (Zhongguo tongji nianjian), 1995, Beijing: China Statistical Publishing House.
6. China State Statistical Bureau, *China Statistics Yearbook* (Zhongguo tongji nianjian), 1997, Beijing: China Statistical Publishing House.
7. Du, J., 1997, "China's Social Security System: Current Situation and Reform Plans", paper presented at seminar on Social Security Funds Management, Beijing, China, April 2-4.
8. Guangdong Finance Department, 1997, interview by author, March.
9. Harbaugh, C. W. and L. A. West, 1993, "Aging Trends - China", Journal of Cross-Cultural Gerontology, No. 8, pp.271-280.
10. Hu, X., 1996, "Reducing State-Owned Enterprises' Social Burdens and Establishing a Social Insurance System", in H. Broadman (ed.), Policy Options for Reform of Chinese State-Owned Enterprises, World Bank discussion paper No. 335, pp. 125-148.
11. Hubei Finance Department, 1996, interview by author, November.
12. Hussain, A., 1994, "Reform of the Chinese Social Security System", in R. Krieg and M. Schadler (eds.), Social Security in the People's Republic of China, Hamburg: Institute for Asian Studies, pp.35-64.
13. Lim, L. L. and G. Sziraczki, 1995, "Employment, Social Security and Enterprise Reforms in China", paper presented at seminar on Changes in China's Labour Market: Implications for the Future, Washington, D.C.
14. Lu H., 1994, "Booming Economy Reshapes Labour", *China Daily (Business Weekly),* 23-29 October, p.8.

15. Ministry of Finance, Department of Social Security, 1998, interview by author, June.
16. Research Team. 1996. "Chengzhen zhigong shehui baozheng zhidu gaige de silu yu fangan", Shehuixue yanjiu, No. 6, pp. 44-53.
17. Shanghai Finance Department, 1996, interview by author, November.
18. State Council, 1995, "Circular on Deepening of Reform of the Pension Insurance System", No. 6, March 1.
19. State Council, 1997, "Decisions on the Establishment of the Unified Basic Pension System for Enterprise Workers", No. 26, July 16.
20. U.S. Social Security Administration, 1997, *Social Security Programs Throughout the World – 1997*', Research report No. 65.
21. Wang J., 1995, "Reform of China's Social Security System", Beijing Review, Vol. 38, No. 31, pp.7-9.
22. World Bank, 1996, China Pension System Reform, Report No. 15121-CHA, Washington, D.C.: World Bank.
23. Xin, R., 1997, "The Situation of Industry Pools", unpublished manuscript.

PART 2
SOCIAL SECURITY FUNDS MANAGEMENT AND TRANSITIONAL ISSUES

CHAPTER 9

PRIVATIZING THE MANAGEMENT: A CHOICE FOR THE PENSION SYSTEM IN CHINA

JASON Z. YIN
W. Paul Stillman School of Business
Seton Hall University
South Orange, NJ 07079, USA
E-mail: yinjason@shu.edu

This paper reviews the pension management system in China and analyzes the pros and cons of the pay-as-you-go and fully funded pension models. It then outlines the institutional framework and organizational structure of a hybrid pension management program for China. The proposed program is composed of a small first-tier defined benefit plan run by the government in combination with a large second-tier defined contribution plan to be managed by private sector. This partially privatized program would provide better incentives for savings and bring market competition into the management of the pension system. The semi-decentralized decision-making structure in the program would eventually be able to maximize the return at a controllable risk level for the pensioners.

1. Introduction

After economic reform for the past 20 years, Chinese policy-makers have found that the existing pension plan, which was established under the socialist planned economy and run by government agencies, has become a major barrier to carry on its economic and social reforms. The goal of the reforms is to transform China's centrally planned economy to a market economy while sustaining rapid economic growth and social and political stability. The concern for the lack of a market-oriented social insurance system has intensified since 1997 when the Asian financial and economic crises began to slow China's export and economic growth. Meanwhile, close to one half of the state-owned enterprises (SOE) were run at a loss and many of them have been *de facto* bankrupted. Tens of multi-millions of workers who have retired or have lost their jobs have little social welfare protection. To transform the old, deteriorating pension program into a market oriented one thus has become not only an economic issue but also a social and political issue that requires immediate attention and policy response.

The central issue was whether privatization is a necessary condition for an efficient social insurance program and how to transform China's current pension program. In essence, it is about how to create an institutional framework (the rules of the game) and its organizational structure (the players) for a social insurance program that will "provide the necessary incentives to encourage decentralized decision-making and an effective competitive market" (North, 1992).

Privatizing pension management has become an attractive option for most countries when they are facing the challenges of an aging population and slow economic growth. Currently many countries have adopted a pay-as-you-go system that was put in place many years ago under more convivial economic and social circumstances. Many problems have surfaced after years of practice and changes in the economic and social environment. One of the problems facing those countries is an aging population. The percentage of the population that is elderly in the US, Canada, Australia and New Zealand today and the percentage projected through 2030 are high. In Western European countries, the elderly comprise a relatively larger share of total population today than they do in the US. In Asia, the Japanese population is older than the US and aging more rapidly. Countries like China (including Taiwan), South Korea, and Singapore, have younger populations today than does the US, but they are expected to have an age structure similar to the US by 2030 (Schieber and Shoven, 1996). Another problem associated with the aging population is the shortage of financial resources to sustain its current pay-as-you-go system. For example, without any change, social security in the U.S. would run short of money by 2030 and would thereafter be able to pay only 75% of the promised benefits (Diamond, 1996). Many countries are moving aggressively to find ways to control the cost of their public retirement programs and to ensure long-term financial stability and economic growth.

Privatization thus becomes a viable alternative to a pay-as-you-go unfunded system that is run by a government agent. It is also of great interest to Chinese policy makers and researchers. A question has been frequently asked: whether the welfare of the pensioners could be improved if all or part of the current pay-as-you-go programs is replaced with private individual accounts managed by the private sector?

2. The Case of China

The pension system in China was established in the 1950s as a pay-as-you-go system for urban areas including government employees and workers in the state-owned enterprises. The political chaos and economic disorder in the 1960s and 70s (the Great Leap Forward followed by three-year natural disaster and ten-year Cultural Revolution) forced the Chinese government to transfer the financial burden of pension payment to the state-owned enterprises whereas the government continued to finance the payment for government employees. The farmers, who account for more than 70% of the population, were totally uncovered by any form of social insurance. Since the economic reform of 1979, the Chinese economy has steadily shifted from the central planning system to a decentralized and market-oriented system and has sustained a 9% growth rate on average. As the reforms in other frontiers proceed well,[1] the demand for establishing a market-oriented pension system becomes urgent.

The Long-term and the Short-term Problems. China, as a developing country with the largest population in the world, is facing more severe and urgent problems than many other developed and developing countries. For the long term, its population is aging more rapidly than many other countries, because of the one-child policy and much increased life expectancy. According to the projection of World Bank (1997),

By 2030 the absolute size of the labor force in China will begin to decline, and by 2050 the ratio of workers to pensioners (age 65 and above) is projected to decline to about 3 to 1 from 10 to 1 ratio. The number of elderly will rise from about 76 million in 1995 to 300 million by 2050.

For the short-term, urgent problems include relatively low and unsustainable social insurance coverage for workers in the state-owned sector and little coverage in the non-state sector. The individual-enterprise-based insurance (pension and health care) system in the state-owned sector has largely collapsed as a large number of state enterprises were run in deficit year after year.[2] Meanwhile, the

---

[1] Significant progress have been made in industrial and financial sectors in Chinese economy, including price reform, commodity and factor market restructuring, tax reform, foreign exchange market, financial market and banking industry transformation, and SOE reform (privatization through corporationalization).

[2] Between 1978, the year before the economic reform, and 1997, the SOEs' contribution to industrial outputs declined from 78% to 28%. Along with the decline in growth rate, the financial performance declined steadily. In 1997, 46% of SOEs ran at loss. And 41% of SOE total workforce was in those money-losing SOEs (China Statistics Yearbook, 1997).

number of pensioners is rising rapidly and has become a burden unbearable for most state-owned enterprises. Farmers and township and village enterprise workers are only partially covered under voluntary pension and health insurance schemes, organized by the Ministry of Civil Affairs. In recent years, pay-as-you-go pension pooling systems were established at the local level. Many localities have separate pools for different ownership forms, e.g. state-owned enterprises, collectively owned enterprises and other population groups. A few provinces have tried to pool pension funds at the provincial level. The development of fragmented local pooling systems is, however, unlikely to provide solutions to the deeply rooted nation-wide problems. A new and sustainable pension system is desperately needed.

The Experiment of A Unified Pension System. Starting from the State Council's meeting on urban pension reform at the end of 1994, the Chinese government has decided to unify the pension system from four aspects --- a unified system with unified standards, unified management, and unified fund usage. In 1995, the State Council selected 49 cities for experiment.[3] Under the unified system, all types of enterprises and workers covered or not covered in the old plans would be brought into a single pension plan with common standards. The management of the pension plan would be transferred from enterprises to government agencies. The administrative management and fund management would be separated. Both employers and employees will contribute to the pension fund. It is expected that the newly founded Ministry of Labor and Social Security will manage the pension program whereas the Ministry of Finance will manage the pension fund.

It has also been decided that, instead of having employers as the sole contributors to pension fund as in the old system, there would be multiple channels of funding. Both employers and workers will make contributions to the fund. It is also affirmed that a multi-tier benefit structure will be implemented.

Private Individual Funded Account. The most important element in the experimentation with a unified pension system is to establish private individual retirement accounts, in combination with the pay-as-you-go system. Establishing individual funded accounts has become a less disputed issue among Chinese policy

[3] A State Council Notice on Deepening Old Age Security Reform in Enterprises was issued as the document of the meeting in December 1994. Two experiment schemes of old age security was announced in 1996 as the State Council 's #6 Announcement. Scheme One emphasizes the contribution of enterprises to the pension fund and social pooling; Scheme Two sheds more lights on the contribution of workers and individual accounts. The Ministry of Labor selected 49 cities for the experiment. In October 1997, the State Council announced its Resolution Regarding Establishing Old Age Security System for Enterprise Employees. (People's Daily, 10/4/97, p.4)

makers. One of the advantages of individual accounts is to smooth the rise in the contribution rate. If the pay-as-you-go system is not reformed, it will require a contribution rate of 39.27% by 2033, according to World Bank's calculation (1997), which is well above the average contribution rate of pension programs in the rest of the world.

According to the State Council Resolution of 1997,[4] each enterprise pays its own workers' pension reserve account in amount equal to 20% of total wages and 3% of the contribution goes to its workers' individual accounts. Each worker will contribute 8% of his/her wage. Thus the individual account for each worker is about 11% of his/her taxable income. The interest rate for individual accounts will be determined by the interest rate for annuity savings accounts.

Table 1: Three Pension Models Under Two Types of Governance

Management Institution	Pay-as-you-go (Defined Benefit)	Partial Funded (Partial Defined Contribution and Partial defined benefits)	Fully-Funded System Accounts (Full Defined Contribution)
Government Agency	Unified publicly managed pool (in most industrial countries, the U.S. Model)	A combination of social pooling and individual accounts (The Model experimenting in some areas in China)	Publicly managed, 100% private individual account (Australia, Western European countries)
Private Investment Corp.	Not an option	Partial privatization plan with a partial private management (Sweden, Mexico)	Privately managed, 100% individual account (Chilean Model)

Under individual accounts, the burden of savings would be shifted from the next generation to the current generation, who would take care of their own retirement costs and plan their contributions during their working time to build up their individualized pension fund. Currently some cities such as Shanghai, are experimenting with individual notional accounts (*minyi jizhang*). A worker's account is set up merely as a bookkeeping device to keep track of contributions plus imputed interest at a rate predetermined by the government. This individualized

[4] The Resolution Regarding Establishing a Unified Old Age Basic Pension System for Enterprise Employees, The State Council of China (document # 26), August 1997.

notional account is different from an individual funded account. There is no actual capital accumulation. It would not generate full benefits for individual or society from maximization of rate of return because the funds are never actually accumulated in these accounts and of course are never invested.

A final decision has not been reached on who and how much the enterprises and their workers should contribute to the pension funds and on how to split the contributions into social pooling and individual accounts. And no final decision has been reached on a unified basic benefit tier either as differences on the design of the program continues.

Briefly, the social insurance reform in China so far has focused on how to shift from the pay-as-you-go system to a mixed system of social pooling and individual accounts.

As shown in Table 1, the new pension program under experiment is somewhere between the pay-as-you-go and fully funded. Although there is a growing consensus on moving toward fully funded individual accounts, the Chinese government has not decided whether China would definitely move into fully funded individual accounts in the near future. Regardless of whether the new system will be a mix of social pooling and individual accounts or fully funded private individual accounts, it has been assumed that the new system will be controlled and managed by government agencies. The possibility of privatizing pension management has not been addressed very much. Therefore, there are two puzzles remaining to be solved:

- Should China adopt substantially or fully funded individual accounts, which will build a direct linkage between contributions and benefits for each individual worker?
- Should the pension funds be managed by the private sector or could the workers be allowed to choose where to invest the funded reserves to support their own retirement?

The next section will discuss the key points in the debate on pension privatization and then discuss what pension model is preferable for China.

3. The Tradeoffs of Privatization

To date, two basic pension models --- pay-as-you-go and fully funded private individual accounts---have generated the most attention in the current worldwide debate on social insurance reform, as shown in Table 2.

Table 2: The Disputes on Defined Benefit Plans versus Defined Contribution Plan

	Pro-Defined Benefit System	Pro-Defined Contribution
Return on Investment	The relative low rate of return is due to the restrictions governing investment of SS reserves, having nothing to do with privatization; A well-managed SS will generate higher return Favorable economies of scale	Private pension plan may yield high rates of return through investment in private stocks and bonds; Better benefit-tax linkage Unfavorable economies of scale
Financial Risks	Risks are shared more broadly across society. At the system level, benefits may not received as what promised	Higher individual financial risks; The returns would vary widely based on timing of contribution and retirement (or when one buys and when one sells)
Political Risks	Inter-generation income distribution is not equitable; Risk associated with "promised" benefits been cut back	Higher risk due to the lack of income redistribution function in the system to reduce the income inequality after retirement
Costs	Lower administrative costs than defined contribution plan	Higher administrative and marketing costs than defined benefit system
Politics of Income Redistribution	Desirable for workers long-term economic and political interests; Provide greater assistance and better protection to low-earners	.Private pension plans empower people to save for their retirement which might benefit the poor more than the rich

Pay-as-you-go: Currently the social assurance programs in most countries are "defined benefit" plans financed by worker payroll taxes, which, in turn, are commonly referred to as the "pay-as-you-go" method. Such plans link worker's retirement benefits to their earnings and years of service. As workers pay their payroll taxes (or the enterprises withhold them), they accumulate benefit credits. They will collect the retirement, disability, or survivor benefits under predetermined terms.

One advantage of these defined benefit programs is that it reduces income inequality among retirees through income redistribution. It provides disproportionate benefits to pensioners --- more benefits to lower-earners and less to higher-earners. The other advantages include lower risk (because it is run by government and government never goes bankrupt) and easy management. The disadvantages include lower rate of return from the pension funds, the possibility of pension deficits, and less incentive to contribute to the fund.

Fully funded. Under fully funded plans, the government sets a mandatory amount from personal income to be saved for each worker's retirement. The workers and their employers contribute a defined amount from their income into the private individual accounts on behalf of each worker. In fact, it is a forced savings plan for retirement. The flow of pension savings will be invested into restricted financial market instruments to maximize the rate of return within the limited risk taken. The retirees will finance their consumption through the sale of assets accumulated. It is also called a "defined contribution" plan.

By design, this plan provides greater incentives to save for retirement through a clear linkage between contribution and benefits. Comparatively, it may bring a higher rate of return through a diversified investment portfolio. For the government, after paying off all the pension debts, it would not have pension debt in the future. The major problem in this system is the individualized risks each pensioner has to bear, which will be further discussed in the following paragraphs.

The Debate. The major departure point in the debate over pension reform is how to solve the projected long term financing problem of the pay-as-you-go pension program. Some people suggest making some improvements to the current system such that the problem can be fixed. For example, Henry Aaron (1997) argues that this long-term deficit is a modest problem, which can be solved "by reforms that entail no serious modification of the basic structure of the program and no payroll tax increases." What we should do is to "tune it up" rather than "trade it in" (1998a). On the contrary, others argue that more fundamental reform is needed, namely "privatizing" some or all aspects of pension (Diamond, 1996; Feldstein, 1996; Gramlich, 1996; Kotlikoff, 1996).

In his analysis of five OECD counties (US, Germany, Italy, Norway, and Sweden), Kotlikoff found three major problems in the current systems. (1) The current fiscal policies for social security in all five countries are unsustainable; and (2) the future generations in the US and Italy, respectively, face financial burdens two and three times as high as those for newborns; and (3) eliminating official debt would still leave a substantial generational imbalance. He concludes that the system needs restructuring.

Laurence Kotlikoff (1996) also found, from his social security privatization simulation, that privatization of social security can generate substantial long-term increases in output, capital stock, and real wages despite the fact that the initial elderly are compensated for their higher fiscal burden arising from the consumption tax. He proposes to privatize the retirement-income portion of the US social security system, i.e., to privatize only contributions to old age insurance (OAI, about 68% of the total pension program), leaving unchanged the contributions made to, and benefits received from, the survivors and disability portions of the social security system.

Chilean Model. The most convincing example for full privatization is the case of Chile. There have been many discussions about the Chilean experience and its relevance to the rest of the world. In fact, the heart of the reform is a privatized mandatory savings plan, together with a market for indexed annuities for conversion of accumulations into a retirement income stream (Diamond, 1996). Workers can choose currently among 21 competing private companies (highly regulated intermediary, referred to as APF) to invest about 10% of their monthly earnings (equivalent to the payroll taxes) in a conservative portfolio of high-rated bonds and equities. In addition, workers are required to purchase term life insurance and disability insurance. The combined contribution covering retirement, life and disability insurance, and administrative expenses are about 13% of their payroll, roughly comparable to the contribution of the US social security benefits.

Upon the retirement, Chileans can choose between a phased withdrawal of their account balances or an inflation-indexed annuity sold by insurance companies. By 1994, pension funds held 55% of government bonds, 62% of mortgage bonds, 59% of corporate bonds, and 11% of corporate equity (Schieber and Shoven, 1996). The gross savings have increased steadily from 9.4% of GNP in 1982, when privatization started to about 25% of GNP by 1997. Economic growth has more than doubled to a 7% average during the years from 1984 to 1997. Seven other Latin American countries, including Argentina, Peru, Colombia, Bolivia and Mexico, have emulated the Chilean example in the past five years. Eastern European countries, including Russia, are considering similar reforms (Jose Pinera, 1998).[5]

It has been largely recognized that pension privatization in Chile has been successful. Policy makers in other countries are trying to imitate the Chilean model. Representatives from 38 countries met in London in 1997 to discuss social security

[5] Jose Pinera, ex-Secretary of Department of Labor and Social Security of Chile, President of the International Center for Pension Reform and Chairman of the Cato Institute's Project on Social Security Privatization. His editorial article entitled "Time to Privatize Social Security," was appeared in Wall Street Journal, April 10, 1998, pp.)

privatization in their countries. Some have referred to this trend as a worldwide social security revolution. A number of scholars have mapped out the design for privatization for other countries. Kotlikoff (1996) proposes four key steps to be taken to privatize social security and to transfer from a pay-as-you-go program to a fully funded program:

(i) Eliminating pension payroll taxes;
(ii) Mandating contributions to private pensions;
(iii) Phasing out pension benefits; and
(iv) Financing pension benefits (including paying out recognition bonds for the Chilean case) during the phase-out (transition) period. It requires deficit financing.

While the advantages of privatization have been recognized, the disadvantages or concerns associated with it also deserve to be fully addressed. There are three major disadvantages or fundamental problems in the privatized pension system. One is that privatized defined contribution plans expose workers/retirees to higher and unshared risk because they allow individuals to invest in the stock market aiming at higher rates of return. The concern is that this plan may not serve the purpose of having a pension plan. The other concern is relatively higher administrative costs of the private pension system than the defined benefit system. And the third is that since the private pension programs would abandon the function of income redistribution inter-generation and intra-generation, then the income inequality among retirees may increase.

Risks of Private Pension Programs. As shown in Table 3, there are variety of risks that may affect pension programs, including economic risks (e.g., inflation and recession), financial risks (e.g., interest rate, return on investment), and personal risks (e.g., lengthy illness, disability, and longevity).

Under defined benefit pension plans, at the system level, a variety of economic and demographic changes, including economic growth, real wage growth, natural birth rates and changes in labor forces, can throw benefit plans out of financial balance. The benefits for current retirees might be cut and the retirement life may have to suffer more than expected. At the individual level, the pension depends on earnings and years of work, as they do under defined contribution plans. The retirement benefits will be lower than average for low-earners and for workers who have a shorter working life. However, the risk is reduced under defined benefit plans because benefits vary less than proportionately with earnings.

In contrast, under private pension plans, workers face a variety of risks individually. Contributions depend on pay level and duration of employment. The accumulated benefits depend on return on investment. Investment, subsequently, depends on interest rates, dividend distribution and appreciation of the assets. These three variables can fluctuate greatly in open market operations from year to year. The pension that a worker will ultimately be able to claim is very sensitive to the timing of contributions and retirement. As shown in some studies, the replacement rates of retirement benefits vary enormously over a relatively short period of time.

Table 3: Types of Risks and Who Bears Them

Risk to benefits		Who bears the risk under		
		Defined Benefit	Defined Contribution	Hybrid Pension Plan
Economic	Inflation	Shared	Individual (1)	Partly Shared
	Recession	Shared	Individual	Partly Shared
Financial	Interest rate	Shared	Individual	Partly Shared
	Return on Invest.	Blend	Individual	Individual
Personal	Extended Illness	Blend	Individual (2)	Blend
	Longevity	Shared	Individual (3)	Depends (3)

(1) Individual bears the risk if he or she has invested in assets other than indexed Treasury Security, first issued in 1996.

(2) The loss of pension is more than four times larger if extended illness is experienced during ones 20s than during one's 50s. under social security the effect on the pension is not age-dependent.

(3) The individual bears longevity risk unless he or she buys an annuity.

Source: Partly from Henry Aaron: "Social Security: Tune It Up, Don't Trade It In", working paper, 1998, except the last column.

Risk is not escapable. The key point is whether the government should expose workers to a relatively higher level of risk and whether the government should let these risks be born by each worker/pensioner alone or should let these risks be shared across society. It is also open for question

The Costs and the Net Return. The more complex an economic system, the more individuals will be engaged in coordinating and operating the system, the more the transaction costs (Coase, 1980; North, 1992). Peter Diamond demonstrates that there would be additional administrative and marketing costs for private individual accounts, including advertisement, record keeping, and verification of deposits and statements. The additional costs may cause a large decrease in returns.

It would be very significant to the size of the accounts built with just a 2% savings rate. These costs indeed have been a major issue in Mexico where 2% SAR accounts have been started on top of the existing pension system (Diamond, 1996). Valdes-Prieto (1994) examined administrative costs for private accounts, converting them into an averaged annual charge. He estimated that the average annual charge per person for the private accounts in Chile is $89.10 per year for 1991, which is 2.94% of the worker's taxable income. However, the US social security administrative cost is $18.70 per person per year on the same basis. It shows that the average administrative cost is much higher in private accounts than in well-run unified government managed systems.

As to whether the net return on the private retirement plans exceed the pay-as-you-go plan, Henry Aaron (1998a) argues that it is not necessarily true for everybody and it might be the opposite for small accounts and for people with little experience with investment or who are particularly adverse to financial risks. In addition, the social security reserves in the US by law must be invested in special Treasury securities with a yield equal to the average return on outstanding Treasury bonds with a maturity of four years or more to keep financial risk to the minimum. But private individual accounts could invest in private stocks and long-term corporate bonds, the yield on which is higher than that of Treasury bonds. Therefore the differential had "nothing to do with Privatization. It is due entirely to the restrictions governing investments of social security reserves." (Aaron, 1998a)

The Redistribution. The way an economic system is organized determines the distribution of the benefits (North, 1992). As mentioned earlier, fully funded individual accounts would increase inequality. This has been the case in Chile. According to Vittas and Iglesias (1992), there was a difference of 3% points in the rates of return to high and low earners in the first ten years of Chilean privatization. Potentially, the inequality of earnings may be a source of social and political instability. It may defeat the goal of a pension system. In addition, as North (1992) argued, it is in the interest of participants to design a privatized system so that it will benefit them, but in so doing there is no assurance that the resulting institutional structure will result in economic growth and will benefit society as a whole.

In brief, the above mentioned concerns, the risk, the return on investment, and redistribution, have shown that fully funded plans or total privatization may not provide a satisfactory solution to the problems associated with a pay-as-you-go plan. Thus it might not be the ideal solution for China to transform its current pay-as-you-go plan to a fully funded plan.

4. Partial Privatization: The Solution for China

Instead of total privatization, a variety of partially funded plans or partial privatization plans have been proposed and some have been implemented or experimented with in various countries. For example, two major changes have been implemented in Sweden's pension reform: (1) To increase the awareness of costs of the system, the contribution is to be split 50-50 between employers and employees. (2) Two percent of the 18.5% aggregate old-age pension contribution will go to an individual retirement account, partially privatizing the pay-as-you-go system. Singapore and many other nations have long provided retirement benefits through a provident fund, a system in which benefits are based on individual deposits plus the overall return on centrally managed investments.

Based on the experiences of pension systems in developed and developing economies and the economic condition in China, it might be preferable for China to take two strategies in establishing its old age pension program. The first strategy is to set up a hybrid pension plan with components from both pay-as-you-go and fully funded plans. The second strategy is to separate the administration of pensions from the management of the funds and let the private sector participate in the management of the funds. These two strategies provide answers to the two crossly linked puzzles mentioned earlier.

The Institutional Framework. As Douglass North pointed out, "...it cannot be emphasized too strongly that a condition for the creation of appropriate organizations and learning in the developing world and the formerly centrally planned economies is the evolution of institutional frameworks that provide the necessary incentives." (North, 1992:17)

The first strategy is essentially to create an institutional framework that provides clear, unambiguous rules and incentives to the relevant agents to faithfully carry out the intentions of the principals. The strategy follows the basic idea laid out in the State Council Resolution of 1997. It calls for creating a relatively small first-tier unfunded defined benefit plan (pay-as-you-go) which is a complement to a relative large second-tier funded, defined contribution plan. According to this program, the enterprise or the employer pays a social security tax to a "social pooling" pension fund equal to approximately 17% of the average earnings in a worker's province, region, or municipality and pays 3% of that to its worker's individual account.. In addition, there is a mandatory second-tier funded, defined contribution savings plan. Therefore, a total of 11% of earnings will be eventually contributed to the individual account. According to this scheme, a worker who is employed and contributes to the pension plan for 40 years will receive a combined pension equal 73% of his/her final earnings (53% from the second-tier benefit), a very high replacement rate. The calculation is based on an annual increase of 3% in real earnings and a 5% real interest rate on deposit. The replacement rate for a 35-year worker will be 66%, which is still a high replacement rate, based on the same assumptions. However, if the inflation rates are high in the later stages of the worker's career, the second-tier benefit can be significantly lower, a risk factor which needs to be considered.

The first-tier pension plan, about 20% replacement rate, will secure the basic need to survive for all pensioners, providing the primary personal security through social risk sharing. It will also redistribute income to reduce the differential among high and low earners. In addition, with the basic welfare in place, it would be easier for China to transform its current pension plan to the new hybrid plan.

The second-tier pension plan will link the contribution of each worker to his/her retirement benefits, creating a better incentive for workers to maximize their capital accumulation through savings and investment plans for their retirement and for their beneficiaries.

Overall, this hybrid plan strikes a balance between return and risk for each individual. It is clear that this plan will expose workers to much less individual risk than the fully funded plan. Meanwhile, the funded plan will bring a better return from the diversified investment portfolio than the defined-benefit pay-as-you-go plan. At the macro level, it will improve social capital accumulation and subsequently economic growth.

However, it is notable that an institution, which is efficient over time, is the one that provides economic and political flexibility to adapt to new opportunities and to avoid unperceived threats. For example, the changes in contribution rates and tax rate (and subsequent replacement rate) are inevitable if economic or demographic conditions change, such as longevity and earnings growth. It would be farsighted to consider enacting provisions that make such adjustments automatic under certain conditions (Aaron, 1998b).

As to the longevity issue, as incomes rise and public health care measures are improved, an increase in longevity in China is virtually certain. This raises a question of the optimal retirement age for Chinese workers. Some suggest that the Chinese government should lift the initial age of eligibility for pensions to 65 years old from the current level of 60 for men and 55 for women. The increase in work life would significantly increase the contribution to and reduce the demand for pension funds of both first and second tiers. However, the longer work life for the workforce has negative implications for unemployment, a major social and political concern for the government.

The Organizational Structure. If institutions are the rules of the game, organizations are the players. Organizations and especially entrepreneurs, are the actors in institutional innovation (North, 1992). The survival and growth of a pension system relies on the efficient management of pension funds. The second strategy suggests that fund management should be separated from pension administration and the government should let private financial institutions participate in the management of the second-tier funds, as in the management structure of the Chilean model.

In a recent study of over 500 companies listed on China's national stock exchange, Xu and Wang (1998) found that there is a positive correlation between performance and ownership concentration. The effect of ownership concentration on firms' performance is stronger for companies dominated by institutional shareholders (each institution has a person as its independent legal representative of ownership) than for those dominated by the state and individuals that are the A-share holders. These findings suggest that state ownership does not improve firms' performance. On the other hand, the small individual shareholders in China do not monitor management well, probably because of the free-rider problem (Grossman and Hart, 1980). In contrast, large institutional shareholders appear to have played a positive role in corporate governance. Entrepreneurs are usually appointed to serve as the legal representatives of the institutions to ensure accountability.

These findings are very important as a guideline for the design of the organizational structure of the pension funds. It becomes clear that the government has an obligation to oversee the pension systems, but it does not mean that the government must provide the fund management service directly. Similar to any other stock companies in China, the pension funds can perform better under the ownership of independent institutions which are staffed with economic and business entrepreneurs and professionals. These findings call for creating a new industry of private institutions (insurance companies) in pension fund management and granting the entrepreneurs of those institutions greater freedom and maneuverability in account management. The workers contract with institutions to receive second-tier pensions in exchange for payments of a periodic premium (retirement contribution). The workers have the freedom of affiliation and the right to change institutions. These institutions, in term, would have to be efficient in order to remain competitive. They would have to endeavor to reduce their administrative costs and obtain an increase in the number of participants through higher benefits and lower commissions.

Nonetheless, the government retains its responsibility to oversee and regulate the industry through, *per se*, its Ministry of Labor and Social Security. An oversight agency needs to be created with a staff of high quality experts with relevant professional training. One of its responsibilities is to select, supervise and control the operation of those competing pension management institutions. Another responsibility is to regulate the operations. For instance, although the introduction of market mechanisms into the pension fund management would ensure efficiency and a better return on pension investment, the open-market operation itself implies a tremendous risk for the insurers. Thus, regulations on investment diversification are needed in order to reduce risk.

When designing a new pension system, the transition problem must be taken into consideration. One of the advantages of the proposed hybrid pension plan is that it makes the transition relatively easier because all workers and retirees are still under the protection of the first-tier defined benefit plan. The workers should be given the option of remaining in the old system or shifting to the new one. Those who agree to join the new system should be granted a "recognition bond' in acknowledgement of their earlier contribution.

5. Conclusion

After reviewing the pension system in China and analyzing the pros and cons of the pay-as-you-go and fully funded pension models, I have outlined the institutional framework and organizational structure of a proposed hybrid pension program for China. This partially privatized and decentralized program would be able to balance the risks and returns to the pension investors. It should be a practical and relatively better choice for China. However, regarding the details of this program, many questions remain unanswered. The detailed design and implementation of an optimal system in China remains a major challenge for scholars and policy-makers. It is important to note that a new social insurance program, no matter how well conceived, could not be the panacea for all of the social security problems a country may face. We should realize that we are dealing with "a complicated set of interrelationships the nature of which take much dedicated work over a long period to discover"(Coase, 1998). However, the first step is to set up proper governance structure including institutions and organizations and then make incremental adjustments and improvements going forward.

References

1. Aaron, Henry J. "Social Security: Tune it up, don't trade it in." *Working Paper*, 1998a
2. Aaron, Henry J. " The Chinese Social Security Reform: Personal Security and Economic Growth," paper presented at *the International Symposium on China's Social Security*, June 23-24, 1998b, Beijing China.
3. Aaron, Henry J. "A Bad Idea Whose Time Will Never Come." *Privatizing Social Security*, Summer 1997.
4. Auerback, Alan, Jagadeesh Gokhale, and Laurence Kotlikoff. "Generational Accounting." *The Journal of Economic Perspective* 8, pp. 73-94.
5. Coase, Ronald. "The New Institutional Economics," The New Institutional Economics. Vol. 88 (2), May 1998, pp.72-74.
6. Coase, Ronald. "The problem of Social Cost," the *Journal of Law and Economics*, 3 (1980): 1-44.
7. Diamond, Peter. "A Framework for Social Security Analysis." *Journal of Public Economics* 8, 1977, pp. 275-298.
8. Diamond, Peter A. "Proposals to Restructure Social Security." *Journal of Economic perspectives*, Vol. 10, Number 3, Summer 1996, 67-88.
9. Feldstein, Martin. "Social Security, Induced Retirement and Aggregate capital Accumulation." *Journal of Political Economy* 82, 1974, pp. 905-926.
10. Feldstein, Martin. "The Optimal Level of Social Security Benefits." *Quarterly Journal Economics* 100, 1985, pp. 303-320.
11. Feldstein, Martin. "The Missing Piece in Policy Analysis: Social Security Reform." *Richard T. Ely Lecture*, May 1996.
12. Ferrara,Peter. "Worldwide Social Security Revolution." Available on the website: http://www.socialsecurity.org/articles/art-14.html.
13. Gramlich, Edward M. "Different Approaches for Dealing with Social Security." *AEA Papers and Proceedings*, May 1996, pp. 358-362.
14. Grossman , Sanford and Hart, Oliver. "Takeover Bids, the Free-Rider problem, and the Theory of Corporation," *Bell Journal of Economics*, 11, 1980: 42-64.
15. Gruber, Jonathan, and David Wise. "Social Security Programs and Retirement around the World." *NBER Working Paper Series* No. 6134, 1997.
16. Hu, Sheng-Cheng. "Social Security, the Supply of Labor, and Capital Accumulation." *American Economic Review* 69, 1979, pp. 274-283.
17. Hussain, Athar. "Reform of the Chinese Social Security System." *Working Paper*, London School of Economics, 1993.

18. Kotlikoff, Laurence J. "Privatizing Social Security at Home and Abroad." *AEA Papers and Proceedings*, May 1996, pp. 368-377.
19. Mitchell, Olivia S. and Zeldes, Setphen P. "Social security Privatization: A Structure for Analysis." *AEA Papers and Proceedings*, May 1996, pp. 363-367.
20. Murphy, Kevin, and Finis Welch. "Social Security: Problems with Proposed Solution." Presented at the *ASSA Meeting in Chicago*, 1998.
21. North, Douglass C. "Transaction Costs, Institutions, and Economic Performance," International Center for Economic Growth: *Occasional Papers* #30, 1992, pp.5-32.
22. Samuelson, Paul A. "An Exact Consumption-Loan Model of Interest with or Without the Social Contrivance of Money." *Journal of Political Economy* 66, 1958, pp. 467-482.
23. Samuelson, Paul A. "Optimum Social Securty in A life-Cycle Growth Model." *International economic Review* 16, 1975, pp. 539-544.
24. Schieber, Sylvester J. and Shoven, John B. "Social Security Reform: Around the World in 80 Ways." *AEA Papers and Proceedings*, May 1996, pp. 373-377.
25. "Social Security 'Privatization'". *News From The Libertarian Party*, 1997, available on the website: http://www.lp.org/rel/970106-Social-Security.html.
26. Statistical Survey of China. Beijing, China: China statistical Publishing House, 1977.
27. Tanner, Michael. "A New Social Security Debate." Available on the website: http://www.socialsecurity.org/articles/art-tanner5.hmtl
28. Wachter, Susan M. "Social Security and Private Pensions." Lexington, Massachusetts: Lexington Books, 1988.
29. World Bank, "Old Age Security, Pension Reform in China." Washington D.C., 1997.
30. Xu, Xiaonian, and Wang, Yang "Ownership Structure, Corporate Governance and Corporate Performance: the Case of Chinese Stock Companies," *World Bank Policy Research Working Paper* No. 1794.

CHAPTER 10

PENSION FUND MANAGEMENT AND CHINA'S FINANCIAL SECTOR

ANJALI KUMAR
The World Bank, 1818 H Street, NW,
Washington DC 20433, USA
E-mail: akumar@worldbank.org
YAN WANG[1]
The World Bank, 1818 H Street, NW,
Washington DC 20433, USA
E-mail: ywang@worldbank.org

This paper first summarizes the *status of pension reform* in China, and the drawbacks of the present system. It points out why, if the government's current plans for pension reform are to succeed, the issue of pension fund management is of importance. The second section discusses *broad regulatory and institutional principles* for pension fund management, in particular, private and decentralized fund management, and describes how such funds operate elsewhere. In the third section, the paper discusses China's present financial *institutions* which could play a role in pension fund management, and current laws and *regulations* pertaining to such institutions. The next section discusses the nature of the financial *instruments* that are available to pension funds for investment, and the structure of the financial *markets* in which they operate. The final section aims to pull together the lessons of the preceding parts and recommend actions necessary, in the financial sector, to pave the way for pension reform. The paper points out that financial market reform must accompany reforms in the pension system, if pension funds are to operate successfully.

---

[1] Senior economists at the World Bank. The conclusions and views expressed here are entirely those of the authors. They do not necessarily represent the view of the World Bank, its Executive directors, or the countries they represent. We are grateful to Xiaoqing Yu, for her inputs for Section 1.

1. Pension Funds in China: Key Issues

The pension crisis has been recognized by the government as a major impediment to enterprise reform, as well as a potentially large and costly unfunded government obligation. The current pension system, covers state-owned enterprises, mostly in urban areas. It is a largely pay-as-you-go system, with defined benefits. Individual accounts, although being initiated in some places, are largely notional, and contain few if any assets, In the past enterprises were individually responsible for paying their own pensioners, but in some places this responsibility has shifted recently to local governments, who pay pension funds from pooled funds, that are regularly replenished by enterprise contributions. There is also some pooling at the sectoral level, with sectors such as railways, civil aviation, and mining, establishing their own pools. Today most public sector workers are covered by such pooling arrangements, which has helped spread risks, and is useful for firms with large pension bills.[2]

Despite these recent attempts at pooling, the current system has a number of drawbacks. For many state enterprises, *contribution rates are high*, with average contribution rates in 1994 of 23.5 percent for thirteen provinces, and 25.9 percent for twelve municipalities – well above the international norm of around 20 percent. Moreover, *the range of contribution rates is highly variable*, from 19 percent in Guangdong and 21 percent in Shenzhen to 28 percent in Henan and 30 percent in Chongqing.[3] Sectoral contribution rates also differ widely and are notably low in some sectors; 8 percent in civil aviation and 10 percent in construction. Differences in the base used to calculate contribution requirements also imply that that *the variance of effective contribution rates is even higher.* [4] High and rising contribution rates have been combined with *falling rates of compliance*. While one reason for declining compliance is the increasing plight of many state owned enterprises, another is the *lack of a legal framework.* China has no social insurance law and the provincial and local authorities managing the funds have limited capacity to enforce their local regulations which at present define contributions and benefits. Recent

---

[2] Most data presented in this paper are dated mid-1998 when we presented this paper at the CES conference in Beijing.

[3] See Table 1.3 in '*Old Age Security: Pension Reform in China*' - World Bank, 1997.

[4] For example, the effective contribution rate in Shenyang is 31.2 percent, calculated as 18 percent of wages plus 40 percent of enterprise pension expenditures. But effective contributions in Jilin are close of 50 percent, based on an enterprise contribution rate of 21.5 percent of both wages plus pensions. See '*Old Age Security*', in '*China 2020*'. World Bank, 1997.

experiments with pooling are still limited, and portability is uncommon.[5] The high degree of fragmentation is mirrored in the *large number of administrative agencies* which have authority over pensions, not only at the central level but also at the local level.[6]

The present system has adverse implications for *state enterprise reform*. Many state enterprises have large pension burdens, although the burden is so variable that it leads to distortions in competitiveness. Some sectors pay less than 15 percent of the wage bill as pension contributions while others pay as much as 30 percent. The *lack of portability* makes enterprise restructuring or closure difficult. The system also implies a loss in terms of opportunities for *term transformation.* Specifically, China's enormous infrastructure requirements could benefit greatly from the participation of pension funds in domestic capital markets. The availability

Figure 1:Required Contribution Rate for Sustainability

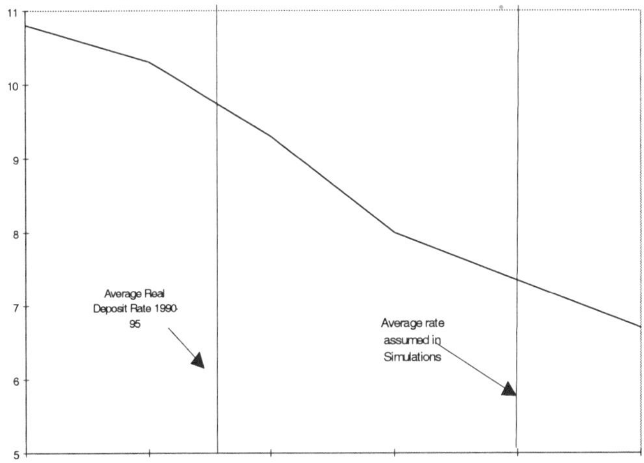

Source: World Bank, *China 2020.*

of long term investible funds through such funds, could help to channel China's high

---

[5] Only nine of the thirty two provinces have experimented with some form of pooling; and of these, only four (the municipalities of Beijing, Tianjin and Shanghai and Hainan province) have reasonably complete provincial pooling, with a uniform plan for all urban workers. The rest have variability across enterprise and locality. Portability across work units within the pool is allowed in some provinces.

[6] Until March 1998, the Ministry of Labor was in charge of pension provision and administration for state enterprise employees, while the Ministry of Personnel fulfilled this role for civil servants. The Ministry of Civil Affairs was in charge of social welfare programs and rural pensions. In March 1998 the National People's Congress announced the establishment of a new Ministry of Labor and Social Security which is charge of administering pension system and other social insurance schemes.

domestic savings to more productive uses than is possible through the present limited array of savings instruments.

But the biggest long run problem with the present system is that the pay-as-you-go nature of present pensions, limited reserves and high replacement rates, combined with China's rapidly aging population, imply that *in the long run, contribution rates are unsustainable.* By end 1996, total pension funds were estimated to have 90 billion yuan in reserves.[7] Given present levels of low real interest rates, current projections indicate rapidly rising contribution requirements, if China is to meet its pension obligations, as the dependency ratio increases (Figure 1). The present pay-as-you-go system is projected to require contribution rates of around 40 percent by the year 2033, when the dependency ratio is estimated to reach its peak.[8]

The government is aware of the shortcomings of the present system and periodically new regulations on pensions have been issued, introducing the recent reforms. State Council Document 26 stipulated a multipillar pension system in the future, and a second pillar which is outside the social pool. The success of the new system, however, will depend on the performance of its pension funds. The rate of returns to funds accumulated can make a major difference to the long term viability and costs of pension reform. Present informal regulations are silent on the subject of pension fund oversight. In terms of the investment strategy permitted for pension funds, they require that 80 percent of pension reserves must be kept in government bonds, and the balance must be kept in bank deposits.[9] Rates of return on these assets have been below the inflation rate in recent years, and thus the reserves which comply with these regulations have had their real value eroded.[10] Yet, several indicators suggest that the real rate of return on capital has been at comfortable

---

[7] Based on a presentation by an official at the State Planing Commission at an EDI conference in January 1998. However, some of these funds are allegedly misappropriated. For 1995, World Bank data indicate reserves of 44 billion yuan. *China 2020*; World Bank, 1997.

[8] China's Research Group for the Social Security System (1995); discussed in '*Old Age Security*', in '*China 2020*'. World Bank, 1997.

[9] State Council Circular, known as Document 26, of July 16, 1997. This supercedes Document No. 6, of March 1, 1995 'State Council Circular on the Deepening of Reforms on the Pension Insurance System', which also prescribed the same guidelines, requiring that the funds should be used to buy special government bond issues for social insurance funds issued by the state. No such bonds were issued, however. In practice, these guidelines have not been adhered to. The state council allegedly undertook a study on 60 pension funds' investments which found a number of irregular practices.

[10] To deal with negative real interest rates in the last few years, the authorities provided 3- to 5-year bank deposits and selective issues of treasury bonds at inflation-indexed rates, and these rates have been recently phased out. The method used for indexation in the last few years needed improvement since it was nontransparent, and it could ensure only a zero real rate of interest. Moreover, these indexed bonds were available only to individuals, not to institutional investors.

positive levels in China. Considering China's high wage growth in the recent years (5.4 percent a year during 1980-93), pension funds face a challenging task in obtaining real rates of return that match or exceed wage growth. However, wage growth is likely to decline, over time, and pension funds which are able to follow a more diversified investment strategy should be able to achieve real rates of return which exceed wage growth.

Figure 2. Real Rate of Return over 1980-1990

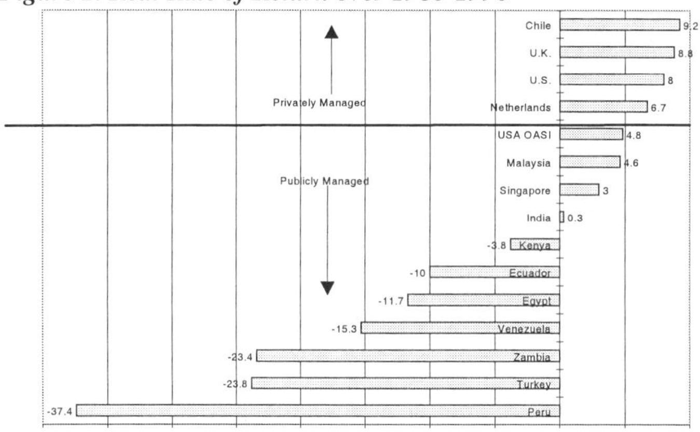

Source: World Bank, *China 2020.*

The stringent limitations placed on pension fund *investment strategy*, in combination with the lack of regulations for pension fund *management* imply that there is also significant non-compliance. Localities invest the funds in local projects, sometimes with higher rates of return, and generally with significantly higher levels of risk. There are incentives to keep funds at the local level, and investment is sometimes non-transparent. Often pension contributions are exposed to risk, as a consequence. Today in China, all pension funds are publicly managed, and there are virtually no options, for an individual worker, for seeking an efficiently managed pension fund, or for an enterprise, to seek better management of its pension assets. There are no privately managed pension funds in China today. Funds remain highly centralized in government hands. Yet, in other countries, privately managed funds have fared well; in many instances better than publicly managed funds (Figure 2).

But effective private fund management requires not only an adequate framework of regulation, and effective supervision and enforcement capacity, but also, the pension fund must operate in a financial market environment which permits it to invest safely in suitable financial instruments. These conditions do not all exist in China today, and authorities seeking success in pension reform must focus on a wide range of actions, not only with regard to pension fund regulation, but also with regard to strengthening financial markets, if pension reform is to be successful.

2. Pension Fund Management: Regulatory and Institutional Frameworks

2.1 Private Pension Fund Management Regulation in the USA

Pension funds are the largest US institutional investor group. Between 1950 and 1994, the assets of pension funds operated by private business entities (private pension plans) and state and local governments (public pension plan) grew from US$17 billion to about US$4.7 trillion. Private pension plans are much larger than public pension plans, amounting to about US$3.5 trillion at year-end 1994, and it is the management of these private pension funds, by financial institutions, that forms the basis of the discussion of this section.

In the US, private pension schemes are highly decentralized. The sponsors of pension plans are subject to a variety of regulations and that have important fiduciary duties regarding the choice of plan investments. Although pooled investment vehicles offered in the form of private pension plans are functionally similar to investment companies, they are specifically exempt from registration and regulation under the US securities laws. Instead, employee benefit plans are regulated by the *Employee Retirement Income Securities Act* of 1974 (*ERISA*) which is the primary law governing the regulation of pension plans and their sponsors. This Act is administered by the US Department of Labor. The *Employee Retirement Income Security Act* of 1974 (*ERISA*) provides basic protection to individual workers for monies invested in private pension schemes. Interestingly, *ERISA* was enacted 40 years after the Federal securities laws and 34 years later than the *Investment Company Act* of 1940. In addition to *ERISA*, state laws governing the responsibility of fiduciaries (i.e., the prudent man rule) provide *guidance on conduct* which is acceptable for those managing money on behalf of others, including pensions, trust departments of commercial banks, and insurance company separate accounts. Public pension schemes, which are administered by state and local governments, are not regulated by *ERISA*, but are subject to the laws and regulations of the states and local jurisdictions which operate such plans.

Under *ERISA*, *two types* of private pension plans are recognized: *Insured and Trusted* plans. Insured pension plans are simply offered through insurance company separate accounts. It does not imply that certain returns are guaranteed to the participants. All other private pension plans must be offered through a trust instrument. Normally, trusted pension plans are offered by bank trust. In this regard, the bank trust department or the insurance company may pool the assets of two or more plans to manage the assets more efficiently and to diversify risk.[11] Although such pooled investment vehicles are functionally similar to investment companies, they are generally exempt from the provisions of the federal securities laws.[12]

Scope of ERISA

Under *ERISA*, pension plan fiduciaries are responsible to discharge their duties solely in the interest of the participants and beneficiaries. *ERISA* requires that 'a fiduciary shall discharge his duties with respect to a plan with the care, skill, prudence, and diligence under the circumstances then prevailing that a prudent man acting in a like capacity and familiar with such matters would use in the conduct of an enterprise of a like character and with like aims.' Consequently, a plan fiduciary must act solely in the interest of the plan participants and such duties must be discharged for the exclusive purpose of providing benefits and with reasonable administrative expenses. Plan investments must be diversified 'so as to minimize the risk of large losses, unless under the circumstances it is clearly prudent not to do so'. *ERISA does not provide quantity restrictions or engage in merit regulation with respect to a specific investment instrument.* This is left to the judgment of plan fiduciaries who, as discussed above, are subject to the requirements of the 'prudent man' rule. Finally, the fiduciary must act in accordance with the documents and instruments governing the plan so long as they are consistent with the requirements of *ERISA*.

ERISA does not require that pensions be made available to workers upon retirement. In the event that such promises are made to workers, it is *ERISA*'s responsibility to make sure that they are kept. *ERISA*'s assurances are accomplished by applying four basic principals. First, workers must become eligible for benefits after a reasonable period of time. Second, adequate funds must be set aside to provide the benefits promised under the retirement plan. Third, persons managing the plan must meet certain standards of conduct. Finally, sufficient information must be made available to determine if the law's requirements are being met. In general, *ERISA*

---

[11]The US securities laws which were enacted in the 1930s contain an exception from coverage for certain pooled investment vehicles, including pension funds. At that time, however, the type of pension plans offered were predominately 'defined benefit plans' offered by large sophisticated employers.

[12]'*Pooled Investment Vehicles for Employee Benefit Plan Assets*', in Chapter 2, '*Protecting Investors: A Half Century of Investment Company Regulation*' US SEC, May 1992.

established time frames for unfunded, or partially funded plans to set aside sufficient funds to become fully funded over a period of time. In addition, *ERISA* applied the prudent man rule to the management of pension plan assets which places limits on the extent to which such plans can hold speculative type investments. Also, *ERISA* created a Federal pension insurance scheme to guarantee a portion of a vested employees retirement benefits. In this regard, defined benefit plans are insured by the Pension Benefit Guarantee Corporation whereas defined contribution plans are not covered by the Federal pension insurance.

Under *ERISA*, plan participants are provided a basic disclosure document that describes the plans benefits and investment objectives. Under *ERISA*, disclosure regulations tend to focus more on the disclosure to participants about the plan itself rather than detailed disclosures about the underlying investments.[13] There is a requirement that each pension fund submit an annual report to the US Department of Labor which includes a detailed balance sheet and investments schedule. Pension funds are required to report this information at market value. The information contained in the annual report, which is rather technical in nature, is also available to plan participants. Unlike mutual funds, there is no requirement that fund assets be valued on a daily basis. In this regard, it should be note that pension plans invest for the long-term retirement needs of plan participants. Mutual funds, on the other hand, must be able to meet the short-term liquidity needs of investors. Consequently, mutual funds must also be able to determine the funds' net asset value at the end of each business day.

2.2 Emerging Markets' Experience with Pension Fund Management Regulation

Pension reform is only beginning to take hold in emerging markets. Chile is most renowned for its efforts to link pension reform with capital market development. In 1981, Chile took actions to replace its bankrupt pension system and to replace it with a private and decentralized fully-funded pension system. Under the new Chilean pension system, the pension scheme is Government-mandated and regulated but the funds are privately managed by specialized companies known as Administradoras de Fondos de Pensiones (AFPs). As a result of the pension reforms, the private pension plans grew very rapidly, totaling US$22.3 billion or 43 percent of GDP by mid-year 1994. In Chile, pension funds are subject to strict upper limits on investments in particular companies and instruments. The Government is responsible for guaranteeing the funding of a certain level of benefits, establishing regulations for the proper operation

[13] *Protecting Investors: A Half Century of Investment Company Regulation*. US SEC May 1992.

of the private pension system, and enforcing the regulations. The regulation of the pension system is the responsibility of the Superintendente de Administradoras de Fondos de Pensiones (SAFP) which reports to the Ministry of Labor and Social Security. The Chief Executive of the SAFP designated by the President of Chile. In administrating the laws and regulations governing the operation of the pension system and the AFPs, the supervisory functions of the SAFP include the following responsibilities:

- Approve the creation of an AFP, its by-laws, and continued existence;
- Supervise the on-going operations of AFPs;
- Ensure AFP compliance with minimum capital and reserve requirements;
- Suggest legal and regulatory reforms to improve the operation of the Chilean pension system;
- Interpret current laws and regulations regarding pensions;
- Provide compulsory general rules applicable to the AFPs;
- Levy fines and, when appropriate, enforce the winding up of the operations of an AFP.[14]

In Chile, credit ratings performed by independent private credit rating agencies play an important role in the administration of the pension regulations. The credit ratings of financial instruments are used to determine the eligibility of a particular instrument for investment by a private pension plan. Thus, only high quality issues are eligible for investment by private pension funds. In 1988, the Chilean Government made it compulsory that all publicly offered securities be rated by at least two private rating agencies.[15] In this regard, both debt and equity securities are required to have continuous and uninterrupted ratings. In most countries, however, it should be noted that only debt instruments are rated. In Chile the rating of shares entails an opinion concerning the 'quality of the stock certificate' taking into account the expected capacity for equity appreciation as well as other characteristics of the instrument. Each authorized credit rating agency must be registered with the Risk Rating Agencies

---

[14] In the event of a cessation of pension payments, or the bankruptcy of an AFP, the Government guarantees certain benefits to every retied person, or beneficiary, or in the case of persons not retired, certain disability and other benefits. See: The Chilean Pension System, Superintendency of Pension Funds Administrator, Santiago, Chile, May 1995.

[15] Under the *Securities Act* of 1981, as amended, the general rating procedures are determined by the Superintendencia de Valores y Seguros. With regard to debt instruments, the risk rating procedures require the rating of issuers in a range of categories (i.e., A through F). Corporate stocks are required to be rated as first or second class, or without sufficient information. Each rating agency is required to register their rating procedures and criteria with the Superintendency.

Register kept by the Superintendencia de Valores y Seguros. They are subject to restrictions intended to insure independence and the professional capacity to conduct the rating business. Today, there are four private credit rating agencies in Chile.

The Government Rating Committee (Comision Clasificadora de Riesgos) plays an important role in the administration of pension regulations by ensuring the adequacy of the rating services provided by the private rating agencies. It has seven members whose task is to determine the eligibility of securities for pension fund investment. The Chilean Government Rating Committee consists of three members appointed by the Government and four members appointed by the private pension funds. Based on ratings provided by the private credit rating agencies operating in Chile, the task of the Committee is to determine eligibility for investment by private pension funds. The Committee cannot change the ratings established by the private credit rating agencies but it has veto power in that it can request to the issuer a third private rating (two are required by law).

Both the US experience with the enactment of *ERISA* in 1974 and the Chilean experience with pension reform in the early 1980s suggest that properly regulated pension schemes managed by NBFIs can contribute to mobilizing capital on behalf of small savers and contribute to the growth and development of the capital market. In contrast, Asia has had only limited experience with private decentralized pension schemes. Most pensions are managed by employee provident funds (i.e., Singapore and Malaysia) or Government sponsored social security systems.[16] In recent years, both Singapore and Malaysia have allowed individual workers to invest their provident fund balances in housing and approved securities. In future years, it is expected that individual workers will be allowed more control over their retirement account investments in line with the further maturation of the financial sector infrastructure and related regulatory systems.

3. China's Regulations Relevant for Pension Fund Management

At present, ***China does not have any regulations specific to pension fund management***, whether public or private. But China did adopt some regulations for investment funds recently and the fund management sector is growing rapidly. This section examines the present institutional structure and its associated regulatory

[16] In Malaysia, for example, the Employee Provident Fund was established in the early 1950s. It is a statutory body under the Ministry of finance with investments managed by an Investment Committee. In the early years, investment by EPF was limited to Government securities but in recent years investments in private money and capital market instruments as well as real estate and infrastructure projects has grown rapidly.

framework, within the financial system, to assess whether these institutions and their regulations are adequate for the establishment of private pension funds. If financial institutional strengthening or financial regulatory reform is required, these needs must be identified and addressed.

As the preceding section discussed, pension funds can invest through other agencies, such as mutual funds, insurance companies, or trust companies. In the USA, the two basic forms of private pension accounts are the Insured and the Trusted accounts. Today, China has a skeletal framework of mutual funds, and very recently, has put in place provisional mutual fund regulations. Given that in the USA, the passage of *ERISA* was more than thirty years after *the Investment Company Act*, conceivably, *pension funds in China could operate under general regulations for investment funds*, if permitted. The present section first discusses the status of investment funds and their regulation in China, and then discusses the situation of Trust companies, and insurance companies. At present, there are drawbacks associated with the participation of institutions as the managers of pension funds, although there are opportunities for strengthening their future role.

3.1 Investment Fund and Mutual Fund Regulation

Although mutual funds in China grew rapidly in number and size over the period 1990 to 1993, the government's attitude towards the development of the mutual fund industry has been one of extreme caution, possibly due to a fear of diversion of deposits out of the banking system. Most (90 percent) are trust funds, with the principles of establishment and operation stipulated in the trust contract. Most management organizations only manage the original fund for which approval was given and therefore it is difficult to achieve economies of scale. A number of informed commentators have suggested that this is inefficient. Ownership of most fund management companies is by large private companies, banks, insurance companies and trust and investment companies, and development is restricted by the parent. Most management companies do not have legal person status and are merely departments of larger institutions, such as Trust and Investment Companies (TICs). Some may have legal person status but may have only one shareholder, which may be in conflict with the Company Law. Some may have legal person status as well as several shareholders, but inadequate management structures. Yet, China's fund managers have tended to be among the more experienced people in the financial services industry. Some domestic funds achieved much better results than the stock market in 1991-1993. The fund issue market has been stable and the launching cost has been low compared to issues on the stock market. All investors are equal and so are the units. Information disclosed about funds tends to be reasonable compared to that disclosed by individual companies. On the Shenzhen and Shanghai exchanges, the share price of most funds is higher than their net asset value.

Regulatory Issues for Investment Funds

Until recently, China's mutual funds operated in a regulatory vacuum, or with locally specified guidelines drawn up at the formal or informal trading centers where such funds were listed, traded or transacted. There were no formal regulations for the listing and trading of such funds and although such listing occurred, it was not formally permitted by the PBoC, the designated supervisory agency for mutual funds. In 1993, the PBoC finally banned the creation of any new funds, pending the promulgation of appropriate legislation. Total mutual fund assets thus account for only a small part of the assets of China's non-bank financial institutions.

In November 1997, the China Securities Regulatory Commission, on behalf of the State Council, issued the long awaited new regulations; the 'Interim Regulations on the Management of Investment Funds'.[17] The regulations are fairly broad in scope and coverage, and they refer specifically to open and closed ended investment funds. However, they do not rule out the management of pension funds. The new regulations are broad in scope, and cover fund establishment, fund managers and trustees, the investment operations of such funds, fund holders rights, and fund supervision.

Some features of the new regulations seem noteworthy and may merit further examination, particularly if applicable to pension funds.[18]

(i) The *fiduciary responsibility* to shareholders, emphasized in most investment fund regulations, are not prominent here, although the fund manager is required to "carry out investments in accordance with the provision of fund covenants." There is no equivalent of the 'prudent man' rule of the *ERISA* regulations of US pension funds.

(ii) The principal *founder* of the fund is designated to be a trust and investment company, a securities company, or a 'fund management company established in accordance with relevant regulations. Thus, the management of investment funds by non-bank financial institutions (NBFIs) such as Trust companies and securities companies is broadly endorsed. As discussed further below, this is problematic. Today, China has no clear legal framework for either securities companies (the draft Securities Law is currently in at least its tenth draft) or for Trust companies (at least

[17] Approved by the State Council on November 5, 1997, and promulgated by the CSRC on November 14, 1997.

[18] The following paragraphs are not a legal opinion and should not be interpreted as such.

six drafts of the Trust law have been formally presented). Both Trust companies and securities companies have had considerable operating problems, many of which stem from the lack of adequate separation of either the operations or the capital requirements, for the multiple roles adopted by such companies.

(iii) In terms of *investment operations*, the Interim Investment Fund regulations specify (a) that investment in stocks as well as bonds should not be below 80 percent of fund assets; that (b) investment in government bonds should not be below 20 percent of fund assets. This regulation appears to allow considerable flexibility to fund investors; more than, say, that permitted currently to insurance companies or to pension funds under the local regulations under which they operate. The regulations also include some prudential ratios, such as (c) asset concentration ratios, so that a single fund manager cannot hold more than 10 percent of the securities of a single firm, and a given fund cannot hold more than 10 percent its net assets in a given firm. Fund managers are prohibited from securities underwriting, real estate investments, and investments with conflicts of interest (d) Liquidity provisions are also specified, although loosely; the regulations require that open ended funds should maintain 'enough cash and bonds' for redemption payments (there is no specified ratio of liquid assets).

In the USA, there are no detailed limits specified for pension fund investments, and it is up to the fund managers to invest prudently within the specified objectives of the pension plan. It must be pointed out however that these rules have been framed against the general backdrop of disclosure-based, rather than merit-based regulation. In many emerging markets (including Chile, as in the example cited above) merit based regulation is more the rule. Also, US regulations for pension funds were drawn up in an era where defined benefit plans tended to predominate, which implied less risk-taking, and the need for less exercise of judgment, on the part of investors. Today, defined contribution plans are tending to overtake defined benefit plans in number. Thus for pension funds in China today, it is likely that more detailed investment guidelines would be called for. With regard to liquidity provisions, the needs of mutual funds, especially open-ended funds, and pension funds, are very different, with high liquidity requirements in the former, and relatively low and predictable liquidity requirements in the latter. The new Interim regulations for investment funds are not very specific on liquidity provisions, and thus could apply to both pension funds and mutual funds. The specification of limits on asset concentration ratios is normally present in both pension fund and mutual fund regulations.

(iv) The *supervision* responsibility of the funds, hitherto entirely under the PBoC, has now been jointly entrusted to both the CSRC and the PBoC 'within their respective terms of reference'. While the CSRC authorizes the establishment of funds, or a fund management company, the appointment or resignation of a fund trustee must be agreed to by both the CSRC and the PBoC. Operating reports are to be submitted to both. This duality in the supervisory structure exists in other areas of capital markets supervision, for example with regard to securities companies, and has been found to render supervision less effective than desirable.

3.2 Trust and Investment Companies

Among the non-bank financial institutions, China's Trust and Investment Companies (TICs) are the most significant group.[19] At end-1995, China's 330 registered TICs accounted for a third of the total assets of the NBFI sector of China.[20] Trust and Investment Companies sprang up to fill a vacuum, in terms of financial sector services, taking advantage of opportunities for regulatory arbitrage in the current framework of financial sector regulation. Initially, many TICs were offshoots of banks, used to circumvent efforts by the State Planning Commission and the People's Bank of China to impose limits on credit expansion. In periods of credit tightening state banks channeled funds to their affiliated Trust and Investment Companies, often classifying the funds so transferred not as loans, which would be subject to the constraints of the credit plan, but in the category "other items net" in their balance sheets. Many TICs were also set up under local governments, used to channel off budgetary funds to favored local projects. Their range of services has grown to include commercial banking, trust services, guarantees, direct investment, funds management, consulting, and project management. Besides economic development projects, some TICs have become a significant force in the securities markets, engaging in underwriting and securities dealing in addition to broking and trading. TICs have been active in real estate development and in the foreign exchange markets.

From 1993, the government restricted TICs' access to finance, due to its growing inability to control credit expansion 'leakages'. With the passage of the Commercial Bank law of 1994 which required the separation of banks and non-banks, the government also made attempts to separate bank-affiliated TICs from

---

[19] The financial situations of TICs have changed since the East Asia financial crisis, and many have been insolvent. This only strengthens our conclusion that TICs are not good candidates as pension fund managers.

[20] At end-1994, the share of non-banks in total financial assets amounted to 10.7 percent. Trust and Investment Companies accounted for 3.5 percent of this share, at RMB 390 billion yuan. *China's Trust and Investment Companies*. World Bank Discussion Paper No: 358, 1997.

their parent organizations. But regularizing TICs has been difficult, due to their wide and ever expanding business scope. As a result, TICs in China do not resemble financial Trust institutions elsewhere in the world. Apart from its heterogeneity, the 'trust business' in China has connections with different levels of government, government agencies or state-owned enterprises (SOEs). In most other countries trust activities serve the private sector, and primarily individuals in the private sector. This has made it difficult for policy makers to find prototypes for defining a framework for legislation or supervision. The lines of business have different risk implications and without any lines of demarcation within the TICs, it is impossible to establish risk-adjusted criteria for sound management. For TICs themselves, the range of services provided is too unwieldy to provide sound management.

Many TICs loans and investments, in early 1996, were illiquid or of questionable quality. The problem has been severe and many of the TICs are thought to be insolvent. One reason is that much of TIC lending is to state-owned enterprises (SOEs), many of which are illiquid and/or insolvent. Loans to insolvent SOEs become frozen on the TICs books. A second reason is the large amount of real estate lending undertaken by the TICs, especially around the boom of 1993. A third reason is the high degrees of risk concentration, not only in real estate or construction but also in other sectors, such as agriculture, which are subject to seasonal fluctuations and natural disasters. TICs do not compute risk concentration ratios.

TIC problems have been compounded by short-term and unstable funding and serious mismatches in asset liability terms. A major source of funding for TICs was the interbank market, where TICs borrowed short, using funds for long term funding, and access to this is now restricted. Recent borrowing activities on the repurchase agreement (repo) market have also caught the attention of the supervisory authorities and their participation in this market has been curbed, through new collateral requirements.

The condition of TICs could be much more serious than their financial statements reflect today. This is because the financial statements of TICs have not disclosed their condition adequately or accurately reflected the operations of their business. This is misleading and additionally makes it difficult to initiate supervisory remedies. Moreover, TICs have increasingly ventured into new high risk areas in the securities business. Initially, TICs restricted themselves to operating as brokers for clients, but are now taking greater risks, dealing on their own account and adopting market positions. Further, many TICs have ventured into underwriting, which, with increasing competition due to the use of 'firm commitment' methods, and a decline in IPO underpricing, also implies increased risks for the underwriter.

Meanwhile, competition from the banking sector has increased. With the government's decision to 'commercialize' the operations of the large specialized banks, these banks are enjoying increased flexibility with regard to client and project selection, and have begun to exercise their new found powers to reject poor projects. Some specialized banks have also requested greater interest rate flexibility, on a pilot basis. These changes are eroding the captive privileges of non-bank financial institutions, notably including the Trust and Investment Companies.

The implications of the preceding observations from the point of view of pension fund management are that although Trust companies in China may be familiar with issues relating to fiduciary responsibility and the management of securities, they are known to have difficulties in terms of the separation of lines of business, with risk management in general, and many have been in a precarious financial condition in the recent past. As such, entrusting pension funds to their management would require, at the very least, careful screening to ensure that the funds are not exposed to undue risk.

Regulation and Supervision of Trust Companies

Regulations governing the establishment and operations of TICs are diffuse, scattered through a series of separate and temporary regulations. A Trust Law has been under preparation for some years now, and has gone through at least six drafts. The most recent regulations that appear to apply to TICs (although this is not explicitly stated) are the *Provisional Regulations for the Administration of Financial Institutions* of 1994. They confirm PBC to be the sole regulatory authority for financial institutions, including TICs. The *Central Bank Law* of 1995 confirms that PBC has a wide range of powers to approve the establishment, changes, termination and business scope of financial institutions. The 1994 regulations pay some attention to the financial requirements for the *establishment* of TICs, but it states only that capital requirements may be prescribed by the PBC, without describing the basis on which they would be determined. Minimum capital requirements for foreign exchange transactions are governed by earlier regulations, and are still defined in terms of level of ownership, rather than riskiness of business.[21]

Shareholder structure and minimum qualifications of senior staff may also be specified by the PBC. The law does prohibit the use of borrowed funds or creditor's

---

[21] In the *Regulations on NBFIs in Foreign Exchange Transactions* (1992) and the *Administration of Foreign Exchange Business Provisions* (1993), in order to deal in foreign exchange, a national TIC must have at least US$15 million of paid up capital in spot exchange or the equivalent of this amount of spot exchange funds in other currencies. Provincial TICs must have US$7.5 million or equivalent.

rights as capital funds. The 1994 regulations also require the separation of banking, trust, insurance and securities business. Thus while the new law does introduce conditions for establishment which approach the principles of capital adequacy and shareholder protection, details are not spelled out. The issue of the multiple forms of business that TICs may undertake and their differences in terms of risk-taking, and hence capital requirement adjustments, are also not addressed. Finally, the 1994 regulations leave ambiguous the issue of the supervision responsibilities of the CSRC, with regard to the securities business undertaken by the TICs. There is no mention of such an obligation. The same ambiguity applies to all non-trust businesses of TICs.

Business Scope, Sources of Funds, and Prudential Ratios

Business scope for TICs is not specified in the 1994 regulations; earlier regulations (*'Provisional Regulations'* of April 1986) define the scope of business of TICs, in addition to trust and entrusted loans and deposits, to include a large variety of financial services, including both banking (custodial services, payments and guarantees) and traditional non-banking services (securities issuance, financial leasing). Loans must be restricted to 'circulating funds', i.e., working capital, with a maximum term of three months; a condition to which violations have been the rule rather than the exception. The *Provisional Regulations* of April 1986 prohibit TICs from operating beyond their business scope unless authorized to do so by the PBC or State Council. This was not strictly enforced. The regulations also emphasize independence from the government (Article 23), (despite continued strong links to government at all levels) but permits trust activities to continue as departments of specialized banks ('in accordance with the division of business for specialized banks') (Article 30). These regulations also require that a TIC may use no more than 60 percent of its total available capital for fixed asset investment, fixed asset loans and leases, but the PBC may adjust this at any time. Yet, the PBC urges TICs to seek the highest rate of return in their operations.

In terms of funding sources, the *Provisional Regulations* of December 1986 established a list of five eligible sources of trust deposits, comprising Government treasuries, Government departments that administer enterprises, labor protection and welfare institutions, research institutions, and academic associations and other foundations. But the trust deposit sources mentioned in the *Provisional Regulations* of December 1986 are barely significant today. TICs are not permitted to receive funds from financial institutions. TICs engaging in foreign exchange transactions are permitted to issues RMB bonds, as approved by the PBC bond issues. The *Provisional Regulations* also permit TICs to issue stock, retain profits, and obtain funds from the local PBC.

Prudential ratios for financial institutions were introduced by the PBC in 1994, and ratios for TICs were specified in the *Notice Regarding the Publication of Provisional Measures of the Financial Trust and Investment Institutions for Asset-Liabilities Ratio Management.* According to these, TICs are required to submit a monthly return to PBC, which measures key financial ratios. The *Notice* of 1994 is the cornerstone of TICs' risk management today. Limits are defined and set for: (a) capital adequacy, (b) & (c) loans to deposits, (d) investments, (e) reserves, (f) shareholder loans, (g) interbank borrowing, (h) overdue loans, (i) asset risk dispersion, and (j) external guarantee restrictions.

Notwithstanding, gaps remain. There are no provisions for consolidated reporting across the businesses, or encompassing all subsidiaries, of a given TIC. As a result, assets or liabilities can be transferred from one business activity to another to manipulate ratios. These ratios lose their relevance as risk management tools for a multibusiness institution with fee-based entrusted business on its own books, particularly as some of them are not very conservative, and some of them are exceedingly so. In their present form they fail to capture the risk structure of the TICs, partly due to the varied nature and business scope of these institutions, partly due to the fact that they do not assess the asset quality nor the liability maturity structure of the TICs.

The Draft Trust Law: An Evaluation of General Principles and Provisions

Aware of the lacunae in the legal framework for its Trust and Investment Companies, China began the drafting of a Trust Law in 1995. The draft has been revised several times and the comments below refer to its fourth version, which was under discussion in early 1996. The draft *Trust Law* identifies many of the problems which TICs have posed to the regulatory authorities, including: (a) the wide scope of business, (b) the lack of standardization in TIC business and operations, (c) the confusion over the roles of TICs versus banks, (d) the lack of rationality in asset structure, (e) the lack of risk control in corporate governance, and (f) the weakness in administration of many of the companies. Yet the law is not adequate to cover the full range of issues confronting these institutions in its present form. Regarding supervision, the draft *Trust Law* states that the new TICs shall be supervised and administered by a specialized department authorized by the State Council, the 'Trust

Supervisory and Administration Department'. It is not clear whether this will be separate from PBC.

The draft *Trust Law* contains some surprising omissions. Elsewhere it is commonly accepted that a trustee owes a fiduciary duty to the trust and to the beneficiaries - the 'the Prudent Investor Rule', also governing the trustee's duties. Generally a trustee is under a duty to exercise all powers over the trust property subject to the 'Prudent Investor Rule,' unless the trust agreement expressly states otherwise. The Prudent Investor Rule requires that: (a) the fiduciary (i.e. trustee or individual who makes investment on behalf of the trust) consider the purposes, terms, distribution requirements and other circumstances of the trust; (b) the fiduciary consider the entire portfolio and not just the one investment; (c) where the trustee has claimed greater skill, the trustee is often held to such higher standards; (d) where receiving a portfolio, the fiduciary has a reasonable time to review existing investments for retention or disposition: it may consider the trustor's or the beneficiary's relationship with certain assets; (e) the fiduciary consider income and safety of capital consistent with impartiality toward the beneficiaries and the purposes of the trust; and (f) that the fiduciary consider all circumstances affecting the trust, as well as other assets of the beneficiaries.

It is particularly questionable whether trust companies should be allowed to act as securities companies. The draft *Trust Law* does not specify what trust companies may or may not do in relation to their concurrent securities business. Since it also does not define trust companies as financial institutions, it is unclear which regulatory authority would be the main regulator of their financial activities

3.3 Insurance Companies and the 1995 Insurance Law

Insurance companies can provide another possible avenue for pension fund management, especially for a third pillar. The insurance industry in China has experienced phenomenal growth since 1979, driven by the radical transformation of the Chinese economy. In 1993, total annual premiums are estimated to have doubled and life premiums trebled. Yet, relative to other countries, including countries in Asia, the industry is still poorly developed (Figure 3) .

There are signs of new competition in the insurance industry, but it is still dominated by the state-owned People's Insurance Company of China (PICC) which in 1993 held around 60 percent of the market.[22] There are a total of 24 domestic companies in China but most of these are regional and are partly owned by PICC. Most were regional branches of PICC that were transformed into separate subsidiaries with partial ownership by local interests, notably banks, during the 1980s. Two independent domestic companies also exist, which are evolving toward competing and innovative nationwide insurers. China Pacific Insurance Company (CPIC), which has its headquarters in Shanghai, is owned by the Bank of Communications, and the Ping An Insurance Company (PAIC) of Shenzhen is jointly owned by a group of banks from Shenzhen and Hong Kong and the Chinese Merchants Group in Shenzhen.[23] In 1993 foreign insurance companies were selectively allowed to enter the market and American International Assurance (AIA) Ltd., a fully-owned subsidiary of American Insurance Group (AIG), was given a license to operate in Shanghai. Tokyo Marine and Fire has also received a full authorization license. In 1997, permission to operate on a limited franchise basis was granted to an additional six to eight foreign or joint venture companies. Meanwhile, Chinese companies are also developing links to international markets.

As in most developing countries, the insurance industry in China is strongly tilted toward nonlife business although the rapid growth of life insurance enabled it to account for 30 percent of the total in 1992. The rapid growth of life insurance is partly explained by rising income levels, but primarily by the growth of group life insurance, for workers in joint ventures, foreign and private companies, and small rural cooperatives, which are not covered by the social pension system but are required to be covered by group policies arranged through insurance companies. *This business could therefore form the core of insured pension schemes, or a third pillar form of pension fund management, in the future.*

[22] Because of the creation of many regional companies in which PICC has a controlling stake, the share of insurance business attributable to PICC seems to have fallen to around 60% in 1993 (31 billion yuan out of a total of 54 billion yuan for the market as a whole). But PICC may still effectively control 90% of the market.

[23] There is also an agricultural insurance company in Xinjiang province and the China Reinsurance Company, an independent subsidiary of PICC responsible for reinsurance both within China and in foreign markets.

Figure 3. China: International Comparison of Insurance Premiums (1992)

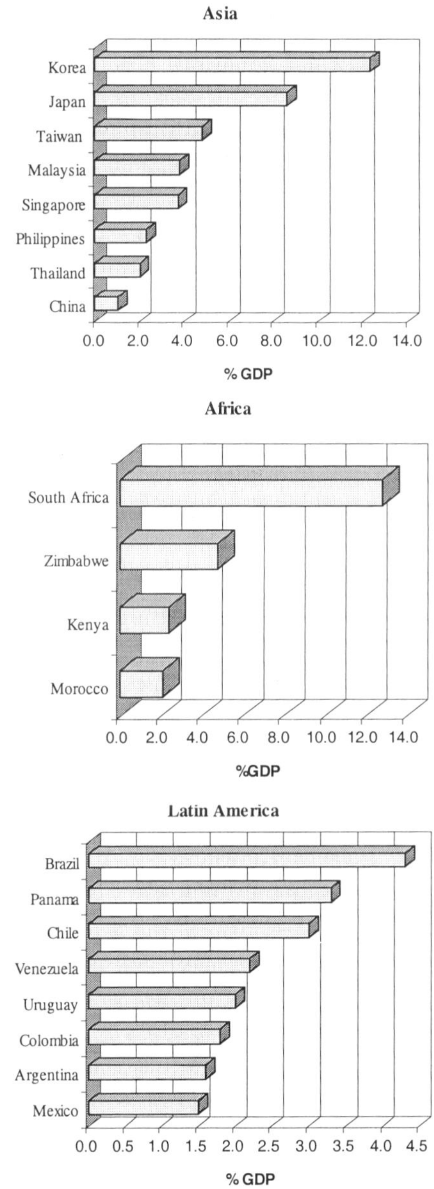

Source: Sigma, World Insurance in 1992, Swiss Reinsurance Company, March.

In terms of financial performance, adding the life and non-life business of PICC, overall performance is weak due to low returns on investments. Nearly 70 percent of income earning assets in 1993 were placed in cash or bank deposits, while the remainder was mostly invested in government bonds, with a nominal average rate of return of just 9.3 percent. The low overall financial returns are a result of the investment rules imposed on PICC, combined with relatively high rates of inflation. But within this financial environment, PICC maintains good control *of its financial affairs.*

Regulatory Reform of the Insurance Industry and Future Prospects

China's insurance law of 1995 is a good start in implementing an internationally acceptable standard of insurance regulation, with management accountability, a strong focus on contract law, emphasizing a balance in protecting the rights of the insured and the insurer, and a strong emphasis on defining the role of the regulator. But in terms of encouraging the development of long term contractual savings and active institutional investors, who could provide a market for infrastructure bonds, the law is disappointingly cautious; more so than its previous draft versions. The investment of funds is limited to bank deposits, government bonds, and other forms of fund application specified by the State Council. Investment in enterprises (presumably including the holding of equity shares or corporate bonds) is explicitly precluded. While this caution is prompted by the regulator's responsibility for safeguarding long term savings, it also eliminates potential support to the offtake of infrastructure bonds. Permitting investment upto certain thresholds, even if low, or subject to certain minimum ratings, would have been preferable.

The new law vests considerable authority in the supervisory body and its capacities. For example, until its passage, insurance premiums were subject to a controlled tariff but with a wide range of variation of 30 percent above or below the approved premiums. The new law states that all basic insurance premium rates shall be formulated by the supervisory body while other rates shall be filed with the supervisory body. This may reduce the discretion permitted to insurance companies to determine premia.

4. Pension Fund Investments: Available Financial Instruments and Markets

Establishing profitable pension funds presupposes that there are an array of relatively safe investment opportunities, which offer reasonably high returns. As discussed above, present regulations in China for both insurance funds and pension funds require that their investment be concentrated in government bonds and bank deposits. The question to examine is, to what extent are safe alternatives available? As the discussion below shows, diversified investment opportunities in domestic capital markets are limited, if high risk investments are to be avoided. If pension funds are to provide profitable future investment opportunities, capital market reform and development will have to go hand in hand with pension reform. Given the long term nature of deposits in pension funds, and the predictability of payouts, in mature economies, pension funds are able to invest in medium to long term debt securities, and also take equity positions in companies, sometimes also contributing to corporate governance by exercising shareholders rights. In China, capital market funding for corporations is limited. Bank financing is still the rule. Most large state enterprises are still owned by the government, and the proportion of a firm's equity that is listed or traded is limited to 20 percent. Shareholding is widely dispersed.

Stock markets tend to be very volatile, and due to wide fluctuations in value, enterprise stock may not be a safe investment for pension funds, unless enterprise and capital market reforms take place.

4.1 Debt Issues and China's Domestic Bond Market

Treasury debt dominates total debt issues, and although total debt on issue in China has grown rapidly, the central role of Treasury issues (i.e., central government debt) has increased over time, rather than decreased, over 1993 to 1996. At least until the present (March 1998), permission to issue debt had been granted only in the context of the aggregate Credit Plan, and it has been difficult for other economic agents to gain permission to issue new debt. Local governments, or provincial governments are not presently permitted to issue their own bonds, due to the center's need to control the creation of aggregate credit. There was a growth in corporate debt until 1992; thereafter the share of enterprise bonds fell from 16.6 percent to 3.2 percent of outstanding issues.

Figure 4. Treasury Bonds and Enterprise Bonds in China (1981–1995)

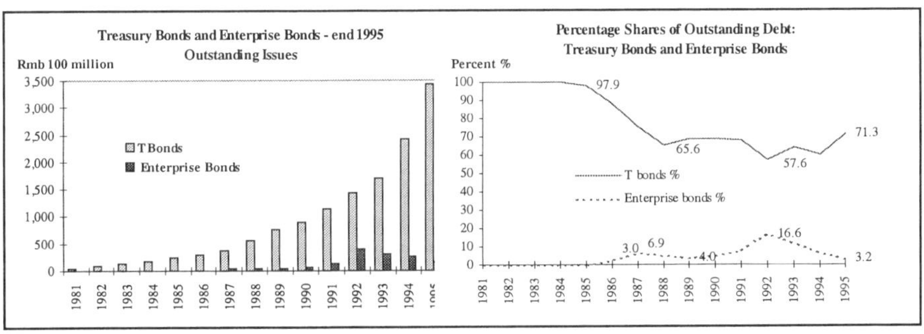

Source: World Bank Data

The decline in the share of enterprise bonds has occurred not only because of the relative increase in volume of Treasuries issued, but also because of an absolute restriction, through the credit quota mechanism, in permitted new corporate bond issues. Annual new local enterprise bond issues, which had increased from Rmb 4.4 billion in 1990 to Rmb 10.5 billion in 1991 and Rmb 25.4 billion in 1992, fell back to Rmb 5 billion in 1993, and to Rmb 4.5 billion by 1995. The result has been an absolute decline in outstanding issues. There has been a similar decline in the issues of short term commercial paper by enterprises. Once issued, enterprise bonds are typically fairly illiquid. Few are listed on the major exchanges of Shanghai and Shenzhen, and as a consequence, are not actively traded. In 1996, only 5 corporate bonds were listed in the Shanghai exchange, and one on the Shenzhen exchange. The principal considerations driving the recent constriction in enterprise bond issues appear to have been (i) the need to maintain tighter macroeconomic control over credit expansion; (ii) increased demand for Treasury funding and some consequent 'crowding out' of investors' demand in the productive sectors; and (iii) problems encountered with early enterprise bond issues, particularly the large spate of issues of 1992. Regulatory authorities have faced problems with enterprise debt issued earlier in this decade. Some of the issuer enterprises are allegedly unable to meet their obligations, now that repayment is due.

Issues of non-government debt are also rendered difficult by other factors; *pricing difficulties* due to the fixed coupon sales of government bonds, irregular issue and (combined with fixed interest rates elsewhere in the economy) lack of benchmark issues. In 1996 for the first time the government auctioned a large part of its debt. However, the largest issues of the year, representing relatively long maturities (3 and 5 year maturities; three issues of Rmb 30 billion each or more) and representing around half of total debt issue by volume, were not auctioned. An increase in the *tradability* and *homogeneity* of debt issued, with a wider range of maturities would also encourage the development of a deeper debt market. The government should also encourage the participation of *wholesale buyers*, such as financial institutions, in bond offtake.

Looking at *secondary markets* for China's debt securities, compared to debt markets in other countries the market remains illiquid; liquidity is not sufficient to meet the transaction needs of larger participants, and pricing and trading practices across different exchanges and trading networks are still to be unified. There are no unified standards for listing bonds in China. Financial and enterprise bonds are listed according to the requirements of the local trading center. The Shanghai stock exchange undertakes to list bonds provided the issue amount is greater than Rmb 100 million, the maturity is greater than two years and the credit rating is A+ or higher. Only five enterprise bonds are listed on this exchange today. Trading, even more than new issues, is overwhelmingly dominated by Treasury bills. Even for Treasury bills, while a bid and offer price is always available, large cash trades can take time to complete. Other debt issues are much less liquid. Annual trading volume, as a percentage of GDP, which had risen to 6 percent in 1992, fell to below 4 percent in 1993, and 2.5 percent by 1994.

An institutional feature critical to the development of a healthy corporate bond market is the presence of widely used and reliable *credit rating agencies*. The development of credit rating agencies has been encouraged since 1991, but so far, the PBoC has approved only two agencies so far, China Chenxing Securities Rating Company Limited and Dagong International Securities Rating Company Ltd. In all, 82 credit rating agencies are said to exist, about 30 of which operate at a national level. However, at present, they are of variable standard, and their credibility is limited.

4.2 Equities and China's Stock Markets

China's equities markets, which de facto began with the legalization of trading in 1991, have grown extremely rapidly since then. By end-1997, 764 companies were listed on the two exchanges of Shanghai and Shenzhen, compared to 658 in Hong Kong, 431 in Thailand, and 303 in Singapore. In terms of annual trading value at US$370 billion, China comfortably exceeded its neighbors except for Hong Kong ($489 billion in Hong Kong, $23 billion in Thailand and $64 billion in Singapore).[24] Yet, despite rapid growth, the market poses problems for investors. Market access by companies has been controlled by a quota process, and companies to be listed are largely selected by political processes, with a relatively limited role played by the regulatory authorities (the China Securities Regulatory Commission) or the securities exchanges where the shares are listed. Disclosure of corporate performance is less than desirable and the submission of periodic reports on corporate performance has been erratic. Limited disclosure has implied that investor behavior has been driven less by fundamentals than by 'events', such as news (not necessarily correct) regarding factors that have a bearing on the market, and markets have displayed extremely high volatility. In many instances, this has been inadvertently aggravated by the government, which has been unaware of the consequences of its own 'announcement effects'.

The limited participation of institutional investors such as pension funds and mutual funds in the domestic A shares market has exacerbated this volatility, and if pension funds were to participate on a significant scale, market behavior is more likely to be driven by fundamentals. This is exhibited by the difference in market performance displayed by the Chinese A (domestic shareholder) and B and H share markets (for overseas shareholders).[25] The fragmented nature of the Chinese share

---

[24] *IFC. Emerging Stock Markets Factbook 1998.*

[25] B shares are securities listed on the domestic exchanges but traded in overseas currencies and purchasable only by overseas nationals; H shares are shares of Chinese companies listed in Hong Kong. It has been shown that the latter markets have lower volatility, and share prices tend to be closer to fundamentals. *China's Emerging Capital Markets.* Anjali Kumar and others, *Financial Time;* 1977.

market has not helped this; although overseas institutional investors largely dominate the B and H share markets, they are not at present permitted to participate in the domestic A share market. Current IPO techniques (and so far all share issues have been IPOs) and the limited amount of new share issues imply that ownership is widely dispersed, and hence a new investor is not likely to have much voice in corporate policy or governance.

5. Summary and Conclusions

Drawing together the lessons of the preceding sections, some broad conclusions can be made about the China's readiness to undertake pension fund management, from the perspective of the financial institutions that could engage in this task, and the financial instruments that such funds could invest in.

The preceding analysis suggests, first of all, that pension reform in China is urgent, and China would do well to move towards a funded, and multipillar system, with components that include decentralized and privately managed pension funds. Yet, today, the existing institutions are not ideally equipped to take on the role as pension fund managers. There are gaps in their regulatory framework, from the point of view of suitability as pension fund managers. Pension funds would also face difficulties in investing, due to the nature and array of instruments presently available on domestic capital markets. If pension reform is to be taken seriously, financial sector reform and capital market reform will have to proceed in parallel. And financial institution-building should be an priority.

The basic difficulty is that China today still lacks a basic social insurance law, and also lacks a law (such as ERISA) which defines the responsibilities of private pension fund managers. In the absence of such regulations, to what extent can existing financial institutions undertake pension fund management? In mature markets, pension funds may manage their investments through other institutions; mutual funds, trust departments of banks, and through insurance companies. The paper examines these three groups of financial institutions, in the context of China, and shows that today, they are not equipped to take on this task.

Of these, the best positioned today is probably the insurance sector, which already has a track record in managing the life insurance plans of workers in certain enterprises. This sector also operates in a relatively clear legal framework, with the Insurance law of 1995. However the insurance law is very cautious in terms of its investment prescriptions, and safety is given clear precedence over high but unsafe returns. The role for active fund management in this framework is likely to be limited.

Trust companies are the least situated to take on additional role as fund managers. Many are in financial trouble as their former lines of business and sources of funding dwindle, and some are undergoing restructuring or liquidation. Their multiple lines of business, often with involvement in risky areas of securities business such as underwriting, and the lack of separate capital requirements, imply that pension funds placed with them could be exposed to risk.

The new regulations for mutual funds are an encouraging step forward, and although the present group of such funds is relatively small and growing, such funds could well provide a group of potential pension fund managers. Yet, present mutual fund regulation would need additional safeguards if it is to be adapted to include the management of pension funds. Such safeguards would include, notably, better delineation of investor protection provisions and fiduciary responsibilities. In the context of China's largely merit-based securities regulation, clearer guidelines on investment policies may also be advisable. Of course, the option of passing new regulation specific to pension funds, and creating new funds, is also an option.

Pension funds in China are also likely to be faced with difficulties in terms of investment, due to the limited array of capital market instruments available to investors, and the limitations of these instruments, at present. Pension funds which wish to invest in domestic securities have a limited choice of debt securities to hold. Treasuries overwhelmingly dominate the market. Corporate debt securities are limited in number, illiquid, and moreover often of questionable quality. In terms of equities, although the choice may appear wider, the associated risks, given the characteristics of market volatility and poor disclosure, are often high. Moreover, trading is highly concentrated in a small proportion of shares, and defacto choice may be narrower than apparent. Thus the entry into this market, for funds entrusted with the management of pensions, will at least initially have to be extremely cautious. From the policy standpoint, it signifies that capital market reform and more broad-based financial regulatory reform will have to accompany pension reform if the objectives of a multipillar system, including some decentralized private fund management, are to be realized.

References

1. Ahmad, Ehtisham, and Athar Hussain. 1991. "Social Security in China: A Historical Perspective." p. 247-301 in *Social Security in Developing Countries*, edited by Ehtisham Ahmad, et al. Oxford: Oxford University Press.
2. Davis, E. Philip. 1995. *Pension Funds, Retirement-Income Security, and Capital Markets: An International Perspective.* Oxford: Oxford University Press.
3. Holzmann, Robert. 1994. "Funded and Private Pensions for Eastern European Countries in Transition?" in Revista de Analisis Economico, 9(1):183-210.
4. James, Estelle. 1997. "New Systems for Old Age Security." Plicy Research Working Paper no. 1766. Policy Research Department. The World Bank, Washington DC.
5. Kumar, Anjali, Nicholas Lardy, William Albrecht, Terry Chuppe, Susan Selwyn,

Paula Perttunen, and Tao Zhang. 1997. China's Non-Bank Financial Institutions: Trust and Investment Companies. World Bank Discussion Paper no. 358.

6. Research Group for Social Security System, Government of China. 1995. *Projection Report of General Program of Basic Pension Insurance for Urban Staff and Workers.* Unpublished manuscript, February.
7. Wang, Yan, 1997. "Managing and Funding the Three Pillars", Chapter 4 in *Old Age Security: Pension Reform in China.* The World Bank. Washington, DC.
8. Social Security Administration, United States. 1995. *Social Security Programs Throughout the World—1995.* SSA Publication No.13-11805, July, Washington DC.
9. Vittas, Dimitri. 1995. "Sequencing Social Security, Pension and Insurance Reform." Policy Research Working Paper no. 1551. Fiscal Sector Development Department. The World Bank, Washington DC.
10. ———. 1995b. "Strengths and Weaknesses of the Chilean Pension Reform." The World Bank, Washington DC. May.
11. World Bank. 1994. *Averting the Old Age Crisis: Politics to Protect the Old and Promote Growth.* Washington, DC: World Bank.
12. World Bank, 1997. *Old Age Security: Pension Reform in China.* In *China 2020* Series. World Bank Publications, Washington DC.

CHAPTER 11

NEW MODELS FOR OLD AGE SECURITY — AND HOW CAN THEY BE APPLIED IN CHINA?[1]

ESTELLE JAMES
Lead Economist, Policy Research Department, World Bank,
1337 30th St NW,
Washington, DC 20007, USA

This paper starts by summarizing the major problems of traditional social security systems, proposals for structural reform, and econometric studies of the impact of pension reform in Chile, which suggest positive effects on growth and efficiency. It then contrasts three variations on the multi-pillar reform model that are being implemented in different countries--the Latin American model (in which individual workers choose the investment manager for their retirement funds), the OECD model (in which employers and/or union trustees choose the investment manager for an entire company or occupation), and the Swedish notional account model (in which there are no funds to invest). Particular attention is paid to ways in which these countries have financed the transition to a multi-pillar system and implications of this analysis for China. A major implication is that allowing pension funds to invest in a diversified portfolio that earns a rate of return consistent with the marginal productivity of capital will go far toward financing the transition in China.

Over the next 35 years, the proportion of the world's population that is over age 60 will nearly double, from 9% to 16% (Figure 1). In China the proportion will jump from 9% to 22%. Due to rapid increases in life expectancy and declines in fertility rates, populations are aging much faster in developing countries than they did in industrial countries. As young working-age people near retirement--around the year 2030--80% of the world's old people will live in what today are developing countries. More than one-quarter will live in China alone. Therefore, China and

[1] This paper was presented at the Conference on China's Social Security Reform in Beijing, June 1998. A slightly different versions was published in the World Bank Research Observer, August 1998.

other developing and middle income countries need to plan for the care of their older populations. And, given their rapid aging, it is essential that they get this right from the start.

Cross-sectional analysis shows that public spending on formal pension plans increases exponentially as populations age. It now exceeds 15% of GNP in some industrialized countries and will do so in many more countries, including China, as the demographic transition proceeds, if systems do not change (Figure 2). With such large sums involved, how this money is generated and spent can affect the entire economy, by influencing factor supplies, productivity and the size of the GNP pie. Therefore, two over-arching criteria should be used to shape and evaluate these programs: they should protect the old (in an equitable way) and they should promote (or at least not hinder) economic growth--which is important both for the old and the young.

In the past, most old age security systems established by governments were pay-as-you-go (PAYG) systems--taxing workers today to pay pensions to old people today. This paper argues that growing old is a predictable life experience that most of us will have with a high probability, so a large part of old age security can instead be provided by self-insurance--people saving for themselves, shifting consumption from their younger productive years to their older years when consumption exceeds income. Myopia among workers may require that retirement saving be mandatory. But relying to some extent on self-insurance and saving may reduce many of the incentive problems associated with tax and transfer PAYG systems, thereby having a positive impact on the over-all economy.

However, another part of old age security systems requires pooling risks and insuring or redistributing across individuals--because some people will have to retire early with disabilities, die young and leave dependents, live longer than average and run out of resources, or earn very low lifetime incomes that are insufficient to support them both for their working and non-working lives. This is the rationale for providing old age security through a combination of *mandatory self-insurance and insurance across individuals--in a multi-pillar system that puts greater emphasis on* saving, has a separate financing and managerial mechanism for redistribution, and shares responsibility between the private and public sectors.

Over the past few years, many countries have indeed been adopting multi-pillar old age security systems. China is also planning to make such a change, although it is facing difficulties in financing the transition. While structural reform is always difficult, the experience of other countries shows that it is possible, that it takes somewhat different forms in different places and it usually involves ingenious ways to cut transition costs.

Part I of this paper briefly describes the almost universal problems in traditional systems and sets forth a recommendation for a multi-pillar system that includes a competitively managed funded pillar to handle peoples' mandatory saving, a publicly managed tax-financed pillar to co-insure and redistribute to low earners and a voluntary pillar for people who want additional protection. Part II summarizes empirical evidence on the positive impact on labor markets, saving, financial markets and growth in Chile, which first adopted a multi-pillar reform in 1980. Part III contrasts three structural reform models that are now being implemented--the Latin American model in which workers choose the investment manager, the OECD model in which employers and/or union representatives control the investment strategy for an entire group, and the Swedish model in which workers have notional accounts with no real savings or investments in them. Part IV analyzes methods for financing the transition in other countries and potentially in China. The Conclusion summarizes these recent developments and their implications for China. A major implication is that allowing pension funds to earn a competitive rate of return consistent with the high marginal productivity of capital in China will reduce transition costs and help to finance them.

1. Problems in Old Systems and Recommended New Systems

Most formal systems of old age security today are publicly managed, pay "defined benefits" according to a formula based on the worker's earnings and years of service, and are financed by payroll taxes on a pay-as-you-go (PAYG) basis--meaning that the contributions made by today's workers are used to pay the pensions of those who have already retired. However, it is now widely recognized that these systems generate many problems, including:

- high and rising payroll tax rates that may increase unemployment;
- evasion and escape to the informal sector, where productivity is lower;
- early retirement, which reduces the supply of experienced labor;
- misallocation of public resources, as scarce tax revenues are used for pensions rather than for education, health or infrastructure;
- lost opportunity to increase long term saving;
- failure to redistribute to low income groups;
- unintended inter-generational transfers (often to high income groups); and
- the growth of a large hidden implicit public pension debt and financing gap, which make the current system non-sustainable in many countries.

As a result, existing systems have not always protected the old, they especially will not protect those who grow old in the future, they often have not distributed their benefits in an equitable way, and they have hindered economic growth. In addition, they are simply not sustainable in their present form.

Now, each of these problems is not found in every country but they are found in most countries, both developing and industrialized. Many are familiar in China. This suggests that they are not accidental but rather inherent in the economics and politics of PAYG defined benefit schemes, which make it easy for governments to promise short run benefits at the expense of large long run costs.

To avoid these dangers, the World Bank has been recommending and many countries (including China) have been moving toward a system that is partially defined contribution, funded and privately managed, rather than exclusively defined benefit, PAYG and publicly managed. Specifically, these new systems contain:

- a mandatory publicly-managed tax-financed pillar for redistribution,
- a mandatory privately-managed fully funded pillar for saving, and
- a voluntary pillar for people who want more protection for old age.

The first pillar resembles existing public pension plans but it is smaller and focuses on redistribution--providing a social safety net for the old, particularly the old whose lifetime income was low. The benefit formula can be flat (uniform for everyone or related to years of covered employment, as in Argentina and the U.K.), means- and asset-tested (as in Australia) or can provide a minimum pension guarantee (as in Chile). The last alternative is obviously cheaper while the first provides additional co-insurance and redistribution to lower middle class workers. In some cases (Australia, Chile) this pillar is financed out of general revenues rather than a payroll tax. Because of its limited scope and broad tax base, tax rates to support this pillar are much lower than the public system requires in most countries today.

The second pillar differs dramatically from traditional systems. It links benefits actuarially to contributions as in a defined contribution (DC) plan, it is fully funded and privately competitively managed. (In a DC plan the contribution rather than the benefit is defined and the future pension depends on accumulated contributions plus investment returns. In a fully funded system assets are always sufficient to cover future liabilities.) Essentially, people are required to save for their old age, and this pillar handles their savings.

A third pillar, voluntary saving and annuities, offers supplemental retirement income for people who want more consumption in their old age.

The second pillar is the most innovative and controversial of the three, so it is worth examining the rationale for its characteristics:

Why mandatory? The rationale here is myopia--a significant number of people may be shortsighted, may not save enough for their old age on a voluntary basis, and may become a burden on society at large when they grow old.

Why defined contribution (DC)? The close link between contributions and benefits in a DC plan should discourage evasion, escape to the informal sector and other labor market distortions, since people are less likely to regard their contribution as a tax. And those who do evade bear the cost in the form of lower benefits rather than passing the costs on to others and undermining the financial viability of the scheme. Since the pension is acquired on actuarially fair terms given the age and accumulation of the worker, DC plans are likely to deter early retirement and to raise the normal retirement age automatically as longevity increases--without a difficult political decision.

Why fully funded? First, pre-funding makes costs clear up front so countries won't be tempted to make promises today that they will be unable to keep tomorrow. Second, it avoids large payroll tax increases that are needed in a PAYG system as populations age. Third, it prevents large inadvertent intergenerational transfers from young people to older workers. Once an unfunded system is set in motion, intergenerational transfers occur automatically as a result of the aging and maturation process, sometimes in ways that people did not expect and would not have chosen after an open discussion. For example, the early generations to be covered (including its rich members) gain, while later generations (including its poor members) lose--even though they did not even have a chance to participate in the political decision that produced this intergenerational contract. Full funding eliminates such undesirable transfers.

Fourth, funding may be used to help build and mobilize long term national saving. These savings can enhance the productivity of future workers, they can be imbedded in consumer durables that provide a stream of future services, and they can be invested abroad, then redeemed to finance an inflow of consumer goods. Thus, saving can be an important ingredient of a long run strategy for providing additional domestic consumption when the dependency rate increases.

Why privately managed? This maximizes the likelihood that economic rather than political objectives will determine the investment strategy, thereby producing the best allocation of capital and the highest return on savings; and it helps countries (especially middle income countries) develop their financial markets. Empirical data show that publicly managed pension reserves typically earn low, even negative returns--largely because public managers are required to invest in government securities or loans to failing state enterprises, at low nominal interest rates that become negative real rates during inflationary periods. The hidden and exclusive access to these funds makes it easier for governments to run large deficits or to spend more wastefully than they could if they had to rely on a more accountable source of funds.

Competitively managed funded pension plans, in contrast, are more likely to be invested in a mixture of public and corporate bonds, equities and real estate, thereby earning a higher rate of return. Private pension funds can enjoy the benefits of investment diversification, including international diversification, that enables them to increase their yield and reduce their risk, by protecting them from inflation and other country-specific risks. They spur financial market development, by creating a demand for new financial instruments and institutions. (But two caveats: countries must have at least rudimentary capital markets before they can put the funded pillar in place, and considerable government regulation and regulatory capacity are need in order to prevent fraud and excessive risk.)

All three pillars co-insure against the many risks that old people face, in particular, against the generalized risk stemming from uncertainty about the future economy or polity--such as breakdowns of the government or the market, changes in relative prices of labor and capital, deterioration in the position of a particular country--by diversifying across types of management (public and private), sources of finance (from labor and capital) and investment strategies (equities and bonds, domestic and international). Risk diversification is especially important given the long time periods and great uncertainty involved. Whatever unpredictable disasters occur in the future--as they surely will--this diversified system is most likely to continue providing protection for the old, according to the old adage--don't put all your eggs in one basket. (See World Bank 1994 for more details about the problems of old systems and the recommended new system. For a quantification of the welfare gains from diversification see Pujol 1996).

2. Efficiency and Growth Effects of Pension Reform: How Large Are They?

The chief theoretical argument for the recommended multi-pillar system is that it will have a positive effect on efficiency and growth, because the old system introduced or failed to remove distortions that will be eliminated by the reforms. A secondary argument is that it will enhance the financial sustainability of the old age system and thereby provide better protection for the old in the long run. And still a third argument is its better distributional effects, especially on inter-generational equity.

Efficiency and growth effects are notoriously difficult to quantify and prove, in part because relatively little experience and data are available and in part because, even if we had the data, it would be difficult to build models that capture all the complex dynamic interactions; that is, it is difficult to specify the counter-factual. In addition, most reforming countries have implemented their reforms within the past 5 years, hardly long enough to judge the consequences. In this section I summarize the econometric research that is beginning to emerge on Chile, which has had its multi-pillar system since 1980. In general, these preliminary data are consistent with the arguments that the shift from defined benefit to defined contribution improves labor markets, the shift from PAYG to funding increases national saving, and private management of these funds enhances financial market development. The sustainability of the old age system improves as a result of the entire set of reforms. However, the impact on equity has yet to be studied empirically, since few people have retired under the new systems (but see Part III and James 1997 for preliminary hypotheses).

2.1 *Shift from the informal to the formal labor market*

A high payroll tax leads workers and employers to escape to the informal sector. Productivity in the informal sector may be lower because firms have less access to product and credit markets, or because technological change is embodied in capital in the formal sector and has an external effect on labor productivity throughout the economy (as in the endogenous growth literature). In addition, regulations that set a minimum wage and other benefits in the covered sector may lead to a wedge between wages and productivity in the formal versus the informal sectors. In hypothetical simulations for a representative economy, Corsetti and Schmidt-Hebbel (1997) show that a payroll tax rate of 20% could cause a massive (47%) shift to the informal sector, thereby reducing the economy-wide growth rate by over 1% annually. In many Latin American countries the informal sector and small firms in the quasi-informal sector do indeed absorb half of the labor force (Schmidt-Hebbel, 1994). Although many other forces are, of course, at work, a shift to a DC system might reduce these incentives for informality, because it closely links benefits to contributions.

What light is thrown on this issue by actual experience in Chile? Between 1980 and 1990, a period when the average share of informal employment in Latin America increased from 26% to 31%, this share dropped from 36% to 31% in Chile. Unemployment fell and wages rose. Edwards (1997) shows that, given reasonable assumptions about the elasticity of labor demand in the two sectors, the shift from DB to DC was responsible for a decline of 2.2%-3.6% in unemployment and a 5-8% increase in wages.

2.2 *Increased long term national saving.*

A major rationale for pension reform that emphasizes fully funded plans is that it will increase long term national saving, hence growth. This is important because empirically we observe that most savings stay in the country of origin and most of a country's productive investment comes from its own saving, despite the global capital markets that supposedly prevail. An increase in saving may simply indicate an inter-generational or life cycle redistribution that does not increase efficiency because it does not make (or have the potential to make) everyone better off. However, such an increase is efficiency-enhancing if the initial saving rate was sub-optimal due to public or private myopia or to a tax wedge between private and social returns to investment, or if new institutions and technologies are developed that facilitate the transformation of short term into long term savings. All these conditions are usually alleged as a justification for mandatory retirement saving plans, in which case they would expand both efficiency and growth.

A number of simulations have been run projecting the impact on saving of a shift to a fully funded scheme in countries that are planning pension reform. Not surprisingly, the results turn out to be highly dependent on the assumptions, especially the assumptions about the crowd-out of voluntary by mandatory saving and the method of financing the transition. Simulations of a hypothetical representative economy indicate that a tax-financed transition to a fully funded system in the presence of credit constraints (implying low crowd-out) will increase output by 22% and welfare by 16% in the long run, while the gain is only 2% without credit constraints (Cifuentes and Valdes-Prieto 1997). If the transition is debt-financed, the effect on saving is also positive if Ricardian equivalence holds so that people save more in anticipation of future tax increases, but if Ricardian equivalence does not hold the impact on saving is negligible (Ayala 1996).

Data from Chile are problematic and the savings ratio is erratic, complicating the analysis of the savings effects of pension reform and making the results highly sensitive to the starting date for comparisons. According to Corsetti and Schmidt-Hebbel (1997), private sector saving as a percentage of GDP increased from almost zero in 1979-81 to 17% in 1990-92 while private consumption decreased commensurately. Their reduced-form two-stage-least-squares regressions attribute half of the decline in the private consumption ratio to the growth of Chile's funded pension plans and correlated developments such as capital market deepening.

Time series regression analyses by Haindl Rondonelli (1996) indicate that pension reform accounts for 6.6 of the 9.9 percentage point increase in the national saving rate in Chile (from 16.7% of GDP 1976-80 to 26.6% 1990-94). Of the 6.6% increase, 3.1% was due to the direct impact of pension saving, 4.2% was due to the financial market deepening impact of pension fund size on other private saving, and the crowd-out effect was .7%--small, because of borrowing constraints.

Using an error correction model, Morande (1996) also finds a significant positive effect of a pension fund dummy on private saving, 1960-95. He speculates that the financial market deepening caused by pension reform may have made voluntary saving less likely to be crowded out by and therefore less sensitive to fluctuations in foreign saving; and made the country's supply of investible resources less dependent on foreign capital.

Providing a somewhat different point of view, Agosin, Crespi and Letelier (1996) find that the main source of increased private saving was private corporations, while voluntary saving of households was negative throughout this entire period. However, forced saving through the new pension system gradually grew to almost 4% of GDP, and this was not offset by greater voluntary dissaving, again suggesting that in Chile crowd-out has been negligible.

While these analyses focus on enhanced private saving, other studies emphasize the impact of pension reform on public saving and dissaving. Chile had to finance a pension transition, in part through deficit finance--which decreased national saving.

The fiscal costs of the transition may have canceled out the positive effect on private saving initially (Agosin et al 1996; Holzmann 1996). But this neglects the disciplining impact that pension reform might have had on other government taxes and expenditures, which ran an increasing surplus over this period, possibly to help cover the transition costs. Since 1987 the consolidated government budget has been in surplus, which quickly exceeded 5% of GDP. In addition, Chile accumulated a large budgetary surplus ex ante in preparation for the reform, thereby reducing its need for deficit finance. While we do not know how large the current or past surplus would have been otherwise, to the degree that the pension reform was financed by increasing general taxes, cutting other public spending or accumulating a prior surplus, transition costs did not decrease public saving. As a result of all these factors, total national saving in Chile is currently much higher than it was pre-reform, despite the decline in foreign saving.

Thus, preliminary evidence indicates that pension reform can have beneficial effects on long term national saving and capital formation--increasing it by 10 to 30% of the ex ante gross rate and even more of the ex ante net rate--especially if it is accompanied by a broader set of policies designed to constrain consumer and government borrowing.

2.3 Financial market development

One reason for favoring private management of pension funds is that this will develop a set of financial institutions--investment managers, insurance companies, and banks--that help to mobilize capital for productive investment and hence are essential for economic development. On the one hand, a funded pillar cannot get started without some minimum financial market capacity, but on the other hand, the funded pillar, if competitively managed and well-regulated, can be instrumental in enabling the financial market to grow in safety, size, depth and complexity. In developing countries, where private saving is already high, one of the main effects of a funded pillar may be to shift these savings out of land and jewelry and into long term financial market investments that are better for the broader economy, because of the development of these financial institutions.

Chile provides strong evidence for this expected growth effect. During the five years preceding the adoption of its new system, Chile prepared the groundwork by organizing a primary market for treasury bonds, reforming its laws governing mutual funds, corporations and securities, privatizing banks, authorizing a price-indexed mortgage bond market and liberalizing the provision of insurance and reinsurance (Valdes-Prieto 1997). After the new system was introduced, this process continued--financial markets became more liquid as the number of traded shares on the stock market and their turnover increased; demand was created for the equities of newly privatized state enterprises; information disclosure and credit-rating institutions developed; the variety of financial instruments including indexed annuities, mortgage and corporate bonds grew; and asset pricing improved. In several of the studies summarized above, financial market deepening associated with pension reform was given credit for the observed increase in private saving.

Econometric analysis suggests that financial market efficiency induced by the reformed pension system (and other factors with which this was closely correlated) increased total factor productivity 1% per year, or half of the increase in total factor productivity, in Chile (Holzmann 1996). This positive impact of pension reform on financial markets together with the impact of financial markets on growth should be of particular interest to China as it plans its economic strategy for the coming years.

2.4 Summary

Given the high correlation between pension reform and other reforms that are often simultaneous, the controversy surrounding the determinants of private saving and labor supply (e.g. how much crowd-out, which variables are endogenous?), the even greater uncertainty about the determinants of public saving (e.g. what is the counterfactual?), and the difficulties in modelling feedback effects, all these econometric and simulation results are highly sensitive to model specification. Moreover, the impact on efficiency and growth obviously depends on key policy decisions such as the question of how high the required contribution rate will be, what proportion of the multi-pillar system will be funded and DC, and how the transition will be financed. Nevertheless, a small but growing body of empirical evidence indicates that pension reform has produced positive efficiency and growth effects in Chile and may be expected to do so in other countries that adopt similar policies.

3. How Have Countries Reformed?

During the past decade, with the pace accelerating during the past five years, several countries have adopted variations on this multi-pillar system. The three major variations are the Latin American (individual account) model, the OECD (employer-sponsored) model and the Swedish (notional DC) model. We have learned from this experience that pension reform is possible, even in democracies, but it takes somewhat different forms in different countries, as a result of their different initial conditions and political economies.

For example, these different conditions led Argentina to choose a relatively large public pillar while Peru did not have any public pillar initially although it eventually introduced a minimum pension guarantee. They led Chile and Australia to choose a much larger private pillar than Mexico and Argentina. They led the UK and Switzerland to build upon a history of employer-sponsored plans, Australia and Denmark to build upon widespread union-negotiated plans. And they led Sweden and Italy to adopt a DC plan in their structural reform, but to keep it largely PAYG. Thus large variations in system design are possible within this broad blueprint for a multi-pillar system.

Table 1: Implicit Pension Debt (IPD) [a] in Developing and Industrialized Countries

Countries that have not Reformed[b]	IPD as % of GDP	Reforming Countries[c]	IPD as % of GDP Pillar[d]
Senegal	27	El Salvador	35
Mali	26	Peru	37
Burkina Faso	15	Colombia	40
Venezuela	30	Mexico	42
Cameroon	44	Bolivia	48
Congo	30	Argentina	86
Brazil	187	Kazakhstan	88
Turkey	72	Chile	100
Albania	67	Australia[e]	115
China	63	United Kingdom[e]	184
Croatia	350	Netherlands[e]	188
Ukraine	141	Denmark[e]	189
Hungary	213	Switzerland	189
United States	113	Sweden	210
Japan	162	Hungary	213
Germany	157	Uruguay	214
France	216	Poland	220
Italy	242	Canada	121

a: IPD is present value of accrued rights of pensioners and workers, under old system

b: *Sources*: Kane and Palacios, Finance and Development, June 1996, p.38 Robert Palacios for Albania Cheikh Kane for Burkina Faso, Congo, Mali Paul Van der Noord and Richard Herd, Pension Liabilities in the Seven Major Economies, OECD 1993 for OECD Countries.

c: Estimated by author based on current public expenditure. Details available upon request. Hungary, Uruguay and Peru are from Kane and Palacios, Finance and Development, June 1996, p.38.

e: Old system featured universal benefits financed out of general revenues not out of earmarked payroll taxes. Hence, the IPD owed as repayment of past contributions, is less applicable.

One of the most important initial conditions that influences the shape of the reform is the implicit pension debt (IPD)--the present value of the pension promises that are owed to current pensioners and to workers according to their years of participation in the old system. The IPD is inherent in PAYG systems, where workers expect to get a specified pension in return for their contributions, but assets are not accumulated to cover this; instead the obligation is covered by implicit IOU's of the government. The IPD exceeds the conventional explicit debt (backed by government bonds) in many countries and exceeds 200% of GNP in some cases (Table 1). It is especially large in countries with high coverage, generous benefits and older populations. Although this debt is not always legally binding, it tends to be socially and politically binding; governments cannot easily renege on these obligations. Reform often converts (part of) the IPD into explicit debt, which creates a barrier to reform in countries that do not want to make their debt transparent. Most developing countries have small IPD's because of their low coverage rates. For example, because until recently only urban workers in the public sector were covered, the IPD in China is less than 50% of GDP. These countries are therefore in the enviable position of being able to change their systems to partial funding before the debt becomes unmanageable.

3.1 The Latin American versus the OECD models

Choice of investment manager: individual choice versus group choice. The Latin American model was pioneered by Chile in 1980 and, bolstered by its initial success, was closely followed by Argentina, Peru, Colombia, Mexico, and Uruguay in the 1990's. It has just been adopted by the first two countries outside the region, Hungary and Kazakhstan. It is now under consideration in Nicaragua, El Salvador and Slovenia and is one of three options proposed by the Social Security Advisory Committee in the United States. In this model, workers get to choose the investment managers of their own individual DC retirement accounts.

By comparison, the OECD model built on the widespread existing employer-sponsored pension plans and made them the foundation for the second pillar. These plans simply became mandatory instead of voluntary in Australia, Switzerland, Denmark (and de facto by collective bargaining in the Netherlands) or an attractive optional alternative to the state plan in the U.K. The employer or a combination of employer and union trustees get to choose the investment manager for each company or occupational group as a whole.

While this system was chosen largely for historical/political reasons in OECD countries, it is reasonable to ask: Which method of decentralization produces a better allocation of capital, higher investment returns and lower administrative costs?

On the one hand, preliminary evidence from Chile indicates that workers are ill-informed, do not make decisions based on investment returns, pension funds incur high marketing costs to lure them, and regulations designed to safeguard the workers lead to inefficient investment strategies, such as herding behavior. On the other hand, the Chilean AFP's have earned an average real return of over 12% gross and 9% net of costs since the inception of the new system, which compares favorably with returns over this period in most other countries.

It has been argued by some analysts that occupational plans (group plans) might have the advantages of economies of scale in decision-making, greater financial expertise of the decision-makers, an improved bargaining position for "wholesale" fees vis-a-vis fund managers, and lower regulatory and marketing costs. (On the existence of scale economies see James and Palacios 1995, Mitchell 1996b). However, occupation plans open the door to financial abuse and more general principal-agent problems, as employers or union representatives make the investment decision while workers bear the risk. Employers might choose investment managers or strategies that benefit them, at the cost of lower returns to their workers. For example, in Switzerland employers tend to choose banks with which they have had long-standing financial relationships, in a relatively non-competitive environment (Hepp 1997). A separation of decision-making from risk-bearing may lead to outcomes that are off the risk-return efficiency frontier. For this reason, workers may ultimately demand more individual choice in OECD countries; group choice alone may not be a political equilibrium.

For example, Australia is now permitting workers to put their retirement savings into special bank accounts. In the U.K. employers were initially permitted to opt out of the state earnings-related plan but subsequently workers were given the right to opt out of their employer's plan in favor of their own personal retirement plan. An extreme case of employer misallocation in the U.K. is exemplified by the Maxwell scandal and an extreme case of worker misinformation is exemplified by the unscrupulous insurance company salesmen who persuaded workers to purchase individual annuity plans when, in fact, they would have been better off staying in the employer's DB plan--leading to lawsuits and a government inquiry (Johnson 1997).

In situations where workers are mobile, part-time or move in and out of the labor force, which is typical of developing countries, an occupational plan may leave them with many small accounts that incur high administrative costs, reducing the resources available for productive investment. This is a problem in Australia, which has a mandatory occupational scheme, and potentially in Hong Kong, which is about to implement such a system. In such cases, a personal saving plan, which would automatically be carried with workers as they change employment status, and which consolidates contributions from many different jobs, may be preferable.

As an alternative that builds on the concept of personal saving accounts but enables scale economies, the government could auction off operating rights to a limited number of investment companies, with an international bidding procedure that specifies risk and other performance criteria, possibly offers a reward for high returns, and chooses the winners based on who charges the lowest administrative costs (similar to the procedure that was recently followed in Bolivia). Initially affiliates and assets might be divided among these companies and workers given the average return, but a timetable could specify that after 2-3 years workers could choose their own companies and entry of additional firms would be permitted. The big danger here is the difficulty in insulating the auction process from political manipulation and corruption. Assuming that this can be accomplished, this procedure may be appropriate for small countries whose markets cannot support many pension companies efficiently or for countries with undeveloped financial markets that want to attract investment expertise but avoid initial excess capacity and marketing expenses. China could consider this procedure as a way of gradually moving from a centralized to a decentralized system.

Transitional costs: add-on versus diversion of contributions. As another important difference between the Latin American and OECD models--most of the OECD countries cited above had a modest public pillar with a small IPD and with little or no payroll tax financing when they started their new system, so they could simply retain it and start the second pillar on top of that. They had no trouble financing the transition because accrued rights were small and/or contributions to the second pillar were added on, rather than being diverted from the first pillar.

For example, Australia had a means- and asset-tested first pillar, financed out of general revenues, to which it simply added a mandatory occupational funded pillar financed out of payroll contributions. Denmark's flat benefit in the public pillar (now being downsized) was also financed out of general revenues while the second pillar is financed out of an additional payroll-based contribution. In the U.K. the state earnings-related pension had just been started a few years earlier when Thatcher decided to end it by encouraging employers and workers to opt out; the accumulated rights were still very small. In Switzerland, employer-run plans that already existed in many firms became mandatory, on top of a modest public pillar which remained.

In contrast, the Latin American countries had bloated benefit promises from and contributions to their public pillars to start out. Thus, to create space for the second pillar, the first pillar had to be downsized and redesigned. When a worker switched to the new system, he was given credit for his past service under the old system, while part of his future contributions were diverted to the new second pillar. These countries had to find the money to continue paying the promised benefits to current pensioners and older workers (the IPD) under the old system, while part of the payroll tax flowing in was diverted to funded individual accounts--a problem that has become known as "financing the transition." Most countries that reform in the future, including China, will have to solve this problem. Part IV discusses how this was done in countries that adopted the Latin American model.

The public pillar in Latin America and OECD. The design of the public pillar varies even more widely than the design of the private pillar. In the Latin American model the minimum pension guarantee is most common (in Chile, Peru, Kazakhstan) although we also find a flat benefit (Argentina) and even a progressive earnings-related benefit (Uruguay, Hungary). Mexico uses an interesting hybrid: a minimum pension guarantee that is partially prefunded by a flat annual contribution to each worker's account by the government. As discussed in Part IV, maintaining a relatively large PAYG public pillar is one way that some of these countries have used to finance the transition. Among countries following the OECD model, the flat benefit is most common (the U.K., Netherlands, Denmark) although Australia uses a means- and asset-tested benefit and Switzerland a very compressed earnings-related benefit. Usually the pension guarantees and means-tested benefits are financed out of general treasury revenues, while the flat and earnings-related benefits are financed out of payroll taxes. These design differences have both equity and efficiency implications and closer examination shows that the devil is in the details, since different countries have chosen different ways to limit costs and target benefits.

For example, in Chile workers are eligible for a minimum pension guarantee of about 28% of the average wage after 20 years of contributions, meaning that the government tops up the benefits of these workers to the guaranteed point if their own accumulation does not suffice. The main beneficiaries here will be low earners who worked only 20 years, disproportionately females who have limited labor market attachment, while workers who remain in the formal labor sector for a full career are unlikely to receive this subsidy. Consequently, evasion may be encouraged once workers reach the 20-year point (although this effect could be mitigated by tying the size of the guarantee to years of service).

In contrast, in Argentina a flat benefit of about 28% of the average wage is paid to all workers who have at least 30 years of contributions. This is a much more costly benefit, since the full 28% is paid to all qualifying workers. But it may also increase system revenues by discouraging evasion until the 30-year point is reached. The main recipients will be workers who spent most of their adult lives in the formal labor sector and women are unlikely to qualify. In the U.K., which pays a flat benefit that is about half the size of Argentina's (as a proportion of the average wage) but does not require 30 years of contributions, the big gainers are people who work few years and live long lives, such as women (for further analysis see James 1997).

Public pillars that are relatvely large and financed by a payroll tax also have the effect of redistributing to regions and industries with many pensioners, hence a high dependency rate, and away from regions and industries with many young workers, hence a low dependency rate. That is, certain well-defined groups will get back more than they put in and vice-versa because of their demography rather than their income, and this may or may not be an equitable transfer. (In Italy, for example, this system results in transfers from the poor South to the rich North). In contrast, the Chilean guarantee is small and will be financed out of general treasury revenues, so it will redistribute modest amounts from rich to poor areas.

This is potentially a big issue for China, given the wide disparity in dependency ratios across localities and the fact that the starting point is a fragmented system. If a country with considerable regional demographic differentiation wants a uniform national system that includes a relatively large PAYG payroll-tax financed pillar, as appears to be the present plan in China, this implies a cross-subsidy from areas with low dependency rates to those with high rates. If such cross-subsidies are deemed unacceptable on political or equity grounds, the consequence will be either differentiated benefits for the same tax rate or differentiated contributions to permit uniform benefits across regions. In that case, ceteris paribus, young workers as well as mobile capital can be expected to move toward localities whose demography allows them to offer higher benefits or lower taxes, even though these are not necessarily the places with the highest marginal productivity of labor or capital.

This dilemma--having to choose between unpopular cross-subsidies and inefficient differentiation--can be minimized by having a small public pillar, preferably financed out of general revenues, and placing greater reliance on the funded DC pillar. As China designs its public pillar, the relative cost, efficiency and distributional effects across individuals and localities of alternative designs should be carefully calculated and taken into account.

3.2 The Swedish model: notional DC plans

What is the NDC? Many countries with large public pillars and implicit pension debts have found it exceedingly difficult to make the transition to a partially funded system with a mandatory private pillar--in part because of the financing problem but also because of the political interests associated with existing institutions. This explains the third group of reforming countries--those that feature notional defined contribution (NDC) plans. I will pay considerable attention to this type of plan because de facto, it is being used in parts of China.

A notional defined contribution plan is one in which the worker has an individual account that is credited with his contributions plus interest. However, the accumulation is notional rather than actual, since the money paid in by workers is immediately paid out to pensioners rather than being invested; i.e. the system remains PAYG. Upon retirement, the notional accumulation is converted into a real annuity, supposedly on actuarially fair terms. Since both the conversion factor and the interest rate are set by the government, the NDC may be thought of as a PAYG DB in which the DB is defined in a new way.

The notional account system was developed by Sweden, although it has not yet been implemented there. It was adopted shortly thereafter by Italy, but with a long transition period. In both cases, the first pillar will be converted into a notional DC plan instead of a traditional DB plan, buttressed by a redistributive flat or guaranteed pension in the "zero" pillar. This will be supplemented by a small (2-2.5%) second funded pillar. The system is also being implemented by Latvia, which hopes to save enough money from reducing evasion and early retirement to eventually start a funded pillar. Poland plans to have a new system with a first pillar that is NDC and a second pillar that is funded. Outside of Europe, China has a notional defined contribution system, de facto. While in principle China wants to start a second pillar made up of funded individual accounts, many municipalities have been unable thus far to finance the transition, so the individual accounts remain largely notional.

Labor market and equity effects. The NDC system was designed to capture some of the advantages described above of linking benefits closely to contributions within each cohort. Most important, compared with most DB earnings-related formulas, it reduces idiosyncratic intra-cohort inequities and labor market distortions, including incentives to evade--providing the notional interest rate is close to the market interest rate. For example, early and late years of contributions receive the same rate of return (the notional interest rate), unlike most DB systems where later years receive a higher return. Similarly, workers with flat age-earnings profiles receive the same rate of return as those with steep profiles, while in most DB systems steep profiles yield a higher return. Most people would consider this a more equitable distributional pattern. In addition, this pattern induces younger workers and workers with flat age-earnings profiles to stay in the system rather than trying to evade. System sustainability is enhanced by uniform returns this avoids the selection problem that occur when high return workers stay in the system and low return people evade.

Further, the NDC discourages early retirement and avoids its negative impact on labor supply and system sustainability, because workers automatically receive lower benefits if they choose to retire early. If the conversion of notional capital to real annuity is on actuarially fair terms, this means that the costs of early retirement are internalized rather than being passed on to others (as occurs in most DB plans), hence fewer workers are likely to retire early. For the same reason, an NDC plan automatically adjusts the retirement age upward (or annual benefits downward) for increased longevity, avoiding the difficult political decision to raise the retirement age that is periodically necessary in DB plans. In Latvia introducing the NDC facilitated raising and (gradually) equalizing retirement ages for men and women.

However, the NDC is not inherently redistributive, so it does not by itself accomplish the first pillar task of protecting low earners. For this purpose, a redistributive "0 pillar" that provides a minimum pension must accompany the NDC. If this redistributive component is large it may override the linkage between contributions and benefits that is responsible for these labor market improvements. In Sweden, given the high level of the minimum pension and its gradual phase-out relative to the average wage, the NDC component will be irrelevant for the majority of workers. In Latvia, the minimum pension for women who retire early partially offsets the incentives to postpone retirement.

Absence of funding and financial market effects. A bigger failing is that the NDC does not capture the benefits of funding, since there are no funds. That is, it does not serve as the (second) funded pillar but rather as the (first) PAYG pillar and, if it is large, it crowds out the opportunity for a funded pillar. That is, intergenerational transfers remain, saving is not augmented and financial markets do not develop. Most important, as the dependency rate increases, the contribution rate would have to increase for newer cohorts, to keep the system solvent in the absence of pre-funding--just as is the case in traditional PAYG DB systems. These younger cohorts may have to notionally "save" for their old age a much larger amount than is optimal for them, in order to cover the benefits that have been promised to older cohorts. In that case, the incentives for evasion and escape to the informal sector would be strong, because their subjective rate of time preference would far exceed the notional as well as the market interest rates.

Sweden plans to build a buffer fund to reduce the need for large tax increases as its population ages. Many Chinese municipalities plan to do the same. But in both cases this buffer fund will be a publicly managed overlay, since the individual accounts remain notional. This raises all the problems (summarized earlier) concerning political manipulation and poor allocation of publicly managed funds. Such a buffer fund will certainly not help China build its private financial markets and may partially crowd out these markets.

Choosing the notional interest rate and conversion rate to annuities. A key factor in NDC plans is--how are the notional interest rate and the conversion rate of notional capital into annuities determined? If the notional interest rate is higher than the market rate, it will be a costly guarantee to the government. If it is less than the market rate, the contribution is more likely to be regarded as a tax so labor market distortions reappear and pressures may arise for an increase. Typically the interest rate is set equal to some exogenous rate, to insulate it from such political manipulation; nevertheless, the possibility remains that a future government will discard this connection and arbitrarily change the rate.

Most commonly thus far, the notional rate has been tied to growth in the covered wage bill (Latvia) or the total wage bill (Sweden)--supposedly an equilibrating device. If the wage bill increases so too do contributions and therefore the ability to impute interest seems to be high. However, this approach does not take account of the lag between timing of contributions and receipt of benefits, under a PAYG system. When the working age cohort is large and growing (e.g. the baby boomers) the imputed interest rate will be high and the IPD will increase rapidly, but when the working age cohort declines (generation X) so too does the notional interest rate. Members of the younger generation must then pay a high contribution rate to cover the large debt owed to the older generation and will themselves receive a low notional interest rate--fertile grounds for evasion and questionable from the viewpoint of intergenerational equity. Thus, using wage bill growth as the notional interest rate does not appear to be an equilibrating device as the dependency rate changes (see Schwarz and Valdes 1998 for a fuller elaboration of this point and a further comparison of DB and NDC).

The conversion factor into annuities supposedly depends on expected longevity upon retirement. However, because the process is notional, it too is highly subject to political manipulation. For example, the government can decide to grant notional credit for non-contributing years (a common problem in old PAYG DB systems), it can impute a low or a high future interest rate into the calculation, and it can fail to adjust the conversion factor when life expectancy increases. Poland plans to impute a 0 real interest rate, which is obviously low, but will guarantee a pension that is indexed to price inflation, thereby providing inflation insurance in exchange for the foregone higher interest that the market would provide; without a market test we do not know whether this is considered a good or a bad deal by the recipients. In general, in the absence of market discipline implicit subsidies or taxes can be included in the conversion calculation, and will interfere with the labor market efficiency effects of the new system.

Despite these shortcomings, the notional defined contribution system is attractive to countries that have very large implicit pension debts, especially those that are unwilling to incur an explicit fiscal deficit to pay off these obligations. It may be a politically convenient way to reduce benefits in inflated programs and to equalize the retirement age for men and women. This may lay the groundwork for savings that eventually enable the growth of a funded second pillar; but until that happens it should be recognized as a very partial reform.

3.3 Summary

Thus, many countries around the world are seeking to diversify their sources of retirement income away from pure reliance on publicly managed PAYG systems. Pension reform has swept through Latin America and several OECD countries now use a multi-pillar system. We are likely to see a domino effect in Eastern and Central Europe and the former Soviet Union over the next few years, following the reforms that have already been adopted in Hungary and Kazakhstan and are on the verge in Poland, Latvia and others. In Asia, where partial funding in a centrally managed or heavily regulated fund is common, the issue is whether governments will relinquish control and we are beginning to see moves toward decentralization in Singapore and Malaysia.

However, countries with large pension debts are having a hard time managing the transition from PAYG to a substantial funded pillar. This summary of structural reforms suggests that the choice of pension systems is highly path-dependent. Once a country starts down the PAYG road, it is very difficult, even impossible, to completely change direction, because of the emergence of the implicit pension debt, transition costs and the entrenched political forces that grow up around the system. Several Latin countries have dealt with this problem by keeping the old systems alive for many years after reform, or by including a large public PAYG pillar in the new system. The danger in both cases is that workers continue to accumulate PAYG credits under arrangements that may not be financially sustainable. Some European countries have dealt with this problem by converting to a notional DC system, which remains PAYG, and carries with it all of the risks discussed above. Thus, the reforms have solved some of the old problems but not all, and they have created some new problems of their own.

The major lesson for developing countries--avoid going down the PAYG road, because it is very difficult to reverse later on. However, a partial reversal is clearly possible and has been implemented in a growing number of countries. Fortunately, China is in a position to reform its system now, before its coverage, IPD and transition costs rise. (For descriptions of the reforms in Latin America see Valdes-Prieto 1997, Cerda and Grandolini 1997, von Gersdorff 1997, Rofman and Bertin 1996, Mitchell 1996a, Queisser 1997, Vittas... On Australia see Bateman and Piggott 1997; on Hungary see Palacios and Rocha 1997; on Sweden see Sunden 1998; on Poland see Rutkowsky 1997; on Italy see Hamman 1997. For another summary of recent structural and piecemeal reforms see Demurgic-Kunt and Schwarz 1997).

4. How Have Countries Financed the Transition?

If countries with a large PAYG pension debt shift to a multi-pillar system that includes a funded component, some of the contribution usually is shifted to the individual accounts. This creates a financing gap between the remaining PAYG revenues and the expenditures needed to cover the implicit pension debt (IPD); some other revenue source must be found to cover this gap. Countries following the Latin American model have faced this transition cost problem, while those following the OECD model have not (because they had small public pillars and did not divert contributions) nor did the NDC countries (because they remain largely PAYG). How did the Latin American countries finance the transition? Three basic methods have been used: cutting the value of the IPD and the financing gap, finding special revenue sources to pay it off, and, finally, resorting to the general borrowing and taxation powers of the treasury. Some of these methods involve critical trade-offs between reducing the cash flow deficit in the short run and reducing the long run pension debt.

Besides summarizing the methods that have been used by other countries, this section briefly suggests which methods might be most applicable to China. In particular, this analysis makes it clear that broader financial market reform, enabling a high rate of return to individual accounts in the new system, simultaneously reduces transition costs and helps to finance them. It cuts the compensation for past service that must be given to workers who switch and also cuts the contribution to the individual accounts needed to provide the target replacement rate.

4.1 Reducing the value of the IPD or the financing gap

(1) Downsize the old system. Before making the transition, reform the old system by downsizing benefits, raising retirement age and penalties for early retirement, tightening eligibility for disability benefits, and changing the indexation method to price indexation, so the outstanding debt, whether implicit or explicit, will be smaller. Chile, Argentina and Uruguay followed this strategy, which may be virtually indispensable to a good pension reform. This cuts the benefits that must be paid to those who stay in the old system, it also cuts the compensation owed to those who switch to the new system, and it increases the probability that they will switch if given the choice. Otherwise, you run the risk of carving in stone benefit promises that never should have been made in the first place, and making it more difficult for the government to escape from these promises.

In the case of China, the benefit formula that was appropriate in the past, based on low and uniform wages and job scarcity, is clearly not appropriate in the future. The government recognizes that a lower replacement rate, higher retirement age and shift to wage rather than price indexation are urgently needed. This will improve the old system and facilitate a transition to the new system.

(2) Recognize past service cautiously. When the transition is made to a new system, workers need to get some recognition for their service under the old system. This can be done through a recognition bond, to be cashed upon retirement, that acknowledges the value of the past contributions (as in Chile) or through the promise of a compensatory pension based on that service (as in Argentina) to each worker who switches to the new system. The compensatory pension postpones the day when cash will be needed, since it is gradually paid off over the entire retirement period of the worker. The recognition bond is paid off somewhat earlier, but it provides another opportunity to reduce the debt: Since it is a legally binding piece of paper it gives the worker greater certainty that the debt will eventually be repaid, and in return for reducing uncertainty the government can downsize the face value of or interest rate on the bond (as with the 0 real interest rate in Peru).

The face value of the recognition bond or the compensatory pension can be reduced further if workers have much more faith in the new than the old system; they (especially young workers) will then be better off even with little or no compensation for their past contributions. For this reason, Mexico grants no prior service credit at all, but gives workers the right to return to the old system at their date of retirement, if this would improve their welfare. The Mexican government apparently expects the new system to fare so well, that few workers (except for older workers already close to retirement) will return. This outcome is uncertain, but if it proves correct, the Mexican government would have saved a large fiscal cost.

Obviously, the higher the expected rate of return on the individual accounts, the lower the compensation needed to keep workers equally satisfied. In effect, the transition can be partially self-financed by building a strong second pillar.

(3) Only partial switch to new system. When the new system is established, keep some workers in the old system. Since those remaining in the old system continue to contribute to it, this reduces the financing gap. This may be accomplished by excluding some workers, such as the military, the police or older workers, from the new system (as in Chile), or by giving all workers a choice but making the new system attractive mainly to young workers (as in Argentina). Colombia has kept the old system operating side-by-side with the new and workers are permitted to switch back and forth (a situation that is fraught with uncertainty and is probably unsustainable). In Uruguay the new funded pillar is made compulsory only for rich and young workers, voluntary for the others.

One advantage of a voluntary switch is that it mitigates opposition to reform from groups most anxious to stay in the old system and permits a low value to be placed on recognition bonds with relatively little political flack. By choosing the minimum terms that are needed to convince the desired number of workers to switch, a government can substantially downsize its recognized debt and transition costs (as in Hungary). These minimum terms will be lower if the expected rate of return on the individual accounts is higher. Thus voluntary switching with low recognition for past service is another potential transition financing mechanism in China and this will work especially well if a competitive investment strategy is followed by the funded pillar.

(4) Retain a PAYG public pillar in the new system, so that some of the revenue inflow continues. Argentina followed this strategy, by utilizing a flat benefit in its new public pillar, rather than the narrower minimum pension guarantee as in Chile. In Argentina, about 60% of the total contribution is attributed to the first (PAYG) pillar. In addition, workers can choose between a funded and a PAYG option for the second pillar. The inflow of funds to the first pillar and the PAYG second pillar helps to cover transition costs in the short run. But if the public pillar or PAYG second pillar offer benefits that are too generous (actuarially unsound), the reform will not be sustainable in the long run--a danger that Argentina faces. This would also raise the spector of politically sensitive cross-subsidies discussed in Part III. Hopefully the PAYG public pillar in the new Chinese system will be small enough to avoid these problems.

4.2 Finding special revenue sources

(1) Social security surplus. If there is a pre-existing surplus in the social security system, it could be used it to pay off part of the debt. While the Latin systems generally did not have a surplus, the U.S. social security trust fund could be used in this way. In China the social security surplus is small in most municipalities and some are running deficits.

(2) Asset-debt swaps. If public enterprises are being privatized, some of the proceeds could be used to pay off the pension debt--a cancellation of long term assets against long term liabilities. This strategy is being followed by Peru and Poland and Bolivia, too, is using privatization assets for pension reform. Similarly, Kazakhstan is using oil revenues to finance the transition. Pension reform is one possible claimant on privatization assets in China. An existing unfunded pension debt generates uncertainty that reduces the market value of enterprises in the process of privatization (as in Indonesia and Japan). If the Chinese government used these revenues to pay off the pension debt, it would receive a higher price as public enterprises are privatized.

(3) Reduce evasion and increase coverage, thereby increasing system revenues. This was part of Argentina's plan; however, the reduced evasion has not yet materialized. China is considering financing the transition by covering all workers at township and village enterprises (TVE's), a rapidly growing group, into the new partially funded system. To the degree that their contributions go into the PAYG pool rather than their individual accounts, such coverage expansion helps to pay off the old IPD in the short run. However, it simultaneously creates a new IPD, which can increase system costs in the long run as the newly covered workers eventually demand their pensions. If future benefits are generous, the short run gain comes at a high long run cost. Moreover, if the PAYG contribution rate is high, evasion will be encouraged among the newly covered workers and their employers, undercutting system sustainability; and if they do not successfully evade higher labor costs may reduce their international competitiveness. Thus, coverage expansion is most useful as a temporary financing device if the PAYG part of the new system, hence the first pillar contributions and future benefits, are small and the newly covered workers will be making most of their contributions to and getting most of their pension from funded individual accounts. It is not clear that the plans in China for expanding coverage to TVE's, at relatively high PAYG contribution rates, meet these criteria.

4.3 Using general borrowing and taxation

(1) Cut other public expenditures to build a primary surplus in the treasury that can be used to pay off part of the pension debt. Chile did this both before and after the reform but most other countries, including China, are burdened with fiscal deficits and/or other fiscal demands that make this remedy inapplicable.

(2) Issue general treasury debt to cover the remaining cash gap in the short run. Because of the fungibility of money we do not know to what extent resources for pension reform have come from debt versus other general revenue sources, but government borrowing has usually increased in the early years of the reform. In countries with a large IPD use of temporary debt finance is almost inevitable so that a heavy double burden of taxation is not imposed on the transition generation of workers. The IPD is low enough in China so that only little and short run debt finance should be needed.

Is this temporary debt finance problematic? Financial markets might react negatively if they were not previously aware of the size of the implicit pension debt, if they believed the obligation to repay it was "soft" and has now become "hard", and if this increases the expected default risk on regular bonds. I offer two pieces of evidence suggesting that, so far, the financial market response has been positive. First, the IMF has recently adopted the position that debt finance earmarked for a pension transition should be allowed beyond the permissible ceiling for other debt, because it is a swap of implicit for explicit debt in the short run and is intended to reduce the over-all debt, hence fiscal solvency, in the long run. Second, Hungary's credit rating from Moody's improved after it adopted its pension reform, even though this required a temporary increase in explicit debt, for much the same reasons.

Where can the government find buyers for these bonds? Some of the new bonds may be sold to the pension funds in the new second pillar; government debt and bank deposits have been the largest initial investments of the new pension funds. All Latin American countries limit international diversification of pension fund investments, which virtually ensures large investments in domestic government bonds. China, too, would easily find buyers of pension debt bonds, from pension funds and related financial institutions. However, the pension funds should not be compelled to purchase government bonds, which therefore must be transparent and pay the market interest rate.

(3) Taxation. Finally, the explicit pension debt should be paid off through taxation, or the object of increasing national saving will not be achieved (additional private saving will be offset by additional public dissaving if the implicit debt is simply changed to an on-going explicit debt). The redemption of debt through tax revenues can be spread over a long period of time to improve political acceptability--but the longer the pay-off the slower the country will receive the benefits of increased national saving for productive investment.

The kind of tax that is used can greatly affect the benefits of the transition (Kotlikoff 1996). In general, a consumption or value-added tax will be least distortionary and most growth-enhancing; but it may also be the most difficult to implement in developing countries and is problematic from an equity point of view if coverage is incomplete. In Argentina the payroll tax paid to the public pillar will also be used to finance the transition, until the population ages further. It has been estimated that if half the current PAYG system were converted to a funded DC system, the financing gap would be paid off by a payroll tax rate of about 1.5% for 70 years in the U.S. (Gramlich 1996). If the mechanisms discussed above were put into effect, this number would be much less in China.

4.4 Financing the transition in China

The big problem in China is not the size of the debt, which is less than 50% of GDP, quite small by international standards, but its uneven distribution. A second big problem is the low rate of return on existing pension reserves, which increases the necessary compensation to middlemen as well as the contribution rate required to achieve the target replacement rate, thereby increasing transition costs and consuming resources that could be used to cover them.

Until now pensions have existed only in urban areas and mainly for employees of government and state enterprises. They have been the responsibility of the enterprise, the industry and/or the municipality, not the national or even the provincial government. Moreover, the magnitude of past obligations, as well as current revenue generating capacities, varies greatly among municipalities. Some municipalities (with few pensioners and many young workers), can easily cover their transition costs and move on to a new multi-pillar system, while others (with declining industries, old non-functioning state enterprises, many pensioners and few young workers) are struggling to cover their bills. Their contribution rates are high and fully spent, leaving little over for the funded pillar. They can either raise their contribution rates to finance the transition or they can remain largely PAYG.

In analyzing how to cover this uneven pension debt, it may be useful to think of it as a remnant of a past political and economic system for the nation as a whole, rather than a consequence of current decisions made by different localities. Having different payroll tax rates for different municipalities simply to cover centrally-determined obligations of the past is inefficient if the costs are borne by employers (as it distorts the location decisions of inflowing capital and new industries) and inequitable if the costs are borne by workers in the form of lower wages. Having a funded system in some municipalities and a PAYG system in others inhibits worker mobility and, by adverse selection, exacerbates the system for the declining municipalities, who will be left primarily with pensioners and older workers as young workers leave. (Also see discussion of public pillar in Part III above). Both for efficiency and equity as well as simple sustainability reasons, therefore, it would seem that the transition costs, i.e. the payment of promised benefits to pensioners and older middlemen, should be borne nationally, through the variety of mechanisms discussed above.

This, of course, will create winners and losers in comparison with the decentralized situation, hence political opposition, unless the losers are compensated in some other way. The challenge for clever Chinese policy-makers is to figure out how to pool the transition costs while compensating the losers enough to dampen their opposition. The above discussion suggests that strategies that make the new system more attractive by allowing the individual accounts to earn returns reflecting the real marginal productivity of capital will help in this regard.

Probably most workers under the age of 40 would prefer the new system even if they received little or no credit for their past service--providing their individual accounts earned returns that reflect the high marginal productivity of capital in China. Yet, in the past investments have been restricted, mainly to government bonds that pay low, even negative, real interest rates. A higher and more competitive rate of return stemming from a new managerial system and a more diversified investment strategy would reduce the necessary compensation to middlemen for past service. It would also reduce the allocation of contributions to the individual accounts needed to provide an adequate replacement rate and would thereby free up more of the current payroll tax for other uses, including financing the transition. As one hypothetical example: Consider a country where the rate of real wage growth is 2% yearly (far below that of China). Then, to fund a 40% indexed replacement rate, a 29% contribution rate is required if the real interest rate is 0, but only a 7% contribution rate is needed if the real interest rate is 5%. In other words, the higher interest rate liberates 22 percentage points, to cover transition costs and important public goods. The Chinese government should thus consider a liberalized investment policy as a way to reduce and cover transition costs, creating more winners, fewer losers and thereby cutting opposition to reform.

5. Conclusion

The World Bank report, *Averting the Old Age Crisis*, argued that old age security systems with a large funded defined contribution component, decentralized competitive management of these funds, and a social safety net, are most likely to promote economic growth, provide acceptable income to the old, and reduce risk by diversification. These recommendations were based on an analysis of the problems observed in pay-as-you-go defined benefit systems and publicly managed funded systems, as well as predictions, based on economic theory, about how the proposed new system would work.

During the past five years, the move toward multi-pillar systems has accelerated around the world, spurred by the same demographic and economic forces that led to the recommendations in *Averting the Old Age Crisis*. With the aging of the world's population, it has become increasingly important to choose a reliable and cost-effective method of old-age support. With economic growth slowing down in many countries and financial markets opening up globally, it has become increasingly important to raise productivity through improved incentives in the labor market and through the accumulation of capital which is then allocated to its most efficient uses. Where income disparities have widened, it has become increasingly important to provide additional protection to low wage-earners who have grown old.

A multi-pillar system that includes a mandatory publicly managed tax-financed defined benefit pillar for redistribution, a mandatory privately managed funded defined contribution pillar to manage peoples' retirement savings, and a voluntary pillar for people who are willing to pay for more security, has seemed to many countries most likely to accomplish these objectives. Thus several Latin American and OECD countries have already adopted multi-pillar systems, and they are under serious consideration in Eastern and Central Europe, Asia and the U.S. Simulations for the United States, Australia and Mexico during the planning phase and econometric analyses of actual results in Chile support the existence of positive growth effects.

China is also planning to adopt a multi-pillar system, although the exact form and speed and adoption is unclear. For China, the interaction between pension reform and financial market reform is particularly noteworthy. Financial market reform will improve the functioning of the individual accounts and thereby reduce transition costs. Pension reform, in turn, can help to build competitive financial markets--and both will feed economic growth.

However, countries with a large PAYG system and accompanying implicit pension debt are having trouble overcoming political opposition and financing the transition to a multi-pillar system. Developing countries are fortunate in that they are at a relatively early stage and can choose the right system almost from the start, before these obstacles arise.

China is somewhere in-between. On the one hand, from a national point of view, its pension debt and total transition costs are low because only a small portion of the adult population is covered, but on the other hand, the distribution of these burdens is very uneven in the current fragmented Chinese system. The challenge is to make the transition before coverage increases and to finance the transition costs in the most efficient, equitable and politically acceptable way--criteria that may not be completely consistent. Allocating these costs differentially according to demography (the status quo) is clearly not going to provide incentives for efficient allocation of capital or labor. Allocating them centrally in some other way will involve cross-subsidies relative to the current decentralized situation. A similar dilemma arises with respect to the question of whether and how to achieve a uniform public pillar.

While these problems are not easy to solve, putting a heavy emphasis on the defined contribution funded pillar and giving fund managers both the permission and the incentive to invest in a diversified portfolio that earns a market rate of return consistent with the high marginal productivity of capital in China will reduce the implicit cross-subsidies and the transition costs, and will thereby move us much closer toward a solution.

References

1. Agosin, M. R., G. Crespi T., and L. Letelier S. 1996. "Explicaciones del Aumento del Ahorro en Chile," Centros de Investigacion Economica, Banco Interamericano de Desarrollo.

2. Ayala, U. 1996. "The Savings Impact of the Mexican Pension Reform," World Bank.
3. Bateman, H. and J. Piggott 1997. "Mandatory Occupational Pensions in Australia." *Annals of Public and Cooperative Economics*, forthcoming.
4. Cerda, C. and G. Grandolini. 1997. "Mexico: The 1997 Pension Reform". EDI Conference volume.
5. Chamorro, C. 1992. Thesis. Catholic University of Chile.
6. Cifuentes R. and S. Valdes-Prieto 1997. "Transitions in the Presence of Credit Constraints," in *The Economics of Pensions: Principles, Policies, and International Experience*, ed. S. Valdes-Prieto. Cambridge: Cambridge Univ. Press.
7. Corsetti, G. 1994. "An Endogenous Growth Model of Social Security and the Size of the Informal Sector," *Revista de Analisis Economico* 9, 1, 57-76.
8. Corsetti, G. and K. Schmidt-Hebbel 1997. "Pension Reform and Growth," in *The Economics of Pensions: Principles, Policies, and International Experience*, ed. S. Valdes-Prieto. Cambridge: Cambridge University Press.
9. Demurgic-Kunt, A. and A. Schwarz. 1997. EDI Conference volume.
10. Feldstein, M. and A. Samwick 1996. "The Transition Path in Privatizing Social Security," NEBR.
11. Friedman, B., E. James, C. Kale & M. Caesar 1996. "How Will China Care for Its Aging Population?" World Bank PRD Discussion Paper.
12. Gramlich, E. 1996. "Different Approaches for Dealing with Social Security," *Journal of Economic Perspectives*, 10, 3, 55-66.
13. Haindl Rondanelli, E. 1996. "Chilean Pension Fund Reform and its Impact on Saving," Universidad Gabriela Mistral, Discussion paper.
14. Hamann, A. 1997. "The Reform of the Pension System in Italy". IMF Working Paper.
15. Hepp, S. 1997. "The Swiss Multi-Pillar System." *Annals of Public and Cooperative Economics*, forthcoming.
16. Holzmann, R. 1996. "On Economic Usefulness and Fiscal Requirements of Moving from Unfunded to Funded Pensions," University of Saarland Working Paper.
17. James, E. and R. Palacios 1995. "Costs of Administering Public and Private Pension Plans." *Finance and Development*.
18. James, E. 1997. "Pension Reform in Latin America: Is There an Efficiency-Equity Trade-off?" IDB Conference and Conference Volume 1997.
19. Johnson, P. 1997. "Pension Reform in the United Kingdom." *Annals of Public and Cooperative Economics*, forthcoming.
20. Kotlikoff, L. 1996. "Privatizing Social Security At Home and Abroad". Discussion paper.

21. Mitchell, O. 1996a. "Social Security Reform in Uruguay," Pension Research Council WP 96-20. Univ. Penn.
22. Mitchell, O. 1996b. "Administrative Costs in Public and Private Pension Systems," NBER Working Paper.
23. Mitchell, O. and A. Sunden. 1994. "An Examination of Social Security Administration Costs in the United States". Pension Research Council WP 94-7. Univ. Penn.
24. Morande, F. 1996. "Savings in Chile: What Went Right?" Inter-American Bank Working Paper Series 322.a
25. Palacios, R. and R. Rocha. 1997. "The Hungarian Pension System in Transition". EDI Conference Volume.
26. Pujol, T. 1996. "Some Considerations on Pay-As-You-Go vs. Fully-Funded Schemes," WB.
27. Queisser, M. 1997. Pension Reforms and Private Pension Funds in Peru and Colombia. WB.
28. Reid, G. and O. Mitchell. 1995. "Social Security Administration in Latin America and the Caribbean," WB Working Paper.
29. Rofman, R. and H. Bertin. 1997. "Lessons From Pension Reform: The Argentine Case". EDI Conference volume.
30. Rutkowsky, M. 1997
31. Schmidt-Hebbell. 1997. EDI Conference volume.
32. Sunden, A. 1998
33. Vittas, D. Citations to be added later.
34. Von Gersdorff, H. 1997. "The Bolivian Pension Reform: Innovative Solutions to Common Problems." WB Working Paper.
35. Valdes-Prieto, S. 1997. "Pension Reform in Latin America: Transition and Implementation Problems." *Annals of Public and Cooperative Economics*, forthcoming.
36. World Bank 1994. *Averting the Old Age Crisis: Policies to Protect the Old and Promote Growth*. Washington DC: World Bank and Oxford University Press.

CHAPTER 12

SOME SUGGESTIONS FROM THE U.S. EXPERIENCE ON HOW TO ESTABLISH A SOCIAL PROTECTION SYSTEM WITH CHINESE CHARACTERISTICS

GEORGE S-F CHU
Department of Economics, University of Nevada, Reno,
NV 89557-0207, USA
E-mail: chu@unr.edu

SHUNFENG SONG
Department of Economics, University of Nevada, Reno,
NV 89557-0207, USA
E-mail: song@scs.unr.edu

DASONG DENG
Department of Economics, Wuhan University,
Wu Han 430072, P.R. China

This paper examines the Chinese social protection system within a broader framework. First, it points out some of the valuable U.S. experience. It then discusses policy implications that are relevant to the current reform in China. From the U.S. experience, ten suggestions are proposed on how to establish a social protection system with Chinese characteristics. Specially, this paper suggests that China (1) reform the social protection system gradually, (2) broaden and improve social assistance and welfare programs, (3) encourage the development of private insurance, (4) establish a social protection system with multiple layers, (5) determine insurance benefits based on basic needs, (6) ensure adequate funds for all social protection programs, (7) establish an income record system, (8) establish a poverty-line system, (9) establish a social protection trust fund commission, and (10) unify the management and administration of social protection programs.

1. Introduction

The social protection system of the United States has been evolving for many years. It has accumulated a vast amount of experience through path-breaking changes and reforms. Some of this experience is general and broad. Although it has emerged in the design of a social protection system of a developed country, it can be used to help formulate social protection policies for developing countries. Therefore, to the extent that the U.S. experience reflects basic principles of social protection, people in China should be able to learn from this in order to shorten the process of trial and error, and thus save a tremendous amount of time and money. In so doing, we should not ignore the differences in each country's social, political, and cultural backgrounds. We need to examine the development of the U.S. social protection system and selectively recommend those elements that are relevant to the special conditions existing in China.

There is a growing literature on the subject of social security reform in China (Deng, 1992; Deng et al., 1997; Hussain, 1994; Liu, 1991; Liu et al., 1994; Song et al., 1998; World Bank, 1997). However, most previous articles have focused on pension system and health-care reforms. Little has been done in other social protection areas such as social assistance, welfare programs, and private insurance. In this paper, we examine Chinese social protection within a broader framework. First, we point out some of the valuable U.S. experience that can help develop a better Chinese social protection system. We then discuss policy implications that are relevant to the current reform in China. From the U.S. experience, we propose ten suggestions on how to establish a social protection system with Chinese characteristics.

2. Reform the Social Protection System Gradually

The U.S. social protection system has evolved gradually over decades. Although politics was involved in the system development and expenditures on some programs at times exerted pressure on government fiscal imbalances, the system has not suffered serious consequences as in many other western countries. This is because the introduction of different types of benefits and the determination of benefit payments in the U.S. have been based on the actual economic status of the country. When the Social Security Act was first promulgated in 1935, for example, retirement benefits were limited to the worker himself/herself. In 1939, the Congress made the Old-Age Insurance system a family program when it added benefits for dependents of retired workers and surviving dependents of deceased workers. Benefits to husbands, wives, and widowers of 65 and over were started in 1950. The scope of the basic national social insurance system was significantly broadened in 1956 through the addition of Disability Insurance. Benefits were provided for severely disabled workers aged 50 or older and for adult disabled children of deceased or retired workers. Benefits to dependents of disabled workers were added in 1958. In 1960, the age-50 requirement for disabled-worker benefits was removed. The 1967 amendments provided disability benefits for widows and widowers aged 50 or older. The 1972 amendments provided for automatic cost-of-living increases in benefits tied to increases in the consumer price index, and created the delayed retirement credit. The 1977 amendments changed the method of benefit computation to ensure stable replacement rates over time. Earnings included in the computation were to be indexed to account for changes in the economy from the time they were earned. The 1983 amendments made coverage compulsory for federal civilian employees and for employees of nonprofit organizations. State and local governments were prohibited from opting out of the system. The amendments also provided for gradual increases in the age of eligibility for full retirement benefits from 65 to 67, beginning with persons who attain age 62 in the year of 2000. The 1994 amendments raised the threshold for coverage of domestic workers' earnings from $50 per calendar quarter to $1,000 per calendar quarter. Adjustments in benefit payments were also made gradually. Retirement benefits are an example. The average monthly payment for retired workers was $22.60 in 1940, $43.86 in 1950, $74.04 in 1960, $118.10 in 1970, $341.41 in 1980, $602.56 in 1990. In December 1995, the average monthly payment was raised to $745 (Social Security Administration, 1997). It is clear that a well developed social security system like that of the United States has been evolving through a long period of time.

Other programs also made gradual advances. In 1937, a public housing program was enacted for low-income people. In 1946, the National School Lunch Program was established for students from poor families. For federal civilian employees, programs were enacted providing group life insurance in 1954 and health insurance in 1959. The government started the Medical Assistance Program for the aged in 1960 and the Food Stamp Program for low-income families in 1964. One of the most important pieces of social legislation was the establishment of the Medicare program under the Social Security Amendments of 1965. The program provided for the medical needs of people aged 65 or older, regardless of income. The 1965 legislation also created Medicaid that provides medical assistance for persons with low incomes and resources. Public health insurance and nursing benefits to students were made law in 1965. In 1972, the State-administered cash assistance programs for the aged, blind, and disabled were replaced by the essentially federally administered Supplemental Security Income (SSI) program. The Women, Infant, and Children program was enacted to improve the nutrition of women, infants, and children. The Personal Responsibility and Work Opportunity Reconciliation Act of 1996 resulted in significant changes to public assistance programs. The Aid to Families with Dependent Children (AFDC) program has been replaced by block grants to the States for Temporary Assistance for Needy Families.

China is a developing country with the largest population in the world. Its per capita capital accumulation and labor productivity are relatively low. In addition, regional and sector differences exist in the level of economic development. Currently, China is moving towards a socialist market economy. Reform has been proceeding in both the economic and political systems. To develop a workable social protection system for China, Chinese characteristics should be recognized. On one hand, insurance coverage and premiums must consider the needs of reasonably protecting people's livelihood. On the other hand, benefits should depend on what can be supported by economic conditions. Policy makers must bear in mind of the unique situation that China is in currently and learn from the experience of the American system that is relevant to Chinese social protection reform. The U.S. social protection system has been evolving for many years. Chinese policy makers should not expect to establish and reform its social protection system hurriedly.

3. Broaden and Improve Social Assistance and Welfare Programs

In the United States, social assistance and welfare is one of the most important social protection programs. Benefit recipients are numerous and payment expenditures are huge. Though some benefits have been cut because of fiscal imbalances, in general the size and scope of the programs have been maintained. Take 1995 as an example, payments were $159.5 billion for Medicaid, $116.4 billion for Medicare, $27.6 billion for SSI, $23.6 billion for AFDC, $22.8 billion for Food Stamps, and $22.1 billion for Unemployment Insurance. These payments add up to a total of $371.9 billion which is 56% of the total expenditure on OASDI (Old-Age, Survivors, and Disability Insurance) (Social Security Administration, 1997). No doubt, the US social assistance and welfare programs are wide in coverage and highly expensive.

In China, social assistance and welfare is not only an important part of the social protection programs, but also an important policy tool for the government to help people overcome hardships and difficulties in their daily lives. It has made considerable strides and achieved admirable results. However, due to various reasons, the extent and level of social assistance are quite limited. In terms of the basic framework, policies, and implementing measures, social assistance and welfare programs are still unsound and incomplete. Many 'three-without' (without children and relatives, income, or a home) people are still left out of the program. Especially in the era of reform, many bottlenecks exist in the economy and society. In many areas the number of 'three-without' has been increasing. Even for those who have received relief, the benefit level is quite low. There is an urgent need to improve further the social assistance and welfare program. In this regard, we believe that China should focus on the following areas: First, the coverage of the social assistance program should be broadened and the assistance level should be increased. Although the basic tenet of this program is still based on the community's mutual support, government within its fiscal capacity should increase its role in this program because community financial resources are usually not adequate.

Second, the base of the social welfare program should be shifted from enterprises to society. In the past in China, a worker's welfare was the responsibility of the enterprise that he/she was working for. It was an enterprise-based insurance, not a social insurance. On the one hand, the welfare program posed a heavy and uneven burden on enterprises. Welfare payments became one of the most important items in an enterprise's cost calculations. This greatly distorted the price structure and the efficiency of the economy. On the other hand, a worker's chance of receiving welfare assistance varied depending on the financial situation of each enterprise. Workers in a financially pressed enterprise might not receive any welfare benefits. Therefore, risks were not spread across enterprises but only within an enterprise. The functions of social protection were absent. Look at the American experience. The welfare programs are broadly based. Programs like minimum income assistance, subsidies to families with children, food stamps, energy subsidies to low income families, and Medicaid, are either nationally financed or/and state financed. Firms are taxed for some programs, such as unemployment insurance and workmen's compensation. Therefore, little cost-distortions and price-distortions have been created for enterprises. Of course, we do not rule out enterprises offering welfare and assistance programs to their workers. All we are advocating is that the critical elements of welfare and assistance programs should not be mandated to the enterprise level but should be taken up at the society level. Firms and individuals pay taxes to support government programs, that is the fundamental function of social protection - spreading risks among all firms and individuals.

Third, facilities for social assistance and welfare need to be renewed and expanded. Many social assistance and welfare facilities have been wearing down. They need to be renewed or replaced. With productivity and economic conditions improving, China is able to build more and better social assistance and welfare facilities for its people. The government should work earnestly with communities to accomplish them.

Fourth, China should develop more workfare programs. Assistance and welfare programs may encourage idleness and laziness. In so far as it is possible, it is reasonable to link assistance or welfare payments to certain services to be performed by recipients who are able to work. In so doing, assistance recipients can get the help they need and also contribute their share to economic growth. These kinds of programs have been studied and tested in many cities and states in the United States.

Fifth, it is important to continue developing social welfare enterprises. In the United States, social welfare enterprises have been well developed. The sometimes called thrifty stores can be found in every city. In China, social welfare enterprises have also existed for many decades. Currently they have reached a considerable scale. By the end of 1995, there were 60,237 social welfare enterprises, employing a total of 2,214,474 of employees, of whom 939,622 were people with disabilities. In 1995, they generated a value-added income of 395.05 million RMB (Deng et al., 1998). With the current economic reform, there is still room for social welfare enterprises to grow and achieve greater economic efficiency. To help social welfare enterprises develop, on the one hand, the government should thoroughly enforce the Disability Protection Act to provide needed assistance, on the other hand, enterprises themselves should also strengthen their management and marketing mechanism, become more cost and price conscious and raise their competitiveness in the emerging market economy.

Sixth, the Chinese government needs to establish more schools for disabled people and provide more qualified teachers for these schools. In the United States, education and vocational training for people with disabilities is called special education. It is one of the most important welfare programs of the federal, state, and local governments. In 1993 there were 5.11 million people with disabilities receiving special education. In 1993, expenditures on special education totaled $2,564 million at the federal level alone. In 1994, it was raised to $3,603 million. In China, education for people with disabilities is also an important assistance program. The Chinese Constitution and the Disability Protection Act clearly state that for people with disabilities, education is both a right and an obligation. Every level of governments should regard education for disabled people as an integral part of the national education program. It should be consistently planned and enforced. The Disability Protection Act further stipulates the purpose, objectives, policies, emphasis, principles, and measures to be applied in special education. However, judging from the current situation of special education, it is clear that what has actually been achieved is far below what is set forth in the Constitution and the Law. Much needs to be done, including building more schools, equipping schools with more and modern facilities, and providing more and better teachers.

4. Encourage the Development of Private Social Insurance and Private Insurance Business

Private social insurance is also an important area of the social protection system. It exists to complement the public social insurance. In advanced countries such as the United States, private sector finance a considerable portion of the social welfare programs. Furthermore, payments received under social protection programs, such as income-maintenance (private as well as public), industrial injury, annuity, and welfare services programs, are often used to purchase medical care, educational services, or residential care, through private insurance companies. Thus, public insurance and private insurance are complementary. The more developed private social insurance, the greater the complementarity between the public insurance and the private insurance. Viewed as a part of Gross Domestic Product (GDP), private social welfare expenditure has gradually but substantially increased from 7.7% in 1972 to 13.3% in 1994. In the latter year, the total private social welfare expenditure was $921,456 million. In 1970, the total private social insurance expenditure was 50.1% of the total public social insurance expenditure. In 1990, this ratio increased to 68.9% (Social Security Administration, 1997, P. 114). No doubt, private social insurance has played a crucial role in social protection in the U.S.

In China, in the near future, due to the limitations of economic development, benefits of public social insurance may not be broad and insurance coverages may be limited. Encouraging more private financing of the social programs and development of private insurance is definitely a meaningful alternative for government policy. China has a tremendous potential for private social insurance and private insurance business to develop and prosper. Take life insurance as an example. First, China has a population of 1.2 billion. In 1995, only 0.37% of the population had life insurance. In 1996, the average premium per capita was a little more than 20 RMB (about $2.50 at the current exchange rate). Second, the real income of the Chinese people has been increasing since general economic reforms started in the late 1970s. According to Chinese statistics, per capita disposable income for urban residents was 1826 RMB in 1992. It increased to 4377 RMB in 1996, an average annual growth rate of 6.8%. Per capita disposable income for rural residents was 784 RMB in 1992. It increased to 1926 RMB in 1996, an average annual growth rate of 5.7%. In the mean time, from 1992 to 1996, savings at banks grew by 2,672 billion RMB, an average annual increase of 668 billion RMB (Deng et al., 1998). The significant increase in per capita income has provided an ample basis for private social insurance and private insurance business to grow. Third, as economic reform deepens, people's reliance on government diminishes. Their desire to protect themselves through alternative means grows. The need for life insurance increases. Fourth, in recent years, several national or regional life insurance companies such as Chung Bao, Ping Bao, Tai Bao, Xing Hua, Tai Kang, and Chung Hong have been established. In addition, several foreign life insurance companies such as Yu Bang and Hong Li have also entered the Chinese market. This shows that the time is now ripe for China to develop a full fledged life insurance industry so that the private personal insurance companies can complement the government's efforts to provide better social protection for the Chinese people.

In order for private insurance to fully and rapidly develop, an adequate environment must be provided. So far as the government is concerned, it should adopt taxation and investment policies that are favorable to the development of the private insurance industry on one hand, and protect the insured through proper supervision and management on the other. On the part of the insurance business, it must establish a pool of professionals with real expertise in private insurance. It must devise special insurance items and design different levels of coverage to meet the needs of the Chinese people. Private insurance must also provide services of high quality and security. It must be able to efficiently utilize the available financial resources to strengthen their ability to pay benefits. Finally, the private insurance market must be made highly competitive in order to achieve both technical and price efficiency.

5. Establish A Social Protection System with Multiple Layers

Social protection involves broad coverage and huge expenditures. Even in the United States, the richest country in the world, the government alone cannot bear the full fiscal burden. Therefore, western countries have tended to establish multiple-layer systems and to encourage the private sector to enter the social insurance business. A multi-channeled and multi-layered social protection system can better spread the risk and reduce the fiscal burden on any layer of protection providers. Take the U.S. as an example. The backbone social insurance programs, such as old-age, dependent, and disability insurance are the responsibility of the federal government. Health and unemployment insurance are shared by federal, state, and local governments. Bodily injury insurance is covered by the states. Communities, individuals, and business organizations are encouraged to participate in the social insurance business. This multi-channeled and multi-layered social protection system enables the Americans to share the responsibility of social protection and to meet the different requirements of various localities.

China is a populous developing country. The fiscal capability of the government is quite limited. The cost of social insurance is so high that neither the government nor the enterprises or workers alone can bear the burden. The American experience can help formulate Chinese social insurance policies. Based on the principle of unified management, the central and local governments, collective and private enterprises, and individual citizens, each should become a part of, and join together to form, a social protection system. As to what insurance items should be introduced in certain areas or localities at what time depends on, in addition to the unified plan of the country as a whole, the special situations of those areas or localities. For example, in poor regions, social welfare programs like productive relief, preferential survival payment, and 'five guarantees' (the guarantees of food, clothes, shelter, medical care, and a decent burial) should be used as the core, old-age insurance and personal insurance can be adopted as the supplement. In big enterprises, state-owned enterprises, and government organizations, old-age, unemployment, medical care, and bodily injury insurance can be the core, and employees' welfare programs can be used as the supplement. Additional annuities insurance, medical insurance, and other personal insurance can also be introduced. Or, in big cities or more developed areas, social insurance and personal insurance can be instituted as the basic items, and society can devote more resources to some other higher forms of social welfare programs. In rural areas or town and village enterprises, old-age and personal insurance can be emphasized, cooperative medical insurance can be continued, traditional social relief and welfare programs can be improved.

6. Determine Social Insurance Benefits Based on the Basic Need

Social insurance payments should be based on the basic needs of the insured. Those basic needs should be broadly defined. They include not just the biological needs, but also the social needs, and the cultural and religious needs. They vary across countries, across localities in a country, and through time (different economic development stages). They are different for people belonging to broadly defined groups. For example, the basic needs of the American people is quite different from those of the Chinese people. Automobile, telephone, and plumbing are necessities in the United States, but they are luxuries in China. The availability of those items should be considered as a part of the basic needs for the Americans, but not for the Chinese, at least at the current level of economic development. Biologically speaking, if a Chinese family can live without plumbing and automobile, so can the Americans. But in America, people live with no plumbing and automobile is a great concern for the government and society. This concern is primarily social. The same holds for China. For example, in big cities, people generally travel much longer distance to work, they have a greater need to attend cultural events, they have a lot more things to catch up with their neighbor - the Jones or the Wangs - than people living in rural areas. Thus, their basic needs for social and cultural activities are greater than that of the rural population. If their social or cultural needs are not satisfied, their health will be endangered. Therefore, their social and personal insurance premiums and payment must be structured differently from that for rural residents.

Social insurance benefits must also reflect and be consistent with the level of economic development. If the social insurance payment is too low, people can not depend on it to maintain a decent and healthy life. If it is too high, this tends to diminish people's incentive to work. In Canada and many European countries where social welfare benefits are set too high, many people do not want to work because the income they receive from social protection is enough to maintain a comfortable life. Once a high level of benefit payments is set, resistence to lower it is almost impossible to overcome. China must learn from the experience of these countries and set a reasonable payment level in the first place.

7. Ensure Funding Resources for All Social Protection Programs

All programs in the social protection system should be adequately funded in order to function appropriately. Funding resources, however, may vary from one program to another. In the United States, for example, the Old-Age and Survivors Insurance is financed by mandatory contributions from employees and employers, while many social assistance programs (such as food stamps and public housing programs) are financed by government general tax revenues.

Generally, social protection includes social insurance, social relief, and social welfare. Social insurance is the first layer and the core of the social protection system. It includes old-age insurance and health insurance. Through legislation, all workers should be required to be covered by social insurance so that their basic livelihood and that of their dependents can be protected. The insurance funds should be primarily financed by contributions of workers and enterprises, with the government playing the last supporting role. Government gets its funds from general tax revenues.

Some members of society are encountering livelihood hardships and difficulties due to natural, social, economic, and individual physiological or psychological reasons. Society needs to provide relief, certain financial and material assistance, in order to help people overcome their difficulties. Social relief is the second layer of the social protection system. It includes natural calamity relief, unemployment relief, relief for disabled people and their dependents, and the five guarantees relief in rural areas. The need for social relief depends on events and locations. Social relief funds should come primarily from the local and central governments through their general tax revenues.

Social welfare includes all welfare payments other than from social insurance and social relief. It also includes all free or low-fee services provided by individuals, enterprises, and government units. Social welfare is the third layer of the social protection system. The funds should come from the same sources as social relief, i.e., from governments. The actual benefits should depend on the level of economic development.

To ensure funding resources, the Chinese government needs to specify responsibilities clearly for different groups. For example, pension contributions to the old-age insurance from workers and enterprises should be clearly stated. In addition, contribution rates should be uniform across various types of enterprises, including state-owned, collective-owned, private, joint, and foreign-owned enterprises. It is also important for the government to have policies to encourage contributions to social protection. For some social protection programs such as old-age and health insurance, benefits should depend on contributions. An individual is entitled to receive a higher pension or greater medical benefits if he/she has made more contributions to this insurance. To encourage contributions, tax incentives could be used. For individual workers, contributions should become tax deductible. For enterprises, contributions should be considered as an item of production costs.

8. Establish an Income Record System

By income record we mean to register and to establish a unified account of all income of beneficiaries such that social protection agencies can use this information to determine benefits. In the United States, some social protection programs are not means tested. For example, retirement benefits are an earned right and are paid regardless of income from savings, pensions, private insurance, or other forms of nonwork income. The benefit level, however, is still related to earnings in covered work. Therefore, the Social Security Administration needs information on worker's past earnings to determine the entitled retirement benefits. There are many welfare programs that are means tested, including Medicaid, SSI (Supplemental Security Income), Food and Nutrition Assistance, Public Housing, and Low-Income Home Energy Assistance. For these programs, both eligibility and benefits are determined on the basis of income. The social welfare administration, based on the documents provided by the beneficiary and information gathered from other sources- mainly taxes, determines the annual income of a beneficiary. If the annual income is higher, his/her benefit payment will be reduced according to a certain formula or he or she must pay a certain amount of income tax. In so doing, on the one hand, the principle of social justice is well served, on the other, peoples work incentive is not impaired. This is experience that China should pay special attention to and learn from.

9. Establish a Minimum Life Protection System (MLPS)

The minimum life protection system means that governments provide social relief to people who are in poverty and who are not covered by the social insurance system so that they can maintain their livelihood. In the United States, the government, based on the level of economic development and peoples basic needs, determines a "poverty line. Specifically, the government estimates a minimum food budget for each type of household and multiplies the food budget by three to get the official poverty line. In 1996, the poverty line for a one-person household was $7,740. The poverty line rose in increment to $2,620 for any additional person in the household. A household with income less than the official poverty line is considered poor. In 1994, 14.5% of Americans were considered poor (Social Security Administration, 1996, pp. 170 and 172).

Providing minimum protection to people below the poverty line is one of the most important social protection policies. To those who have been determined, through investigation (including income and property), to be below the poverty line, governments provide relief. Relief takes many forms, including cash subsidies, material supplies, food stamps, free or low charge medical care, housing subsidies, job training, and employment arrangements. For example, to be eligible for the Food Stamp Program, households may have no more than $2,000 in countable resources such as bank accounts and net income must be 100% or less of the federal poverty line ($20,280 for a family of four in 1997). A family is issued a monthly food stamp allotment that is equal to the maximum allotment for that household's size, less 30% of the household's net income. MLPS is the last defense in the social protection system and has provided a high degree of stability to the American society. Social protection has not been well developed in China. The coverage of social protection is still quite limited, especially in small cities or towns and in rural areas. As the Chinese economy continues to grow, more should be done in this area. In broadening social protection in this direction, the following consideratons must be specially noted. (1) Beneficiaries of the minimum life protection programs are people who are not covered by the social insurance system. When natural, social, and other events occurs, these people are fully exposed and completely helpless. It is the responsibility of various governments to provide this relief. (2) The funds to provide such relief should generally come from local governments. In some special cases when a local government is facing fiscal difficulties, the central government should provide the funds. (3) The relief standard for the minimum life protection program should be set according to the actual situation of each locality. It should be enough for a person in that locality to maintain his/her basic needs. (4) The forms of relief should be broad. They may include cash, food, cooking oil, fuel, clothing, or other materials that can enhance productivity. If possible, medical and health assistance should be provided. (5) The MLPS should be efficiently managed and strictly supervised. Objective criteria should be adhered to in providing relief.

10. Establish a Social Protection Trust Fund Commission

In the United States there is an agency in charge of the Social Security Trust Fund, the Board of Trustees (the Secretary of the Treasury as the Managing Trustee). Social security taxes are collected from employees and employers and deposited into trust funds. Benefits are paid from the trust funds. The Board manages and invests the social security trust fund for the Social Security Administration. Any money not required for current benefit payments is loaned to the federal government, which issues interest-bearing bonds to the trust funds. The government pays interest on the bonds and redeems the bonds when they mature. Interest earnings, as well as proceeds from maturing bonds, that are not required for benefit payments are invested in additional bonds. In future years when then-current Social Security taxes are inadequate to pay benefits, interest earnings and the proceeds from the maturing bonds will be used to make benefit payments. Such investment produces tens of billions of dollars revenue from the hundreds of billions dollars in the trust funds every year. In 1995, for example, investment of Old-Age and Survivors Insurance Trust Funds produced a net interest of $32.82 billion and the accumulated trust fund was $458.52 billion at the end of 1995 (Social Security Administration, 1996, p. 178).

In China, a similar organization should be established. The purpose is to put the huge trust fund into productive uses such that it grows through time. Investment of social security funds must be based on the principle of security, liquidity, high yield, and public interest. In addition to the traditional ways of depositing it in government banks and buying government bonds, funds can be invested in some high-yield and secure projects, like real estate and large-scale infrastructure (Song and Chu, 1997). They can also be invested in some higher-yield and higher-risk options, like domestic corporate bonds and securities, and even in international financial markets. To make these investments more efficiently, the Chinese government needs not only to provide a better investment environment but also to attract and train more professionals. The latter should be considered as an important government task. China needs more professionals who have expertise financial disciplines.

11. Unify the Management of Social Protection Programs

The core of the social protection programs is important actions that a government takes to protect its people. Coverage is very broad and contents are quite comprehensive. Management is complicated. Implementation is sophisticated. Therefore, social protection programs need a specific government agency to plan, enforce, coordinate, guide, and administer the various programs. In China, the social protection programs have emerged from the bottom. In the past, state and private enterprises, government agencies, party organizations, labor unions, each initiated its own protection programs. The management and administration of these programs was fragmented among five groups: labor, personnel, administration, insurance companies, and professions and trades. There were overlaps, omissions, and competitions. The whole social protection system was ineffective and inefficient. In view of this, the government established a Ministry of Labor and Social Security in 1998. Its main purpose is to coordinate and consolidate the various social protection programs into a unified network to improve the effectiveness and to reduce inefficiencies in the programs. This is a milestone in the Chinese social protection history.

Drawing on the experience of the United States, we would like to offer the following organizational recommendation. Under the Ministry of Labor and Social Security, three agencies should be established: (1) a Social Security Reform Commission (or Bureau), whose primary responsibility is to provide vision, enact and revise social protection laws and regulations, engage in long term and short term plans, and guide and coordinate various programs and among various groups; (2) a Social Security Administration, whose primary responsibility is to administer the various programs, and (3) a Social Security Trust Fund Commission (or Bureau) whose primary responsibility is to gather, invest, and manage the social protection trust funds. With these three agencies, policy making, administration, and fund investment can be separated. This separation, in turn, would make each of them function more effectively and efficiently.

12. Conclusions

As Chinese economic reform proceeds, Chinese economic development is advancing. The Chinese government has been increasing its attention to the social protection of its people. It has determined to adopt an old-age and medical insurance system that combines both social pooling and individual accounts, to improve and broaden its unemployment insurance and social relief programs. Yet, the Chinese social protection system is still in a formulation stage. There is a long way to go in order to achieve a meaningful, workable, effective, and efficient social protection system.

In this paper, we have examined the U.S. experience in this field to offer some suggestions to the Chinese authorities in formulating their social protection policies. Specifically, this paper suggests that China (1) reform the social protection system gradually, (2) broaden and improve social assistance and welfare programs, (3) encourage the development of private insurance, (4) establish a social protection system with multiple layers, (5) determine insurance benefits based on the basic need, (6) ensure funding resources for all social protection programs, (7) establish an income record system, (8) establish a poverty-line system, (9) establish a social protection trust fund commission, and (10) unify the management and administration of social protection programs. We believe that these suggestions can help China achieve a better social protection system.

References

1. D. Deng, *Comparative Social Insurance* (Chinese Financial Press, Beijing, China, 1992).
2. D. Deng, G. Chu, and S. Song, "The Taxing System of the Chinese Social Security and Strategies for Its Reform", in *Tax Reform in China*, eds. D. Xu and J. Li (Chinese Economic Press, Beijing, China, 1997).
3. D. Deng, S. Song, and G. Chu "Lessons from the US Experience and Suggestions to China's Social Security Reform", presented at the International Conference of the Chinese Economists Society and Chinese Academy of Social Sciences, (Beijing, China, June 22-24, 1998).
4. A. Hussain, "Social Security in Present-Day China and Its Reform", *American Economic Review* 84(2), pp. 276-280, (1994).

5. L. Liu, "Social Security for State-Sector Workers in the People's Republic of China: The Reform Decade and Beyond", *Social Security Bulletin* 54(10), pp. 2-16 (1991).
6. G. Liu, X. Liu, and Q. Meng, "Privatization of the Medical Market in Socialist China: A Historical Approach", *Health Policy* 27, pp. 157-174 (1994).
7. Social Security Administration (SSA), *Annual Statistical Supplement to the Social Security Bulletin*, (SSA Publication No. 13-11700, Washington D.C., 1996).
8. Social Security Administration (SSA), *Social Security Programs in the United States*, (SSA Publication No. 13-11758, Washington D.C., 1997).
9. S. Song and G. Chu, "Social Security Reform in China: The Case of Old-Age Insurance." *Contemporary Economic Policy* 15(2), pp. 85-93 (1997).
10. S. Song, G. Chu, and D. Ding, "Reform of the Social Security System in the People's Republic of China", in *China's Tax Reform Options*, eds. T. Fulton, J. Li, and D. Xu (World Scientific, Singapore, 1998).

PART 3
HEALTH CARE REFORMS, RURAL SOCIAL SECURITY, AND SOCIAL WELFARE

CHAPTER 13

SOCIAL SECURITY FOR THE RURAL ELDERLY IN CHINA

D. GALE JOHNSON
Office of Agricultural Economics Research
The University of Chicago, 1126 East 59 Street,
Chicago, IL60637, USA
E-mail: dg-johnson@uchicago.edu

This paper discusses various issues involved in the establishment of social security systems in rural farm areas in China. After reviewing the current economic status of the rural elderly and programs of rural social security, the author assumes that (1) a pension should be equal to 40 to 50 percent of the income at the retirement age; (2) the contribution should be about 5,000 yuan per couple, and (3) the age when the pension begins should be 65. The author also argues that whether the rural pension system should be compulsory or voluntary, it depends on the guarantee of a reasonable positive real rate of return on invested funds and responsible behavior of the government.

Formal systems of social security have a somewhat different role in rural farm areas than in urban areas. In most countries, especially the industrial countries, the farm elderly have substantially more assets than do urban people. Generally speaking farm families not only own some or all of the land they farm but in addition have substantial investments in livestock and machinery that can be liquidated if necessary. However, even in high income countries where most farm people own their own farms, farm and other rural people are now included in formal social security systems.

The situation in China today differs from the above brief description. Farm people do not own their land and cannot sell that asset to provide for their needs when they are elderly. But this does not mean that the rural elderly are left without support for their later years. This support comes within the structure of the extended family - nearly all rural elderly live in households that include two or three and occasionally four generations. But there are strong reasons to consider strengthening and expanding the existing forms of social security for rural people. The rapid decline in fertility in rural areas during the past four decades will mean that more and more elderly will either live alone or only with their spouses in the decades ahead. In addition, the rural elderly's connection with farming will decline over time.

Based on data from the State Statistical Bureau's rural household surveys for 1990 for Sichuan and Liaoning Provinces, 8 percent of the population was elderly in 1990. If the average family size is 5, as it approximately was, then in a village of 1,000 there would be 200 families. If a third of the elderly were widows or widowers and two thirds had spouses, 54 families would have had one or more elderly. This would mean that 27 percent of the households had one or more elderly members. But if the percentage of elderly in the population increases to 20 percent, as it well could within a quarter century, and if the same distribution of the elderly between those living with a spouse and those not prevails, then 135 households or 65 percent of all households would have at least one elderly member.

In the recent past, as well as currently, most elderly could rely not only on the household members with whom they live, but probably one or more additional sons that did or could contribute to their needs. As the percentage of the population that is elderly increases, it seems inevitable that an increasing percentage of the rural elderly will live alone or with only their spouse. In the late 1980s only 6.4 percent of the elderly lived alone or only with their spouses in Sichuan but in Liaoning, with its higher average income, 12.7 percent did. It seems inevitable that these percentages will increase as the number of sons per family declines. As that happens, for many people the family support that currently or recently existed will not be available. In this setting formal social security will have a much larger role in providing for the rural elderly.

1. Current or recent economic status of the rural elderly

Based on data from the rural household surveys for Sichuan and Liaoning for 1990, I concluded that the rural elderly had levels of income or consumption that did not differ significantly from those who were not elderly. This conclusion rests on the assumption that within the multiple generation households in which they lived they shared in the available consumption expenditures in an equitable manner. This does not necessarily mean that they shared equally with other adults in per capita expenditures since the needs of the elderly differ somewhat from that of other adults. From the data available to me I cannot determine if this assumption is accurate, but from personal observations in villages and from my understanding of rural family life, I believe that it is a reasonable assumption.

Households were classified in various ways - by average age (greater or less than 60) and by whether the household included persons 60 years and older. In Sichuan the per capita incomes were essentially the same for households with an average age less than 60, greater than 60 or in households with persons aged 60-64 or 65 and over. The average income for households with an average age of less than 60 was 506 yuan in 1990; for those with an average age greater than 60, 563 yuan. Households with persons aged 60-64 had per capita incomes of 500 and those with persons 65 or older, 480 yuan. These differences are very small.

Another look at the Sichuan data indicated that families with no elderly had per capita incomes of 536 yuan compared to incomes of 494, 516 and 462, respectively, for families that had an elderly member who was 60-64, 65-69 and 70 and older. Again these differences are very small.

In Liaoning there were important income differences between families with no elderly and those with elderly. Families with no elderly had per capita incomes of 833 yuan in 1990 and the average for families with elderly was about 675 - a difference of almost 20 percent. However, Liaoning data on per capita consumption expenditures indicate significantly smaller differences for households without elderly and with elderly - the former had per capita expenditures of 601 and the latter 547, a difference of 10 percent. The per capita expenditures on food were nearly identical - 321 and 327. For Sichuan there were no apparent differences in per capita expenditures, either for all living or food expenditures - if anything, families with elderly spent slightly more in total and for food. The expenditures on food include home produced as well as purchased food. In Liaoning it seems that savings were adversely affected by the presence of elderly in the household.

In 1990 the data indicate that families with elderly members received very little from the state budget - the families had to get by with their own resources. Income from the state budget averaged about 2.5 percent of the income of households with elderly and half of that came from participation in the rural household survey! So transfers from the state budget accounted for little more than 1 percent of the income of households with elderly. In Sichuan receipts from the public benefit fund of the collectives were nil - zero for households with average age greater than 60 and less than 1 yuan for 350 independent elderly households.

It should be remembered that most of the rural elderly make significant contributions to the income and welfare of the households in which they live. This contribution ranges from continued full-time work on the farm to taking care of children.

In 1987 there was a large Sample Survey of China's Aged Population. It is not possible to make direct comparisons with respect to income with the data in the rural household surveys. The Sample Survey attributes income to individual household members, but in the publication available to me there is no indication how this attribution was made. The Sample Survey indicated that pensions provided 4.7 percent of the income of the rural elderly while support from children provided 38 percent. The household surveys found that the elderly households in the two provinces received almost nothing from urban relatives. However, I assume that the support from children found in the Sample Survey includes assistance from children living in rural areas, presumably often in the same household.

I conclude from the data from the rural household surveys, insofar as Sichuan and Liaoning are representative of rural China, that as of the beginning of this decade the circumstances of the elderly were quite similar to that of other members of their families. In other words, where incomes were relatively high, the elderly also had relatively high levels of consumption; where incomes were relatively low, the elderly shared in the deprivation on approximately the same basis as other members of the household. My conclusion is that as of 1990, the traditional Chinese family, as it existed in rural areas, met the needs of the elderly quite well, given the income level of the family. It may, in fact, require some very imaginative social engineering to duplicate what existed in 1990 if the rural extended family is adversely affected by the rapid decline in fertility and by the large increase in the percentage of the elderly in the rural population that will occur in the coming decades.

2. The need for knowing more

Before there is a major revision of the current rural pension program or a major effort to promote it, it is important that knowledge of the status of both the current and future elderly be substantially strengthened. There is much that is unknown about the current rural elderly with respect to health status, work activity, and sources and amount of financial resources. While much can be learned from the rural household surveys, and this source should be fully exploited, the survey does not provide information on health status or work activity. It will either require additional surveys of a sample of the current elderly to provide an adequate basis for more fully understanding their circumstances, such as the percentage living in poverty, or who are or should receive extensive medical care, and the contribution of their work to their own support or the addition of a small number of questions to the State Statistical Bureau's rural household surveys.[1]

The need for knowing more is supported by an important study of social security that was completed after the first draft of this paper was written (Benjamin, Brandt and Rozelle 1998). Drawing on different sources, they reported that in 1995 approximately a third of the households in Hebei and Liaoning Provinces lived alone (p. 11). They found that in 1995, contrary to the results given above, the elderly had significantly lower levels of income or consumption than did the nonelderly. However, they also reported that in another survey with data for 1989 the elderly had essentially the same incomes as nonelderly adults (p. 24). I doubt if the difference in the conclusion was due to the difference in dates. These contradictory results reenforce the need for knowing more.

While it is important to better understand the circumstances of those who are now elderly, neither the current nor a reformed rural pension system will have a significant impact on the current elderly. Unless contributions are made over an extended period - at least three decades - the accumulated funds will provide only modest pensions. In fact, it is primarily the rural population that is now 30 years old or younger who would participate in a rural pension program and realize anything like its full potential for providing financial support for the elderly. The circumstances of those who will be elderly in 2030 are likely to be significantly different from those who are now elderly. As noted earlier, a larger percentage is likely to live outside an extended family, either alone or with their spouse.

It is important to anticipate the sources of current income of the elderly some three decades in the future in order to determine what percentage of the income they receive at the time of retirement should come from the pension. In what follows, it is assumed that a pension equal to 40 to 50 percent of income at the time of retirement would be appropriate. This assumes, however, that the rural population will still retain a

---

[1] The value of the rural household surveys could be significantly increased in terms of understanding the efficiency with which rural resources are used if there were questions concerning the allocation of labor. The data now available from the surveys are inadequate for a production function analysis of resource use since there is no measure of the amount of labor applied to farming. It is also important to have data on the allocation of time between farming and nonfarming activities and such data are not now available. Identification of the health status of the elderly, as well as other members of the household, would not require asking such questions in the same time pattern as the other detailed data are collected, but could be done on a quarterly basis.

significant connection with the land, at least to the extent of maintaining a garden plot and producing some poultry and pigs for their own consumption and, perhaps, receiving rent from their land use rights or for land actually owned, if the current policy of collective ownership of land were to be abolished.

But since by 2030 the percentage of the rural labor force primarily engaged in agriculture is likely to be less than half what it now is, the above assumptions may not be valid and need to be tested against the expected experiences of today's young rural people.

3. The current program of rural social security

There is a social program of welfare houses for the elderly who cannot take care of themselves and have no children to do so. These now provide for a very small percentage of the rural elderly, a percentage so small that the Sample Survey of the rural elderly did not include such institutions as a separate category.

In some of the higher income rural areas adjacent to large cities, part of the rural population has participated in various pension systems for some years. Starting in 1993 a rural pension system administered by the Ministry of Civil Affairs has become available in most rural counties. This pension system was tried as an experiment in Shandong Province in 1991 and was made available nation-wide in 1993. As of the end of 1997 there were 82 million who had paid some funds into the system but the average amount of the payment was very small, 231 yuan (less than $30 at the current rate of exchange). Thus there has been limited experience with the rural pension system and I believe that everyone involved with it recognizes that major modifications are required, if it is to meet the needs of the rural elderly well into the 21st Century. What I shall say may appear to be quite critical of what is now being done, but that is not my intent. Instead my intent is to make suggestions for improvement of the pension program as well as to suggest that there are other changes in national policies that would assist in meeting the needs of the rural elderly.

It needs to be recognized that for at least the next two decades the annual pensions derived from the current pension program will be so modest as to require that most of the needs of the elderly be met by the extended family or from the resources controlled by the elderly. If 10 percent of a couples' annual income of 5,000 yuan is paid into the pension fund and if the real rate of return is 4 percent, the accumulated value at the end of 20 years would be about 11,000 yuan. This would provide for an annual annuity for the couple of 950 yuan, equal to 18 percent of their estimated income 20 years hence. It is assumed, in this example, that their real earnings increase at 4 percent annually.

4. Ratio of pension payment to earnings at time of retirement

I do not believe that the percentage of income at the time of retirement that would be provided by a pension payment need be as high as what is often believed to be desirable for urban workers. Rural people, including those who hold nonfarm jobs, have access to earnings possibilities that many can pursue during the years they are receiving a pension. These include continued work in agriculture, including producing food for home consumption as well as for sale, assisting in the raising of grandchildren, thus freeing the time of family members, and the cushion provided by the return on the land that they have rights to. Land would have greater security value if farm people owned it. But it will have considerable security value if the use rights are for a long term (say 50 years) and there is a competitive rental market for land use rights.

Consequently I have assumed that the objective should be for a pension to equal 40 to 50 percent of the income at the retirement age. This is on the assumption that the individuals still have a significant connection with agriculture, either on a full-time or part-time basis. In this case, the elderly will generally have other sources of income in the form of home produced food as well as cash income generated by their activities. For those rural residents who have severed all or nearly all of their connections with farming - they may continue to live in a village but have given up all land other than that related to their house - the retirement income should probably be a larger percentage of income at time of retirement - perhaps of the order of 65 percent or so. These individuals should be encouraged to purchase additional annuities, hopefully with rates of return that reflect the real rate actually earned on investments in the Chinese economy.

5. The rate of return

The annual payment from a pension fund is a function of four variables - the number of years payments are made, the amount of the periodic payment, the rate of return earned by or attributed to the money paid into the fund, and life expectancy when the payment from the fund starts. In the longer run, it is reasonable to expect that most individuals would pay into the fund for approximately the same number of years - if retirement is at age 60, it would be reasonable to assume that rural individuals would start paying by the age of 20 or earlier if they have a job that pays wages. However, it may be that the pensions should not start until age 65 since by the third or fourth decade of the next century, life expectancy at birth in China should approach 75 year and life expectancy at age 60 would significantly exceed 15 years. In this case, payment into the fund might be expected to occur for 45 years with a significant impact on the value of the fund at the time of retirement.

If most people pay for approximately 40 or 45 years, then the two most important variables affecting the amount of the retirement payment are the amounts contributed and the real rate of return on the investment. The nominal rate is largely irrelevant since the nominal rate reflects, in part, the rate of inflation. A nominal rate of return that was just equal to the rate of inflation would mean that the pensioner would simply get back the real value of what he or she paid into the fund. If they paid in 10 percent of their income for forty years, then as a pension they would receive an amount equal to approximately 7.5 percent of what their income was immediately before they retired or started to receive their pension. They would have gained nothing, in real terms, from having contributed 10 percent of their income for so many years. As the examples that will be presented clearly show, how much the expected value of the pension, in real terms, exceeds the payments made depends on the real rate of return on investment.

While the real rate of return on investment and the percentage of income paid will determine the absolute magnitude of the pension, the percentage of pre-pension income covered by the pension depends also on the relationship between the rate of return and the rate of growth of income. If the rate of return is less than the rate of growth of earnings, the outcome is that the amount of the pension will be a low percentage of earnings at the time the pension starts unless a high percentage of earnings is paid into the fund each year. Conversely if the rate of return is greater than the rate of growth of income, then the pay out relative to pre-pension income will be significantly higher, assuming the same percentage of income contributed. Consequently, an important consideration in the establishment of a pension system is the relationship between the growth of income and the real rate of return on the invested funds. Experience indicates that the real rate of return on investments exceeds the rate of growth of wages. This has been true in the United States, even where the real rate is derived from the return on government bonds. The World Bank (1997, p. 58) reports that in China for 1980-1993 that real wages increased at an annual rate of 5.4 percent, while the pre-tax earnings to asset ratio was estimated to be 13 percent for 1986-1995. But in 1996 this ratio was only 6 percent.

The experience of China's rural pension program since its inception makes it very clear that the government has made no commitment concerning the rate of return to be earned on the money that rural people pay into the fund. It is evident that for the period from 1993 through 1997 the real rate of return on the money paid has been **negative**. In other words, the real value of the accumulated fund for an individual who had made equal payments in each year from 1993 through 1997 would have been less than the real value of the money paid in. In 1997 and this year the rates of inflation are below the return on investment, but it remains true that for the entire period that the real rate of return has been negative. This is hardly a propitious start for a pension program.

6. Amount of annual contribution

In the discussion that follows, it is assumed that an individual or rural couple pay a fixed percentage of their current earnings into the fund each year. In the examples, I have used the rural household surveys to estimate the average income of each rural labor force participant for 1995. The estimate that I derived was 2,500 yuan per person or 5,000 yuan per couple.[2] The current rural pension program depends on payments made by individuals or couples and assumes that the only payments credited to the fund are made by the individuals, either personally or on their behalf by the local collective or village. For the time being, it is assumed that participation is voluntary. In most social security or pension systems that exist participation is not voluntary and, at least pro forma, only part of the payment is made by individual. In fact, of course, regardless of who sends the check to the pension agency, the employee is paying the cost since the wage reflects the fact that the employer is paying part of the cost of social security. But at least there is the appearance that someone else is paying part of the cost.

I do not know what advice the Ministry of Civil Affairs is giving rural people concerning the relationship between the amount of the payments and the pension that will be received and the amount of annual payment, as percent of income, that would be required to provide a pension that represented, say, 40 to 50 percent of their income at the time of retirement. I do know that in my own country the politicians have not been forthcoming about how modest are the levels of payment from our social security system.[3] While never quite saying so, the impression has been left that the pension is

[2] The 2,500 yuan was derived by taking the per capita net income in rural households as given in the rural household survey for 1995 and multiplying it by the number of persons supported by each laborer (SSB 1997). Thus income from all sources is included in the estimated income per worker.

[3] After the above was written, the current president of the United States in a discussion of ways to reform the social security system before it goes bankrupt informed his listeners that they needed personal savings to

adequate to meet the needs of the elderly, even though it is unlikely that many persons of modest means would receive a pension that would approach 50 percent of their income at the time of retirement.[4]

There are an enormous number of combinations of real rates of return on the investments, real rates of increases of income during the period of payment, the number of years that payments are made into the fund, life expectancy at the age of retirement, and the amount of payment as a percentage of one's income. I will not bore you with all of the many combinations that were estimated, but will provide a small number that indicate the effects of variations of some of the variables that should be taken into account in devising a pension program.

Let us assume that the objective is to provide an individual or a couple with a pension equal to 40 to 50 percent of the income at the time of retirement. It is also assumed that payments are made for 40 years, that real incomes increase at 4 percent annually, and that life expectancy at age 60 is 10 years. If the real rate of return on the funds were 4 percent, it would require an annual payment of 10 percent of income to achieve the stated income objective. Holding other variables constant, if the real rate of return were 6 percent, then an annual rate of contribution of 6 percent would be adequate to provide a pension equal to 50 percent of income at the time of retirement. But if life expectancy at age 60 were 15 years, as it almost certainly will be 40 years hence, it would require an annual rate of payment of 7.5 percent of income if the real rate of return were 6 percent.

---

supplement social security payments.

[4] If you call the Social Security system, you will be told the probable size of your pension, but you must take the initiative.

Suppose the government is willing to commit itself only to a 2 percent real rate of return on investment. Then paying 10 percent of annual income for 40 years, with life expectancy of 10 years at age 60, would provide a pension equal to 31 percent of income at time of retirement. If life expectancy were 15 years, the pension would be 21 percent of income at time of retirement.

As expected, the real rate of return has a large effect on the size of the pension for a given annual rate of payment and is a critical feature of any rural pension system and one that requires prompt attention by the appropriate governmental officials. It is not a decision that can be long delayed.

How can an appropriate real rate of return be determined? The funds that are accumulated over time can be invested in real resources, earning on average a positive real rate of return. Since such investments have an element of risk, the actual real rate paid might be some relatively large fraction of the actual real return. The long term real rate of return in the economy of the United States as measured by the difference between the yield on low risk bonds and the rate of inflation is of the order of 3 percent. As measured by returns on common stocks over the past half century, the long run rate of return has been about 9 percent. This is for a long period prior to the recent sharp increase in stock prices. The real rates of return in China should be this high, if not higher, for the foreseeable future. If this is a correct surmise, then a commitment to a 4 percent real rate of return would not be one that would impose real costs on the rest of the economy.

If the pension system is to be voluntary and succeed in including a high percentage of the rural population, it would need a guaranteed return of this order to be at all competitive with other potential uses of funds. As capital markets develop in China over the years, private mutual funds will emerge that will offer expected positive returns on investments. And given the expected profitability of capital investments in China for decades to come, the private funds would certainly be competitive with the rural pension fund if the latter paid significantly less than a real return of 4 percent. It is worth emphasizing that if the program is voluntary, it will need to compete with the alternatives facing rural people. These alternatives include investments in agriculture and in nonfarm enterprises as well as any private annuity programs that may develop over the years. Consequently if participation is to cover a significant percentage of the population, the rate of return on the investment must be reasonable compared to that from the available alternatives.

7. Age when pension begins

Most of the above discussion assumes that the payout from the pension would start at age 60. Serious consideration should be given to increasing the age to 65. If this were done, under reasonable assumptions concerning the rate of return and its relationship to the rate of growth of income, annual contribution rates of 7.5 percent would result in pensions equalling 40 to 50 percent of income at the time the pension began. This might well make the rural pension system more attractive to rural people, especially to those with relatively low incomes.

8. Rate of real return and annual growth of income

The size of the accumulated fund available to pay for the pension depends on the variables noted above - the amount of the annual payments, the real rate of return, and life expectancy at the at the age payments begin. There is another variable that affects the relationship between the amount of the pension and the percentage of income at the time of retirement. This is the annual rate of growth of income during the period of accumulation. If the real rate of return is less than the income growth rate, then the pension will be relatively small compared to income at the time of receiving the pension payment. If the real rate of return exceeds the rate of growth of income, the pension will be significantly larger relative to income than when the two rates are equal.

9. Investment of funds

If participation in the pension fund approached 100 percent, the flow of funds would be very large. Assuming an average income per worker of 2,500 yuan in 1995 prices, a 10 percent payment and 400 million rural workers, the annual payment into the fund would be 100 billion yuan. These payments, however, would not represent a net addition to existing savings. In fact, the payments would probably largely supplant or replace savings in other forms, such as in savings deposits at the Agricultural Bank. In 1994 the savings deposits in the Agricultural Bank increased by 138 billion yuan. The pension fund would be unlikely to add substantially to the supply of funds available for investing in the economy. But it would add something if a significant positive real rate of return were guaranteed. Currently there is considerable uncertainty about the real rate of returns on either bank deposits or government bonds. If the return on the pension funds were set at 4 percent in real terms, there would be no net cost to the government budget if the funds were invested in activities that yielded at least 4 percent. This is certainly possible in the Chinese economy if funds are invested where they will yield the highest return. However, this would require a change in governmental policy, a change that is now underway. Investment has been subsidized by low interest rates, interest rates that were often negative in real returns. If the nation's resources are to be used efficiently, the interest rates charged and paid should reflect the productivity of invested funds. In China currently and for some time to come a real rate of return of 4 percent appears to be one that could be readily sustained. What is required, of course, is that investments go to those activities that will yield the highest returns. If this were done, guaranteeing a 4 percent real return would not require a subsidy from the budget.

Several countries have issued substantial amounts of indexed bonds, notably the United Kingdom and Israel. Some 18 percent of the former's marketable debt is in indexed securities, while 79 percent of the Israeli marketable debt is indexed to changes in the price level. The United States introduced indexed bonds in January 1997, which then yielded a real return of 3 3/8 percent per annum. An advantage of indexed bonds is that they force monetary and fiscal authorities to consider an additional impact of the indexed bond compared to bonds and other securities that are not indexed. When governments issue securities that are not indexed, the government can reduce the real value of its outstanding debt through inflation - in other words, pay off part of its debt to its people by an inflation tax. But where indexed bonds are involved, this cannot be done. If there is inflation, the government is committed to find the resources required to compensate the security holders for the inflation. This may well be an important reason why indexed government debt securities have seen limited use. But clearly this is an alternative that the Government of China could and should consider. As long as inflation is held in check, there is no cost to the government and considerable benefit to those who hold the securities.

10. Employees of TVEs

Implicit in the above discussion is that the income earned by employees of rural nonfarm enterprises would be included, alongside any income earned from farming, in determining the contribution to be made for the pension fund. There is a possibility that the employees of TVEs might be included in the national pension program designed primarily for the benefit of urban workers. In the World Bank's *Old Age Security* it is made clear why employees of at least the township enterprises[5] might be included in a

[5] It is noted a number of times in *Old Age Security* that the employees of the township enterprises might be

unified pension system: "If the system is unified and coverage is extended to the nonstate sector (including township enterprises), **substantial resources would be generated that could be used to fund the transition**." (emphasis supplied)

The transition referred to is the period during which a new pension system that might include a low level of pension for all (Pillar 1)[6], supplemented by a compulsory individual account, that would exist alongside the current unfunded system for as long as individuals covered under that system continued to receive pensions and to cover the cost for employment service for individuals working at the time the unified system might be inaugurated.

In other words, as is true in so much that occurs in China, people living in rural areas would be called upon to pay for a benefit that will go primarily to urban people. It is not only that the rural employees would contribute extra funds to pay for the transition costs, but since it is highly probable that the average age of township and village enterprise employees is less than that of urban employees, they would continue to pay taxes into Pillar 1 that would exceed the benefits they would receive for many years to come.

11. Supplements to rural pensions

As shown above, unless the rate of return on the accumulated funds, both during the period of contribution and when the pension is received, is at a significant positive real

---

included in the unified national system. However, the employment data for 1994 given in Table 3.2, page 39, in a column labelled "Employment in township enterprises" is exactly the same figure that is given in the *China Statistical Yearbook, 1996* for township and village enterprises. The Yearbook employment figure apparently covers all nonfarm employees in rural areas, including those employed in private firms as well as in enterprises actually owned by the townships and villages. Employment in the private sector is now about the same as in the township and village enterprises.

[6] Pillar 1 is the universal and low level of support for a pension system now under discussion in China. This pillar would provide a poverty-level income for all who had participated in the system for 40 years and could be either universal or based on a means test. Pillar 1 would be financed either through general taxes or payroll taxes. The payment would be about 24 percent of average wages. Pillar 2 would be a mandatory individual account system that would be fully funded, financed equally by employer and employee. If the annual contribution were 8 percent of wages, after 40 years the pension would equal 36 percent of wages if the rate of return and the growth of wages were the same (World Bank 1997, p. 45). Pillar 3 is a voluntary supplementary individual retirement account. It is assumed that there would be licensed pension fund management enterprises that would offer such accounts.

rate of at least 4 percent, the pension will fall well short of meeting the needs of the retired, if those needs are defined as 40 to 50 percent of the income at the time of receiving the pension. One way in which pensions could be supplemented is to transfer ownership of farm land to farmers. As a land market developed, the owners could use the land to supplement their pension in one of two ways. The first would be to sell it and invest the funds and the other would be to rent it and use the rent to supplement the pension and any other assets.

Since the opposition to farmers owning land continues as a strong political force, an alternative is to provide farmers with an iron clad lease of the land for a long period of time, such as 50 years, with the lease being continuously extended at decade intervals during the lifetime of the farm operator.[7] An iron clad lease means that the lease cannot be abrogated by local or other officials by such means as land reallocations based on demographic changes in the village or for any other reason. If this were done, then the lease would have a capital value and could be sold to help finance a family's requirements during retirement. Or the land could be leased to someone who would farm it and the rent used to supplement the pension. But perhaps the most important contribution of land to the income of rural residents, especially those living in an extended family, would be its contribution to income.

How much is land worth? Except for transfers of land to nonagricultural use, I know of no data on the value of farm land. The prices paid for transfers to nonagricultural use, since they occur primarily in areas in or near cities, do not represent the value of land for farm purposes. A rough estimate of the current value of land for farm purposes as an average for all of China can be made by attributing a certain percentage of farm income to land. The appropriate percentage is unknown but a figure ranging from a third to 40 percent seems reasonable. On the basis of the income per household from agriculture in 1995, this would mean that the return to land

[7] Rights to use land for a defined period, that is only renewed as it expires, offers declining security as time passes. Assume that the rights are for 50 years for land in a household that includes an individual who is 20 years old. If that person starts to receive a pension at age 65, the period for the land use rights would have but 5 years to run. The value of the rights for 5 years is modest. And if the individual has ceased agricultural production, there would probably be no guarantee that the rights would be renewed at the end of the period. What the present system of allocating land use rights for a long but defined period ignores is that the value of those rights diminishes over time and that this has a number of effects on resource use as well as on the value of the rights as a supplement to a pension. This is but one of the numerous issues that need to be resolved if land is to continue to be collectively rather than individually owned.

would have been from 1,800 yuan to 2,200 yuan for an average area of 0.6 hectare. If the real rate of return is assumed to be 4 percent, this gives a land value of 75,000 yuan to 90,000 yuan per hectare.[8]

Over time, of course, the size of farm operating units will increase as the number of farm households declines as economic growth occurs and labor is transferred out of agriculture. Forty years from now the average size of farm operating units will be well in excess of a hectare - perhaps as much as two hectares. Thus owning land would provide an important asset that could be used to provide funds for retirement, if needed. Forty years hence the value of a hectare of land would be significantly greater than the accumulated value of payments of 10 percent of annual income at 4 percent real rate of interest. This sum is approximately 50,000 yuan, in 1995 prices. But the capital value of farmland is not likely to be used for retirement, but only the rental value, since most of the land will be transferred to the next generation. But it would provide a significant degree of security in case it were needed.

12. Concluding comments

I have not addressed the issue of whether the rural pension system should be compulsory or voluntary. Most basic pension systems in the world are compulsory. Persons meeting certain criteria must make payments into the systems, whether they want to or not. An argument in favor of compulsion exists when society accepts the responsibility for providing a minimum level of financial aid for those who for a lack of foresight or bad luck have insufficient means to prevent real hardship when they are no longer able to work.

But there are clear disadvantages to compulsory systems. Such systems permit governments to behave irresponsibly.[9] This is illustrated by the difficulties that

---

[8] This is probably a conservative estimate of the value of cropland in China. Converted to U.S. dollars at an exchange rate of 8 yuan per dollar, this is a value per hectare of about $1,000. In the United States the average value of land is now about $3,500 per hectare in the very productive Corn Belt.

[9] Let me cite three examples related to the social security system of the United States; the first two are based on my own experience. The U.S. government has made commitments that permitted the value of pensions to far exceed the accumulated value of all payments made into the system. I am the beneficiary of two of these. The first is that millions of people have been added to the system, not when they started to work but at a later date and treated as though they had made payments when they started to work. I did not enter the system - start making payments - until I was 36 years old yet my social security payment is essentially the same as if I had started making payments when I was 21. The second is that during the 1970s a significant

confront many social security or pension systems that now exist. The theory of such systems, actual or implied, has been that when a young person pays money into the system, that money is invested and eventually used to provide the pension for that person. In fact, what exists in nearly all governmental systems is that a large part, if not all, of what the young person pays is used to pay the pension for someone who is now retired and is not invested and committed to his or her pension. In other words, most systems are on a pay-as-you go basis and a large share of what is paid in is not invested but is used to pay current pensions. Under these circumstances the young person must assume or hope that when he or she retires there will be enough workers to pay into the fund in order to provide the pension that he or she thought had been earned.

Compulsory systems need not work this way. Chile has devised a system, now being copied elsewhere, of individual retirement accounts that significantly limits the role of the government. The government collects funds from each participant, including any contribution made by the employer, and then turns the money collected from each individual over to a private enterprise that invests the funds for the individual. The participant chooses among a number of such enterprises and the government imposes certain rules of behavior on the enterprises. If a particular firm performs poorly over a period of time in terms of returns on its investments, that firm can be forced into liquidation and its assets and obligations transferred to other firms according to the wishes of those owning the retirement accounts.

---

error was made in calculating the ratio of benefits to payments made. The benefits were double indexed for several years - they were increased currently and prospectively both for changes in the cost of living index and the increase in the average wage paid. Since part of the increase in wages reflected the change in the cost of living, this amounted to counting the change in the cost of living twice. It took several years for the government to recognize its error. But the Congress and the President were unwilling to admit that a mistake had been made and the formula for the payout for a particular group of participants who had not yet retired was not adjusted when the formula for calculating benefits was corrected. I was the beneficiary of both of these decisions.

The President and the Congress have congratulated themselves on their success in balancing the federal budget. The budget balance depends on counting the $101 billion excess of social security receipts over social security expenditures as budgetary income for the 1998 fiscal year. This is spending the same money twice. The excess of current social security receipts over current payments are committed to future social security payments. Spending the excess now means that some time in the future it will have to be replaced to meet commitments that are now known to exist. If the budget were really balanced, the $101 billion of excess social security receipts would be invested in securities that would generate earnings to pay for commitments that we now know exist. And the $101 billion would also be available instead of being currently spent.

It would be difficult to argue today that the state of capital markets or the regulatory structure exists for the privatization of the rural pension system in China. If this is the case, it is incumbent on the government to be very forthright concerning how it will handle the funds that rural people trust to it. This includes a commitment to a positive real rate of return.

Whether the rural pension system is compulsory or voluntary, a critical component is the guarantee of a reasonable positive real rate of return on invested funds. If the system is compulsory, equity requires such a commitment. If the system is voluntary, its success in obtaining participation of a large percentage of the relevant population depends on the expected real rate of return and the degree of confidence in that return. One argument for a voluntary system is that it requires responsible behavior by the government if there is to be a high rate of participation.

References

1. Benjamin, Dwayne, Loren Brandt and Scott Rozelle, "Aging, Well-being, and Social Security in rural North China." Unpublished paper.
2. State Statistical Bureau (SSB 1997), *China Statistical Yearbook 1997* Beijing: China Statistical Publishing House.
3. World Bank (1997), *Old Age Security: Pension Reform in China*. Washington,
4. D.C.: The World Bank.

CHAPTER 14

SOCIAL WELFARE AND TRANSITION TO A MARKET ECONOMY IN CHINA

ATHAR HUSSAIN
Asia Research Center,
London School of Economics
Houghton Street, London, WC2A 2AE, UK

This paper outlines various social welfare programs in the broad context of socio-economic changes. It discusses socio-economic changes with implications for social welfare. It analyzes arrangements for income maintenance in rural and urban areas and their reform, including old-age pensions, unemployment insurance and poverty relief in rural areas. The emphasis is on the current situation and the likely trend of changes over 25 years taking 1995 as the benchmark.

1. Introduction

Social welfare is taken here in its broad meaning covering the protection of the population from deprivation and the development of its capabilities. A few simple questions underlie the discussion here:

- How free is the Chinese population from the threat of destitution?
- What are the arrangements for income maintenance in old age and unemployment and how effective are they?
- Does the population have access to adequate medical care in case of illness and how far has China succeeded in abolishing the incidence of preventable diseases?
- How successful has China been in banishing illiteracy and raising the education level of its population?

In terms of the current level of human development indicators, China stands out among low-income economies (those with an annual per capita income of less that $700), which China is in terms of GNP if not PPP statistics; it resembles middle--income economies. Its population enjoys a comparatively high life expectancy of 69 years and a low infant mortality rate; and its illiteracy rate of 12% (1995 figure) is lower than in any low-income economy except Sri Lanka and Vietnam (WDR 1996). Compared to populous developing economies covering a large territory, the percentage of the population living in poverty is low 9% (World Bank 1992). Apart from the famine brought on by the upheavals of the Great Leap Forward compounded by natural disasters in 1959-61, China has been remarkably successful in protecting its population from the threat of starvation and destitution. The map of deprivation for China differs from that for many developing economies in two respects. One is the absence of abject poverty in cities. Two, extreme rural poverty is largely concentrated in sparsely populated regions (in the Northwest and Southwest). However, the first is changing with growing urban immigration and, lately, lay-offs by state enterprises in urban areas; rural poverty has yet to be fully investigated, it may be more widespread in densely-populated regions than generally believed.

However, China's outstanding record in human development is losing its lustre. Over the reform period since 1978, improvements in indicators of human development have not been as sustained and dramatic as growth in per capita income, which underscores the point that rapid economic growth alone is not sufficient to banish deprivation. A concerted policy is also needed. Following a sharp drop in the population in absolute poverty from 33 to 12% between 1978 and 1985, progress in reducing poverty has since been very slow, if not negligible (World Bank 1992b). The downward trend in the "under-five mortality rate" (the indicator of child health recommended by WHO) in evidence until the early 1980s, seems to have come to a halt or even risen in some of the poorer provinces (World Bank 1996). The rates are particularly high in some of the interior provinces. Though the illiteracy rate has dropped from 23% in 1980 to 12% in 1995, school attendance still varies widely between urban and rural localities and between boys and girls and drop out rates are high in some rural localities.

Looking ahead 10 to 15 years, the appropriate comparators are not low- but middle-income economies whose ranks China is expected to join in the near future. In health indicators and educational attainment, China lags behind a number of Asian countries. Its under-five mortality rate of 43 per 1,000 live births is higher than those in Malaysia, Thailand and Sri Lanka and several times those in Hong Kong, South Korea and Singapore (UN: Human Development Report 1996). The incidence of preventable diseases such as viral hepatitis is high. The average length of schooling is significantly shorter and the drop out rates before the completion of basic schooling is higher than in Malaysia, Thailand, Sri Lanka, let alone South Korea. The percentage of school leavers going into higher education is very low even compared to low-income Asian countries. What these gaps suggest is that without a concerted effort in improving child and maternal health and raising the educational level of its population, China would in the near future begin look like a laggard amongst East and Southeast Asian economies. Not only important in their own right, these measures are also widely recognized as essential in sustaining rapid economic growth.

The purpose of this paper is to outline various social welfare programs in the broad context of socio-economic changes. It is structured as follows. By way of background, Section 2 discusses socio-economic changes with direct implications for social welfare. Section 3 analyzes arrangements for income maintenance in rural and urban areas and their reform, including old-age pensions, unemployment insurance and poverty relief in rural areas. Section 4 presents a brief outline of the rural social security system. Section 5 focuses on health-care and health insurance and Section 5 concludes. For reasons of space, education is not discussed. The emphasis here is on the current situation and the likely trend of changes over next 25 years taking 1995 as the benchmark.

2. Three Transitions

Issues concerning social welfare in the present-day China are shaped by three transitions it is currently undergoing:

- demographic ;
- low to a middle-income economy;
- command to a market economy.

The first consists in a change from the demographic regime of high fertility and low life expectancy to one of low fertility and high life expectancy with a non-rising population. Its salient features are a deceleration in the growth rate of the population and a changing age structure. The second transition is accompanied by the usual processes of a steady flow of labor out of farming coupled with a shift from self to wage employment, and a rising population movement within and out of the countryside to cities. The main feature of the third transition is the shrinkage of the state sector, which has been the mainstay of urban social security.

2.1 Demographic Transition

The Chinese population is currently just over 1.2 billion (21% of the world total) and growing at around 1.1% per year, similar to the rate in the US but low compared to 1.8% in India and the average rate of 1.4% for middle-income economies (WDR 1996). The key prospect for the future is a decelerating growth towards a non-rising population total of between 1.5 to 1.6 billion in 2145-50, i.e. 350 and 400 million more than the 1996 total. Given the asymptotic growth pattern, most of this increase will take place over the next 20 to 25 years, and that will be accompanied by a radical change in the age-structure. Given the mortality pattern, population growth depends on the number of women of child-bearing age (broadly 15 to 45) and the total fertility rate (the number of children per woman on average). The first depends on the fertility rates over 15 to 45 years ago: i.e., in 1997, on the rates between 1952 and 1982, when it ranged between 3 to 6. The current total fertility rate is less than 2, just below the number needed for the population to replace itself. It is likely to fall further given the determination of the leadership to maintain mandatory birth control. Therefore population growth in China will in the coming years, as now, be driven not by the above-replacement fertility rate, but by the rising number of women of child-bearing age as a result of the carry over effects of the above-replacement fertility rates up to the end of the 1980s, which will take around 50 years to peter out completely.

Both the increase in the population and the change in age structure have implications for social welfare, especially the latter. The former because of two reasons: first, creating employment for additional members of the labor force, and, second, pressure on environment and natural resources. The age structure matters because it determines the ratio of producers to dependants in the population. Given the already huge size of the Chinese population, even a low growth rate translates into a large number (currently just over 12 million per year). Though China covers a vast territory, much of its population is densely concentrated in a comparatively narrow corridor along the eastern seaboard and the Yangtze river basin. With urbanization proceeding apace, the population will in the future be even more concentrated than now, raising further the pressure on an already strained environment. As is well-known, the ratio of cultivated area to the population in China is low: 78 hectares per 1,000 people; and the projected increase in the total population of between 300 and 400 million will lower it even further. How serious a problem does this pose for China or the rest of the world? Together with rising per capita income, this will require an adjustment in farming in and perhaps also outside China but it does not imply a catastrophic grain shortage. Such prophesies (Brown 1995) rest on flimsy evidence and faulty arguments. The potential for raising grain yields, especially wheat and coarse grain, which China imports, and extending the cultivable area is far from exhausted in China, let alone outside China.

The ramifications of the changing the age-structure of the population for social welfare run wide and deep. What this change will consist, of is brought out by a comparison with the population profile in 1995 and 2020 (Table 1).

Compared with the 1995 pattern, the median age of the population in 2020 will be 9 years higher, and, proportionately, there will be fewer younger people and more elderly people. The age profile of the population will look more like a cylinder than a pyramid, as it did at the time of the last census in 1990, and would resemble that in the present-day developed economies. Because of an extra-ordinarily rapid demographic transition, China will have to adapt to an aging population at a much lower level of per capita income than has been the case in the present-day developed economies. The economic consequences of the changing age-structure depend on three factors: first, not only the ratio of the elderly, on which much of the discussion in China tends to be focused, but also on the ratio of children in the population, second, their respective needs and labor productivity, and, third, the pattern of financing of their support. It is important to point out that, although the ratio of the elderly will be higher in 2020, the dependency ratio will be lower than that in 1995. Thus in the aggregate, the cost of supporting the rising numbers of elderly persons will be partially offset by the declining numbers of children, not only relatively but also in absolute numbers. The extent of the offset will depend on the respective requirements of children and elderly persons.

Table 1: **Population Profile 1995 and 2020**

	1995	2020
Total (1,000)	1,236,696	1,479,223
Median Age	29	38
Ratio of Children to the Population[1]	26.7%	21%
Ratio of the Elderly[2]	6.7%	11%
Dependency Ratio[3]	50.2	45.1

Notes: 1. Aged (0-14);
2. Aged (654);
3. {(0-14)+ (65⁺)}/(15-64). The 1995 figures are from China *Population Yearbook 1996*; those for 2020 are from a World Bank projection which should be taken as illustrative.

An exclusive focus on the ratio of the elderly as the index of the burden of old-age support can be misleading for two reasons. First, it concentrates on the adverse side and neglects the bonus provided by declining fertility. Accruing first, the latter will continue to outweigh the former until 2025, if not later. The implication is that China has more time to adjust to the aging population than is generally believed. Second, it gives a distorted picture of the geographical distribution of the burden of supporting the elderly population. In terms of the ratio of the elderly alone, coastal provinces appear to carry a higher burden of supporting the elderly population, but most of these also have a lower ratio of children to the population because of their lower fertility rates. As a result the total dependency ratio, including both children and elderly persons, is generally lower in richer coastal than in the poorer interior provinces. For a proper analysis of the economic impact of the changing structure of the population, one needs to weight children, adults and elderly persons by their respective consumption needs and also to take into account at labor productivity, which has the same effect as the rise in the working population relative to dependants (Cutleretal, 1990).

Both children and elderly persons are supported by the working population, but their respective requirements are different. Children have to be educated and found jobs at the end of schooling, and elderly persons make an extra demand on medical care. In 2020, there will be 16 million fewer school-age children (5-14) than in 1995, but 80 million more elderly persons (65+). The changing age structure will require an adjustment in the schooling system, old-age support and medical care. As the sources of financial support and personal care of children and of elderly persons differ, the impact of the changing age-structure will vary with institutions. Much of .the financial cost and personal care of children falls on families, but a large part of their cost of education is met from public resources, though over the reform period the cost borne by parents has risen. Currently the financial support for elderly persons in China is split between families society (which in the Mainland parlance means the government and enterprises), with the former carrying the main burden. Only a percentage of the elderly (around 24.6% of above-60) receive pensions and most of them are in urban areas. The rural elderly making up the majority of the elderly population depend on their children, predominantly sons. There are now collective (community) pension schemes in rural areas, but these are still in the initial stage and cover only part subsistence.

Under the current arrangements, the government, enterprises and families will all feel the impact of the changing age-structure of the population. In urban areas the cost of the rising ratio of the elderly will fall on enterprises (including their employees), the government and families. For the latter two it will be offset by the declining ratio of children, though not necessarily completely. State enterprises, which already carry a heavy burden of pensions, will be most adversely affected by the change as they will receive none of the dividends of the falling ratio of children. Currently, around 78% of retirees are ex-state employees (China Labor Statistical Yearbook_1996: 441); and a vast majority of new retirees over the next decades will also be from the state sector, the median age of their labor force being higher than that of non-state enterprises. In rural areas the economic impact of the changing age structure will be largely on families, given the low coverage of old-age pensions there. Though with the development and extension of rural collective pension schemes a part of the cost will be shifted to the community or the local government.

As increasingly realized in China, the current heavy reliance on the family for old-age support goes against the grain of the demographic trend and socio-economic changes. The financial support and personal care of elderly persons by their children have traditionally rested on co-residence or residence in close proximity. An increasing number of young couples prefer nuclear households and migration increasingly rules out multigenerational households. In the future not only will working adults be supporting larger number of elderly but also for a longer period. An extreme example is a future hypothetical family comprised at 2 earners and 5 dependants, consisting of a working couple (both single children themselves), their single child and their four elderly parents. Given the usual trend of falling in mortality rates, life expectancy at 65 in 2020 would be 3 years higher for women and be 2 years higher for men than in 1995.

Thus a crucial issue facing China is the progressive replacement of family support with social support for elderly persons. Though the focus of current policy discussions is on pensions in urban areas, the problem is far more serious in rural areas. There not only are old-age pensions rare, but the ratio of the elderly to the working population is higher than in urban areas (Table 2).

Table 2: Age Structure 1995 (%)

	Cities	Towns	Rural Areas
Children/Labor Force	29.3	33.5	44.5
Elderly/Labor Force	9.7	8.7	10.3
Total Dependency Ratio	3.9	42.2	54.8

Notes: Children: [0-141;.Labour Force: [15-64]; Elderly: [65+]
Source: *China Population Yearbook 1996*

In fact, compared to cities and towns, rural areas are handicapped in three respects: not only do they have a higher ratio of the elderly because of the emigration of working adults but also a higher ratio of children because of their higher fertility rate; moreover, their average per capita income is lower. The low ratio in towns is due to the recent immigration of working adults. The adverse gap in the age pattern between the urban (cities and towns) and rural areas is likely to widen over time with further emigration which consists mostly of working adults.

The near doubling of the number of elderly persons (from 83 to 163 million) and changes in the family structure put three items on the reform agenda:

- an overhaul of the pension system to extend coverage and to provide it with a sound financial basis;
- expansion in medical care geared to elderly persons;
- expansion of personal services for the elderly, which are currently limited.

2.2 Process of Development

The focus of this section is on how economic development is altering the sectoral distribution of the labor force and its terms of employment which are of central importance for social welfare. Particular emphasis is given to the shift from self- to wage employment because of the close link between the latter and the form of social security system (labor insurance) in China. The current labor force of 624 million divides 72:28 between rural and urban, which in China are more administrative than economic categories. Because of restriction on migration, which have diminished in rigour but not disappeared, and the explosive growth of town and village enterprises (TVEs), rural is increasingly not synonymous with agricultural, nor is urban with urbanization. The proportion of the labor force in farming is 52% (20 percentage points less than the rural population share), and around 29% of the rural labor force is engaged full-time in non-farming activities (*Statistical Yearbook of China 1996*).

Table 3: Sectoral Distribution of Labor Force (%s)

	1995	2020
Farming	52.2	12
Industry	23.0	31
Services	24.8	57

Source: China Labor Statistical Yearbook 1996: 12

The sectoral distribution of the labor force in China presents some anomalies, which wereeven more marked at the outset of economic reforms. The 52% share of labor in farming is similar to that in low-income and some low middle income economies. Associated with this, natural disasters (floods and draught) remain a major contingency for a large majority of the population. But the share in industry in China (23%) is comparatively high, and the share in services is comparatively low 25%. The period since 1978 marks a break from the pre-reform period in two respects: first, a sharp acceleration in the transfer of labor out of farming, and, second, a steady shift of labor towards services in the non-farming sector. In the 17 years 1978-1995, the share of labor in farming has dropped by 18 percentage points, more than twice as rapid as the mere 13 percentage drop in the 26 years from 1952 to 1978 *(China Labor Statistical Yearbook* 1996: 12). From 1991 China has entered a new development phase of declining agricultural labor, which has since fallen by 19.4 million. A side effect of the single-minded emphasis on industrialization and bias against services in the pre-reform period was to put brakes on the transfer of labor out of farming, thus dampening the rise in per capita income. The period since 1978 has also seen a steady shift of non-farm employment towards services: its share in total employment has more than doubled from 12 to 25%. In part, this represents compensation for the neglect of the service sector in the pre-reform period, when the share of services rose by a mere 3 percentage points in 26 years and all but a small proportion of the labor outflow from agriculture was towards industry. If, as seems likely, the change in the sectoral distribution of employment between now and 2020 follows the same pattern as it has since 1990, the share of labor in agriculture would fall at the rate of just over 1.6 percentage point per year, and for every percentage point drop, the share of labor in services would rise by 0.8 percentage point and the share of industrial labor by 0.2 percentage points. The result would be that services would have the largest share followed by industry and agriculture, the exact reverse of the ordering in 1978. The distribution would be very similar to the distribution in the present-day South Korea (Table 3).

What are the social welfare implications of the sectoral re-distribution of the labor force? One way of *answering this* question is to examine how this would alter the working life of individual members of the labor force and the contingencies facing them. At present, a modal member of the rural labor force is self-employed in farming combined with some side-line activity, resident in the place of birth and regards children as source of support in old-age. A modal member of the urban labor force has worked for the same unit (most likely in the state sector) since entering the labor market and has little, if any, experience of unemployment. By 2020, most likely earlier,. a modal member of the labor force in rural and urban areas would be wage-employed on a terminable contract in either industry or services. If middle-aged, he or she would have experienced several job changes, including adapting to a very different occupation, spells of unemployment and also a change in the place of residence since entering the labor force, most likely from a village to a town or a city. He or she would also face the prospect of retirement at some age and may have only one child. This already holds true for increasing numbers, not only in urban but also in rural areas.

In sum, in tandem with the re-distribution of the labor force, the following interrelated changes with a direct bearing on social welfare are under way:

- shift from self to wage employment;
- the prospect of unemployment;
- migration and increased labor mobility;
- retirement at a particular age.

A major problem is that the current legal and administrative framework and the social security system are geared to individuals with the first rather than the second type of working life history. The designation "formally employed" (*zhigong ren*) is reserved for the urban labor force and does not apply to the rural labor force despite the fact that 28.5% (128.6 million) of them are wage-employed in TVEs. Regarded as "self employed", neither labor insurance (discussed below) nor many labor laws apply to wage-employees in rural areas, nor are they counted as unemployed when laid off or entitled to a retirement pension. Moreover, although migrant labor ("floating population") currently totals between 50 to 70 million (between 7 to 10% of labor force), labor migration is still largely treated as a temporary rather than as a permanent phenomenon. As elsewhere, migration in China is driven by the gap between urban and rural incomes, which since the mid 1980s has been widening and is now wider than in 1978, and is further fuelled by the construction boom in cities. Rural migrants are allowed to take up temporary or casual employment in cities but not allowed to settle permanently without permission, which is hard to obtain in large cities such as Beijing and Shanghai, though not any longer for small towns. Migration contributes to an increase in income in rural areas, but it also has implications for social security. Not being allowed to settle, a large percentage of migrants do not have permanent housing and are largely excluded from urban social security. Provisions for the portability of the old-age pensions and unemployment insurance either do not exist or are rudimentary.

Both the growth in wage employment in rural areas and rural out-migration, though massive, have yet to be incorporated in the Chinese social security system, which is still based on the anachronistic assumptions that rural labor is self-employed in farming and is immobile. Government policy is only slowly beginning to recognize labor migration as an irreversible feature of economic development. A tangible policy change is the emphasis on the proliferation and development of medium and small-towns and a loosening of restrictions on immigration into them.

2.3 Transition to a Market Economy

Economic reforms have brought in their wake a rapid and sustained growth rate and unprecedented rise in living standards, but they have also had a profound impact on labor insurance. Even though the Chinese economy has managed to skip the downward part of the J-curve of the transition from a command to a market economy, it is undergoing changes similar to those in transitional economies of Eastern Europe. In the present context, of special importance are the following:

- the growing replacement of permanent employment with terminable employment and the possibility of enterprise bankruptcy;
- the rapid growth of a non-state (including private) sector, and of wage employment in rural areas, which, for the most part, are outside the labor insurance umbrella ;
- growing incompatibility between the traditional social welfare responsibilities of enterprises and their economic role.

The proportion of employees on terminable as opposed to life-long contracts has risen from mere 2% in 1984, when it began to be introduced, to 41% of formal wage employees *(zhigong ren),* which excludes rural wage employees. These included in the total, a large majority of the wage-employed labor force that is now employed on terminable contracts. This trend away from permanent towards terminable employment and the possibility of an enterprise going bankrupt (still rare) are necessary for furthering efficiency and are central features of market economy. But they also create contingencies such as unemployment. The total number of registered urban unemployed (which excludes migrants from the countryside) which dropped sharply in the early 1980s has since 1985, except for a dip in 1991, been rising steadily. The "open" unemployment rate which fluctuated until 1992 has since risen. It would have risen even further had enterprises been allowed to shed surplus labor and state sector employees who are kept on the books and paid only a part of their wages also been counted. The true unemployment rate in urban areas is reckoned to be two to three times the actual rate. The prospect of large urban unemployment haunts the Chinese leadership.

Correlated with the rise in "visible" unemployment in recent years is a marked shift in the composition of the unemployed by status. From 1983 to 1991, new entrants to the labor force accounted for over 80% of the unemployed. In just two years from 1992 to 1994 their percentage has fallen by 20 percentage point due not to a fall in their numbers (which has slightly risen in recent years) but a steep rise in the numbers of laid-off workers *(China Labor Statistical Yearbook 1996:* 10). Unlike new entrants to the labor force, they are eligible for unemployment benefit. The shift in the composition of the unemployed towards laid-off workers will in the future accelerate as state enterprises are forced to shed their surplus labor, which is estimated to be between 10 to 20% of their labor force. This trend will be further re-enforced by a fall in new entrants to the labor force due to the fall in the school-age cohorts. This has two implications. First, the numbers receiving unemployment insurance would continue to rise, which requires an overhaul of the system. Second, because prospects for finding a job diminish with the age of the unemployed, China in the future may have a significant problem of long-term unemployment, particularly in some regions such as the Northeast.

The labor insurance system inherited from the pre-reform period has been founded in urban enterprises (especially stateowned) . Two changes linked directly with the transition to a market economy are eroding its foundations: first, the diminishing importance of the state sector as source of employment, and, second, the growing incompatibility between the extensive social welfare role of enterprises carried over from the pre-reform period and their adaptation to a market economy. The proportion of state-sector employees amongst total wage-employees has fallen steadily. The drop is a modest 5 percentage points if the proportion is only with respect to those officially termed as "formal employees", but a dramatic 24 percentage points if employees of TVEs are also included, as they should be. On the second count, the proportion of state-sector employees has fallen from 64% in 1978 to 40% in 1995. Of the total number of new jobs created since 1978, the state sector accounts for only 22% and of the remaining 78 percentage points, TVEs alone account for 66 percentage points (calculated from *China Labor Statistical Yearbook* 1996). As TVE employees are almost completely excluded from labor insurance, this development amounts to a massive shrinkage in the proportion of the wage-employed labor force covered by labor insurance. The trend is expected to continue because in the future most of the new jobs will be in TVEs or in non-state urban enterprises outside the umbrella of labor insurance, such as private enterprises and foreign-invested enterprises. In the future, the state sector rather than creating is likely to be losing jobs.

The extensive social welfare role of enterprises is a source of problems for both social security and enterprise reforms. Problems for social security, because it makes the coverage dependent on the financial position of the enterprise, eroding its uniformity and reliability. With the worsening financial position of state enterprises, many of them are not able to meet their labor insurance obligations. Problems for enterprise reform, because it forces the government to subsidize loss-making enterprises for reasons of social welfare. Firms in market economies also play an important social welfare role, which is extensive in some economies such as Japan. The problem in China is not that enterprises have social welfare responsibilities but that these date from when enterprises were "government agencies" and were not financially independent. These responsibilities were not decided either by or for enterprises in today's Chinese economy. Moreover, they have grown since the beginning of the reforms, for example, the increased number of pensioners enterprises have to support. The basic dilemma of enterprise reform in China is that strict adherence to the financial autonomy of enterprises erodes the coverage of labor insurance, which, in principle is independent of the employment unit. Conversely, the efforts to uphold labor insurance coverage through subsidies seriously comprises the principal aim of reform i.e., to make enterprises responsible for their profits and losses.

3. Social Security System and Labor Insurance

The Chinese social security system has two central features (for detailed discussion see Hussain, 1993). First, it consists of two separate sub-systems, urban and rural (discussed in Section 4), with different organizations and benefits - a common feature in developing economies. Second, the urban system remains segmented according to the ownership status of the employment unit (work unit in China), though not as tightly as before. Both features are anomalous, carry-overs from the pre-reform period. Employees of the government and state-owned enterprises (SOEs), almost all in cities, benefit from the comprehensive Labor Insurance, providing disability and old-age pensions, maternity and sickness benefits, medical care and, since 1986, unemployment benefits as well. There is a parallel, but less generous Labor Insurance for urban collectively-owned enterprises (COEs), also publicly-owned but of a lower status than SOEs. The anachronistic distinction between SOEs and COEs still survives and is carried over into Labor Insurance. A unified system for all urban employees is planned but only slowly being implemented, with some localities such as Shanghai taking steps towards unification of the system. The plan is to have a unified pension system for all employees by the turn of the century. Another problem is a minimal provision for those outside the umbrella of Labor Insurance, such as migrants.

3.1 Labor Insurance

Labor Insurance is characterized by three interlinked features: first, the absence of a specialized administration and fragmented management, second, a wide variation in benefits within the same scheme in some cases, and, third, highly decentralized and *ad hoc* financing. In the case of Labor Insurance, day-by-day administration rests largely with units of employment (work units or *danwei),* performing social welfare functions which in other economies would be performed by social security agencies. The government's role consists mainly of supervision and coordination, which is split between different government organizations. Whilst the Central Ministry of Personnel and Provincial or Municipal Personnel Bureau are responsible for government employees, employees of nongovernmental work units such as collective and state-owned enterprises are the responsibility of the Central Labor Ministry and Provincial or Municipal Labor Bureau. Recently some localities, such as Shanghai, Xiamen, Shenzhen and Hainan, have taken steps towards overcoming the split supervision and management of Labor Insurance by establishing a unified 'Social Security Administration'. However, the central leadership has yet to decide on the administrative framework for social security.

Although Labor Insurance is governed by national regulations, the details of organization, benefits and financing have come to vary widely due to the piecemeal and decentralized reforms in the 1980s. Variations across cities or work units are particularly marked in two areas: the financing of old-age pensions and the terms and financing of health insurance. In certain aspects, variations in Labor Insurance are likely to widen with the current trend towards provinces and municipalities each drawing up their own blue-prints for a radical reform of the Labor Insurance system. Strictly speaking, local and piecemeal attempts to sustain and reform Labor Insurance do not have a firm legal basis, and there is a growing need for comprehensive social security law.

Many of the distinctions which apply to the social security systems in Western countries do not apply to the Chinese system. In market economies there is an important distinction between 'Public' (or ‘socialized', as commonly termed. in China) social security schemes and welfare provisions by units of employment, such as old-age pensions and health care (termed 'occupational' welfare) (Titmuss: Ch.2). The distinction does not hold in the Chinese context. Given the central role of work units in its functioning, Labor Insurance is organized like 'occupational welfare'. But unlike 'occupational welfare' in market economies, the range of benefits under Labor Insurance are mandated by the government and in principle meant to be fairly uniform across work units. Moreover, as with social insurance, the government carries the ultimate financial responsibility for maintaining Labor Insurance. The distinction between ' financed from the government budget' and 'financed by employers' is therefore highly blurred in the Chinese context. A large majority of the labor force covered by Labor Insurance is in government organizations or state-owned enterprises, and lossmaking enterprises are kept afloat by subsidies from the government. In sum, the current Chinese social security system is a hybrid between variable 'occupational welfare' and relatively uniform social insurance. As pointed out earlier, the current social welfare role of enterprises dates from the pre--reform period and is a source of problems for both Labor Insurance and enterprise reforms. The problem is all the more serious because Chinese enterprises are not "naturally selected" for profitability, many of them in their present form are nonviable.

Labor Insurance consists of three main schemes:

- old-age and disability pensions;
- unemployment insurance (introduced in 1986);
- health care and maternity benefits.

The first and the third date from the 1950s, when Labor Insurance was introduced. The absence of unemployment insurance in the past reflected partly the ideological assumption that unemployment was a characteristic of capitalist economies, and partly the employment and recruitment policies. Employment was for life and the government carried responsibility for finding employment for the urban labor force. There have been periods of comparatively high urban unemployment in the past, but these were dealt with either through job creation or the return of the redundant labor force from the cities to the countryside (as during the period following the Great Leap forward). Until recently notably absent from the above list has been a wide-ranging social assistance scheme in urban areas aimed at guaranteeing a minimum living standard regardless of the employment record. Faced with growing unemployment and lay-offs in cities, the government has now introduced a means-tested social assistance scheme.

The above three schemes differ greatly in management and administration, financing and the problems they face. Old-age pensions and health insurance are large programs in terms of numbers covered and expenditure, which has risen sharply in the 1980s. Their management is in the hands of work units, which are also responsible for their financing, in the first instance at least. Whilst pension costs of employees of state-owned and collective enterprises are pooled, health care and maternity benefits still continue to be financed individually by units of employment, though recently some cities have begun to pool health care costs for major illnesses. In contrast, unemployment insurance is managed not by work units but by Provincial or Municipal Labor Bureaus and is financed by a payroll tax. It comes closest to being a 'public or socialized' social security scheme. All three schemes face major problems arising from the three transitions and the legacy of the Cultural Revolutionary period.

3.2 Old-Age Pensions

Pensions are a percentage of the last 'basic wage' (excluding bonuses) in employment and pensioners have also their health care cost covered by their ex-work unit. Unlike the cost of pensions, it is not pooled and, as we shall see, its coverage may vary greatly across work units. Pensions are based on a national schedule, ranging between 75 to 100% of the 'basic wage', and depend upon the years of employment and the date of recruitment. The ratio of average pensions to the average wage is 84% (1995 figure). Pensions are uprated with inflation, but a standard procedure for indexation has yet to emerge.

The management of old-age pensions still rests almost entirely with work units. They keep records of the parameters relevant to determining pensions, disburse pensions' of their ex-employees and are also responsible for their personal care. This highly decentralized system raises two sets of problems: first, its viability and efficiency and, second, the scope for abuse of the system. This system, which worked reasonably well when the number of pensioners was small, is under strain and will become increasingly cumbersome as the number of pensioners rise relative to the labor force. The disappearance of enterprises due to mergers, which are increasing, and bankruptcies, will compound the problem. Further, the keeping of records of employment and wages by enterprises makes it easier for them to abuse the system, and makes it more difficult for the authorities to prevent abuses. From the point of view of both efficiency and reducing the abuses, and ensuring a uniform service to pensioners, there are strong arguments in favor of transferring the management of the system from work units to a specialized social security agency.

Currently pension expenditure is financed almost entirely by employers on what is generally termed a 'pay-as-you-go' basis. Employee contributions exist in some cases and are likely to become common in the future. The pension costs of ex-employees of state-owned and collectively owned enterprises are pooled, separately in most cases. Enterprises participating in a pooling scheme devote a set percentage of their wage bill to pensions; both the percentage and the definition of the wage bill vary across localities and schemes. Contribution rates vary between 16 to 26% of the total wage bill. Since it is not the pool but enterprises which disburse pensions, the pooling arrangement works by an ex-post redistribution. Enterprises spending more than the percentage claim the difference and, conversely, those spending less pay the difference into the pool. Contributions to the pensions pool are not based in law, and compliance is significantly less than 100 and falling (World Bank 1996a).

The current pooling arrangements are a make-shift response to the problem of a wide variation in the ratio of pensioners to the labor force across work units.

The old-age pension scheme in China currently covers around 141 million employees and 31 million retirees, making it one of the largest in the world, and the numbers are expected to rise rapidly over the next two decades. But there is a wide mismatch between its size and its organization, which is highly fragmented and is only suitable for handling small numbers of pensioners. A series of piecemeal changes to the scheme since 1979, such as pooling, have. prevented it from collapsing, but they have also created new problems. The scheme suffers from a variety of problems, but it seems that the creation of a specialized and unified administrative structure (at least at the municipal level) has priority over other measures. Without this, it would seem very difficult to effectively address the other problems from which the scheme suffers, such as the abuse of the system and the absence of long-term planning of benefits and finances.

3.3 Unemployment Insurance

Unemployment insurance was introduced only in 1986 and has until now been a very limited scheme. It was originally confined to employees of state-owned enterprises, though in a number of cities larger collective enterprises are also included in the scheme. Only the following are eligible for unemployment insurance (for details see, Fu, Hussain, Pudney and Wang, 1992):

- those laid off due to bankruptcy, a major restructuring of the enterprise on the verge of bankruptcy, or disciplinary offences.
- contract workers on the expiry their contract.

As the first has been rare, the scheme may be regarded as simply a complement to employment on short-term contracts, which until now has been confined to newly recruited blue-collar employees only. A notable omission from the above list of the unemployed qualifying for benefits are "workers laid off for being surplus to the requirements of the enterprise". Until now they have been few in number, even though "surplus labor" is reported to be substantial. Enterprises rather than dismissing their surplus employees are supposed to deal with the problem internally. In effect, parallel to the 'social' unemployment schemes, enterprises run their own specific unemployment insurance schemes, retraining and job creation and placement schemes.

The unemployment insurance benefit is equal to a percentage of the average basic wage (excluding bonuses) over last two years in employment. The replacement percentage ranges between 50 and 75%, and depends on the years of employment. The recipients have their health care costs covered on a cost-sharing basis, for example, in Shanghai their share is 30%. The recipients are allowed to remain in their existing dwellings, but at present there is no separate allowance for house rent. This may pose a problem in the future as house rents are raised. Unemployment benefits are also uprated periodically in line with the cost of living index. Unlike a number of OECD economies, the receipt of benefits does not include requirements such as training or 'actively searching for a job'. The main categories of the unemployed not entitled to benefits include new entrants to the labor force or those who have exhausted their benefits. There is no special provision in the scheme for the long-term unemployed, which may be needed in the future. Currently 2.6 million out of the total of 5.2 million registered unemployed (around 50%) receive unemployment benefits, which is higher than the percentage in the US and UK (figures from *China Labor Statistics Yearbook 1996*: 91 & 428).

All enterprises or work units participating in the scheme are supposed to pay 1% of their total wage bill into the unemployment insurance fund. But this is the maximum and the rates are lower in some cities. Notwithstanding the low rate, the unemployment insurance fund has been in surplus but this is likely to change with increasing unemployment. The purpose of the unemployment insurance scheme in China is very different from those in market economies. It is not a response to (registered) urban unemployment, which is low by international standards. Rather it is intended first to encourage labor mobility, which has been exceptionally low in China, and, second, to make it possible for enterprises to adjust their labor to their needs, in particular to reduce 'surplus labor'. Given that the scheme is a necessary complement to employment on short-term contracts, it has contributed to increased labor mobility. However, the scheme has had little or no effect on the second count.

Unlike the old-age pension scheme and health insurance, the unemployment insurance scheme does not seem to suffer from major design problems. The main problems are that it is restricted to a section of the labor force, and the receipt of benefits is not linked retraining or to job search.

4. Rural Social Security

In contrast, to elaborate social security benefits enjoyed by most of the urban population, social security provisions in rural areas are sparse and highly variable. Labor Insurance does not apply to Town and Village Enterprises. The rural social security system consists of means-tested social relief to poor areas and households financed by the central and provincial governments and disaster relief. In addition, there are also locally organized and financed partial old-age pensions. Rural medical care now largely takes the form of a fee for service, though some localities have cooperative health insurance (discussed in Section 5). The sparseness of social provisions in rural areas would suggest that China's success in preventing deprivation in rural areas is due more to households having opportunities for earning a living either through farming and non-farming activities rather than to social security schemes.

The rural social security schemes and natural disaster relief come under the purview of the Civil Affairs Ministry or Provincial or County Civil Affairs Bureau, which are also responsible for neighbourhood committees in urban districts which perform a variety of functions, including the provision of residual social relief. The organization and the administration of rural social security schemes rests with the county and township governments (the lower tiers of government in rural areas) . Variations in rural social security schemes are even greater than in Labor Insurance because they still lack the foundation of regulations. Except for poor areas, the structure and the financing of social security is almost entirely left to counties and township governments, and differences can be large even amongst neighbouring rural counties within the same province or municipality.

The pronounced urban bias in social security provisions is not particular to China. It is found in many developing economies. Historically social insurance has been tied to wage labor in two senses (see Atkinson 1991). First, two of the principal contingencies usually covered by social insurance: retirement at a particular age and unemployment, are directly related to wage employment. Second, social insurance in most economies is typically financed by contributions from the wage-employed and their employers. Therefore the proportion of the labor force covered by social insurance depends crucially on the proportion in wage-employment. Although inequitable, to a degree it is unavoidable, given the problems in designing and financing social insurance schemes for the self- or the informally-employed even in developed economies.

The main problem does not lie with the differential treatment of the agricultural and non-agricultural labor force, but with the administrative distinction between the urban and the rural population, which is increasingly not consistent with the division between the wage-employed and the self-employed labor force. With the rapid growth of "town and village enterprises" in the 1980s, the numbers of the wage-employed amongst the rural labor force has risen sharply. For example, in 1991, TVEs employed around 128.5 million (29%) out of the total rural labor force of 450 million. The present administrative distinction between the urban and rural population is particularly anomalous in the case of the labor force in the rural counties within the precincts of cities, a substantial part of which may be wage-employed.

5. Health Status and Health Care

5.1 Health Situation

There are three aspects of the current health situation which deserve attention and call for a concerted policy for reversal: first, slow improvement or retrogression in child health over the reform period, second, persistence of wide interprovincial variations, and third, significant, and in some cases even a rising incidence, of easily preventable infectious and parasitic diseases, especially in rural areas.

One indicator of the health situation is the causes of death, which vary between rural and urban China (Table 4) and, following the usual convention, divide into three groups:

Group 1: Communicable, maternal, perinatal and nutritional conditions
Group 2: Non-Communicable diseases
Group 3: Injuries and Toxicosis

Emblematic of poverty and lack of adequate health care, the first group of diseases claim virtually all of their victims from developing countries. But, contrary to the usual presumption, non-communicable diseases are neither diseases of affluence nor necessarily of old-age. In China (rural and urban areas taken together) these diseases cause around 73% of deaths, more than four-and-half times as many as those due to Group 1 diseases. In the age group 30-44, these diseases are responsible for 57% of male deaths and 60% of female deaths (Global Burden of Disease; Health Financing: 96-97). Thus China, like other developing economies, is burdened with both communicable and non-communicable diseases.

Table 4 : Cause of Death in Urban and Rural China

	Urban Areas	Rural Areas
Group 1	6.6	8.2
Group 2	85.8	79.5
Group 3	7.6	12.3

Source: *Statistical Yearbook of China 1996*: 720-721.

With the pattern of death akin to that in middle-income economies, China is in the final stages of the "epidemiological transition" from the prevalence of deaths from Group 1 to the Group 2 diseases as the main cause of death. However, epidemiological transition is still far from completed. Communicable diseases still take a substantial and avoidable toll. Their incidence is much higher than suggested by their rank in causes of death both in rural and in urban areas. A survey in Sichuan revealed as many as 40% of infectious ailments in rural areas go unreported (Chen 1989).

Looking forward over the coming decades, how would the disease pattern change and what implications would it have for health care? Already the biggest killer, non-communicable diseases would rise further in importance as the main cause of death, as would their incidence especially amongst the elderly population. The pattern of causes of death in urban areas, if not in rural areas, will approach that in developed economies. The speed of elimination of infectious diseases will depend crucially on the implementation of the existing plan for the elimination of infectious diseases *(Agenda 21)*. Moreover, the narrowing of the gap between rural and urban areas will depend on widening access to health care by raising the health insurance coverage in rural areas and reducing inequality in health-care provision. The growing importance of non-communicable diseases suggests the need for campaigns for a healthier life-style and an additional tax on tobacco, a major cause of such diseases. With the aging of the population, the need for long-term care will rise.

5.2 Health-Care Provision

Comprised of three loosely connected strands, two large and one nascent, China's health care system involves of a large infrastructure and employs a huge number of personnel. There are in total 190, 000 health establishments and 4.3 million medical personnel, including doctors of both Western and Chinese medicine, nurses and paramedics (SYC 1996). Most of the doctors are employees of either public health departments or work units, the proportion of the self-employed (private practitioners) is small but growing. At the core of the health-care system are 68,000 hospitals housing 2.8 million beds. Hospitals vary widely in size and services provided; around 53,000 of them are rural (located in townships and villages, excluding those in county seats). As well dispensing in-patient care, hospitals also provide outpatient care.

The central role played by hospitals in the Chinese health care system is linked with the fact that an overwhelming majority of doctors are employees rather than self-employed. Countries where self-employment among doctors is common tend to have a more diversified institutional structure consisting of hospitals, clinics and small surgeries than China has. The role of hospitals raises the issue of a trade-off between efficiency and access. Typically, hospitals provide a diverse range of curative and diagnostic services, ambulatory care being just one of them, though many of the establishments in rural China are probably no more than clinics with a few beds. Some -of these services, such as in-patient and specialized care and diagnostic services, are subject to significant economies of scale, although not basic ambulatory care. On efficiency grounds, hospitals should be large, providing a diverse range of curative and diagnostic services; and should therefore be few in numbers and preferably located in densely populated areas so as to ensure a high utilization rate. But to ensure easy access, hospitals should be geographically dispersed and therefore large in numbers and comparatively small. The first implies a lower cost than the second but at the cost of being beyond easy reach of the rural population, which is of special relevance in a low-income country such as China with a large rural population and a underdeveloped transport and communication network. Analysis of household data indicates a dampening impact of distance on the use of medical care (WB:1996b) Currently, a balance between efficiency and broad access in China is achieved through a mix of hospitals of different sizes with a diverse range of services.

There are three separate health-care networks, each fairly decentralized and with loose connections. One is public, the second is "occupational" and the third is private. The distinction between them consists in the supervising agency, the source of funding and their clientele. By far the largest is the "Public Health Network", which performs the dual function of serving government employees and also the population at large and covers both rural and urban areas. It is not free at the point of service and only partially subsidized by the government. It is "public" in the sense that its staff are employees of departments of public health from the central down to the county level, which also act as supervisory agencies and partially subsidize operational and capital expenditure. Allied to it is the rural network of clinics and hospitals run by townships (the lowest government tier in rural areas) and villages (a communal rather than a governmental unit), which cover a large proportion of townships but as yet not all. Except in some regions, their staff are not employees of public health departments.

The "occupational" network is run by state-owned and larger collective enterprises, the armed forces, prisons and a range of other institutions. It is mainly urban and extensive, comprised of a disparate range of facilities each serving a restricted category of patients, to whom it is predominantly free at the point of service. The network is predominantly financed by "work units" and its staff are not employees of public health departments but of the parent unit. The third is the private medical service, which is more prevalent in rural than in urban areas. There are 172,000 private medical practitioners in urban areas and 930,000 "village doctors", who are the main source of primary medical care in rural areas (SYC 1996: 717; *Agricultural Yearbook 1995:* 321). Unlike their peers, private practitioners are not employees but self-employed. Their proliferation is a post-1978 development and prompted, in rural areas, by the collapse of cooperative health insurance and, in urban areas, by the rise in the number of people without health insurance.

Aside from curative services, there are three networks of preventive and early diagnostic services. These include the Epidemiological Prevention Services (EPS), Maternal and Child Health Service (MCH) and Family Planning Service (FPS) which receive their budgets from provincial and county government. But increasingly they have come to depend on fee-for-service, which has had a deleterious effect on preventive and early diagnostic services in some rural areas. Operating relatively independently each other, these networks provide overlapping services, which suggests scope for raising efficiency through administrative coordination and consolidation.

5.3 Medical Provision in Rural Areas

Compared to urban areas, two features mark out medical provision in rural areas: it is more sparse and more variable from locality to locality. There still remain many villages without any medical facility; the plan is to have a clinic in most villages by the year 2,000 *(Agenda 21:* 67). The 72% of the population classified as rural is served by a three-tiered medical network. The first tier consist of around 930, 000 "village doctors", 414,000 paramedics (health workers) and 381,000 midwives (Agricultural yearbook 1995: 321). Village doctors, an evolved form of "barefoot doctors" of the pre-reform period, are the first port of call for rural inhabitants needing primary medical care and channel patients to township health center hospitals. They engage in medical practice either full-time or part-time, as a side-line to farming. Except in a few localities where "Rural Cooperative Health Insurance" still survives, they charge fee-for-service and also receive a mark-up on (typically about 15%) prescriptions, which provides an incentive to over-prescribe drugs, an incentive which pervades the Chinese health-care system.

The second tier consists of 52,000 rural health center/hospitals with 732,000 beds (25 percent of the total), that are staffed by just over one million junior doctors and other medical personnel (1994 figures, *Agricultural Yearbook* 1995: 318). They operate on fee-for-service basis, but a part of their costs are covered by the rural local government. The extent of subsidies varies widely depending on local revenue. Richer localities with developed TVEs tend to have better facilities than poorer ones. The first two tiers are local and not an integral part of the public health network, though they are supervised by county health bureaus. The top tier of the system is made up of county hospitals, numbering around 4,000 with one million beds, these dovetail into urban hospitals. These hospitals are usually the last point of referral for rural patients, since a few can afford the services of large specialized city hospitals.

The urban-rural gap in health-care provision is wide, and, more serious, rather than narrowing since 1985 it has become wider. Whilst since 1985 the number of hospital beds and medical personnel (doctors, nurses and paramedics) has been rising in urban areas, it has been falling in rural areas (at the county level). Among medical personnel, the number of doctors and nurses has slightly risen, the number paramedics has been fallen sharply. A part of the decline in hospital beds in rural areas is due to the consolidation of facilities in urban hospitals which are more intensively used than rural hospitals and increasingly used by the rural population. But for most rural inhabitants for whom county hospitals are the medical facility of last resort, the reduction in number of hospital beds in rural areas represents a reduction in accessible medical facilities.

5.4 Health Care Financing - Sources and Uses

Currently, China devotes 3.8% percent of GDP (1993 figure) to health care, which is up from 3.0% in 1978 and is comparatively high for a low-income country. The reported percentage would be higher but for comprehensive government price controls on medical treatment and drugs, and may be an underestimate due to under-reporting of out-of-pocket expenses. Extrapolating from international trends, this percentage will rise driven by two factors: first, the aging of the population, second, rising cost per treatment as a result of rising wages of medical personnel and increasing non-labor costs.

Turning to sources of health care expenditure, their importance derives from their implication for the distribution of the demand for medical care and its cost. For example, under financing through fee-for-service (without any insurance), the burden falls entirely on patients and is distributed according to medical care dispensed. This usually means that a proportion of those stricker with illness either purchase medical treatment at the cost of slipping into poverty or cut down and forego treatment but pay the price in ill health and a higher risk of avoidable death. Either choice creates a vicious circle between inadequate medical care and poverty. Fee-for-service is particularly inequitable when it is mostly confined to the relatively poor section of the population, as it is in China. While most of the urban population is covered by health insurance, all but a small proportion of the rural population is subject to fee-for-service. In contrast, financing through insurance (commercial or non-profit) by spreading the burden widely over the covered population rather than just patients, loosens the link between payment and medical care, the extent of loosening depending on the terms of insurance. An inevitable consequence of health insurance is a higher demand and expenditure on medical care. A part of this increase is justified and fits in with the social purpose of health insurance: to provide medical care to those in need but forced to forego it under the fee-for-service arrangement. But there is also a part which is wasteful. However, the main problem is that it is not easy to distinguish between justified increase in demand and waste.

The three main sources of financing for health care in China are government subsidies, the health insurance schemes and individuals (termed "out-of-pocket" expenses) . Over the reform period the first two have diminished in importance, shifting a greater burden of financing to the third. Government financing for health is channelled in two forms: first, subsidies on curative and preventive services for the population at large (here termed "spending from the budget") and, second, re-imbursement under the "Government Health Insurance Service" (GIS). Grouping the latter with the other employee health insurance scheme (Labor Insurance), the composition of health financing in selective years of the reform period is shown in Table 5. Out-of-pocket expenses cover a variety of payments by individuals with different distributive implications. These include "full" fee-for-service, co-payment and registration fee (which fall entirely on those receiving treatment), on the one hand, and individual contribution towards insurance (which falls on all those covered under the scheme). The latter is only common in rural cooperative schemes but still rare in the occupational schemes covering the urban population.

Table 5: Sources of Health Financing (%)

	1978	1986	1993
Government Budget[1]	28	32	14
Insurance Schemes[2]	30	33	36
Rural Insurance Schemes	20	5	2
Out of Pocket[3]	20	26	42
Others	2	4	6
Health Expenditure, % of GDP	3.0	3.2	3.8

Note: 1. Excludes insurance expenses for government employees.
2. Includes the insurance schemes for government employees (GIS) and Labour Insurance (LI).
3. Includes both user fee, co-payment and fee-for-service

Source: World Bank 1996b

In the past 15 years the composition of health expenditure has undergone a major change with highly adverse implications for the distribution of medical expenditure by income groups and between the ill and healthy. In the 8 years between 1978 to 1986, the principal change consisted of a huge reduction in the share of rural cooperative insurance schemes and a significant rise in the share of out-of-pocket expenses, most likely, due almost entirely to the shift to fee-for-service in rural areas. The following 7 years saw change as large as that in the preceding 8 years, but this time it consisted largely of a shift of expenditure from the government budget to the pockets to urban as well as rural patients. The share of out-of-pocket expenses is likely to be an under-estimate because it excludes under-the-table or side-payments to medical personnel, which are improper or illegal and therefore go unreported. Circumstantial evidence suggests that these have risen in importance. The main cause of the changed pattern is a sharp fall in the ratio of government revenue to GDP, which forced the government to cut subsidies on health care. A particular casualty of this squeeze is the Epidemic Prevention Service (EPS), which until 1985 was entirely funded from the budget. The proportion covered by the budget has since fallen to half of the total costs. As a result, field visits have fallen sharply in frequency and nonremunerative services have been neglected.

5.5 Health Insurance Schemes

Compared to developing economies in Asia, China has a high proportion of its population with health insurance, mostly noncontributory in urban areas and contributory in rural areas. Given its high rate of growth and its experience with health insurance, among large developing economies, China has great potential for extending health insurance cover to a large majority of the population in the near future. There are three types of public (non-commercial) schemes for covering the cost of health care, and private and commercial health insurance is rare or non-existent. These include labor insurance, the "government employee scheme" (GIS) and the cooperative medical care schemes. The first two are occupational schemes tied to employment, and the third is village-based, which after a period of decline is undergoing a revival.

A schematic outline of the three health insurance schemes is shown in Table 6. Broadly, the main issues in reform of health insurance are two: first, increasing the proportion of the population with a health insurance umbrella, especially in rural areas, and, second, an overhaul of LI and GIS which in terms of numbers are large schemes. The two aims are partially interrelated.

As pointed out earlier, both LI and GIS are a part of a wider social welfare package which includes retirement and disability pensions. Neither is an integrated scheme. Both fail to use adequate risk pooling. In particular, LI consist of arrangements whereby work units either provide or cover the cost of health care for their respective labor forces and retirees. In contrast, the rural cooperative health insurance is standalone, not part of a wider social welfare package. Moreover, LI is organizationally separate from GIS even though it is almost identical in design to GIS and is anchored in SOEs. It differs from occupational health schemes in market economies in that, being an inheritance from the pre-reform period, it is not designed for enterprises in a market economy.

As increasingly recognized in China, Labor Insurance in the present form has a limited life expectancy. The main reason is that health insurance is underwritten by enterprises, each for its own employees, and there is, as yet, no systematic co-insurance mechanism for pooling risks across enterprises, other that the government may provide subsidies when the enterprise is unable to meet insurance claims and some localities, such as Beijing, have introduced a pooling for major medical expenditures. The highly decentralized risk-bearing by enterprises is unsustainable when risks are unevenly distributed because of wide differences in the age composition of the labor force and the ratio of retirees to the labor force. Added to this, the financial position of enterprises is deteriorating. The occupational insurance schemes suffer from the fundamental flaw of insufficient risk pooling to be viable. Without a complete overhaul of the present health insurance arrangement under LI, there will be a progressive reduction in the numbers covered and a steady and an uncertain erosion of benefits for those who remain covered. The latter has been happening. Although in principle uniform, medical benefits under labor insurance have come to vary widely depending on the financial health of the work units. Enterprises in financial difficult delay reimbursement or cut down on the proportion of re-imbursed costs. A revision of the benefit schedule is needed but the problem is that it is undergoing a piecemeal revision forced by the financial position of the enterprises often with damaging implications for the quality of health- insurance cover. Labor Insurance is increasingly becoming like an umbrella with holes. Among urban workers, the mounting health care costs now rank as the prime concern well ahead of the fear of unemployment and the security of old-age pensions (Beijing Review, No. 3, 1997: 21).

Table 6: Health Insurance Schemes

Features/Scheme	Labor Insurance Scheme	Public Service Scheme	Cooperative Scheme
Membership	SOE & COE employees (current & retired) & their dependants	Government and other public employees & dependants	Village residents
Noose Covered	44 million & a % of 31.5 in COE and their dependants	69 million & dependants	10% of the rural population: 86 million
Geographical focus	Urban	Urban	Rural
Medical care Providers	Enterprise clinics and designated hospitals	Institutional clinics and designated MOH hospitals	Rural doctors; Township/ village Health Centers; county hospitals
Financed by	Mostly enterprises	Government budget	Beneficiaries and collective welfare funds
Managed by	Enterprises and the government	Institutions and local public health authorities	Villages and townships
Cost Containment	Piecemeal measures by work units	Piecemeal	Built into the design of the scheme

The last few years have seen a series of piecemeal reforms. These include the progressive amalgamation of GIS and LI and the introduction of a health budget, as in Shanghai, selective pooling of major medical costs across enterprises in a number of cities, such as Beijing, and the introduction of experimental schemes in Zhenjiang and Jiujiang. The major feature of these schemes is, first, the introduction of joint funding by work units, the governments and beneficiaries, second, the allocation of risk bearing between beneficiaries and the insurance schemes, and, third, the introduction of a mechanism for cost-containment. This experiment has now been extended to 50 locations. By now China has accumulated enough knowledge about feasible options for a reform of health insurance in urban areas. The main task for the coming years is the formulation of a national framework drawing on experimental reforms.

5.6 Rural Cooperative Health Insurance

Rural cooperative health insurance developed as an off-shoot of collective agriculture. A part of collective income went into the establishment and the running of health station (cooperative medical care clinics) at the brigade (village) level. These were staffed by local inhabitants with elementary medical training on top of primary education, known as "barefoot doctors" (now termed rural doctors) They were paid by the collectives on the remuneration system used to pay farmers. The system was partly financed by the collective, partly by pre-payment and co-payment. The system received a boost during the Cultural Revolutionary period and by the mid 1970s covered around 90% of villages.

The decollectivisation of the rural economy unravelled the cooperative health insurance schemes with which it was intertwined. Its collapse was due to three factors: first, the disappearance of the administrative foundation of the schemes, second, a decline in collective funds which subsidized the schemes, and, third, the erosion of cooperative ideology. The scheme as inherited from the pre-reform period suffered from major defects. The quality of service varied widely and it involved coercion. But it served an important function of bringing medical care to villages, albeit elementary. Commitment of cooperative health insurance schemes still remains; an important index of which is the survival of cooperative schemes in many localities, which, according to field studies, are more widespread than previously believed. A notable step towards a revival rural cooperative health insurance schemes is the "Sichuan Rural Health Experiment". The experimental scheme was organized in 1989-90 and covered a sample of 26 villages and 40,443 individuals. There are now a wide range of cooperative health insurance schemes in rural areas, but most of these are in relatively prosperous areas.

6. Conclusions

The Chinese social security system is still marked by pre-reform distinctions, even though changes brought about by the economic reforms have cut the ground from underneath them. In particular, the assumption that 'rural' corresponds to 'self--employed' and urban to 'employed', in the state or the collective sector, which underlies the segmentation in the social security provision between urban and rural areas. The urban and rural areas are no longer separated by a wall of administrative restrictions as they were pre 1978. There are a large number of immigrants who live and work in urban areas. Migration poses a special problem for the Chinese social security provisions which still remain premised on the assumption that the population is immobile. Not only has rural-urban migration increased but there is also a significant increase in rural to rural migration.

A combined social security system for urban and rural areas, although desirable, is not feasible in the immediate future for financial and administrative reasons. Nor is a substantial narrowing of the gaps in provision. The tax system these require is decades in the future. The urban and the rural systems have to be reformed separately. However, there would seem to be little reason to regard reform of rural social security as a task for later, which is the current official position.

Current reform proposals envisage each province having its own Labor Insurance schemes. National Labor Insurance is precluded by the wide economic differences amongst provinces and their divergent interests. It would involve substantial transfers between provinces, given the wide variation in the ratio of pensioners to the labor force covered by labor insurance. A mechanism to secure such transfers is absent; the reform of fiscal relations between government is under way and has yet to be completed. However, what seems feasible is a 'federal framework' which, while permitting provincial variation, provides for the transferability of welfare rights, especially pension rights, across the country.

Reform of Labor Insurance requires that work units shed most of their mandated social welfare obligations and transfer these obligations to social security agencies and their financing to a combination of social security contributions and general taxes. The case for such reform is strong. The present enterprise population is not 'naturally selected' for a market economy. Many are insolvent, unable to meet their liabilities from own funds; their social welfare obligations are either financed in disguise by the government or not met as expected. The present system has elements of both and creates uncertainty for employees and disguises the true cost of Labor Insurance.

Reform of Labor Insurance also requires reassessing benefits in terms of what can be financed and eliminating the status distinction between the state-sector and the non-state sector employees, which is a barrier to labor mobility and has become a huge handicap for the state sector.

In rural areas, reform requires the institution of a parallel labor insurance scheme financed by employer and employee contributions at least in larger rural enterprises. The benefits, should be determined on the basis of what can be financed, rather than modelled on Labor Insurance. There is also a need for reform of social security schemes for farming households and the informally employed to ensure at least minimum provision, presently ill-defined. This will require the institution of an adequate rural local taxation system and a mechanism of transfer to poor areas, and also a further development and the systematization of existing cooperative social welfare schemes.

In health care and health insurance, major issues in urban areas are:

- widening the range of risk pooling by spreading costs and contribution across enterprises and a progressive elimination of fragmentation according to the status of the work unit (government agency, SOE, COE and non-state enterprises);
- a progressive disengagement of the provision of medical services from the financing of health insurance;
- a re-definition of benefit entitlement and a division of benefits between those available to all regardless of the work unit and those left to the discretion of the work unit;
- the introduction of payment by beneficiaries through a generally applicable schedule of pre-payment, deductibles and co-payments.
- forward-looking financial planning and the introduction of a system of cost-containment and monitoring of services delivered by providers.

Main issues for the establishment of a community healthcare insurance in rural areas are the following:

- The source of finance for the subsidization of the scheme, except in some prosperous areas the scheme cannot be financed by premia and co-payments alone. Thus an extension of the scheme will require additional government expenditure by various tiers of the government.
- An administrative organization for collecting premia and making payments to providers.
- A mechanism to keep administrative and medical costs in check and formulation of a budget.
- Transparency in the operation of the scheme and accountability to beneficiaries.

The fourth is of central importance for collective action to set up and sustain a cooperative scheme. However, it does pose the problem of a village being too small to allow sufficient pooling of the risk of catastrophic illness. A possible way out is a coinsurance scheme at the township or the village level. China now has in place elements for a widespread introduction of cost-effective rural cooperative health insurance schemes. First, much of the rural population is familiar with cooperative health insurance schemes and does not need conversion to benefits of health insurance. The establishment of elected village councils in recent years provides the foundations for an administrative structure for the operation of schemes. Besides, the existence of village doctors and a network of village/township health posts and hospitals means that many of village dispose of the medical infrastructure for such operation of the schemes.

References

1. Agenda 21 (1994): China's Agenda 21 - White Paper on China's Population, Environment, and Development in the 21st Centur Beijing.
2. Atkinson, Anthony B. "Social Insurance", Welfare State Programme Discussion Papers, No. 65, London School of Economics, 1991.
3. BR (Beijing Review), Vol. 36, No. 47, November 22-28, 1993
4. Barr, Nicholas. " Economic Transfers in Russia: Problems and Some Policy Directions", Economics of Transition, 1 (3), 1993, 317344.
5. Brown, L (1995): Who Will Feed Chain? Wake-Up Call For A Small Planet, New York: Norton.
6. Chen,G.C: (1989): Medicine in Rural China, University of California Press.
7. Cutler, D.M.; Poterba, J.M.; Sheiner, L.M.; Summers, L.H. (1990): "An Aging Society: Opportunity or Challenge", Brookings Paper on Economic Activity, I.
8. Dr6ze, J. and Sen, A.K. Hunger and Public Action, Oxford: Oxford University Press, 1989.
9. Howes, Stephen. "Income Inequality in Urban China in the 1980s: Level, Trends and Determinants", Economic Transformation and Public Finance Discussion Papers, No.3, London School of Economics, 1993.
10. Global Burden of Disease, Harvard Institute of Public Health, World Bank and WHO.
11. Howes, Stephen and Hussain, Athar. "Regional Growth Patterns in Rural China", mimeo, London School of Economics, 1993.
12. Hussain, Athar. and Stern, Nicholas. "Economic Transition on the Other Side of the Wall - China", mimeo, London School of Economics, 1993.
13. Hussain, Athar (1993). "Reform of the Chinese Social Security System", China Programme Discussion Papers, No.27, London School of Economics, 1993.
14. Peng, X. "Recent Trends in China's Population and Their Implications", mimeo, London School of Economics.
15. SSB (State Statistical Bureau) (1996): Statistical Yearbook of China 1996, Beijing.
16. SSB (State Statistical Bureau) (1996): China Labour Statistical Yearbook 1996, Beijing.
17. SSB-(State Statistical Bureau) (1996): China Population Yearbook 1996, Beijing.
18. Titmuss, R. (1992): Essays on the 'Welfare Sate, London: Allen and Unwin.
19. UN (1996): Human Development Report 1996, New York.

20. World-Bank (1992): China - Strategies for Reducing Poverty in the 199s. Washington, D.C.
21. World Bank (1996): World Development Report 1996. Washington, D.C.
22. World Bank (1996a): China: Pension System Reform. Washington, D. C.
23. World Bank (1996b): China: Issues and Options in Health Financing. Washington, D.C.

CHAPTER 15

CHINESE RURAL SOCIAL SECURITY AND LAND HOLDING

YAOHUI ZHAO
China Center for Economic Research, Peking University
Beijing 100871, P. R. China
E-mail: yhzhao@ccer.pku.edu.cn

G. JAMES WEN
Department of Economics, Trinity College
Hartford, CT 06106, USA
E-mail: jwen@mail.trincoll.edu

After examining the institutional background of land holding and old age support in rural China and the supporting mechanisms for the elderly under the collective and household responsibility systems, the paper analyzes the mechanisms for old-age support. Several hypotheses are derived regarding the effects on the need for savings from a few factors, namely, the changes in the management system, fertility rate and livelihood of elderly. All these changes lead to a greater demand for alternative instruments for saving.

1. Introduction

Chinese rural institutions have undergone dramatic transformations since 1949, most notably collectivization in the 1950s and de-collectivization in the early 1980s. The social security system also changed dramatically. In this paper, we analyze the shift of the means of old age support in rural China as a result of economic reform and the adequacy or inadequacy of the system as it stands now and in the future.

We argue that during the period of collective management of land, with the elimination of private land ownership, intergenerational transfer within the whole collective replaced intergenerational transfer within the family as the primary means of old age support. With the reinstatement of household responsibility for land, support for the elderly fell back onto the shoulders of families thus increasing the need for individual savings as a vehicle for inter-temporal transfer. However, because of incomplete de-collectivization, namely, the continued ownership of land by collectives and the lack of investment alternatives that can yield reasonable rates of return, the savings of rural people have been inadequately rewarded.

Specifically, this paper addresses the following questions:

(1) How do intergenerational transfers perform under the household responsibility system as compared to collective management? Or, why is the model of inter-temporal transfer more appropriate in describing post-reform consumption behavior?

(2) What factors affect the need for private savings in inter-temporal transfers in rural China and why is the propensity to save higher under the household responsibility system and expected to increase further in the future?

(3) What types of savings instruments are available and what returns are being offered? Why is the current land collective ownership inadequate in providing support for the rural elderly?

The paper is organized as follows. The first section discusses the institutional background of land holding and old age support in rural China. The second section examines the supporting mechanisms for the elderly under both the collective and household responsibility systems in terms of pure intergenerational transfers in the absence of saving. The analysis shows how a feasible mechanism under the collectives became infeasible under a decentralized system. The third section examines the mechanisms for old-age support by introducing savings into the picture to show how inter-temporal consumption can be smoothed. Several hypothesies are derived regarding the effects on the need for savings from a few factors, namely, the change in the management system, fertility rate and whether the elderly live alone. All these changes lead to a greater demand for alternative instruments for saving. The fourth and the fifth sections then discuss the viability of various means of savings, paying special attention to land ownership. Conclusions and comments are presented in Section six.

2. Rural land holding and old-age support—the institutional background

Because of the lack of social security programs and security in private property rights in traditional China, the family was been the major source of support for the rural elderly. The support was secured through two means: one, high fertility and efforts to foster of filial piety; the other, the accumulation of physical and financial resources as insurance against non-filial behavior. A typical traditional family model was multi-generations housed under one roof, with the most senior controlling the resources.

Land was one of the most important forms of resources protecting against old age poverty in traditional China. The oldest male in a family usually held the land; while his sons served as laborers and managers whose incomes supported the parents. The land was distributed among sons only after the death of the oldest male. The prospect of losing the inheritance right was a powerful deterrent to non-filial behavior and fostered the intergenerational transfer of income within the family. In the case of the death of all of the children, the elderly could still live on the rent, or on the income received from selling the land and other assets. This is equivalent to an inter-temporal transfer. Therefore, the traditional system of old-age support was a combination of intergenerational and inter-temporal transfer of wealth, with emphasis on intergenerational transfers. The land, by its very nature, played a crucial role in making such a system workable.

However, in the mid-1950s, as a result of the collectivization movement, the private ownership of land and other means of production was eliminated, thus depriving people of the ability to accumulate assets. New social institutions were consequently invented to substitute for the old. One was the involvement of the collective in family matters to help maintain intergenerational income transfers within a family. For example, a family had to get approval from the collective in order to divide family assets among the sons (Wang 1995). Another was to guarantee the minimum living standards of the elderly by distributing part of the collective produce on a per capita basis. This system was an insurance against the risk of having no children at old age. It is equivalent to an intergenerational transfer across all members of the collective. This new institutional arrangement effectively reduced the need for asset accumulation by any individual member. In the jargon of economics, old-age support in this period was mostly intergenerational transfers across a larger pool of people.

In the early 1980s, the great agricultural reform returned the management of land to farm households while keeping the collective ownership of land intact. The task of providing support for the elderly fall back onto farm households. However, without private ownership of land, the ability of people to accumulate assets is severely limited. This gives rise to two problems. First, there is no effective means to ensure that children will provide for their parents because the elderly do not have important financial leverage such as land. Second, the ability of people to make inter-temporal transfers as a means to reduce the risk of not having the support of their children is also strained. In addition, there are new challenges facing the rural elderly, namely, the reduction in the number of children, and the increasing uncertainty brought about by the shrinkage of family size, the migration of the young to the cities, etc.

3. A system of old-age support via Intergenerational transfer and its institutional requirement

During the collective period, production and income allocation was centralized at the collective level (production team, usually the size of a natural village). After the harvest, part of the output was delivered to the state as a tax and part was retained by the collective to pay for administrative costs and welfare expenditures. The remainder was distributed among the households. The primary basis for income distribution was population, the rest labor. It is commonly agreed that the distribution to labor was mostly based on labor participation, instead of work effort, either because difficulties in monitoring or the lack of a mechanism for penalizing lack of efforts (Lin 1990).

Let Y(N, L) be the output of the collective production, where N is the total number of laborers in the collective and L is total land. Let M be the total number of elderly, defined as those who do not participate in work because of poor health or the general weakness.[1] Assuming constant returns to scale, output can also be expressed as a function of per capita inputs Y=(N+M) $y(\hat{N}, \hat{L})$, where $\hat{N}=\frac{N}{N+M}$ is the proportion of working population and $\hat{L}=\frac{L}{N+M}$ is per capita land. A proportion a (0<a<1) of the output is distributed based on population and the rest (1-a) is distributed based on labor. Therefore, non-labor income available to everyone is ay, and labor income for each laborer is (1-a) $\frac{N+M}{N}$ y.

Denote the number of workers and the incapacitated elderly in a family as n and m respectively. Assume that incomes are allocated among family members in an egalitarian manner. Since total labor income in a household is n(1-a) $\frac{N+M}{N}$ y, each member within a family is entitled to $\frac{n}{n+m}$ (1-a) $\frac{N+M}{N}$ y, which is what each worker or elderly person receives in addition to non-labor income determined at the village level, where m is the number of elderly in the household and $\frac{n}{n+m}$ the share

[1] Young children born into the family are considered pre-determined in the model. The number of young children is not explicitly treated in the model because they are dependents just like the elderly. One may think of M as being the sum of dependents who need support.

of working population among all members of a family. Denote $\hat{n} = \frac{n}{n+m}$, thus each worker contributes a proportion (1-$\hat{n}$) of his income to the elderly.

Assume that a person lives for 2 periods: he works in period 1 then becomes an incapacitated elderly person in period 2. Let C_1 be his consumption in period 1 and C_2 in period 2 and denote y_1 as per capita income of the collective in period 1 and y_2 as that in period 2. Applying the same system of notation to the proportion of working people in both collective and household, under our assumption, the budget constraints for a person during the two periods are:

$$C_1 = a\, y_1 + \hat{n}_1 (1-a) \frac{1}{\hat{N}_1}\, y_1$$

$$C_2 = a\, y_2 + \hat{n}_2 (1-a) \frac{1}{\hat{N}_2}\, y_2$$

Since savings are not permitted in this model, consumption in each period is entirely determined by the available resources. For an elderly person, consumption is determined by his own allocated income and by sharing the returns to laborers in the family.

Now let us introduce uncertainty into the picture. The uncertainty of consumption in the second period comes from the possible infertility, mortality of children, or the unwillingness of children to support their parents.[2] All these cases can be considered as if there are no supporting children. Therefore, the variable n is defined as the number of supporting children and the uncertainty is summarized by the variable $\hat{n}_2$, which takes the value of larger than 0 at a probability p and 0 at a probability (1-p). Denote consumption in these two possible states of nature as C_2^1 (when $\hat{n}_2$>0) and C_2^2 (when $\hat{n}_2$=0). In case of no supporting children, the consumption of an elderly person would be financed solely by income from collective distribution:[3]

$$C_2^2 = a\, y_2$$

[2] When the grown children live in separate households, the probability that they do not provide for their parents increases. In the collective period, the collectives were capable of forcing the children of the elderly to support the parents because the collectives controlled income allocation. Under the household responsibility system, the enforcement becomes less feasible.

[3] In case the elderly has no surviving children and no other source of income, and has lost the ability to work, the rural collective is supposed to provide necessary living arrangements to them. The social welfare system was established in 1956 right after the popularization of rural collectives and later developed into a system of "five guarantees" which guarantees food, clothing, housing, medical care and burial in case of death and education for orphans. The system provided for the minimum level of living arrangements for the most destitute elderly.

The difference in incomes in the two states of nature is

$$C_2^1 - C_2^2 = \hat{n}_2 \ (1\text{-a}) \frac{1}{\hat{N}_2} \ y_2 .$$

If $\hat{n}_2 = \hat{N}_2$, i.e., the share of young workers in a family equals the overall proportion in the village, then

$$C_2^1 - C_2^2 = (1\text{-a}) \ y_2 .$$

It shows the larger the share of income distributed based on population, the better off the elderly in the case of no support from their children.

Since the early 1980s, the household responsibility system has replaced collective production. Land is allocated to each individual household. After paying taxes and meeting procurement quota requirements, the household is free to dispose of the rest of the output.

Assuming that the household production technology is constant returns to scale, the value of output takes the form

$$Z(n,l)=(n+m)z(\hat{n},\hat{l}),$$

where $\hat{l}$ is per capita land in the household. z(.) is the value of per capita output. Assuming that the output is shared equally among all members of a household, and denote z_1 as per capita household income in period 1 and z_2 in period 2, the budget constraints are

$$C_1 = z_1$$
$$C_2 = z_2 .$$

If an elderly person had the misfortune of not getting support from any children, the only possible source of income would be rental income from leasing out his land, R($\hat{l}_2$), where $\hat{l}_2$ is his land size at old-age. Under this setting the difference between the two states is

$$C_2^1 - C_2^2 = z_2 + R(\hat{l}_2).$$

To summarize the above discussion, let us compare the consumption levels for the elderly person with and without supporting children under the collective and household responsibility systems.

3.1 The consumption of the elderly with supporting children

For a family with supporting children, if its labor share is the same as the whole village, then the consumption of the elderly is equal to per capita output under both systems. However, because the labor productivity is much higher under the household responsibility system than collective management, the elderly with supporting children are clearly better off under household responsibility system than under collective management. Many authors (McMillan and Zhu 1989, Lin 1992) have shown that labor productivity increased by at least 40 percent after management was privatized.

3.2 The consumption of the elderly without supporting children

Consumption under collective management was a fixed share of per capita output of the collective. The share was normally set at 70 percent in most rural collectives (Bai 1998).

$$C_2^2 \,|\text{collective}= \text{a}\, y_2 .$$

Consumption under the household responsibility system is the rent from the land.

$$C_2^2 \,|\text{household}= \text{R}(\hat{l}_2).$$

Since the land is distributed according to population, the land of an elderly is equal person to per capita land in the village, which averaged 0.1 hectare in 1995 for the whole country. There are no available statistics regarding the amount of rent being commanded by land, but according to some anecdotal evidence, it is rather insignificant, and in some developed areas even negative. (Add reference.) Under such circumstances the rent alone is not sufficient for providing old age support.

Based on the above analysis, the consumption of the elderly without any supporting children is clearly less under the household responsibility system than under the collective system. Thus, if rural people approaching retirement age had expected to rely on the collective as the last resort for old age support and thus had saved little, they were worse off if for some reason support from their children is unavailable. There is no insurance against the situation of no supporting children. In the event of death or incapacitation of the children, there is little life insurance in rural China. In the case of children refusing to provide support for their parents, the village cadres can do little because the power of income allocation is no longer in their hands. The welfare system that had provided minimum support for the childless rural elderly has also become less reliable with the dismantling of the collective.[4] The rural people soon realize that they must rely on their own savings to

[4] When explaining the definition of "the census of five-guarantee households," *The Encyclopedia of China's Social Security System* compiled by the Ministry of Civil Affairs (editorial committee 1995) says (pp. 943-44): "Since the 3rd Plenum of the 11th Central Committee meetings, various rural policies have brought about a rapid development of rural economy and a large improvement in the living

prevent poverty at old age.

4. A model of old-age support with possibilities of inter-temporal transfer

Denoting savings in the first period by a person as S_1, the individual budget constraint under collective management is

$$S_1 = a\, y_1 + \hat{n}_1 (1-a) \frac{1}{\hat{N}_1} y_1 - C_1$$

$$C_2 = (1+r) S_1 + a\, y_2 + \hat{n}_2 (1-a) \frac{1}{\hat{N}_2} y_2 .$$

The inter-temporal budget constraint can be expressed in terms of the tradeoff between consumption in the two periods:

$$C_2 = (1+r)[\, a\, y_1 + \hat{n}_1 (1-a) \frac{1}{\hat{N}_1} y_1 - C_1] + a\, y_2 + \hat{n}_2 (1-a) \frac{1}{\hat{N}_2} y_2 .$$

When there is uncertainty with respect to the number of supporting children in the old age, and assuming that the household labor share is the same as the village as a whole, i.e., $\hat{n}_1 = \hat{N}_1$ and $\hat{n}_2 = \hat{N}_2$ then the inter-temporal budget is reduced to

$$\text{p: } C_2^1 = (1+r)[\, y_1 - C_1] + y_2$$

$$\text{1-p: } C_2^2 = (1+r)[a\, y_1 - C_1] + a\, y_2$$

Similarly, the budget constraint for an individual under household responsibility system is:

$$S_1 = z_1 - C_1$$

$$C_2 = (1+r) S_1 + z_2 .$$

Combining the two and expressing the result in terms of inter-temporal tradeoff, the budget constraint can be expressed in one equation:

$$C_2 = (1+r)[\, z_1 - C_1] + z_2 .$$

With uncertainty in having supporting children at old age, the budget is written as

$$\text{p: } C_2^1 = (1+r)[\, z_1 - C_1] + z_2$$

$$\text{1-p: } C_2^2 = (1+r)[\, z_1 - C_1] + R(\hat{l}_2).$$

The utility function representing inter-temporal preference is assumed to take the form

---

standards of rural people. This is advantageous for our work on the rural 'five guarantee' households. However, many places have not given out new certificates of 'five guarantee' household for many years, which made it unclear as to how many 'five-guarantee' households there should be. Some places have not acted in response to the changed management and income allocation system in rural areas, which has caused inadequate living conditions for existing 'five-guarantee' households."

$$\underset{C_1, C_2^1, C_2^2}{Max}\ U(C_1)+ßpU(C_2^1)+ß(1-p)U(C_2^2),$$

where 0<ß<1 is time preference. At optimal choice, the following condition is satisfied for both the collective and the household responsibility system (Appendix A.1):

$$U'(C_1)=ß(1+r)[pU'(C_2^1)+(1-p)U'(C_2^2)].$$

With savings opportunities, the consumption in the second period increases by the amount of savings for both the collective and the household responsibility systems.

Comparative statics with respect to the share of incomes distributed according to population show that (Appendix A.1):

$$\frac{dC_1}{d\alpha} > 0,$$

which means that the higher the income distributed regardless of labor, the more the worker will consume, leaving less for savings. On the other hand, the less equal the distribution across individuals who work and who do not work, the more the worker will save. This analysis implies that as the population-based distribution of income was abolished as a result of the replacement of the commune system by the household responsibility system in the early 1980s, household savings are expected to increase. This hypothesis is consistent with general observations. (Add evidence.)

If there is at least one child providing for elderly parents, it can be shown (Appendix A.1) that as the number of children increases, a rural worker will consume more in the first period and save less, i.e.,

$$\frac{dC_1}{d\hat{n}_2} > 0.$$

The hypothesis about the relationship between the number of children and savings is based on the assumption that children are a substitute for savings--when there is no opportunity for saving financial assets, having more children is an alternative. Many people argue that Chinese farmers do not have extra resource to save. We believe that this is not true, because raising children also requires resources. Presumably a farmer can put the resources in the form of savings by having less children.

In China, the protection of private property rights is never adequate; thus savings accumulated for retirement purposes have not been safe. This is probably one of the reasons why children, especially sons, have traditionally been considered by many to be the most secure form of investment for old-age support. With the introduction of retirement programs for urban workers, together with lower mortality rates, higher labor force participation, and education for women, the fertility rate in urban China for the period of 1980-85 was only one quarter of the 1950-55 level. The fertility rate in rural areas saw a similar drop, but at a much smaller magnitude partly because the old-age provision is much less generous than in urban areas (Johnson 1998). Nevertheless, the fertility rate decreased from 6.25 in 1950-55 to 4.97 in 1975-80 and 2.83 in 1980-85 (Johnson 1994). The declining fertility rate since the early 1980s might be partly attributable to the one-child family planning policy instituted in the early 1980s, but economic factors should have played a role, especially the expanded non-farm employment opportunities and the resultant increase in the value of time. In any case, with the declining fertility rate, there is a larger demand for other sources of saving.

Another interesting result from comparative statics analysis deals with the relationship between the demand for savings and the probability of having supporting children. It shows that (Appendix A.1):

$$\frac{dC_1}{dp} > 0,$$

i.e., the likelihood for a person to have no supporting children will discourage the person for consuming more when young and working. Thus he will save more.

Given the number of surviving children in a household, there is a possibility that the children may refuse to support their parents. There is no definite rule that can be used to predict who will and who will not treat their parents well, but it is generally true that the ability to enforce the support from children is correlated with whether the elderly parents live in the same household with the children, and whether the children live close or far away.

Two recent developments in terms of living arrangements between the elderly and their children are worth noting. One is the increased independence of children from parents. As income goes up, increasingly households can afford to build additional houses, therefore, more and more children live separately from their parents as soon as they are married. This partly explains the decline in average household size(from 5.54 in 1980 to 4.42 in 1996). This trend is continuing. Even though the oldest child is supposed to live with the parents in the same compound, very often the elderly have separate living arrangements—separate housing, kitchen, and income sources. When there is more than one child, the task of providing for the elderly parents is often negotiated between the children. Since providing for the parents is a public good (bad) for the children, the amount of care given to the elderly parents could be under-supplied. Some children may even refuse to support their parents.

Another development is increased rural-to-urban migration. As is true in other parts of the world, those that migrate from rural China are mostly young, and the elderly parents seldom move with their children (Zhao 1998). Although the current migration is largely temporary, permanent migration at a large scale is going to happen in China sooner or later. Migration may bring more incomes to children, but when the children are far away physically, it is less feasible to require them to provide support.[5]

With the increasing independence of children either in the form of living separately in the same village or moving to another place, the probability of the rural elderly not getting support from their children also increases. According to our analysis, this leads to a greater demand for alternative investment opportunities.

The above discussions regarding fertility and family structure imply that raising children is becoming a less attractive means of investment for old age security—the children may be away or not willing to provide support. Therefore, the demand for a safer investment vehicle is stronger. We now turn our attention to the availability of other means of savings and their returns.

5. The types of savings available in rural China

The models specified in Section III treat savings as a homogeneous product that can be freely chosen. In reality, savings can take many forms: aside from investing in children as we discussed in the previous section, there are bank deposits, securities, property, pension plans, etc. We will show below that not all are available as a viable means of savings, in fact, rural people have very limited ability of generating reasonable returns to their savings for old-age security.

5.1 Bank deposits and bonds

Interest rates on bank deposits have been set at levels far below the equilibrium since the 1950s as part of the industrialization strategy to encourage the growth of heavy industries (Lin's 1997). Since the early 1980s, real interest rates have been mostly negative with the exception of a few years. (Add figure) With low or

[5] Although this paper mainly considers income support from the family members toward the elderly, physical care is also important for the elderly, especially at times of illness and handicap. When the children is away, the amount of care from the children is decreased.

negative interest rates, putting money in a bank is not a profitable undertaking. The Chinese government started issuing treasury bonds at rates slightly better than bank interest rates in the mid-1980s (verify), but real interest rates are still low and very often negative (until very recently).

5.2 *Investment in financial or physical capital*

Financial markets are located in large cities and thus not accessible to most rural people. Even if they are, it is hardly a good choice for long-term investment because the markets are extremely thin, and hence volatile.

The Chinese farmers started to set up village enterprises in the mid-1980s. Although these brought fortunes to some rural people, they are hardly a viable choice of investment for ordinary rural persons. First, opportunities for rural industries are spread very unevenly across China: It is relatively easy in the coastal areas, but very difficult in the hinterland. Second, direct investment in a local enterprise is too risky for the purpose of old-age support because the risk is not diversified at all.

5.3 *The rural pension program by the Ministry of Civil Affairs*

In response to the demand for a savings vehicle, the Ministry of Civil Affairs experimented with a rural social pension scheme in the late 1980s and started promoting the program in 1991 nationwide. Unlike the urban pension system, which has both pay-as-you-go and funded elements, this pension scheme is an entirely funded system with personal accounts. However, because government regulation requires that the funds be used to buy treasury bonds or put in banks as deposits, the rates of return have been too low to attract voluntary participation (Johnson 1998).[6] By the end of 1997, there were only 82 million participants, accounting for 10.4 percent of all rural people, and the overall accumulated payment was 13.9 billion yuan, which is 169 yuan per person, or 11 percent of 1996 rural net per capita income.[7] As pointed out by Johnson (1998), the program would have to offer a real rate of return of at least 4 or 5 percent in order to be adequate in providing for the

---

[6] At times of high rates of inflation, the real rates of return were even negative. In 1997, the nominal rate of return was 6.8 percent, while the inflation rate was 3 percent as was reported by the State Statistical Bureau.

[7] Source: interview with an official at the Ministry of Civil Affairs. It should be noted that part of the participation were compulsory, as in the case of

elderly support, and only that would attract the voluntary participation of the rural people.

5.4 Other sources of support

We have argued in this section that there are few means of investment that rural people can use to protect themselves against old age poverty. What are other alternative choices that have been made by the rural people?

The first alternative is to invest in property. There are few types of private property that are accessible to farmers and can serve the purpose of old-age support. Semi-durable goods such as tractors have limited life spans and thus are not suitable for old-age savings. The only two major types of private property available for old-age support are houses and trees planted on the homestead. It is evident that farmers have invested heavily in housing since the mid-1980s. Wen (1995) observes that many farmers have constructed houses far beyond the normal need for living space and that consumption is not the only return to housing construction. What would be the return to the housing investments? As migration takes place at a large scale, which we believe would occur sooner or later, the value of the houses would probably decrease because demand for housing would decrease in rural villages. So the housing investment may turn out to be another risky investment.

6. Land holding as a possible means of saving

Our previous discussion shows that investment in none of the following can lead to secure and reasonable returns: children, banks, capital markets, TVEs, housing or the government sponsored pension program. This leaves us with the last alternative: land.

Many people in the government hold the view that there is no need for a social pension program in rural areas because rural people have land as a means of old age support. But as indicated earlier, the amount of rent that the land is getting is not enough to guarantee subsistence if rent is the sole source of income.

The main reason for the low level of rent is because land is not transferable. The rural collectives own the land, and the transfer of use rights was not permitted until 1993. However, evidence shows that very few transfers have taken place (add reference). The primary reason is thought to be the lack of security of rental rights: When a household rents the land out, it becomes an indicator that the household does not need the land. When land is redistributed among households, the household may lose its use rights to the land. As a result, the rental mainly takes place between friends and relatives; some plots are even left idle as people engage in non-farm jobs. Because the number of people who are available to take in the land is limited to friends and relatives, the rent is greatly depressed.

What is the potential value of land rents? According to Johnson's (1998) method of estimation, assuming that a third to 40 percent of the per capita income is derived from land, the return to land was from 636 to 770 yuan per person. This can be achieved only when the rental rights are completely secure. Under such conditions, the returns to land can be further increased because of the improvement of land quality as a result of having more incentives to invest in the land. Under current insecure rental rights, farmers are unwilling to make land-specific investments in land that has long-term returns because the returns would not be realized if reallocation occurs. There is evidence that land readjustment does take place frequently in many places (Prosterman et al. 1998). Recent findings show that land productivity would increase significantly if the disincentive to investment were removed (Carter and Yao 1998).

How do we make the use rights more secure? Clearly, if the land is privately owned, then the farmers should naturally have the freedom to dispose of the land. If it is infeasible politically, then granting farmers the right of perpetual use is an alternative.

Land has some unique characteristics as a safer and more profitable investment for old age security in rural China. Because of these characteristics, investing in land would have been even more attractive to farmers if farmers were to be allowed to own their land or to permanently use their land and to leave the land to their children.

First, the value of land rises in general because of population growth and the rise in its productivity. Secondly, land provides food security to its owners or users. In this sense, land is a risk free long-term investment. In addition, land, as a valuable asset controlled by the elderly, can provide old age security by acting as credible leverage against non-supporting children. The traditional China did not have capital markets, or a banking system or pension system in today's sense. Land played a very special role in meeting the demand for old age security.

Nevertheless, under the current responsibility system, land is collectively owned; thus every member of the collective has an equal right to use the land. Reallocations or readjustments among villagers take place frequently in response to population changes in the village. Because of the collective ownership of land, it is the local authorities, not the elderly, that the younger generation will turn to when they need land for living or for building houses after getting married. The old generation has lost their leverage over their children at a time when they need such leverage most because of the vulnerability that the elderly are facing after the dismantling of the commune system.

7. Conclusions and discussions

China has an urgent need for finding a viable means of support for the rural elderly. This paper examines the reasons for the absence of such a system.

Before the rural economic reform that took place in the early 1980s the collectives shouldered a large part of the burden of supporting the rural elderly. With the dismantling of the collective management of land and income allocation the responsibility for old age support was returned to the rural households. With this shift of responsibility for the elderly support, the demand for savings increased. The reform has created many new opportunities for earning higher incomes and thus has contributed to increased savings for the old age support. This paper employs an intergenerational transfer model to show the inadequacy of the method after the economic reform, and then uses an inter-temporal transfer model to shows how various factors affect the demand for savings during working life. Underlying both cases is an uncertainty facing a rural person: that he may end up with no support from his children. We demonstrate that the intergenerational transfer worked better under the collective management than under the individual household responsibility system. Furthermore, as the number of children declines and the rural elderly increasingly live without the support of children as the result of the independence of children, the need for alternative means of savings also increases. Children as providers of old age security will be even more risky in the future as fertility drops further and large-scale outward migration takes place.

We then examine the availability of alternative forms of savings and investment as viable means of old age support—bank deposits, investments in capital markets, social pension funds, and property. We conclude that none provides an attractive rate of return that the Chinese capital market should be able to provide given China's stage of development.

How do people react to the low returns to investment? This is a difficult question. One possible response is to save excessively to compensate for the low returns in order to guarantee a minimum standard of living at old age. Another way is to work beyond one's normal working life in order to save more. Casual observation shows that Chinese rural elderly continue to work until he or she becomes disabled by illness. This is true not only of the elderly without children, but also those living with children. This is clearly an undesirable solution.

Based on our analysis, there are three possible solutions. One is to relax the restrictions on fertility and increase the ability of people to rely on their children for old age support. The second is to increase the rate of return to pension programs. This can be done through two ways. One is to issue inflation-indexed government bonds with higher rates of return. As Johnson (1998) argues, the real rate of return in the Chinese economy should be much higher than what has been offered. The second way is to increase competition in the pension market. If the government is the sole provider of pension insurance, there is no incentive to lower the cost of management and increase the rates of return.

The third possible solution is to give farmers permanent tenancy rights, or even to privatize the land. By doing so, land will reassume its role as a device for inter-temporal and intergenerational transfers within rural households. This can provide to a significant extent the urgently needed old age security at a time when the government can do very little financially, and the rural elderly feel very vulnerable after the dismantling of the commune system. Such policy will not cost the government anything, but will significantly improve security for the rural elderly.

References

1. Bai, Nansheng. 1998. "The Determinants of Household Income during the Period of Collectivization," unpublished manuscript.
2. Carter, Michael R. And Yang Yao. 1998. "Property Rights, Factor Proportions, and Land Productivity: Theory and Evidence From China," paper presented at the Workshop for Land Tenure, Land Markets, and Productivity in Rural China, May 15-16, Beijing.
3. Editorial Committee. 1995. *The Encyclopedia of China's Social Security System.* China Democracy and Law Publishing House, Beijing.
4. Johnson, D. Gale. 1994. "Effects of Institutional and Policies on Rural Population Growth with Application to China," Population and Development Review, Volume 20, No. 3, September, pp. 503-531.
5. ----1998. "Social Security and Rural Elderly," unpublished manuscript.
6. Lin, Justin Y. 1992. "Rural Reforms and Agricultural Growth in China," *American Economic Review*, vol. 82, March, pp. 34-51.
7. ---1990. "Collectivization and China's Agricultural Crisis in 1959-1961," Journal of Political Economy, vol. 98 (December), pp. xx.
8. ---- and F. Cai and Z. Li. 1996. *The China Miracle: Development Strategy and Economic Reform*, The Chinese University Press, Hong Kong.
9. McMillan, J. Whalley, and L. Zhu. 1989. "The Impact of China's Economic Reform on Agricultural Productivity Growth," Journal of Political Economy, vol. 97, no. 4, pp. 781-807.

10. Prosterman, Roy, Tim Hanstad and Brian Schwarzwalder. 1998. "Implementing the Legal Framework for Rural Land Tenure: Evidence and the Way Ahead," paper presented at the Workshop for Land Tenure, Land Markets, and Productivity in Rural China, May 15-16, Beijing.
11. Wang, Sibin. 1995 "An Aggressive Response to Social Transformations: A look at the Rural Social Old-Age Insurance from the Viewpoint of Sociology," in *A Collection of Evaluation Papers on the Basic Plan for Rural Social Pension Insurance*, December. Unpublished manuscript.
12. Wen, James G. 1995. "The Land Tenure System and Investment Mechanism: The Case of Modern China," Asian Economic Journal,...
13. Zhao, Yaohui. 1998. "Labor Migration and Income Differences in Rural China," in Economic Development and Cultural Change (forthcoming)

Appendix A.1 Optimization in inter-temporal and intergenerational transfer

1. Decentralized household responsibility system

$$\underset{C_1, C_2^1, C_2^2}{Max}\ U(C_1)+ßpU(C_2^1)+ß(1-p)U(C_2^2)$$

s.t. $C_2^1=(1+r)(z_1 - C_1)+ z_2$ and $C_2^2=(1+r)(z_1 - C_1)$.

The maximization problem is reduced to

$$\underset{C_t^i(t)}{Max}\ U(C_1)+ßpU((1+r)(z_1 - C_1)+ z_2)+ß(1-p)U((1+r)(z_1 - C_1))$$

F.O.C.: $U'(C_1)-pß(1+r)U'(C_2^1)-(1-p)ß(1+r)U'(C_2^2)$

S.O.C.: $U''(C_1)+pß(1+r)^2U''(C_2^1)+(1-p)ß(1+r)^2U''(C_2^2)<0$.

Take derivative of the F.O.C. w. r. t. p:

$$U''(C_1)\frac{dC_1}{dp}+pß(1+r)^2U''(C_2^1)\frac{dC_1}{dp}-ß(1+r)U'(C_2^1)$$

$$+(1-p)ß(1+r)^2U''(C_2^2)\frac{dC_1}{dp}+ß(1+r)U'(C_2^2)=0.$$

Rearrange terms,

$$\frac{dC_1}{dp}=\frac{\beta(1+r)U'(C_2^1)-U'(C_2^2)}{D}>0.$$

The denominator is the expression in the left-hand side of the S.O.C. and is therefore negative. The numerator is negative because $C_2^1>C_2^2$, thus the whole expression is positive.

2. Collective management

$$\underset{C_1, C_2^1, C_2^2}{Max}\ U(C_1)+ßpU(C_2^1)+ß(1-p)U(C_2^2)$$

s.t. $C_2^1=(1+r)(y_1 - C_1])+ y_2$ and $C_2^2=(1+r)(a\,y_1 - C_1)+a\,y_2$

The problem can be rewritten as:

$$\underset{C_1, C_2^1, C_2^2}{Max}\ U(C_1)+ßpU((1+r)(y_1 - C_1)+ y_2)+ß(1-p)U((1+r)(a\,y_1 - C_1)+a\,y_2)$$

F.O.C.: $U'(C_1)-pß(1+r)U'(C_2^1)-(1-p)ß(1+r)U'(C_2^2)$

S.O.C.: U"(C_1)+pß$(1+r)^2$U"(C_2^1)+(1-p)ß$(1+r)^2$U"(C_2^2)<0.

Take derivative of the F.O.C. w. r. t. a:

$$U''(C_1)\frac{dC_1}{d\alpha}+p\beta(1+r)^2U''(C_2^1)\frac{dC_1}{d\alpha}+(1-p)\beta(1+r)^2U''(C_2^2)\frac{dC_1}{d\alpha}$$

$$-p\beta(1+r)U''(C_2^2)((1+r)y_1+y_2)=0.$$

$$\frac{dC_1}{d\alpha}=\frac{\pi\beta(1+r)U''(C_2^2)((1+r)y\ +y_2)}{D}>0.$$

The denominator is negative by the S.O.C., the numerator is negative because U"<0.

3. Number of children greater than 0.

$$\underset{C_1,C_2}{Max}\ U(C_1)+\beta U(C_2),\ \text{s.t.}\ C_2=(1+r)(z_1-C_1)+z_2$$

The problem can be rewritten as

$$\underset{C_1}{Max}\ U(C_1)+\beta U((1+r)(z_1-C_1)+z_2)$$

F.O.C.: U'(C_1)-ß(1+r)U'(C_2)=0.

S.O.C.: U"(C_1)+ß$(1+r)^2$U"(C_2)<0.

Comparative statics w.r.t. $\hat{n}_2$:

$$U''(C_1)\frac{dC_1}{d\hat{n}_2}+\beta(1+r)^2U''(C_2)\frac{dC_1}{d\hat{n}_2}-\beta(1+r)U''(C_2)\frac{dz_2}{d\hat{n}_2}=0$$

$$\frac{dC_1}{d\hat{n}_2}=\frac{\beta(1+r)U''(C_2)\,{}^{dz_2}\!/_{d\hat{n}_2}}{U''(C_1)+\beta(1+r)^2U''(C_2)}>0.$$

The denominator is negative from the S.O.C., the numerator is negative because U"<0.

CHAPTER 16

CONFLICTS BETWEEN SOCIETY'S DESIRES AND INDIVIDUAL RESPONSIBILITY: FINANCING ISSUES IN CHINA'S URBAN HEALTH INSURANCE REFORM*

WEI YU
Department of Medicine, Boston University,
720 Harrison Avenue, Boston, MA 02118, USA
E-mail: wyu@bu.edu

With a review of the demographics, the health care system, and facilities in 57 experimental cities and China's reform on health care financing, the paper analyzes employers' incentives in the new health insurance system and practical problems associated with individual health care accounts.

1. Introduction

Since China initiated economic reform 20 years ago, its economy has been growing rapidly. While the market system continuously stimulates economic growth, the structural transition of state-owned enterprises (SOEs) under the market system also generates social instability, especially in urban areas where SOEs are concentrated. Under such circumstances, an effective social safety system is needed to smooth the transition.

As a socialist country, the Chinese government established a Labor Health Insurance (LHI) for SOE employees and a Government Health Insurance (GHI) for employees of government agencies in 1950s. Both programs worked effectively for 30 years. Economic reform breaks the LHI and GHI into working-unit-based insurance programs, which considerably weakens their capability to spread financial risk.

Starting in 1995, the government conducted a series of experiments in health insurance in 57 cities. This paper examines the financial problems encountered in these experimental cities. It focuses on: 1) effects of economic reform on the LHI and GHI programs; 2) incentives of employers and employees in financing a Community-Based Health Insurance System (CBHIS); and 3) problems with a financing policy that combines an individual health care account with a social risk pooling account.

The paper is organized in five sections. The next section provides general background on demographics, the health care system, and facilities in the 57 experimental cities. Section 3 reviews effects of China's economic reform on health care financing. Section 4 analyzes employers' incentives in the new health insurance system, and section 5 examines practical problems associated with individual health care accounts. The last section presents some concluding remarks.

2. Experiment of Health Care Financing in the 57 Cities[1]

The State Council and the Ministry of Health started health care reform in Zhenjiang, Jiangsu province and Jiujiang, Jiangxi province in 1995 and extended the reform to 57 cities in 27 provinces later. Cities in China usually include some suburban counties. People who worked on farms in those suburban counties are classified as agricultural residents[2]. In the 57 cities, about 30% of the population are agricultural residents and 46.8 million are non-agricultural residents accounting for 13% of the total non-agricultural population in the nation. Among the 57 cities, 25 have populations of less than 2 million, 20 have populations between 2 and 5 million, and 12 cities have more than 5 million people (1995 data).

2.1 Coverage rates by LHI and GHI

Proportions of urban residents covered by LHI or GHI in the 57 cities are summarized in Table 1.. Since agricultural residents live in rural counties and are covered by

---

[1] Data and statistics used in this section are obtained from the survey conducted by the Department of Legal and Policy, the Ministry of Health in China and Hu et al[1].

[2] China had a strict regulation that separated residents between rural and urban areas before economic reform. Rural residents were counted as agricultural population . Rural residents are covered by a Medical Cooperative System (MCS) which is under a separate plan. The MCS is financed by residents in each village and has very limited coverage.

different health care program, the rates reported in Table 1 are the proportions of urban residents (non-agricultural population) covered by either LHI or GHI. Table 1 shows that rates of insurance coverage across cities vary substantially with median around 50%. The level of insurance coverage depends on the industrial structure in each city. Rates of insurance coverage are higher in cities where the proportions of residents who work in SOEs are higher.

Table 1: Distributions of Insurance Coverage by City Size for Urban Residents in 1995

City population	25 percentile	Median	75 percentile
< 2 million (25 cities)	20.30	49.40	56.50
2 - 5 millions (20 cities)	29.30	45.10	57.50
> 5 million (12 cities)	36.01	61.80	66.00

Source: Hu, Ren, et al[1].

2.2 Medical Expenditures and Utilizations

For people covered by LHI and GHI, LHI paid 61% of the total medical expenditure, GHI paid 23%, and individuals paid 16%. The distribution of average medical payment per person by city size and source of payment is tabulated in Table 2. People in small cities pay more out of pocket than people in large cities. A possible explanation for this difference is that SOEs in large cities are managed by higher level government agencies (province or ministry) and their benefits are usually better than companies managed by county or lower level governments.

In 1995, the average number of outpatient visits for people covered by LHI and GHI is 10 times and the average rate of hospitalizations is 16.3%. The average length of hospital stays is 15.5 days (Table 3). However, there are considerable variations of using both outpatient and inpatient services among these cities. The proportion of people hospitalized in high-use cities is about three times of that in low-use cities and hospitalized patients in high-use cities stay twice longer than those in low-use cities. The number of outpatient visits is also doubled in high-use cities.

Table 2: Distribution of Average Annual Medical Expenditure per Person and as Percent of Annual Average Wage in 1995

(in RMB yuan)

City population	25 percentile	Median	75 percentile
Paid by LHI (percent of wage)			
< 2 million (25 cities)	223.0 (5.5)	451.5 (7)	576.5 (9)
2 - 5 millions (20 cities)	224.0 (6.0)	327.0 (7)	467.0 (9)
> 5 million (12 cities)	289.5 (6.0)	515.0 (10)	713.0 (13)
Paid by GHI (percent of wage)			
< 2 million (25 cities)	220.0 (5)	345.5 (7)	499.0 (3)
2 - 5 millions (20 cities)	262.0 (8)	354.0 (9)	394.0 (10)
> 5 million (12 cities)	352.0 (7)	547.0 (10)	634.0 (12)
Paid by individuals (percent of wage)			
< 2 million (25 cities)	25.0 (1)	107.0 (2)	136.0 (2)
2 - 5 millions (20 cities)	25.5 (1)	33.5 (1)	45.0 (1)
> 5 million (12 cities)	25.0 (1)	37.0 (1)	90.0 (2)

Source: Hu, Ren, et al[1].

Table 3: Utilization of Medical Services by People Covered under LHI and GHI in 1995

	25 percentile	Media	75 percentile
Number of annual average outpatient visits	6.0	10.2	13.8
Percent of people hospitalized	9.7	16.3	29.5
Average length of hospital stays	10.1	15.5	21.0

Source: Hu, Ren, et al[1].

2.3 Hospital Revenue and Expenditure

Due to price regulation, hospitals use profit from drugs to offset costs of medical services. On average, more than 50% of total revenue (either inpatient or outpatient services) is from drugs (Table 4). Hospitals at all levels lose money from medical services and make profit from drugs (Table 5). Among province-managed hospitals, for example, 41% of total revenue is from medical services, but medical services account for 53% of total cost. This directly affects efficiency in using medical resources.

Table 4: Sources of Hospital Revenue (yuan) in 1995

Sources of Revenue	**25 percentile**	**Median**	**75 percentile**
Outpatient fee (per visit)	22.4	31.1	44.0
Drugs in outpatient (per visit)	14.5	20.4	29.0
Hospitalization (per stay)	639.4	1173.5	1854.7
Drugs per hospitalization stay	475.3	720.0	1205.0

Source: Hu, Ren, et al[1].

Table 5: Percent of Revenue and Costs from Drugs and Medical Services by Hospital Rank*.

	Province	City	District	County
Revenue: Medical Services	40.8	33.1	31.4	37.5
Drugs	50.6	62.5	63.9	52.0
Cost: Medical Services	52.7	43.5	42.1	47.6
Drugs	46.0	56.2	57.4	50.0

Source: Hu, Ren, et al[1].

* Hospitals are classified and managed by different levels of governments in five ranks: province, city, district, county, and others.

3. Effects of Economic Reform on Health Care Financing

To understand health insurance reform in urban China, it is necessary to review the effects of economic reform on existing LHI and GHI programs. Under the centrally-planned system, behavior of consumers and medical service providers are much less complicated than under the market system. The reform, however, brings the market system into health care services which creates many incentives for consumers and the providers. To understand these changes, we have to understand special characteristics of medical services.

3.1 Characteristics of Medical Services

Medical care has a strong component of social welfare. In almost every country, regardless of its institutional structure and economic system, the government always plays an important role in financing medical care. Medical services also have very special characteristics in resource allocation under a market system. First, providers have the power to affect demand because there is significant informational asymmetry on medical services between the supply and demand sides. Second, as medical services are usually paid by a third party (an insurance company), patients may consume more than they would have if they paid for the services by themselves (moral hazard). With these factors, a market-oriented and private-owned medical care system can easily push medical expenditures up to an unaffordable level. Third, as medical services are highly technical and specialized, it is very costly to manage the system. The experience in U.S. is a good example. Based on the 1988 data, commercial insurance spent 26.9% of the total premiums for management while the Medicare only spent 2.3% and Canadian national health insurance program spent 3%.

3.2 China's Health Care System before the Reform

China's health care system before economic reform was very effective. With limited resources (per capita GDP in 1978 was only 915 yuan), life expectancy at birth increased dramatically between 1950 and 1981[3] from 35 years to 68 years in 1981. In addition to significant improvement in nutrition, China's health care policy during that period was also an important factor in the achievement. First, the government funded a series of projects to improve public health such as cleaning drinking water, processing sewage, providing free immunizations for children, and preventive care for pregnant women. Second, it established affordable health insurance systems in both rural and urban areas. China achieved this mainly through a very centralized policy in finance and resource management. This policy, however, has been considerably weakened by economic reform.

3.3 Effects of Economic Reform on Health Care System

Economic reform has affected China's health care system so dramatically because policy makers do not fully realize the weakness of a market system in health care. The aim of China's economic reform is to improve efficiency in state-owned enterprises. Therefore, tying personal interest to working effort so that people have an incentive to work hard becomes a key principle of the reform. Economic profit is often the only measurement of performance for enterprises, including hospitals.

Economic reform affects China's health care system in two respects. The first is

[3] There is no statistics for the life expectance at birth before the establishment of the People's Republic of China except a survey conducted by a student at Jinling University in 1931. That survey showed that the life expectancy at birth was 35 years. Because there was little improvement in nutrition and health care services from 1931 through 1949 and there were two wars during that period, the life expectancy is believed to be at the similar level (35 years) in 1949.

on the insurance system, especially the Labor Health Insurance (LHI) which covered 140 million employees of SOEs[4] in 1992. Before economic reform, LHI was backed by the government and costs of medical care were strictly controlled. It functioned effectively for almost 30 years. Economic reform shifted financial responsibilities to SOEs, including pension and health insurance. This policy changed the government-supported health insurance program into an enterprise-self-insured system. When the LHI is independently financed by individual enterprises, several problems immediately emerge. First, financially insolvent SOEs cannot pay health care bills for their employees. Second, small enterprises have much higher risk. A severe illness can quickly bankrupt the insurance fund. Also, SOEs with a large proportion of retired employees have much higher costs for health care than other enterprises.

The second effect is on hospitals. Before reform, salaries of hospital employees (doctors, nurses, and managers) were set and paid by the government and had no relation with hospitals' profit or performance. Since economic reform, profit is directly connected to employees' income. Under the old system, hospital employees did not have an incentive to work hard. Shirking and poor quality were major problems. The market system has effectively improved hospital services in both quality and quantity. It, however, also creates another problem - inefficient use of medical resources. For example, since the government still controls prices, selling drugs and ordering certain tests (such as CT and MRI) are more profitable than other services. As a result of this price regulation, physicians are more likely to order profitable tests and prescribe more profitable drugs than the level that is clinically necessary.

In general, China's urban health insurance reform touches the interests of three entities: the government, business enterprises, and hospitals. When many people lose their health insurance, they put strong pressure on the government to reestablish an effective health insurance system. Managers in business enterprises must consider how to keep the balance between the social responsibility to finance medical services for their employees and the business responsibility to compete in the market. With limited support from the government, hospital directors must seek a balance between hospital profit and efficient use of medical resources.

Economic reform has raised a couple of important questions on health care for China's policy makers. Under the central-planned system, policy makers were not concerned with financing problems. For any health care project, they just made a plan and wrote a budget. Now, they must decide how to raise funds reasonably for health

---

[4] Data obtained from the Ministry of Health.

care services and how to allocate resources efficiently. Because both questions are subject to value judgements, arguments on health care policies are inevitable. The general conflict is between the society's desire to have a universal health care system and an individual or an employer's responsibility to finance such a system.

4. Employers in the CBHIS

The immediate objective of the CBHIS is to replace the collapsing LHI and GHI programs. Since both programs were completely paid by employers, they still pay most of the premiums for the CBHIS to smooth the transition. Therefore, employers' incentives under the new health insurance program are important to carry out the CBHIS successfully.

4.1 Employers' Attitudes to the CBHIS

As SOEs are now all financially self-responsible, employers act like individuals and try to minimize their cost for health insurance. It is also possible that employers may maximize their own interest, not employees' benefit. Financially, enterprises and government agencies participating in the CBHIS can be generally divided into four categories: the loser, the winner, the unaffordable ones, and those that just break even.

The winners benefit from the CBHIS in two aspects. Some employers benefit financially from the CBHIS because they pay less than actual costs. SOEs with a large number of retired employees are likely to be in this group. Another type of benefit from the CBHIS is risk spreading. By pooling resources in a large group, many small and middle sized enterprises have considerably reduced the financial risk posed by catastrophic diseases. SOEs that cannot afford to pay premiums may have to be subsidized by the government through other financial channels. In Jiujiang, for example, about 20% of the enterprises could not afford the CBHIS. Losers have a strong incentive against the CBHIS. If these enterprises do not participate, the CBHIS could not succeed. Hence, it is important to justify their behaviors and adjust policy accordingly.

4.2 Reasons not to Join the CBHIS

Unwillingness to join CBHIS are associated with four factors. First, employers are concerned with rates of contribution. The premium is calculated as a fixed percentage of total wage bill or budget of a firm. Thus, companies with better financial status and higher salaries pay more than others. Second, companies with healthy employees (usually new ones with younger employees) pay more than their actual health care expenditures. Third, desire to control health care funds and maintain the privilege of using the resource. Last, many large enterprises have their own clinics, even full size hospitals. If they join the CBHIS, they may not fully use their own facilities.

Among the four types of problems, the third one is a typical agency problem though it sometimes can be a major factor in decision making. The last factor is associated with reorganization of the medical industry. A considerable number of hospitals are owned by large SOEs and industrial ministries. In 1997, 39% of outpatient visits and 31% of hospitalizations were provided by those industrial-owned clinics and hospitals. Therefore, any adjustment to those industrial hospitals should be done carefully. If these large enterprises can provide reasonable health care to their employees, it may be more efficient to let them self-insure. The first two factors, however, deserve more discussion.

4.3 Social and Moral Standards for Health Care Financing and Distribution

The common argument for enterprises that have either higher salary level or healthy employees will be that joining CBHIS costs them more money and provides less for their employees. They believe that it is not fair for them to subsidize others for health insurance. As fairness in financing health care services is related to many social factors such as cultural background and social standards, it is hard to establish criteria which can be accepted by everyone. However, two principles in health care policy are commonly accepted by many nations with different cultural backgrounds and economic capacities. First, the level of contribution to health care services is more related to income than health status. Second, the distribution of medical resources depends more on health condition than ability to pay.

These two common principles reflect the evolution of social attitudes towards medical services. Even in the very early days, doctors often charged patients based on their ability to pay. With social and economic development, financing health care is gradually taken over by government as a public program. Some countries have universal health insurance financed through either general or specific taxes such as the U.K. and Canada. Others have commercial insurance financed jointly by employers and employees with the government taking care of the poor and the elderly as in the U.S. system. Regardless of different financing methods, the premium or tax paid by individuals is never based on health status. These financing methods are different from the financing principles in commercial insurance. It reflects the social standard for health care financing.

4.4 Enterprises with Better Financial Status

If we agree with the two common principles in financing health insurance, then it is not difficult to answer questions raised by enterprises that have higher levels of salaries and wages. The rule to collect premiums based on the total salary of an enterprise is consistent with the social agreement that people that have higher incomes should contribute more.

However, since the way to calculate salary among different types of enterprises is quite different, using salary as a base to calculate premiums may not reflect the actual income level of employees in the enterprise. It also introduces an incentive to report less salary by shifting compensation into other categories. With these problems, the financing method may punish more efficiently operated and honorably reporting companies.

4.5 Enterprises with Healthy Employees

Many newly established companies such as foreign-invested or jointly-invested companies hire young and healthy employees. Therefore, medical expenditures for these new enterprises are much less than older SOEs. When these new companies join the CBHIS, they are more likely to pay more than their actual medical expenditures. If we agree with the principle that health insurance premiums should not be based on individuals' health status, it may not be desirable to the society to charge more to enterprises with a large proportion of old employees and retirees. In the short run, enterprises with young employees pay more than they get from the insurance program. In the long run, however, employees in these companies will get older and medical cost will go up. Paying the same rate for health insurance for young employees can be considered as meeting a responsibility to society for employing young workers. By averaging health care cost of hiring old and young workers, this policy also avoids discrimination in employment against age.

In many cities, attracting foreign investment is a major policy to stimulate local economic growth. Therefore, local governments often set special policies for foreign invested companies. If attracting foreign investment is indeed good for the local economy, it is worth considering how to transfer the benefit from the economic growth to public programs such as health insurance. When foreign investment increases economic growth, a share of the growth should be transferred into social safety programs.

4.6 A Feasible Financing Method

A possible financing method is that every employer pays the same premium which is only based on the number of employees insured. For those that cannot afford health insurance, the government may subsidize those employers through consumption tax. Since consumption, especially luxury consumption is closely related to individual income, using a consumption tax to subsidize low income families for health insurance is consistent with social standards. Another source to subsidize health care may be the cigarette tax. It is widely assumed that smokers will cost more for health care. Since it is difficult to collect higher premiums from smokers, a sales tax may prove to be a satisfactory alternative.

5. Individual Health Account

To participate in the CBHIS, employers contribute 10% of total salary and individuals contribute 1% of personal salary[5]. The fund is then divided into two accounts: the social pooling account and the individual account. Savings in the individual account are accumulated over time for each person. When a person needs medical care, money in his individual account is used first. Once the person's medical expenditure has depleted his individual account, the social pooling account will take over with cost sharing and deductions. Using individual accounts to finance health insurance in China, however, has several problems.

5.1 Extra Burden to Employers

One of the important goals for China's urban health reform is to ease the financial burdens of SOEs. With individual accounts, employers have to pay more unless they can significantly reduce medical consumption. China's individual accounts are paid

[5] These rates are based on the experiment in over 50 cities. According to recent policy, the employers' share may be reduced and individual contribution may increase.

mainly by the government and employer, and the personal contribution only accounts for a very small proportion. Table 6 shows the shares of health insurance funds in four cities which are applying CBHIS on an experimental basis.

Table 6: Rates* of Contributions by Employer and Employees and for Individual Accounts in Four Cities with CBHIS

City	Employer	individual	Percentage deposited into the individual account
Zhen-jiang[1]	10%	1%	age <= 45: 5%; age >45: 7%; retired: 5%
Jiu-jiang[2]	10%	1%	age <= 45: 4% age >45: 5.5%; retired: 5.5%
Yang-zhong[3]	10%	1%	age <=45: 5%; age >45: 7%; retired 5%
Hai-nan[3]	10%	1%	age <= 40: 4%; age 41-50: 5%; age >50 (not retired): 6%; retired: 8%

Sources: 1. Gu[8]; 2. Tu[9]; 3. Ma, Zhang, and Dai[10].

*All rates for individuals are based on personal annual wages in the previous year. For employers, the rates are based on last year's total wage and salary as well as pensions for retired persons.

Table 6 shows that about half of the health insurance funds are deposited into individual accounts. Zhenjiang's individual accounts took 48.5% of the total health insurance fund (1995 data), and Hainan's individual accounts took 64.2% (1996 data). Because a large proportion of medical expenditure is spent by a small group of people, a considerable amount of money in the individual accounts will not be used. In 1995, 17.7% of the total health insurance fund was left in the individual accounts in Zhenjiang, and 15.7% left in Jiu-jiang. These numbers suggest that employers would have to pay about 1.5% of total wages to the health insurance fund which is left in individual accounts. Furthermore, both cities have deficits in the social pooling account (4.5% in Zhenjiang and 5.9% in Jiujiang in 1995) which were covered by borrowing from individual accounts. Including the deficits, employers' contribution increased about 2% of total wages which were due to the saving in the individual account (numbers in the above paragraph come from Wang and Yang.

5.2 Limited Power to Control Cost

By using the individual accounts, policy makers hope that people will not overuse medical services. Individual accounts are used in Singapore and Chile to finance social safety programs, including pensions and health insurance. Individual accounts are more appropriate when used for pensions. It can ensure that every person has certain amount of saving after retirement. However, it is not effective to control medical cost. First, a small proportion of people consume a large proportion of medical resources. In the United States, for example, 10% of the population consumes about 60% of total medical resources. China has a similar situation. According to the survey of Yangzhong, Jiangsu province, the 1995 annual medical expenditure is 998 yuan for the retired and 380 yuan for employees. For those who used a large proportion of medical resources, the individual accounts have no impact on their demand. In Yangzhong CBHIS, 71% of the retired have entered into the social pooling account and only 17% of employees entered the social pooling account. Therefore, the power to control medical cost by an individual account is very limited. Second, the share of resources used for chronic diseases is increasing over time. Shangdong Medical University Lei et al. simulated the growth of medical cost for chronic diseases. Their study indicates that total medical expenditures for chronic diseases accounted for 29% in 1994 and would grow at 18% per year. When chronic diseases account for a large part of medical expenditures, individual accounts have very limited power to control cost.

Individual accounts also induce illegal activities. In the cities in which the CBHIS is established, it is observed that when a person's individual account is depleted, he may lend his card to his relatives or friends. Because hospitals also want to increase revenue, such violations are not seriously monitored. In Gaoqing country of Shangdong Province, to encourage saving in an individual account, 50% of the money left in an individual account can be withdrawn at the end of the year. This, in fact, still does not have an impact on controlling costs for those who have chronic diseases or severe medical problems. It may further encourage illegal behavior under the system.

5.3 Investment of the Saving in Individual Accounts

When there are long-term savings in the individual account, investment becomes important, especially for the young. Financing health care through an individual account is actually self-insurance during the lifetime. When a person is young with little medical expenditure, money is accumulated in his or her individual account. When the person is old, the saving accumulated in his or her individual account will be used to pay medical services. For a healthy young person, the period of accumulation may take 20 or 30 years before he starts heavily using the money for medical services. In this case, the rate of return becomes very important.

Suppose a young man has an annual income of 10,000 yuan, and each year, 5% (500 yuan) of his wage is deposited in his individual health insurance account. Assume that he is healthy between age 25 and 55, and his average annual medical expenditure during the 30 years is only200 yuan. In this case, he will save 300 yuan each year for 30 years. If the real rate of return is 0%(return just equals to inflation), 3%, and 5% respectively, the accumulated amount in his individual account will be 9,000 yuan, 14,727 yuan, and 19,931 yuan by the time he reaches age 55. Therefore, it is very important to have a good return in individual accounts. If the saving in the individual account is used for high-risk investments, it may lose everything.

Currently, savings in individual accounts in most cities do not have positive real returns, and some savings are actually used to cover deficits in social pooling accounts. When the debt from individual accounts is accumulated and the saving does not have real return, the individual account will not have adequate funds for healthy people to withdraw for other purposes that is designed to attract saving. When people realize that the individual accounts are actually empty, the very limited incentive to control cost will disappear too.

5.4 Portability

Still another practical problem for China to establish an individual account is portability. Differing from Singapore and Chile, China has a large difference in income level among provinces. The per capita gross domestic income in rich provinces such as Shanghai and Guangdong provinces is much higher than that in poor provinces such Gansu and Qinghai. Therefore, under the market system it is almost impossible for China to establish a national system for health insurance. Without individual accounts, moving from place to place will be relatively easy. When only some cities have an individual-account system for health insurance, however, carrying the savings from one area to the other under different systems is a problem. For example, if city A has an individual account and city B does not. If a worker moves from city A to city B, he may simply withdraw his money and deposit it in his personal account in city B. However, it may raise some concerns if a worker moves from city B to city A. Because he does not have any savings in his individual account, he will have to immediately use the social pooling account to pay for health care for him and his family. If a city has a large number of new workers moving in (such as rural workers), the social pooling account will be used more than expected.

Another potential problem in China's case is that healthy people have an incentive to leave the system when they retire. Because they are healthy, they must have accumulated a large amount of savings in their individual accounts. When reaching the retirement age, they are free to determine where to live. If these people can withdraw their savings on individual accounts and move to a place that has no individual accounts, they then can obtain a large amount of cash for other consumption. This will have two effects on the health care system:

First, this behavior will severely affect the financial situation of a local health care system if the system regularly borrows money from the individual account to cover the deficit of the social pooling account. In this case, the insurance administration has no choice but restrict withdrawals from the individual accounts. This, in turn, will completely destroy any incentive to save money in individual accounts.

Second, this behavior will also affect the total health expenditures in the nation. If retired healthy persons with accumulated savings in their individual account move into cities without individual account systems, they can immediately spend their savings for other consumption. They can pay a premium to join the new health insurance or stay uninsured. The problem is that when these people get sick later, they will consume extra resources transferred from society. In this case, the major purpose of the individual account, which is self-insurance during life time, completely disappears.

6. Concluding Remarks

A general feature of China's economic reform is to tie benefit closely to individuals' effort. When this principle is applied to policies in health insurance programs, it induces personal behavior that is in conflict with society's desire. An individual's decision to purchase health insurance is affected by three factors: income level, health status, and willingness to bear risk. Financing health care will be much simple if everyone has the same level of income, same status of health, and same preferences for risk. Unfortunately, people differ from each other and conflicts appear.

Economic theory predicts that the optimum level of insurance coverage one will buy is equal to expected loss and the premium is the product of the probability of being sick and the expected loss while being sick. If everyone is charged by the insurance rule, the elderly, the sick, and the disabled must pay a much higher level of insurance premium for health care, which is not consistent with socially accepted standards.

This conflict between society's desire and individual responsibility can be extended to employers. The difference between an employer and an individual with respect to purchasing health insurance is that an individual bears the loss of being sick directly and an employer bears the loss of sick employees indirectly. Employers are often restricted by their responsibility to employees and act passively to protect employees from financial hazards due to sickness.

This difference, however, only affects the level of coverage an employer would like to purchase. It does not affect an employer's behavior regarding to the payment for health insurance. The premium which an employer is willing to pay is the product of the coverage and the probability of being sick (the average level), which is closely related to the average level of health status of his or her employees. Employers probably have less incentive to subsidize the poor than individuals. Therefore, the conflict between society's desire for health care and employers' responsibility may be more pronounced.

In summary, the development of civilization suggests that health care should be provided at a reasonable level (usually determined by the economic level) to everyone in society. However, each person or employer has a strong incentive to achieve an optimum level of risk sharing, which is generally not consistent with the society's desire. Such conflict may have to be balanced by the government's redistribution policy. Hence, a tax-based redistribution is needed to achieve the socially desired health care system.

References

1. Hu Shanlian, Ren Minghui, et al. "General Report about Basic Health Care System for the 57 Experimental Cities in Health Care Reform (Quanguo Zhigong Yiliao Baozhang Zhidu Gaige Kuoda Shidian Chengshi Jiben Zhuangquang Fenxi Baogao), " *Chinese Health Economics*, Vol 16, No. 5, 1997, p44-48.
2. Arrow, Kenneth J. Uncertainty and the Welfare Economics of Medical Care, *American Economic Review* 53: 941-973.
3. Brandon, Robert M., Michael Podhorzer, and Thomas H. Pollak. Premiums without Benefits: Waste and Inefficiency in the Commercial Health Insurance Industry, *International Journal of Health Services*, Vol. 21(2), 1991, pp 265-283.
4. China Annual Statistics, 1986, Beijing: China Statistics Publication House.
5. China Annual Health Statistics, 1992, Beijing: The People's Health Publication

House.

6. Yu Wei and Ren Minghui. "The Important Part of State-Owned Enterprises Reform: Employee Health Insurance (Guoyou Qiye Gaige de Zhongyao Yihuan: Gongfei Yiliao Baoxian), in Reform of China's State-Owned Enterprises (Zhongguo Guoyou Qiye Gaige), edited by Xu Dianqing and Wen Guanzhong, China Economics Public House, Beijing: June 1996, p 433-458.
7. China Annual Health Statistics, 1997, Beijing: The People's Health Publication House.
8. Gu Xiandan. "Important Theoretical and Policy Issues in China Employee Health Insurance Reform (Woguo Zhigong Yiliao Baoxian Zhidu Gaige Zhong Ying Zhuzhong de Ruogan Wenti)," *Chinese Health Economics*, No. 2, 1997, P25-27.
9. Tu Zixian "Brief Introduction of Jiu-jiang Health Care Insurance Reform (Jiu-jiang Shi Yiliao Zhidu Gaige de Jiben Neirong)," *China Health Economics*, No. 9, 1995.
10. Ma Lishun, Zhang Yongjun, Dai Jinfeng "Discussion on Share of Individual Medical Account (Yiliao Geren Zhanghu Bili Chutan)," *China Health Economics*, No. 11, 1996, p53-54.
11. Wang Huanqing. "Thoughts about the Combination of the Social Pooling Account and the Individual Account in Health Insurance (Guanyu Yiliao Baoxian Shehui Tongchou yu Geren Zhanghu Jiehe Fangshi de Sikao), *China Health Economics*, No. 3, 1997, p21-22.
12. Yang Huayou. "Effects, Problems, and Policies of Jiujiang's Health Care Reform (Jiujiang Yiliao Baoxian Zhidu Gaige de Chengxiao, Wenti, he Duice), *China Health Economics*, No. 10, 1996, p 27-28.
13. Lei Haichao, Liu Xingzhu, and Bian Ying. "Effects of Increasing in Chronic Diseases on China's Total Health Expenditure and Macro Economy (Manxingbing Zhengjia Dui Woguo Weisheng Zongfeiyong ji Hongguan Jingji de Yingxiang Yanjiu).
14. Zhong Aifen and Wang Xinyao. "Review and Future of China's Employee Health Care System (Woguo Zhigong Yiliao Baojian Zhidu de Huigu yu Zhanwang), *China Health Economics*, No. 11, 1996, p49-50.
15. Folland, Sherman, Allen C. Goodman, and Miron Stano. The Economics of Health and Health Care. Prentice Hall, Upper Saddle River, NJ 07458, 1997.

CHAPTER 17

FINANCING HEALTH CARE IN DEVELOPING ECONOMIES: SIMULATIONS FOR CHINA

AKE BLOMQVIST
Department of Economics, University of Western Ontario,
London N6A 5C2, Canada
E-mail: Akeb@julian.uwo.ca

SUSHENG WANG
Hong Kong University of Science and Technology

LIJING ZHU*
Hong Kong University of Science and Technology

The paper illustrates the consequences of different health policy choices by means of computer simulations based on a simple general equilibrium model in which labor is the only production factor. The results of the simulations of hypothetical policy alternatives are discussed.

1. Introduction

Financing services that contribute to population health typically is one of the public sector's most important responsibilities, in both poor and rich countries.

There are several reasons for this. For certain kinds of preventative services, the case for government intervention arises because they have significant external effects so that competitive markets will tend to underprovide them. This argument is relevant to any activity that reduces the incidence of infectious (contagious) disease, including the provision of clean drinking water and waste disposal facilities, as well

* A more detailed version is available in the form of a working paper (Blomqvist, Wang, and Zhu 1998). Financial support from Hong Kong Research Grants Council project HKUST548/95H is gratefully acknowledged.

as vaccination programs and public health measures generally. Such activities are likely to account for a relatively large portion of the total cost of health-related programs in countries with low income.

In most countries, however, government also typically has a major role in the financing and provision of those curative health services for which external effects are less important. In part, this is because government financing of health services is seen as an effective way to promote equity.

The equity argument has several elements. First, public financing can be seen as a way of redistributing real income in favour of groups at high risk of illness. Such groups would be disadvantaged even in the presence of a well-functioning system of private insurance, but they will be especially badly off if private insurance is unavailable or very costly.

Second, however, in low-income countries with weak tax and transfer systems, the usual arguments against redistribution in kind (rather than in cash), may be reversed: Programs of redistribution in cash may be so administratively costly that certain types of redistribution in kind may be more efficient, in spite of the conventional arguments against in-kind transfers. If that is so, redistribution in favour of the poor through government provision of services such as health and basic education is likely to be favoured.

While the above line of reasoning relates principally to low-income countries, government typically is responsible for most of the cost of health care in high-income countries as well. In such countries, however, the reasons for government financing are somewhat different. In particular, the argument that public financing of health is a relatively efficient way of redistributing income in favour of the poor has much less force in high-income countries with well developed tax and transfer systems.[1] Moreover, programs intended to reduce the incidence of infectious disease typically account for a much smaller share of total spending in high-income countries than in low-income ones, so that the efficiency argument for government intervention aimed at correcting for external effects is less significant in the former group.

If government does not take responsibility for financing the cost of health care, most people will want to have some type of private health insurance to make sure that they will be able to pay for health services if they should become seriously ill and need expensive treatment. However, evidence from a number of countries,

---

[1] The argument that public financing is a good way of redistributing toward those with high risk of illness may still apply, however. For a formal analysis, see Blomqvist and Horn (1984).

particularly the United States, suggests that systems of private health insurance may be inefficient and costly to administer. Citizens in many high-income countries with a high degree of public financing are firmly convinced that they have a much more efficient health care system than that in the United States, where the high cost and imperfect availability of private health insurance for many population groups are seen as major shortcomings.[2]

Thus, somewhat different but nevertheless compelling arguments in favour of predominantly public financing of health care are well established for countries at both the high end and the low end of the per-capita income scale. In contrast, the principal point of the present paper is that for countries at intermediate levels of per capita income, there is a strong case for a system of *mixed public and private financing* and provision of health services.

Specifically, the paper focuses on "transitional" countries where the process of per capita income growth is well established. Empirical evidence, starting with the work of Kuznets, has shown that in such countries there is a strong tendency for measures of income inequality to rise, as significant portions of the population reach intermediate or high levels of per capita income.

In countries with rising income inequality, those responsible for health policy face a dilemma. The emerging middle class will gradually become dissatisfied with the standard of health care that the public sector provides for the broad classes of the low-income population. However, with average income remaining relatively low, the cost of raising the standards of health care provided *for everybody* to a level that would satisfy the middle class, is likely to be prohibitively high, particularly if the tax system is not highly developed and there are many other demands on public-sector revenue.

Several responses are possible to this dilemma. The worst outcome probably is when political pressure from the middle class causes a reallocation of resources *within* the health care system, away from the services of particular importance to the (rural and urban) poor, and in favour of those demanded by the middle class. This response clearly is inconsistent with any reasonable definition of equity, and may

[2] For a discussion of the high administrative cost of financing health care through private insurance in the United States, see Woolhandler and Himmelstein (1991). A large amount of material exists on the differences between the mixed public-private U.S. system and the much more centralized "single-payer" system in Canada. See, for example Evans (1986), Evans et al. (1989), and Fuchs and Hahn (1990).

also lead to substantial inefficiency, especially if the reallocation in favour of the middle class is accomplished through informal or corrupt mechanisms.[3]

Another response is to allow and encourage the development of voluntary insurance-based financing mechanisms for those who want a higher level of service than is provided in the public sector, while using most of the public-sector health care funds to serve the needs of the low-income population.

A mixed system of this type is sometimes criticized on the grounds that it implies a "two-tiered" health care system: a lower tier (the public one) for the poor, another tier (the private one) for the rich. In many countries, there is widespread support for the view that preventing the emergence of a two-tiered system should be regarded as a high policy priority, on the grounds that such a system is inherently inequitable.

In this paper, we argue against this view. Specifically, we suggest that in an economy where a weak tax system limits the government's ability to raise funds, a policy of ruling out a two-tiered system may implicitly be very costly. Moreover, we argue that it may sometimes also be inequitable in the sense that a single-tier health care system represents an inefficient way of helping the poor.

We illustrate the consequences of different health policy choices by means of numerical simulations based on a simple general equilibrium model in which the only factor of production is labour, but in which income inequality is generated by differences in the productivity of different individuals' labour. A person's demand for health services depends on a stochastic health state parameter that is unknown *ex ante*, and individuals are risk averse so that there are *ex ante* efficiency gains from (public or private) insurance. The implicit high cost (the so-called excess burden) of public funds results from the assumption that the only kind of tax is a progressive (linear) income tax, and that individuals reduce their work effort when taxes rise.

While the analysis and results are meant to be representative of a "typical" country at an intermediate stage of development, our interest in these issues originated with the case of China, whose health services system is now undergoing major changes. These changes result in part because of the reduction in the role of the state-owned firms that previously were responsible for financing the cost of their employees' health care, and in part because of the dismantling of the communes that

---

[3] Ho (1995) quotes statistics and estimates indicating that large numbers of people in China's rural areas have no guaranteed access to publicly financed health services, and that in the 1980s, as many as half the patients needing hospital treatment could not be admitted because of bed shortages. At the same time, there were complaints that the patients who *were* in fact admitted, were staying in hospital much longer than strictly necessary.

had this role in rural areas. The question of what mixed system of public and private financing will ultimately emerge as a replacement is an important part of the current policy debate in China.

The rest of the paper is organised as follows. In section 2 we specify the basic model, and explain how the quality of publicly financed health care is represented, as well as the way the model's equilibrium depends on individuals' choices between public or private health services. Section 3 contains a brief description of the procedures used to calibrate the model. In section 4, we describe the results of a number of simulations of hypothetical policy alternatives, and section 5 contains concluding comments.

2. The Model

We consider a model in which total output is determined by the aggregate input of one input only, labour. A fixed amount of output G must be used to produce a public good which does not directly enter consumers' utility functions. (It can be thought of as the cost of general government services such as maintaining law and order, for example.) Each remaining unit of output may either be consumed or used to produce one unit of health services. (Thus the price of one unit of health services is constant at unity.)

There are N consumers. Each one has the same amount T of total time which can either be used to produce labour or consumed in the form of leisure. Different consumers' time has different productivity: The maximum amount of output that the i'th consumer could produce is $w_i T$, where w_i is interpreted as either a gross wage rate or simply as a productivity parameter. The differences in w_i imply that different consumers have different realised income.

During each time period, the consumer will be in one of two states s, $s = S,B$, where S stands for the "healthy" state in which the consumer does not suffer a serious illness, while B is the state in which the consumer *does* suffer a serious illness. To begin with, the consumer does not know which state he/she will be in, but the probability π_B that he/she will be in state B is known. Each consumer has the same *ex ante* utility function $E(c_{iS}, \cdot_{iS}, h_{iS}, c_{iB}, \cdot_{iB}, h_{iB})$ whose value depends on the state-specific values of consumption, c_{is}, leisure $\cdot_{is}$, and health services h_{is}, where the subscript i refers to the consumer and $s = S,B$ refers to the state. The individual's objective is to maximize E subject to the relevant budget constraints.[4]

[4] For details on the functional form of E and the budget constraints, and a list of parameter values, see the Appendix.

Government expenditure consists of G plus whatever amount the government spends to finance health care in those cases where it is involved in this activity. For simplicity, government revenue is supposed to be raised through a progressive linear income tax. That is, the net amount of tax revenue r_{is} collected from individual i in state s is given by

$$r_{is} = -a + t \cdot w(T - \, ._{is})$$

where a is a "demogrant" and t is the (constant) marginal tax rate applied to the consumer's income.[5]

We now introduce health services in the model. To start with, consider the case where the government is not involved in financing health care. In this case, individuals either pay for health services directly out of their own pockets, or through privately acquired health insurance. To keep the analysis as simple as possible, we model private health insurance as a state-specific lump-sum payment. This assumption, and the assumption that the probabilities of each state are known and identical for each individual, rules out explicit consideration of certain inefficiencies that tend to arise in real-world private insurance markets.[6] The efficiency losses caused by these problems are represented instead as a fixed cost f associated with each private insurance contract; f also includes the administrative cost of providing insurance. The insurance market is assumed to be competitive which implies that the premium for each contract is equal to f plus the expected value of the insurer's payments under the policy.

Even though private insurance in this form is available, it is possible that an individual's *ex ante* utility may be higher without insurance than with insurance. In equilibrium, individuals choose the insurance status (insured or uninsured) that gives them the highest *ex ante* utility, given the optimal choices of consumption, leisure and health services, in each case. Given government non-health expenditure G, equilibrium for the economy as a whole also requires that one of the two fiscal parameters a, t be chosen such that the government budget is balanced. When consumers obey their budget constraints and the government budget is balanced, the economy's aggregate resource constraint is automatically satisfied.

---

[5] The assumption that all tax revenue comes from an income tax is made for convenience only. Since other types of taxes also have distortionary effects that, in the context of this model, are similar to those of an income tax, the principal conclusions of the model should not be affected by this assumption in a major way.

[6] We refer here to the problems of moral hazard and adverse selection. For descriptions based on U.S. experience, see, e.g., the textbook by Folland, Goodman and Stano (1997).

Next, consider the case where the government *does* involve itself in financing health care. We model this case as follows. First, we introduce the variables h_{GS}, h_{GB} which represent, respectively, the quantity of health services offered by the government to a person in state S, and to a person in state B. (For concreteness, h_{GS} may be thought of as the services provided in institutions such as rural health centres or urban outpatient clinics, while h_{GB} are services provided in government hospitals.)

We assume that these services are exogenously given policy parameters, the same for all patients who use the public system, regardless of income, and that they are provided at zero out of pocket cost to the patient. We also assume that persons who choose to use publicly provided health services, in either state, cannot supplement the quantities provided by the government through purchasing additional services in the private market. (However, as explained below, we do not rule out the possibility that a person may choose to use private-sector health services in one state, while relying on those provided by the government in the other state.)

A common feature of government-provided health services in developing countries is that they involve various forms of quantity rationing. In the case of outpatient services, rationing often manifests itself in long waits before a patient is seen by a doctor or other professional; the desire to avoid the long wait is one reason why those who can afford to, often prefer to use the services of private doctors. In the case of treatment for major illness, quantity rationing may consist of long waiting lists before a person can have an appointment for specialist treatment or services such as non-emergency surgery.[7] (In the case of certain kinds of disease, these waiting lists may obviously imply not only prolonged pain and suffering, but also the death of some patients whose treatment is delayed.)

In the model, we represent quantity rationing in state S as the loss of a fixed amount of time, denoted by $\cdot_{G}$, for each patient who receives government services h_{GS}. For state B, we represent rationing by postulating that only a fraction of those seeking treatment in the government system in state B will in fact be treated, while the remainder will receive no treatment. The fraction receiving treatment is denoted π_{GB}; clearly, $\pi_{GB} \leq 1$.

When government health services are available, the individual has several additional options in maximizing *ex ante* utility. Two options remain as before: the

[7] Recall the information from Ho (1995) quoted in footnote 3 above regarding the patients who could not be admitted to hospital because of bed shortages.

option of buying private insurance and using privately provided services, in both states; and the option of having no insurance but still using privately provided services in both states. Under both of these options, the quantities h_{iS} and h_{iB} are chosen by the individual. A third option is to use government health services in both states. Under this option, we have $h_{is} = h_{Gs}$, $s = S,B$, where the quantities h_{GS} and h_{GB} are exogenously determined. Finally, we allow two "mixed" options: to use government services in either state S or state B, and privately provided services in the other state.[8] Equilibrium in the model is defined as before. However, the government budget constraint must now be modified to include the cost of publicly provided health services.

3. Parameter Value and Functional Form

The parameters of the model were chosen in such a way as to generate an initial equilibrium that, in certain relevant respects, was similar to data for the Chinese economy in the early 1990s.[9] Government spending on goods and services (G) was set at approximately 15% of initial GDP. The demogrant a was set at a level equivalent to 4% of per capita GDP. Given these parameters, the marginal tax rate t necessary to balance the government budget is 19%.

We considered five income classes, that is, five different values for the productivity parameters w_i. They were chosen such that the (uncompensated) labour supply elasticity was +.075, and the before-tax distribution of income by quintile was similar to that reported for China in the early 1990s. With respect to health services utilization, we assumed that on average, those in state B use 15 times the amount of health services of those in state S. Combining this with the assumption that China spends about 5% of GDP on health services,[10] we set average health services spending by those in state S (assumed to constitute 93% of the population)

---

[8] In this model, private insurance is only relevant for those who use privately provided services in state B. That is, it will never be optimal for an individual to use private insurance to finance health services utilized in state S. For the case where individuals use publicly provided services in state S and private ones in state B, we assumed that they used private insurance to finance the latter.

[9] For further details regarding the calibration method, see the Appendix and Blomqvist, Wang and Zhu (1998).

[10] The World Bank (1993, p. 210), gives a lower figure (3.5% of GDP) for China in 1990. We have used a somewhat higher figure to calibrate the model, partly because we think the World Bank figure still reflects the failure of the rural health care system to recover from the reduction of resources it suffered under the impact of economic reforms in the 1980s, partly because other countries at a similar stage of development (such as India) show a substantially higher percentage. On the former point, see Ho (1995).

to the equivalent of roughly 2.5% of per capita GDP, while those in state *B* were assumed to have annual spending of some 3/8 of per capita GDP.

To estimate health services use by income class, we assumed that the income elasticity of health services spending by those in state *S* was unity (that is, health services spending by those in state *S* was proportional to disposable income).[11] The income elasticity for those in state *B* was implicitly assumed to be much lower.

In solving the model, we assumed that the consumers' preferences could be described through a utility function similar to that described in Selden (1978). As a reference point for the simulations below, we chose parameters characterizing private and public insurance so as to produce the following pattern of health services financing and utilization. Those in the lowest income quintile (Q1) used the public system in both illness states. Individuals in the second and third quintiles also relied on the public system, but only in state *B* (that is, if they suffered a major illness); in state *S*, they relied on the services of private providers, which they paid for out of their own pocket. Those in the fourth and fifth quintiles used the services of private providers in both illness states, but the method of financing was different: Individuals in Q4 relied on private insurance, while individuals in Q5 paid for all health services out of their own pockets.

TABLE 1: **Reference Solution, Parameters and Endogenous Variables**

Parameters	$h_{GS} = .1$ $\cdot_{G} = .1$ $h_{GB} = 5.4$ $\pi_{GB} = .95$ $a = .55$; $G = 2.0$
Variables	GDP = 13.46 Gov. Exp. = 2.784 $t = .2068$ $\Sigma\Sigma h_{iS} = .6688$ $\Sigma_i h_{iS} = .2994$ (Gov't share: 6.2%) $\Sigma_i h_{Ib} = .3695$ (Gov't share: 58.3%)

[11] For a discussion of the income elasticity issue using international cross-section evidence, see Blomqvist and Carter (1997).

The equilibrium values of the principal variables in the model in the reference solution, and the parameter values relating to the government and private insurance plans that generated this equilibrium, are shown in Table I.

The value h_{GS} = .1 was equivalent to assuming that those individuals with minor illness (s=S) who used the public system would receive services costing only about .75 of one percent of per capita GDP each year. If, for simplicity, we use the round number 5000 yuan as the order of magnitude of per capita GDP, this would be equivalent to annual spending of 37.5 yuan per capita, and is about equivalent to the amount that an individual in the first (poorest) quintile would voluntarily spend if no public services were available. (Following the assumption that the income elasticity of demand for health services in state S is about unity, however, 37.5 yuan is considerably less than individuals with higher income would spend voluntarily. In the reference solution, average spending by all individuals in state S on health services is equivalent to about 120 yuan per year.) Moreover, the value . $_{G}$ = 0.1 is equivalent to assuming that those who use the public health services system in state S would incur a time cost of approximately six days per year over and above the time cost incurred by those using the services of private providers (primary-care doctors).[12] Thus the assumptions in the reference solution implied that government services in state S were of relatively low quality both in the sense of a low level of service and long waiting times. Finally, the value f = .02 is equivalent to an annual cost of less than 10 yuan per private insurance policy, over and above the actuarially fair premium. This amount may be compared to the actuarially fair premium of a policy that pays the cost of health care to the 7% of the population who are seriously ill (that is, who are in state B) each year: This premium would be about 130 yuan per year.

4. Policy Simulations

In this section, we use the model described above to illustrate the consequences of changing certain model parameters, particularly those that relate to the quality of the health care provided in the public sector. At the aggregate level, we look at the effects on aggregate health care spending and on the share of total health services provided by the public system (that is, on the cost to the government), as well as on the impact on economic efficiency as measured by the sum of the compensating variations (relative to the reference solution) for gainers and losers. We also

---

[12] In the time units used in the model, average work time is about 3.5 per year; assuming 200 working days, .1 equals about .1/3.5 times 200, or approximately 6, days.

consider the impact of each change on equity, by computing the (approximate) compensating variation (CV) for each of the five income classes Q1 (lowest) to Q5 (highest). Results of five such policy simulations are shown in Table II, and we briefly discuss each of them below.

TABLE 2: Simulations

Solution No.	(0) Ref.	(1) $h_{GS}2$	(2) $h_{GS}2\,.\,{}_{G}0$	(3) $\pi_{GB}85$	(4) $\pi_{GB}100$	(5) pub100
$\Sigma\Sigma h_{iS}$ (% change)	--	+1.5%	+1.0%	1.1%	0.9%	-1.8%
% Government Funding	35.00	37.6	48.4	2.7	58.7	100
Tax Rate t (%)	20.68	20.99	21.44	18.91	22.06	24.34
Σ_iCV/GDP (%)	--	-0.15	0.0	1.20	.97	.31
CV_{Q1} (%)	--	1.54	3.20	-4.87	2.58	4.93
CV_{Q2}	--	0.32	2.07	0.0	2.52	3.83
CV_{Q3}	--	-0.34	1.01	2.05	2.58	4.93
CV_{Q4}	--	-0.39	-0.94	2.20	1.36	0.66
CV_{Q5}	--	-0.39	-0.94	2.20	-0.03	-2.36

Financing Patterns:
Reference solution: G2, GB, GB, P2i, S
Solution 1: G2, G2, GSi, P2i, S
Solution 2: G2, G2, G2, P2i, S
Solution 3: GSi, P2i, P2i, P2i, S
Solution 4: G2, GB, GB, GB, GB
Solution 5: All G2

Legend: "G2" means "use of government services in both states"; "GB" means "use of government services in state *B*"; 'P2i" means "use of private services in both states, with insurance"; "*S*" means "use of private services in both states, no insurance"; "*GSi*" means "use of government services in state *S*, with insurance for state *B*".

4.1 Raising the standards of primary care

In the reference solution, the government provides only a limited extent of primary care (that is, care to those in state *S*). Only those in the lowest quintile used the public system for their primary care, while everyone else used private providers. An increase in the quality of the primary care provided in the public system could be expected to raise the public-sector share as more people use the public system.

Column (1) in Table II shows the effects of raising the parameter h_{GS} from .1 to .2 (or from about 37.5 to 75 yuan per person per year). Intuitively, such a change could consist of providing more advanced pharmaceuticals, raising the ratio of doctors to nurses in health clinics, etc. (Note, however, that the parameter $\cdot_G$ stays the same. That is, the waiting time in public clinics is assumed unchanged in this experiment.)

In the model, this policy change causes income classes Q2 and Q3 to switch from private providers to the public system for primary care (in state *S*). The model predicts a small increase (of 1.5%) in aggregate spending on health care, and an increase in the government's share of total health care costs. The increased government expenditure necessitates a tax increase (by approximately 1/3 of one percentage point). The effect on economic welfare as conventionally measured, is negative, but the size of the aggregate welfare loss is only about 0.15 of one percent of GDP. The equity effect is progressive, in the sense that welfare increases for income classes Q1 (by the equivalent of about 1.5% of its income) and Q2, but there are welfare losses (essentially because of the higher taxes) for the middle and high income groups.

In Col. 2, it is assumed that the standard of primary care in the public system is further improved, in the sense that the system's capacity is expanded sufficiently so that waiting times are eliminated. This change was represented by changing the parameter $\cdot_G$ to $\cdot_G = 0$. (The parameter h_{GS} was set at .2, as in Col. 1.) With this reform, the increase in aggregate spending on health care is somewhat smaller than in Col. 1, but there is now a substantial increase in the government's share (to over 48%), as the model predicts that income classes Q1, Q2, and Q3 will use the public system in both states under this experiment. In comparison with the reference solution, there is now a tax increase of about 3/4 of one percentage point. The aggregate efficiency effect of this hypothetical reform package is approximately zero.

From an equity point of view, Col. 2 implies that this policy package has a substantial progressive effect, with the lowest income class showing a real income gain of more than 3%. Groups Q2 and Q3 also show positive gains, whereas for groups Q4 and Q5 there are net losses as their taxes rise.

4.2 Secondary/tertiary care

Columns 3 and 4 show the results of hypothetical changes to the standard of health care the government provides to those with serious illness (in state B). In particular, they show the results of simulations in which the parameter π_{GB} is changed from its value in the reference solution. As discussed above, this parameter can be thought of as representing the extent to which the government creates waiting lists for access to the treatment in hospitals for serious illness, by limiting the capacity of the hospital system. In the model, it equals the probability that an individual who relies on the public system in state B will in fact be treated (receive h_{GB}); those who are not treated will die (be assigned a utility of zero).

In Col. 3, the value of π_{GB} has been reduced to .85 from .95, its value in the reference solution. That is, waiting lists have been allowed to be so long that 15% of those who rely on the public system in state B will not receive treatment. With this assumption, the model predicts that almost everyone will switch to health care from the private sector: Only those in income class Q1 will continue to rely on the public sector in state S; in state B, all income classes seek care in the private sector, with all but income class Q5 relying on private insurance to finance their care in state B.[13]

Lines 4 to 9 in Col. 3 illustrates the fundamental tradeoff between equity and efficiency that is involved in public financing of health care. Line 4 shows that the effect of virtually eliminating public-sector health care is a substantial efficiency gain, equivalent to 1.2% of GDP in the model. Intuitively, this result reflects the reduced efficiency loss as reduced public health care costs make possible a reduction in taxes. However, the impact on equity is highly regressive: Income class Q1 suffers a loss equivalent to almost 5% of their real income, while groups Q3, Q4, and Q5 experience gains equivalent to more than 2% of their real income, as their taxes fall.

While Col. 3 shows the effect of reducing the standard of care in the hospital sector, Col. 4 shows the effects of *raising* the standard, in the sense that the government expands the hospital system sufficiently so that there are no waiting

[13] The income in class Q5 is sufficiently high in relation to the cost of care in state B so that even with the relatively low loading cost of insurance (the parameter f), individuals in this class are better off self-insuring. In a separate experiment (not shown in Table II), the parameter f was raised from .02 to .05. The result was that income classes Q4 and Q3 then switched to self-insurance, but the two lowest income classes continued to rely on private insurance to finance their care in state B.

lists. In the model, this is represented by setting $\pi_{GB} = 1$.[14] With this assumption, everyone will rely on the public sector for treatment when they are seriously ill.

4.3 *A single-payer system*

Although the solution in Col. 4 had no private health insurance (since everyone used the public system in state *B*), it still corresponded to a "mixed" system in which privately financed health services accounted for about 40% of the total costs of health care. In the simulation in Col. 5, in contrast, the public-sector parameters were set at levels that made it optimal for every income class to choose public-sector care in both states. (In the health policy debate, a system in which the public sector pays for 100% of the cost of health care is sometimes referred to as a "single-payer" system.) Specifically, the waiting time parameters were set at . $_G = 0$ and $\pi_{GB} = 1$, respectively (that is, it was assumed that there were no waiting time for access to public-sector primary care, and no waiting lists for hospital care). The parameter h_{GB} was set at the same value as in the reference solution, and h_{GS} was raised (in increments of .05) until it was high enough so that everyone would seek primary care in the public-sector system. This occurred at $h_{GS} = .3$.

With a public-sector share of 100%, a tax rate of 24.3% (or about 3.6 percentage points higher than in the reference solution) was necessary to finance aggregate government expenditure, although (in comparison with the reference solution) there was a small decrease in aggregate spending on health care. Again relative to the reference solution, there was an aggregate efficiency gain, though only by about 0.3% of GDP. From an equity point of view, the model shows a move to a single-payer system to be highly progressive: The lowest income class is shown as gaining the equivalent of as much as 5% of real income, and the only class with a net loss is Q5 where the loss corresponds to more than 2% of real income.

5 Concluding Comments

In a rapidly changing society such as China's, the formulation of government policy in the health sector involves an exceedingly complex set of questions. An exercise

[14] It is implied by the assumptions of this model that no one dies from serious illness provided they receive treatment at least equal to θ_B in state *B*. In reality, of course, many people die from serious illness even if they receive immediate treatment. Thus the extent to which the parameter π_{GB} differs from unity should be thought of as the *excess* mortality among those who rely on the public sector, when waiting lists for treatment exist in the public sector but not in the private sector.

with a small stylized model of the type used above can obviously only focus on a small subset of them.

In the present paper, the objective is to illustrate an issue that arises in a situation where the standard of publicly financed health care is the same for everyone (rich or poor), who uses the public system, but where those who so desire are free to use privately provided health services instead. If public-sector health care is financed through a progressive tax system, there will then be an equity-efficiency trade-off.

Raising the quality of publicly provided care will have a favourable impact on equity. By increasing the quality of care for the (predominantly low-income) users of the public system, it tends to raise their real income; if the tax system is progressive, most of the incremental tax revenue that must be raised to pay for the increase in quality will be born by those with relatively high income. However, with a positive income elasticity of demand for health services, inducing people with different incomes to utilize the same level of health services has a negative effect on efficiency, as conventionally defined. The reason is that, at the same level of health services utilization, those with higher levels of income have a higher willingness to pay, at the margin, for additional health services, than those with a lower income. The results of the simulation exercises bring out this equity-efficiency trade-off quite clearly.

As is usual in static general equilibrium models, the calculations in this one yield aggregate efficiency effects that seem relatively modest.[15] To what extent they should be used as guidelines for actual policy-making, therefore, depends on whether longer-term dynamic efficiency effects would go in the same direction as the calculated ones. The same caution, of course, applies with respect to the estimated effects on equity.

Subject to the preceding qualifications, the results in Section 4 are nevertheless interesting in several respects. Consider first the comparison of the reference case with solutions (1) and (2) which involve different levels of improvement of the standard of publicly provided primary care (care in state *S* in the model). Both solutions are shown as raising the real income of the low-income groups that use publicly provided primary care. However, solution (1) shows a negative aggregate efficiency effect, and solution (2) is estimated to yield an aggregate efficiency effect of approximately zero, even though it involves the elimination of the resource waste

[15] Note that even the largest of the aggregate efficiency effects in Table II is equivalent to a little over one percent of GDP, which is only a fraction of the amount by which China's GDP has been growing each year in the last two decades.

associated with waiting times in publicly provided care. On the other hand, consider the effects in solution (3) of a hypothetical policy of *reducing* the quality (through allowing increased waiting times) of publicly provided care for those with serious illness. Surprisingly, the simulation indicates that such a policy would have a substantial *positive* aggregate efficiency effect, even though it would be equivalent to reducing the real income of the bottom quintile by some 5%. Both of these comparisons highlight the nature of the trade-off that policy makers face.

Comparison of the reference case with solutions (4) and (5) illustrates the same principle in a different way. In solution (4), an improvement of the quality of publicly provided care to those with serious illness (loosely, those needing hospital care) results in *both* an aggregate efficiency gain, *and* an improvement in equity. In solution (5), the standard of publicly provided care has been improved (in comparison with the reference case) for both primary care and for those with serious illness. Even though solution (5) still shows an efficiency gain (in comparison with the reference case), it is smaller than the efficiency gain in solution (4) which involves a lower quality of primary care. Taken together, these calculations suggest the following question: Should a second-best policy be limited to providing a relatively high standard of care for those with serious illness, while supporting those with low incomes through cash transfers rather than through publicly provided primary care?

References

1. Blomqvist, Ake, and Henrik Horn (1984), "Public health insurance and optimal income taxation", *Journal of Public Economics*, 24, pp. 353-373.
2. Blomqvist, Ake, and Robin Carter (1997), "Is health care really a luxury?", *Journal of Health Economics*, 16, pp. 207-29.
3. Blomqvist, Ake, Susheng Wang and Lijing Zhu (1998), "Financing Health Care in Developing Economies: A Simulation Approach", unpublished working paper, 1998.
4. Evans, Robert G. (1986), "Finding the levers, finding the courage: Lessons from cost containment in North America", *Journal of Health Politics, Policy and Law*, 11, pp. 585-615.
5. Evans, Robert G. et al. (1989), "Controlling health expenditures: The Canadian reality", *New England Journal of Medicine*, 320, pp. 571-77.
6. Folland, Sherman, Allen C. Goodman, and Miron Stano (1997), *The Economics of Health and Health Care*. (Second Edition.) Upper Saddle River, N.J.: Prentice Hall.

7. Fuchs, Victor R., and James S. Hahn (1990), "How does Canada do it?", *New England Journal of Medicine*, 323, pp. 884-90.
8. Ho, Lok Sang (1995), "Market reforms and China's health care system", *Social Science and Medicine*, 41, pp. 1065-72.
9. Selden, Larry (1978a), "A new representation of preferences over 'Certain x Uncertain' consumption pairs: The 'Ordinal Certainty Equivalent' hypothesis", *Econometrica*, 46, pp. 1045-60.
10. Selden, Larry (1978b): "An OCE analysis of the effects of uncertainty on saving under risk preference independence", *Review of Economic Studies*, 46, pp. 73--82.
11. Woolhandler, S., and D. U. Himmelstein (1991), "The deteriorating administrative efficiency of the U.S. health care system", *New England Journal of Medicine*, 324, pp. 1253-1258.
12. World Bank (1993), *Investing in Health: World Development Report 1993*. Oxford University Press for the World Bank.

APPENDIX

The utility function used (following Selden (1978a,b)) was

$$E_i = \left[\delta_c (E(\tilde{c}_i - \hat{c})^\alpha)^{\beta/\alpha} + \delta_\ell (E(\tilde{\ell}_i - \ell)^\alpha)^{\beta/\alpha} + \delta_h (E(\tilde{h}_i - \tilde{\theta})^\alpha\right]^{\frac{1}{\beta}}$$

(A1)

Here $\tilde{c}$ denotes the random variable:

$$\tilde{c}_i = \begin{cases} c_{Bi} \text{ with probability } \pi_B \\ c_{Si} \text{ with probability } 1-\pi_B \end{cases}$$

(A2)

and $\tilde{\ell}_i$, $\tilde{h}_i$ and $\tilde{\theta}$ are similarly defined. The parameters δ_c, δ_ℓ, δ_h, $\tilde{c}$, $\tilde{\ell}$, α, and β are state-independent. The two illness severity parameters θ_s, $s = S,B$ are state-dependent, with $\theta_B > \theta_S$.

Since private insurance in this model is equivalent to a state-contingent contract, a privately insured individual faces a single budget constraint given by

$$\sum_s \pi_s (c_{is} + h_{is}) + f \le a + w_i (1-t) \sum_s \pi_s (T - \ell_{is})$$

(A3)

For individuals who use private health care but have no insurance, the (state-dependent) budget constraints are

$$c_{iS} + h_{iS} \le a + w_i (1-t)(T - \ell_{iS})$$

(A4)

$$c_{iB} + h_{iB} \le a + w_i (1-t)(T - \ell_{iB})$$

(A5)

For individuals who use government services in state S, (A4) is replaced by

$$c_{iS} \le a + w_i (1-t)(T - \ell_{iS} - \ell_G)$$

(A6)

in state S. For individuals who use government services in state B, the relevant budget constraint is:

$$c_{iB} \le a + w_i (1-t)(T - \ell_{iB});$$

(A7)

In equilibrium, individuals choose the option (i.e., whether to use private or public health services, in either state, and, if they use private services in state B, whether or not to be insured) which gives them the highest *ex ante* utility, given the optimal choices of c_{is}, $\cdot\ _{is}$, h_{is}, $s = S,B$ in each case. Given G, equilibrium for the economy as a whole also requires that one of the two fiscal parameters a, t be chosen such that the government budget is balanced:

$$G + \sum_{i \in \Omega_S} h_{GS} + \pi_{GB} \sum_{i \in \Omega_B} h_{GB} = \sum_i \sum_s r_{is} = -N \cdot a + t \cdot \sum_i \sum_s w_i (T - \ell_{is})$$

(A8)

where Ω_s, $s = S,B$, represent the subsets of individuals who use government health services (rather than privately provided services) in the respective states.

The parameter values used in the simulations were as follows (for further explanations of how these values were chosen, see Blomqvist, Wang and Zhu (1998)).

TABLE 3: Parameter Values

$\alpha = 0.2$	$\theta_S = 0.0$
$\sigma = 0.85$	$\theta_B = 5.0$
$\pi_B = 0.07$	$T = 8$
$\delta_c = .442$	$w_1 = 1.0$
$\delta = .551$	$w_2 = 1.937$
$\delta_h = .007$	$w_3 = 2.2915$
$\hat{c} = -.2$	$w_4 = 4.354$
$\hat{\ell} = -1.2$	$w_5 = 8.1$

CHAPTER 18

GROWTH AND SECURITY UNDER WELFARE-CORPORATE CAPITALISM AND MARKET SOCIALISM

MYRON J. GORDON[1]
Rotman School of Management, University of Toronto,
Toronto, ON 5S1V4, Canada
E-mail: gordon@mgmt.utoronto.ca

The essential differences between a pure capitalist and a pure socialist economy are private vs. public ownership of capital and reliance on the market vs a bureaucracy to administer the economy. Under the theory of each pure system it is a utopia, while the reality in each case has been closer to a hell on earth. A pure capitalist system at best provides growth without economic security, while the opposite is at best true of a pure socialist system. Feasible alternatives are welfare capitalism and market socialism.

When the security provided by the transition from feudalism to capitalism ended, about 1850 in Western Europe, continued growth required the security provided by the rise of welfare capitalism. That in turn has been reversed by the rise of corporate capitalism. The modern corporation engages in a wide range of non production activities in the pursuit of the profits from monopoly power. These activities enable corporations to participate in all of the worlds important markets and move production from one country to another at will. Most impressive is their ability to move beyond the traditional domain of the market to make profitable growth industries of utility services, public services such as education and health, and the culture industries. That plus the international mobility of capital has reduced greatly the ability of countries to manage their economic affairs. Whether this decline in welfare capitalism is cyclical or secular remains to be seen.

---

[1] An earlier version of this paper was presented at the International Symposium on the Establishment of a Market-Oriented Social Security System in China, June 23-25, 1998, Beijing, China.

In China the transition from the security without growth of bureaucratic socialism to market socialism began about 1980. In agriculture and in bringing industry to the countryside it has been immensely successful, but that success is creating problems of further development that threaten the viability of continued state ownership and control. These problems have existed from the start in urban state enterprises. There it has been most difficult to reconcile modernization, profitability and growth with security and equality. China's leaders appear determined to close the gap over time between China and the West in productivity and per capita consumption. Whether the means to that end is the continued development of market socialism or the transition to welfare-corporate capitalism remains to be seen.

1. Growth and Security Under Welfare-Corporate Capitalism and Market Socialism

The two things that people want most from their country's economic system are growth in their income and security in their income. To the degree that workers find security in capitalist countries, it has been obtained in large measure, but not solely through social security -- old age pensions, unemployment compensation and other benefits, financed through the tax system and managed through government. Social security contrasts with the private capitalist arrangement for security-portfolio wealth. A third source of security is the corporation. Pensions and other benefits provided by the corporation have grown relative to social security over the last 25 years.

In socialist countries, the government guarantees economic security to its workers, but it delegates immediate responsibility for the security of their income and other benefits to the enterprise or other work unit. Now, it is proposed that the immediate responsibility for pensions and other benefits be transferred to government. To arrive at a policy with regard to social security under each type of system, it is useful to understand how security is provided in general and to understand the tradeoff between security and growth.

This paper will review the historical development and examine the main current features of welfare-corporate capitalism and market socialism in providing growth and security. Welfare-corporate capitalism and market socialism are the systems that we now enjoy or suffer depending on your point of view, and variations on them are what the future is likely to bring. Our understanding of these two systems is served by first considering four other economic systems. Two are the theories of a pure capitalist system and a pure socialist system. The other two are the actual performances of pure capitalist and pure socialist systems. Our examination of market socialism will rely on China, for the obvious reason that China is the country where market socialism has the longest history and richest development.

The two main distinguishing features of a pure capitalist system are a) private ownership of the means of production, and b) reliance on markets for the administration of the economy. By contrast, a pure socialist system has a) public ownership of the means of production, and b) reliance on a bureaucracy to administer the economy. Neoclassical, that is establishment economists, have constructed a theory of a perfectly competitive capitalist system that is a utopia. Everyone is free to buy, produce and work at whatever she wants. All wage and profit rates are fair. There is no unemployment, insecurity, etc. Similarly, utopian socialists, anarchists and Marxists in the capitalist world, and establishment socialist economists in the former Soviet Union have constructed various theories of a pure socialist system that also are utopian in nature.

Establishment economists here and in the former Soviet Union have recognized that the real world falls short of their respective utopias. Neoclassical economists tell us that the gap is due to market imperfections. In doing so some of them offer us a more attractive vision of the future than the great theologians. The latter, with few exceptions, recognize that human imperfections make a heaven on earth practically impossible, but some neoclassical economists assure us that heaven on earth requires only that we overcome market imperfections. I presume that the establishment economists in the former Soviet Union claimed that their utopia required only that imperfections in the bureaucracy be overcome.

In fact, neither pure system has existed in practice for any length of time, and neither is a viable option for the future. Each pure system soon proves to be closer to a hell than a heaven on earth. The worldly function of pure systems is largely ideological. The human desire for perfection makes it attractive for the champions of capitalism to compare the theory of a pure capitalist system with the reality of pure socialist systems in order to reject socialism, while socialist radicals compare the theory of a pure socialist system with the reality of pure capitalist systems in order to justify the call for the end to capitalism. To see why neither pure system is a viable option for the future, and to understand what options we really have, we must look at each of these systems within the context of their historical development.

However, the rationale for the above conclusions that will be presented in what follows can be summarized quite briefly. A pure capitalist system at best provides growth without security, while a pure socialist system at best provides security without growth. People require both security and growth, so that either extreme is intolerable for any length of time. Welfare-corporate capitalism and market socialism can be more or less successful in providing both, so that the survival of each in any country may depend solely on a variety of circumstances surrounding its existence at a particular time and place. There is, however, a difference between the two systems. The dominant, if not the sole distinguishing feature is the ownership and control of wealth. In one, the private ownership of wealth is predominant, while in the other it is collective or public ownership. Perhaps, the private ownership tips the balance between growth and security in favour of growth, while the dominance of public ownership and control has the opposite effect. Whether or not that is true, and if it is true, whether it makes one system more or less attractive and more or less successful in the competition between the two are questions of considerable interest and importance.

2. Transition from Feudalism to Capitalism

European capitalism had its origins in feudal society. Feudalism there arose in the centuries following the fall of the Roman Empire, in order to provide security against the raids of marauding tribes. Tribalism was the alternative economic system at the time. The typical feudal manor was a closed system that also provided economic security through its technology of production and social arrangements. However, the agricultural surplus that increased with the progress of feudal society could not be realized very effectively by employing artisans in the feudal manor for the production of the wide range of manufactures, including armaments and ornaments, that were being produced in the towns. A far more profitable use of this surplus was its sale to the towns, that is by becoming involved in market transactions and the rise of capitalism. Nowhere is the contradiction in the development of a system more vivid than the role of capitalism in the development of feudalism. The towns made possible the realization of the surplus being produced on the feudal estates, but they did not merely embellish feudal life by providing it with more attractive products for consumption. The size of the feudal armies, the period of time that they could be mobilized for war, and the quality of their armaments all depended on the development of the towns and their activities. Where the towns were suppressed or failed to develop for other reasons, feudal power stagnated and became vulnerable to defeat.

The towns, however, financed the rise of national monarchs and eventually nation states; so that the progress of feudal society undermined its foundations. The contradictions in this process transformed, corrupted and ultimately destroyed feudal society. It culminated in the transition to capitalism between the 15th and 18th centuries, a unique and remarkable event, since that transition did not take place under roughly similar circumstances in other places[2]. One striking example is 17th Century China.

Capitalism can be a very effective engine of economic growth, but it is also a terrible engine of economic insecurity, and without high growth the insecurity is intolerable. This insecurity was moderated during the transition from feudalism to capitalism, both by the growth made possible by the transition, and by the cushion provided by the underlying feudal society. That transition was completed in Great Britain by about 1850, and by that date the country was to come as close as it ever was to having a pure competitive capitalist system. Feudalism was gone and the welfare state had not been established. About 1850, Charles Dickens's novels and Karl Marx's *Capital*, each in its own way, described the consequences of that system for the mass of the people. Marx drew his information from the reports of parliamentary committees on child labor, the employment of women, and the housing and health of the people. These reports warned that unless drastic corrective action was taken, the British working class would be physically destroyed by the competitive capitalist system that was in place.

3. The Rise of Welfare Capitalism

Over the years 1850 to 1950, the leading capitalist countries suffered both the privation and insecurity of fluctuations in employment and output, and periodic wars of increasing scale. However, the dominant story was the rise of the welfare state, the extraordinary growth in productivity and in prosperity for both capitalist and worker, and the phenomenal growth in the managerial and professional middle class. The private arrangements to find economic security proved to be inadequate, and social security was found in numerous ways, including trade unions, pension plans, unemployment compensation, socialized medicine and public housing. Progressive taxation and employment expenditure policies, undertaken to increase aggregate demand, were among the other features of the welfare state. With corporate income taxed at rates of about 50%, with marginal tax rates on personal income in excess of 50%, and with the proceeds employed for social welfare, it may have appeared to many capitalists that the peaceful transition to socialism was all but complete.

---

[2] This evolution and its theoretical framework are presented in greater detail in the last chapter of Gordon (1994).

However, the rise in the welfare state is understood better as a Marxist contradiction in the development of capitalism. With the end of feudalism at home, the growth made possible by its elimination and the security provided by its continued existence had to be replaced. Technological progress and imperialism provided continued growth, but that was not enough: the continued development of capitalism required its gradual elimination. Social democracy seemed to be no less effective an instrument for expropriation than socialism.

During the Great Depression, the establishment economic rationale for the welfare state and its related developments were explained with greater rigour and authority than ever before by John M. Keynes and M. Kalecki. The formal recognition and adoption of the welfare state, due in large measure to Keynes, made the years 1945 to 1970 a golden age in capitalist development. It was a period of stability and growth, rising expectations and their realization, at least in the industrialized countries.

4. Corporate Capitalism

The 1970's, however, inaugurated a reversal in the rise of the welfare state, that was due in large measure to the development of the modern corporation over the prior 100 years.

The 18th and 19th century manufacturing enterprises described by Adam Smith and Karl Marx were engaged predominantly if not solely in production. Competition was dealt with by means of price wars, mergers and cartels, instruments that did not require a large corporate bureaucracy. Typically, factory and office were located in the same or in adjoining buildings, and managing one or more other factories elsewhere in the same country was a challenging task. Over the last century the progress in travel, transportation, communication, data processing and in the practice of management have resulted in the global corporation. It participates in all of the world's important markets, while moving production almost at will from one low wage country to another in order to minimize production cost.

The distinguishing feature of the modern corporation is that it engages primarily in a wide range of non-production activities in pursuit of monopoly power. These activities include research and development for the purpose of improving existing products, discovering new products and reducing production costs. They include selling and advertising to differentiate products, thereby increasing sales and increasing the mark up of price over production costs. They include labor relations to persuade or intimidate workers to produce more or accept lower wages. They include political contributions, lobbying and corruption of government officials in order to obtain natural resources on favorable terms and other favors of government. They include the employment of lawyers, accountants and financiers to avoid and evade taxes and to influence tax legislation. I could go on. These activities may be harmless apart from their cost and their consequences for the distribution of income. They may also be beneficial or malignant in their immediate consequences for society. Regardless, what they all have in common is the pursuit of the profits to be gained from monopoly power.[3]

A useful measure of a firm's monopoly power, called the degree of monopoly, is the ratio of value added to the wages of production workers. Value added is sales volume, less the cost of the materials used in production. The Annual Survey of Manufactures of the U.S. Bureau of Census collects this data. Over the years 1899 to 1949, the degree of monopoly power in the manufacturing sector of the US economy fluctuated in a narrow range around 2.5. Over the years 1949 to 1994, it rose dramatically to 5.2, so that production cost accounted for only 20¢ of every dollar of profit in 1994. Profit on capital and the cost of monopoly activities absorbed the other eighty cents. The process is simple: corporate growth takes place to the degree that expenditure in the pursuit of monopoly power generates a rise in monopoly power, and the increased profits that result provide the funds for a further rise in the expenditure for monopoly power.

The importance of these monopoly activities is illustrated quite dramatically by looking at the financial statements of Microsoft, a leading high technology company. In the year ending June 1997 it had sales revenue of $11,358 million, while the labor and material cost of producing the products sold was only $1,085 million. The cost of research and development was $1,925 million, while sales and marketing expenses were almost 50% greater at $2,856 million. General and administration expenses came to $362 million, and income before deducting income taxes was $5,314 million. Notice that the total labor and material cost of producing the output sold during the year was less than 10% of the value of the goods sold, while the expenditures to maintain and increase its monopoly power came to 45% of sales revenue, and profits amounted to 47% of sales revenue. The profit of over $5

---

[3] The pursuit of monopoly power and its rise in the U. S. manufacturing sector are described in greater detail in Gordon (1998). Schumpeter (1942) in large measure anticipated these developments. Competition takes form of the search for monopoly power that also involves according to Schumpter the process of "creative destruction" that results in the elimination of monopoly power. The development of the modern corporation is recognised and interpreted in different ways in Chandler (1977) (1990), Galbraith (1967), Sherer and Ross (1990), Simon (1976) and Williamson (1985).

billion was earned with an investment in inventory, equipment and buildings of less than $2.0 billion. The market value of Microsoft's common stock was over $160 billion, reflecting the extraordinary opportunities for profitable growth created by its monopoly power. Microsoft is only a somewhat extreme example of the costs incurred and the profits generated in the pursuit of monopoly power by the large modern corporation.

5. Welfare-Corporate Capitalism

Individually and collectively, General Electric, Disney, Merck, Sony, Toyota, Intel, Siemens and all of the other great multinational corporations of the world are magnificent institutions. No less marvellous an accomplishment is the countless small growth enterprises that spring up in response to every opportunity for profit. Most disappear in bankruptcy, many are absorbed by and reinvigorate the great corporations, while a few grow into mighty corporations themselves.

The genius of corporate capitalism is illustrated most vividly by its ability to discover or create opportunities for profit beyond the traditional areas where the market has ruled. The authority and role of government and the threat to corporate power that it represents are thereby being reduced drastically. Government ownership or regulation had been the rule in electricity, telecommunications and other services that are provided by public utility companies, on the grounds that they are natural monopolies and the public interest is served through the widest possible access. These industries are now being privatized and deregulated with the claim that efficiency and progress are served through the rule of the market[4]. Concentration of ownership in a few multi-national corporations is not considered a problem. Similarly, health care, education, prisons and other services for which externalities and important public purposes have justified reliance on government or non-profit institutions are now being privatized and made profitable.

Most remarkable has been the transformation of television, newspapers, and book publishing, music, sports, and all other expressions of art and culture. They are being transformed into great industries dominated by multinational corporations

---

[4] In the telecommunication and electricity industries, profitability is increased by raising the price for basic services, in particular access to the service, since the demand for access is price inelastic. In addition, basic services are exploited to subsidize exotic services to the rich for which demand is price elastic. Analogous exploitation of the price system takes place in health care and education. Inequality of income and marginalization of the poor, by reducing their access to these services, is thereby increased.

such as Disney and Time Warner and extreme right-wing individuals such as Rupert Murdoch and Conrad Black. These new growth industries offer dazzling prospects for profitability. In addition, they convert capitalist control of society from a costly and sometimes ugly burden (Chile, Nicaragua, Angola) to a highly profitable growth industry. For the most recent developments in the corporate control of agriculture and its threat to the survival of peasants in the third world, see Kahn (1999).

The most brilliant and mystifying consequences of the technological and institutional developments that have given rise to corporate capitalism is the internationalization of financial capital. Money, bonds, shares and other forms of nominal wealth now move from one country to another with the speed of light, at practically no cost, in enormous volumes, and beyond the knowledge and control of government. That, combined with the World Bank, the IMF, the World Trade Organization and the unchallenged leadership of the United States has reduced drastically the power of governments relative to corporations. Felix (1998) describes how the international mobility of financial capital is making increasingly difficult the national use of fiscal policy, monetary policy or industrial policy to influence economic performance. Tax avoidance, tax evasion, tax havens and investment incentives are making personal and corporate profits free of taxation. Even the World Bank and the IMF are now raising questions about the international mobility of capital.

Unfortunately, that is not the whole story. The leading capitalist countries have experienced varying combinations of high unemployment rates, high inflation rates, unprecedented government deficits, and increasing inequality and insecurity of income. Now more than ever, the rich get richer and the poor get poorer. See Barnet and Cavanagh (1994), Danzinger and Gottschalk (1995), Gordon (1996), Harrison (1994), Korten (1995) Mishel and Bernstein (1993) and Rifkin (1995). All but a few of the third world countries at the end of World War II have experienced the same ills with even greater force, particularly in Africa and Latin America. In a number of African countries, the breakdown of civil society makes genocide a reality or a likely prospect. In practically all of the other third world countries foreign investment and loans to corporations and governments is a necessary but frequently not a sufficient condition for development. Even when development takes place, a large fraction of the money is diverted to the U.S. dollar accounts of generals, politicians and capitalists. When questions are raised as to how well the money has been used, capital flight forces terrible hardships on the mass of the population, as has taken place in Mexico, Indonesia, Russia and other countries. The flight of money from developed (Japan, Canada, and Western Europe) as well as developing countries to the United States, the depreciation of their currencies and the buying of their industries at fire sale prices is a new form of imperial tribute[5].

The system we now live in may be called welfare-corporate capitalism. However, the role of the state in providing for the welfare of the population has gradually diminished over the last 25 years, while the role of the corporation in generating growth, monopoly profits, inequality and unemployment has expanded. It is to be hoped that this process is cyclical and not secular, and a desirable balance between the two forces can be achieved. Recent election results in the leading capitalist countries suggest that is what the people want, and it is to be hoped that the democratic process can overcome the increasing corporate influence on the media, the universities and the other means by which corporations control society. The only force capable of destroying capitalism is capitalism itself, and the international capital movements described above make that a real possibility.

6. Bureaucratic Socialism

Let us now consider the historical development of market socialism in China, the place where it has achieved its greatest development to date. For over 100 years prior to 1949, when a socialist government came to power in China, rule by imperialist foreign governments and provincial warlords had reduced the country to a state of poverty, corruption, violence and degradation that defied description. Over the next five years, the new government moved rapidly towards a pure socialist system. Ownership of practically all wealth was transferred to the government, and a bureaucracy determined the production and distribution of output. These changes accomplished wonders in terms of equality of income, full employment, and

---

[5] Over the last decade there has been a more or less steady rise in the United States Trade deficit. Among the reasons for that deficit has been the flight of money from the rest of the world, first for the safety and then for the profitability as well of holding U.S. dollar assets, particularly shares of stock. In 1996 before the collapse of the Asian Tigers, the deficit had reached a high of $195 billion. The preliminary figure for 1997 is $264 billion. (See the Survey of Current Business, May 1998). As the currencies of the rest of the world depreciate in response to this flight, more and more of their resources and cheap labor must be exported to earn a dollar. The private wisdom and the national folly of this flight to the dollar is confirmed by the soaring U.S. stock market, and the decline -- collapse, in some cases -- of the foreign economies. In addition, foreign multinationals recognize that they must have a large presence in the U.S., one that can only be satisfied by acquisitions such as the acquisition of Chrysler by Daimler-Benz of Germany. To the extent that Chrysler shareholders want to keep their money in U.S. shares, the rise in the U.S. stock market and U.S. dollar are both accelerated.

improvements in education, health care and other services. Production of basic commodities such as grain, cloth and steel also increased significantly.

However, the progress that took place under this centralized bureaucratic system made further progress increasingly more difficult. A modern economy requires hundreds, no, thousands of different types of steel, and even greater variety in cloth, food, and other classes of products. Growth and technological progress required change. A central bureaucracy could not possibly acquire all of the information needed to administer the economy effectively. This was particularly true under the primitive state of Chinese technology in travel, communication, data processing and enterprise management. It also could not bring about a high rate of technological progress, since central control required that workers and managers do only what they were told to do: the freedom and motivation to improve, innovate, or work harder would disrupt the system. The Great Leap Forward and the Cultural Revolution were disastrous attempts to catch up with the West within the framework of a pure socialist system.

In 1978 China decided to expand the role of the market in administering the economy without giving up government ownership. It also decided to acquire technology and to some degree capital from the West through joint ventures, wholly owned foreign companies, private enterprise, and by "opening to the outside world" in other ways. What were the consequences of this decision?

MARKET SOCIALISM IN THE COUNTRYSIDE

In agriculture the household responsibility system was adopted. Under it the use of the land but not its ownership was distributed among the peasant households in a remarkably egalitarian and equitable manner. Each household was then required to make deliveries to the state in kind or in cash, and beyond that the household could produce what it wished for market and enjoy the proceeds therefrom. Maintaining state ownership made it impossible to separate a peasant family from the income from its plot of land, so that the most populous system of social security in the world was thereby created. Combining the security of state ownership with the material incentives of the market produced spectacular results. Prior to 1978 the growth rate in agricultural production was about 2.1%, little more than the population growth rate. Since then the growth rate has been over 6.0%, and now all but a small fraction of the Chinese people eat well. The high rate of "hidden unemployment" that existed in the countryside made it possible to achieve this increased growth rate in agricultural output, the growth in rural industry to be described shortly, and a large migration from the countryside to the cities. Prior to the eighties migration to the cities was prohibited in order to prevent the runaway urban population growth in other third world countries. Now peasants are free to go to the city: they go seasonally or stay if they make out and return to their plot of land if they don't. This freedom is of immense value, material as well as non-material.

Increasingly over the last decade and more so in the future, productivity growth in agriculture will require more technology, a rising capital-labor ratio and better trained farmers. These developments make small scale family farming increasingly inefficient, and the lure of non-farm employment makes staying on the land increasingly unattractive. Hence, an increasing fraction of peasant households are leasing their plots to professional farmers. What this will do to the social security system represented by the socialized collective ownership and democratic sharing in the income from the land remains to be seen. The modernization of agriculture and of industry in the countryside must take place, and that may prove to be a more serious threat than corruption to the survival of market socialism in the countryside.

7. Township and Village Enterprises

More spectacular than the improvement in agriculture has been the growth of nonfarm employment in the countryside. Prior to the eighties, the low rate of growth in farm output, the high infrastructure investment required to expand urban industry, and the low productivity of urban industry made it unprofitable to expand urban industry at a higher rate than the natural growth rate in the urban population. The inputs would exceed the outputs. Consequently industry was brought to the countryside, where hidden unemployment and the housing along with other infrastructure assets, made the marginal cost of increased employment in nonfarm activities close to zero. Anything earned by the family members that went to work in the township and village enterprises (TVEs) was an addition to family income, and any TVE profit was a net addition to township and village (TV) income. Another factor in the growth of TVEs was the change in the nature of their output. Prior to 1980 they were engaged largely in the manufacture of agricultural inputs -- e.g. tools for farming and fertilizer -- in order to maximize self-sufficiency in the countryside. After 1980, the growth in TVEs was mainly in light industry, where the production of consumer goods contributed significantly to exports and the standard of living in China.

Employment in TVEs rose from 28 million in 1978 to 135 million in 1996. Gross output value, not value added, rose from 32.5% of the figure for urban state enterprises in 1984 to 138% in 1996. The quality and quantity of the output have improved correspondingly. In bringing industry to the countryside Deng Xiaoping succeeded where Mahatma Gandhi and Mao Zedong failed. With about 200 million peasant households in the countryside, about one in two now have income from the land plus income from TVE employment. The increased prosperity of the peasant families near the big cities and along the costal plain has been stunning. They now have little material incentive to go to the cities in search of employment. Peasants in the interior with little access to TVE are now free to go to the city for seasonal or permanent employment, so they also share somewhat in the increased prosperity.[6]

In most TV's there is still comparatively little inequality of income and democratic control over local officials remains strong. See Ho (1994), Rozelle (1994), Findlay, Watson, and Wu (1994), and Byrd and Qinsong (1990). However, the expanded role of the market and the relaxation of central control have contributed to increased inequality of income. See Griffin and Zhao (1993), World Bank (1997), and Kahn and Riskin (1998). Furthermore, it is now also possible for the officials and managers in TVs to capture the income and power of landlords and small merchants in third world capitalist countries. In Guangdong, the province that serves as Hong Kong's workshop, severe sweatshop conditions have become a serious problem. In some TVs growth has been so great as to require the employment of peasants from the interior. Since they don't enjoy the same rights as "citizens" of the TV, they can be and are exploited more easily. In addition, local officials and Hong Kong capitalists conspire to capture and transfer to Hong Kong a large fraction of the value added in TVEs, so that the foreign exchange enterprises generate for China's economic development is reduced materially. The story with regard to technology transfer is mixed, in that China has acquired the capacity to manufacture a wide range of low technology but modern consumer products that are useful to the country, while progress in the capacity to innovate and to market abroad comes much more slowly.

The problems for market socialism raised by the modernization of agriculture are also being encountered with TVEs. Regardless of whether these enterprises are privately or collectively owned, the people who manage them, the TV officials, the TV employees and the TV as a whole, share in the profits and in the control of the enterprises in varying degrees. In fact, ownership is commonly far from clear, and for various reasons it has not been necessary nor desirable to resolve the ownership

---

[6] Poverty imposes hard choices. Prior to the 1990's, peasants were not allowed to go to the cities. That avoided the terrible urban slums, with their vices, child labor, etc., that are found elsewhere. But if you were born a peasant, you knew that you would die a peasant, unless you were lucky. Now peasants are free to go to the city, where they may find prosperity, sometimes by participating in its vices. However, those who don't succeed can return to their farm in the countryside.

question. However, as the comparative advantage of small scale production with low labor and infrastructure costs declines, the TVEs will require increasingly sophisticated technology and a rising ratio of capital (including human capital) to production labor. Whether or not these developments are compatible with continued local ownership and control of enterprises remains to be seen. The passage of time will also create increasing pressure for the clarification of ownership rights in the TVEs. In the West, the appearance of the term "stakeholder" reflects the increasing complexity of ownership rights under a system of welfare-corporate capitalism. But that is nothing compared to the problem of ownership in the transition from a pure socialist to a market-socialist system. As long as everyone is making money, clarification and finalization of the laws governing the process does not have the highest priority.

8. China's State Emterprises

The modernization of China's economy depends critically on the performance of its urban state enterprises, and progress there has been far less impressive than in agriculture and in TVEs. Technology in 1980 in practically every industry was 25 to 50 years behind the West. An enormous range of products introduced and made popular in the West over the prior 25 years were still not produced in China. Practically every industry, therefore, required 1) new equipment that could only be imported, 2) the recruitment of an engineering staff with the training needed to use the equipment, 3) advice for staff and workers on how to use the equipment in producing the range of products for which it was designed, 4) foreign exchange to buy the equipment, and 5) foreign enterprises able and willing to provide the equipment and the advice. Perhaps an even greater barrier to the desired technology transfer was the institutional structure of Chinese industry. Socialist principles of equality and stability were strongly entrenched in the state enterprises and in the government bureaucracy. The spread in compensation rates between unskilled workers and enterprise managers was extremely narrow, and all workers shared in generous benefits, that included free education and health care, practically free housing and utilities, subsidized food and retirement at 80% or more of pre-retirement pay. The prime responsibility of management in these state enterprises was to maintain this privileged status for the enterprise and its employees. The term "iron rice bowl" accurately described the security and mentality in state enterprises.

Over the next 15 years a series of reforms were adopted in order to make enterprises more market oriented and thereby overcome the above institutional barriers to improving their technology and productivity. Initially the enterprises were allowed to produce for market after satisfying the production plan, and keep the profits for investment. Gradually over time production plans determined by the state were abandoned, enterprises bought materials and sold output on the market, kept profits after taxes, and management shared in good performance. However, unprofitable enterprises and their workers could attribute their difficulties to an irrational price structure and other conditions beyond their control. They were subsidized through loans that governments required the banks to make, and through purchase of their output, so that they were not forced to fire unneeded workers or go bankrupt.

The formidable obstacles to modernization and market orientation made one-half of the state enterprises by number unprofitable. However, the profitable ones have been profitable enough so that the industrial sector has been reasonably profitable in aggregate, and aggregate output has grown at an annual rate of about 8% over the last 15 years. It should be added that unprofitability has been largely concentrated in certain industries, coal, oil, textile and heavy machinery in particular, where new technology has not been introduced or product prices have been depressed by government policy to encourage growth and exports. See Gordon (1998), pp. 255-75.

It is quite remarkable that about half of the state enterprises by number and much more than half in terms of value added have been able to overcome obsolete technology, poor management, an excessive work force and high compensation rates, so that the manufacturing sector in aggregate has been reasonably profitable. Over the last decade the government has experimented with various new ways to deal with the unprofitable enterprises, among them the forced merger of small ones with large successful ones, forced because redundant workers and managers are still not dismissed easily, and neither party welcomes the merger. An increasingly common practice has been to make surplus workers stay at home at reduced pay but with housing and other benefits. Sooner or later many find other jobs, so that hidden unemployment falls, while open unemployment, which excludes peasants who can return to the countryside, did not for a long time climb above three percent of the urban population[7].

---

7 There is another solution when the loss enterprise has been located on a choice piece of urban land due to the absence of a rational real estate market. The land is sold for what it is worth, and the proceeds are distributed among the former employees. Enterprise debt here as in other liquidations is for the most part cancelled. When the Tianjin Bohai Brewery was declared bankrupt in 1994 with debts of 183 million yuan, its assets were sold for 54 million yuan. Of that amount, 16 million yuan were devoted to retraining programs and separation pay for the workers equal to 3 times annual earnings.

Unemployment in China is a difficult and contentious subject. Prior to the economic reforms, there was no open unemployment such as exists in the West. It was then claimed that there was "hidden" unemployment, in that 30% or more of the people employed on the farms and in the cities could be removed without reducing output. Now peasants come to the city looking for work when the crop is in, and they return to their farms if permanent employment in the city is not found. Should they be counted as unemployed? The extent of urban unemployment is also difficult to measure, since welfare in China is provided through the enterprise. Does a worker become unemployed when he is told to stay at home at one-half pay with housing and other benefits continued? Nonetheless, there is evidence that unemployment is rising in China, because the government is using it to an increasing degree to motivate economic development.

China's leadership has not been satisfied with the rates at which technological progress and the transfer of surplus workers to productive employment are taking place. The 15th Party Congress which ended recently put this problem at centre stage, and measures were announced to transform or eliminate the unprofitable enterprises will be employed more intensively in the coming years, but it remains to be seen how much the radical restructuring of industry will take place through large scale bankruptcies and large scale unemployment. The recent decline and collapse of the economies of many Asian countries has not had a material impact on employment in China, perhaps because China has strong controls on international capital movement. Consequently, it is possible that a higher rate of growth in productivity can be achieved without a massive increase in open unemployment.

A related problem that is gaining increased recognition and gradual solution is the development of an institutional structure that recognizes rights and obligations of the various stakeholders in state enterprises, including government in its role as government and as owner. It is well known in the West that the separation of ownership and control has forced stockholders to share enterprise profits with management in varying degrees. In fact, stockholders are expropriated to the degree that they lose control of the enterprise. China is still trying to find a solution to the problem of state ownership other than wholesale privatization, loss of control to enterprise managers or continued bureaucratic inefficient and paternalistic control by old line ministries.

An increasing fraction of bank debt becomes unsupported by sound loans, but bank debt is really government debt, which in total is not large relative to GNP.

China explores every possible option in the quest for modern technology. Western principles and institutions in management, education, government and other areas of life are imported and experimented with in the same way as technology in industry is imported. See Guthrie (1998). Joint ventures and private enterprises have grown faster than state enterprises, and they lead the way in importing foreign technology. State enterprises are being transformed into "limited liability" corporations, with shares being offered to private investors at home and abroad. However, these state corporations are not being privatized as in the West, where majority ownership and control are placed in private hands. The most significant growth in the private sector will be the continued integration of Hong Kong, Taiwanese and overseas capital into the Chinese economy. A substantial public sector did not put an end to capitalism in the countries of Western Europe, and a significant but relatively small private sector and private portfolio investment in state enterprises need not spell the end of market socialism. There is no evidence that China's leadership and people has an ideological commitment to socialism regardless of its cost. On the other hand, the experience of Russia, Eastern Europe, Southeast Asia and the other poor countries of the world is no reason to become integrated in the world capitalist order.

9. Conclusion

In aggregate, the prosperity of China's urban as well as its rural population is increasing at an impressive rate. Civil rights as well as human rights have also improved significantly over these years. Of course, China is still a poor country, and its people do not have the civil rights that exist in wealthy capitalist countries. Furthermore, the inequality of income, crime, prostitution and corruption that we find in capitalist countries have also increased considerably. However, their levels still do not approach what we observe in Indonesia, India, Mexico Egypt, Brazil, Russia, Ukraine and other large Third and Second World countries. Most important, China does not have the widespread grinding poverty and degradation, and the private and unofficial violence against the urban as well as the rural poor that exists in so many countries.

What is going on in China may, as some claim, be nothing more than a transition to capitalism, so that within 25 years it will be quite impossible to distinguish between China's economic system and the range of economic systems in which private ownership is predominant and the term welfare-corporate capitalism is appropriate. It is also possible that China and some other countries will find market socialism an attractive long-run alternative to welfare-corporate capitalism. Perhaps the differences between the two systems will become negligible over time, with both serving society well. That would be nice, but it cannot be taken for granted. China's leadership seems convinced that both national independence and popular support require substantial progress over the next 25 years in per capita GNP and in consumption. What remains to be determined is whether the high growth rate needed to realize that objective requires: (1) the large scale privatization involved in the transition to welfare-corporate capitalism; or (2) the continued ownership and control of the economy by government that is involved in the further development of market socialism.

References

1. Barnet, R.J. and John Cavanagh. 1994. *Global Dreams: Imperial Corporations and the New World Order.* New York: Simon and Schuster.
2. Byrd, William A. and Lin Qingsong, eds. 1990. *China's Rural Industry: Structure, Development, and Reform.* New York: Published for the World Bank [by] Oxford University Press.
3. Chandler, Alfred. 1990. *Scale and Scope: the Dynamics of Industrial Capitalism.* Cambridge, Mass.: Harvard University Press.
4. Chandler, Alfred. 1977. *The Visible Hand: The Managerial Revolution in American Business.* Cambridge, Mass.: Harvard University Press.
5. Danzinger, Sheldon and Peter Gottschalk. 1995. *America Unequal.* New York: Russel Sage Foundation; Cambridge, Mass.: Harvard University Press.
6. Felix, David. "Asia and the Crisis of Financial Globalization". Forthcoming in Baker, D., G. Epstein, and R. Pollen, eds. *Globalization and Progressive Economic Policy.* New York: Cambridge University Press.
7. Findlay, Christopher, Andrew Watson and Harry X. Wu, eds. 1994. *Rural Enterprises in China.* New York: St. Martin's Press.
8. Galbraith, John Kenneth. 1967. *The New Industrial State.* Boston: Houghton Mifflin.
9. Gordon, David. 1996. *Fat and Mean.* New York: Martin Kessler Books.
10. Gordon, Myron J. 1994. *Finance Investment and Macroeconomics: The Neoclassical and Post Keynesian Solution*, Aldershot, England: E. Elgar.
11. Gordon, Myron J. 1998. "Monopoly Power in the United States Manufacturing Sector, 1899 to 1994". *Journal of Post Keynesian Economics,* 20(3), 323-35.

12. Gordon, Myron J., Yue Li, and Zhilong Tian. 1998. "The Future of Market Socialism in China," in Donald Brean, ed., *Taxation in Modern China*. New York and London: Routledge.
13. Griffin, Keith and Renwei Zhao, eds. 1993. *The Distribution of Income in China*. New York: St. Martin's Press.
14. Guthrie, Doug. 1998. "The Declining Significance of *Guanxi* in China's Economic Transition," *The China Quarterly* 154 (June) 254-282.
15. Harrison, Bennett. 1994. *Lean and Mean: The Changing Landscape of Corporate Power in the Age of Flexibility.* New York: Basic Books.
16. Ho, Samuel P.S. 1994. *Rural China in Transition: Non-agricultural Development in Rural Jiangsu, 1978-1990.* Oxford: Clarendon Press.
17. Kahn, A.R., and Carl Riskin. 1998. "Income and Inequality in China; Composition, Distribution and Growth of Household Income, 1988 to 1995." *The China Quarterly* 154 (June): 221-253.
18. Kahn, Jenifer. 1999. "The Green Machine." *Harper's* 298 (April): 70-73.
19. Kalecki, M. 1954. *Theory of Economic Dynamics.* New York: Rinehart.
20. Korten, David C. 1995. *When Corporations Rule the World.* West Hartford CN: Kurmarin Press, and San Francisco: Bernett-Koehler.
21. Mishel, Lawrence and J. Bernstein. 1993. *The State of Working America, 1992-3.* Armouk N.Y.: M.E. Sharpe.
22. Rifkin, Jeremy. 1995. *The End of Work.* New York: G.P. Putnam Sons.
23. Rozelle, Scott. 1994. "Decision-making in China's Rural Economy: the Linkage Between Village Leaders and Farm Households." *The China Quarterly* 137 (March) 99-124.
24. Scherer, Frederic and David Ross. 1990. *Industrial Market Structure and Economic Performance.* 3rd ed. Boston: Houghton Mifflin.
25. Schumpeter, Joseph A. 1942. *Capitalism, Socialism and Democracy.* New York; Harper and Row.
26. Simon, H. A. 1976. *Administrative Behavior.* 3rd ed. New York: Free Press.
27. Williamson, Oliver. 1985. *The Economic Institutions of Capitalism.* New York: Free Press.
28. World Bank. 1997. *Sharing Rising Incomes.* Washington, D.C.: The World Bank.

PART 4
SOCIAL SECURITY REFORM IN THE WORLD: LESSONS FOR CHINA

CHAPTER 19

THE STRUCTURAL PENSION REFORM IN LATIN AMERICA: COMPARATIVE DESCRIPTION AND EVALUATION OF PERFORMANCE, TESTING OF ASSUMPTIONS, AND LESSONS

CARMELO MESA-LAGO
Economics and Latin American Studies
University of Pittsburgh, 1902 Beechwood Blvd,
Pittsburgh, PA 15217, USA

The paper provides a comprehensive comparative analysis of the pension reforms introduced in eight Latin American countries from 1981 to 1997. It identifies and discusses seven principal issues in the world debate on pension reform, the two universal paradigms, and how the pension systems in the region fit into the model. It then evaluates the performance of the eight reforms. The lessons of the reforms for the region and the world are also discussed.

1. Introduction

One of the most important social policy issues at the end of the 20th Century is the social security crisis and, within it, the issue of reform of pensions (Although an equally important debate is occurring on health-care change, considerably fewer reforms have been actually implemented in that area). In the United States, a Presidential Commission has recently released a report on social security reform, and the members of the Commission split their votes in three different positions. In Europe, France, Germany and Spain are confronting serious problems with their pensions and other entitlement programs. Japan has an enormous pension debt which is complicating its efforts to structure a sustainable recovery. It is reported that in the OECD countries, pension unfunded liabilities total US$30 trillion (Hsiang

1997). In this crucial field, Latin America has already accumulated considerable experience over the last 16 years, as eight countries have introduced structural pension reforms of various types. In the past, Latin America copied models for social security from the developed countries; now those countries can and are learning from the region's pioneering rich and varied experience in this area, its accomplishments, errors and unresolved problems. Currently, Hong Kong, Hungary, Poland and other countries are considering Latin-American models of pension reform; and some members of the above-cited U.S. Commission, favored elements taken from those models.

This paper provides a comprehensive comparative analysis of the pension reforms introduced in the eight Latin American countries from May 1981 to May 1997: Argentina, Bolivia, Chile, Colombia, El Salvador, Mexico, Peru and Uruguay (for background see Mesa-Lago 1994, 1996b, 1997). The first part of the paper identifies and discusses seven principal issues or dichotomies in the world debate on pension reform, the paradigms developed by the two principal international organizations, and how the pension systems in the region fit into these paradigms. The final section analyses the lessons to be drawn from the reform in the Latin American region for China and the rest of the world.

2. Crucial Issues and Paradigms in the World Debate on Pension Reform

This section firstly identifies and summarizes two opposing positions in the international debate concerning the essential features of pension reform; secondly, it contrasts the two international paradigms on the three "pillars" of a pension system; and thirdly, it places the eight Latin American reforms within the two international paradigms.

In the last decade, an important international debate has emerged on nature of the pension reform. Until the 1990s, the controversy was confined to social security experts and administrators of pension programs. Since the early 1990s, however, several international organizations have taken a prominent role in the debate with conflicting stands: the International Labor Organization (ILO) and the International Social Security Association (ISSA) on one side, and the World Bank (WB) and the International Monetary Fund (IMF) on the other side (for the former see ILO 1993 and Beattie and McGillivray 1995, and for the latter see WB 1994, IMF 1995 and James 1996). Regional institutions, such as the United Nations Economic Commission for Latin America and the Caribbean (ECLAC) and the Inter-American Development Bank (IDB), have also done studies in this field but without clearly taking positions in the debate (see Mesa-Lago 1996a).

2.1 Seven Issues or Dichotomies on the Nature of the Pension Reform

Some issues or dichotomies can be identified in the debate on the nature of pension reform. These are summarized in Table 1. It should be noted, however, that the positions are not always extreme or "black and white" and hence, in some points, we refer to the priority or preference given by each side. The analysis also shows that, occasionally, the dichotomy is false or presented in an incomplete fashion because there are more than two alternatives.

TABLE 1: SEVEN DICHOTOMIES IN THE WORLD DEBATE ON PENSION REFORM

Points of Debate	ILO, ISSA	World Bank, IMF
1. Overall goal	Social	Economic
2. Financial System	Pay-as-you-go, Partial-funded-collective	Fully-funded- individual
3. Contributions	Not Defined	Defined
4. Benefits	Defined	Not defined
5. Administrator	Public (social security)	Private
6. Political Independence	Permeability	Immunity
7. Type of Reform	Non-structural	Structural

Source: Based on Mesa-Lago 1996a.

(1) Overall Goal: Social Versus Economic. The traditional goals of social security pension systems were essentially social: income maintenance in old-age, disability and death, intra and intergenerational solidarity, and so forth. The field was fundamentally handled by international technicians (ILO, ISSA), managers, lawyers and actuaries of pension programs, and scholars (usually jurists). Economists did occasional work in the field but macroeconomic issues were not central to it. The economic and social security crises in the developing world in the 1980s (particularly in Latin America), combined with structural adjustment programs sponsored by international financial organizations (WB and the IMF), raised their interest in social security, and economists began to play an increasingly important

role in the field. From the outset these financial groups argued that social security ("public" thereafter) pension programs suffer from serious flaws such as high payroll contributions, poor compliance (evasion and payment delays), regressive fiscal subsidies to the middle class, inefficient investment, heavy and growing actuarial (and sometimes financial) pension debt, adverse effects on the fiscal deficit and inflation and, as a result, have negative impacts on national savings, economic growth and employment. From this perspective, the substitution of "private" for "public" pension systems, would eliminate such problems and promote national savings, capital markets, real positive investment yields, economic growth and employment creation, which in turn, would guarantee adequate and equitable pensions.

Against the above contensions, the ILO and ISSA have argued that the risks resulting from the proposed reforms would be higher than the current risks: uncertainty because the pension amount would depend on unpredictable macroeconomic factors (e.g., economic growth, inflation, capital return), complexity especially as relates to the decision to select a pension option at the time of retirement, insufficient minimum pensions to satisfy basic needs, introduction of inequalities by age and sex, and double burden on current active insured in order to finance their own pensions and the deficit associated with the transition. In addition, they objected to the mixing of pension and economic reforms (while the other side argued that the two reforms are inseparable), and argued that public pension systems were not designed and could not solve problems of underinvestment and low economic growth, and that the negative impact of "private" systems on the economy, productivity, national savings and employment would be nil or very small.

In spite of apparent unreconcilable differences between the two sides, they have mollified their stands somewhat. The ILO (1993) has begun to accept some economic goals of pensions, and the need to place them in a macroeconomic context. The WB (1994) has begun to emphasize social aspects such as equity. There is no conclusive evidence that the two overall goals reinforce or conflict with each other, hence, the debate continues.

(2) Financial System: Pay-as-you-go Versus Fully Funded. Pensions can be financed by pay-as-you-go (PAYG) or capitalization systems. Within the former we may distinguish between simple systems (without reserves) and systems with a contingency reserve, while the latter have important variants such as fully funded individual systems (FFI) and partially funded collective systems (PFC). In the simple PAYG system, the contributions of the present generation of insured finance current pensions while the contributions of future generations of insured finance the pensions of the current insured. As the system matures and the population ages,

there is a need to increase the contributions, often to very high levels and forcing the state to finance rising deficits (PAYG with a small reserve may deal with short-term but not medium- and long-term imbalances). This system, therefore, is based on intergenerational solidarity and may have intragenerational solidarity as well, through transfers of revenue from high-income to low-income insured. The latter might be in the law or spirit of the system but may not necessarily be implemented in practice (a common criticism from the WB). The FFI system is based on a fixed-uniform premium (defined contribution), and current and future insured finance their own respective pensions through the deposit of their contributions (and, in some cases, their employers' as well), in an individual account which is invested and its yield added to such an account. This system lacks solidarity as it holds a strict relationship between contributions and pensions.

The WB-IMF, some regional financial organizations and several scholars (see, among others, Guérard and Kelly 1997; Macías 1997) have induced confusion into the debate on this issue by creating a false dichotomy between PAYG and FFI, thus omitting the PFC system, which is often based on the scaled premium method (SPM). This method accumulates reserves from insured's and employer's contributions in the starting period (e.g., 15 or 20 years), such reserves are then invested and generate a yield which, together with forthcoming contributions, should finance pensions in that period. An actuarial evaluation should determine if the current contribution (plus the investment yield) is sufficient or must be increased to finance pensions in the next period (the latter is usually the case, hence, the name "scaled"). This system is collective, rather than exclusively individual, because it should apply the solidarity principle to pay a minimum pension to low-income insured and set a maximum pension also. Individual insured' s accounts should also be maintained, as the pension must be legally related to years and amount of contributions. The SPM shares features of both PAYG (intra and intergenerational solidarity, increasing premium--but more spread and gradual) and FFI (reserves that are invested, individual accounts and some relationship between contributions and pensions--but lesser than in the FFI). It should be noted that, in practice, the essential principles of the SPM method have often been not followed or distorted, hence, leading to serious imbalances.

James acknowledges that there is no evidence as to the adverse effects of PAYG on national savings, but asserts that FFI has a positive impact on the capital market and national savings provided that three conditions are met: (a) the government can not benefit from the pension fund, (b) an incipient capital market should exist before the FFI system starts to function, and (c) strict state regulation is essential to prevent excessive risks and fraud. She adds that, when the domestic market is incapable of absorbing all the capital flow from the pension funds, part of it may be invested abroad, which also helps to diversify the portfolio. The WB acknowledges that, in the long run, saturation of the international capital market might occur, which would result in a decline in the investment yield.

The ILO and ISSA respond that there is no proof that, in developing countries, the FFI has had a positive impact on national savings, and that it is difficult in these countries (specifically in Latin America) to build large and efficient capital markets (see IV-H-2). Furthermore, the liberalization of rules to invest part of the pension funds abroad might stimulate a flight of capital and provoke domestic disinvestment. Another point is that the evaluation of the impact on national savings should not be limited to the FFI alone, but embrace the pension reform as a whole which, may lead to a deficit in the old system and a surplus in the FFI; the key question is whether the net outcome is positive, negative or neutral.

(3) Contributions: Not-Defined Versus Defined. In "public" pension systems, contributions are not defined (i.e., they are neither fixed nor uniform) because they tend to rise in the long run, more rapidly in PAYG and more gradually in the PFC. As these programs have been in operation for more than a century, we can ascertain their long-run trends. In the beginning, when there are few pensioners, the contribution is small but, as the pension system matures and the population ages, the contribution must be raised. Countries with both young populations and pension programs, usually have low contributions, while countries with both old populations and pension programs face very high contributions. The latter promotes evasion, payment delays and underdeclaration of taxable income.

Conversely, it is assumed that in the FFI system the contribution is defined or fixed-uniform, hence it should not increase thus apparently providing infinite certainty to the program (the age of both the population and the program should not affect the contribution). But these systems have been in operation for a short period and those assumptions have to be tested by the passage of time and demographic changes. For instance, as life expectancy expands, in order to maintain the same pension level (with unchanged contributions but longer passive life), future pensioners will face either a reduction in benefit levels, an elevation in retirement age or an increase in contributions (mandatory or voluntary); another alternative would be tax exemptions or other fiscal transfers. A more reasonable assumption, therefore, is to say that the effect of raising life expectancy should probably be milder on FFI than on PFC and PAYG, but it is unrealistic to argue that there will be no impact whatsoever (Nitsch and Schwarzer 1997). The WB also argues that the defined contribution avoids the problems of non-compliance; for instance, if an insured evades, delays the payment of the contribution and you fails to declare income, he/she would reduce or lose the pension, and this would neither affect the system nor the other insured. And yet, as we will see later, the experience of all countries with pensions reforms in Latin America shows that half of the insured are not active contributors.

(4) Benefits: Defined Versus Non-Defined. In "public" systems the benefit (pension) is regulated by law which establishes its minimum and maximum, provides a formula to calculate the pension according to the years and amount of contributions, and may even specify its adjustment to the cost of living. If the system functions well it has the advantage of certainty in the amount of the pension and permits solidarity to operate. The WB properly notices that in many countries those legal rules are not applied in practice (particularly in old programs): the real value of the pension decreases over time due to inflation, the minimum pension does not cover basic needs, and solidarity does not function because certain groups of the population (in the middle-income bracket) enjoy pensions much higher than most of the population (particularly in the low-income bracket) or who are not covered at all.

In the FFI system the benefit is not-defined because the insured gets the pension resulting from his/her contributions. As more is accumulated in the individual account (and usually there is the possibility for voluntary additional contributions), more will be invested and the higher the pension would be, and vice versa. But the role of inflation and real investment yield are crucial for the final amount of the pension to be collected and those are uncertain factors. So far, virtually all pension reforms in the region have generated high positive investment yields but, once again, this favorable situation may change over time. Finally, although it is true that the FFI system does not allow for endogenous solidarity, it can provide it exogenously; for instance, the state often guarantees a minimum pension by financing the needed amount to those insured who have not accumulated enough funds in their individual accounts to finance such a pension. This guarantee, however, may be an incentive for free riders: as will be explained later, it appears that the low degree of compliance in FFI programs in the region can be partly explained by insured deliberately minimizing his/her contribution in order to maximize the state subsidy.

(5) Administration: Public Versus Private. The FFI system is normally identified in the literature as "private" because it is often managed by private for-profit corporations of "exclusive dedication", e.g., organized specifically and only for that function. (Also it is frequent in the literature to equate public administration with PAYG and private administration with FFI; see as an example Uthoff 1995). But many FFI systems can be alternatively owned and managed by private corporations, private not-for-profit organizations, public institutions (including social security ones), banks, insurance companies, cooperatives, mutual-aid funds, trade unions,

family-allowance funds, etc. The "private" nature of the system has been questioned (see, among others, Gillion and Bonilla 1992) in view of four crucial state functions included in it: compulsory enrollment, strict regulation and supervision, considerable subsidies and transfers, and other guarantees to be discussed later.

The WB argues that private administration is superior to traditional social security ("public"), because competition among private corporations to attract the insured produces the following beneficial outcomes: increase in the efficiency of administration, reduction of costs and maximization of investment yield. In order to achieve these effects some basic requirements are needed: minimum access to information, transparency and a regulatory-supervisory framework. And yet the WB acknowledges that, due to the mandatory nature of the system, there might be concentration of insured in a few pension administrators (particularly in those countries where the number of insured is small).The ILO-ISSA add that access to information does not guarantee that the insured have the capacity or skills to make a rational selection of administrator, especially when such information and the options are complex. In Latin America, there is significant concentration of the insured in the operating pension systems (private and otherwise), and salesmen and publicity appear to play a more significant role in selecting an administrator than low commissions and high yields.

(6) The Political Independence of the System: Permeability Versus Immunity. The WB and some scholars (see Diamond 1996; Mitchell and Zeldes 1996) affirm that FFI-privately-administered systems are insulated from political interference and manipulation (a historical practice amply observed in the old public systems) due to the insured's ownership of the individual account and the private nature of the administration. The WB nevertheless recognizes that no system is completely immune and all would function better if the government behaves properly. And yet, in the social security arena, most governments in Latin America have behaved improperly: not fulfilling their financial obligations as employer and third party, forcing the pension fund investment into public securities with little or no value, and/or ordering such funds to be deposited in the central bank without adjusting the principal to inflation and paying no interest at all or negative real interest. The state, therefore, has contributed to the social security crisis in the region and it is reasonable to be concerned whether the government would turn that negative role into a positive one after pension reform.

As a privately administered system that requires the state to play an important role to function properly, FFI systems may open the door to government interference. According to Beattie and McGillivray and others (Mesa-Lago 1996a), this is plausible in an scenario of widespread public protest when real pensions (particularly the minimum) decline below the amount required to satisfy basic needs, or if the investment of the pension fund negatively affects fiscal and monetary policy or if the government needs the funds to finance the costs of the transition for a very long period thus impeding the proper diversification of the portfolio.

(7) Type of Reform: Non-Structural Versus Structural. There is a consensus between the two sides of the debate on the need for the reform but a significant disagreement on the type of reform to be implemented. There is no consensus either on the diagnosis of the public system but here the gap has been reduced. James believes that such systems have failed and are beyond repair, while the ILO-ISSA rejects that conclusion. And yet, the latter have acknowledged many of the public system flaws: excessive centralization, lack of coordination with macroeconomic policies, low level of pensions (sometimes below the poverty line) and lack of adjustment of pensions to inflation, high administrative costs, inefficient registration and control of compliance (hence high levels of evasion and payment delays),financial and actuarial disequilibria, and complex and delayed granting of pensions. Such flaws have often created disenchantment with public systems and the perception that alternative models of reform are better and more efficient (ILO 1993; Iyer 1993; Beattie and McGillivray 1995).

In view of the lack of agreement between the two sides both on the diagnosis and the six crucial issues of reform previously discussed, the type of transformation proposed is different. The ILO-ISSA favor "perfecting" the public system in order to correct its acknowledged flaws (non-structural reform): making entitlement conditions more strict (e.g., raising the retirement age, expanding the years of contribution required to gain the right to a pension), eliminating privileged regimes and too generous benefits, reducing administrative expenditures, tightening control of evasion and payment delays, reestablishing the financial and actuarial equilibria, improving efficiency and paying adequate pensions. (The ILO has also accepted a role of the private sector but centered in supplementary pension programs). The WB judges these changes as positive but insufficient to solve the fundamental (economic-financial) problems in the long run, therefore, it proposes a radical, structural reform to substitute the public system for a FFI privately administered one. James also believes that a non-structural reform of the public system is not politically viable due to the resistance of interest groups, but the other side argues that a structural reform would confront similar or more formidable barriers.

2.2 *Two Universal Paradigms on the Three Pillars of a Pension System*

Both the ILO and the WB have developed paradigms of supposedly universal application on the ideal features of a pension system. The two organizations identify three "pillars" in such a system: the first is at a basic level and assistance in nature, the second is the core of the pension program and provides the fundamental benefit, and the third is supplementary. There may be differences in the three pillars in terms of: their legal nature (mandatory or voluntary), financial system (PAYG, PFC or FFI), contributions (non-defined or defined), benefits (defined or non-defined) and administration (private, public or multiple).

(1) The ILO Paradigm. The ILO first paradigm, developed in 1992, was very schematic and had many lacunae (Gillion and Bonilla 1992). The second was developed in 1993 and it is more detailed and concrete (Iyer 1993).

The ILO notes that it is not possible to design precise strategies and structures with world-wide application, due to differenences in resources and the needs of the countries, but offered the following three-pillar paradigm:

The first pillar is mandatory, based on PAYG, financed by taxes, provides a universal subsistence pension based on need, and is administered by the state. The second pillar is mandatory, based preferentially on PFC, financed by employers and insured contributions (with the state guaranteeing certain benefits), provides defined benefits, and is administered by social insurance; this pillar should be reformed to become unified, extend its population coverage, improve its administrative efficiency, increase its autonomy vis-a-vis the state, maintain financial equilibrium, raise investment yield, and pay adequate pensions. The third pillar is voluntary (but regulated by the state), based on FFI (but without completely excluding other methods), financed by defined contributions (from the insured and/or the employer), provides non-defined benefits (supplementary pensions), and is administered by competitive private institutions. In the overall interrelationship between the second and the third pillar, more weight could be assigned to the latter when considered necessary by public opinion.

The administration of the three pillars should be separated but coordinated, regulated and supervised by an autonomous institution with tripartite representation in its administration. The state should be responsible for the transition costs, inflation risks, legal structure of the system, guarantees in case of insolvency, and incentives to develop the third pillar (ILO 1993; Iyer 1993).

(2) The WB Paradigm. The WB developed its paradigm of three pillars in a study published in 1994, with some important differences with the ILO paradigm. The first pillar has insurance and redistribution goals, it is mandatory, based on PAYG, financed by taxes, guarantees a minimum and uniform benefit, and is administered

by the public sector. The second pillar has insurance and savings goals, it is mandatory, based on FFI, financed by defined contributions (either through an individual saving plan paid by the insured alone or by an enterprise plan financed by the employer and the employee), provides non-defined benefits, and is administered by the private sector but regulated by the state. The third pillar has a saving goal, it is voluntary and similar to the second pillar in the remaining features (WB 1994).

According to the WB there should not be only a first pillar, because it might not be financially viable in the long run (as the system matures and the population ages) and, in addition, could distort the labor market, promote evasion and obstruct the development of the capital market. In order to avoid these problems, the WB offers four alternatives, each one combining a public system and a saving plan, both mandatory: (a) public system of uniform pension with individual saving plan; (b) public system that guarantees a minimum pension with individual saving plan; (c) public system of uniform pension with enterprise saving plan; and (d) public system of pension conditioned to need with an enterprise saving plan.

The WB warns that its paradigm is not simple, unique and applicable to all countries, hence there might be different combinations in each pillar, considerable variation in the relative proportions of the mandatory pillars, and diverse rhythms in the implementation of the system. The structural reform proposed by the WB is specially recommended for countries that are starting a new pension program and for those with old programs in a precarious situation (James 1996). Such specification excludes all countries of Latin America, except the pioneers: Argentina, Brazil, Chile, Cuba and Uruguay (only Brazil and Cuba have not introduced a reform yet).

(3) Similarities and Differences in the Two Paradigms. As shown in Table 2, the paradigms of the ILO and the WB fully coincide in the first and third pillar, but profoundly differ in the second pillar, due to their different diagnoses, objectives and features of the reforms proposed by each organization. The second pillar is mandatory in the two paradigms but in the ILO it is based on PFC, financed by non-defined contributions paid by the insured *and* the employer, provides defined benefits, and is administered by social insurance (public). Conversely in the WB paradigm, the second pillar is based on FFI, financed by defined contributions paid by the insured *with or without* the employer's, provides non-defined benefits, and is administered by the private sector. The two paradigms, therefore, are unreconcilable because of the fundamental disagreement regarding the second, central pillar.

TABLE 2: COMPARISON OF THE PARADIGMS OF THE ILO AND THE WORLD BANK

PILAR	ILO	WORLD BANK
First		
Legal Nature	Obligatory	
Financial Regime	Pay-as-you-go	
Contributions	Taxes	
Benefits	Uniform minimum (based on need)	
Administration	Public (state or social insurance)	
Second		
Legal Nature	Obligatory	
Financial Regime	Partially-funded-collective (PFC)	Fully-funded-individual (FFI)
Contributions	Non-Defined (insured and employer)	Defined (insured w/wo employer)
Benefits	Defined	Not defined
Administration	Public (social insurance)	Private
Third		
Legal Nature	Voluntary	
Financial Regime	Fully-funded and individual (FFI)	
Contributions	Defined (individual w/wo employer)	
Benefits	Not Defined	
Administration	Private	

Source: Mesa-Lago 1996a

(4) Placing the Eight Latin American Pension Reforms in the Two Paradigms. In spite of the apparent flexibility of the ILO and the WB paradigms and the disclaimer that they are not exclusive, in practice they aspire to guide the shaping of a pension system or its reform in an universal way. But there are close to 200 countries in the world with enormous differences among them; such a wide gamut includes, on one

extreme, developed countries in Europe (with centennial pension systems) and, on the other extreme, very poor countries in Africa and Asia which lack even basic pension systems. Even within the confines of Latin America, the differences are immense: at one extreme are Argentina, Chile, Costa Rica, Cuba and Uruguay (socially developed countries with pioneer universal pension programs that have as much as 73 years in operation) and at the other extreme Haití, Honduras and the Dominican Republic (poor countries with either no pension program or of recent introduction and extremely limited population coverage).

Table 3 fits the eight Latin American countries with structural pension reforms into the WB paradigm, and notes as well their conformance with the ILO paradigm. The table shows that all the eight countries have three-pillar systems but with considerable differences among them and much more diversified features than those typified by the WB and the ILO.

First Pillar: A minimum or basic pension is provided in all countries but with important differences among them: in Chile, El Salvador and Mexico it is paid by the government to those in the FFI system; in Bolivia it is paid by the state in the old public system but not in the FFI system; in Argentina and Uruguay it is paid by social insurance to those in the public reformed system and in the public component of the mixed program; in Colombia it is provided in either the public reformed system or the FFI depending on which of the two the insured is (paid by social insurance with state subsidy); and in Peru it is paid in the public system by social insurance, while in the FFI it has been left for future legislation hence not implemented yet. This pillar is not based on PAYG but on PFC in Colombia and Peru; it is mainly financed by contributions in the public systems, and partially by taxes in Chile. Alternatively, a social assistance pension (means tested) paid by the state is offered to the non-insured in Argentina, Chile and Uruguay (and perhaps in Colombia); it is not available in Bolivia, El Salvador, Mexico and Peru (Bolivia, nevertheless, offers a solidarity bonus but regardless of income).

TABLE 3: WORLD BANK'S THREE PILLARS AND PENSION-REFORMED SYSTEMS IN LATIN AMERICA

COUNTRY	PILLARS		
	MANDATORY PUBLICLY MANAGED PILLAR	MANDATORY PRIVATELY MANAGED PILLAR[a]	VOLUNTARY PILLAR[b]

ARGENTINA	Yes, universal basic pension in the reformed public program and in the public component of the mixed program (but not in FFI), or social assistance pension (means-tested)	Yes, in the FFI when the insured choose the mixed program. The FFI can be publicly managed. The insured can choose the public system and collect a defined pension[a]	Yes, in the FFI when the insured choose the mixed system.
BOLIVIA	Yes for old public system, not for new FFI; but an insured age 65 whose pension is less than 70% of the minimum wage, can monthly withdraw that % from his/her fund. An annual bonus is paid to those 65 if were 21 at end of '95. No social assistance pension.	Yes, all the new FFI system.	Yes, in the new FFI system.
COLOMBIA	Yes, minimum pension for those who choose the public program, or in the FFI or social assistance pension (means-tested)[c]	Yes, when the insured choose the FFI system; the latter can be publicly managed (or by coops, etc.). The insured can choose the public system, and collect a defined pension[a]	Yes, in the FFI when the insured choose this system.

CHILE	Yes, minimum pension guaranteed by the government (through the FFI), or social assistance pension (means-tested)	Yes, all the FFI system.	Yes, in the FFI system.
EL SALVADOR	Yes, minimum pension guaranteed by the government, no social assistance pension.	Yes, all the new FFI system.	Yes, in the new FFI system.
MEXICO	Yes, minimum pension guaranteed by the government, no social assistance pension.	Yes, but FFI system can be also publicly managed (one by the social security institute) or mixed. Old insured can choose between defined and nondefined pension.[a]	Yes, in the new FFI system.
PERU	Yes, minimum pension for those who choose the public system, or minimum pension from FFI (only envisaged in '95 but not yet paid), no social assistance pension.	Yes, when the insured choose the FFI system. The insured can choose the public system and collect a defined pension[a]	Yes, in the FFI for those who choose this system.
URUGUAY	Yes, minimum pension in the public program or social assistance pension (means-tested), but no minimum pension from FFI.	Yes, in the FFI when the insured choose the mixed system. The FFI can be publicly managed. The insured can choose the public system.[a]	Yes, in the FFI if the insured choose the mixed system, but only for those who have high salaries.

[a] Countries which deviate from private administration (World Bank) and have public administration or the possibility to choose it (ILO).

[b] Only insured contributions.

[c] Not clear if social assistance pension is paid in practice.

Source: Elaborated by Fabio Bertranou and Carmelo Mesa-Lago based on World Bank 1994 and legislation of the eight countries.

Second Pillar: According to the WB paradigm, the second pillar exists in the FFI of Bolivia, Chile, El Salvador and Mexico; the FFI component of the mixed system in Argentina and Uruguay (not in Argentina if the public system is chosen); and in the FFI alternative in Colombia and Peru for those who choose this system. The administration of this pillar is private in Bolivia, Chile, El Salvador and Peru (in the latter there is a parallel public system); but it is multiple in the other four countries. The employer contribution has been eliminated only in Bolivia, Chile and Peru, but not in the remaining five countries. With the exception of Chile (and to considerably less extent Bolivia, El Salvador and Mexico) the second pillar in the eight countries does not fit the WB paradigm; and in Argentina and Uruguay (and in the alternative public programs of Colombia and Peru) it is much closer to the ILO paradigm. In the 12 Latin American countries that have not undertaken pension reforms, this pillar conforms with the ILO paradigm.

Third Pillar: The third pillar exists in the FFI of all countries, but in Argentina and Uruguay only if the mixed system is selected (not if the public system is chosen), and in Colombia and Peru only if the FFI system is selected (not if the public system is chosen).

In summary, among the eight countries with structural pension reforms, only Chile fully conforms with all the features of the WB paradigm, while three other countries (Bolivia, El Salvador and Mexico) meet some of the WB features, two countries (Colombia and Peru) could be in one or the other paradigm (depending of what system is chosen), and two countries (Argentina and Uruguay) are closer to the ILO paradigm than to the WB. All the remaining countries of the region so far conform with the ILO paradigm, but this may change if they undertake reforms.

3. Findings and Lessons from the Reforms

In this final section we summarize our findings and derive lessons from the eight pension reforms. At least nine countries in Latin America are considering pension reforms: Brazil, Costa Rica, Ecuador, Guatemala, Honduras, Nicaragua, Panama, Paraguay and Venezuela. These countries should learn from the accumulated experience to have a better future reformed system. In addition, countries which already have a reform in operation or are about to start one, should consider a "reform of the reform" in order to improve their systems.

3.1 Universal Model or Multiplicity of Models

In none of the eight countries are reforms the same, even specific cases within a general reform model are different. For instance, the four countries that follow the substitutive model (Chile, Bolivia, El Salvador and Mexico) show significant variations in their systems: the "closing" of the old system, the options given to the current insured to stay in the old system and move to the new, the freedom to change administrators, the employer and insured contributions, the recognition bond, the minimum pension, the type of administration of the FFI system, the state guarantees, etc. Such differences are even wider among the substitutive, mixed and parallel models. The pretense that there is an universal model of reform is therefore rejected.

The author of the Chilean model, José Piñera, asserted in 1994 that such model is universal and has three essential elements: (a) the FFI, (b) private administrators exclusively dedicated to pension management, and (c) full freedom of election among administrators (AFPs). He argued that the three countries that had reforms at that time (Argentina, Colombia and Peru) followed the Chilean model and applied its three essential elements, but reality proved that argument to be incorrect. Piñera later acknowledged that there were "distortions" in the reforms of those countries (imposed by political reasons) but predicted that those systems would fail and be replaced by the pure Chilean model (for sources see Mesa-Lago 1996a). In 1997, when four more diverse reforms had been enacted (Bolivia, El Salvador, Mexico and Uruguay), Piñera radically changed his initial stand, saying: "The transition [reform] can be done in any country in the world, but it must be different, adapted to the local economic, social and political conditions. It is a complex challenge and each country has to face it in its own manner... All [current reforms in Latin America] are well oriented...The model that I support is the individual account, that is the essential element" (AIC Conferences 1997, author's notes).

Countries considering pension reform should not be led by the false pretense that there is an universal and perfect model of reform. They should, instead, study the various types of reforms in existence as well as their performance, and structure a reform according to their circumstances and needs, and should reduce the transition costs as much as possible.

3.2 Population Coverage and Compliance

Actual coverage of the EAP in the eight countries ranges from approximately 80% (Argentina, Chile and Uruguay) to 12% (Bolivia) but, in the first group of countries, that coverage was the same or close to it prior to reform. In Chile, coverage of the self-employed is voluntary and only 11% of the total number of workers in this occupational category is affiliated. The percentage is considerably higher in Argentina and Uruguay where coverage of that group is mandatory. In all these three countries, the percentage of the EAP which is self-employed and informal is a minority, but in the remaining countries they constitute the majority of the labor force. The high contributions of the insured in the FFI system (particularly if the employer contribution has been eliminated) makes it almost impossible to extend coverage to a majority of the EAP.

Our studies disproved the assumption that ownership of the individual account and strict relationship between contributions and pensions in the FFI model (elimination of solidarity transfers) provides incentives for workers to register, punctually pay their contributions and declare their full salary-income, in order to increase their individual account and achieve a higher pension at retirement. We found that the contributor/affiliate ratio averages 54% and ranges from 45% (Peru) to 67% (Uruguay). This seems to be the result of several factors including double counting of the same insured in two or more administrators, temporary or permanent withdrawal from the labor force, and manipulation of low-income insured to minimize their contributions and maximize the state subsidy to guarantee a minimum pension. Depending on the importance of each explanatory factor, either effective coverage is smaller or freedom to move creates serious administrative problems or the cost of the minimum pension (and moral hazard) would be much higher than initially estimated.

Countries in which the majority of the labor force is self-employed, informal and/or agricultural will confront severe limitations to extend coverage with the FFI system, and only half of the affiliates could be active contributors. Alternative measures to extend coverage should be incorporated in the reform, e.g., the 1% contribution for that purpose introduced in Colombia. Another possibility would be to create a Solidarity Fund with partial proceeds from privatization of public enterprises (as in Bolivia) but earmarked to expand coverage among those special groups of the labor force instead of paying a benefit regardless of income and lack of social protection. State payroll contributions (as in Mexico) should be partially assigned to subsidize the incorporation of low-income self-employed. All these groups should be given flexibility to choose coverage of individuals risks, including the three types of pensions as well as health care. A better system of control of compliance should be introduced, perhaps through a centralized collection agency, in order to remove from the registry workers who have abandoned the labor force, eliminate double counting (multiple individual accounts by the same insured), and reduce the number of free riders who fail to declare their income. This will also allow a more accurate estimate of the labor force really covered by the system and the elimination of statistical distortions.

3.2 *Standardization of Entitlement Conditions and Elimination of Privileges*

The assumption that reform standardizes all entitlement conditions and eliminates privileges, thus reducing costs has only proven to be partially (but mainly) validated by empirical analysis. In general, costs are reduced in virtually all countries because of those reforms and the tightening of entitlement conditions. Homogenous conditions, nevertheless, are enforced within the reformed system but there might be two systems in operation with divergent conditions, either temporarily or permanently, as well as groups of insured (although a minority) excluded from reform and allowed to keep their preferential systems: the armed forces in all countries (except in Bolivia which also eliminated 51 programs, most of them with divergent entitlement conditions, contributions, etc.), federal and provincial employees, oil workers, etc. Another assumption is that fiscal resources are reassigned to avoid subsidies to middle-income insured and target low-income ones, thus improving the equity of the system. In fact, in at least five of the eight countries, significant fiscal resources are or will be deployed to consolidate the new system covering a minority of the labor force (normally in the middle-income group) when they could be more fairly used in reducing poverty in the majority of the population.

Standardization of and more adequate (strict) entitlement conditions as well as eradication of privileges are unavoidable ingredients in any type of reform, in order to improve equity and financial viability, but countries considering reform should be aware that those conditions will not be universally imposed and that there might be regressive use of fiscal resources to consolidate the reform. Public pressure should be put on those excluded from the new system to join it, providing a transitional period in which old entitlement conditions would be applied but making mandatory the affiliation of new entrants in the labor force. Bolivia's reform should be an example to follow in this area.

3.3 *Market, Private Administration, Freedom of Choice and Competition*

The market, private administration and freedom to select administrators do not necessarily secure competition, compliance, and reduction in administrative costs as is usually assumed. We discussed in section B the low ratio of contributors vis-a-vis affiliates but, so far, the highest ratio is found in Uruguay, where there is a multiplicity of administrators, and the lowest ratio is in Peru's FFI, despite government additional reforms to make it more attractive to the insured. Our studies also show that there is a very high concentration of insured in the three major administrators: 100% in Bolivia and El Salvador; from 69% to 73% in Chile, Peru and Uruguay; 58% in Colombia and 40% in Argentina. Note that the two countries with the lowest concentration ratios do not have a substitutive model and exclusive private administration, but mixed and parallel models instead, combined with a multiplicity of administrators in the FFI system/component. The selection of the administrator is not mainly based on their charging lower commissions and paying higher capital returns but on the activities of salespersons and publicity. The latter two take the overwhelming majority of administrative expenditures. The premium paid to insurance companies shows a declining trend in most countries with a system in operation, but the commission charged by the administrators has increased, and the combination of the two has either been stagnant or rising. The high costs of operation (ranging from 25% in Chile to 32% in Peru over the total contribution) substantially reduces the amount deposited in the individual account. With only one exception (Uruguay), the number of administrators is positively related to the size of the insured body: 17 and 21 in Mexico and Argentina (that have the largest number of insured) and 2 or 3 in Bolivia and El Salvador (that have the lowest number). In the last two countries there is a duopoly and, hence, no competition but, even in countries with a large number of administrators, the high degree of concentration creates a sort of oligopoly, and the trend setters are the largest administrators (the three biggest in Chile have a combined pension fund equal to 20% of GDP). In Chile, which has a fairly large number of insured and the longest period of operation, the number of administrators has remained basically stable in the long run in spite of a relative low starting capital required and due to the high administrative costs of operation. Unlimited freedom to move (Chile) conveys a high price in turnover, administrative costs and confusion in individual accounts. To avoid or reduce these flaws, most countries have established a limit of one or two changes per year, create incentives to stay and penalties to move. In Bolivia, the government distributed the insured between the two administrators and does not allow any changes until the year 2000; this limitation reduces the problems noted above but eliminates competition which is supposed to be the foundation of the FFI system.

Countries with a small number of insured should be careful to establish a FFI system; an exclusively private administration faces significant barriers and a multiplicity of administrators is probably more viable; opening the market to other financial intermediaries should be considered particularly in these countries. In all cases, limitations on the freedom to change administrators are needed (one per year), tougher control of salespersons and publicity should be established, and incentives/penalties created (a surrender fee for transfer, a bonus for those who stay more than one year in the same administrator) to avoid/reduce the problems noted above. There is a serious and urgent need to better inform and help the insured to understand the reasons for the selection of administrators and carefully control the number of salespersons (and their activities) as well as publicity. Data on commissions charged by the administrators and their investment yields should be made homogenous, simple to understand and compare by the average insured, and widely diffused in order to facilitate a learned selection. A central collection agency will reduce paperwork among small administrators and cut down system expenditures. All these measures should improve competition and reduce administrative costs.

3.4 Investment Yields, Capital Markets and National Savings

Obviously the creation of a FFI system does not automatically generate a dynamic and relatively safe capital market and high investment yields. Countries with low insured populations and lack of or incipient non-regulated capital markets and insurance industries will face significant barriers to diversify the portfolio and find profitable financial instruments. In the four Latin countries in which the reform has operated for sometime, the average gross real investment yield ranges from 7% to 16%, which is quite impressive, but all of the four have relatively large insured populations and regulated capital markets (with some previous history in Argentina and Chile). Those yields are not necessarily going to be achieved by countries with different conditions. Chile, pioneer of the reform and the country with the longest and most successful record, is facing difficulties to place the growing capital flow in an increasingly saturated capital market, and the real investment yield sharply declined in 1995-1996; projections for that yield are now from one-third to one-half of the previous average since inception. Furthermore, the net investment yield (after deducting the administrative commissions) in Chile was lower that the interest paid by bank deposits during the first 14 years of operation of the FFI system, and only after that period the net yield has become slightly higher (similar results were found in Peru in the first three years of operation). The state guarantee of an annual minimum investment yield is a laudable safety measure for the insured but create distortions: long-term risks are avoided (including investment abroad), the largest administrators become trend setters, and the portfolio composition tends to be alike among all administrators to ensure they do not fall outside the limits. The 5-year right of the Superintendency in Bolivia to determine the minimum and maximum of the pension fund to be invested on 15-year treasury bonds (with a US dollar cap) largely to finance the transition, mainly places the success of the system on the government ability to pay a high real yield. Mexico's rigid rules on investment in an attempt to maximize safety for the insured also conspire against high yields.

Contrary to the widespread assumption that FFI generates an expansion of the capital market and national savings, an econometric study of Chile, sponsored by the IMF, found that: (a) there is no proof that FFI has been the decisive factor or even an important component in the development of financial markets; and (b) in 1981-1995 FFI did not influence net savings and the reform as a whole had a negative impact on savings. Another study on the impact of the Chilean pension reform (combining fiscal costs and generation of savings for the same period) shows that the net balance was negative in each year (although declining) and it averaged -2.6% of GDP in the entire period. Similar data are not available in other countries, although there are estimates and projections on the fiscal cost of the transition.

Countries contemplating pension reform (whatever its model) which neither have a capital market nor an insurance industry or lack state control, should enact first the corresponding laws to introduce and/or strengthen those markets, establish a superintendency of securities and insurance, and allow a reasonable period for their consolidation, before passing a pension reform law. Those countries with reform in place or about to begin, should flexibilize investment regulations, empower the superintendency of pension administrators to push for portfolio diversification and provide incentives for investment in long-term instruments, extend from one to three years the period of time where the mandatory minimum yield is measured, lift the prohibition to invest abroad, support the creation of new financial instruments, and allow some flexibility--within certain safety parameters--to tailor the insured's portfolio according to their needs (for instance, young insured are willing to take more risks while those close to retirement want to reduce volatility). Administrators must be obliged to publish net investment yields and provide simple and understandable monthly statements of the individual accounts; the superintendency should lead an educational campaign to educate the insured on the reading of the statement and the investment yields. There is an urgent need to carefully evaluate the pension debt and the fiscal costs of the transition, as well as the net balance of the pension reform. As the assumption that the FFI system fosters national savings has been so far rejected by evidence, the principal goal of pension reform should not be that, but other more viable, priority goals such as standardization and elimination of privileges, expansion of coverage and so forth. In order to reduce transition costs, very serious consideration should be given to the following measures: selection of a mixed or parallel versus a substitutive model, maintenance of the employer contribution, limitations to the recognition bond (not granted in a mixed system, and in the FFI system submitted to a ceiling, minimum years of previous contributions, reasonable adjustment to the cost of living but no interest or at low rate), and conditions to the minimum pension (minimum years of contribution and adequate control to reduce moral hazard). It is better to carefully assess *a priori* the cost of the reform and the granting of the above benefits without limitations, than to find after the reform that the transition costs are considerably higher than anticipated, that the state cannot honor some or all of those benefits, and that the reform is not financially viable.

3.5 Income Redistribution and Gender Inequality

While we have discussed the effects of a pension reform on income distribution, serious studies evaluating many of those effects are lacking. Establishing homogenous entitlement conditions in the old and new systems, and eliminating privileges should be starting measures in all pension reforms to infuse equity and progressive effects. In countries with a very low coverage of the labor force (concentrated in middle-income salaried workers) fiscal subsidies to consolidate the system for the minority covered have regressive effects, as such resources should be geared to extend coverage to low income groups or help the poor who are the majority. The FFI system is "neutral" and lacks solidarity, hence, it reproduces existent income inequalities at best or has regressive effects; to mitigate those adverse effects and introduce some solidarity in the system, the state must guarantee minimum and social assistance pensions, and a reasonable adjustment of pensions (including the minimum or basic) to the cost of living. Mixed systems combine elements of public social security (with solidarity) and the FFI system and, hence, should have more progressive (or less regressive) effects than the substitutive system, provided they are financially viable in the long run to secure those positive effects. Public systems are "gender neutral" because they have defined benefits and solidarity and, hence, set equal replacement rates for female and male insured, assuming those systems are financially viable in the long run. FFI systems are "gender differentiated" because their benefits are non-defined and they lack solidarity; as insured women often retire earlier and live longer than men (and also have lower salary and density of contributions), their replacement rates are considerably lower. Mixed systems reduce the gender gap in replacement rates because they combine a public component (which provides equal rates) with a FFI component (which does not), hence, the net outcome is less differences in such rates.

To reduce the sex gap in substitutive systems, the state should provide some solidarity in order to increase the women insured's replacement rates (fixing the same age of retirement attenuates but does not eliminate the gap). Fixed commissions should be eliminated to correct the regressive effect on low-income insured, while commissions on contributions could be changed to commissions based on assets managed. These measures would improve equity among insured with different incomes, eliminate subsidies of active contributors to inactive affiliates, and create incentives to reduce evasion and payment delays

3.6 The Role of the State

The role of the state has been crucial in all types of reform even in the substitutive ones with private administration, because the government has made the system mandatory, financed its transition, established a superintendency (in most countries financed with public resources) that strictly regulates and supervises the system, and provided multiple guarantees to the system and the insured. Without such state actions, reform would not have been successful in Chile, to cite the country with the longest experience. Historically the state has "behaved properly" fulfilling its obligations in Argentina, Chile, Colombia, Mexico and Uruguay, before and after the reform. Conversely, in El Salvador and Peru (and the majority of Latin America) the state played a negative role in social security prior to reform: not paying its contributions as employer and third party (generating a huge debt that was eroded and even vanished by inflation), and forcing social security institutions to place their reserves in the central bank or in public securities without indexation of the principal and paying (if at all) negative real interest rates (hence depleting the reserves). The state intervention in these systems was, therefore, a principal factor in their disequilibria and crises. One of the assumptions of the FFI model is that insured's ownership of the individual account will prevent such adverse intervention of the government in the pension system and, so far, the 16 years of operation of the Chilean system confirms that assumption. And yet, once again, the Chilean state acted positively before reform, regardless of the ideology of the administration in power. The key question is whether that positive role will occur in those countries where the state played an adverse role before reform. The case of Peru raises some serious questions, as the state owns more than US$200 million to the FFI system for non-payed contributions as employer, has issued recognition bonds to only 1% of those insured who moved to that system, and has not met its promise to regulate and guarantee the payment of the minimum pension. What would happen to current and future pensioners if the state does not meet its obligations to finance the deficit of the public system?

Regardless of the type of pension reform (public-reformed, substitutive, mixed, parallel), therefore, it is essential that the state "behaves properly" and fulfills its obligations as employer and third party in order to secure the success of such a reform. This is perhaps the most important lesson learned, not only from the ongoing pension reforms, but from 73 years of operation of social security in Latin America.

CHAPTER 20

SOCIAL SECURITY REFORMS IN TAIWAN

SHENG CHENG HU
Institute of Economics, Academia Sinica
Taipei 11529, Taiwan
E-mail: shu@ieas.econ.sinica.edu.tw

This paper describes the current social security reforms in Taiwan and discusses their implications for the sustainability of social security in Taiwan and in Mainland China. Since the stage of economic development and demographic structure in Taiwan in the early 1960s when it first established a social security system were similar to those of Mainland China, Taiwan's experience and the current reform efforts would provide useful references for Mainland China.

1. Introduction

Taiwan's social security system was established in the late 1950s and early 1960s, when the per capita income was low and the population was young. The system is fragmented and it covers only about two thirds of the population. The existing system is financed on the pay-as-you-go basis, achieving old age security by intergenerational transfers. Such a system works well in an economy where the population growth rate is high and the ratio of the elderly population to the total population is low.

Since the early 1990s, the Taiwan government has been planning to establish an economy-wide social security system by the year of 2000. The main purposes of the reforms are to expand the coverage of the social security system to the entire population in response to the rapid aging of the population. The side benefit of the reforms is the streamlining of the existing system. The planning process was completed recently and the proposed system was tentatively approved by the Cabinet (the Executive Yuan). The objectives of the reforms are not only to expand coverage to the entire population but to streamline the outdated existing system.

As in other countries, there is concern in Taiwan about whether the proposed social security system will adversely affect the performance of the economy, particularly the saving incentives.[1] The saving propensity in Taiwan has been high but declining since the mid 1980s. The personal savings rate was 29% in 1986, but it fell to 18% in 1993 and further to 17% in 1997, without an end to the decline in sight. One of the main reasons that the country has been able to weather the current Asian financial crisis is because it has a huge foreign exchange reserve made possible by the country's high saving propensity. The importance of aggregate saving for the economy is further underscored by Krugman (1994) and Lau (1998). They have argued that it is the rapid accumulation of the factors of production, not the growth in total factor productivity, that contributes to the rapid growth of the newly industrialized countries in Asia. Thus, a high propensity to save is necessary for continued rapid growth of the economy. The declining saving propensity implies not only a possible slowdown in the economy but that the elderly will have fewer financial resources for retirement consumption.

The purposes of this paper are to review Taiwan's existing social security system, describe the current social security reforms, and discuss their implications for the sustainability of social security in Taiwan and in mainland China. Since the stage of the economic development and the demographic structure in Taiwan in the early 1960s when it first established a social security system were similar to those of mainland China, Taiwan's experience with the social security system and the current reform efforts provide a useful lesson for mainland China.

The plan of the paper is as follows. Section 2 describes the current economy and demographic situation. Section 3 reviews the current social security system. Sections 4 considers the experience of the current social security reforms, and Section 5 the economic effects of the reforms and their implications for the sustainability of social security. Section 6 is the concluding section.

2. The Economy and Demographic Transition

The Taiwan economy has sustained a long period of rapid economic growth,

---

[1] Needless to say, there is also concern that the proposed social security might affect the incentive to invest and lead to exodus of firms to mainland China and other countries. Some businesses did make vague threat of this possibility. However, a survey by Su, Yang, Chang and Hu (1996) suggests the effect of social security on investment is not as large as its effect on savings, because much of the social security tax to businesses will be shifted to workers.

high savings propensity, near full employment and stable prices. The economy is dominated by small- and medium-sized firms, which are export-oriented, mobile, flexible and resilient. Between 1982 and 1992, almost half of the enterprises employed less than 10 persons. Employees in enterprises with more than 5000 employees accounted for less than 5% of the working population. The industrial sector (manufacturing, mining, construction and utilities) accounted for 38%,while the service sector (commerce, transportation, government and finance) 60%, of Gross Domestic Product (GDP). In recent years, the manufacturing sector has been successfully transformed from low-skilled labor intensive to skilled labor and capital intensive industries. For example, it is now the third largest producer of computer-related products in the world.

Although Taiwan's social security system is not as well developed as those of industrial countries, Taiwan's income distribution has been quite equitable. The poverty rate among the elderly is higher than other age cohorts, but it is relatively low compared with those in other countries and has been declining in recent years. For example, the poverty rate among the cohort of age 65-70 was 16 per thousand (‰) in 1981. It declined to 14 ‰ in 1984, 11.5 ‰ in 1990, and further to 9 ‰ in 1993. The poverty rate among the cohort of age 70-75 was 22 ‰ in 1981. It rose to 26 ‰ in 1984, but then declined to17.5 ‰ in 1990, and further to 12.5 ‰ in 1993. (See Wang and Liu (1997).) On the other hand, the elderly have increasingly relied on themselves rather than their children or pensions for retirement consumption. According to a survey by the Directorate General of Budget, Accounting and Statistics (DGBAS), the fraction of living expenses of the elderly provided by children fell steadily from 65.8 percent in 1985 to 53.3% in 1993 and further to 48% in 1996.

The rapid growth of the economy has led to a decline in both birth and death rates. The birth rate was 45.3 per thousand (‰) in 1955 and declined steadily to 14.98 ‰ in 1997. According to a projection by the Council for Economic Planning an Development, the government's planning agency, it will fall to 12.04 ‰ by 2010, and further to 12.15 ‰ in 2030. (See (CEPD (1996).) The death rate also fell from 8.6 ‰ in 1955 to 5.93 ‰ in 1997. But it is projected to rise to 6.96 ‰ in 2010, 9.17‰ in 2030. As a result of the declines in both birth and death rates, the population in Taiwan is aging more rapidly than those in industrial countries. The life expectancy at birth for females (males) is likewise projected to rise from 78.34 (72.3) years in 1997 to 80.12 (74.26) years in 2010 and 82.66 (77.78) years in 2030. The population aged 65 and older accounted for 8.1% of the total population in 1997 and is projected to rise to 9.85% by 2010 and 19.6% by 2030. The dependency ratio, defined here as the ratio of the population aged 65 and older to the population aged 15-64, is projected to rise from 11.8% in 1997 to 14.1% in 2010 and further to30.95% in 2030.

The aging of the population alters the way we think about caring for the elderly. In the traditional society, it is the responsibility of the family to take care of its elderly members. As the population ages and the dependency ratio increases, this practice has become more difficult. As noted above, the elderly are now increasingly dependent on themselves rather than their children for retirement consumption. In the same manner, the question is raised about the viability of the pay-as-you-go social security system that relies on intergenerational transfers to provide old-age security.

From the aggregate point of view, the increased life expectancy implies that if the current standards of living are to be maintained, productivity must grow more rapidly than in the past to produce additional output for increased retirement consumption. Otherwise, workers will have to work longer and retire later, or save more while young.

3. Existing Social Security Programs

Against the above described background, Taiwan began the process of planning a national pension program in 1993. The planning task was initially undertaken by the Department of Social Affairs, the Ministry of Interior, but was subsequently taken over by the Council for Economic Planning and Development. After two stages of planning and research, the process was completed in June, 1998. The proposed national pension program was tentatively approved by the Cabinet shortly afterwards.

Taiwan's proposed social security system does not begin from scratch. There are already two public insurance programs that provide for retirement and other benefits. The Public Employees Insurance Program covers all regular government employees, and the Labor Insurance Program cover most workers in the private sector. In addition, there is a social assistance program that provides assistance to the elderly poor. These public insurance and social assistance programs constitute the first pillar of old age security. The second pillar consists of pension plans mandated by the Basic Labor Law (for workers) and the Public Employees Retirement Law (for public employees). The third pillar of old age security consists of individual savings and commercial annuities.

3.1 First Pillar of Old Age Security

The Public Employees Insurance Program, established in 1959, provides retirement, survivors' and disability benefits to regular government employees. Each insured person who has been enrolled for at least 5 years is eligible for a one-time retirement benefit. The one-time retirement benefit is equal to 5 times the last working month's wage for each retiree who has been insured for five years, plus one additional month's wage per additional year's insurance coverage for 6 to 10 years, an additional two-months' wage per additional year's insurance coverage for 11 to 15 years, an additional three-months' wage per additional year's insurance for 16 to 20 years, and the maximum 36 times the last working month's wage for more than 20 years of insurance coverage. In other words, there is a penalty on working for more than 20 years. This stipulation encourages early retirement by government employees who have employment opportunities in the private sector.

The program was established in 1958 when the economy was poor and the government was unable to pay its employees competitive wages and salaries. Therefore, government employees' insurance was designed as delayed compensation, funded on a pay-as-you-go basis. The insurance premium is heavily subsidized and the government's share of cost is financed by its operating budget. The implicit debt of the program is now between NT$80 to NT$100 billion (or equivalently between US$2.5 to US$3.125 billion at US$1 = NT$32.)

The Labor Insurance Program was established in 1960. It also provides retirement, survivor's and disability benefits to the insured persons. It covers workers in enterprises that employ at least 5 persons, professionals and non-regular government workers. Each insured person is eligible for a one-time retirement benefit upon reaching age 60 (55 if female), or upon reaching age 55 (50 if female) if he has been insured for at least 10 years, or upon completion of 25 years of service with the same employer. Each retiree receives one (last working) month's wage per year of insurance coverage for the first fifteen years, and two months' wage per year of insurance coverage in excess of fifteen years. The maximum amount of benefit is 45 times the last working month's wage. Those who work beyond age 60 are allowed to receive up to additional 5 months' wage. Thus, the practical maximum is 50 times the last working month's wage. The insurance premium is between 6.5 and 11 percent of the worker's monthly wage, of which 20% is borne by the worker, 70% by his employer and 10% by the government. The program is on a near pay-as-you-go basis. It has now accumulated NT$300 billion (or US$9.375 billion) of assets, but has an implicit debt at least three times as large. The final responsibility for the pension debt is borne by the government.

3.2 Second Pillar of Social Security

The second pillar of social security consists of the pension plans mandated by the public employees' retirement law and the basic labor law. The latter stipulates the basic relationships between employers and their employees, including working conditions and the retirement benefit that employers must offer their employees. There is no room for negotiation between employers and their employees regarding the level of retirement benefit. In contrast, in industrial countries, these pension plans are usually sponsored by employers as a result of the negotiations between the employers and their employees (or their unions).

According to the basic labor law, a covered worker is eligible for a one-time retirement benefit if he reaches age 55 and has been working for the same firm for at least 15 years, or regardless of his age if he has worked for the same firm for at least 25 years. The retiree is entitled to two units of benefit per year of work for the first fifteen years of service (with the same employer), but one unit of payment per year of service beyond the fifteenth year. The maximum amount of retirement benefit is 45 units. Each unit of benefit is equal the last working month's average wage. The law requires the employer to fund the promised retirement benefit at a rate stipulated by law (between 2 and 15% of the worker's wage at the employer's discretion).

The Public Employee Retirement Law provides retirement benefit to public employees who have been employed for at least five years and have reached age 60, or who have been employed for 25 years. Each employee is eligible for a one-time retirement benefit which is 1.5 units per year of service. Each unit of benefit is equal to two times the last working month's basic wage, or roughly 1.4 times the last month's wage. The maximum amount of retirement benefits that the employee is entitled to is 53 units or about 74 times the last month's wage. Those who have worked for more than 15 years are eligible to choose among a one-time benefit, an annuity, and some combination of the two. The premium is between 8 and 12 percent, of which 35% is borne by the employee and 65% by the government. However, the government has the final responsibility for the pension debt. That is, if the reserve is inadequate for funding the retirement benefit, the government must pay the balance.

3.3 Third Pillar of Old Age Security

The third pillar of old age security consists almost entirely of individual savings. Taiwan's annuity market began in September 1997, when the Ministry of Finance approved the first annuity contract. As expected, the market is small and is not expected to expand too rapidly, primarily because people choose to self insure against uncertain life-span with the family. Parents who live too long are supported by their children and those who die unexpectedly leave their children with additional bequests. Commercial annuities are therefore not in great demand.

Table 1: Three Pillars of Old Age Security: The Existing System

	First Pillar	Second Pillar	Third Pillar
Mandate	Public Employee Insurance Program Labor Insurance Program National Pension Program	Public Employee Retirement Law Basic Labor Law	Voluntary
Objective	Redistribution Coinsurance	Saving Coinsurance	Saving Coinsurance
Benefits	One-time Benefits and Annuities	One-time Benefits	
Financing	Contributions by Employees and Employers Government subsidy	Contributions by Employees and Employers	Personal Saving Commercial Annuities
Funding	Partially Funded	Partially Funded	Fully Funded
Management	Publicly Managed	Privately Managed	Privately Managed

Although Taiwan does not have devices such as individual saving accounts that encourage long-term saving, the tax law already exempts interest earnings up to NT$270,000 (or US$8,438) from income tax liabilities per household. Thus, interest earnings are practically tax free for most middle and lower income families as well as young families, whose wealth is less than NT$4.5 million (US$14,0000) assuming that the interest rate is 6%. This may explain why personal savings constitute the most important source of workers' retirement income. However, as mentioned above, Taiwan's savings rate has been declining in recent years, although it remains high by comparison with the

US standard. The declining saving rate implies that the third pillar of old age security is not as strong as before, and the responsibility of the first two pillars is becoming more important.

3.4 Need for Reform

The World Bank recommends that the first two pillars of old age security should provide 60% of income replacement. According to this criterion, in theory, the two pillars of old age security in Taiwan should provide adequate income security. Take a long-time worker who is covered by the basic labor law and the labor insurance law as an example. He is eligible for a one-time retirement benefit equal to 90 times the last working month's wage. Now assume that the worker lives for 15 years (or 180 months) after retirement at t_0. Let R be the income replacement rate, $R = b(t)/y(t)$, where b(t) is the retirement benefit and y(t) is the monthly income if he works at time t. We can convert the one-time retirement benefit into an annuity that is indexed according to productivity growth at the rate of g, so that $y(t) = y(t_0)(1+g)^j$, where $j = t-t_0$.

$$90\ y(t_0) = \sum_{j=0}^{180} b(t) \left(\frac{1}{1+r}\right)^j = \sum_{j=0}^{180} R\ y(t) \left(\frac{1}{1+r}\right)^j .$$

Assume that the growth rate of productivity is g= 2% per annum. The income replacement rate is

$$R = 90 / \sum_{j=0}^{180} \left(\frac{1+g}{1+r}\right)^j \approx 60\%$$

if the real rate of return on assets (r) is 8% and is around 50% if r = 7%. Thus, the income replacement rate is close to the rate recommended by the World Bank.

Under the Public Employees Insurance Program and the Public Employees' Retirement Law, a government employee is entitled to a total of 100 times his or her last months wage. This translates into an income replacement rate of 55% to 65%, better than that expected by a worker.

However, as of the end of 1993, only two thirds of the population aged 25 and older was covered by the first pillar of old age security: 10.8 % by Public Employees' and related insurance, 59.3% by Labor Insurance and 2.9 % by social assistance programs. And as of November 1997, only 47% of workers were employed in enterprises that funded pensions according to the stipulations of the basic labor law. Moreover, a number of changes have to be made to ensure that the first pillar offers adequate old age security.

First, both existing public employees and labor insurance programs were established in1959 and 1960, respectively, when Taiwan had only a per capita GDP of US$1230 (1960 figure) at 1997 prices and a life expectancy at birth of 62.3 for males and 66.7 for females (1962 figures). As a result, the normal retirement age was set at 60 rather than the 65 that is typical in social security programs in industrial countries. The low normal retirement age has helped the economy during the period of rapid structural changes. Those who were unemployed due to skill obsolescence were encouraged to retire early and replaced by new and more skillful workers. However, now that life expectancy is 71.95 years for males and 77.83 for females (1997) and is projected to increase rapidly, retirement at age 60 has become too early.

Second, the one time payment of retirement benefits in both programs does not offer old-age security because the money is frequently lost because of unwise portfolio management and unexpected inflation.

Third, pensions are not portable between the private and public sectors. This stipulation hampers the mobility between the two sectors and, more importantly, the government effort to privatize state enterprises and downsize the government sector.

Finally, because the economy is dominated by small and medium-sized firms, a large number of workers are either self employed or employed in family enterprises or small business (with employees less than 5 persons). Their wages are not easily determined. As a result, the Labor Insurance Program covers only those who work in enterprises which employ at least five persons. This explains why one third of the adult population is without public pension coverage, while in countries such as the U.S., employment –based social security systems cover more than 90 percent of the population.

Even the second pillar of old age security needs changes. First, the basic labor law requires a long vesting period. It takes 25 years with the same employer, while the average life of small or medium-sized firms is less than 13.3 years and the average years of service with the same company are only 8.3 years. Furthermore, in 1997, since the penalty on the failure of firms to fund their pensions is light, only 13.71% of nearly 190 thousand firms covered by the basic labor law actually funded their pensions. The long vesting requirement also provides firms with an incentive to renege on their obligations by firing workers right before the workers' retirement benefits become vested. In sum, the probability that workers will actually receive their retirement benefits upon retirement is not good, particularly in small and medium-sized firms.

Second, the one-time retirement benefit is based on the last working month's average wage. This not only makes the retirement benefit too closely tied to the cyclical movements in wages but also is subject to moral hazard. If a firm raises the wage of the worker in his last working month, the firm has to pay not only for the raise itself but the accompanying increase in retirement benefit (up to 45 times the pay raise). Therefore, it provides the firm an incentive to reduce the worker's pay.

4. Social Security Reforms

Social security reforms undertaken by the government consist primarily of expanding the and improving coverage of the first pillar of old age security to the entire population. There have also been attempts to reform the pension stipulations in the basic labor law, but further progress is pending. In September 1997, the first commercial annuity contract was introduced in the market.

An easy way to expand the first pillar of old age security is of course to extend the coverage of the public employees and the labor insurance programs to those who have not been covered. However, as mentioned above, both public employees and labor insurance programs need to make changes that cannot be easily carried out. Therefore, it was decided to retain and revise these two existing programs, but to create a new national pension program to cover the one-third of the adult population that is not yet insured by the two programs. Those who are insured by the existing programs are allowed to choose between staying in the current programs and joining the new one, although all new workers in both public and private sectors will be required to join the new national pension program. Administratively, the national pension program and the existing public employees and labor insurance programs will be managed by separate organizations although their benefit levels will be unified. Retention of the existing programs enables the government to avoid settling the implicit debts owed by the two existing programs.

The proposed plan contains the following features.:

(1) The national pension program is a defined benefit program. All retirees receive an identical lump-sum annuity that provides for only basic living expenses. All insured persons pay a lump-sum monthly premium. The full benefit level at the program inception is set equal to 65% of the average consumption expenditures for the preceding two years, or around NT$9100 per month. The minimum guaranteed benefit level is $2000 per month. The benefit is indexed for subsequent years on the basis of consumer prices (50%) and the real wage rate (50%).

(2) Insured persons who have reached age 65 and have been insured for 40 years are eligible for full benefit. Each insured person who is aged 26-39 at program inception will receive a fraction 1/(65-A) of benefit per year of

insurance coverage if they have been insured for at least ten years, where A is their current age. Thus, they are eligible to receive full benefit if they have been insured for 65-A years. Each insured person who is 40 and older at program inception will be entitled to 1/25 of full benefit per year of insurance coverage if they have been insured for at least ten years. Each insured person who is 55 years and older will be eligible for (65-A)/25 of full benefit after having been insured for 65-A years.

(3) Those who are 65 and older at program inception are eligible for a retirement *subsidy* in the amount of NT$2000 per month without having to pay any premiums.

In deciding the premium, one of the concerns of the planners was to avoid resistance to the new program, so the premium cannot be too much higher than those charged by the existing programs. It was decided to set the lump-sum premium equal to 10% of the full benefit level, i.e., NT$910 per month. Part of the premium is subsidized by the government, financed by raising the value-added tax by one percentage point.

The premium structure will result in partial funding of the retirement benefit. It is expected to maintain the financial soundness of the new national pension program for the next 25 years. A provision is included to allow an automatic rise in the premium when revenue falls short of expenditures. This is a step forward compared with the existing programs in terms of maintaining the financial soundness and avoiding negative impact on the economy.

Because of the difficulty in determining the wages of those who are not yet covered by the existing programs, the premium and the retirement benefit are stipulated as lump sum. It implies that lower-income workers will have to pay a larger share of their incomes toward retirement. In other words, they are over insured compared with those who are better off. Such a stipulation, however, can be justified by the fact that fewer of these people are covered by the second pillar of old age security.

In conjunction with the establishment of the new national pension program, there will also be changes in the two existing public insurance programs. The goals of the changes are first to unify the retirement benefits and premiums across programs. Second, retirees will be allowed to choose between an annuity and a one-time benefit. Third, pensions should be portable across the three programs. The main differences among the three programs will be the additional features that each program provides. For example, the labor insurance program will provide pregnancy and injury insurance benefits which are not included in the national pension program.

5. The Economic Effects of Social Security Reforms

As mentioned above, from the aggregate point of view, an increase in life expectancy means that workers have to either postpone retirement or save more. Thus, if social security is to be sustainable, it not only has to be financially sound, but avoid distorting the saving incentive. This section considers how the proposed national pension program interacts with demographic changes to affect aggregate saving decisions.

How social security affects aggregate savings depends on the way it is funded, the number of the population who are myopic and the age structure of the population. According to the permanent-income/life-cycle hypothesis, a rational person plans his consumption on the basis of his life-time resources. Social security affects his consumption by causing a change in his life-time resources:

$$\Delta C(t) = \gamma \Delta Y(t),$$

where ΔC is the change in consumption, ΔY is the change in life-time resources brought about by the proposed national pension program, γ is the marginal propensity to consume out of life-time resources, and t is the current age.[2] If social security is fully funded and actuarially fair, then it does not affect individual consumption because it leaves lifetime resources unchanged. If social security is on a pay-as-you-go basis, then the rate of return on social security expected by an individual can be different from the market rate of return on assets. In general, the rate of return on social security is higher the higher the population growth rate and the older the individual. For those individuals for whom the rate of return from social security is higher (lower) than the market rate of return on assets, social security increases (reduces) their consumption by causing a rise (fall) in their life-time resources. [3]

However, not all individuals plan their consumption according to their lifetime

---

[2] The marginal propensity to consume out of social security wealth can be shown to be:

$$\gamma = \frac{1 - 1/(1+r)}{1-(1/(1+r))^{T-t+1}}$$

where γ is the subjective discount rate. (See Hu, Chen and Chen (1998) for derivation.)

[3] If individuals had bequest motives, then they would take into account the burden of social security transfers on their offspring. As a result, the marginal propensity to consume out of social security wealth would be zero, and social security leaves the total savings of the rational population unchanged. (See Barro (1974)

resources. There are individuals who are unable to plan for their retirement because they either are short sighted, or do not have information to do future planning, or face credit constraints, or find information too costly, or are unable to carry out life time planning. These individuals can be called myopic in the sense that their behavior is better described by Keynes' current income hypothesis than by the permanent-income/life-cycle hypothesis. A study by Deaton and Paxson (1993) indicates that the permanent-income/ life-cycle hypothesis is the best but not the perfect theory to describe Taiwanese consumer behavior. A study by Chan and Hu (1997) suggests that about 30 percent of the population (income weighted) is myopic. Social security reduces consumption of myopic workers by causing a fall in their current disposable income while it increases consumption of myopic retirees by augmenting their current disposable income. The net effect of social security is to increase the total saving of the myopic population provided that the former effect dominates.

Table 2 provides a simulation of the saving effect of the proposed national pension program. We use the demographic tables for 1995-2035 projected by the CEPD (1996). We assume that the existing Public Employees and Workers Insurance Programs remain unchanged and cover the same percentage of the population, so that the new national pension program affects only 27% of the population. We assume that 30% of the population is myopic and that their marginal propensity to consume is 100%. (See Chan and Hu (1997).) Rational individuals have logarithmic instantaneous utility functions and their subjective discount rate is 4%.[4] The real rate of interest is set equal to 6%. These calculations do not allow for induced changes in the interest rate and the wage rate, because we consider Taiwan as a small open economy.

We see from the first row that the proposed program described in the preceding section would result in a fall in aggregate saving by NT$20 billion in the first year or a fall in the savings rate by 0.21 percentage points (of Gross Domestic Product). The fall in the savings rate would rise to 0.59 percentage points by 2010 and further to 2.68 percentage points by 2035. This amount is not as small as it appears to be. The reason is that the proposed national pension program affects only 27% of the population. A full-scale program would result in a fall in the savings rate by 9.93 percentage points, or equivalently more than

[4] A logarithmic utility function implies a relative risk aversion coefficient of 1. Studies of the U.S. data suggest that the relative risk aversion coefficient is about between 2 and 4, while the study by Chan and Hu (1997) seems to suggest the relative risk aversion coefficient is much lower. We cannot even exclude the possibility that the coefficient may approach 0.

60% in aggregate savings. This result is consistent with results obtained by Feldstein (1995, 1974).[5]

Table 2 : The Effects of the Proposed National Pension Program on Aggregate Savings

Units: Millions of Constant NT Dollars

(% of real GDP)

Year	2000	2010	2035
Projected Demographic Change	-20,299 (-0.21%)	-77,825 (-0.59%)	-738,677 (-2.68%)
Current Demographic Scenario	-20,299 (-0.21%)	-54,023 (-0.41%)	-223,113 (-0.81%)

Data Source: Hu, Chen and Chen (1998)

Second row, Table 2 demonstrates what would happen if there were no demographic change. The decline in aggregate saving due to the proposed national pension program would be 0.21 percentage points (of GDP) for 2000, 0.41 percentage points for 2010 and 0.81 percentage points for 2035, respectively. A comparison with the first row shows that population aging aggravates the adverse saving effect of social security only slightly for the first ten years but to an increasing extent afterwards. By 2035, it will exacerbate the adverse saving effect by as much as 3 times (2.68 vs. 0.81 percentage points), because of the rapid change in the dependency ratio beginning in 2010. In conclusion, the interaction between population aging and social security could have a large impact on aggregate savings over time, even if social security is partially funded.

6. Concluding Remarks

This paper describes the current social security system in Taiwan and the proposed reforms undertaken by the government since 1994. The existing

[5] Feldstein (1974, 1995) did not explicitly consider whether there is myopic population, but the coefficient of disposable income (YD) in his regression equations implicitly takes into account myopia.

social security system consists of three pillars. The first two pillars, if fully realized, will provide around 60% of income replacement, about the level recommended by the World Bank. However, there is still a large segment of the population that does not have pension insurance. Even those who are insured are not ensured of old age security because of a number of outdated stipulations. The reforms undertaken by the government are to make social security a universal annuity. It also tries to increase the funding ratio in order to ensure the financial integrity of the system and to avoid distorting aggregate saving.

Economic development in mainland China requires privatization of its state enterprises. Cooperation of workers is crucial for its success and requires that government honor the obligations of state enterprises. A social security system to take over the pension obligations of state enterprises ensures that workers' old age security is not affected by the privatization of state enterprises. As Taiwan's experience has shown, funding social security on a pay-as-you-go basis is less costly to the government at this stage of economic development and demographic transition, since it allows the spread of all pension obligations throughout future generations. However, the pay-as-you-go system will have a negative effect on capital accumulation. And the negative effect can be exacerbated by rapid aging of the population. Such a system is not viable in the long run.

Full funding of social security reduces the distortionary impact of social security on capital accumulation and thereby economic growth. On the other hand, in a fully-funded system, pension assets will grow with the maturity of the system and aging of the population. On the basis of Taiwan's experience (Chu, Huang, Yang and Hu (1994)), the pension assets are potentially very large, possibly as large as 2.5 times the country's GDP. If the government controls this huge amount of pension assets, it will become a huge financial force as well as an indirect owner of the enterprises that it tries to privatize. The original intent of privatization could be defeated. A possible solution is either to partially fund or to privatize social security.

References

1. Atkinson, Anthony, 1995, "The Welfare State and Economic Performance," *National Tax Journal*, 68: 171-98.

2. Barro, Robert, 1974,"Are Government Bonds Net Wealth," *Journal of Political Economy*, 82:1095-117.

3. Chan Vei-Lin and Sheng-Cheng Hu, 1997, "Financial Liberalization and Aggregate Consumption: The Evidence from Taiwan," *Applied Economics*, 29:1525-1535.

4. Chu, Cyrus, Ting-Yuan Huang, Cheng-Chen Yang and Sheng-Cheng Hu, 1994, "The Effect of National Pensions on Government Finance, " *Taiwan Economic Forecast and Policy*, 25.2: 35-68

5. CEPD (Council for Economic Development and Planning, the Executive Yuan), 1996, *the Projected Population for the Taiwan Area, Republic of China*. (In Chinese.)

6. Deaton, Angus and Christine Paxson, 1993, "Saving, Growth and Aging in Taiwan," *National Bureau of Economic Research Working Paper* #4330.

7. Feldstein, Martin S., 1995, "Social Security and Saving: New Time Evidence," *National Bureau of Economic Research Working Paper* No. 5054.

8. Feldstein, Martin S., 1974, "Social Security, Induced Retirement and Aggregate Capital Accumulation," *Journal of Political Economy*, 82:905-26.

9. Hu, Sheng-Cheng, Kuo-Mei Chen and Lii-tarn Chen, 1998, "Demographic Transition and Social Security, " Presented at the International Conference on Economic Aspects of Demographic Transition: The Experience of Asian Pacific Countries, Institute of Economics, Academia Sinica, Taipei, Taiwan.

10. Krugman, Paul, 1994, "The Myth of Asia's Miracle," *Foreign Affairs*, 73:62-68.

11. Lau, Lawrence, 1998, "The Sources of Asian Economic Growth," in Gustav Ranis, Sheng-Cheng Hu and Yunn-Peng Chu (ed.) *The Political Economy of Development in Taiwan*, Cheltenham: Edward Elgar.

12. Wang, Temu and Chao-hsien Liu, 1997, "Population and Poverty in Taiwan," in Te-Hsiung Sun, Li Chi, Mei-Lin Lee (eds.), *Population Aging and Care of the Elderly*, ROC Population Association. (In Chinese.)

13. World Bank, 1994, *Averting the Old Age Crisis*, Oxford: Oxford University Press.

14. World Bank, 1997, *Old Age Security: China 2020*. Washington, D.C.: The World Bank.

CHAPTER 21

VIETNAM'S OLD AGE SECURITY SYSTEM: RECENT TRANSFORMATIONS AND THEIR RELEVANCE FOR UPCOMING CHANGES IN CHINA

DANIEL GOODKIND
Bureau of Census, University of Michigan,
Washington, DC 20233-8860, USA
E-mail: Daniel.M.Goodkind@ccMail.census.gov

TRUONG SI ANH
Institute for Economic Research, Hai Ba Trung Street,
Ho Chi Minh City, Vietnam

BUI THE CUONG
Institute of Sociology, 27 Tran Xuan Soan,
Hanoi, Vietnam

As policy makers consider how to reform China's old age security system, they can benefit from knowledge about similar reforms in other countries and the challenges they have met. We examine such reforms in Vietnam, a neighboring country with a social, economic, and demographic profile quite similar to China's. Prior to 1995, pension and disability benefits, the primary source of public support, were usually available only to state workers through an internal pay-as-you-go system (heavily subsidized with general government revenues). In 1995, a new Social Security Administration was formally established which expanded such coverage to employees of non-state firms. Under the new system, employer contribution rates were raised, wage deductions added, and wage replacement ratios reduced to 75 percent or less of final wages. We explore financial, ideological, and demographic reasons for these reforms as well as challenges to the new system, many of which are related to Vietnam's market-oriented transition. Along the way, we compare similarities and differences between the Chinese and Vietnamese contexts. Our analysis draws upon survey data, reviews of public documents, and interviews with public officials.

1. Introduction

As policy makers consider reforms in China's old age security system (Krieg and Schadler, 1994; West, 1996; World Bank, 1997), they can benefit from information about similar reforms in other countries and the challenges they have met. Such knowledge can assist them in anticipating possible outcomes of current reforms in China. We explore reforms in the old age security system of Vietnam. Although smaller than China, this neighboring country shares a similar cultural and demographic profile: a Confucian cultural heritage, a populace that is about 80 percent rural, and an ethnic minority composing 12-13 percent of the population. But the Vietnamese case is most instructive because recent changes in its old age security system are similar to those now being considered in China. Moreover, the general pace and scope of their transitions from central planning to more market-oriented economies are similar.

Like China and other developing countries, Vietnam has relatively limited public resources available to ensure the well-being of its elderly citizens. As has been the case for untold generations, most elderly Vietnamese remain dependent on their children and other family members for their care and welfare (Dang, 1994; ICDS, 1997; Truong et al., 1997). Nevertheless, public pensions have been available in the past, primarily to those retiring from the state sector, and a new Social Security System established in 1995 is attempting to extend old age benefits to employees of non-state firms. The new system, as before, relies on a combination of government subsidies and pay- as-you-go financing, although now with expanded employer contributions and new payroll deductions.

Our report examines financial, ideological, and demographic reasons for these reforms. In particular, we show how a rapidly aging workforce within the shrinking state sector has rendered it demographically incapable of caring for future pensioners through an internal pay-as-you-go system. In addition, we detail other challenges facing the government as it renegotiates its old age security system. Along the way, we highlight regional variations in public support within Vietnam. We also compare similarities and differences between the Chinese and Vietnamese contexts.

2. Data Sources and Multi-Method Research Strategy

This paper relies primarily on data from the 1992/93 Vietnam Living Standards Survey (VLSS, 1994), a nationally representative survey of 4,800 households. That survey was undertaken by the State Planning Committee and General Statistical Office with support from several international organizations. We also refer briefly to a pair of surveys of the elderly in the northern and southern sub-regions of Vietnam centered around Hanoi and Ho Chi Minh City which included 930 and 840 elderly people, respectively (Truong et al., 1997). Our analysis of Vietnam's reformed old age security system is based not only upon these surveys but also other public documents, such as the new set of labor and pension guidelines established by the Ministry of Labor, Invalids, and Social Affairs (MOLISA, 1996), as well as discussions held in 1997 with policy specialists in MOLISA and the new Social Security Administration.

3. The Reformed Old Age Security System (1995): Towards an Expanded Pay-as-you-go System

As part of its administrative restructuring under market reforms (*Doi Moi)*, Vietnam decided in 1990 to set up a national Social Security Administration to take over from the Ministry of Labor, Invalids, and Social Affairs (MOLISA) the task of administering pensions and other social benefits[1]. Five provinces (including Hanoi and HCM City) were selected to begin implementing the pilot programs of the new agency. Incremental changes, beginning with Decree 43CP in 1993, culminated in 1995 with Decree 12/CP (26 January 1995; MOLISA, 1996), although the system continues to evolve.

The most basic change concerns who is covered. The prior pension system covered only state workers (and members of most high ranking non-agricultural cooperatives, which were considered to be operating almost as if they belonged to the state sector). The new system has been expanded to include all state and non-state enterprises with more than 10 employees. Remaining uncovered are the self-employed and those working on family farms, who together constitute 80 percent of working Vietnamese. As before, the system relies on pay-as-you-go financing (with

1 Prior to that time, MOLISA had been in charge of pensions, disability and survivors benefits, whereas the Vietnamese Confederation of Labor had been in charge of pregnancy, illness, and accidents. Official responsibility for all of these benefits were transferred to the new Social Security Administration.

heavy government subsidies making up for funding shortfalls), although the contribution scheme has been altered somewhat to increase revenues. In years prior to 1995, state enterprises contributed between 5 and 13 percent of their wage bill to MOLISA and/or the Vietnam Confederation of Labor. The new system requires all enterprises to contribute 15 percent of their wage bill, along with a new 5 percent payroll deduction, to the new Social Security Administration[2]. Moreover, the maximum wage replacement ratio was reduced from 95 to 75 percent of final wages for both pre- and post-1995 retirees[3].

The new system features nationally uniform defined benefits within the state sector (MOLISA, 1996[4]), but unlike before, they are now pegged collectively to the minimum wage to protect against inflation. Some healthy enterprises may also have their own benefit plans to supplement the national one. Such supplements may also be provided by provincial and other regional authorities based on local conditions[5].

Unlike Vietnam, China has yet to establish a nationally uniform pension system. In the past, state enterprises have been responsible for both funding and administering pensions for their own retirees, but China is now encouraging benefit schemes and resource pooling across geographic sub-regions (West, 1996; World Bank, 1997). Such pools evidently are not widespread, nor even required, in Vietnam. That such a strategy is not required may have something to do with scale. Since Vietnam is comparable to Sichuan province in terms of its and population, it has been easier to establish national standards there. In addition, our impression is that Vietnamese state enterprises have tended to be less autonomous and less involved in all aspects of daily life than those in China, which may have

---

2 In addition, given the inefficiency and bloated size of state-owned enterprises, as well as expected future layoffs in that sector, Decree #59/CP (3/10/96) stipulated that another 5 percent of after tax income be applied to pay for unemployment insurance. Maximum receipt of such benefits for any workers was to be 6 months at full salary level.

3 In order to avoid the discontent that would have occurred among current pensioners after such a reduction, a pension supplement was instituted to recompense pre-1995 pensioners for early military service or various revolutionary activities. Under this system, the government awarded a fixed amount for each year of such service. In our discussions with pensioners in Vietnam, we found that this supplementary pension award was very close to the amount that they had lost due to the reduction in the wage replacement rate.

4 National pension guidelines existed before the mid 1990s, but due to administrative disorganization following reunification in 1975, regional authorities evidently adjusted these rates to local conditions.

5 There are some issues that have yet to be fully resolved. Evidently, MOLISA requires contributions to be based on wages only, but the Security Administration prefers to withhold based on a combination of wages plus other benefits, the latter of which still vary by region. There are also uncertainties about how the transitional fund will operate for hose contributors retiring after 1995.

further facilitated the establishment of nationally uniform standards and administration.

According to our conversations with officials in Vietnam's Social Security Administration, contributions to the social security system appear to be running fairly well within the state sector. Yet, even now, only about one third of all current pension outlays are being generated by the pay-as-you-go system, a proportion they expect to rise as the proportion of pre-1995 retirees among all pensioners declines and progressively more employees and their employers pay into the system. However, there are many challenges ahead before the system can sustain itself. One problem is that many state enterprises remain unprofitable.[6] Just as in the past, they will have to rely on government subsidies if social security contributions are to be made. The required subsidy might even increase if the higher contribution rate leads to an increase in non-compliance. Moreover, the current pay-as-you-go system is not likely to be viable in the long run due to the rapid aging of the state sector (to be discussed shortly).

Thus, economically inefficient state enterprises threaten to undermine the very purpose of the new system; to create a pay-as-you-go system independent of government subsidies. The collection of social security contributions from private sector enterprises is just as problematic. Although firms that survive free market competition are more likely to be financially healthy than their state-owned counterparts, their concern with profits may encourage them to avoid contributing to the new system. Moreover, since contributions are tied to the wage bill, private enterprises may have an incentive to claim that they have fewer employees (or a lower wage bill) than they actually have.

In addition to these challenges regarding revenue collection, the new Social Security Administration faces a variety of other problems. For instance, public confidence in the system is rather low. Workers know that the value of monthly pensions have declined in real terms. That decline was steepest in the 1980s when adjustments due to inflation were made irregularly. Pension rates are now tied to the minimum wage[7], yet that erosion has continued. The inflation rate between 1992-96 was 40 percent, but over the same period the minimum wage was increased by only 20 percent. Moreover, state workers became skeptical about public support

---

6 One recent report suggested that only 22 percent of state enterprises were unprofitable as of 1996 (Bao Dau Tu, 1998), although knowledgeable observers consider that number to be unrealistically low.

7 The monthly pension rate is now based on three factors: the minimum wage, a Amultiplier (1-10; based on occupation, rank, and experience) and the wage replacement rate (55-75 percent; based on years' experience).

in general because of negative experiences with a new national health insurance system[8].

There are also a host of administrative difficulties, such as those described to us by a representative of MOLISA's Social Insurance Division. Hundreds of disputes are filed each month regarding the amount of pensions being received. The resolution of these disputes is slow, in part because the system has only recently been computerized. Prior work records exist only on paper and are cumbersome to locate and verify[9]. Another general problem concerns the lack of managerial and technical experience. These include insufficient skills for projecting relative numbers of contributors versus pensioners to assess the future viability of the system. Lastly, although the government eventually would like to expand coverage of the social security system to the self-employed (including family farming households, given the poverty of many of these workers and the difficulty of collecting contributions, extending this system to the self-employed remains a distant hope.

4. The Demographic Rationale for Recent Reforms

Why exactly did Vietnam expand social security coverage to private sector enterprises? A primary reason we heard about during our discussions with government officials was the desire to cover a larger portion of citizens. The current system is inequitable because it is limited to the state sector, and given that this sector is now shrinking relative to the private sector, even greater inequality would result if coverage remained limited to the state sector[10]. Another reason,

---

8 Membership in this government-sponsored health system ostensibly entitles one to certain services. In practice, however, inclusion within this system guarantees little. Given the very low salaries among health personnel and a lack of medical supplies, service cannot be expected unless private payments are made to doctors, nurses, and hospital attendants. Moreover, the system has been plagued by poor management, corruption, and bad attitudes among health workers towards their patients. However, some of these problems have been reduced in response to mounting criticisms printed in newspapers and discussed in he Vietnamese parliament.

9 The list of current pensioners as well as their prior work records have been largely computerized, in part with the financial and technical assistance of the International Labor Organization (ILO), although the total labor pool of future pensioners has not.

10 The VLSS (1992-93) corroborates the regressiveness of the public transfer system. It found that he poorest 20 percent of households receive only 7 percent of total pension and disability payments as well as only 13 percent of all other transfers whereas the wealthiest 20 percent receive 39 and 27 percent of these benefits, respectively (World Bank, 1995). A separate analysis of government expenditures found that over 80 percent of all government transfer payments involve retirement

stated in very general terms, was that the prior system was increasingly nonviable because required outlays were increasing at the same time that collected revenues were shrinking (as were available government funds to subsidize the system).

Demographic perspectives help to clarify further these financial difficulties.

One issue concerns the age structure of the *working* population in the state sector. That structure is illustrated in Figure 1, which shows the number of workers enumerated in the VLSS (1992/93). As is well known, a pay-as-you-go system based on payroll deductions can only work well when the proportion of current workers to retirees is relatively high (e.g. population structure truly resembles a pyramid). Of course, over time, as fertility and mortality drop and the population ages (as is happening in Vietnam), population pyramids become more rectangular, rendering a pay-as-you-go system less viable unless workers and employers are willing to contribute ever larger proportions of their incomes to the system.

Figure 1: Combined Age Structure of Workers in the State Sector (inner figure) and Non-State Firms (10+ Employees)

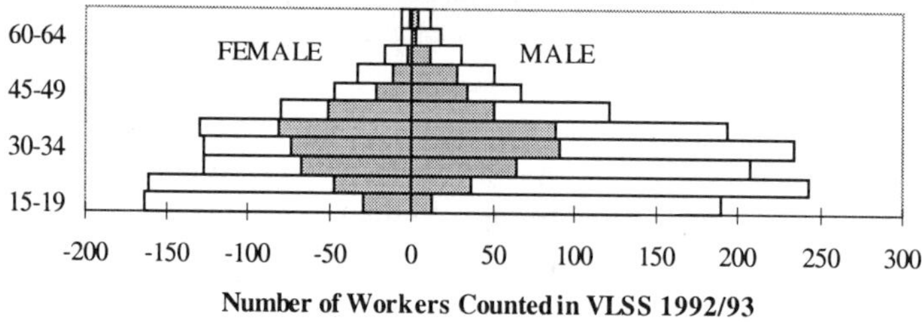

However, the age structure within Vietnam's state sector has *already* lost its pyramid shape. Figure 1 shows a large bulge of workers between ages 30 and 44, with sharply attenuated cohorts of younger workers below those ages, in part due to hiring reductions in the state sector in the wake of *Doi Moi*. For instance, the percentage of state workers among Vietnam's total work force has fallen steadily from 14.8 to 8.7 percent between 1985 and 1994 (Statistical Yearbook, 1992-96), and other survey evidence suggests that these reductions in state hiring (at least

pensions and other benefits for state workers, even though such workers constitute only 45 percent of the population overall (ibid. Pg. 62).

through 1992) have come primarily at the expense of young workers (McCarty, 1993).

Thus, due to the age structure of the working population, the state sector would be demographically *incapable* of supporting its future elderly retirees through a pay-as-you-go system unless contribution rates were raised sharply (or retirement ages raised or wage replacement rates reduced further). The rationale for expanding social security coverage to private enterprises is thus readily understood. When one adds together workers in state and non-state enterprises (Figure 1), their combined populations transform dramatically into the pyramid shape which makes a pay-as-you-go system possible (at least temporarily).

By region, the deficit of younger workers in the state sector is worst in the Red River delta. Figure 2 shows the ratio of younger to older state workers. In the Red

Figure 2: Ratio of Younger Workers to Older Workers Within Vietnam's State Sector (source VLSS 1992/93)

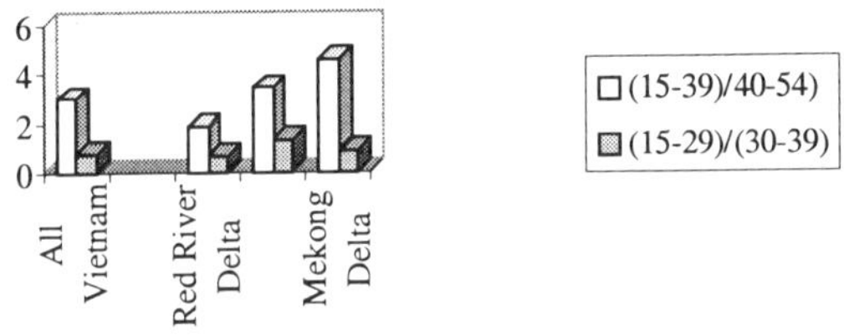

River Delta, there are only 1.8 younger workers, aged 15-39, for each worker aged 40-54 (the standard retirement age is 55 or women and 60 for men), whereas this ratio is above 3.5 and 4.5 in the Southeast (HCM City and provinces east of it) and Mekong Delta regions, respectively[11]. This regional discrepancy is due to the fact that central planning had been pursued in the northern region since national partition in 1954, whereas it was instituted in the southern region only after reunification in 1975, a temporal discrepancy resulting in a greater proportion of older state workers

11 These three sub-regions overlap geographically with our surveys f the elderly (to be discussed shortly). Vietnam contains sever official sub-regions altogether. Data from the other sub-regions (Northern Highlands, North Central, Central Coast, Central Highlands) display congruent patterns to Figure 2 based on their location vis a vis the pre-1975 boundary between northern and southern regions (not shown)

in the northern area[12]. The top-heavy age structure in the northern region is also a consequence (perhaps even a cause) of the greater reduction in hiring of younger workers there --even when one considers only those workers below age 40, the proportion of those below 30 to those 30-39 is lowest in the Red River area.

This regional discrepancy is due to the fact that central planning had been pursued in the northern region since national partition in 1954, whereas it was instituted in the southern region only after reunification in 1975, a temporal discrepancy resulting in a greater proportion of older state workers in the northern area. The top-heavy age structure in the northern region is also a consequence (perhaps even a cause) of the greater reduction in hiring of younger workers there --even when one considers only those workers below age 40, the proportion of those below 30 to those 30-39 is lowest in the Red River area.

An even more immediate problem concerns the declining ratio of workers to pensioners. Although we do not have precise measures of this ratio over time, indirect evidence suggests that the decline has been substantial. In the northern area, where the state sector expanded greatly during the late 1950s, the proportion of state workers achieving the 20 years experience necessary to earn a pension likely jumped suddenly in the 1980s and then continued to increase, just as in China, where the worker/pensioner ratio correspondingly plummeted from 30.3 in 1978, to 12.8 in 1980, to 5.1 in 1994 (West, 1996: p. 3)[13]. In the southern area, which was not reunified until 1975, many state workers did not have enough years experience to earn a pension by the time the VLSS was taken (1992/93). As a result, older southern state workers have been less likely to expect a pension in the past, but younger ones are more likely to expect one in the future. Figure 3 confirms this assertion. In the Red River Delta, similar percentages of both younger workers aged 30-44 and older workers aged 45-54 expected a pension (about 89 percent)[14].

---

12 We limited our calculations in this figure 2 to workers below age 55 because a reduced size in workers above that age may not signify a lesser dependency on younger workers but more (e.g. they may currently be pensioners). Note that state sector workers in he Red River delta shows a top-heavy age pyramid relative to the southern areas *despite* the fact that higher proportion have retired there at younger ages (not shown). Thus, regional discrepancies of pensioners to workers are likely as severe, if not more so, that those suggested by the worker ratios shown in by Figure 2. Regrettably, we cannot readily calculate pensioner/worker ratios with VLSS data because pension receipts were queried only at the household level.

13 An official at Vietnam's Social Security Administration suggested hat the current ratio of workers to pensioners in 1997 was about 4 to 1.

14 The sharp drop off in percentages of workers under age 30 who expect a pension likely reflects the uncertainty of this group regarding future employment within the state sector.

However, in the Southeast (HCM City and several provinces to the east) and Mekong River Delta areas, larger percentages of younger cohorts, who were aged

Figure 3: Percentage Vietnamese State Sector Workers Who Expect to Receive a Pension, by Age (source, VLSS 1992/93)

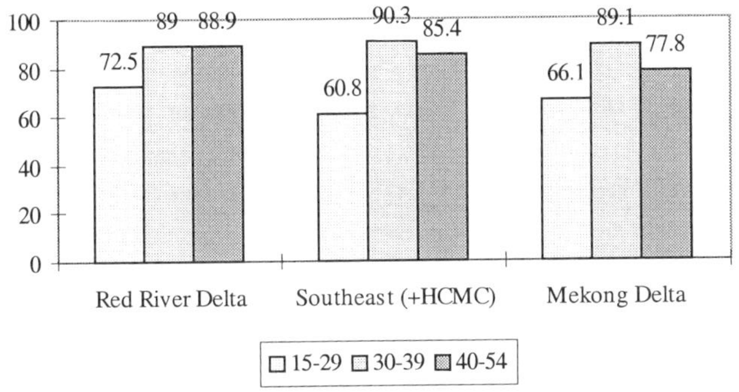

13-27 at the time of Vietnam's reunification, expected a pension (90.3 vs. 85.4, and 89.1 vs. 77.8 percent, respectively).

Thus, demographic patterns within the state sector reveal that the Red River Delta region is currently least capable of supporting its elderly through a pay-as-you-go system. The Red River Delta is also the region where state sector employment remains most prevalent. Figure 4 shows the proportion of elderly (60+) receiving monthly pension or disability benefits based on our aforementioned surveys of the elderly in northern and southern sub-regions, which were conducted by the authors during 1996 and early 1997 (Truong et al, 1997; note that the VLSS did not ask about pensions among *individual* elderly). Within these sub-regions, clusters were randomly selected from three major sectors: districts of each primal city, other urban townships, and all rural districts[15].

The proportion of pension recipients varied from well over half of all elderly in the urban Red River delta, to under 12 percent in the southern area. Again, this reflects the legacy of Vietnam's partition and reunification. State sector employment in the urban north expanded greatly following partition in 1954, but such expansion did not occur in the southern area until after reunification in 1975, and even then it did not occur to the same extent as in the north (Ngo, 1988).

15 About 30 elderly respondents within each cluster were randomly selected from lists of the elderly in the north and household registers in the south. The data each sub-region were weighted to be representative of the elderly populations within them.

Figure 4: Percentage Elderly Vietnamese Receiving Monthly State Pension or Disability Compared to Percentage Whose Last Primary Occupation was in the State Sector (source, authors' surveys 1996/97)

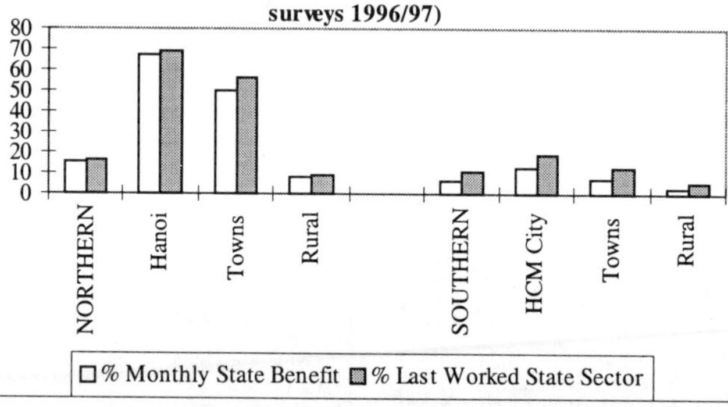

Indeed, Figure 4 shows a fairly close relationship between the frequency of monthly public benefits and the proportion of those whose last worked in the state sector[16].

5. Concluding Summary - Relevance for China

This report examined the changing system of public support to the elderly in Vietnam. A new Social Security Administration was created as part of Vietnam's market-oriented reforms and is responsible for old age security. The most significant change is that the former pension system, an ostensibly pay-as-you-go system designed for (and exclusively benefiting) state sector workers, now attempts to cover enterprises in both the state and private sectors (whether contributions are being made fully remains uncertain). Such changes have been enacted due to financial constraints and concerns for increasing social equity. Underlying demographic realities also render these changes necessary because the state workforce is both shrinking and aging rapidly, leaving it incapable of providing for the welfare of its own retirees through an internal pay-as-you-go system. The Red River Delta in Vietnam's northern region, where central planning was pursued longest and most vigorously following the 1950s, is the region where state enterprises are currently least capable of taking care of their own retirees.

16 Our questionnaire asked respondents to identify their primary occupation during several key historical periods -- prior to 1995, 1995-75, 1976-89, and since 1989; the southern survey further divided the 1955-75 period in half.

The demographic and financial problems facing Vietnam as it renegotiates its old age security system are quite similar to those facing China, which faces a congruent set of problems in the wake of its own free market transition (Krieg and Shadler, 1994; West, 1996; World Bank, 1997: FEAER, 1997). China is now considering similar reforms, such as the extension of coverage to the non-state sector and the reduction in the wage replacement ratio from .95 to .75 (World Bank, 1997).

One notable difference between Vietnam and China is that the former has a more unified pension system in regard to national standards and centralized administration. In contrast, Chinese state enterprises are still apparently more directly responsible for their employees, not only regarding pensions, but also for education, housing, and other benefits. Since economically healthier state enterprises tend to employ larger proportions of younger workers, and since those younger workers are required for a healthy pay-as-you-go system, Chinese authorities hope to coax them into regional pools which include less healthy enterprises with older age structures (ibid.). Nevertheless, whatever the causes of these national differences, our analysis of regional differences in Vietnam has similar implications for China. Old age reforms will be most problematic in those areas where the state sector was previously most prevalent (and where the proportions of state retirees are currently greatest).

In both national contexts, it will be important to augment the pay-as-you-go system. Even with the expansion of coverage to the non-state sector, some privatization of individual accounts is required if these systems are to remain viable in the long run amidst the continued aging of the population, inflation, and other economic conditions (World Bank, 1997). In addition to the above concerns, there are also many day-to-day administrative challenges facing Vietnam's new Social Security Administration. To the extent that these and other challenges hinder revenue collection, the social security system will remain reliant on central government subsidies. The government, in turn, due to increasing financial constraints and the drift away from central planning, may have to reduce benefits further or pass responsibility for the elderly back to individual families.

Indeed, this brings us back to the critical issue of *familial* support that we glossed over earlier in this paper. Most Vietnamese elderly remain financially dependent on their children, and they are least dependent on their children's income in the Red River Delta, where pensions are most prevalent (Cuong, et al., 1999; Goodkind, et al, 1999). This finding might reflect a simple inverse mathematical relationship (that is, pension availability within any given *household* renders the contribution of children's income less important).

Yet, there could be a more dynamic relationship between private and public support to the elderly. Could the increased availability of public support systems (in China, Vietnam, and elsewhere) be viewed by families as a substitute for their own support and thereby itself accelerate the breakdown of traditional family support over time (e.g. Chan and Cheung, 1997)? In the past, could this breakdown in family support have been greatest in urban and other areas where central planning was most aggressively pursued, rendering the elderly there especially vulnerable if social safety nets now fray in the wake of free market reforms? Or has familial support continued regardless, and will it continue to do so in the future? Put another way, how do old age security systems truly contribute to *net* improvements in the welfare of the elderly? These crucial questions remain open for future investigations.

References

1. Bao Dau Tu (Investment Review). 1998. Hoat Dong cua cac Doanh Nghiep Viet Nam: Thuc Trang va Van De Dat Ra (Activities of Vietnamese Enterprises: Realities and Emerging Problems). 26 February.
2. Chan, Angelique and Paul Cheung. 1997. *The Interrelationship between Public and Private Support of the Elderly: What Can We Learn from the Singaporean Case?* Research Reports - Comparative Study of the Elderly in Asia. No 97-41.
3. Bui, The Cuong, Truong Si Anh, Daniel Goodkind, John Knodel, and Jed Friedman. 1999 (forthcoming). Vietnamese Elderly Amidst Transformationa in Social Welfare Policy, in David Phillips (ed.) *Ageing in the Asia-Pacific Regions: Issues and Policies*; also issuing as Research Report, Population Studies Center, University of Michigan.
4. Dang Thu. 1994. *Local Level Policy Development for Integrating the Elderly into the Development Process in Vietnam.* New York: United Nations, ESCAP, Asian Population Studies Series No. 131-F.
5. Far East Asian Economic Review (FEAER). 1997. The Burden of Age, 23 October: 82-84.
6. Krieg, Renate, and Monika Schadler, eds. 1994. *Social Security in the People's Republic of China.* Institut fur Asienkunde: Hamburg.

7. Goodkind, Daniel, Truong Si Anh, and Bui The Cuong. 1999 (forthcoming). Reforming the Old Age Security System in Vietnam, in *Southeast Asian Journal of Social Science*, Vol. 27, No. 2: 139-162.
8. McCarty, Adam. 1993. Industrial Renovation in Vietnam, 1986-91, pp. 97-143 in *Vietnam's Dilemmas and Options*, edited by Mya Than and Joseph L.H. Tan. Singapore: Institute for Southeast Asian Studies.
9. Ministry of Labor, Invalids, and Social Affairs (MOLISA -- Bo Lao Dong Thuong-Binh va Xa Hoi; BLDTBXH). 1996. System of Current Laws and Regulations Regarding Labor, Invalids, and Social Affairs *(He Thong Van Ban Phap Luat Hien Hanh Ve Lao Dong-Thuong Binh Va Xa Hoi*). Hanoi. In Vietnamese.
10. Ngo, Vinh Long. 1988. Some Aspects of Cooperativization in the Mekong Delta, pp. 161-173, in *Postwar Vietnam: Dilemmas of Development*, edited by David G. Marr and Christine P. White. Ithaca: Southeast Asian Program.
11. *Statistical Yearbook* (Nien Giam Thong Ke Viet Nam). 1992-96. Hanoi. Truong Si Anh, Bui The Cuong, Daniel Goodkind, and John Knodel. 1997. Living Arragements, Patrilineality, and Sources of Support Among Elderly Vietnamese, *Asia Pacific Population Journal* 12 (4): 69-88.
12. Vietnam Living Standard Survey (VLSS). 1994. *Vietnam Living Standards Survey: 1992-1993.* Hanoi: State Planning Committee and General Statistical Office.
13. West, Loraine A. 1996. *Pension Reform in China: Preparing for the Future.* Washington, D.C.: U.S. Bureau of the Census, International Programs Center (No. 83).
14. World Bank. 1995. *Vietnam: Poverty Assessment and Strategy.* Report No. 13442-VN. Washington, D.C.: World Bank.
15. World Bank. 1997. *Old Age Security: Pension Reform in China.* Washington, D.C.

CHAPTER 22

CHOICE OF SOCIAL SECURITY SYSTEMS: SINGAPORE'S EXPERIENCE

DING LU
Department of Economics, National University of Singapore,
10 Keat Ridge Cresent, Singapore, 119260
E-mail: ecslud@leonis.nus.edu.sg

This paper discusses the principles of Singapore's social security system. We first examine the rationale for Singapore to have chosen a fully funded scheme. We then look into the institutional structure of the scheme and introduce its social-economic functions. Finally, we comment on the relevance of the Singapore experience to China's development of a market-oriented social security system.

1. Introduction

Social insurance programmes provide benefits to individuals and families for loss of income due to retirement, disability, illness, and unemployment. "Old Age, Survivors and Disability Insurance" is the official name of social security in the US. In industrialised countries, the social insurance programmes mainly consist of three areas of coverage, i.e., publicly mandated pension funds (such as the social security system in the US), publicly mandated medical insurance (such as Medicare in the US and public medical welfare in some European countries), and unemployment insurance.

In Singapore, the backbone of the social security system is the Central Provident Fund (CPF), a fully funded pension scheme first established in 1955. The primary objective of the scheme was to provide financial security for workers in their retirement or when they are no longer able to work. Over the past several decades a variety of modifications have expanded the CPF into a comprehensive social-security savings scheme, which not only takes care of a member's retirement, home ownership and healthcare needs, but also provides financial protection to CPF members and their families through its various insurance schemes. Apart from being the main vehicle for provision of social security, the CPF has also been the single most important financial intermediary in the city-state. When there is a sharp economic downturn, the CPF can even serve as a macroeconomic instrument to save jobs by cutting labour costs.

This paper discusses the principles which underlie Singapore's social security system. We first examine the rationale for Singapore to have chosen a fully funded scheme. We then look into the institutional structure of the scheme and highlight its social-economic functions. Finally, we will comment on the relevance of Singapore's social security experience for China.

2. Rationale for a Fully Funded Social Security System

2.1 Types of social safety net

Nowadays there are mainly four types of social safety nets in market economies. The first is the social welfare system directly financed by taxation or other forms of state-mandated income redistribution. Most social welfare benefits in industrialised countries are financed in this way. Social welfare provision is uniform for all those who are qualified. Therefore it provides universal coverage. The second measure is a combination of compulsory saving, social insurance, and income redistribution, such as the US social security system.

Both the first and second measures share the feature of pay-as-you-go (PAYG) financing. Under PAYG, benefits are paid to current retirees or beneficiaries from the contributions of the current generation of workers in payroll taxes or in other forms of taxes (Figure 1). Both measures are meant to provide social insurance through intra-generation and intergeneration redistribution of income. The US social security system, however, is a more personalised PAYG scheme with better accountability. Social security benefits vary from person to person depending on earnings history, age, and other personal conditions.

Figure 1: PAYG Cash Flows

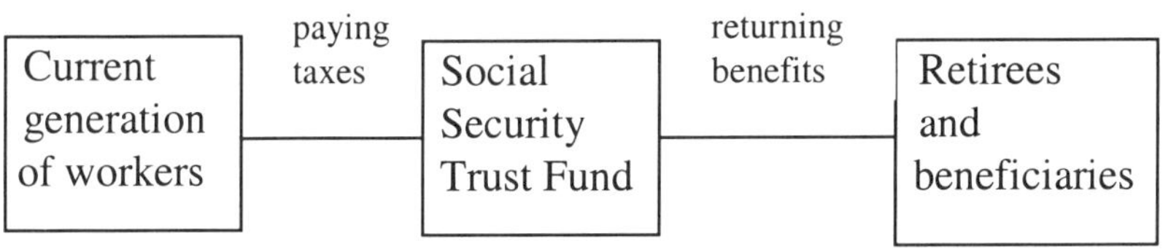

A third measure combines compulsory insurance participation and income redistribution. The unemployment insurance schemes in the American states represent such a model. Under this system, an insured worker who loses his/her job can receive benefits for a stipulated period (usually no more than 26 weeks) before he/she finds the next job. The average weekly benefit to unemployed workers amounted to about 45 percent of average earnings. The unemployment insurance trust fund is built on the basis of unemployment insurance taxes collected from employers, which are similar to insurance premiums.

The fourth scheme to provide a social safety net is compulsory or semi-compulsory personal savings. The scheme involves reserve (or actuarial) funding (RF) for social insurance. In principle, the RF scheme is a fully funded system like a private pension fund. The mechanism of a pension fund is based on cash inflows and outflows. Workers make contributions (inflows) to the pension fund that provides the money for future pension benefits (outflows) to workers during retirement years. The pension fund invests workers' pension contributions and, upon their retirement, returns to them accumulated pension contributions plus interest earned from investment (Figure 2). Pension funds may disburse benefits in a lump sum or as a stream of payments. Many pension policies also offer life insurance that covers death, disability, and major illness. In such cases, disbursement of benefits may occur prior to retirement if the contributor dies or becomes disabled or severely ill.

Figure 2: Cash Flows of Fully Funded Pension Funds

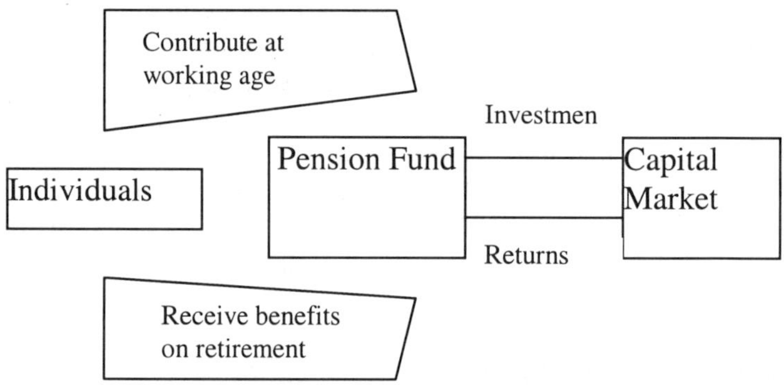

Liabilities of a pension fund are its projected promised future payments to contributors. The value of liabilities depends on the actuarial assessment of life expectancy, retirement age of contributors, and projected retirement benefits. On the other hand, the value of assets depends on the size and frequency of contributions and the expected rate of return on the fund. Pension funds are fully funded or solvent when future pension payments are guaranteed by contributions that are invested or saved until recipients collect retirement benefits [Table 1].

Table 1: Assets-Liabilities of a Pension Fund

Assets	Liabilities
Fund capital, depending on	Projected promised future payments to contributors, depending on
➢ size and frequency of contributions	➢ the actuarial assessment of life expectancy
➢ the expected rate of return on the fund	➢ retirement age of contributions
	➢ projected retirement benefits

Publicly mandated RF schemes differ from private pension funds only in a few aspects. First, they are compulsory or semi-compulsory. The government mandates the participation and contribution rates. Under semi-compulsory arrangements, individuals may chose more than one contribution rate. Second, RF schemes usually mandate contributions from both the employer and employee to build up an individual's retirement fund. For private pension funds, contributions often come from the employees themselves. Finally, withdrawal of money prior to retirement may be possible if the contributor migrates or for permitted uses.

2.2 Singapore's choice

The current Central Provident Fund in Singapore was established in 1955 when Singapore was still under British rule. As a fully funded pension scheme, the primary goal of the CPF was to provide financial security for workers in their retirement or when they are no longer able to work.

In the early years of self-government (after 1959), there were proposals made by various committees to convert the scheme into a PAYG system. The Singapore government, however, firmly rejected these proposals. While expanding the scheme into a comprehensive social safety net since then, Singapore's policy makers have consciously retained the scheme's main feature of being a fully funded RF system. This reflects a principle that the Singapore government has adhered to over the years of economic development, i.e., to steer clear of the Western state welfarism.

The social welfare system directly financed by government's fiscal budget has the advantage of providing universal protection. It has proved to be the most expedient one for the administration to mobilise resources and target needy groups. However, it is vulnerable to the abuse of political power for the sake of political popularity and all kinds of social-economic diseases related to the welfare state. In many industrialised economies, political leaders over the years granted generous eligibility for welfare benefits on the basis of political expediency.

The result is a massive social security system that provides a safety net for people "from womb to tomb" (especially, in some Western European countries). The benefits range from governmentally financed general education, vocational training, and health care to direct payments in cash or in kind for children, the sick and disabled, and the unemployed. The lack of transparency and accountability of social security finances, combined with inefficient administration, have made countries like Sweden and the Netherlands suffer from absenteeism and low productivity growth (Lundberg 1989). The massive welfare system has undermined people's sense of self-reliance and self-respect. The cost burden of the expensive welfare payment falls on the working people in the form of excessive marginal tax rates, which kills incentives to work and make money. The vicious cycle of welfarism, high tax rates, and stagnant economic growth has trapped the Western welfare states in a situation of high unemployment and declining competitiveness (Winsemius 1993).

The US type PAYG social security system has much better accountability than a state welfare system. It has two trust funds: old-age and survivors insurance and disability insurance. The US system, however, is not a fully funded pension system. In the US treasury, payroll taxes are indistinguishable from all other revenues of the federal government. Payroll taxes are not directly deposited in social security trust funds. The Social Security Administration only receives credits in the form of non-marketable Treasury securities (or IOUs) when payroll taxes are collected [Marlow (1995, p. 340-345)]. In other words, only paper credits (IOUs) reside in the trust funds. In contrast to fully funded pension funds, the social security system is required only to have funds sufficient to meet its obligations to pay beneficiaries in the current year (Figure 1).

Because of this partial funding feature, the US-type social security does not require that inflows be equal to outflows over the life of the pension fund. No future obligations are required to be met. Consequently, the average rate of return on the social security pension funds tends to be equal to the growth rate of the social security tax (payroll tax) base. The latter is proxy for the combination of the working age population's growth rate and the real economic growth rate.

The partial funding feature makes it possible for the government to set up supporting funds for the programme when necessary. Starting as a system of retirement insurance, the US social security has evolved into a primary source of transfer from citizens to the federal government to the citizens [Marlow (1995, p. 346)].

Over its history, the US-type social security system has struggled to be a compromise beween two competing objectives. One is individual equity, which refers to the degree to which an individual's benefits are related to taxes paid. It requires higher benefits for those who have contributed more. Under this principle, a member's monthly pension benefits are linked to his/her average monthly income over his/her working life. The other is social adequacy, which refers to the welfare objective of ensuring adequate benefits, regardless of the taxes paid. As a result, the benefit formula redistributes income among the retired population from those who had high earnings to those who had low earnings.

These effects inevitably have implications for people's incentives to work and decisions on retirement and savings. Income redistribution through the system should yield similar disincentives to work as taxed on income. On saving decisions, the wealth substitution effect is likely to dominate. Individuals would treat their contributions to social security as savings and reduce their personal savings. In particular, the expectation of paternalist subsidies or transfers from the government may further discourage private savings. On the other hand, the retirement effect refers to the possible earlier retirement under social security and consequent increased saving for longer retirement life. Intergenerational transfers may also have influenced people's savings through a bequest effect. Although the issue remains controversial whether and how much the US-type social security has reduced private savings, it is difficult to believe that savings have not been negatively affected by social security to a significant degree.[1]

In the long term, a PAYG system focuses potential financing crises. As the economy matures, economic growth tends to slow down, as happened in most industrialised countries. Economic growth also results in the changing demographics, in particular, the ageing population. All this makes PAYG less sustainable.

Since the reserve funding (RF) system is fully funded, the system has no redistributing function and is therefore not a charge on the government budget. Every member has an explicit personal account and full claim to his/her contributions without expectation for state subsidies or transfers. It therefore may not distort individuals' work incentives and saving behaviour. Advocates for RF system often claim that the system can generate additional savings and hence contribute to capital formation, a feature of considerable importance to developing countries. We must be aware that the system's potential for savings mobilisation depends on many factors, including the coverage of the scheme, the rate of contribution and ceilings on contributions, tax benefits for contributions, growth of income and employment, etc. A less controversial point is that a RF system may give the state access to non-inflationary funding through its investment in government bonds. It also should be recognised that a RF system can adapt better to changing demographics than a PAYG system thanks to its full funding nature. A big challenge to RF schemes, however, is to preserve the

[1] See Feldstein (1972), (1977), and Browning and Browning (1994), p. 221.

real value of the funds collected through appropriate fund management, particularly when inflation is a problem.

In Singapore, the RF system is preferred because of its reliance on family savings rather than on societal insurance and income redistribution. During the years of Singapore's economic takeoff, the government clearly put its first priority on job creation and economic growth over income redistribution. In other words, the priority has been to make a bigger pie of economic wealth rather than a more evenly cut pie. The system's potential contribution to capital formation was certainly a plus.

A RF system, by its very nature, does not provide universal coverage. No earnings, no savings; low earnings, low savings. A prolonged period of high unemployment and low wages would jeopardise the accumulation potential of the scheme for both the individual and the state. Neither is a pure RF system designed to provide insurance against catastrophic events. Therefore, over the years, a variety of modifications have expanded the CPF into a comprehensive social-security savings scheme, which not only takes care of a member's retirement, home ownership and healthcare needs, but also provides financial protection to CPF members and their families through its insurance schemes.

3. Structure of the CPF

In Singapore essentially all working citizens or permanent residents who are not self employed must be members of the CPF. Self-employed persons used to be encouraged to be members only on a voluntary basis. Now they are required under statutory rules to contribute to Medisave, a special account in the CPF for hospitalisation needs.

3.1 Contribution

Starting as a compulsory saving scheme, the CPF requires contributions from both the employee and the employer. The CPF board sets contribution rates, which are defined as percentages of the employee's monthly salary. In addition, the Board also sets a salary ceiling for calculating the amount of the contributions. When a member's monthly earning exceeds the ceiling, his/her actual contribution rate will be less than the stated contribution rate.

Initial rates of contribution started at a modest level of 10 percent (with 5 percent each for the employee and the employer) in the period from 1955 to 1967. From 1968 to 1984 the CPF board progressively raised the contribution rate to a peak of 50 percent. Since 1987, lower contribution rates were set for persons above 55 years old to encourage continued employment for older workers. By 1998, the CPF contribution rate was 40 percent for workers 55 years old and below. Monthly contributions are subject to a maximum of S$1,200 each for the employer and the employee, based on a salary ceiling of S$6,000 a month, beyond which no CPF is payable. The contribution rates for different age groups are given in Table 2.

Table 2: Singapore CPF Contribution Rates (as of 1998)

Age Group	Contribution Rate (including both the employer and the employee)
age 55 years and below	40 %
above 55 to 60 years	20 %
above 60 to 65 years	15 %
above 65 years old	10 %

Source: CPF web site.

3.2 Accounts

As an RF scheme, every dollar in the account belongs to the individual him/herself. Each CPF member has three accounts with the Fund - the Ordinary, Medisave and Special Accounts.

- Ordinary Account savings can be used for housing, approved investments, insurance, education and transfers to top-up parents' Retirement Accounts.
- Medisave Account savings are for meeting hospitalisation expenses and certain approved outpatient treatments such as Hepatitis-B vaccinations, Renal Dialysis and Chemotherapy. It can also be used to buy MediShield or MediShield Plus and approved private medical insurance under Private Medical Insurance Scheme (PMIS).
- Special Account savings are reserved for old age and contingency purposes.

  By 1998, of the total contribution rate of 40 percent, 30 percentage points were for the member's Ordinary Account, 6 percentage points for his/her Medisave Account and the remaining 4 percentage points for his/her Special Account. For members aged 35 to 44 years, the Medisave Account receives 7 percentage points and for those aged 45 and above, it receives 8 percentage points with a corresponding decrease in the Ordinary Account. There is also a Retirement Account for members who after withdrawing their CPF savings at 55 need to set aside a Minimum Sum in the account for their old age.

The CPF scheme was further extended to all self-employed persons earning a net trade income of more than S$2,400 a year in July 1992. By contributing 6 percent to the Medisave Account, the self-employed are able to enjoy the same healthcare benefits as other members.

3.3 Withdrawal

CPF members can withdraw their CPF savings when they reach 55, after setting aside a Minimum Sum in their Retirement Accounts for old age. Members can also withdraw their CPF savings if they emigrate permanently or become permanently incapacitated.

When the member reaches 55, he/she may withdraw savings from his/her Ordinary and Special Accounts after putting aside a certain amount, known as the Minimum Sum, in his Retirement Account for old age. He/she must also retain a certain amount in the Medisave Account. If he/she continues to work after 55, he/she must still contribute to the CPF, but at a lower rate. Part of the contribution will go into the Medisave Account until the maximum is reached. Savings after 55 may be withdrawn every three years. From 1 July 1995, if the amount set aside is less than the Minimum Sum, half of his withdrawals after 55 have to be set aside until the full Minimum Sum is reached.

A distinctive feature of this compulsory saving system is its various withdrawal schemes to allow members to withdraw funds for approved uses before they reach old age. These schemes are listed in Table 3.

These approved uses of funds can be classified into the following categories:

(a) Medical expense: A member can use all of his/her savings in Medisave Account to pay for in-hospital charges and certain outpatient treatment. He/she can also use the money to pay premiums for MediShield and MediShield Plus, the two catastrophic illness insurance schemes for CPF members and their dependants.

(b) Housing: A member can use all his/her savings in Ordinary Account to purchase housing for residence.

(c) Education: A member may use savings in Ordinary Account to pay for tuition fees for full-time degree and diploma courses at approved tertiary institutions for him/herself or his/her children. The use is subject to 80 percent of one's CPF savings in excess of the Minimum Sum amount

(d) Investment: Non-bankrupt CPF members may use up to 80 percent of their CPF savings in excess of the Minimum Sum amount to invest in financial instruments. They can also use all savings to invest in non-residence properties.

(e) Nest-egg savings for family members: A member can top up his/her spouse or parents' Retirement Accounts.

4. Social-Economic Functions of the CPF

From the above description of the CPF scheme, we conclude that the institution has evolved from a single faceted to a multi-faceted scheme over the years. It, however, retained its main feature of being a fully funded RF system.

It must also be noted that the government has not managed the CPF in a rigid manner. Instead, it has introduced a number of insurance "plug-ins" to cover members and their families from catastrophic needs, such as MediShield, Dependent Protection Scheme, Home Protection Scheme, Minimum Sum Scheme, etc. Having a public agency such as the CPF board provide such insurance services is desirable because of certain market failures associated with a private insurance market.

4.1 Rectifying market failures in insurance market

In market economies, private insurance protections against certain catastrophic risks are perceived to be inadequate in some areas, in particular, for retirement and health needs of the low-income families and for unemployment. One reason is *adverse selection*, which occurs when an insurance policy meant to cover average risk of the public attracts only those at greatest risk. When an insurance policy is offered, customers who have a higher risk of incurring the catastrophic event (such as a type of disease or unemployment) will find it a good deal since the premium is calculated on the average risk of the public. On the other hand customers who are less likely to incur such events will find the premium too expensive and therefore will not buy the policy. Adverse selection thus creates a lopsided risk pool characterised by a high ratio of high-risk policyholders. This prospect prevents private insurance companies from providing adequate protections in these areas.

Table 3: Major CPF Usage Schemes

Scheme	Nature and Mechanism	Use
Use before age 55		

Medisave	A portion of a member's CPF contributions is deposited into his monthly Medisave Account. When he is below 35, the amount is equivalent to 6% of his monthly salary. Between the ages of 35 and 44, it is 7%, and at 45 and above, it is 8%. Currently, members only need to set aside up to S$20,000 in their Medisave Accounts. Persons registered as partners, sole-proprietors and self-employed are required to contribute.	To be used at approved hospitals for ward charges, doctor's fees, fees for surgery and operating theatres, medical treatments and supplies, rehabilitation services, maternity expenses, etc. Medisave also covers certain outpatient treatment.
MediShield (1990) and MediShield Plus	A catastrophic illness insurance scheme for CPF members and their dependants. The annual premium is deducted automatically from the member's Medisave Account, unless he or she decides not to be insured.	To help members meet the high medical costs of prolonged or serious illnesses.
Public Housing Scheme (1968)	CPF members can use their savings to buy Government-built flats from the Housing & Development Board (HDB). They can also use their CPF to pay for the cost of upgrading incurred under the HDB Main Upgrading Programme for older housing estates. Family co-owners may pool their CPF savings to buy the flat.	When buying a new flat, all the savings in the CPF Ordinary Account may be used to pay the 20% deposit as well as the balance of the buying price. For a resale flat, CPF savings may be used to pay either the purchase price or its market value as determined by a valuer appointed by the Housing Board, whichever is lower. If a housing loan is taken out, future monthly contributions may be used to pay the instalments. The savings can also pay for stamp duty and legal fees incurred in the purchase.

Residential Properties Scheme	CPF members can use their savings to buy private residential properties in Singapore to live in or to rent out.	All of the savings in the Ordinary Account and future monthly contributions paid into the same account may be used to buy the property, or to pay the instalments on the housing loan, as well as the stamp, legal and survey fees incurred in the purchase.
Dependent Protection Scheme (1989)	This is a term-life insurance scheme for members under 60. It provides CPF members or their families with financial help to tide over the first few years in the event of an insured member's permanent incapacity or death.	Should the member die or become permanently incapacitated, his family will receive up to $36,000 to tide them over the first few years. The premium for 12 months, depending on the member's age, varies from $36 for those under 35 years to $360 for those 55 to 59 years old. It can be deducted from his Ordinary Account or paid by cash.
Home Protection Scheme (1981)	This Scheme protects members and their families from losing their homes bought under the Public Housing Scheme if the insured member were to become permanently incapacitated or die. The balance of his outstanding housing loan would be paid by the CPF Board based on the amounts insured.	When applying for the scheme, the member may indicate the proportion of the loan for which he wishes to be insured. If he is the sole owner, he should be insured for 100% of the loan. For co-owners, the total coverage should add up to not less than 100% of the loan.
Investment Scheme (1986) (1993)	Any member aged 21 and above who is not a bankrupt and has enough CPF savings may invest in financial instruments.	CPF members may use up to 80% of their CPF savings in excess of the Minimum Sum amount to invest in trustee shares, loan stocks of trustee companies and approved unit trusts.

Non-residential Properties Scheme	CPF funds can be used to buy office premises, shop units, factories and warehouses in Singapore. The property must be on land which is freehold or has a remaining lease of at least 60 years.	The full 100% of the total savings in the Ordinary Account and all future monthly contributions to it may be used. However, the total amount used by a single member or the joint buyers may not be more than 70% of the value or the purchase price, whichever is lower.
Education Scheme (1989)	A member may use his savings to pay for tuition fees for full-time degree and diploma courses at approved tertiary institutions in Singapore.	CPF members may use up to 80% of their CPF savings in excess of the Minimum Sum amount for the tuition fees. The student must repay the funds plus interest starting a year after graduation.
Topping-up of the Minimum Sum (1987)	A member can volunteer to top up his parents' Retirement Accounts if the parents are 55 and above and have a re-grossed balance of an amount less than the minimum sum. The member may use either cash or transfer from his own CPF account. If his parents do not have Retirement Accounts, he may open the accounts for them. He may also top up his own or his spouse's Retirement Account.	The member may deposit it in one lump sum or in smaller annual amounts. If he is using his own CPF funds, he must first have at least twice the Minimum Sum in his own account. If the member tops up his own Retirement Account using cash, it is subject to a ceiling which is the difference between the Minimum Sum and the balance in his CPF Account at age 55. A member can claim tax relief of up to $6,000 per calendar year for the top-up.
Use after age 55		
Lump Sum Withdrawal	CPF members can withdraw their CPF savings when they reach 55, after setting aside a Minimum Sum in their Retirement Accounts for old age.	
Minimum Sum Scheme (1987)	A Minimum Sum is held in the Retirement Account. This sum pays a monthly amount from age 60, which helps to meet their basic needs on retirement.	Alternatively, the sum may be used to buy a life annuity with an insurance company or deposited with a bank that will yield a monthly income.

Source: CPF web site.

Another reason is *moral hazard*, which refers to policy holders' lax efforts to avoid the risk being covered by the insurance. In areas where moral hazard problems are serious, provision of private insurance tends to be inadequate. Moral hazard behaviour may increase the average risk of policyholders and make the insurance policy insolvent.

Provision of certain insurance services through the private sector may be inefficient due to high transaction costs arising from a fragmented market. The insurance business displays economies of scale. Administrative cost per head tends to decrease as the size of the insured group rises. Studies have shown that, in industrialised countries, administrative costs average about 12 percent of outlays for private health insurance while only about 5 percent for public health insurance [Browning and Browning (1994, p. 199)]. As for retirement insurance, the administrative costs in the US social security system are less than 2 percent of benefits paid while private insurance companies spend one dollar in administrative costs, dividends, and taxes for every two dollars in benefits paid [Goodsell (1983, p.52)]. On top of that, competition in the private insurance market may generate excessive marketing costs for insurers and searching costs for individuals.

Finally, some insurance services are under-provided in the market simply because there is not sufficient demand thanks to individuals' poor vision of their catastrophic and retirement needs. All individuals in the real world are not as rational as assumed in economic models. They may not be farsighted enough to save enough or buy sufficient insurance for their own good. Paradoxically, this "irrationality" may be argued by some economists as the individual's "rational expectation" of being bailed out by the state or society when they run out of savings or face uncovered catastrophic events.

The insurance schemes (MediShield, Dependent Protection Scheme, Home Protection Scheme, Minimum Sum Scheme) provided through the CPF can effectively rectify these market failures to a large extent. First, the member will be automatically covered if he or she does not opt out by signing required forms. Premium payments are automatically deducted from the member's CPF account if no action has been taken by the member to opt out. This procedure minimises the likelihood of adverse selection.

Second, the compulsory nature of the CPF savings works together with the automatic coverage procedure to ensure a near-universal coverage of these insurance policies. These publicly mandated insurance umbrellas have sheltered those who would otherwise not be farsighted enough to purchase these policies on their own.

Third, compared with private insurance, the administrative costs of the CPF-attached catastrophic insurance policies are very low. On top of existing administration of members' CPF accounts, very little additional work is necessary to handle these policies. The CPF's near-universal coverage also unifies the otherwise segmented insurance market and hence maximises the benefits from economies of scale.

As for the market failure arising from moral hazard, the Singapore government has been very diligent in preventing it by regulating the health care services. With third-party payment provided by the insurance policies, inefficient use of resources can easily to occur in the medical service market. Covered by medical insurance, a patient would not be too concerned about controlling the cost of medical treatment. The asymmetric information about medical services also tends to induce service suppliers to take advantage of the situation by driving up costs. Consequently, both insurance premiums and average treatment costs end up in an up-spiralling cycle. Such supply-driven cost increases under third-party payment schema are a major factor behind the breathtaking rate at which health care costs have been increasing in some industrialised countries.

In Singapore, "health care financing is based on individual responsibility, coupled with government subsidies to keep basic health care affordable." "To avoid the pitfall of 'free' medical services stimulating insatiable demand, patients pay directly for part of the cost of medical services which they use, and pay more when they demand a higher level of services" [Ministerial Committee (1993)]. Following this principle, since the early 1990s, the regulatory authority has restricted the coverage of all medical insurance policies to 80 percent of the medical expense under co-payment schemes. On top of that, the government regulates the provision of hospital beds and the overall number of doctors and specialists. Mandatory classification of wards caters for hospitalisation needs of different income groups. Non-emergency specialist services are provided only for referred patients. Medical services and prices are monitored by the health authorities. The managed health care system has been introduced to oversee demand for medical service. All these measures have helped contain the rise of health care costs.

4.2 Financing economic development

A major advantage for choosing the RF mechanism for financing social security is the generation of non-inflationary funds to finance economic development. The bulk of the CPF funds have been required by law to be invested in long term government securities. Compared to financing public expenditures by taxation, the CPF mechanism has, among other factors, helped Singapore obtain a competitive tax structure.

There is a statutory requirement that the CPF Board has to invest all its surplus funds in government securities or place them as advanced deposits with the Monetary Authority of Singapore for the purchase of the on-coming issues of government securities [Ng (1996)]. The government has used CPF savings mainly in two ways: to finance development projects, especially the construction of public housing, and to acquire foreign reserves and assets.

From the 1960s to the 1980s, development of the massive public housing programme was part of Singapore's nation building strategy. Through the program, Singapore has achieved one of the world's highest home ownership ratios in a matter of some twenty years. Behind this "miracle" was government's calculated management of demand and supply in the public housing market. On the supply side, the compulsory land acquisition for urban redevelopment in the early years has kept down the land cost of public estate development. Thanks to massive construction with limited number of standardised models, the supply of public estates has achieved great cost-efficiency based on economies of scale. Careful planning of urban land use also has contributed to the control of supply cost of public estates.

On the demand side, the Central Provident Fund has provided the majority of Singaporeans a financial leverage towards home-ownership. Individuals' CPF savings plus the low-interest housing mortgage loans provided by the Housing Development Board have greatly facilitated personal purchase of home-estate, particularly for lower-income citizens. In an economic sense, the CPF savings have helped overcome an important market failure in the private housing market. Lack of collateral of low and middle class families could prevent the underdeveloped private financial market from providing sufficient loans to finance housing demand. Studies have shown that, among other factors, changes in CPF contribution rates have had the largest influence on demand for public housing. The availability of CPF financing has induced individuals to become homeowners at an early age with some consequences for non-housing expenditure [Tyabji (1996)]. It is one of the most important factors that have made Singapore successful in providing home ownership to almost the entire citizenry in one generation's time.

4.3 Maintaining social values

"Family as the basic unit of society" is one of the five "Shared Values" officially endorsed by the Singapore Parliament in 1991.[2] A distinctive feature of Singapore's public policy is its emphasis on strengthening the family. In the words of the Minister for Community Development, Abdullah Tarumugi, "We believe that the state of our families, the building blocks of society, determines

---

[2] The five Shared Values are: Nation before community and society above self; Family as the basic unit of society; Community support and respect for the individual; Consensus, not conflict; Racial and religious harmony.

not only the moral tone of the society but its economic health as well." Cohesive families are thought to be a "basic tenet of Singapore's progress".[3]

To some extent, the CPF scheme serves as a vehicle to maintain such values. Compared with other forms of social safety net existing in the Western industrialised countries, Singapore's CPF system is purely a personal compulsory saving account. CPF benefits extend not only to members but also to their immediate family members in many different ways. Every dollar in the account belongs to the individual him/herself and his/her family. The system is more reliant on family savings rather than on societal insurance and income redistribution.

Like the structure of a traditional extended family, most CPF schemes cover three generations, enabling members to care for themselves, their spouses and children, parents and even siblings where necessary. CPF savings may be used to pay for one's home, the family's medical bills, and to buy a home and medical insurance for immediate family members. Through topping-up Minimum Sum (see details in Table 3), the CPF has allowed intergeneration and intra-generation transfers but confined them within the family. Members' investment in education for themselves or their children is encouraged by the introduction of the Education Scheme (also ref. to Table 3). With these plug-in features, the CPF has demonstrated over the years its advantages to provide a safety net without jeopardising work incentives and the values of self-reliance, thrift, and family-cohesiveness.

4.4 Managing aggregate savings and labour costs

CPF compulsory savings also have important macroeconomic implications. A possible role is to ensure a high saving rate that can sustain long term growth. From 1975 to 1993, Singapore achieved a national saving rate (defined as savings over GDP) of 34 percent. Of the national savings, 13 percent came from the private compulsory savings in the form of net savings in CPF accounts [Han (1996)]. Although there has not been a definitive econometric estimate of the size of the CPF's impact on domestic savings, many believe and non-econometric studies strongly suggest that the CPF has played a role in increasing domestic savings [Lucket et al. (1994)]. It is, however, unlikely that the CPF system has led to an excess of compulsory savings. This can be attributed to the prudence in fund management and selective privatisation of fund uses by introducing various investment schemes, housing schemes and insurance schemes [Han (1996)].

---

[3] *Straits Times* (Singapore), 11 March 1995

It is interesting to note that changes of CPF contribution rates have been an important macroeconomic policy instrument in Singapore. Employees' contribution rate directly affects individuals' disposable income and the permitted uses of the CPF savings influence the structure of aggregate demand. The steadily rising employees' contribution rate from 1950s to the mid-1980s probably played a role in restraining aggregate demand and suppressing inflation [Ng (1996)].

Changes in employers' contribution rate have a significant impact on unit labour costs. When the economy encountered a deep recession in the mid-1980s, the Singapore government prescribed a strong medicine to reduce business costs and expedite economic recovery. This included suggesting a wage freeze over two years to employers and cutting employers' contribution to the CPF from 25 percent of wages to 10 percent. These measures amounted to a 12-percent reduction in workers' wages. The bitter medicine was administered speedily and effectively. Together with some tax cuts and counter-cyclical infrastructure expenditure, the measures helped the economy to recover in 1987 and by 1988 wages had started to grow by 6 percent per annum in real terms.

In the second half of 1998, Singapore entered its first recession in 10 years under the contagion effect of the 1997-98 Asian financial crisis. In June 1998, the government released a $2 billion package of off-budget measures to help lower business costs and improve Singapore's competitiveness, which had been eroded by the sharp fall in other regional currencies. This was further bolstered by a second $10.5 billion package in November 1998. Among tax rebates, lower rentals and duties, a crucial component of the package was a 10 percentage-point cut in employers' CPF contribution rate (from 20 percent to 10 percent of monthly wages). Together with a suggested 5-8 percent cut in wages, these measures were expected to reduce business costs by about 15 percent and help Singapore recover from the crisis.[4]

4.5 Social security beyond the CPF

Like any RF system, Singapore's CPF is inherently weak in providing universal coverage. To ensure social adequacy, some supplementary welfare supports are necessary.

For instance, patients who are unable to pay their hospital bills can seek help from Medifund, an endowment fund set up specially to help poor and needy Singaporeans pay for their medical care. Medifund was started in 1993 with an initial endowment of $200 million from the Government. $100 million a year was injected into the Medifund over the last 2 years by the Government,

---

[4] *Report of the Committee on Singapore's Competitiveness*, the CSC Press Conference, Singapore, 11 November 1998.

bringing its balance to $400 million. Only the interest income from the endowment fund is used to pay hospital bills of the poor. The interest income is distributed to public sector hospitals. Every public sector hospital has a Hospital Medifund Committee appointed by the Government to consider applications and allocate funds.[5]

The aged poor (above 60 years old), the totally disabled, chronically ill and vagrant may receive a moderate welfare benefit from the government. However, the benefit is less than 70 percent of the official poverty line [Tyabji (1996)]. The broad principle is to confine such assistance only to the unemployable. Instead of providing unemployment insurance, the government has insisted on encouraging and assisting all employable persons to obtain gainful employment.

In the area of social welfare, the Singapore government has been keen to steer clear of the Western state welfarism. The welfare policy of Singapore is compassionate to the disadvantaged but will not provide for a person what the family can provide. The approach has been designed to (a) tackle the root cause of a problem (such as disadvantaged families) not just the symptoms; (b) focus on preventive and developmental services; (c) help the disadvantaged become more independent by training them for jobs; and (d) motivate the underclass to get out of the poverty trap through a variety of incentive programs.[6]

The Small Families Improvement Scheme illustrates the approach. It helps upgrade low-income families by providing a housing grant and educational assistance to children. Besides income qualifications, this scheme requires that families stay intact and small. If the family breaks up or gives birth to more than two children, the couple will stop receiving the grants. A purpose of these requirements is to "prevent a proliferation of single-mother families" as observed in some Western welfare states. Another purpose is to prevent low-income families from being trapped in the burden of raising too many children.[7]

The Singapore government also subsidises community-based care and support systems for the elderly and the poor. For approved community-based charity programmes, the government has a "dollar-to-dollar" subsidising policy to match the amount raised by non-government organisations by the equal amount of public money. The conditional subsidising policy again is to ensure minimum free-riding on government support.

In recent years, with concern regarding the low CPF balance of many aged members, the government has topped up these members by transferring funds from its coffer. These topping-up transfers are made in lump sum and an unpredictable manner to minimise their possible disincentives for work and saving.

---

[5] Ministry of Health (Singapore)'s web site on Medisave, Medishield, Medifund.

[6] *Sunday Times* (Singapore), 12 September 1993, p. 1.

[7] *Straits Times* (Singapore), 16 August 1993.

5 Concluding Remarks

In China's transition toward a market-based economy, an emergent task is to establish social insurance programmes compatible with the new economic environment. This task has caught the attention of China's policy makers and was written into several important official documents, including the Chinese Communist Party (CCP)'s *Decision on Several Issues of Establishing Socialist Market Economic System* (1993) and the National People's Congress (NPC)'s *Outlines of the Ninth Five-year Plan for National Economic and Social Development and the Long-term Target for the Year 2010* (1996). In recent years, the government has taken concrete steps to establish China's social security system.

As a late developer of a social security system, China has the opportunity to learn from other countries' experience in managing social insurance and to choose among the existing systems the one best fit to its social context. In this procedure, it is important to follow sound economic principles and judgement in introducing institutional reforms into the social security system. Under the mounting pressure of unemployment due to rapid economic transition and structural changes, it is too easy for China, in a haste to develop a social safety net, to fall into the pitfalls of state welfarism that has caused undesired social-economic consequences in many industrialised countries.

In this regard, the Singapore experience appears highly relevant. Singapore, with its majority population of Chinese, has inherited a heritage of Chinese culture. The Singapore leaders have, in particular, upheld Confucian values as distinct elements in their social policies. The common cultural roots of the two economies make Singapore's social security experience particularly appealing to China.

In both societies, the family has a traditional role in providing personal safety net. From the perspective of economic efficiency as well as cultural continuity, maintaining family cohesiveness and its role in social stability is desirable in both societies in their modernisation process. Besides, China nowadays is undergoing rapid economic growth and structural changes like Singapore experienced in the 1960s-70s. Like Singapore in its early stage of development, China is also hungry for social capital to finance public projects necessary for sustaining economic growth. In these aspects, the unique social-economic functions of Singapore's system may bring in some helpful tips for China in developing a market-oriented social security system. From the above discussion, we may summarise the principles of a Singapore-type social security system as follows:

First, the publicly mandated social security programmes should play a supplementary role to the protections existing in the private insurance market and family-community institutions. They should target market failures and aim to improve efficiency in insurance provision.

Second, of different types of publicly mandated social security programmes, reserve funding (RF) should be the backbone system. It has the advantages of a fully funded system that does not rely on the government budget and provides non-inflationary financing for development projects. Of all types of social safety nets, it results in minimum distorting effects on work and saving.

Third, a reserve funding social security system should have the flexibility of installing insurance "plug-ins" to expand coverage. Social insurance policies for personal catastrophic needs must also be fully funded by premium payments and should not mingle with state welfare subsidies and transfers. Meanwhile, cautions should be extended to minimise the moral hazard behaviour of the insured persons.

Fourth, the RF system should confine intra-generation and intergeneration transfers within families. This preserves not only the crucial feature of a RF system but also the values of family cohesiveness.

Fifth, permitted uses of RF savings may be designed to encourage demand for merit goods, such as housing and education, and other efficient uses of savings.

Sixth, the mandated contribution rates of the RF system may play the role of a macroeconomic policy instrument that adjusts disposable income and labour costs.

Finally, where it is necessary to supplement the RF system with welfare assistance in transfer payments, free welfare benefits should be confined to the unemployable and incentives should be provided to encourage all the employable to upgrade themselves through education and gainful employment.

References

1. Browning E. K. and J. M. Browning. 1994. Public Finance and the Price System. Englewood Cliffs, NJ: Prentice Hall.
2. Central Provident Fund Board's web site, http://www.cpf.gov.sg
3. Han, Kang Hong. 1996. Savings and Investment in Singapore, in Lim Chong Yah ed. *Economic Policy Management in Singapore*, Singapore: Addison-Wesley Publishing Company.
4. Feldstein, Martin. 1974. Social Security, Induced Retirement and Aggregate Capital Accumulation, *Journal of Political Economy*, 92(5).
5. Feldstein, Martin. 1977. Social Security and Private Savings: International Evidence in an Extended Life Cycle Model, in M. Feldstein and R. Inman eds. The Economics of Public Services, New York: Halsted Press.
6. Goodsell, Charles T. 1983. *The Case for Bureaucracy*. Chatham, NJ: Chatham House Publishers.

7. Luckett, Dudley G., David L. Schulze, and Raymond W.Y. Wong. 1994. *Banking, Finance & Monetary Policy in Singapore*, Singapore: McGraw-Hill.
8. Lundberg, Erik. 1989. The Rise and Fall of the Swedish Model, in: Bornstein, Morris ed. *Comparative Economic Systems: Models and Cases.* Homewood, IL: Irwin, pp. 79-97.
9. Marlow, Michael L. 1995. *Public Finance: Theory and Practice*, Orlando, FL: Harcourt Brace & Company.
10. Ministerial Committee. 1993. *Affordable Health Care : A White Paper*, Singapore : Singapore National Printers [for] Ministry of Health.
11. Ministry of Health (Singapore)'s web site on Medisave, Medishield, Medifund, http://www.gov.sg/moh/mohiss/hlthfin.html.
12. National People's Congress (NPC). 1996. Outlines of the Ninth Five-year Plan for National Economic and Social Development and the Long-term Target for the Year 2010. Beijing: Peoples Press.
13. Ng, Beoy Kui. 1996. Bank Liquidity Management and the Implication on Exchange Rate Policy in Singapore, in Lim Chong Yah ed. *Economic Policy Management in Singapore*, Singapore: Addison-Wesley Publishing Company.
14. Tyabji, Amina. 1996. Financing Social Security, in Asher, M. and A. Tyabji eds, *Fiscal System of Singapore: Trends, Issues, and Future Directions*, Singapore: National University of Singapore.
15. Winsemius, Alfred. 1993. Economic Effects of Dutch Welfare System, in: Goh Chok Tong's Speech on Singapore's National Day Rally, Straits Times (Singapore), 16 August, p. 24.

CHAPTER 23

FROM THE PUBLIC PENSION SYSTEM TO THE PRIVATE PENSION SYSTEM: WHAT CHINA COULD LEARN FROM OTHER COUNTRIES' EXPERIENCES

ELLEN YING YAN
Key Corperation, 127 Public Square -0501
Cleveland, OH 44114-1306, USA
E-mail: Ellen_Ying_Yan@keybank.com

This paper analyzes PAYGO, private, and two-tier pension systems. A detailed comparison is made regarding pros and cons of different pension systems. The important issues, as well as pension system transition problems, of private pension system are discussed. Some suggestions are proposed regarding China's current social security reform.

1. Introduction

As the world's population ages, pay-as-you-go (PAYGO) public pension systems begin to face severe financial problems globally due to their inadequate link between contributions and benefits. PAYGO public pension systems define the cash benefits to be paid after retirement but not the contribution amount of the participants. Therefore, PAYGO systems lack appropriate incentive mechanisms. PAYGO pension funds are usually managed by government.

The method of PAYGO system finance is under serious debate. PAYGO systems take income from younger generations and give them to older generations, while placating the young with promises of repayment. This financing method not only reduces national saving, but also saddles the next generation with the debt obligation to meet (Kotlikoff 10). As populations age, the problems with PAYGO become more severe. Population aging has two components: increased longevity, which extends the proportion of life spent in retirement, and decreased fertility, which reduces the growth rate of the labor force. These two changes make PAYGO systems hard to sustain.

China's current social security system generally follows the PAYGO scheme (Song and Chu14). Thus, it has all the shortcomings that a PAYGO system has. Moreover, China's social security faces much more serious aging problem due to its one-child policy. China's one-child policy has created a unique family structure: one child has two parents and four grandparents. This has dramatically increased the social security dependency ratio and makes it unsustainable at the current benefit level. It has also imposed enormous fiscal burdens on the working generations and impeded current economic reforms. As China's economy shifts from central planning to market discipline, the labor force has become more mobile. There is a huge demand for a more portable and more incentive compatible social security system. Thus, social security reform in China is very imperative and important.

The private pension system in Chile is a very efficient scheme and successfully supports the increasingly elderly society by avoiding the problems that PAYGO systems have. The private pension plan specifies the amount that participants contribute but not the benefit payoffs. In private pension systems, contributions are usually a predetermined fraction of salary. The pension fund consists of a set of individual investment accounts, one for each covered participant. The pension participant's benefits are determined by his total accumulated value of contributions and the earnings on those contributions. The fund can be used to purchase an annuity, or become accessible as a lump sum upon participants' retirement.

Chile and Mexico are the two countries that have replaced an existing PAYGO scheme with a private pension system.[1] The government-mandated retirement saving schemes in Chile and Mexico give pension participants a retirement income that is closely tied to the contributions they made. This scheme also avoids the labor supply distortion that PAYGO systems have, with which people try to minimize their contributions while maximizing what they could get out of it. The mandatory savings scheme serves the dual purpose of providing capital formation and meeting retirement income need. It makes the link between contributions and benefits

---

[1] Malaysia, Singapore, India, Indonesia and some other countries have national mandated provident funds to manage the social security.

transparent. It also reinforces the property rights of participants to their accumulating assets.

However, it is well known that financing the transition from a public PAYGO system to a private pension system is very difficult due to the "paying twice" problem. During the transition period, the transitional working generation needs to set aside savings to fund its own future benefits, while at the same time having to pay for the retirement of the previous generation due to the existing PAYGO system. Since Chile has transited very successfully, Chile's experience is highly valuable to China and other countries that are intending to reform their social security systems.[2]

This paper provides detailed comparisons between PAYGO system and other social security systems, including the public managed provident pension funds, private pensions, and two-tier pension systems. The special features of China's social security system are analyzed. Several proposals are made, aiming to improve the current social security reform in China.

This paper is organized as follows. Section 2 compares the institutional differences between a PAYGO system and a private pension scheme. Section 3 discusses the pros and cons of centralized pension versus the decentralized managed pensions and some important regulatory issues of the private pension system. Section 4 discusses the issues of financing the transition and its relevance to economic reforms. Section 5 introduces alternative two-tier pension systems of the United Kingdom and Japan. Section 6 analyzes the problems in China's social security system and some proposals are made to improve the current social security reform.

2. The Comparison of PAYGO Scheme and the Private Pension System

There are two basic types of pension plans: defined benefit (DB) and defined contribution (DC) plans. DB plans specify formulas for cash benefits to be paid after retirement but not the contribution amount of the participants. PAYGO is a typical DB plan. The pension fund of a DB plan is either managed by government or by employers. Since the benefit formula of a DB plan is determined by the years of

---

[2] Mexico's social security reform began in July of 1997, whether it is successful or not still need to be seen.

service and the level of salary of the participants, it absorbs the investment risk and guarantees the participants' benefits regardless of participants' longevity.

A DC plan specifies the amount that participants contribute but not the benefit payoffs. Since every participant has his or her own individual investment account, the participant usually has some choice over the way the account is invested. The retirement account is fully funded by nature rather than by regulations. The employer has no legal obligation beyond making periodic contributions to the account. DC plans do not have portability problem nor do they inhibit labor mobility. On the contrary, they foster long-term savings and capital market development. However, the participants have the responsibility to bear all the investment risk and longevity risk.

The advantage of a DB plan is that it can provide a secure and predictable source of income to the retirees. DB benefits do not depend on the rate of return available in the financial markets, thus, the participants are insured against market risk. Besides, DB benefits are annuities, paid out at a constant rate until the retiree dies, so participants are also insured against longevity risk. However, DB plans usually do not offer explicit inflation insurance and they are subject to political risk. The government, because it has the power to legislate changes in the law, can find ways to repudiate social security obligations by reducing the promised benefit level without obvious penalty.

The advantage of a DC plan is that it offers participants more portable and flexible retirement savings. The benefit of the DC plan is totally determined by the participant's contribution and its earnings. The participants to a DC plan do not have the same degree of retirement income security that DB plans provide. However, DC plans allow participants to customize retirement saving to suit their tastes and their own financial circumstances. The direct line between contribution and benefit gives DC participants strong incentive to perform. The decentralized managed pension plan, the private pension scheme, seems more successful than the publicly managed provident funds because private pension gives participants more freedoms. The participants in a private pension system choose the pension funds they prefer to invest in and they have certain control over how the accounts are managed.

However, private pension systems have their own problems. Privately managed pensions fail to insure participants against poor investment performance. The problem could be severe if most participants have had little financial experience or information about the investment. In addition, private pensions do not protect low-wage workers with interrupted careers, such as women, who may never accumulate enough pensions to support themselves in old age. Along similar lines, the pensions may fall below subsistence standards because of inflation or low investment returns. Therefore, sole private pensions can leave considerable old age poverty. Some of these problems can be handled without public transfers if the purchase of private disability insurance and term life insurance is compulsory. Beyond that, government could alleviate poverty and extreme investment risk by guaranteeing a minimum pension based on years of employment--or by redistribution social assistance programs as they did in Chile.

The DB form of pensions dominates in most countries around the world. However, the trend now is to select the DC form when staring new plans. There are two kinds of DC plans, centralized or decentralized mandatory saving schemes. The difference between them is elaborated in the next section.

3. The Important Issues of Private Pension System

3.1 The Centralized vs. Decentralized Mandatory Saving Plans

Two kinds of schemes exist for DC plans: the centralized provident funds and decentralized private pension funds. The centralized provident funds are run by the national government. The government determines the use of the fund and sets the rate of return. Centralized provident funds usually have low cost because of economy of scale. Singapore, Malaysia, India, and Indonesia all have national provident funds for their social security systems. However, the centralized managed plans could create capital and labor market distortions and capricious redistribution similar to those in PAYGO systems. This is because provident funds' required contribution rates can be high and returns relatively low. If government has exclusive access to the funds and invests them inefficiently, then the potential advantage of mandatory saving schemes are lost. Since their capital allocations are not subject to any competitive market test or even public scrutiny, the rate of return of those funds are usually low. Between 1980 to 1990, the average rate of return of Zambia's centralized provident funds is -23.5%, Kenya's -3.8%, India's 0.3%, Singapore's 3%, Malaysia's 4.6% (World Bank [1994]).

Nevertheless, in a decentralized managed pension system, participants pick their pension company from a small number of authorized funds, presumably based on their record of returns and risks. Staying competitive, the private funds usually do well in terms of maximizing returns and minimizing risks. Furthermore, the privately managed pension schemes have fewer labor supply distortion effects and are insulated from political pressure to misallocate capital. Therefore, the decentralized funded plans have earned much higher returns than centralized plans, reflecting their competitive nature and efficient capital allocations. Chile, the country that has fully implemented a decentralized mandatory saving scheme, had an average real rate of return 9.2 percent between 1980 and 1990, much higher than those of the centralized provident funds. Several other Latin American countries (e.g., Peru, Mexico, and Argentina) are in the process of introducing private pension plans.

3.2 More Regulatory Issues of the Private Pension Plans

In spite of all of its advantages, a decentralized plan requires a complex regulatory structure to ensure financial soundness and the integrity of funds managers. This includes the fiduciary standard of pension companies, the safety of their investments, the range of products offered and information disclosure, the size of fees and commissions, the guarantees provided by government, and clear regulatory rules that penalize malfeasance. Extensive regulation is needed since participants often lack the expertise needed to make their decisions wisely. Chile set up a separate identity Administradoras De Findoes De Pensiones (AFP), which is both legally and financially independent from pension funds, to do the regulation. Pension funds need to have minimum capital margins and fund managers must be monitored by the supervisory authorities. The shortage of local expertise in developing countries like China could provide a case for using foreign fund management companies in joint ventures with local firms.

One way to protect the participants is to have those pensions disclosure fund information regularly to participants. Another way to protect the investors is to set investment rules, such as to set percentage limitations on investments in corporate equities, foreign securities, bank deposits, or government bonds. Those rules should focus on two principles: safety and profitability. While safety ensures the investments are properly diversified and invested in the approved assets, the profitability implies that fund managers are free to seek the highest returns subject to these rules.

There are two approaches that could be used in regulating pension funds. The first approach, used by the US and UK, is called "prudent man rule." This approach has few specific restrictions on allowable investments. Instead, this rule requires fund managers to invest properly as would be done by a prudent person acting in such circumstances. Failure to perform may result in civil or criminal charges.

The second approach, used by Chile, Japan, and many other countries, specifies maximum and minimum restrictions on the percentage of a pension portfolio that may be invested in certain types of assets. This approach, although less flexible, is simpler for regulators. The fund managers should be allowed to invest a portion of the assets in real estate, foreign assets, equities, or indexed bonds to hedge against inflation.

Whether government should provide plan termination insurance for pensions is also a controversial issue. According to Pseudo12, insurance provided by government for pension funds is necessary. First, pension participants do not have the chance to diversify this risk and the default of pension funds could be extremely serious for them. Second, corporate bankruptcies are highly correlated due to the systematic risk inherent in macroeconomic fluctuations. So, too, are the returns to pension assets. For this reason, private markets may not be able to provide plan termination insurance, even if demand for this insurance exists at premium rates that are commensurate with risk. "Market failure" is the primary reason for the government providing the insurance for pension funds. However, if the premium charged by government is not market-based, there exist opportunities for strategic behavior. That is, the pension managers might take too much risk that threatens the long-run solvency of the insurer.

The contribution rate is one of the most important factors that needs to be determined in mandatory saving plans. According to James and Vittas9, a normal mandatory saving scheme-- with a real rate of return of two to three percentage points higher than the growth rate of real earnings, a passivity ratio of one-half with the price or wage index-- requires a contribution rate of 10 to 15 percent to cover a 40 percent replacement rate (the ratio of social security benefits to that average taxable wage) and plan expenses. The contribution rate needs to be higher when people retire early or the real rate of return is lower than the growth rate of earnings, or if other objectives are pursued in addition to retirement savings. The contribution rate is as high as 22% in Malaysia and Sri Lanka and 35% in Singapore, but only 13% in Chile. The contribution rate in the U.S. is fairly comparable, despite being a PAYGO scheme. The trust pension funds in the U.S. are administered by the Pension Benefit Guaranty Corporation (PBGC) and Thrift Savings Plan (the latter is for federal employees). For employees, who work 45 years and retire at age 65, therefore, have a passivity rate of about 1/2.5, receive benefits that have a median of 43 percent of pay Grubbs4.

Investment risk and inflation risk should not be ignored. The level of interest rate is critical when the participants use their accumulated assets to purchase the annuity. One way to reduce this risk is to require participants to purchase small annuity contracts periodically once they reach a predetermined age, such as age of 50. By reducing the lumpiness of the purchase, participants could diversify the interest rate risk. Another way to mitigate the interest rate risk is to allow participants to purchase a variable annuity but this would bring in the investment risk for them throughout retirement. The inflation-indexed annuity, if it is available and financed through inflation-indexed bonds, is an ideal vehicle to hedge the inflation and investment risk Grubbs5.

4. Financing the System Transition and its Relevance to the Economic Reform

The transition from a PAYGO system to a funded private pension system is generally difficult because of the "paying twice" problem. The "paying twice" problem is that the during the transition period, the working generation have to pay for the social security of the previous generation because of the existing public pension system and, at the same time, they have to save for their own future benefits under the new private pension system.

The double payment burden can be eased when the government issues bonds to finance the transition, as in Chile. The bonds are given to those workers having past service credits in the old social security system. The bonds are interest bearing but no payment can be made until the workers reach retirement Turner and Rajnes15. Those bonds are financed out of general revenues. A surplus of the government general revenue is very helpful to ease the transition. The Chilean government, in anticipation of costs of transition from PAYGO to the private pension system, purposely accumulated a government surplus in its general revenues.

However, Mexico plans to adopt both debt financing and financing through taxation, which in principle should allow the reform to have a positive impact on national saving. Debt financing implies that in the short-run, national saving and the capital stock will be only marginally affected, and primarily by magnitudes those depend on the net efficiency gains of the financial system as well as on voluntary saving. On the other hand, if these future fiscal deficits are financed through taxation, this will essentially combine pension reform with tighter fiscal policy. This strategy would imply a transfer of resources from current to future generations, encouraging a higher rate of saving and, thus, capital stock formation Carstens1.

In Chile, all new entrants to the labor force, except the self-employed, must establish an individual account pension plan to which they contribute a minimum of 10 percent of their salary, up to a maximum level of earnings that is roughly five times the average salary of all covered workers. The self-employed can participate voluntarily. Participants in the old social security system have the option of continuing in the old scheme or joining the new system.

The private pension system is an important instrument for accelerating capital market development; increasing long-term saving, boosting investment in productive capital formation, and monitoring corporate performance. In 1981, when Chile established its mandatory saving scheme, Chile had few financial assets in which pension funds could invest and it did not permit international investments. However, the subsequent demand for financial securities by Chilean pension funds encouraged development of a successful stock market.

The mandatory saving scheme can generate substantial long-term financial savings in a relatively short time. In Singapore the resources of the Central Provident Fund rose form 28 percent of GDP in 1976 to 76 percent in 1991. In Malaysia the balance of the Participants Provident Fund increased from 18 percent of GDP in 1980 to 41 percent in 1987 (World Bank17). In Chile, total assets have grown rapidly from less than 1 percent of GDP in 1981 to 25 percent in 1990 and 43 percent in 1994 (Schieber and Shoven13). The mandatory saving scheme also provides an opportunity to stimulate capital markets and expand the supply of productive capital. By 1994, the pension funds held 55 percent of government bonds, 59 percent of corporate bonds, and 11 percent of corporate equities in Chile (Schieber and Shoven13).

The Chilean pension system has stimulated the development of Chilean financial market and other institutions and practices. These include modern bank supervision, new security and corporation laws, increased disclosure requirements for public companies, risk classification agencies for bonds, a long-term corporate bond market and a second stock market, new types of mortgage bonds, and improved regulation of insurance companies.

Mexican social security reform is also expected to produce a significant long-term increase in the availability of financial resources to the Mexican economy. The reform will promote further financial specialization and the creation of new financial instruments, in particular, medium- and long-term securities that are urgently needed in Mexico, since most of the lending now in Mexican is tied to short-term interest rates with maturity less than a year in most cases. Reform is also estimated to double the financial savings in Mexico within 25 years (Garstens1). The availability of these resources will promote financial deepening and long-term investment, which should have a significant impact on growth.

Mandatory pension funds, if invested in the private sector, could be become major stockholders and could exercise voting rights and power over corporate management. This could have serious implications. This channel could allow pension funds to have far-reaching influence on the economy with pension funds being able to exercises a monitoring function to encourage good performance from corporations.

Privatization of other industrial sectors-- the transfer of state property to private ownership--presents unique opportunities for the development of private pensions, since the sales revenue of the state properties can be directly used for financing the pension system transition or pension funds could invest in newly privatized enterprises.

Pension funds can play an important role in privatizing an economy, as they did in Chile, because of their financial expertise and because their funds create a demand for a financial market.

It is argued that a reliable legal system needs to be established to govern prudence, self-dealing, and other aspects of fiduciary behavior, settlement of property disputes and bankruptcies procedures (Korczyk11).

5. The Two Tier Pension System

Although the public and private pension systems are quite different, they are not mutually exclusive. Many countries adopt a DB plan as a "primary" plan, in which participation is mandatory, and supplement them with voluntary DC plans.[3] Those plans have the benefit of both public and private pension systems and they are more feasible for China. Therefore, they deserve closer scrutiny.

Both Japan and the United Kingdom permit contracting out of the social security system. In these countries, the participants can reduce their social security

---

3 A variation on this design is a "floor" plan, which is a DC plan with a guaranteed minimum retirement annuity determined by a DB formula.

tax payments, and in exchange, the employer provides the employees a private pension plan that meets certain requirements. All employers in the United Kingdom are permitted to contract out. However, in Japan only large employers may do so if they meet profitability and other requirements.

In the United Kingdom, the social security system (first tier) provides a flat rate basic pension that does not depend on earnings. The maximum amount is payable only if contributions have been paid for 90 percent of the working lifetime, from age 16 to state pension age (65 for males and 60 for females). However, proportionately reduced pensions are payable to those with incomplete contribution record, provided that contributions have been paid or credited for 25 percent of the working lifetime. The additional pension (second tier) is based on earnings between the lower and the upper earnings limits, revalued to the level appropriate at the time of retirement. This additional earnings-related pension permits employers to contract out their participants, who are members of an adequate DB occupational pension plan. Those plans must undertake to provide members and their surviving spouses with guaranteed minimum pensions that are broadly equivalent to the earnings-related additional pension to which they would have been entitled if they had not been contracted out. The effect of this form of contracting out is to substitute earnings-related benefits provided by occupational pension plans for the earnings-related benefits that would otherwise have been payable through the social security system on a PAYGO basis. Almost half of the work force in the UK is contracted out through membership in such DB occupational pension plans (Daykin2).

The Japanese pension system consists of social security, private pension plans, and individual saving plans. Basically, it is a two-tier structure: the first tier is composed of the National Pension plan that provides a flat benefit related to years of working but not earnings. This tier of benefits includes an old age pension, a disability pension, and a survivors pension. The second tier includes five plans that cover different groups of workers. It is related to both years of working and earnings. In Japan, private pension plans have been traditional DB plans. The DC plans are considered as individual saving plans. There are three types of plan in Japan: the tax qualified plan, the DC plan for the self-employed participants, and the participants' pension fund plans which are contract-out plans. Contrary to the regulation of the U.S., Japanese private pension plans are not required to be managed independent of the sponsoring company (Watanabe16).

However, with the dramatic population aging in Japan, their social security system has increasing problems. Most of their problems are associated with their basic PAYGO approach. The system has an adverse impact on the inter- and intra-generation allocation of resources, and it discourages private saving as well as the labor supply of the aged and women. Therefore, Japan is considering reforming their pension system to make it a more fully funded private pension (Horioka6).

6. The China's Social Security Reform

China's current social security has two separate subsystems: one for the employees of government and state-owned enterprises (SOE) and another less generous one for the employees of urban collectively owned enterprises (COE). This non-unified system is obsolete and has been undergoing reform since 1984. The reform tries to establish a three-tiered old-age insurance system. The first tier provides a basic pension to all employees in urban sectors. The second tier consists of enterprises' additional contributions to the basic pension and depends on availability of enterprise bonus and welfare funds. The third tier is mandatory individual pension accounts layered on top of the first two tiers.

However, the pensions of the first two tiers are primarily PAYGO. Thus, they have all the problems that PAYGO system have. Besides, even for the first two tiers, there is no uniformed regulation to govern them. Each province or autonomous region sets its own contribution rate and reports to the State Council. The local government establishes a committee to manage the pension fund. The pension pools, however, vary from place to place, as permitted by the central government (Song and Chu14) For the third tier, employees contribute 3 percent of their wages to their individual supplementary pension funds. The contribution is deposited into special bank accounts and they are not appropriately invested.

Thus, China's social security needs further reform due to the increasing pressure brought upon by the dramatic development of China's economic, financial, and banking reforms. The continuing high growth rate of China has brought about increasing income inequality between occupational groups in the cities and people in the rural areas. The bigger income differences also showed up between people in coastal cites and the interior provinces (Howes7). Due to the gradual overhaul of the residence registration system, the labor force has become more mobile. There are two kinds of major migration trends in China now: the migration from the interior areas to the special-economic districts in the coastal cities and the migration from rural areas to urban areas. Those migrations have created a huge demand for a more portable and more flexible social security system. The rising population migration also erodes family support for the elderly. Old-age support has become a social-welfare problem rather than just a family affair. Moreover, the privatization of the state-owned enterprises in China has abolished most of the employment guarantees, which they had for decades. This has contributed to the rapid growth of private sector and self-employment. The growing private sector also demands a more uniform and reliable social security system.

In contrast to Hussain8, I think that building up a unified social security system is very important for China as economic reform goes deeper. Establishing a governmental agency to supervise and manage a basic "floor" pension for all employees is imperative to provide a secured and essential foundation for retirees, especially in China's dynamic economic environment.

There are six suggestions I would propose to compliment China's current social security reform and make it more tilted towards a defined contribution plan.

(1) The mandatory contribution rate of the individual pension account should be increased. A higher mandatory contribution rate of individual pension account may increase national savings. More domestic capital accumulation will reduce all the risk associated with foreign borrowing.

(2) Those personal pension accounts should be defined contribution accounts. The defined contribution scheme is always fully funded. Those accounts should be actively managed and the management results should be distributed to pension participants periodically. The actively managed and well-communicated individual pension accounts will increase individuals' sense of ownership of their social security rights. It also allows them to see the direct link between their contribution and their pension benefits.

(3) The proportion of the benefit from the personal pension account, in terms of all pension benefits, should be gradually increased while the portion of government guaranteed social security benefit should be gradually reduced. This change will reduce government forbearance successively and harmonize to the further development of China's economic reform.

(4) The employer-based pension should also be defined contribution instead of defined benefit. This not only will free the employers from the heavy burden of increasing proportion of retirees but also provide the pension participants the right incentive to work, thus, reducing the labor supply distortions.

(5) The Chinese government should set up an independent agency to regulate pension management. The social security system needs to be unified in order to

provide a basic pension floor for all the pension participants to reduce the poverty problem in the barren areas.

(6) It seems that a publicly managed pension scheme is more feasible for China than an immediate shift to a private pension system. This is because in China most people lack of experience with a market oriented system and financial matters. However, the final system that China should adopt for its social security should be the private pension scheme.

This paper analyzes different pension systems and provides a general view of these systems and their shortcomings. Some problems in China's social security system resemble the problems that other PAYGO systems have. However, China's system is not a complete PAYGO system yet and has quite some special problems of its own. Therefore, more caution is needed to exercise the appropriate action. I hope that this paper could induce more interesting debate about China's social security reform.

Acknowledgements

The early version of the paper was written when author was a visiting economist at Federal Reserve Bank of Cleveland. The paper was presented at the international symposium on Establishing a Market-Oriented Social Security System in China, Organized by Chinese Economist Society. The suggestions from the symposium attendees are appreciated. The author also want to thank David F. Gates (the referee), Jason Yin (the editor), and an anonymous referee for their helpful comments.

References

1. Carstens, A.G., 1997, The Reform of Social Security in Mexico, In S. A. Sass and R.K. Triest eds. Social Security Reform Conference Proceedings, Federal Reserve Bank of Boston.
2. Daykin, C. D., 1996, Occupational Pension Provision in the United Kingdom, In Z. Bodie, O.S. Mitchell, and J.A. Turner eds., Securing Employer-based Pensions: An International Perspective. Philadelphia: University of Pennsylvania Press and The Pension Research Council, 33-68.
3. Gramlich, E.M., 1996, Different Approaches for Dealing with Social Security, American Economic Review 86, 358-362.

4. Grubbs, D. S. Jr., 1996, Comments, In Z. Bodie, O.S. Mitchell, and J.A. Turner eds., Securing Employer-based Pensions: An International Perspective. Philadelphia: University of Pennsylvania Press and The Pension Research Council, 187-192.
5. Grubbs, D. S. Jr., 1983, Vesting and a Federal Portable Pension System, Journal of Pension Planing and Compliance 9, 5.
6. Horioka, C. Y., 1997, Japan's Public Pension System: What Is Wrong with It and How to Fix It, In S. A. Sass and R.K. Triest eds., Social Security Reform Conference Proceedings, Federal Reserve Bank of Boston.
7. Howes, S., 1993, Income Inequality in Urban China in the 1980s: Level, Trends and Determinants, Economic Transformation and Public Finance Discussion Paper No. 3, London School of Economics.
8. Hussain, A, 1994, Social Security in Present-Day China and Its Reform, American Economic Review 84, 276-280.
9. James, E. and D. Vittas, 1996, Mandatory Saving Schemes: Are They Answer to the Old Age Security Problems?, In Z. Bodie, O.S. Mitchell, and J.A. Turner eds., Securing Employer-based Pensions: An International Perspective. Philadelphia: University of Pennsylvania Press and The Pension Research Council, 149-181.
10. Kotlikoff, L., 1996, Privatizing Social Security at Home and Abroad, American Economic Review 86, 368-372.
11. Korczyk, S., 1993, Prospects for Private Pensions in Poland, the Former Czech and Slovak Federal Republic, and Bulgaria, Washington DC: Report to the US Department of Labor Pension and Welfare Benefits Administration.
12. Pesando, J. E., 1996, The Government's Role in Insuring Pensions, In Z. Bodie, O.S. Mitchell, and J.A. Turner eds., Securing Employer-based Pensions: An International Perspective. Philadelphia: University of Pennsylvania Press and The Pension Research Council, 286-305.
13. Schieber, S. J. and J.B. Shoven, 1996, Social Security Reform: Around the World in 80 ways, American Economic Review 86, 373-377.
14. Song, S.F., and G. S. Chu, 1997, Social Security Reform in China: The Case of Old-Age Insurance, Contemporary Economic Policy 15, 85-93.
15. Turner, J.A., and D. M. Rajnes, 1996, Private Pension Systems in Transition Economies, In Z. Bodie, O.S. Mitchell, and J.A. Turner eds., Securing Employer-based Pensions: An International Perspective. Philadelphia: University of Pennsylvania Press and The Pension Research Council, 193-210.

16. Watanabe, N., 1996, Private Pension Plans in Japan, In Z. Bodie, O.S. Mitchell, and J.A. Turner eds., Securing Employer-based Pensions: An International Perspective. Philadelphia: University of Pennsylvania Press and The Pension Research Council, 121-142.
17. World Bank, 1994, Averting the Old Age Crisis: Policies to Protect the Old and Promote Growth, Washington, DC: World Bank and Oxford University Press.

CHAPTER 24

PENSION REFORM IN HUNGARY

ANTAL DEUTSCH[1]
Department of Economics, McGill University,
855 Sherbrooke St. W
Montreal, Quebec, H3A 2TT, Canada

Hungary was the first transitional economy to legislate the operation of private pension funds. This paper describes both the setting and the process of pension reform in Hungary. The problems in transferring from the old system to the new one are also addressed. The early Hungarian experience may be useful for China.

1. Introduction

Pension reform is now at or near the top of the economic agenda practically everywhere. Traditional arrangements based on those working paying those who are now old (PAYGO), have run into difficulties in industrialized, as well as the transforming countries. People, for whatever reason, have decided some years back to have fewer children. That in turn leads to an ever-increasing burden on those now working: this economic burden has been transmitted to the political mechanisms. Reformers seek to relieve the rising burden by calling for increased self-provision, those resisting reform argue for recognition of acquired rights. The result is high political drama in France and Italy, and dignified grumbling in Sweden.

All this is related to the increasing unwillingness of nearly everyone to accept government deficits financed by debt and printing money. These are the sources heavily relied upon to finance failing public pension schemes. Hungary, having become the first transforming economy to undertake a thorough-going reform of its social security system, represents an example of both the problems and potential solutions.

---

[1] Antal Deutsch is Professor of Economics at McGill University and an advisor to the Hungarian Ministry of Finance. His work in Hungary is supported by the Canadian International Development Agency.
An early version of this paper was published in the October 1997 issue of *World Economic Affairs*.

This paper attempts to describe, in a footnote-less user-friendly fashion, both the setting and the process of reform in Hungary. The lessons for China depend on both the present decentralised state of pension arrangements in the PRC, and the degree of political determination to proceed to a multi-pillar system. One complicating factor is the multiplicity of local pension arrangements that now exist in China. A reconciliation of many local interests may be necessary before a Hungarian-style reform becomes universally acceptable.

2. The World of Pension Plans

Pensions are replacement income for those too old to work. "Funded" pension plans have a pool of assets large enough to meet their future liabilities. "PAYGO" plans have little or no assets, and rely on future payments into the plan to finance benefit pay-outs. There are two kinds of pension benefits: "Defined benefit" plans (DB), promise a monthly income calculated on the basis of previous earnings and years of service. In order to run a DB scheme, the plan need not be funded, but there has to be a solvent guarantor. By contrast, "Defined contribution" (DC) plans simply accumulate a savings account which will buy whatever annuity is available on the market at the time of retirement. DC plans require assets and safeguards, but no guarantor of a promised level of benefits, because there is no such promise.

Government sponsored plans in most major industrial countries are based on PAYGO arrangements. Such pensions provide the institutional potential to include elements of income redistribution. These typically run not only from rich to poor, but surprisingly, also from later generations of contributors to the initial generations of recipients. Defined benefit arrangements transfer wealth from men with short life-expectancies at retirement to women with long ones. It is always seductive politically to deliver something apparently for nothing. How much redistribution there is in a plan and in which direction, are political decisions constrained by the availability of resources.

There are successful and unsuccessful pension plans. The major success criteria are 1) solvency, and 2) a rate of return on his/her investment to the typical contributor which is competitive with returns available elsewhere. To help the latter, sometimes favoured tax treatment is provided by government. Success or failure is ultimately measured by the ability of the system to provide pensions, and the feeling of the participants that they are getting their money's worth. While all participants in pension plans are unlikely to be financial wizards, there will be an intuitive understanding of the individual's benefits and costs. You can not fool all of the people all of the time...

Private pensions, be they DB or DC, are legally required to have dedicated assets to cover their liabilities. A major scandal of recent vintage in the United Kingdom, where assets were simply stolen, has alerted pension regulators generally to the need for more serious security arrangements. One major exception to the specific funding requirements is the practice in the German Federal Republic, where the funds for the company pension plan remain within the sponsoring firm. There is a government backed guarantee for solvency of these plans.

Public schemes, by contrast, are most often of the PAYGO variety. This means that everyone's pension is paid by other people down the road. The theory of successful PAYGO plans presumes that the working population as a proportion of the total will grow (or at least not decline!). The theory also presumes that labour productivity in the economy (usually as a result of somebody else's capital investment!) will also grow. If these conditions do not hold, the solvency of the plan will be threatened.

To the extent that public pensions represent actual and potential government outlays, they are in conflict with all other government expenditures. As a politically astute way of restraining overall pension expenditures, governments often earmark a payroll tax to cover the ongoing expenditures of the PAYGO system. In years of surplus, benefit increases are granted, while in the inevitable years of shortfalls, an instant "crisis" is created. Attempts to increase the yield on this payroll tax by raising the rate or by broadening the tax base, will in chronic cases lead to no increase or to an actual decrease in the amounts collected. The required supplement from general funds gives the government both the need and the excuse to reduce benefits.

Benefits may be reduced in three ways:

1) The formula used in determining the initial pension may be made less generous.
2) The retirement age may be raised.
3) Inflation may not be fully compensated.

The first two of these measures affect future pensioners who may not be fully aware of the impact on them at the time of enactment. The third measure affects the population of present pensioners immediately: for this reason, it is less popular with governments.

3. Pension Reform

Heaven for pension plan designers is to start with a country that has none. Unfortunately, such opportunities are rare. One interesting pioneering design, initiated in Asia, evolved from the retirement system of the British Colonial Civil Service. This is the Central Provident Fund of Singapore (CPF). The CPF requires the setting aside of 40% of everyone's current wage in a personal account. These compulsory savings pay for retirement, the ownership of flats, and health care expenses. The existence of CPF is credited with the provision of the modern housing stock of Singapore, as well as all the other good things that flow from having what must be one of the world's highest savings rates. Singapore pension savers' money is centrally administered by the Government.

The Chilean pension system, widely imitated in Latin America, requires 10% of wages to go into dedicated private accounts. The funds are managed by highly regulated competing private investment firms. Both the Singaporean and the Chilean schemes have been obtaining high real rates of return and are generally thought of as providing satisfaction to the participants.

Reform is usually an exercise in the design of a new system, while the liabilities are left over from the old one. The twin goals of reform are usually to reduce the budgetary cost to the taxpayer, as well as to increase benefits to the retirees. All this is constrained by the need to pay ongoing pensioners, and to meet the benefit promises accruing to those contributing to the old scheme.

Looking at the recent experience of public pension schemes around the world, it seems clear that pension reform in the late 90's means redesigning the scope of the public pillar (PAYGO) by reducing benefits. Many PAYGO schemes also carry the cost of late-in-life unemployment reclassified as early retirement, and of disability pensions. For the latter, cost reduction can only be obtained by tightening eligibility conditions.

The second aspect of reform is to redirect funds previously going to the PAYGO system to privately owned and managed contribution accounts which are fully funded. These are attractive, because they confer a sense of ownership on the pension saver and if competently managed, promise much better returns to the typical participant than can be obtained by putting the same funds into the PAYGO arrangement.

For the other aspect of the diversion, specifically the gap in PAYGO receipts, the Hungarian case described below should prove enlightening.

4. The Case of Hungary

Hungary's population totals 10 million and is, slowly declining. The birth rate is low, and the death rates of middle-aged men are spectacularly high. The causes of the latter are the incidence of smoking, alcoholism, generally bad diet, and a great deal of stress. The retired population is overwhelmingly female, aging, and in need of ever-increasing medical expenses. The labour force is 4.5 million, of whom about .7 million are officially unemployed. There are 2.9 million pensioners including those on early retirement and disability benefits. Hungary has had a funded social security system since 1928. There was also a complete body of legislation governing the operation of funded, private, employer-sponsored pension plans. Many of the assets in these were lost during World War II and in the hyper-inflation of 1945-46. Whatever was left, was sequestered. A Soviet-style social security system was in place by the late 1940's, as part of the newly introduced planned economy. (See Appendix 1)

Following the changes of 1989, it was clear to all that pension reform was needed. Pensions are low, the payroll-tax in 1997 was high: 30.5% of wages. The initial step was a resolution passed by Parliament in October 1991 pointing to the desirability of a four pillar system consisting of a base amount payable to all aged citizens, plus a service and earnings related public pillar, complemented by voluntary employer/employee pension plans, as well as individual savings schemes. It was quickly recognized that the resource requirements of the "base amount payable to all" make the resolution a wish list, rather than a program.

Following two years of intense preparatory work, the Hungarian Parliament passed in the Fall of 1993, legislation enabling the establishment and functioning of private pension plans. The government pension-scheme remained untouched at this stage. A period of rapid growth of the private funds in terms of both membership and assets followed. By September 1998, there were 300 funds in existence, with total membership of 700,000 and total assets of US $300 million.

After the relatively non-controversial private pension funds came into being, it was time to address the larger issues of social security. Demographic studies for Hungary show that the dependency ratio on the shrinking number of those economically active is very low, and will continue to deteriorate for the foreseeable future. It is in this context that the reform of the PAYGO pension system become inevitable, but difficult.

The particular generation undertaking the change to a funded system will have to bear the ongoing costs of PAYGO, as well as the burden of the investment required to establish the new system. The older view of this problem was that the obstacles are insurmountable.

Fortunately, a new way of looking at this problem has evolved. It is assumed that the burden of PAYGO is a given and will have to be paid regardless of what happens. In this way, the future obligations of PAYGO at a point of time may be viewed as an implicit form of the national debt. When the current portion of this implicit debt is paid, and thereby enhances the current budget deficit, it becomes part of the explicit national debt. Thus with pension reform, the total debt is the same as before, but more of it has become formally written down. The incremental current budgetary deficit caused by reform becomes an accounting identity without much economic significance.

In the age of Maastricht, budget deficits and debts are considered to be bad. For this reason, it appears to makes sense for a government to keep the rate of conversion from implicit debt to explicit at a low percentage of GDP. (However, it is difficult to provide a rational explanation for the caution, because smart bond-raters know all about implicit debt!)

The specific reform arrangements in Hungary are:

1) The retirement age is to advance in stages, from 55 and 60 for women and men respectively, to a unisex 62 years, by 2008.
2) The annual indexing of ongoing pensions will follow the Swiss indexing formula (Box 2).
3) The payroll tax financing of pensions will extend its base to capture all wage-like incomes.
4) In the initial year of 1998 and in 1999, 6% of wages; in 2000 and thereafter, 8% of the current employee share to the Social Security Pension will be diverted to individual retirement accounts for those participating in the new system. These contributions will be deductible from the income and social security tax bases. PAYGO benefits will be adjusted accordingly, with a lessened redistribution between income groups.
5) Participants in the new plan will include all those entering the labour force after July 1998, plus anyone wishing to switch to the new system. Persons born in 1952 or before who switch, run the risk of having a lower aggregate pension than without the reform. Switchers born since 1952 have their pre-reform level

of aggregate pensions guaranteed. There is no ceiling on the annuity obtainable from the new second pillar. There will be a two-year election-period.

The measures have been fully enacted, with the exception of the Swiss indexing, which is supposed to take effect after 2000. That issue has run into heavy political fire.

The expectations attached to these reforms are:

1) they will reduce the scope of the PAYGO program, hence the Government's deficit in the long-run;
2) they will increase substantially the stock of domestically-owned savings;
3) the level of pensions will be more closely related to the level of earnings on which they are based;
4) the private DC pension will more than offset the cut in the government DB pension, thus leaving future pensioners better, some hope, much better off.

5. Some Tough Issues

The expectations of the reformers clashed with the activities of the anti-reform lobby. Some of the latter are motivated by a dislike of substituting private activity for government activity. In other cases, there is a well-established self interest in the status quo, resulting in income streams that are likely to be reduced following successful reform. Neither of these positions make for promising arguments in the public arena. The rhetoric actually employed by the anti-reform lobby invoked threats to present pensioners by the diversion of funds to individual accounts. There is also the "foreign devils" argument, usually associated with causes supported by the World Bank and the International Monetary Fund. (In the Hungarian case, it is not easy to defend a Soviet-imposed institution against the weight of Western experience.) The final, but understandable, anti-reform argument is the assertion that the money going into private pension accounts will simply be stolen. Given the historical record, it is not easy to meet this particular argument by invoking the existence of state institutions designed to protect property rights.

The Hungarian PAYGO system promises identical wage and service determined monthly benefits to both men and women. Gender-neutral as this may appear, the benefit has a greater value to women, because they live longer to collect it. This is typical of PAYGO systems the world over. What is important to remember here, is that real resources are required to pay pensions, and the gender-composition of beneficiaries matters significantly in determining the aggregate cost of a DB pension plan.

It is with defined contribution schemes such as the new Hungarian pension savings accounts, where a finite sum of money is turned into an annuity at the time of retirement, that this relative longevity problem becomes visible. With any given accumulation in a pension account, a life payout would result in lower monthly payments for women of a given age, simply because there are more months in their remaining lives. Annuity markets reflect the actuarial fact of longevity: at a given age, for a given amount of capital, men get more per month, women less.

There have been political pressures from some women's groups directed to the use of unisex annuity tables. These tables, in principle, simply ignore the gender of the future pensioner in establishing the amount of the monthly pension. Unfortunately, that cannot be the end of the story. If every pensioner has his/her annuity determined on the basis of the female mortality experience, monthly *pensions will be low* and because of the predictable early mortality of men, there will be a *surplus* in the plan. Conversely, using male rates in determining pensions will yield *higher pensions*, but on account of the predictable female longevity, a *deficit* in the annuity scheme will inevitably arise.

Accordingly, the ratio of genders within the scheme becomes a critical variable in choosing the policy on establishing annuities, and remaining solvent. If pension funds allow the lump sum withdrawal of pension accounts, males disadvantaged by the use of female rates will move to gender distinct arrangements with insurance companies and the like. That would leave unisex annuity programs overwhelmingly populated by females, and the unisex rates would be very close to female rates.

Maintaining unisex rates above the female rates under these circumstances requires additional resources. With defined benefit schemes, the issue does not usually emerge explicitly, where it is the guarantor of the plan whose resources become committed. Where overall costs are constrained, the costs of unisex rates are paid by lower overall benefits accruing to pensioners of both genders. The Hungarian government in putting forward its reform legislation has stated that women's monthly pensions originating with the DC pillar shall not be "disadvantaged" by the fact of their gender. In the next few years, provision will have to be made for the resource requirements of this promise. (Please note that even spectacular investment performance will not provide the resources required, because investment gains accrue to both sexes equally. To run a truly unisex arrangement, special funding will be required for women only.)

Another set of issues involve the establishment of the taxation policies for the new system. It is a stated intention of the reform program to have the contributions to private accounts count as a deduction from the income tax base and the social security tax base, and the emerging annuities as additions to taxable personal income. It is also understood that pension funds will not be taxed on their earnings.

Contributions to pension plans are deductions from disposable income. Pension benefits are additions to disposable income. For this reason, many countries prefer to allow a deduction (within limits) of contributions to pension plans, but tax the emerging annuity. By extension of this principle, the income accruing to the pension plan during the years of accumulation remains free of tax.

Where rates of return to pension plans are higher than the marginal borrowing rate on the national debt, and income tax rates are not very steeply progressive, it may turn out that the net worth of the taxing government is increased by allowing the tax-base deduction of contributions to pension plans. The value of future income taxes on deferred pension arrangements may be thought of as an implicit offset to a country's national debt. Actual practice, which varies from country to country, is usually colored by short-term treasury thinking. The tax expenditure lost from current tax collections looms larger than the potential collections on the horizon, no matter how big.

With Soviet-type systems where there was traditionally no explicit income tax, the practice of not including pension income in the tax base has grown up. Part of the reform effort in transforming economies is to persuade makers of tax policy to follow the practice announced by the Hungarian reform programme, to take full effect in 2013.

The major puzzle now is the proportion of persons who will actually opt to transfer to the new system. That number can only be guessed at, but so far it is 1.2 million. The Government hopes that the proportion will be low enough to accommodate the resulting shortfall in the cash flow of the PAYGO system to within one percent of GDP. During the first three months of 1998, the number of those electing to switch has been more than double the original estimate for all of 1998. It follows that the expected cash shortfall should be at least twice the original estimate.

6. In the Window

Hungary was the first transitional economy to legislate the operation of private pension funds. Hungary is again the first transitional economy to have legislated thorough-going social security reform. Because a large number of countries will be evaluating the early Hungarian experience, the story is of much more than local significance. Since the first draft of this paper was written, Poland has enacted similar reform legislation to take effect on January 1, 1999.

Some specific questions to be answered for the decision-makers of the other transforming economies are:

(1) Will the individual pension accounts produce a suitable real rate of return?
(2) Will the book-keeping costs of the transformation, if badly underestimated, cause some kind of crisis?
(3) Will the public sector evolve a system of record-keeping of a more complex system fast enough to avoid serious problems?

While there are weighty reasons to be optimistic on all counts, the reader must by now suspect that pension reform is far more than an abstract exercise in public finance.

Appendix 1

ON THE SOVIET-TYPE ECONOMY AND ITS PENSION SYSTEM

An immense amount of nonsense has been written about the Soviet-type economy. (An excellent description of how this system actually worked may be found in János Kornai, *The Socialist System, The Political Economy of Communism*, Oxford University Press, Princeton University Press, 1992.) The Soviet version of the planned economy was based on compulsion. All capital assets were sequestered, and legislation was passed requiring every able-bodied citizen to find state-approved employment. Compliance was mixed. Enthusiastic cooperation cannot be legislated and the natural human tendencies to trade, truck and barter kept resurfacing. This was one economic reason for the eventual change in the economic system.

In a macroeconomic sense, the system worked by centralising all significant cash-flows in the hands of the government, and maximizing or optimizing nothing in particular. (A socialist "reform" literature grew up, keeping economists busy developing the idea of "optimization", as a way to improve things.) The key to the planning process was an allocation of the available cash flow between the government and consumers. There was also a need to supply goods to match the cash flow (adjusted for changes in the stock of savings). The planners, not surprisingly, never managed to get the saleable and desired mixture of goods right, so as to match both resource constraints and consumer demand. Everyday life was characterized by shortages and unsold surpluses. This inevitably translated to consumer dissatisfaction, as did above all, the aggregate level of resources available for consumption. The resulting mess was managed by imports financed through Western borrowing in the "soft" dictatorships such as Hungary and Poland, and by police repression in the "hard" dictatorships like Czechoslovakia and Romania. (Following the change in economic systems, the former were left with large external debts, while the latter were not.) The narrowing constraints on acceptable levels of consumer deprivation, repression and foreign borrowing accounted for another set of major reasons for the changes of 1989. Pension systems were virtually identical throughout the entire Soviet Empire. One major characteristic was the low retirement age: 55 for women, 60 for men. This had two important functions. It reduced the pervasive hidden unemployment, and provided a stream of consumer services to families by able-bodied, active grandparents.

For reasons explained above, the planned economy was characterized by much standing in line. The able-bodied grandparent could stand in line for bread, milk, or meat, while the parents in the same household could go to work. The implicit babysitting services also had considerable value to the family. All this was facilitated by a disastrous shortage of the housing stock, forcing a very large proportion of families to crowd into multi-generational households.

The pension system itself aimed for a replacement rate of about 40% of the average wage. Pensions were miserably low, but not unreasonable as an increment to the cash income of the multi-generational family unit. The implicit egalitarianism of this pension system was broken by an unabashed tendency to provide generous bonuses over and above the base pensions to those favoured by patronage. Medals awarded for services to the government automatically carried pension add-ons.

The pension system was characterized by minimal to non-existent record-keeping on potential claimants, hence no serious planning of the expenditure level was or could have been undertaken. As a major allocation of governmental resources, pension systems became an unfunny parody on the idea of planning the economy.

Appendix 2

HOW TO INDEX PENSIONS FOR INFLATION

What follows is a discussion repeated in the context of PAYGO pensions in an inflationary environment. (The indexing of funded pensions in the real world is heavily influenced by resource availability.)

There are two ways to look at indexing of pensions. The consumption base suggests compensating for increases in the consumer price index annually, or more frequently where warranted. The logic underlying this practice is that the pensioner has established a standard of living. CPI indexing maintains that standard in the face of inflation.

The other approach is to index pensions in line with the average industrial wage. Here, the objective is that public pensioners should participate in national income changes. It is further assumed that average wages are a reliable index of prosperity, or lack thereof.

On closer scrutiny, both of these approaches fail the stated intent. In most countries, their consumption basket used for the indexing of consumer prices is representative of the preferences of some specific group of the population. Even where a special price index is developed for the typical consumption patterns of pensioners, individual variations in consumption habits are likely to be large. In plain English, inflation, as measured by the CPI, may be very different from that experienced by a particular pensioner household. Much is being made of the upward bias, implicit in all conventional consumer price indexes, from ignoring the offset available by substituting relatively cheap goods for those that have become relatively dear. This theory deals with the type of situation where the price of coffee might go up, while the price of everything else (including tea) stands still. Where there is broad and general increase in all prices, as in the transforming economies, the implicit overstatement of inflation in the index by failing to account for substitutions becomes irrelevant.

The case for using average wages is even less convincing. Average wages, by definition, measure the average pay of those who happen to be employed as of a point in time. Changes in observed values incorporate, on top of the wage changes of the on-going working population, the following:

(1) Decreasing tendencies in the observed average wage on account of the current retirement of relatively senior, and highly paid workers.
(2) Another decrease in the average wage on account of the hiring of relatively junior, thus low paid, workers.
(3) Increases in the average wage on the account of bad business conditions causing the layoff of relatively junior workers.
(4) Decreases in the average wage on account of prosperity caused hiring of relatively junior workers.

It is fair to conclude that the average industrial wage has many factors influencing it, and if the intent is to make the adjustment representative of the rate of change in economic activity only, the other factors at work may very well make the total effect perverse.

One compromise, which solves none of these problems, is what is known as "Swiss Indexing". This simply involves taking half the change in the consumer price index, and combining it with half the change in the industrial wage. By altering these proportions, a very large set of indexing possibilities emerge.

SUBJECT INDEX

SUBJECT INDEX

SUBJECT INDEX